THE COLLECTED WORKS OF
SAMUEL TAYLOR COLERIDGE · 16

POETICAL WORKS

General Editor: KATHLEEN COBURN
Associate Editor: BART WINER

THE COLLECTED WORKS

THE COLLECTED WORKS OF

Samuel Taylor Coleridge

Poetical Works

I

Poems (Reading Text): PART 2

EDITED BY

J. C. C. Mays

�֍ BOLLINGEN SERIES LXXV
PRINCETON UNIVERSITY PRESS

This edition of the text by Samuel Taylor Coleridge is
copyright © 2001 by Princeton University Press

The Collected Works, sponsored by Bollingen Foundation,
is published by Princeton University Press, Princeton, New Jersey
ISBN 0-691-00483-8
LCC 00-021206

Library of Congress Cataloging-in-Publication Data

Coleridge, Samuel Taylor, 1772–1834.
Poetical works / edited by J.C.C. Mays.
p. cm.—(Bollingen series; 75) (The collected works
of Samuel Taylor Coleridge; 16)
Includes bibliographical references and index.
Contents: v. 1, pt. 1. Poems (reading text)—v. 2, pt. 1.
Poems (Variorum text)—v. 3, pt. 1. Plays
ISBN 0-691-00483-8 (v. 1, pt. 2: alk. paper)—
ISBN 0-691-00484-6 (v. 2, pt. 2: alk. paper)—
ISBN 0-691-09883-2 (v. 3, pt. 2: alk. paper)
I. Mays, J.C.C. II. Title. III. Series.

PR4470 .F84 vol. 16   821'.7–dc21

The Collected Works constitutes
the seventy-fifth publication in Bollingen Series

The present work, number 16 of the Collected Works,
is in 3 volumes, this being 16:1 pt 2

Princeton University Press books are printed on acid-free paper and meet
the guidelines for permanence and durability of the Committee on
Production Guidelines for Book Longevity of the Council on Library Resources

Typeset by John Waś, Oxford, UK

Printed in the United States of America
1 3 5 7 9 10 8 6 4 2

THIS EDITION
OF THE WORKS OF
SAMUEL TAYLOR COLERIDGE
IS DEDICATED
IN GRATITUDE TO
THE FAMILY EDITORS
IN EACH GENERATION

IN THE PREPARATION OF
THESE VOLUMES THE EDITOR IS
INDEBTED FOR SPECIAL KNOWLEDGE
AND CO-OPERATION
TO
Lorna Arnold
Joyce Crick

CONTENTS

───────────■ I ■───────────

vii

Contents

Contents

Contents

LIST OF ILLUSTRATIONS

221. EPITAPH ON A BAD MAN, PERHAPS AFTER VICESIMUS KNOX

[May–Sept 1799]

C copied out lines 3–4 in a notebook (*CN* I 625 f 120ᵛ), as part of a sequence of more than thirty such epigrams, mostly adapted from the German. The full version was published in *M Post* (22 Sept 1801), under the signature "Εστησε" (=STC), and four ms versions date from 1830 and after. The lines were never published over C's own name or collected.

EHC (*PW* II 961n) suggests that C's lines derive from an antithesis to be found in the second stanza of an epigram called *Posthumous Fame* in Vicesimus Knox's *Elegant Extracts* (1790) 283–4 at 284:

> If on his spacious marble we rely,
> Pity a worth, like his, should ever die!
> If credit to his real life we give,
> Pity a wretch, like him, should ever live.

C's source could have been John Owen's *Epitaphium Athei*, in *Epigrammatum Libri Tres* (2nd ed 1606) 1.28 p 5:

> Mortuus est, quasi victurus post funera non sit,
> Sic vixit, tanquam non moriturus erat.

This appears in a German translation by V. Löber as *Des Gottlosen Grabschrift*, collected in *Epigrammatische Anthologie* ed J.C.F. Haug and F. C. Weisser (10 vols Zurich 1807–9) IX 130:

> Ich starb, als lebt' ich nach dem Tode nimmer;
> Ich triebs im Leben so, als lebt' ich immer.

However, neither Owen nor Löber mentions the gorgeous tomb and "credit"— which might be held to be slight hints for C's first couplet.

Such a background bears on C's remarks following a ms version dated 11 Nov 1832:

> This epitaph I published some 3 & 20 years ago in the Morning Post, without consciousness of being either a Plagiarist or a Translator. But in the Saturday Magazine, Novʳ 10ᵗʰ, 1832, I find

Epitaph on an Infidel
(FROM THE LATIN)

Beneath this stone the mouldering ashes lie
Of one to whom Religion spoke in vain:
He liv'd as tho' he never were to die,
He died as tho' he ne'er should live again.
—M.

Now this seems to me most ingeniously to combine the three gifts of slandering, stealing, and flat'ning ~~/ or instead of M it should be M / Hm / alias Hum.~~, in Mr. Min's Em.[1]

The epitaph does indeed appear on p 183 of the issue C cites, with variations of capitalisation, punctuation, etc. While it could be a fresh translation from John Owen's Latin, or might derive from a German source, the source closer to home in Knox was probably what prompted the charge of plagiarism.

In two of the four late mss the title names Hazlitt, who died on 18 Sept 1830, and another names the dead man as an atheist. C also added a prose note on Hazlitt to one of the ms texts:

> With a sadness at heart, and an earnest hope, grounded on his misanthropic strangeness when I first knew him, in his 20 or 21st year, that a something existed in his bodily organism that in the sight of the All-merciful lessened his responsibility—and the moral imputation of his acts & feelings. (Notebook 47 [=BM Add MS 47542] f 1^v; *CN* v)

Although Hazlitt's last words were "Well, I've had a happy life", his end was sad and lonely. Only two mourners—one of them CL—followed his body to the graveside.

The six texts differ from one another in minor ways. The *M Post* version is given here; the first text differs from the others in a major way, lacking the first couplet.

Of him, that in this gorgeous tomb doth lie,
This sad brief tale is all that Truth can give—
He liv'd, like one who never thought to die,
He died, like one who dar'd not hope to live!

[1] C allows the sound of the signature "M" to drift into *um*, *h'm*, and *humbug* before replacing it with a typographic pun on *Mr Insignificant's M*. A min is a small size of type and an em is a horizontal measure of type—here the length of the rule before the printed signature.

222. TWO VERSIONS OF AN EPIGRAM ON LYING, FROM LESSING

[May–Sept 1799]

C copied out the first version in a notebook (*CN* I 625 f 121ʳ), as part of a sequence of more than thirty such epigrams, mostly adapted from the German. He gave the second version to Joseph Cottle, and published it soon afterwards in *Annual Anthology* II (1800), the version given here. The original epigram by Lessing ultimately derives from the Stoic paradox of the Cretan Liar: *Sinngedichte* No 45 *Auf einen Lügner*, in *Sämmtliche Schriften* I 28:

> Da magst so oft, so fein, als dir nur möglich, lügen:
> Mich sollst du dennoch nicht betriegen.
> Ein einzigmal nur hast du mich betrogen:
> Das kam daher, du hattest nicht gelogen.

A two-line rendering of the same German original, but apparently unconnected with C, appeared anonymously, with others, in *The Courier* (9 Nov 1799):

> Not one of all his tales I swallow,
> Once he spoke truth, and dup'd me hollow.

(*a*)

Say what you will, ingenious Youth!
You'll find me neither Dupe or Dunce.
Once you deceived me, only once—
Twas then when you told truth.

(*b*)

If the guilt of all lying consists in deceit
Lye on—'tis your duty, sweet Youth!
For believe me, then only we find you a cheat
When you cunningly tell us the truth.

223. EPIGRAM ON AN OXFORD
BROTHELHOUSE,
ADAPTED FROM LESSING

[Before Sept 1799]

C copied out the lines in a notebook (*CN* I 625 f 121ʳ), as part of a sequence of more than thirty such epigrams, mostly adapted from the German. They were published anonymously in *M Post* (4 Nov 1799), the version given here, but not collected in his lifetime. They derive, like most of the items in the same notebook entry, from Lessing's *Sinngedichte*, here No 50, *Auf einen Brand zu* * *, in *Sämmtliche Schriften* I 31:

> Ein Hurenhaus gerieth um Mitternacht in Brand.
> Schnell sprang, zum Löschen oder Retten,
> Ein Dutzend Mönche von den Betten.
> Wo waren die? Sie waren— —bei der Hand.
> Ein Hurenhaus gerieth in Brand.

> An Oxford brothel-house caught fire.
> At midnight, from their peaceful pillows
> Up leapt a dozen rev'rend Fellows,
> And quench'd the conflagration dire.
> This brave, this truly christian band,   5
> Where were they?—Oh! they were at hand—
> It was a brothel-house caught fire.

224. EPIGRAM ON A LADY'S TOO
GREAT FONDNESS FOR HER DOG,
FROM LESSING

[May–Sept 1799]

C copied out the lines in a notebook (*CN* I 625 f 121ʳ), as part of a sequence of more than thirty such epigrams, mostly adapted from the German. He gave a copy to Joseph Cottle, and the epigram was published in RS's *Annual Anthology* II (1800), the version given here. Two other transcripts exist in the hand of SC, with notes which suggest that C connected the epigram with Mrs Leckie, after he had seen her with her dog in Malta. An unsigned, slightly different, version was published in *M Chron* (18 May 1813). It was never collected by C.

C's original is Lessing's *Sinngedichte* No 66, *An die Dorilis*, in *Sämmtliche Schriften* I 39 (which in turn follows, perhaps, Martial 1.83):

> Dein Hündchen, Dorilis, ist zärtlich, tändelnd, rein:
> Daß du es also leckst, soll das mich wundern? nein!
> Allein dein Hündchen lecket dich:
> Und dieses wundert mich.

> Thy lap-dog, Rufa, is dainty beast,
> It don't surprise me in the least
> To see thee lick so dainty clean a beast.
> But that so dainty clean a beast licks thee—
> Yes—that surprizes me.   5

225. EPIGRAM ON MIMULUS, FROM LESSING

[May–Sept 1799]

C copied out his translation in a notebook (*CN* I 625 f 121ᵛ), as part of a sequence of more than thirty such epigrams, mostly adapted from the German, but appears never to have published it. It derives from Lessing's *Sinngedichte* No 56, *Grabschrift auf ebendenselben* (tr "Epitaph on the same man", referring to the original of **226** *Epigram on Paviun*), in *Sämmtliche Schriften* I 34:

> Hier faulet Mimulus, ein Affe.
> Und leider! leider! welch ein Affe!
> So zahm, als in der Welt kein Affe;
> So rein, als in der Welt kein Affe;
> So keusch, als in der Welt kein Affe;
> So ernst, als in der Welt kein Affe;
> So ohne Falsch. O welch ein Affe!
> Damit ichs kurz zusammen raffe:
> Ein ganz originaler Affe.

> Here moulders Mimulus, an Ape—
> Alas, alas! O what an Ape.

So tame, as in the world no other Ape—
So clean, as in the world no other Ape—
So chaste, as in the world no other Ape—   5
So grave, as in the world no other Ape.
So loving true—! O what an Ape!
In short, that I may all together scrape—
He was, in truth, quite an Original Ape.

226. EPIGRAM ON PAVIUN, FROM LESSING

[May–Sept 1799]

C copied out the lines in a notebook (*CN* I 625 f 121ᵛ), as part of a sequence of more than thirty such epigrams, mostly adapted from the German, but appears never to have published them. The poem derives from Lessing's *Sinngedichte* No 55, *Auf den Tod eines Affen*, in *Sämmtliche Schriften* I 33:

> Hier liegt er nun, der kleine, liebe Pavian,
> Der uns so manches nachgethan!
> Ich wette, was er itzt gethan,
> Thun wir ihm alle nach, dem lieben Pavian.

The change of name in C's version helps his rhyme but loses the joke on Pavian, German for "baboon".

Here lies he now, the pretty Paviun,
Who after us so many things has done.
I lay a wager, what he now has done,
We all do after him, the pretty Paviun.

227. EPITAPH ON AN INSIGNIFICANT, ADAPTED FROM LESSING

[May–Sept 1799]

C's lines began as they ended, as an adaptation of Lessing's *Sinngedichte* No 52, *Grabschrift des Nitulus*, in *Sämmtliche Schriften* I 32:

Hier modert Nitulus, jungfräulichen Gesichts,
Der durch den Tod gewann: er wurde Staub aus Nichts.

Tr "Here Nitulus [=Little Nothing] moulders, of the girlish face, who was victorious in death: from nothing he became dust." C's first notebook drafts are in four lines (*CN* I 625 ff 121^v–122^r), but later versions and the version published in *PW* (1834) were pruned to two. The text given here was copied out for JG in *Omniana*, along with some other humorous epigrams (*CM*—*CC*—III 1071; cf **37** *Epigram on my Godmother's Beard*; **201** *Epigram on Goslar Ale*; **562** *The Pun Polysyllabic*).

Tis CYPHER lies beneath this crust,
Whom Death *created* into Dust.

228. EPIGRAM ON MARRIAGE, FROM LESSING

[May–Sept 1799]

C's lines are imitated from Lessing's *Sinngedichte* No 93, *An den Trill*, in *Sämmtliche Schriften* I 55:

Bald willst du, Trill, und bald willst du dich nicht beweiben:
Bald dünkt dichs gut, bald nicht, ein Hagestolz zu bleiben.
Ich soll dir rathen? Wohl! Thu, was dein Vater that:
Bleib frey; heirathe nichte!—Da hast du meinen Rath.

C copied out his translation in a notebook (*CN* I 625 f 122^r), as part of a sequence of more than thirty such epigrams, mostly adapted from the German. He appears never to have published it, unless he is the author of what amounts to a drastic revision—a version which appeared anonymously, with other epigrams, in *The Courier* (9 Nov 1799) and was reprinted in *The Poetical Register for 1802* II (1803) 372, which reads as follows:

EPIGRAM,
FROM THE GERMAN OF LESSING

You hesitate if you shall take a wife:
Do as your father did—live single all your life.

Bob now resolves on marriage schemes to trample
And now he'll have a wife all in a trice—

Must I advise?—Pursue thy Dad's Example
And marry not. There hast thou my advice.

229. EPIGRAM ON MAIDS AND ANGELS, FROM LESSING

[May–Sept 1799]

C's lines derive from Lessing's *Sinngedichte* No 108, *Auf Lorchen*, in *Sämmtliche Schriften* I 63:

> Lorchen heißt noch eine Jungfer. Wisset, die ihrs noch nicht wißt:
> So heißt Lucifer ein Engel, ob er gleich gefallen ist.

He drafted his version in a notebook along with many other such adaptations of German authors (*CN* I 625 f 122ʳ), but appears never to have published it.

> We still call Bet a maid—perchance, from this,
> That a fallen Angel still an Angel is.

230. EPIGRAM TO A VIRTUOUS ŒCONOMIST, FROM WERNICKE

[May–Sept 1799]

C's lines are adapted from Wernicke *Epigrams* 1.32 *An den sparsamen Irinus*, in *Christian Wernickens Überschriften, nebst Opitzens, Tschernings, Andreas Gryphius und Adam Olearius epigrammatischen Gedichten* ed Ramler 17; also in *Blumenlese deutscher Sinngedichte* ed Joerdens 110:

> Du liebst das Geld, Irin, doch so, daß dein Erbarmen
> Der Arme fühlt; du fliehst die Armuth, nicht die Armen.

C drafted his lines in a notebook (*CN* I 625 f 122ʳ), as part of a sequence of more than thirty such epigrams, mostly adapted from the German, and they were published anonymously in *M Post* (28 Oct 1799), the version given here. He transcribed them for at least two autograph hunters later in his life, but never included them in a collection.

You're careful o'er your wealth, 'tis true,
Yet so that of your plenteous store
The needy tastes and blesses you—
For you flee Poverty, but not the Poor.

231. EPIGRAM ON GRIPUS, FROM LESSING

[May–Sept 1799]

C copied out his lines in a notebook (*CN* I 625 f 122ᵛ), as part of a sequence of more than thirty such epigrams, mostly adapted from the German, but he appears never to have published them. His source is Lessing's *Sinngedichte* No 123, *Auf Muffeln*, in *Sämmtliche Schriften* I 71:

Freund Muffel schwört bey Gott und Ehre,
Ich kost' ihn schon so manche Zähre.—
Nun? frommer Mann, wenn das auch wäre;
Was kostet dich denn deine Zähre?

Old Gripus shakes his head, & swears
That I have cost him many tears.
Grant, pious Gripus this, were this true—
Pray, how much might your tears cost you.

232. ON THE SICKNESS OF A GREAT MINISTER, FROM LESSING

[May–Sept 1799]

C's lines are adapted from Lessing's *Sinngedichte* No 119, *Auf die Genesung einer Buhlerinn*, in *Sämmtliche Schriften* I 69:

Dem Tode wurde jüngst vom Pluto anbefohlen,
Die Lais unsrer Stadt nach jener Welt zu holen.

Sie war so alt doch nicht, und reizte manchen noch,
Durch Willigkeit und Scherz in ihr gemächlich Joch.
"Was?" sprach der schlaue Tod, der ökonomisch denket,
Und nicht, wie man wohl glaubt, den Wurfpfeil blindlings schwenket:
"Die Lais brächt' ich her? das wäre dumm genung!
Nein! Aertz' und Huren—nein! die hol' ich nicht so jung!"

The first version C copied out in a notebook (*CN* I 625 f 122ᵛ) is closer to the original, which is about the recovery of a harlot. The adapted version given here was published anonymously in *M Post* (1 Oct 1799)—although Pitt's health, which was continually bad, was no worse at this time than at any other. C never included the lines in any of his collections.

Pluto commanded Death to bring away
BILLY.—Death made pretences to obey,
And only made pretences; for he shot
A headless dart, that struck, but wounded not.
The ghaunt Economist, who, tho' my grandam   5
Thinks otherwise, ne'er shoots his darts at random,
Mutter'd, What? put my BILLY in arrest?
Upon my life, that were a pretty jest.
So flat a thing of Death shall ne'er be said or sung:
No! Ministers and Quacks! them take I not so young.   10

233. EPIGRAM TO AN AUTHOR,
FROM LESSING

[May–Sept 1799]

C's lines are given here as he copied them into his notebook (*CN* I 625 f 122ᵛ). The first two lines, at least, derive from Lessing's *Sinngedichte* No 15, *Die Ewigkeit gewisser Gedichte*, in *Sämmtliche Schriften* I 11:

Verse, wie sie Bassus schreibt,
Werden unvergänglich bleiben:—
Weil dergleichen Zeug zu schreiben,
Stets ein Stümper übrig bleibt.

When the lines were first printed in *M Post* (24 Jan 1800), they were adapted to apply (in the words of the title), "*TO MR. PYE*, I On his Carmen Seculare (a title which has, by various persons who have heard it, been thus translated, A

Poem, *an age long*)." Pye was poet laureate, and his *Carmen Seculare for the Year 1800* had appeared late in 1799. When C printed the lines over his own name in *BL* (1817) and *PW* (1834), they were addressed "To the author of the Ancient Mariner". Both applications are afterthoughts.

A curious parallel to C's lines, in an epigram said to have been composed by Matthew (?) Hole (d 1730), is cited by S. W. Singer "More Borrowed Thoughts" *N&Q* II (36) (6 Jul 1850) 82–3.

> Your Poem must *eternal* be,
> Dear Sir!—It cannot fail:
> For tis incomprehensible
> And without head or tail.

234. THE LETHARGIST AND MADMAN: A POLITICAL FABLE, AFTER THE *GREEK ANTHOLOGY*

[Aug–Sept 1799]

C copied out the lines in a notebook (*CN* I 625 f 123^{r-v}), as part of a sequence of more than thirty such epigrams, mostly adapted from the German, and they were published anonymously in *M Post* (19 Sept 1799), the version given here. He never published them over his own name or included them in a collection.

The poem expands a six-line anonymous epigram in the *Greek Anthology* (9.141):

> κοινῇ πὰρ κλισίῃ ληθαργικὸς ἠδὲ φρενοπλὴξ
> κείμενοι ἀλλήλων νοῦσον ἀπεσκέδασαν.
> ἐξέθορε κλίνης γὰρ ὁ τολμήεις ὑπὸ λύσσης
> καὶ τὸν ἀναίσθητον παντὸς ἔτυπτε μέλους.
> πληγαὶ δ' ἀμφοτέροις ἐγένοντ' ἄκος, αἷς ὁ μὲν αὐτῶν
> ἔγρετο, τὸν δ' ὕπνῳ πουλὺς ἔριψε κόπος.

Tr Paton (LCL) III 73 "A man in a lethargy and a maniac lying in one bed ridded each other of their respective maladies. For the one, made daring by his madness, leapt from the bed and belaboured the insensible man all over. The blows cured both, waking up the one, and his great exertion throwing the other into a sleep."

C's immediate source for the Greek was probably Lessing, who quotes and translates the epigram in his essay *Zerstreute Anmerkungen über das Epigramm* in *Sämmtliche Schriften* I 119–20. Lessing deprecates the epigram for its inconclusiveness, a trait C turns to political advantage with his moral. The LCL text and translation do not differ from Lessing's in essentials. In view of C's interest in epigrams, it is worth noting that the now standard version of the *Greek Anthology*, derived from the Palatine ms (with poems found only in the Planudean ms as an appendix or as bk 16), was not published until 1813–15. In the earlier "Planudean" anthology (the standard edition until the 19th century) the reference for this poem (as given by Lessing) is 1.45. In the first printed edition of the "Palatine" anthology, in Brunck's *Analecta Poetarum Graecorum* (3 vols Strasburg 1772–6), it appears (vol III p 238) as No 411 of the anonymous poems, again in a form which does not essentially vary from the text given above; Brunck's edition is rearranged by author rather than by subject or class (the norm in other editions). In 1808 (*CN* III 3276 f 72ᵛ) C took Brunck as the standard, with which he proposed to compare J. de Bosch's edition of the Planudean anthology, of which three volumes had so far been published (1795–8).

In good King OLIM's reign, I've read,
There lay two Patients in one bed.
    The first, in fat, lethargic trance,
Was wan, and motionless as lead:
    The other, like the folks in France,   5
Possess'd a diff'rent disposition;
    In short, the plain truth to confess,
The man was madder than MAD BESS!
Yet, so it chanc'd by Heaven's permission,
Each prov'd the other's best physician.   10

Fighting with a ghastly stare,
Troops of despots in the air,
    Obstreperously jacobinical,
The madman froth'd and foam'd and roar'd;

1. King OLIM] The personification of the Latin adverb *olim* "once upon a time", commonly found at the beginning of narratives, would have been understood by all English readers with a rudimentary knowledge of Latin. The Germans had been using the word as a proper name ("in Olim's time" etc) since the 17th century, and C would have met with it in Bürger—in a passage he annotated (*CM—CC—*

I 829)—and Schiller, and no doubt in conversation. He mentioned King Olim again in an early draft of **640** *Romance* and in a notebook entry of 1825 (*CN* IV 5232 f 39ʳ), linking him there with Jack the Giant-killer to illustrate the tendency of nations to exaggerate the antiquity of their origins.

8. MAD BESS] I.e. a Bess o'Bedlam.

His neighbour snoring octaves cynical,   15
Like good John Bull in posture clinical,
Seem'd living only while he snor'd.

The Jacobin, enrag'd to see
This fat insensibility,
Or tir'd with solitary labour,   20
Determin'd to convert his neighbour.
So up he sprung, and to't he fell,
Like Devil piping hot from Hell,
With indefatigable fist,
Belabouring the poor Lethargist;   25
Till his own limbs were stiff and sore,
And sweat-drops ran from ev'ry pore.
Yet still, with "flying fingers sweet,"
Duly accompanied by feet,
    With some short interludes of biting,   30
He executes the self-same strain.
Till the slumb'rer woke for pain,
    And fiercely girds himself for fighting,
That moment that his mad colleague
Sunk fast asleep thro' pure fatigue.   35

THE MORAL.

The Allies and the French * * *
Ye Fable-mongers in verse or prose;
By all your hopes of Cash or Laurel,
Save, O save us from the Moral.

28. "flying fingers sweet,"] The phrase "flying fingers" (in the note-book, "'flying fingers' fleet—") is probably quoted from Collins *The Passions* 89, but it also appears in Dryden and in Rowe.

235. EPIGRAM TO A CRITIC, WHO EXTRACTED A PASSAGE FROM A POEM

[May–Sept 1799]

C copied out the lines in a notebook (*CN* I 625 f 124^r), as part of a sequence of more than thirty such epigrams, mostly adapted from the German. They were published anonymously in *M Post* (16 Dec 1801), the version given here, where the title continues: "WITHOUT ADDING A WORD RESPECTING THE CONTEXT, AND THEN DERIDED IT AS UNINTELLIGIBLE." The poem was republished over C's name in *The Keepsake for 1829*, but he never collected it. The context in the notebook suggests that they might have a German source, but this has not been traced. However, the previous lines in the notebook make up a version of a poem composed some time before most of the surrounding poems (**193** *On an Infant Who Died before its Christening*), and the present one might likewise be a recollection, in this case from another source.

C wrote another version of the lines, in not quite metrical rhyming prose, in a marginal note on RS's *Life of Wesley* (2 vols 1820), now at NYPL (Berg Collection); cf *IS* (1979) 197. For another criticism of critics see **521** *Contemporary Critics*.

> Most candid Critic!—what if I,
> By way of joke, pull out your eye,
> And, holding up the fragment, cry,
> Ha! ha! that men such fools should be!
> Behold this shapeless Dab! and he,   5
> Who own'd it, fancied it could *see!*—
> The joke were mighty analytic;
> But should you like it, candid Critic?

236. NAMES, FROM LESSING

[May–Aug 1799]

C copied out the lines in his notebook (*CN* I 625 f 124^v) while he was in Germany, or very soon after his return, in 1799. They adapt Lessing's *Die Namen*, in *Sämmtliche Schriften* I 309:

Ich fragte meine Schöne:
Wie soll mein Lied dich nennen?
Soll Dich als Dorimene,
Als Galathee, als Chloris,
Als Lesbia, als Doris,
Die Welt der Enkel kennen?
Ach! Namen sind nur Töne:
Sprach meine holde Schöne.
Wähl' selbst. Du kannst mich Doris,
Und Galathee und Chloris,
Und—wie du willst mich nennen;
Nur nenne mich die Deine.

C's poem was published anonymously in *M Post* and *Courier*, and pseudonymously in *The Poetical Register for 1803*. SH also transcribed it in her album *SH's Poets*. The lines were first published over C's name in *The Keepsake for 1829*, and first collected in *PW* (1834).

The several ms and printed versions differ from each other, as if C took literally the protest the poem makes, that any name would serve if it fitted the line. The version given here is from *M Post* (27 Aug 1799), although the title derives from *PW* (1834).

I ask'd my fair, one happy day,
What I should call her in my lay;
By what sweet name from Rome or Greece,
Iphigenia, Clelia, Chloris,
Laura, Lesbia, or Doris,   5
Dorimene, or Lucrece.

Ah! replied my gentle fair,
Beloved, what are names but air?
Take thou whatever suits the line,
Call me Clelia, call me Chloris,   10
Laura, Lesbia, or Doris—
Only, only, call me thine.

237. EPIGRAM: ALWAYS AUDIBLE, FROM KÄSTNER

[May–Sept 1799]

C copied out the lines in a notebook (*CN* I 625 f 124ᵛ), as part of a sequence of more than thirty such epigrams, mostly adapted from the German, and the poem was published in *M Post* (19 Dec 1801), the version given here. It was not republished or otherwise circulated or collected during C's lifetime. The poem derives from an epigram by Abraham Gotthelf Kästner, *Zweimal eilf Uhr* (dated 1761), in *Vermischte Schriften* II 483:

> Um eilf Uhr in der Nacht, könnt ihr zum Damon gehn;
> Und er wird euch, bey ihm zu bleiben flehn:
> Um eilf Uhr Vormittag, dürft ihr soviel nicht wagen,
> Ihr möchtet ihn sonst aus dem Bette jagen.

> Pass under J A C K 's window at twelve at night,
> You'll hear him still: he's roaring!
> Pass under J A C K 's window at twelve at noon,
> You'll hear him still—he's snoring!

238. OVER THE DOOR OF A COTTAGE, AFTER LOGAU

[May–Sept 1799]

C copied out the lines in a notebook (*CN* I 625 f 125ʳ), as part of a sequence of more than thirty such epigrams, mostly adapted from the German. He made a fair copy, perhaps as late as 1827, which the present text reproduces, but he appears never to have published the lines. EHC (*PW*—EHC—II 997 No 3) suggests that C's source is Lessing's *Sinngedichte* No 104 *Auf die Hütte des Irus*. Much more likely is Logau's *Die beste Arzeney*, in *Sinngedichte* ed Ramler and Lessing 2.42 p 46; also in *Blumenlese deutscher Sinngedichte* ed Joerdens 95:

> Freude, Mäßigkeit und Ruh
> Schleußt dem Artz die Thüre zu.

The Pleasures sport beneath this Thatch,
But Prudence sits upon the watch,
Nor Dun nor Doctor lifts the Latch.

239. THE DEVIL OUTWITTED
OR, JOB'S LUCK,
AFTER LOGAU AND JOHN OWEN

[May–Sept 1799]

C copied out the lines in a notebook (*CN* I 625 f 125ʳ), as part of a sequence of more than thirty such epigrams, mostly adapted from the German, and the poem was published in *M Post* (26 Sept 1801), the version given here. It was printed again in poetical albums in 1827 and 1829, and circulated in ms, before being collected in *PW* (1834).

The first stanza is adapted from Friedrich von Logau's *Hiob's Weib*, in *Sinngedichte* ed Ramler and Lessing 3.90 p 89:

> Als der Satan gieng von Hiob, ist sein Anwald dennoch blieben,
> Hiobs Weib; er hätte nimmer einen bessern aufgetrieben.

The second stanza is adapted from the same author's *Auf den Hornutus*, in *Sinngedichte* 1.68 p 25:

> Hornutus las, was Gott Job habe weggenommen,
> Sey doppelt ihm hernach zu Hause wiederkommen:
> Wie gut, sprach er, war dieß, daß Gott sein Weib nicht nahm,
> Auf daß Job ihrer zwey für eine nicht bekam!

The original of C's and Logau's lines is an epigram by John Owen, *Epigrammatum Libri Tres* 3.199 p 86, which C might have came across in his reading for the projected **50.X1** *Imitations from the Modern Latin Poets*:

> Miseria Iob.
>
> Diuitias Iobo, sobolemque, ipsamque salutem
> Abstulit, hoc Domino non prohibente, Satan.
> Omnibus ablatis, misero tamen una superstes,
> Quæ magis afflictum redderet, uxor erat.

There are several imitations of this in French, three of which are given in *Épigrammes choisies d'Owen* ed N. Le Déist de Kerivalant (Lyons 1819). An English version, signed "S. W. I.", appeared in *The Poetical Register for 1806–*

1807 VI (1807) 97; and another English version, anonymously, claiming to be a translation from Wernicke, in *The London Magazine* IX (Mar 1824) 239.

Sly Beelzebub took all occasions
To try JOB's constancy and patience.
He took his children, took his health,
He took his honour, took his wealth,
His servants, horses, oxen, cows—   5
And the *sly* Devil did *not* take his spouse!

But Heav'n, that brings out good from evil,
And loves to disappoint the Devil,
Had predetermin'd to restore
Twofold all, JOB had before,   10
His servants, horses, oxen, cows—
Short-sighted Devil *not* to take his spouse.

240. EPIGRAM ON THE SPEED WITH WHICH JACK WRITES VERSES, AFTER VON HALEM

[May–Sept 1799]

C copied out the lines in a notebook (*CN* I 625 f 125ʳ), as part of a sequence of more than thirty such epigrams, mostly adapted from the German. They were published in *M Post* (23 Sept 1799), the version given here, and in RS's *Annual Anthology* II (1800), but never collected by C. They probably derive from an epigram on the Leipzig publisher Weigand by G. A. von Halem, *Hinz und Kunz*, in *Blumenlese deutscher Sinngedichte* ed Joerdens 426:

Hinz.

Sieh! alle die gedruckten Sachen
Hat Fix gemacht; das ist ein Mann!

Kunz.

Noch mehr! er soll sie schneller machen,
Als Weigand sie verkaufen kann.

In a letter to Samuel Rogers in 1813 (*WL—M* rev—II 70) WW applied the lines to Walter Scott.

Jem writes his verses with more speed
Than the Printer's boy can set 'em.
Quite as fast as we can read,
But not so fast as we forget 'em.

241. EPIGRAM ON A BAD SINGER, AFTER PFEFFEL AND MARTIAL

[May–Sept 1799]

C copied out the lines in a notebook (*CN* I 625 f 125ᵛ), as part of a sequence of more than thirty such epigrams, mostly adapted from the German. They were published in RS's *Annual Anthology* II (1800), the version given here, and F. R. Reynolds's *The Keepsake for 1829*, before being collected in *PW* (1834). They perhaps derive from G. K. Pfeffel's *Apoll und sein Schwan*, in *Poetische Versuche* (3 vols Basle 1789–90) III 36:

> Vor seinem Tode sang der Schwan
> Sein erstes Lied und auch das letzte.
> Apoll, den das Gekreisch ergötzte,
> Nahm ihn zu seinem Vogel an:
> "So sollten es, rief er mit Lachen,
> Die Poetaster alle machen."

Or they might derive from another German source, ultimately dependent on Martial's epigram (13.77) on the dying swan:

> Dulcia defecta modulatur carmina lingua
> Cantator cygnus funeris ipse sui.

Tr W.C.A. Ker (2nd ed 2 vols LCL 1968) II 419 "The swan gives forth its sweet measured song with failing tongue, itself the minstrel of its own death."

Swans sing before they die—'twere no bad thing
Should certain persons die before they sing.

2. 'em] Not simply the letter "m" but, in printing, a unit of measure, traditionally the horizontal space occupied by the letter "M". The version remembered by WW has "'en", which suggests an alternative typographic measure (2 ens = 1 em).

242. EPIGRAM ON A JOKE
WITHOUT A STING

[May–Sept 1799]

C copied out the lines in a notebook (*CN* I 625 f 125ᵛ), as part of a sequence
of more than thirty such epigrams, mostly adapted from the German, and they
were published in RS's *Annual Anthology* II (1800), the version given here.
There are two late transcripts in other hands, but the lines were never published
by C over his own name or collected by him. They might have evolved out of
the epigram preceding them in the notebook and the *Annual Anthology* printing
(**241** *Epigram on a Bad Singer*), or they might derive from an untraced German
original.

A joke (cries Jack) without a sting—
Post obitum can no man sing.
And true, if Jack don't mend his manners,
And quit the atheistic banners,
Post obitum will Jack run foul   5
Of such *Folks* as can only *howl*.

243. TO A LIVING NINON D'ENCLOS

[May–Sept 1799]

C copied out the lines in a notebook (*CN* I 625 f 125ᵛ), as part of a sequence of
more than thirty such epigrams, mostly adapted from the German. He bracketed
the first six lines, drew a line underneath, and wrote: "Something more humor-
ous I instead of this.—" He appears never to have published the lines or given
copies. They probably derive from a German source which has not been traced.

Anne Lenclos, who called herself Ninon de L'Enclos (c 1620–c 1705), was
a famous French courtesan, whose active career spanned a particularly long
period.

2, 5. *Post obitum*] "After death".

Thy Charms, O Nina, are not flown,
And mine was ne'er a heart of stone.
I pay'd my suit, it is most true,
And saw with Joy that you preferr'd me—
And that I did not marry you—   5
Indeed, twas not *your* years deterr'd me!—
But your Son, that grey-hair'd Prig—
O wherefore wore he not a wig?

244. EPIGRAM ON A MAIDEN MORE SENTIMENTAL THAN CHASTE

[May–Sept 1799]

C copied out the lines in a notebook (*CN* I 625 f 126ʳ), as part of a sequence of more than thirty such epigrams, mostly adapted from the German. They were published along with another of his poems in *M Post* (9 Dec 1799), the version given here, over the pseudonym "LABERIUS." (see **162** *Parliamentary Oscillators* headnote), but C never republished or collected them. Woodring 229 suggests that C might have assumed the pseudonym "out of bitterness toward the satiric depths he had fallen to" (Latin *labi* "to fall").

"Tho' forc'd to part from my sweet WILL,
   "From my sweet true love forc'd to part,
"Thank Heav'n! I *bear* his *image* still—
   "'Tis in my *heart!*

These words, in tender tones, said NANCY,   5
   And NANCY best the *truth* must know;
Else I confess that I should fancy,
   It were an inch or two *below*.

245. THE EXCHANGE OF HEARTS

[May–Sept 1799?]

C copied out the lines, under the title "Timorous Love", in a notebook (*CN* I 625 f 126ʳ), towards the end of a sequence of more than thirty such epigrams, mostly adapted from the German. There are many English analogues, e.g. Craddock's lines [=Joseph Cradock (1742–1846)?] which were set as a medal-winning glee for five voices by S. Webbe in 1776:

> You gave me your heart t'other day,
>   I thought it as safe as my own;
> I've not lost it,—but, what can I say?
>   Not your heart from mine can be known!
>   (*The Words of the Most Favourite*
>   *Pieces, Performed at the Glee Club,*
>   *the Catch Club, and Other Public So-*
>   *cieties* comp Richard Clark—1814—
>   389)

The lines were published in *Courier* (16 Apr 1804), the version given here, over C's initials, in *The Literary Souvenir* (1826), over his name, and elsewhere, but they were not collected during his lifetime. Whether they derive from another author has not been established. They might even comprise a fragment of another narrative: for example, allowing the substitution of "father" for "mother" in line 5, they might have been left over from **155** *Continuation of "The Three Graves"*. In the notebook they form a second set of verses numbered "30", and, if they are understood as a recasting of the first set (**244** *On a Maiden More Sentimental than Chaste*), the exchange has an added dimension (the lover made his maiden pregnant).

> We pledg'd our hearts, my Love and I,
>   Me in her arms the Maiden clasping;
> I could not guess the reason why,
>   But oh! I trembled like an aspen!
>
> Her father's leave she bade me gain;   5
>   I went, but shook like any reed!
> I strove to act the man—in vain!
>   We had exchang'd our hearts indeed.

4. Cf **146.X1** *Osorio* II ii 97EC.

246. EPIGRAM ON A SUPPOSED SON

[May–Sept 1799; Jan–Feb 1800]

C copied out the lines in a notebook (*CN* I 625 f 126ᵛ), towards the end of a sequence of more than thirty such epigrams, mostly adapted from the German. They were published in *M Post* (5 Feb 1800) over the signature "J. P.", the version given here. The lines were not circulated or reprinted during C's lifetime.

If KC is correct in her assessment that the complete notebook entry was written at one time, the present lines might well derive from a German original which has not been traced. A sodden autumn in 1799 was followed by an icy winter, which led to a number of emergency measures to conserve corn, including different standards for wheaten bread (see John Ehrman *The Younger Pitt: The Consuming Struggle* (1996) 277–93). Eventually, following a second failure of the harvest in 1800, the unpopular so-called Brown Bread Act was passed. If the lines have to do with this, Billy ("Brown") Pitt is like his father, who, as the recently created Lord Chatham, faced similar grain shortages in 1766; and the reason for the signature "J. P." is that Justices of the Peace had responsibility, which some of them deplored, for enforcing the standards for bread.

> Billy Brown, how like his Father!
> Mr. Brown, indeed, says No.
> Mrs. Brown too, who knows better,
> Says the same—*but thinks not so!*

247. PONDERE, NON NUMERO, FROM LOGAU

[May–Sept 1799 or later]

C copied out the lines in a notebook (*CN* I 625 f 127ʳ), at the end of a sequence of more than thirty such epigrams, mostly adapted from the German. They were published anonymously in *M Post* (26 Dec 1801), the version given here. Although there are fair copies in C's hand dating from 1810 and 1830, the poem was not published over his name or collected during his lifetime.

C copied the German original on to an earlier page of his notebook (Notebook 3½ f 52ᵛ = *CN* I 432), where it is the twenty-first of a sequence of thirty such pieces in English and German:

Freunde muß man sich erwählen
Nur nach wägen, nicht nach zählen.

See Friedrich von Logau *Sinngedichte: Zwölf Bücher, mit Anmerkungen über die Sprache des Dichters* ed Ramler and Lessing 2.65 p 53; also in *Blumenlese deutscher Sinngedichte* ed Joerdens 79.

Friends should be *weigh'd*, not *told:* who boasts to have won
A *multitude* of Friends, has ne'er had *one*.

248. LINES COMPOSED IN
A CONCERT-ROOM

[Sept 1799?]

The first known version of the poem appeared anonymously in *M Post* (24 Sept 1799). A revised version was included in *SL* (1817), which was afterwards reprinted in *PW* (1828, 1829, 1834). The poem is an odd mixture of personal and literary references. Thus, the Harlot, Priest, Captain, and Lady recall Della-Cruscan circles of the early 1790s, and "our old Musician", Edmund, and Anne interpret C's own background in literary terms. Many features of the poem— its manner and attitude—suggest that its elements might date from some time before it was first published. It appears to unite fragments from several backgrounds, which C might have found at Stowey or Ottery after his return from Germany.

Specific references are obscured, it would seem, because of the way in which earlier meanings are differently applied in the new, altered context. For example, in a letter of 5 Jul 1796 (*LL*—M—I 42) CL appears to identify "the proud Harlot" of line 3 with Mrs Gertrude Elizabeth Mara (1749–1833), the great German singer who sang at DL between 1790 and 1802 (see James Broaden *Memoirs of the Life of John Philip Kemble*—2 vols 1825—II 52, 64–5). A later reference by C to Madame Mara is, by contrast, conspicuously respectful (*CL* I 635: to W. Godwin 13 Oct 1800).

Again, when the poem was published in *M Post*, it continued for a further eighteen lines, as follows:

> Dear Maid! whose form in solitude I seek,
>   Such songs in such a mood to hear thee sing,
>   It were a deep delight!—But thou shalt fling
> Thy white arm round my neck, and kiss my cheek,
> And love the brightness of my gladder eye,

The while I tell thee what a holier joy
It were, in proud and stately step to go,
  With trump and timbrel clang, and popular shout,
  To celebrate the shame and absolute rout
Unhealable of Freedom's latest foe,
  Whose tower'd might shall to its centre nod.
When human feelings, sudden, deep and vast,
As all good spirits of all ages past,
  Were armied in the hearts of living men,
Shall purge the earth, and violently sweep
These vile and painted locusts to the deep,
  Leaving un ———— undebas'd,
  A ——— world, made worthy of its God.

Readers of the poem in *M Post* would have taken "Freedom's latest foe" to be France, and the "absolute rout" to be Suvorov's victory over Joubert at Novi on 15 Aug 1799—even though C's private attitude towards Suvorov and the Russians seems to have been different (*CL* I 529: to TP 16 Sept 1799; 539: to RS 15 Oct 1799; see Woodring 239–40). The invocation of the Maid, and properties like the timbrel and "popular shout", are none the less confusing, and they suggest that the lines might originally have been written about the fall of quite opposite forces of "tower'd might", like the Bastille.

The supposition that the *M Post* version was cobbled together *ad hoc* may explain why it is not entirely regular in its rhyming. C told RS in Dec 1799 that he meant to improve the metre (*CL* I 550), but he included the poem in his later collections with few changes beyond omitting the concluding eighteen lines. The version given here is from *SL*.

Nor cold, nor stern, my soul! yet I detest
  These scented Rooms, where, to a gaudy throng,
Heaves the proud Harlot her distended breast,
  In intricacies of laborious song.

These feel not Music's genuine power, nor deign   5
  To melt at Nature's passion-warbled plaint;
But when the long-breath'd singer's uptrill'd strain
  Bursts in a squall—they gape for wonderment.

Hark! the deep buzz of Vanity and Hate!
  Scornful, yet envious, with self-torturing sneer   10
My lady eyes some maid of humbler state,
  While the pert Captain, or the primmer Priest,
  Prattles accordant scandal in her ear.

O give me, from this heartless scene releas'd,
  To hear our old musician, blind and grey,   15
(Whom stretching from my nurse's arms I kist,)
  His Scottish tunes and warlike marches play,
By moonshine, on the balmy summer-night,
  The while I dance amid the tedded hay
With merry maids, whose ringlets toss in light.   20

Or lies the purple evening on the bay
  Of the calm glossy lake, O let me hide
    Unheard, unseen, behind the alder-trees
Around whose roots the fisher's boat is tied,
  On whose trim seat doth Edmund stretch at ease,   25
And while the lazy boat sways to and fro,
  Breathes in his flute sad airs, so wild and slow,
That his own cheek is wet with quiet tears.

But O, dear Anne! when midnight wind careers,
  And the gust pelting on the out-house shed   30
    Makes the cock shrilly in the rain-storm crow,
    To hear thee sing some ballad full of woe,
Ballad of ship-wreck'd sailor floating dead,
  Whom his own true-love buried in the sands!
Thee, gentle woman, for thy voice remeasures   35
Whatever tones and melancholy pleasures
  The Things of Nature utter; birds or trees
Or moan of ocean-gale in weedy caves,
Or where the stiff grass mid the heath-plant waves,
Murmur and music thin of sudden breeze.   40

249. HEXAMETRICAL TRANSLATION
OF PSALM 46

[Sept 1799]

C copied out his version in a letter to GC of 29 Sept 1799 (*CL* I 532), introduc-
ing them with a report of a conversation with RS:

We were talking of Hexameters while with you. I will for want of some-

thing better fill up the paper with a translation of one of my favourite
Psalms into that metre, which allowing trochees for Spondees as the nature
of our Language demands, you will find pretty accurate in Scansion.

The reference is to Psalm 46 (in eleven verses in the AV), and C provides a
metrical analysis of lines 1–2 and 6 as follows:

> Gōd ĭs ŏur Strēngth ănd ŏur Rēfŭge: thērefŏre wĭll wĕ nŏt trēmblĕ,
> Thō' thĕ Ēarth bĕ rĕmōvĕd, ănd thō' thĕ pĕrpētŭăl Mōuntăıns

and

> Thē Īdōlătĕrs rāgĕd, the Kingdoms were moving in fury—

On the present occasion C finds that only occasional phrases from the AV will
fit the metre, but in his lecture of 24 Nov 1811 (*Lects 1808–1819—CC—*I 223)
he is reported to have demonstrated the frequency of dactylic hexameters in the
AV translation of the Psalms. In *Lesson in English Prosody* (*SW&F—CC—*
201–6 at 202) and in marginalia on Esaias Tegnér *Die Frithiofs-Sage* (Stuttgart
& Tübingen 1826) +1–+3 in BM C 126 b 10 (*CM—CC—*v), he quoted the same
altered version of Ps 47.5. He quoted his version of Ps 46.4 as an instance of "a
fine *Hexameter*" when he annotated Lacunza's *The Coming of the Messiah* in
1827 (*CM—CC—*III 479). Cf also **256** *Hexametrical Version of Isaiah.*

God is our Strength and our Refuge: therefore will we not tremble,
Tho' the Earth be removed, and tho' the perpetual Mountains
Sink in the Swell of the Ocean! God is our Strength & our Refuge.
There is a River, the Flowing whereof shall gladden the City,
Hallelujah! the City of God! Jehova shall help her.   5

The Idolaters raged, the Kingdoms were moving in fury—
But He utter'd his Voice: Earth melted away from beneath them.
Halleluja! th' Eternal is with us, Almighty Jehova!

Fearful the works of the Lord, yea, fearful his Desolations—
But *He* maketh the Battle to cease, he burneth the Spear & the Chariot.   10
Halleluja! th' Eternal is with us, the God of our Fathers!—

250. EPIGRAM ON SIR RUBICUND NASO

[Sept 1799]

C sent the epigram to RS on 30 Sept 1799 (*CL* I 536), and it was published anonymously in *M Post* (7 Dec), the version given here. It was never acknowledged by C or collected by him. In a subsequent letter to RS of 24 Dec 1799 (*CL* I 552) C made it clear that the poem describes Sir John William Anderson (c 1736–1813), MP for London, Lord Mayor in 1797–8, and alderman, sycophant, alarmist, and supporter of Pitt. The joke about red-nosed Pittites was endemic in Opposition circles, and served to counter ministerial satires on the famous glow of Sheridan's drunken nose (see *CL* I 110: to RS [26 Sept 1794]; **11** *The Nose: An Odaic Rhapsody*, on William Gill; Woodring 232–3). The condition of talk *sub rosa*—"in confidence", but here involving bribery by George Rose, Secretary to the Treasury—turns the epigram into a kind of bull: "Whenever you talk indiscreetly, you're safe because you're on the ministry payroll."

The suggestion that C is indebted to a particular source in Lessing (*PW*— EHC—II 958 No 23) is altogether misleading.

Speak out, Sir! you're safe! for so ruddy your nose,
That talk where you will, 'tis all *under the Rose*.

251. TO DELIA

[Oct–Nov 1799?]

The poem is something of a mystery. It exists in a single ms thought to be in C's hand, and is addressed "To Mr Humphry —— I from the Author—". However, the paper is of a sort rarely used by C, indeed perhaps without parallel, and the identification of the hand is uncertain.

Mr Humphry is unknown to fame, which is odd in view of the many sources of information available to throw light on C's acquaintance. In the absence of other explanations, it is possible that the dash following the name—which is written more like a diagonal—might stand for Davy. If it does, the poem is likely to have been given to him in the early days of his friendship with C, which began in Bristol or Upcott in Oct 1799 (Cottle *E Rec* II 46, *Rem* 274; *CL* I 539: to RS 15 Oct 1799; Lawrence Hanson *The Life of S. T. Coleridge: The Early Years*—1938—361) and which continued in London through the following months. The phrase "from the Author—" is less usual for C than a signature or initials, and may be another indication of a new acquaintanceship. Alternatively, the unusual acknowledgment of authorship may point to the poem being a pastiche. It is clearly a plausible essay in a poetic kind, but it does not communicate how seriously it should be taken. Several writers in C's own day addressed sonnets and elegies to Delia—among poets known to C, William Cowper, John Bampfylde, Rev John Swete, Thomas Russell, Lucy Aikin (Mrs Barbauld), and RS, whose "Abel Shufflebottom" parodies of Della-Cruscanism were written at Westbury in 1799. If C wrote the poem, it might have some connection with Davy or RS, and might have been written impromptu for a specific occasion now beyond recovery; or it might resemble **248** *Lines Composed in a Concert-room*, in having been found among old papers at this time.

> O Thou whose love-inspiring Air
>   Delights, yet gives a thousand Woes—
> My Day declines in dark Despair,
>   And Night hath lost her sweet Repose.
>
> Yet who alas! like me was blest,   5
>   To others e'er thy Charms were known,
> When Fancy told my raptur'd Breast
>   That Delia smil'd on *me* alone?
>
> Nymph of my Soul, forgive my Sighs:
>   Forgive the jealous Fires I feel;   10
> Nor blame the trembling Wretch who dies
>   When Others to thy Beauties kneel—
>
> Lo! theirs is ev'ry pleasing Art,
>   With Fortune's Gifts unknown to Mc:
> I only boast a simple Heart   15
>   In love with INNOCENCE & THEE.

252. COUPLET ON GROSVENOR BEDFORD

[Dec 1799]

The couplet represents a very doubtful attribution. C copied it into the Gutch Notebook under the heading "Gros Bedford" (*CN* I 252). Grosvenor Bedford (1773–1839) was a lifelong friend of RS. They were at Westminster School together, and from 1792 to 1803 Bedford was a clerk in the Exchequer Office. He had contributed a parody, *The Rhedycinian Barbers*, to the *Monthly Magazine* III (May 1797), which was reprinted by RS in *Annual Anthology* I (1799); and he printed privately a translation of Musaeus' *Hero and Leander*, also in 1797.

The application of the lines to Grosvenor Bedford refers to his failure to marry (despite the frequent urging of RS), and obliquely to his character: he was genial and sociable, but apparently inefficient and dilatory. See *SL* (Curry) II 481–2. However, it is quite possible that C is applying to Grosvenor Bedford lines he had found elsewhere applied to a duke of Bedford: Francis Russell, fifth duke (b 1765), was interested in crossing breeds of cattle and was to die unmarried in 1802 (*DNB*). Some play on the duke's parallel situation is doubtless involved, even if C wrote the lines himself.

By crossing despair of improving this Breed,
And wearied to Bedfordshire hasten indeed.

253. LOVE

[Nov–Dec 1799]

The poem was inspired by C's first visit to Sockburn in Oct–Nov 1799, when he met and fell in love with SH. Feelings roused at Sockburn were shaped by fantasy and projected against a Stowey background, though the feeling and the sense of background are of a kind which have misled many readers. Genevieve is a figure of wish-fulfilment, as in the Christ's Hospital sonnet of that name (poem **17**), whatever innocent trifles passed between C and SH in 1799 (see *CN* I 578, 1575). Although there is a recumbent statue of an armed knight (of the Conyers family) at Sockburn, as well as a famous "Grey Stone" nearby, the ruined tower midway on a mount, with a statue of a figure alongside ("tall" and "rudely carved" in the ms), more obviously pictures the folly and statue halfway up the hill at Cothelstone Park, in the part called Tilbury on the flank of Bagborough Hill, near Stowey.

A brief description and an illustration of the Bagborough tower and statue (which, it should be added, are some 300 yards apart) are given by Barbara Jones *Follies and Grottoes* (2nd enlarged ed 1974) 383. Edward Blore's drawing of the effigy in Sockburn Church, which has undoubtedly affected C's presentation of the Bagborough statue, is in BM Add MS 42014 f 11ʳ.

Other earlier experiences, in Germany as well as in the Quantocks, are incorporated. Compare *CL* I 499: to Mrs C 17 May 1799 with lines 9–10, *CN* I 230 and *CL* I 504: to Mrs C 17 May [1799] with the cancelled stanza between lines

44 and 45, etc. For evidence of how the central imagined experience recurred in C's mind see **347** *Phantom* 4–5. WW's objection is worth recording: he told Tom Moore that "there was too much of the sensual in it" (*Journal of Thomas Moore* ed Dowden IV 1661, under 20 Feb 1835).

C drafted the poem as an "Introduction to the Tale of the Dark Ladie" (poem **182**), on which he had been working since Stowey days, and which had failed, like *Christabel*, to move forward. The present poem was published with this title ("Introduction . . .") in *M Post* (21 Dec 1799). It is introductory in the sense that it celebrates energy of the kind needed to complete the *Dark Ladiè*—i.e. a sense of emotional renewal for C himself—but otherwise its relation is oblique. C pruned the opening and closing stanzas and made a few other revisions when he included it as an independent poem, re-entitled *Love*, to replace WW's *The Convict* in *LB* (1800). The revised form was included in *SL* (1817) and later collections with only minor changes. The version reproduced here is that of *SL*, taking in C's own erratum.

The originally drafted "Introduction to the Tale of the Dark Ladie" and the later, pruned version, *Love*, were popular from the first, and were frequently reprinted in newspapers and anthologies in C's lifetime. Walter Scott told the actress Sarah Smith, "The verses on Love . . . are among the most beautiful in the English language" (*Scott L* III 400); and John Gibson Lockhart described the poem as "better known than any of its author's productions . . . many hundreds of our readers have got it by heart long ago, without knowing by whom it was written" (*Bl Mag* VI (31)—Oct 1819—12; repeated in similar terms ibid XI (65)—Jun 1822—670; cf also [J. G. Lockhart] *Peter's Letters to his Kinsfolk*—"2nd ed" 3 vols Edinburgh 1819—II 220–1). The artist George Dawe exhibited a large picture based on *Love* at the Royal Academy in 1812, which he entitled *Genevieve* (exhibit 220). This has led to both versions on occasion being described as "Genevieve"—a title never employed by C. C placed it first among the "Love Poems" section in his later collections, and told Allsop (probably c 1820): "The 'Ancient Mariner' cannot be imitated, nor the poem, 'Love'. *They may be excelled; they are not imitable*" (Allsop I 95).

The following stanzas appeared in the earlier form of the poem, when it was an "Introduction to the Tale of the Dark Ladie", in *M Post* (21 Dec 1799):

⁻1   O leave the Lilly on its stem;
        O leave the Rose upon the spray;
        O leave the Elder-bloom, fair Maids!
        And listen to my lay.

        A Cypress and a Myrtle bough,
        This morn around my harp you twin'd,
        Because it fashion'd mournfully
        Its murmurs in the wind.

        And now a Tale of Love and Woe,
        A woeful Tale of Love I sing:

Hark, gentle Maidens, hark! it sighs
And trembles on the string.

But most, my own dear Genevieve!
It sighs and trembles most for thee!
O come and hear what cruel wrongs
Befel the Dark Ladie.

Few sorrows hath she of her own,[1]
My hope, my joy, my Genevieve!
She loves me best whene'er I sing
The songs that make her grieve.

44[+]   And how he cross'd the Woodman's paths,
Thro' briars and swampy messes beat;
How boughs rebounding scourg'd his limbs,
And low stubs gor'd his feet;

80[+]   I saw her bosom heave and swell,
Heave and swell with inward sighs—
I could not choose but love to see
Her gentle bosom rise.

96[+]   And now once more a tale of woe,
A woeful tale of love I sing:
For thee, my Genevieve! it sighs,
And trembles on the string.

When last I sang the cruel scorn
That craz'd this bold and lonely Knight,
And how he roam'd the mountain woods,
Nor rested day or night;

I promis'd thee a sister tale
Of Man's perfid'ous cruelty:
Come, then, and hear what cruel wrong
Befel the Dark Ladie.

End of the Introduction.

All thoughts, all passions, all delights,
Whatever stirs this mortal frame,
All are but ministers of Love,
And feed his sacred flame.

---

[1] This stanza became the fifth in the   below.
later version of the poem, lines 17–20

Oft in my waking dreams do I   5
Live o'er again that happy hour,
When midway on the mount I lay,
    Beside the ruin'd tower.

The Moonshine, stealing o'er the scene,
Had blended with the lights of eve;   10
And she was there, my hope, my joy,
    My own dear Genevieve!

She leant against the armed man,
The statue of the armed knight;
She stood and listen'd to my lay,   15
    Amid the lingering light.

Few sorrows hath she of her own,
My hope! my joy! my Genevieve!
She loves me best, whene'er I sing
    The songs that make her grieve.   20

I play'd a soft and doleful air,
I sang an old and moving story—
An old rude song, that suited well
    That ruin wild and hoary.

She listen'd with a flitting blush,   25
With downcast eyes and modest grace;
For well she knew, I could not chuse
    But gaze upon her face.

I told her of the Knight that wore
Upon his shield a burning brand;   30
And that for ten long years he woo'd
    The Lady of the Land.

I told her how he pined; and ah!
The deep, the low, the pleading tone
With which I sang another's love,   35
    Interpreted my own.

She listen'd with a flitting blush,
With downcast eyes, and modest grace;
And she forgave me, that I gazed
   Too fondly on her face!   40

But when I told the cruel scorn
That craz'd that bold and lovely Knight,
And that he cross'd the mountain-woods,
   Nor rested day nor night;

That sometimes from the savage den,   45
And sometimes from the darksome shade,
And sometimes starting up at once
   In green and sunny glade,

There came and look'd him in the face
An angel beautiful and bright;   50
And that he knew it was a Fiend,
   This miserable Knight!

And that unknowing what he did,
He leap'd amid a murderous band,
And sav'd from outrage worse than death   55
   The Lady of the Land!

And how she wept, and claspt his knees;
And how she tended him in vain—
And ever strove to expiate
   The scorn that crazed his brain.   60

And that she nursed him in a cave;
And how his madness went away,

41, 60. scorn] The same word re-
curs significantly in **146.X1** *Osorio*,
WW's *The Borderers* and *Lines Left
upon a Seat in a Yew-tree*, and many
other poems by both authors. It sug-
gests that the knight's peculiar af-
fliction here is intellectual pride or
alienation, which WW and C associ-
ated with Godwinian rationalism. Cf
182 *The Ballad of the Dark Ladiè*
20EC.
   44⁺. The extra stanza printed in *M
Post* (see the headnote) does not ap-
pear in any of the earlier ms versions.

When on the yellow forest-leaves
A dying man he lay.

His dying words—but when I reach'd   65
That tenderest strain of all the ditty,
My faultering voice and pausing harp
Disturb'd her soul with pity!

All impulses of soul and sense
Had thrill'd my guileless Genevieve;   70
The music, and the doleful tale,
The rich and balmy eve;

And hopes, and fears that kindle hope,
An undistinguishable throng,
And gentle wishes long subdued,   75
Subdued and cherish'd long!

She wept with pity and delight,
She blush'd with love, and virgin-shame;
And like the murmur of a dream,
I heard her breathe my name.   80

Her bosom heav'd—she stept aside,
As conscious of my look she stept—
Then suddenly, with timorous eye
She fled to me and wept.

She half enclosed me with her arms,   85
She press'd me with a meek embrace;
And bending back her head, look'd up,
And gazed upon my face.

'Twas partly Love, and partly Fear,
And partly 'twas a bashful art,   90

81. Her bosom heav'd] The *M Post* version reads "Her wet cheek glow'd", following on from the stanza at 80⁺ (given in the headnote) which was later dropped, and which in the ms draft was at the centre of a passage which C considerably reworked.

That I might rather feel, than see,
The swelling of her heart.

I calm'd her fears, and she was calm,
And told her love with virgin-pride.
And so I won my Genevieve,   95
My bright and beauteous Bride.

254. ODE TO GEORGIANA, DUCHESS OF DEVONSHIRE, ON THE 24TH STANZA IN HER *PASSAGE OVER MOUNT GOTHARD*

[Dec 1799]

The duchess, whose private life was somewhat scandalous, was active in the
Foxite Opposition. She published *The Passage of the Mountain of Saint Goth-
ard*, a thirty-stanza poem, in the Opposition papers of 19 and 20 Dec. The Aus-
trians and French (and later the Russians) had been fighting over the St Gothard
Pass since May, but the timeliness of the poem stems from fears that Austria
would secede from the war and that St Gothard and Piedmont would revert
to the French. The poem was dedicated "To my Children", and Rousseauistic
nursing of her own children was a frequently noised fact about the duchess.
Woodring 119–23 gives references, and describes how the ode chimes with C's
changing attitude towards Fox, Sheridan, and the Whigs. One year later the
duchess, like Fox, received a copy of *LB* (1800) from C (see *CL* II 665: to TP
19 Jan 1801).
    C's poem was first printed (he said badly) in *M Post* (24 Dec 1799), and soon
afterwards in vol II of RS's *Annual Anthology* (Bristol 1800). It was included in
subsequent collections with very few revisions. The text given here is from *SL*
(1817), with some slight adjustments to the pattern of indentation. In line with
the title, the epigraph does indeed derive from the 24th stanza of the duchess's
poem.

"And hail the Chapel! hail the Platform wild!
Where Tell directed the avenging Dart,
With well strung arm, that first preserv'd his Child,
Then aimed the arrow at the Tyrant's heart."

Splendor's fondly fostered child!
And did you hail the Platform wild,
  Where once the Austrian fell
  Beneath the shaft of Tell?
O Lady, nurs'd in pomp and pleasure!   5
Whence learnt you that heroic measure?

Light as a dream your days their circlets ran,
From all that teaches Brotherhood to Man
Far, far removed! from want, from hope, from fear!
Enchanting music lull'd your infant ear,   10
Obeisant praises sooth'd your infant heart:
  Emblazonments and old ancestral crests,
With many a bright obstrusive form of art,
  Detain'd your eye from nature: stately vests,
That veiling strove to deck your charms divine,   15
Rich viands, and the pleasurable wine,
Were your's unearn'd by toil; nor could you see
The unenjoying toiler's misery.
And yet, free Nature's uncorrupted child,
You hail'd the Chapel and the Platform wild,   20
    Where once the Austrian fell
    Beneath the shaft of Tell!
  O Lady, nurs'd in pomp and pleasure!
  Whence learnt you that heroic measure?

    There crowd your finely-fibred frame,   25
      All living faculties of bliss:
    And Genius to your cradle came,
      His forehead wreath'd with lambent flame,
        And bending low, with godlike kiss
        Breath'd in a more celestial life!   30
    But boasts not many a fair compeer
    A heart as sensitive to joy and fear?
And some, perchance, might wage an equal strife,
Some few, to nobler being wrought,
Co-rivals in the nobler gift of thought.   35
        Yet *these* delight to celebrate
        Laurell'd War and plumy State;
        Or in verse and music dress
        Tales of rustic happiness—

Pernicious Tales! insidious Strains!   40
   That steel the rich man's breast,
   And mock the lot unblest,
  The sordid vices and the abject pains,
    Which evermore must be
  The doom of Ignorance and Penury!   45
But you, free Nature's uncorrupted child,
You hail'd the Chapel and the Platform wild,
   Where once the Austrian fell
   Beneath the shaft of Tell!
O Lady, nurs'd in pomp and pleasure!   50
Where learnt you that heroic measure?

—You were a Mother! That most holy name,
   Which Heaven and Nature bless,
  I may not vilely prostitute to those
   Whose Infants owe them less   55
  Than the poor Caterpillar owes
   Its gaudy Parent Fly.
You were a Mother! at your bosom fed
  The Babes that lov'd you. You, with laughing eye,
Each twilight-thought, each nascent feeling read,   60
Which you yourself created. Oh! delight!
  A second time to be a Mother,
   Without the Mother's bitter groans:
  Another thought, and yet another,
   By touch, or taste, by looks or tones   65
O'er the growing Sense to roll,
The Mother of your Infant's Soul!
The Angel of the Earth, who, while he guides
  His chariot-planet round the goal of day,
All trembling gazes on the Eye of God,   70
  A moment turn'd his awful face away;
And as he view'd you, from his aspect sweet
  New influences in your being rose,
Blest Intuitions and Communions fleet
  With living Nature, in her joys and woes!   75

68–77. C deleted the lines in the   response to CL, who poked fun at
Yale copy of the poem, probably in   them (*LL*—M—I 224–5).

Thenceforth your soul rejoic'd to see
The shrine of social Liberty!
O beautiful! O Nature's child!
'Twas thence you hail'd the Platform wild,
Where once the Austrian fell   80
Beneath the shaft of Tell!
O Lady, nurs'd in pomp and pleasure!
Thence learnt you that heroic measure.

255. THE SONG OF DEBORAH TRANSLATED

[Dec 1799]

C's lines are a version of Judges 5.1–11. The only known version is bound into
a large contemporary folio, along with letters home from Germany to Mrs C and
TP. It may well reflect C's reading of this form of "translation" during his time
in Germany, an interest which was renewed upon his return in collaboration
with RS. The full ms title is as follows:

> The Song of Deborah, translated in the *parallelisms of the Original/ (*that
> is, so that each Line or member of a sentence is counter-balanced by the
> following, [?]either by difference, or similitude, or by the repetition of the
> same thought in different words or with a different Image.—)

WW added a long note on repetition in poetry to *The Thorn* in *LB* (1800) and
after, which ended with a reference to the same passage in Judges (*WPW* II
512–13). Cf C's later comments on the sublimity of the Song of Deborah in
Lects 1808–1819 (CC) I 267, 310; *BL* ch 17 (*CC*) II 57; *CN* III 3247 f 5ᵛ, 4113
f 18ʳ, 4116.

Repetition and parallelism had been discussed as a feature of the poetic style
of the Old Testament by 18th-century critics like Lowth and Monboddo. But
C's literary interest is likely to be mixed with a theological one. He returned to
the story of Deborah in letter 3 of *Confessions of an Inquiring Spirit* (*SW&F*—
CC—1135–6), making literary appreciation part of his argument against a fun-
damentalist reading of the Bible.

Then sang DEBORAH,
And Barak, Abinoam's Son,
On that day sang they thus:

That the Leaders of Israel led on,
And the People willingly followed   5
Praise ye the Lord!

1

Ye Monarchs, hear!
Give ear, ye Princes!
I sing to the Everlasting,
To the Everlasting will I play & sing praises,   10
To the Lord God of Israel.

2

Lord God, Eternal!
When thou marchedst out from Seir,
When thou marchedst on thro' Edom,
The Earth trembled,   15
The Heavens dissolved,
The Clouds poured,
Mountains melted away from the Lord,
Mount Sinai from before the face of Jehovah,
The Lord God of Israel.   20

3

In the days of Samgar, the Son of Anath,
In the days of Jael lay waste the High roads,
The Travellers went not save by crooked by-ways
Suspended were the Assemblies of Israel,
They ceased, till I arose, Deborah,   25
Till that I arise, a Mother in Israel.

4

To themselves they had chosen strange Gods;
And close to their gates came War.

1–6. C wrote alongside, in the RH margin: "This is a mere announciation, a *giving out* of the Hymn, which begins with 'Ye Monarchs!' &c—".

Not a Shield was there seen, nor a Spear
Among the twice twenty Thousand of Israel. 30

5

My Heart, it swells high to the Rulers of Israel,
O ye, who offered yourselves freely among the People,
Praise the Everlasting One.

Ye that ride on white Asses,
Ye that sit on seats of costly Coverings, or embroidered Seats 35
Ye that walk on the High-roads, frame a Song.

A Song for the Voice of herdsmen, who beside the Draw-wells
Draw water for the Herds & Flocks!
For there will they sing the Deeds of Jehovah,
His Deeds will the People of Israel praise. 40

256. HEXAMETRICAL VERSION OF ISAIAH

[Dec 1799? Aug–Oct 1802?]

C frequently praised the poetry in Isaiah, especially the first chapter (*Lects 1808–1819—CC*—I 69, 223; *BL* ch 14—*CC*—II 14–15; *TT* 24 Feb 1827, 14 Aug 1833—*CC* I 64, 417). In a note on *TT* 14 Aug 1833 HNC reports C repeating "a great deal of Isaiah by heart, and he delighted in pointing out the hexametrical rhythm of numerous passages in the English version"; HNC then quotes the AV version of Isa 1.2–3 (*TT*—1835—II 228–9n). The present version is of verses 2–17 of the same first chapter. It differs from the AV translation by omitting words and changing phrases. Cf **249** *Hexametrical Translation of Psalm 46*; **695** *Adaptation of Isaiah 2.7*.

The text exists in a single ms. It might date from the later part of 1799, at a time when C was occupied in hexametrical projects with RS (which were overtaken by other interests in early 1800). Or it might date from Aug 1802 or afterwards, when C told William Sotheby that he had discovered "that the poetical Parts of the Bible . . . are little more than slovenly Hexameters . . . The Thing is worth an Experiment" (*CL* II 857). Some punctuation is supplied in the text given here.

The text is preceded by a metrical memorandum in C's hand, as follows. The unorthodox alternative feet illustrate his remark as to the admissibility of a trochee substituted for a dactyl in English (see **249** *Hexametrical Translation of Psalm 46* headnote; **257** *Hymn to the Earth*):

C allows himself the liberties he sets out for the English hexameter, as opposed to the classical or the German, in his comments quoted in **185** *English Hexameters* headnote and **216** *Mahomet* headnote.

Line 31 is partially scanned:

Yōur nĕw-/ mōōns, yŏur ăppōīntĕd/ Fēasts hăth mў/ Sōūl ĭn ăbhorrence

Hear, O ye Heavens! give ear, O Earth, for the Lord God hath spoken.
Lo! I have brought up Children and they have rebelled against me.
The brute Ox knoweth his owner, the Ass the crib of his Master.
Israel doth not know, my People, doth not consider.—
Ah the sinful People, a Folk with iniquity laden,   5
Seed of unrighteous Doers, children corrupt and corrupters,
They have forsaken the Lord God, they have provoked the Holy
One of Israël to Anger, yea, they have gone away backward.
Wherefore should ye be any more stricken? Ye will be revolting
More and more: the whole Head is sick and faint is the whole Heart.   10

From the Sole of the Foot to the Head no Soundness is in it—
But Wounds, and bruises, and noisome Sores, that have not been closed,
Have not been closed, nor bound not, nor ever assuaged with ointments.
Desolate lies your Country, with fire your Cities are wasted;
Your Land, lo! Strangers devour it even in your presence,   15
Hosts unknown have pass'd o'er it, each in its path of destruction.—
And the daughter of Zion is left, as a Cot in a vineyard,
As a Lodge in a garden, of Gourds, as a City besieged.
But that the Lord with us had left a very small remnant,
We should have been as Sodom, we had been like to Gomorrah!   20
Hear the Word of the Lord, give ear ye rulers of Sodom!
Hear the Law of our God, give ear ye men of Gomorrah!
What boot they, your myriad of victims to me, saith the Lord God—
I am full of the offerings of Rams, and the burnt fat of fed beasts,
And I delight not in blood of Bullocks, or Lambs, or of He-goats.   25
When ye appear before me, who this at your hand hath required,

That ye may tread my Courts? Ah! bring no more vain Oblations!
Incense is grown an abomination unto me, the new-moons,
Yea, the sabbaths, th' appointed Assemblies, I cannot away with
It is iniquity all, all, even your solemn Meeting! 30
Your new-moons, your appointed Feasts, hath my Soul in abhorrence.
They are a trouble unto me. O! I am weary to bear them,
And when ye spread forth your hands, I will hide mine eyes from
    beholding.
Yea, when ye make many prayers, I will not hear you: your hands are
Stain'd with blood.—O wash ye, be pure, and cease to do evil.— 35
Learn to do well, seek Judgment, relieve the Oppressed,
Judge the fatherless Child, & plead for the shelterless widow.—

257. HYMN TO THE EARTH, FROM STOLBERG

[Dec 1799?]

C's hexameters are a free translation (unacknowledged in the only printed ver-
sion) of the first 25 lines of F. L. Stolberg's *Hymne, an die Erde*, in C and F. L.
Stolberg *Gedichte* 267–9 (the poem continues to p 284), also in hexameters:

Erde, du Mutter zahlloser Kinder, Mutter und Amme!
Sei mir gegrüßt! sei mir gesegnet im Feiergesange!
Sieh, o Mutter, hier lieg' ich an deinen schwellenden Brüsten,
Lieg', o Grüngelockte, von deinem wallenden Haupthaar
Sanft umsäuselt, und sanft gekühlt von thauenden Lüften!
Ach, du säuselst Wonne mir zu, und thauest mir Wehmut
In das Herz, daß Wehmut und Wonn', aus schmelzender Seele,
Sich in Thränen und Dank und heiligen Liedern ergießen!

Erde, du Mutter zahlloser Kinder, Mutter und Amme!
Schwester der allfreuenden Sonne, des freundlichen Mondes,
Und der stralenden Stern' und der flammenbeschweisten Kometen,
Eine der jüngsten Töchter der allgebärenden Schöpfung,
Immer blühendes Weib des Segen träufelnden Himmels!—
Sprich, o Erde, wie war dir, als du am ersten der Tage
Deinen heiligen Schooß dem bulenden Himmel enthülltest?
Dein Erröthen war die erste der Morgenröthen,
Als er, im blendenden Bette von weichen schwellenden Wolken,
Deine gürtende Binde mit siegender Stärke dir löste!

Schauer durchbebten die stille Natur, und tausend mal tausend
Leben keimten empor aus der mächtigen Liebesumarmung.
Freudig begrüßten die Fluten des Meeres neuer Bewohner
Mannigfaltige Schaaren; es staunte der werdende Wallfisch
Ueber die steigenden Ströme, die seiner Nasen entbraußten;
Junges Leben durchbrüllte die Auen, die Wälder, die Berge,
Irrte blöckend im Thal, und sang in blühenden Stauden, . . .

For other translations by C from Stolberg see poems **212, 258, 259, 281.**

C's lines are known in only one version, published in *Friendship's Offering
for 1834*, where they are introduced by the following initialled note:

> It may not be without use or interest to youthful, and especially to intel-
> ligent female readers of poetry, to observe, that in the attempt to adapt
> the Greek metres to the English language, we must begin by substitut-
> ing *quality* of sound for *quantity*—that is, accentuated or comparatively
> emphasized syllables, for what, in the Greek and Latin verse, are named
> long, and of which the prosodial mark is ‐ ; and *vice versâ*, unaccentuated
> syllables for short, marked ˅. Now the hexameter verse consists of two
> sorts of *feet*, the spondee, composed of two long syllables, and the dactyl,
> composed of one long syllable followed by two short. The following verse
> from the Psalms, is a rare instance of a *perfect* hexameter (*i.e.* line of six
> feet) in the English language:—

> Gōd cāme l ūp wĭth ă l shōut: ōūr l Lōrd wĭth thĕ l sōūnd ŏf ă l trūmpĕt.

> But so few are the truly *spondaic* words in our language, such as Ēgȳpt,
> ūprōār, tūrmōīl, &c. that we are compelled to substitute, in most instances,
> the trochee, or ‐˅, *i.e.* such words as mērrȳ, līghtlȳ, &c. for the proper
> spondee. It need only be added, that in the hexameter the fifth foot must
> be a dactyl, and the sixth a spondee, or trochee. I will end this note with
> two hexameter lines, likewise from the Psalms.

> Thēre ĭs ă l rīvĕr thĕ l flōwĭng whĕre l ōf shāll l glāddĕn thĕ cītȳ,
> Hāllĕ l lūjăh thĕ l cĭtȳ ŏf l Gōd! Jē hōvăh! hăth l blēst hĕr.

The versions of Ps 47.5, 46.4 appear to be C's own. In an emended set of
loose sheets of *Friendship's Offering* he completed the metrical analysis by
inserting foot-dividers to read "thĕ l cītȳ" and "Jē l hōvăh!" And he added at
the foot of the page: "P.S. To make any considerable number of Hexameters
feasible in our monosyllabic, trochæo-iambic langu⟨a⟩ge, there must, I fear, be
yet other Licences granted—in the *first* foot, at least, ex.gr. ań superfluous ˅
prefixed in case of particles, such ⟨as⟩ Of, And & the like—likewise, ‐˅‐, when
the stronger Accent is on the first Syllable." Cf **249** *Hexametrical Translation
of Psalm 46.*

In the same set of loose sheets C also made a number of corrections in the

verse lines (for details see vol II), and these are incorporated in the text given
here.

Earth! thou mother of numberless children, the nurse and the mother,
Hail! O Goddess, thrice hail! Blest *be* thou! and, blessing, I hymn thee!
Forth, sweet sounds! from my harp; my voice shall float on your
    surges—
Soar aloft, O my soul! and bear up my song on thy pinions.

Travelling the vale with mine eyes—green meadows; and lake with
    green island,   5
Dark in its basin of rock; and the bare stream flowing in brightness;
Thrilled with thy beauty and love, on the wooded slope of the mountain,
Here, Great Mother, I lie, thy child with its head on thy bosom!
Playful the spirits of noon, that creep or rush through thy tresses;
Green-haired Goddess! refresh me; and hark! as they hurry or linger,   10
Fill the pause of my harp, or sustain it with musical murmurs.
Into my being thou murmurest joy! a tenderest sadness
Shed'st thou, like dew, on my heart! till the joy and the joy of the sadness
Pour themselves forth from my heart in tears, and the hymn of
    thanksgiving.

Earth! thou mother of numberless children, the nurse and the mother,   15
Sister thou of the Stars, and beloved by the Sun, the rejoicer!
Guardian and friend of the Moon, O Earth, whom the Comets forget not,
Yea, in the measureless distance wheel round, and again they behold
    thee!
Fadeless and young (and what if the latest birth of Creation?)
Bride and consort of Heaven, that bending hangs o'er thee enamoured!   20
Say, mysterious Earth! O say, great Mother and Goddess!
Was it not well with thee then, when first thy lap was ungirdled,
Thy lap to the genial Heaven, the day that he wooed thee and won thee!
Fair was thy blush, the fairest and first of the blushes of morning!
Self-upgather'd thou shrankest! the blissful Shudder thrill'd thro' thee!   25
Mightier far was the joy of thy sudden resilience: and forthwith

25. Originally two lines:

Deep was the shudder, O Earth! the
  throe of thy self-retention:
Inly thou strovest to flee, and didst
  seek thyself at thy center!

C deleted the lines and wrote "Shrink-
ing and inly self-gather'd", which he
in turn deleted before writing out the
present version of the line.

Myriad myriads of lives teemed forth from the mighty embracement.
Thousand-fold tribes of dwellers, impelled by thousand-fold instincts,
Filled, as a dream, the wide waters: the rivers sang on their channels:
Laughed on their shores the hoarse seas: the yearning ocean swelled
    upward: 30
Young life lowed through the meadows, the woods, and the echoing
    mountains,
Wandered bleating in valleys, and warbled in blossoming branches.

       *   *   *   *   *   *

258. TO A CATARACT, FROM A CAVERN NEAR THE SUMMIT OF A MOUNTAIN PRECIPICE, FROM STOLBERG

[Dec 1799?]

The poem exists in a ms version dating from 1799, in two ms versions copied out for correspondents in 1833, and in a version published in *PW* (1834). The earliest ms version is closest, especially in its first seven lines, to F. L. Stolberg's *Der Felsenström*, in C. and F. L. Stolberg *Gedichte* 124–7:

> Unsterblicher Jüngling!
> Du strömest hervor
> Aus der Felsenkluft
> Kein Sterblicher sah
> Die Wiege des Starken;
> Es hörte kein Ohr
> Das Lallen des Edlen im sprudelnden Quell!

Stolberg's poem continues for another 39 lines, and C's version alters the emphasis of the German entirely, although it does expand hints to be found there, e.g. Stolberg's lines 18–21:

> Dich kleidet die Sonne
> In Stralen des Ruhmes!
> Sie malet mit Farben des himlischen Bogens
> Die schwebenden Wolken der stäubenden Flut!

For other translations by C of Stolberg see poems **212, 257, 259, 281.**
    The first of the two 1833 versions describes the poem as "A fragmentary

recollection of an Ode, in which the Writer attempted an accomodation of the regular Pindaric Scheme of Metrical correspondence, by Strophe, Antistrophe, and Epode to a Language in which, as in the English, *Accent*, or the comparative *Stroke* of the voice [?]on the Syllables, is substituted for the *Quantity*, or comparative *prolongation* of the Sounds." Cf *CL* vi 944–5: to Mrs J. G. Lockhart 26 Jul 1833, where C continues with one of his lessons on "simple" feet, with English words as examples. Cf also the notes quoted at **185** *English Hexameters* headnote and **257** *Hymn to the Earth* headnote. The text follows; beside the first seven lines is a metrical analysis in the margin:

$$- - \cup \cup -$$
$$- - \cup \cup -$$
$$\cup - \cup \mid \cup - \cup \mid \cup - \cup - \cup$$
$$- \cup - \cup -$$
$$\cup - \cup \mid \cup \cup \mid - -$$
$$- \cup \mid - \cup \mid -$$
$$\cup - \cup \mid \cup \cup \mid - -$$

C concludes this version with the comment: "| &c &c | *Meant* to have been finished, but *somebody* came *in*, or some*thing fell* out,—& tomorrow—alas! tomorrow! | S. T. C."

The second 1833 version begins with a separate metrical analysis, following the part of the ms which comprises a letter. Thus:

Strophe

The text of the poem is concluded by a row of five asterisks, followed by the comment: "Cætera desunt.[1] Some*thing* fell *out*, or some*body* came *in*—& so

[1] Tr "The rest is lacking."

Tomorrow—alas! the Sunset gorgeous Horizon. the inarrivable Horizon of that
Hope-Lie, Tomorrow! I S. T. Coleridge I August, 1833—i.e. of every Man's the
Year—Novr. 30th, of *his* Life!"

This is C's only known attempt at an English approximation to a truly Pin-
daric ode, although he described **24** *Translation of Euclid* as a "Pindaric Ode"
and applied the terminology "Strophe" etc to sections of **142** *Ode on the De-
parting Year*. The attempt ends with only 7 out of 17 lines of the antistrophe
completed and no epode. He has not achieved exact correspondence in strophe
and antistrophe between lines 1 and 18, 5 and 22, and 7 and 24. Lines 3 and 20
do correspond, but the metrical analysis is inaccurate at the end.

C gives a plausible impression of the controlled irregularity (as it was then
understood) of Pindar's metrical schemes, and has even, in his shortest lines,
produced exact equivalents of Pindaric lines as they appeared in pre-1811 edi-
tions. As he implies in the notes referred to above, metrical patterns involving
two or more stressed syllables in succession do not come naturally in English,
and to produce long sequences of these, such as Pindar used, would be quite
impracticable. Lines 1 and 2 match the sixth line (in contemporary editions) of
successive epodes of *Olympian Ode* 6 (μάντιν τ' ἀγαθόν—now *Olympian* 6.17)
or the fifth line of strophes and antistrophes in *Pythian Ode* 3 (Οὐρανίδα γόνον
εὐ- —now *Pythian* 3.4); and lines 4 and 6 match the ninth lines of strophe and
antistrophe in *Pythian Ode* 11 (-μασε Λοξίας—now *Pythian* 11.5).

The lineation of Pindar's *Odes* was changed in 1811, when August Böckh
published his edition, based on a deeper perception of metrical intricacies and
following the evidence of ancient critics against division of words at line-
endings. When C commented on Pindar's metre in 1806 (*CN* II 2835) he seems,
though obscurely, to be referring to such word-division. For a more general
fragment on Greek metre written c 1820 see *SW&F* (*CC*) 861–4. At an early
date C must at least have had access to Erasmus Schmied's edition of Pindar
(Wittenberg 1616), in which the metrical schemes are set out. For this and other
editions of Pindar see **520** *Specimen Translation of Pindar* headnote. His anno-
tations to the 1616 edition (in *CM*—*CC*—IV 118–21) do not touch on metre.

C does not state explicitly, though it is implied in his comments on the
scansion of English verse—passim in *CM* (*CC*), as well as in his various dis-
cussions of writing dactylic hexameters in English—that stressed syllables in
English differ from long ones in Greek in that they are variable and movable. In
Greek, long and short are fixed for purposes of scansion, with few exceptions, a
main one being that a short vowel followed by a mute consonant and a liquid in
another word may be either long or short. On this lengthening "by position" cf
C's comments given at **48** *Sors Misera Servorum* 2EC. For his questions about
the actual pronunciation of Greek poetry, which he justifiably felt cannot have
been so invariably regular as the ancient writers on metre imply, see the frag-
mentary introduction to an essay on Greek metre, presumably to be written in
collaboration with HC, in *SW&F* (*CC*) 861–4.

The text given here follows the second 1833 ms version (but restoring "the" before "Rock" in line 8). None of the four versions indicates the relation to Stolberg, and after C's death the lines were taken by James Ferriar in support of a charge of plagiarism in *Bl Mag* XLVII (1840) 287–99 at 298–9 and n—a charge which WW vigorously countered on C's behalf (*WL—L* rev—IV 50).

STROPHE

Unperishing Youth!
Thou leapest from forth
The Cell of thy hidden Nativity!
Never Mortal saw
The Cradle of the Strong One;   5
Never Mortal heard
The Gathering of his Voices—
The deep-murmur'd Charm of the Son of the Rock
Which is lisp'd evermore at his slumberless Fountain.
There's a Cloud at the Portal, a Spray-woven Veil 10
At the Shrine of his ceaseless Renewing:
It embosoms the roses of Dawn;
It entangles the shafts of the Noon;
And into the bed of its stillness
The Moonshine sinks down, as in slumber— 15
That the Son of the Rock, that the Nurseling of Heaven,
May be born in a holy Twilight.

ANTISTROPHE

The Wild goat in awe
Looks up and beholds
Above thee the Cliff inaccessible!   20
Thou at once full-born
Mad'nest in thy Joyance,
Whirled, shatter'd, split'st,
Life invulnerable!

259. TELL'S BIRTH-PLACE,
IMITATED FROM STOLBERG

[Dec 1799?]

C's poem is an imitation of F. L. Stolberg's *Bei Wilhelm Tells Geburtstätte im Kanton Uri*, in C. and F. L. Stolberg *Gedichte* 114–15):

Seht diese heilige Kapell!
Hier ward geboren Wilhelm Tell!
Hier, wo der Altar Gottes steht,
Stand seiner Eltern Ehebett!

Mit Mutterfreuden freute sich
Die liebe Mutter inniglich,
Gedachte nicht an ihren Schmerz,
Und hielt das Knäblein an ihr Herz!

Sie flehte Gott: er sei dein Knecht;
Sei stark und muthig und gerecht!
Gott aber dachte: ich thu' mehr
Durch ihn, als durch ein ganzes Heer!

Er gab dem Knaben warmes Blut,
Des Rosses Kraft, des Adlers Mut,
Im Felsennacken freien Sinn,
Des Falken Aug' und Feuer drin!

Dem Worte sein und der Natur
Vertraute Gott das Knäblein nur;
Wo sich der Felsenstrom ergeußt
Erhub sich früh des Helden Geist.

Das Ruder und die Gemsenjagd
Hat seine Glieder stark gemacht;
Er scherzte früh mit der Gefahr,
Und wußte nicht, wie groß er war!

Er wußte nicht, daß seine Hand,
Durch Gott gestärkt, sein Vaterland
Erretten würde von der Schmach
Der Knechtschaft, deren Joch er brach!

For other translations of Stolberg by C see poems **212, 257, 258, 281**.

The poems which inspired **254** *Ode to Georgiana, Duchess of Devonshire* had praised Tell's defiance of an Austrian despot, in a stanza that C quoted as epigraph to his own poem. C had been reading and translating Stolberg earlier that same year, but the present lines differ in being a much closer, line-for-line translation, and were perhaps dashed off, prompted by thoughts of Tell in the poem he had just written. See also Woodring 119. C's lines were not published until *SL* (1817), the version given here, and the subsequent collections included them with only a few changes of punctuation. For his later, different interest in Tell see *CN* IV 5371 and n, 5375.

I.

Mark this holy chapel well!
The Birth-place, this, of WILLIAM TELL.
Here, where stands God's altar dread,
Stood his parents' marriage-bed.

II.

Here first, an infant to her breast,   5
Him his loving mother prest;
And kiss'd the babe, and bless'd the day,
And pray'd as mothers use to pray.

III.

"Vouchsafe him health, O God! and give
The child thy servant still to live!"   10
But God has destined to do more
Through him, than through an armed power.

IV.

God gave him reverence of laws,
Yet stirring blood in Freedom's cause—
A spirit to his rocks akin,   15
The eye of the Hawk, and the fire therein!

V.

To Nature and to Holy writ
Alone did God the boy commit:
Where flash'd and roar'd the torrent, oft
His soul found wings, and soar'd aloft!   20

VI.

The straining oar and chamois chase
Had form'd his limbs to strength and grace:
On wave and wind the boy would toss,
Was great, nor knew how great he was!

VII.

He knew not that his chosen hand,   25
Made strong by God, his native land
Would rescue from the shameful yoke
Of *Slavery*—the which he broke!

260. A CHRISTMAS CAROL

[Dec 1799]

In a letter to RS sent on 24? Dec 1799 C described the poem as "in as strict a sense as is *possible*, an Impromptu" (*CL* I 552). There is no reason to disbelieve him. The suggestion in *PW* (JDC) 624A that the poem was "probably inspired by the passage of Ottfried" which C probably translated in Feb–May 1799 (=poem **191**) is unconvincing: the poem shares as much with the **254** *Ode to Georgiana, Duchess of Devonshire*.

The carol was published in *M Post* (25 Dec 1799), and was included in RS's *Annual Anthology* II (1800), in *SL* (1817), and in the later collections. A few improvements were made in the *Annual Anthology* text, which was further refined in an annotated copy, and this is the version given here. The *M Post* and *Annual Anthology* versions, as printed, ended with the following, ninth stanza:

> Strange prophecy! could half the screams
>   Of half the men, that since have died
> To realize War's kingly dreams,
>   Have risen at once in one vast tide,
> The choral music of Heavens multitude
> Had been o'erpower'd and lost amid the uproar rude!

I.

The Shepherds went their hasty way,
    And found the lowly stable shed,
Where the Virgin Mother lay:
    And now they check'd their eager tread,

For to the Babe, that at her bosom clung,   5
A Mother's song the Virgin Mother sung!

II.

They told her how a glorious Light,
    Streaming from an heavenly Throng,
Around them shone, suspending night!
    And sweeter than a Mother's song,   10
Blest Angels heralded the Saviour's birth,
Glory to God on high! and PEACE ON EARTH!

III.

She listen'd to the tale divine,
    And closer still the Babe she press'd;
And while she cry'd, The Babe is mine!   15
    The milk rush'd faster to her breast:
Joy rose within her, like a summer's morn;
PEACE, PEACE ON EARTH! the Prince of Peace is born!

IV.

Thou Mother of the Prince of Peace,
    Poor, simple, and of low estate;   20
That Strife should vanish, Battle cease,
    Oh why should this thy soul elate?
Sweet Music's loudest note, the Poet's story,
Didst thou ne'er love to hear of Fame and Glory?

V.

And is not WAR a youthful King,   25
    A stately Hero clad in mail?
Beneath his footsteps laurels spring,
    Him Earth's majestic Monarchs hail
Their Friend, their Playmate! and his bold bright eye
Compels the Maiden's love-confessing sigh.   30

VI.

"Tell this in some more courtly scene,
    "To Maids and Youths in robes of state!
"I am a Woman, poor and mean,

"And therefore is my soul elate.
"War is a ruffian Thief with gore defil'd,   35
"That from the aged Father tears his Child;

VII.

"A murderous Thief, by fiends ador'd,
    "He kills the Sire, and starves the Son;
"The Husband kills, and from her board
    "Steals all his Widow's toil had won;   40
"Plunders God's world of Beauty, rends away
"All safety from the night, all comfort from the day!

VIII.

"Then wisely is my soul elate,
    "That strife should vanish, battle cease:
"I'm poor, and of a low estate,   45
    "The Mother of the Prince of Peace!
"Joy rises in me, like a summer's morn:
"PEACE, PEACE ON EARTH! the Prince of Peace is born!"

261. IMPROMPTU: ON CANDLES
BEING INTRODUCED WHILE A
YOUNG LADY WAS SINGING

[Dec 1799?]

The only known version of the poem was published in *M Post* (1 Jan 1800),
over the signature "J. P." The same signature is attached to the epigram *On a
Supposed Son*, which appeared in *M Post* (5 Feb 1800) and which is incon-
trovertibly by C (poem **246**). The signature has no obvious explanation, unless
it was supplied by Daniel Stuart to suggest a variety of contributors, and this
leaves a small element of doubt concerning C's authorship.

Wherefore, wherefore, most unwise,
    Did you bring the candles here?
Why remind us we have eyes,
    When we wish'd to be *all ear*?

262. TALLEYRAND TO LORD GRENVILLE:
A METRICAL EPISTLE

[Jan 1800]

The official translation of Talleyrand's letter to Grenville of 25 Dec 1799, introducing a proposal of negotiations for peace from Napoleon to George III, together with the text of Grenville's reply of 4 Jan 1800, was published in *M Post* (7 Jan 1800), immediately provoking protest from the Opposition. C's lines appeared, unsigned, in the same paper three days later. The "remainder"—promised in the last line for the following day, a Saturday—never appeared, and the lines were never reprinted or collected by C.

The background is described by Woodring 149–51 and in Erdman's notes to *EOT* (*CC*) I 92–7, some of which are repeated here verbatim. William Wyndham Grenville, created Baron Grenville in 1790, was Secretary of State for Foreign Affairs between 1791 and 1801. C parodies the logic of his reply to Talleyrand, which brusquely made clear that negotiations could not be entered into until the Bourbons were restored. The operative device throughout C's lines is to portray Grenville as the ministerial image of Talleyrand, accumulating coincidences and implying further similarities.

To the EDITOR of The MORNING POST.

MR. EDITOR,

    An unmetrical letter from Talleyrand to Lord Grenville has already appeared, and from an authority too high to be questioned: otherwise I could adduce some arguments for the exclusive authenticity of the following metrical epistle. The very epithet which the wise antients used, "*aurea carmina,*" might have been supposed likely to have determined the choice of the French Minister in favour of verse; and the rather, when we recollect that this phrase of "*golden verses*" is applied emphatically to the works of that philosopher, who imposed *silence* on all with whom he had to deal. Besides, is it not somewhat improbable that Talleyrand should have preferred prose to rhyme, when the latter alone *has got the chink?* Is it not likewise curious, that in our official answer,   ⁻1.5   ⁻1.10

⁻**1.7–11.** "*aurea carmina,*" . . . *silence*] The *Golden Verses*, metrical maxims of Neopythagoreanism, were sometimes attributed to Pythagoras himself, whose disciples had to keep silent for five years.   ⁻**1.13.** *has got the chink?*] Talleyrand's belief in graft as the silent ingredient of all negotiation was notorious.

no notice whatever is taken of the Chief Consul, Bonaparte, as if ⁻1.15
there had been no such man existing; notwithstanding that his ex-
istence is pretty generally admitted, nay, that some have been so
rash as to believe, that he has created as great a sensation in the
world as Lord Grenville, or even the Duke of Portland? But the
Minister of Foreign Affairs, Talleyrand, *is* acknowledged, which, ⁻1.20
in our opinion, could not have happened, had he written only that
insignificant prose-letter, which seems to precede Bonaparte's, as
in old romances a dwarf always ran before to proclaim the ad-
vent or arrival of knight or giant. That Talleyrand's character and
practices more resemble those of some *regular* Governments than ⁻1.25
Bonaparte's I admit; but this of itself does not appear a satis-
factory explanation. However, let the letter speak for itself. The
second line is supererogative in syllables, whether from the osci-
tancy of the transcriber, or from the trepidation which might have
overpowered the modest Frenchman, on finding himself in the act ⁻1.30
of writing to so *great* a man, I shall not dare to determine. A few
Notes are added by

Your servant,

GNOME.

P.S. As mottos are now fashionable, especially if taken from out ⁻1.35
of the way books, you may prefix, if you please, the following
lines from Sidonius Apollinaris:

Saxa, et robora, corneasque fibras
Mollit dul ciloquâ canorus arte!

⁻**1.15–16.** as if there had been no such man existing;] The Opposition press consistently made play of min- isterial policy to ignore or deny that Bonaparte was the *de facto* leader of the French nation.

⁻**1.24.** knight or giant.] C returned to the same image of Napoleon as gi- ant a few weeks later, in the same newspaper (*EOT—CC—*I 112).

⁻**1.34.** GNOME.] *M Post* (4 Jan 1800) included—in an address to the author of a satirical series "To the Sylphid"—a prayer of "the green-eyed Gnome, whom mortals Envy call, and gods, Rodonte." If C's in- troductory letter intends an allusion to this previous issue, it asks us to see the envy, by transfer, as Grenville's.

⁻**1.38–9.** Sidonius Apollinaris *Phoebus to his Well-beloved and Own Particular Thalia* 20–1, in *Letters* 8.11.3 tr W. B. Anderson (2 vols LCL 1936–65) II 461 "By the tuneful ut- terance of his sweet-voiced art [he] charms rocks and oaks and hearts of horn."

TALLEYRAND, MINISTER OF FOREIGN AFFAIRS
AT PARIS, TO LORD GRENVILLE, SECRETARY OF
STATE IN GREAT BRITAIN FOR FOREIGN AFFAIRS,
AUDITOR OF THE EXCHEQUER, A LORD OF TRADE,
AN ELDER BROTHER OF TRINITY HOUSE, &c.

¯1.40

My Lord! tho' your Lordship repel deviation
From forms long establish'd, yet with high consideration,
I plead for the honor to hope, that no blame
Will attach, should this letter *begin* with my name.
I dar'd not presume on your Lordship to bounce,   5
But thought it more *exquisite* first to *announce!*
My Lord! I've the honour to be Talleyrand,
And the letter's from *me!* you'll not draw back your hand
Nor yet take it up by the rim in dismay,
As boys pick up ha'pence on April fool-day.   10
I'm no Jacobin soul, or red-hot Cordelier,
That your Lordship's *un*gauntleted fingers need fear
An infection, or burn! Believe me, 'tis true,
With a scorn, like another, I look down on the crew,
That bawl and hold up to the mob's detestation   15
The most delicate wish for a *silent persuasion.*
A *form long establish'd* these Terrorists call
Bribes, perjury, theft, and the devil and all!
And yet spite of all that the *Moralist prates,

* This sarcasm on the writings of Moralists is, in general, extremely just;
but had Talleyrand continued long enough in England, he might have found an
honourable exception in the second volume of Dr. Paley's Moral Philosophy: in
which both Secret Influence, and all the other *Established Forms*, are justified,
and placed in their true light.   5

2. forms long-establish'd] The
person-to-person way in which Tal-
leyrand brought Napoleon's offer of
peace did not conform to accepted
diplomatic practice and was the sub-
ject of comment.

6, 16, etc. Phrases in italic come
either from Grenville's reply or from
reports of his recent speeches.

10. Alluding to the custom of show-
ering hot coins among tricksters on
1 April, among which were coins of

little worth.

11. red-hot Cordelier] The Corde-
liers district in Paris had been a hotbed
of popular radicalism, politically to
the left of the Jacobins and led by such
figures as Danton and Marat.

12. *un*gauntleted] One of two words
in the poem (the other is line 68 "en-
tempests") which C appears to have
coined for the occasion.

19fn. On secret influence and
William Paley's *Principles of Moral*

'Tis the keystone and cement of *civiliz'd States*.   20
Those American **Reps!* And i' faith, they were serious!
It shock'd us at Paris, like something mysterious,
That men, who've a Congress—But no more of't! I'm proud
To have stood so distinct from the Jacobin crowd.

My Lord! tho' the vulgar in wonder be lost at   25
My transfigurations, and name me *Apostate*,
Such a meaningless nickname, which never incens'd me,
Cannot prejudice you or your Cousin against me:
I'm Ex-bishop. What then? Burke himself would agree,
That I left not the Church—'twas the Church that left me.   30
My titles prelatic I lov'd and retain'd,
As long as what *I* meant by Prelate remain'd:
And tho' Mitres no longer will *pass* in our mart,
I'm *episcopal* still to the core of my heart.
No time from my name this my motto shall sever: 35
'Twill be *"non sine pulvere palma"*† for ever!

Your goodness, my Lord! I conceive as excessive,
Or I dar'd not present you a scroll so digressive;
And in truth with my pen thro' and thro' I should strike it;
But I hear that your Lordship's own style is just like it.   40
Dear my Lord, we are right: for what charms can be shew'd,
In a thing that goes straight like an old Roman road.
The tortoise crawls straight, the hare doubles about,

* A fashionable abbreviation in the higher circles for Republicans.—Thus
Mob was originally the Mobility.

† *Palma non sine pulvere*—in plain English, an itching palm, not without the
yellow dust.

---

and *Political Philosophy* see *Lects
1795 (CC)* 69 and n 5.

28. your Cousin] Grenville's cousin
was Pitt; both had recently used a
scandalous amount of "secret influ-
ence" to purchase the votes for Irish
Union; both had once favoured parlia-
mentary reform.

30. Edmund Burke (1729–97) thus
viewed his split with Fox and other
fellow Whigs who did not share his

alarm about the French Revolution
and would not join him in 1792 in
support of Pitt and war with France.
Talleyrand had indeed been a bishop.

36 and fn. *non sine pulvere palma*]
Tr "The [victor's] palm is not won
without dust." A proverbial expres-
sion (cf Horace *Epistles* 1.1.51), here
jokingly mistranslated as referring to
the hand held out to receive a bribe.

And the true line of beauty still winds in and out.
It argues, my Lord! of fine thoughts such a brood in us,   45
To split and divide into heads multitudinous,
While charms that surprise (it can ne'er be deni'd us),
Sprout forth from each head, like the ears from King Midas.
Were a genius of rank, like a common place dunce,
Compell'd to drive on to the main point at once,   50
What a plentiful vintage of initiations*
Would Noble Lords lose in your Lordship's orations.

My fancy transports me! As mute as a mouse,
And as fleet as a pigeon, I'm borne to the house,
Where all those, who *are* Lords, from father to son,   55
Discuss the affairs of all those, who are none.
I behold you, my Lord! of your feelings quite full,
'Fore the woolsack arise, like a sack full of wool!
You rise on each Anti-Grenvillian Member,
Short, thick, and blust'rous, like a day in November!†   60
Short in person, I mean: for the length of your speeches,
Fame herself, that most famous reporter, ne'er reaches.

* The word *Initiations* is borrowed from the new Constitution, and can only mean, in plain English, introductory matter. If the manuscript would bear us out, we should propose to read the line thus—"What a plentiful *Verbage*, what Initiations!" inasmuch as Vintage must necessarily refer to wine, really or figuratively; and we cannot guess what species Lord Grenville's eloquence may be   5 supposed to resemble, unless, indeed, it be *Cowslip* wine. A slashing Critic, to whom we read the manuscript, proposed to read, What a plenty of Flowers— what Initiations! and supposes it may allude indiscriminately to Poppy Flowers, or Flour of Brimstone. The most modest emendation, perhaps, would be this— For Vintage, read Ventage.   10

† We cannot sufficiently admire the accuracy of this simile. For, as Lord Grenville, though short, is certainly not the shortest man in the House, even so is it with the days in November.

44. An allusion to the sinuous Hogarthian "line of beauty", and thereby to Grenville's bland justification of ugly ministerial policies.

48. Asses' ears sprouted from Midas. See Ovid *Metamorphoses* 11.146 et seq.

51fn. The "new Constitution" was proclaimed on 13 Dec 1799, following Napoleon's overthrow of the Directory and the establishment of the Consulate. "Poppy Flowers" are associated with sleep and oblivion, while "Flour of Brimstone" is burnt stone or sulphur. The word "Vendage" means vending, selling.

Lo! Patience beholds you contemn her brief reign,
And Time, that all-panting toil'd after in vain,
(Like the Beldam who rac'd for a smock with her grandchild),   65
Drops and cries—were such lungs e'er assign'd to a manchild?
Your strokes at her vitals pale truth has confess'd,
And zeal unresisted entempests your breast!*
Tho' some noble Lords may be wishing to sup,
Your merit self-conscious, my Lord! *keeps you up*,   70
Unextinguish'd and swoln, as a balloon of paper
Keeps aloft by the smoke of its own farthing taper.
Ye SIXTEENS† of Scotland, your snuffs ye must trim;
Your Geminies, fix'd stars of England! grow dim,

* An evident Plagiarism of the Ex-Bishop's from Dr. Johnson.

"Existence saw him spurn her bounded reign,
"And panting Time toil'd after him in vain:
"His pow'rful strokes presiding Truth confess'd,
"And unresisting Passion storm'd the breast."   5

† This line and the following are involved in an almost Lycophrontic tene-bricosity. On repeating them, however, to an *Illuminant*, whose confidence I possess, he informed me (and he ought to know, for he is a Tallow-chandler by trade), that certain candles go by the name of *sixteens*. This explains the whole, the Scotch Peers are destined to burn out—and so are candles! The English are 5 perpetual, and are therefore styled Fixed Stars! The word *Geminies* is, we confess, still obscure to us; though we venture to suggest, that it may perhaps be a metaphor (daringly sublime) for the two eyes, which noble Lords do in general possess. It is certainly used by the Poet, Fletcher, in this sense, in the 31st stanza of his *Purple Island*.   10

"What! shall I then need seek a patron out,
"Or beg a favour from a mistress' eyes,

68. entempests] See line 12EC. Cf **335** *The Pains of Sleep* 45 "entempesting".
68fn. *Prologue Spoken by Mr. Garrick at the Opening of the Theatre Royal, Drury Lane, 1747* 5–8 (var) (*B Poets* XI 843).
70–2. A prose version of the lines had been drafted in the Gutch Notebook: "Grenville's merits ought to keep him up but the sense of his own merit, as a paper balloon | Kept aloft by the smoke of its own farthing

Candle—" (*CN* I 253).
73. SIXTEENS of Scotland,] The sixteen compounding Scottish peers, kept in the Grenvillean camp by control of patronage in the hands of Pitt's manager, Henry Dundas, on whom see *M Post* (22 Jan 1798) in *EOT* (*CC*) I 18 n 2.
73fn. Lycophron (b c 320 B.C.), author of *Alexandra*, was proverbial for obscurity. The verse quotation is from Phineas Fletcher *The Purple Island* I 31 (var) (*B Poets* IV 385).

And, but for *a form long establish'd*, no doubt,   75
Twinkling faster and faster, ye all would *go out*.

Apropos, my dear Lord! a ridiculous blunder
Of some of our Journalists caus'd us some wonder:
It was said, that in aspect malignant and sinister,
In the Isle of Great Britain a great Foreign Minister   80
Turn'd as pale as a Journeyman Miller's frock coat is,
On observing a star that appeared in BOOTES!
When the whole truth was this (O those ignorant brutes!)
Your Lordship had made his appearance in boots.
You, my Lord, with your star, sat in boots, and the Spanish   85
Ambassador thereupon thought fit to vanish.
But, perhaps, dear my Lord, among other worse crimes,
The whole was no more than a lie of *The Times*.
It is monstrous, my Lord! in a civilis'd state,
That such Newspaper rogues should have licence to prate.   90
Indeed, printing in general—but for the taxes,
Is in theory false and pernicious in praxis!
You and I, and your Cousin, and Abbe Sieyes,
And all the great Statesmen, that live in these days,
Are agreed, that no nation secure is from vi'lence,   95
Unless all, who must think, are maintain'd all in silence.

"To fence my song against the vulgar rout,
"And shine upon me with her *geminies?*"

82. BOOTES!] C's astronomical punning may have been inspired by the identification of other ministers in Pitt's government with stars in the anonymous "Ode, Pindarico-Sapphico-Macaronica . . . in Guilielmi Pittii . . . laudem" rpt from *M Chron* in *The Spirit of the Public Journals for 1800* IV (1801) 295–304 at 297 and 303, though it is George Rose who is Boötes and there is no mention of boots. On the negotiations with Spain see *M Post* (16 Dec 1799); *The Spirit of the Public Journals for 1800* 295–304; *The Spirit of the Public Journals for 1801* V (1802) 37–8; etc.

85–6. The punctilious Spaniard was upset by Grenville's lack of decorum.

93. The Abbé Siéyès (1748–1836) had been active in revolutionary politics from the inception of the movement. He was a member of the provisional consulate until Dec 1799 and helped Napoleon draft the new constitution.

96. The Newspaper Act of Apr 1799, putting proprietors and printers on record, and the continued suspension of Habeas Corpus, subjecting them to imprisonment without trial, gave the government strong legal control. Unofficial control through the

This printing, my Lord—but 'tis useless to mention,
What we both of us think—'twas a cursed invention,
And Germany might have been honestly prouder,
Had she left it alone, and found out only powder.   100
My Lord! when I think of our labours and cares,
Who rule the department of foreign affairs,
And how with their libels these journalists bore us,
Tho' Rage I acknowledge than Scorn less decorous;
Yet their presses and types I could shiver in splinters,   105
Those Printers' black Devils! those Devils of Printers!
In case of a peace—but perhaps it were better
To proceed to the absolute point of my letter:
For the deep wounds of France, Bonaparte, my master,
Has found out a new sort of *basilicon* plaister.   110
But your time, my dear Lord! is your nation's best treasure,
I've intruded already too long on your leisure;
If so, I entreat you with penitent sorrow
To pause, and resume the remainder to-morrow.

262.X1. THE PICCOLOMINI

[Feb–Mar 1800]

See vol III.

---

granting or withholding of subsidies had already severely circumscribed the independence of British journalism. In France most of the newspapers were still controlled by the royalists, many by Jacobins, but Napoleon would shortly (17 Jan 1800) close 60 of the 76 existing papers. On 27 Feb 1799 the *Moniteur* had been constituted the official government organ.

106. Printers' devils were boys who removed newly inked sheets from the printing press and whose hands and faces, as a result, were habitually black with ink.

110. *basilicon* plaister] A plaister or drug supposed to possess "sovereign" (βασιλικός "royal"), i.e. powerful, virtues.

PASSAGE DU GRAND S.^T BERNARD EFFECTUÉ PAR L'ARMÉE DE RÉSERVE.

9. Lithograph by H. C. Müller of the French army crossing the Great St Bernard Pass on its way to the Marengo campaign in 1800. The French Revolutionary and Napoleonic Wars of 1792–1815, unprecedented in scale, produced economic and political consequences of the most profound kind for English society

263. A COUPLET ON TANNING

[Feb–Mar 1800]

The lines appear in a notebook only (*CN* I 692), and are undoubtedly connected with one of C's tanning friends, TP or Samuel Purkiss; they might even have been given to C by one of them. C dined with Purkis in London at the time KC suggests the notebook entry was made, and was in correspondence with TP about a house at Aisholt (*Poole* II 4, 6; *CL* I 562: to TP [Jan 1800]; etc).

A Brown, for which Heaven would disband
The Galaxy, & all the Stars be tann'd.

263.X1. THE DEATH OF WALLENSTEIN

[Mar–May 1800]

See vol III.

264. LINES FOR HARTLEY COLERIDGE

[Before Jun 1800]

The lines were recorded by HNC in the *Table Talk* Workbook, under 14 Aug 1833, with a prose explanation (see *TT—CC—*I 415):

I always made a point of associating images of cheerfulness & lightsomeness with death & the grave, when instructing my children. To be sure, I believe little H. did astonish a party of very grave persons, his mother's aunt's connections, who asked him if he had learnt any hymns—by replying affirmatively saying that Papa had taught him a pretty Resurrection Hymn—wch he repeated with great glee as follows:

One has to suppose the occasion taking place before the family, including the precocious HC, moved north.

Splother! splother! splother!
Father & mother!

Wings on our shoulders—
And Up we go!

265. TWO LINES ON THE STARS
AND THE MOUNTAINS

[Jul 1800]

The lines were written into Notebook $5\frac{1}{2}$ (*CN* I 766), which continues thereafter: "July 25, 1800—a grey whiteness all over them, [. . .] they looked black thro' a grey gauze of mist—". Then C adds the phrase "The Intenebrants & Nephel-ηκeka-lummenists."—i.e. "the dwellers in darkness" and "persons who have adopted the practice of veiling themselves in cloud", referring to obscurantists with words coined from Latin and Greek derivations.

And tho' the Stars were many & bright in Heaven,
There was a hoary Twilight on the Mountains—

266. ON THE POET'S EYE

[Aug 1800]

When C drafted the lines in Notebook 21 (*CN* I 791), he set the scene in his Keswick study: "11 ° clock at night—that conical Volcano of coal, half an inch high, ~~sending~~ ejaculating it's inverted cone of smoke—the smoke in what a furious wind, this way, that way—& what a noise!" When the lines were printed in *Bl Mag* (Jan 1822), the metre and tone were modified. They were never collected and the version given here is from the notebook, ignoring a superseded version of line 3 and laying out the lines as verse.

The poet's eye in his tipsy hour
Hath a magnifying power
His soul emancipates his eyes
Of the accidents of size/
In unctuous cones of kindling Coal   5
Or smoke from his Pipe's bole

His eye can see
Phantoms of sublimity.

267. THE TWO ROUND SPACES ON THE TOMBSTONE: A SKELTONIAD (TO BE READ IN THE RECITATIVE LILT)

[Sept–Oct 1800]

C liked to maintain that the origins of the poem were accidental. "Mackintosh was taken slightly ill in passing through Grasmere; the snow was deep, & I remember being tickled, as I looked on the humble church-yard, with the thought that if he, a great lawyer & a Scotchman should die, his burial there with a great tombstone in the middle of the ground would be an odd circumstance" (VCL S MS 20 Clutch 1 = ms for *TT* 31 Mar 1833—*CC*—I 352–3 var). There is, however, no record of Mackintosh passing through Grasmere, nor of snow falling before C had already sent a copy of the poem to Davy. C's comments on the poem are complicated by a sense of its lack of charity and, after it began to circulate, a fear that it would offend. It was associated in his mind with **214** *The Devil's Thoughts*, and he appears not to have discouraged rumours of RS's authorship (see vol II TEXT MS 3), for similar reasons. However, although RS is credited with stanza 16 (pillorying the Scots) in the 1834 version of poem **214**, he was in Portugal when the present poem was written.

The object of C's lampoon is James Mackintosh (1765–1832). C assumes that he is dead and that, until the world ends and Christ returns—according to the old belief, "About the same hour that he came last", i.e. at Epiphany— "The Dev'l and his Grannam" will spend the daybreak of every Epiphany at Mackintosh's tomb, to claim him when the last trumpet sounds. The terms of the attack are political. Mackintosh had repudiated his earlier attitude towards the French Revolution by his friendship with Burke and in *A Discourse on the Study of the Law of Nature and Nations* (Feb 1799), for which he was excoriated by the radicals. C seems even to apply the specific and famous condemnation of Mackintosh by his former friend, the unrepentant Whig Dr Parr, giving equal emphasis to his being a Scot, a lawyer, and an apostate (P. W. Clayden *The Early Life of Samuel Parr*—1887—381).

But ideological differences were less pronounced than C liked to pretend, and his motivation is instinctive and visceral, indeed unfair. There is an autograph letter at PML, dated London 17 Nov 1797, addressed by Mackintosh to C, offering to assist him financially and asking him to write for *M Post* (MA 1857 R–V No 8). The fact that Mackintosh introduced C to Daniel Stuart (his brother-in-law by his first wife), and was related by his second marriage to C's patrons the Wedgwoods, appears to have exacerbated rather than assuaged C's hostility. C disliked Mackintosh because he was a Scot, and disliked Scots because of the qualities they shared with Mackintosh. A series of letters from Stuart to C at PML (MA 1857 Nos 4, 5, 12) show that Stuart was evidently not on good terms with his brother-in-law, and he evidently helped set C against him.

A Skeltoniad (not in *OED*) is a satirical poem like *The Dunciad* or *The Rosciad*. Modelled on the verse of John Skelton (c 1460–1529), it consists of irregular lines with frequent repetition of the same rhyme. Although C had projected such a poem some months before (*CN* I 386), and though the lavatorial images are anticipated in letters in which more reasoned objections were becoming clearer (e.g. *CL* I 588: to W. Godwin 21 May 1800, *CN* I 634), the attack was possibly triggered by suspicions that Mackintosh had moved or would move in to help Stuart while C remained in the north. C had been detained by work on the second edition of *LB*, and six months later told Godwin that he expected Mackintosh to have been talking against WW's poetry in London (*CL* II 737: 23 Jun 1801). Mackintosh admitted to Fox in 1807 that "Coleridge is well known to have (copiously enough) disliked me" (*Memoirs of Sir James Mackintosh*—2 vols 1836—I 326; and see also *BL*—1907—I 228–9n, *CN* II 2468n).

The present text follows a fair copy in C's hand, being a slightly revised version of that sent to Davy in Oct 1800 and soon afterwards published (in part) in *M Post*. The title derives from the earlier ms and the *M Post* versions. At least eight other versions are recorded, of varying authority and all differing slightly and differently coinciding, although C did not acknowledge the poem until *PW* (1834). The variations between texts for the most part concern single words and phrases and the division of lines. The original meaning is muffled in some versions by substituting 5 or 7 Jan in line 20, and by moving line 25 to follow line 32.

The Devil believes, that the Lord will come
Stealing a March without Beat of Drum
About the same hour that he came last,
On an old Christmas Day, in a snowy Blast.
Till he bids the Trump sound, nor Body nor Soul stirs: 5
For the Dead Men's Heads have slipp'd under their Bolsters.

Ho! Ho! Brother Bard! In our Church-Yard
Both Beds and Bolsters are soft and green:
Save one alone, & that's of stone,
And under it lies a Counsellor keen: 10

7. Brother Bard] WW.

Twould be a square Tomb if it were not too long,
And tis rail'd round with Irons tall, spearlike, & strong.

This Fellow from Aberdeen hither did skip
With a waxy face & a blabber lip
And a black tooth in front, to shew in part   15
What was the colour of his whole heart.
This Counsellor sweet! this Scotchman complete!
The Devil *scotch* him for a snake!
I trust, he lies in his Grave awake!

On the 6th of January   20
When all is white both high & low
As a Cheshire Yeoman's Dairy,
Brother Bard, ho! ho! Believe it or no,
On that tall tomb to you I'll shew
Before Sun-rise & after Cock-crow   25
Two round spaces void of snow.
I swear by our Knight & his forefathers' Souls
That in shape & in size they are just like the Holes
    In the house of Privity
    Of that ancient Family.   30

On those two spaces void of snow
There have sate in the night, for an hour or so,
He kicking his Heels, she cursing her Corns,

13–19. Stuart omitted these lines when he published the poem in *M Post*. Mackintosh was a lawyer from Aberdeen and, as Stuart afterwards explained, "had had one of his front teeth broken and the stump was black" ("Anecdotes of the Poet Coleridge" *Gentleman's Magazine* NS IX—May 1838—485–92 at 486).

18. The Devil] The earliest ms version has Apollyon, the Greek name for Abaddon, king of hell and angel of the bottomless pit. The specific allusion to Rev 9.11 strengthens the Apocalyptic-Epiphanic motif.

19. In one ms C wrote alongside "a *humane* Wish." The reason is—despite his real horror of "lying in a dark, cold place", awake in the grave (*BL* ch 22—*CC*—II 141)—that the alternative supposed here for Mackintosh is hell.

27. our Knight] A poetic licence; Mackintosh was not knighted until 1803.

31 et seq. The doom to which Panurge consigns the soul of the old poet Rominagrobis for his heretical sarcasms on the monastic order, at the close of Rabelais *Œuvres* (Paris 1567 etc) bk 3 (Pantagruel) ch 22.

All to the tune of the Wind in their Horns,
    The Dev'l and his Grannam   35
    With a snow-blast to fan 'em,
Expecting & hoping the Trumpet to blow,
For they are cock-sure of the Fellow below!

268. SIX LINES ON A KESWICK HOLIDAY

[1800?]

The lines were drafted in Notebook 4 (*CN* I 899), and never published.

    Upon a sunny Holiday
    When the Bells were ringing merrily
    I looked from my window
    On the dazzling Lake that twinkled
    Thro' the dancing Leaves of   5
    The Trees on the Margin

269. THE MAD MONK

[Sept–Oct 1800]

The poem was published in *M Post* (13 Oct 1800), over the signature "CAS-SIANI, jun."; and in a posthumous collection of Mrs Robinson's poems, as by "S. T. COLERIDGE, Esq." It resembles **168** *The Old Man of the Alps* and **172** *Lewti* in that it is a revision and expansion of earlier lines by WW, although, significantly, it is differently signed.

Although the *M Post* version can be supposed to have been reworked by C, it none the less contains many anticipations and echoes of poems by WW. In particular, the second stanza resembles the first stanza of the *Intimations Ode*, and the whole poem resembles *'Tis Said, that Some Have Died for Love* (*WPW* IV 279, II 33–4). The relative contributions of WW and C have therefore been much debated, as well as the spirit in which the revision was made. Neither poet acknowledged authorship of the poem, or collected it. On internal grounds, it has been read as the work of each of them separately and as a parody of WW. Unless further external evidence comes to light, it is impossible to decide between the alternatives; and it is unsurprising that it is given both here and in the Cornell Wordsworth (*"Lyrical Ballads", and Other Poems, 1797–1800* ed James Butler and Karen Green—Ithaca 1992—802–6). The final version appears to be a mixture of borrowed material, parody, and genuinely attempted imitation (by C), a mixture characterised by a distinctive tone of uncertainty.

If the revision was made with parody in mind, the parody was not primarily of WW. The subtitle in the *M Post* version is "AN ODE, in Mrs. RAT-CLIFF's manner", but the poem recalls Mrs Robinson too, and even hints at Joseph Cottle. There is a situation in Mrs Radcliffe's *The Italian* (1797: III 222–34) where the monk Schedoni, "nearly frantic", confesses to the murder of his beloved when jealousy came and lit his "passions into madness"; or again, C's (or WW's) second stanza echoes sentiments expressed by St Aubert and the Count de Villefort in Mrs Radcliffe's earlier *Mysteries of Udolpho* (1794: III 337–8, 362–3). C reviewed *The Italian* for the *Critical Review* (*SW&F— CC*—79–82). There are similarly Gothic situations in Mrs Robinson's writing, e.g. in her *Anselmo, the Hermit of the Alps* and *The Murdered Maid*. More important, she has the same gentle elegiac note that pervades *The Mad Monk* and accompanies its drama. Last of all, CL had written to C on 26 Aug 1800 about his reading in Joseph Cottle's *Alfred*: "I got as far as the Mad monk the first day & fainted. . . . His terrific scenes are indefatigable" (*LL—M—*I 236). C remembered and quoted CL's response in a letter to Josiah Wedgwood on 1 Nov (*CL* I 645), and this, as well as the scene in Cottle's poem (*Alfred: An Epic Poem, in Twenty-four Books*—1800—II 214–330), appears to lie behind the occasion of the poem's composition.

The idea of imitating the kind of writing attacked in the Preface to the 1800 *LB*—"frantic novels, sickly and stupid German Tragedies . . . idle and extravagant stories in verse" (*W Prose* I 128)—probably occurred while the edition was being prepared. WW, who was not above joking at his own work about this time, might even have taken a hand in the early stages of the poem's development. A more specific occasion joins the Mad Monk of Cottle's poem and CL's response to it in a crude burlesque entitled "Imitation of Modern Poetry, An attempt at the simple," signed "H" in *M Post* (2 Oct 1800). C remarked on its crudity at the same time as he praised its drollness, on 7 Oct, and asked Daniel Stuart who the author was (*CL* I 629; "H" was in fact William Jerdan). It is possible that the same fragmentary letter to Stuart—which C filled out "with a few Poems", one of which was **192** *Alcaeus to Sappho* (a revision of WW) and another of which might have been **267** *The Two Round Spaces on the Tombstone*—contained the text of *The Mad Monk*.

The *M Post* pseudonym is in line with C's practice of signing poems he took over from WW, although this particular signature was not used elsewhere. It might hint at WW as hermit, since there was an austere, mad 4th-century hermit named Johannes Cassianus; possibly at C himself, through Giuliano Cassiani, the Italian nationalist poet who had written somewhat in the manner of *The Mad Monk* before his death in 1778; possibly at the satiric-parodic intention, via an

allusion to Bayle's note on Cassius Longinus (Lucius)—"It is from the judicial
severity of this Cassius, that very rigid Judges have been called *Cassiani*" (*A
General Dictionary, Historical and Critical . . . of Mr. Bayle*—10 vols 1734–
41—IV 166).

The same letter to Stuart of 7 Oct, which could have enclosed the text of *The
Mad Monk*, commented also on Mary Robinson's illness (she died on 26 Dec
1800). A text was also sent to Mrs Robinson, probably about the same time as
the one to Stuart. The fact that C sent it to her proves that he intended imitation
as much as parody; and this joins with echoes of several of his poems (for
example, line 45 recalls the Ancient Mariner's "O let me be awake, my God! |
Or let me sleep alway") as a reminder of the mixture of motives and tone.

The present text is the slightly improved one sent to Mrs Robinson. The *M
Post* text differs in its title (*The Voice from the Side of Etna; or, The Mad
Monk*) and in the phrasing of individual lines. It also has a different division
into stanzas (8⁺, 16⁺, 24⁺, 32⁺, 37⁺, 45⁺), and continues after line 47 as follows:

> The twilight fays came forth in dewy shoon,
> Ere I within the cabin had withdrawn,
> The goat-herd's tent upon the open lawn.
> That night there was no moon!!

I heard a voice from Etna's side;
   Where, o'er a cavern's mouth
   That fronted to the south,
A chestnut spread its umbrage wide:
A hermit, or a monk, the man might be;   5
But him I could not see:
And thus the music flow'd along,
In melody most like to old Sicilian song:

"There was a time when earth, and sea, and skies,
   The bright green vale, and forest's dark recess,   10
With all things, lay before mine eyes
   In steady loveliness:
But now I feel, on earth's uneasy scene,
   Such sorrows as will never cease;—
   I only ask for peace;   15
If I must live to know that such a time has been!"
A silence then ensued:

---

9. Echoed, in a different mood,   *1809.*
in **456** *Couplet Written in November*

Till from the cavern came
A voice;—it was the same!
And thus, in mournful tone, its dreary plaint renew'd: 20

"Last night, as o'er the sloping turf I trod,
   The smooth green turf, to me a vision gave
Beneath mine eyes, the sod—
   The roof of ROSA's grave!
My heart has need with dreams like these to strive;   25
   For, when I woke, beneath mine eyes, I found
   The plot of mossy ground,
On which we oft have sat when ROSA was alive.—
Why must the rock, and margin of the flood,
   Why must the hills so many flow'ret's bear,   30
   Whose colours to a *murder'd* maiden's blood
     Such sad resemblance wear?—
I struck the wound,—this hand of mine!
For Oh, thou maid divine,
   I lov'd to agony!   35
The youth whom thou call'dst thine
   Did never love like me?

"Is it the stormy clouds above
   That flash'd so red a gleam?
   On yonder downward trickling stream?—   40
'Tis not the blood of her I love.—
The sun torments me from his western bed,
   Oh, let him cease for ever to diffuse
   Those crimson spectre hues!
Oh, let me lie in peace, and be for ever dead!"   45

Here ceas'd the voice. In deep dismay,
Down thro' the forest I pursu'd my way.

270. INSCRIPTION FOR A SEAT BY A ROAD SIDE, HALF-WAY UP A STEEP HILL, FACING THE SOUTH

[Aug–Oct 1800]

The only known text was printed over the signature "VENTIFRONS" in *M Post* (21 Oct 1800) rpt *Cambridge Intelligencer* (8 Nov 1800). The signature renders literally "Windy Brow", the farmhouse on Latrigg above Keswick once owned by the family of WW's friend and patron Raisley Calvert. It is not clear whether the poem should be ascribed wholly to WW, or should be considered a revision by C of earlier lines by WW. The second alternative is more likely, although the evidence is circumstantial. C's use of an early WW poem in **192** *Alcaeus to Sappho* pub *M Post* (24 Nov 1800) may be seen as a close parallel.

The first version of the poem in octosyllabic couplets is to be found in WW's Windy Brow Notebook (DCL MS 10 ff 18ᵛ, 19ᵛ; *WEPF* 271–2), where it follows on the beginning of **169** *Translation of a Greek Song*. It is dated between Apr and mid-May 1794 by Reed I 25, 152. The second version of the poem, on which the *M Post* version is based, was drafted in WW's Racedown Notebook (DCL MS 11 ff 21ᵛ, 22ʳ, 30ʳ–31ʳ, 33ʳ–35ʳ; *WEPF* 294, 300–1, 303–5) some time between spring/summer 1796 and spring 1797. The same notebook carried a version of **168** *The Old Man of the Alps* and WW's beginning of **155** *The Three Graves*.

It used to be thought that the untitled fair copy on ff 33ʳ–35ʳ was in WW's hand with additions in the hand of MH. Carol Landon and Jared Curtis guess that it was made by DW (*WEPF* 279–80, 750–1) and, in a separate article, Curtis speculates that C and DW might have played a part in arriving at this version (" 'Poem Hid in a Tin Box': Dorothy Wordsworth and the *Inscription for a Seat by the Pathway Side Ascending to Windy Brow*" *Bucknell Review* XXXVI—1992—156–72). It reads as follows:

> Thou who with youthful vigour rich & light
> With youthful thoughts dost need *no rest*—to whom
> The plain & mountains breast alike present ~~an~~
> A path of ease if chance thy careless eye
> Glance on this ~~spot~~ Turf—here stop & think on ~~these~~em
> The ~~houseless~~ weary homeless vagrants of the earth
> Or ~~of~~ that ⟨poor⟩ man the rustic artisan
> Who ~~lo~~aaden with his implements of toil
> Returns at night to his far-distant home
> And having plodded on through rain & mire
> ~~h~~His ~~limbs~~ frame oer ~~wearied~~ laboured weak with feverish heat
> And chafed & fretted by December's blasts

Here pauses thankful to recruit his strength
And mid the sheltering warmth of these bleak trees
~~Doth find a grateful calm /~~ A grateful quiet finds or think on them
Who in the Spring to meet the warmer sun
Crawl up this steep hill side that double bends
Their bodies bowed by age or malady
And having gazed at last the wished for ~~spot~~ seat
Repose & well-adm*i*onished ponder here
On final rest. & if a serious thought
Should come uncalled ~~that~~ how won each motion light
Thy balmy spirits & thy ⟨now⟩ fervid blood
~~Will~~ Shall change to mournful feeble cold & dry
Cherish the wholesome sadness. *i*And wher'eer
The tide of life impel thee   Oh be prompt
To lend thy strength to be the staff of all
That need support so   shalt thou give
To youth the sweetest joy that youth can know
And for thy future*s* self thou shalt prepare
Through every change of years & pain that balm
Which 'mid a tossing world shall soothe thy heart
Even till thou sink beneath the waves to Peace—
                    (cf *WEPF* 755, 757; also *WPW* I 301–2)

The Racedown Notebook drafts are evidence of WW's difficulty with the poem, and his disinclination to publish the fair copy is evidence that he was not sure he had solved the problems. In addition, he never included the *M Post* version in any of his own collections—in contrast to his inclusion of other poems which he published in the same newspaper and which were subscribed, differently, "W.W." or "MORTIMER." Therefore, although RS was inclined to attribute the *M Post* version to WW simply (a worn cutting from the newspaper is preserved at Waterloo University, Ontario—Bertram Davis Collection—with WW's initials subjoined in what might be RS's hand), it is more probably a revision by C. C is known to have been especially interested in the seat at Windy Brow from early Aug 1800, as well as in other garden seats at the same time (*DWJ* I 55, 58; *CN* I 830); and he is known to have been interested in writing poems on the naming of places in Sept–Oct (*WL—E* rev—304–5). He made use of other WW juvenilia in which WW had no further interest to meet his commitments to *M Post* at this time, signing them with a variety of apposite pseudonyms like the one here, and *CN* I 830 suggests that he worked on WW's poem after 10 Oct.

Thou, who in youthful vigour rich, and light
With youthful thought, dost need no rest! O thou,
To whom alike the valley and the hill

Present a path of ease! Should e'er thine eye
Glance on this sod, and this rude tablet, stop!   5
'Tis a rude spot; yet here, with thankful hearts,
The foot-worn soldier and his family
Have rested, wife and babe, and boy, perchance,
Some eight years old or less, and scantly fed,
Garb'd like his father, and already bound   10
To his poor father's trade! Or think of him,
Who, laden with his implements of toil,
Returns at night to some far distant home,
And having plodded on through rain and mire
With limbs o'erlabour'd, weak from fev'rish heat,   15
And chaf'd and fretted by December blasts,
Here pauses, thankful, he hath reach'd so far;
And 'mid the shelt'ring warmth of these bleak trees
Finds restoration. Or reflect on them,
Who, in the spring, to meet the warmer sun,   20
Crawl up this steep hill side, that needlessly
Bends double their weak frames, already bow'd
By age or malady; and when at last
They gain this wish'd-for turf, this seat of sods,
Repose, and, well admonish'd, ponder here   25
On final rest. And if a serious thought
Should come uncall'd—how soon thy motions light,
Thy balmy spirits, and thy fervid blood,
Must change to feeble, wither'd, cold, and dry,
Cherish the wholesome sadness! And where'er   30
The tide of life impel thee, O be prompt
To make thy present strength the staff of all,
Their staff and resting place: so shalt thou give
To youth, the sweetest joy that youth can know,
And for thy future self thou shalt provide   35
Through ev'ry change of various life a seat,
Not built by hands, on which thy inner part,
Imperishable, many a grievous hour,
Or bleak, or sultry, may repose; yea, sleep
The sleep of death, and dream of blissful worlds,   40
Then wake in Heav'n, and find the dream all true!

270.X1. THE SPELL
OR, LAUGH TILL YOU LOSE HIM!

[1800–15]

See vol III.

271. A STRANGER MINSTREL

[Nov 1800]

The poem was printed only twice in C's lifetime—in Mary Robinson's *Memoirs* (1801) and in her *Poetical Works* (1806). It was doubtless written in response to her *Ode Inscribed to the Infant Son of S. T. Coleridge, Esq. Born Sept 14, at Keswick, in Cumberland*, which appeared in *M Post* (17 Oct 1800).

Mary "Perdita" Robinson (1758–1800) was an actress who became the mistress of the Prince of Wales. Abandoned by the prince, she contracted the beginnings of a slowly paralysing illness and about the same time turned to literature. C reviewed her novel *Hubert de Sevrac* in *Critical Review* NS XXIII (1798) 472 (cf *CL* I 318: to W. L. Bowles [16 Mar 1797]; *SW&F—CC—*82), but their friendship began only in the last year of her life. It was based on an admiration for her as a poet, sympathy for her political views, and a deepening respect for her as a woman, as well as a degree of self-identification. The exchange of poems between the two has been excellently described by Susan Luther "A Stranger Minstrel: Coleridge's Mrs. Robinson" *Studies in Romanticism* (Boston, Mass) XXXIII (Fall 1994) 391–409. However, see C's letter to her daughter of 27 Dec 1802 (*CL* II 903–6), where he also protests against the printing of his "silly" poem; and also **269** *The Mad Monk*, where Mrs Robinson's poems may be among those which are parodied.

As late on Skiddaw mount I lay supine
Midway th' ascent, in that repose divine,
When the soul, center'd in the heart's recess,
Hath quaff'd its fill of Nature's loveliness,
Yet still beside the fountain's marge will stay,   5
   And fain would thirst again, again to quaff;—
Then, when the tear, slow travelling on its way,
   Fills up the wrinkle of a silent laugh;
In that sweet mood of sad and humorous thought—

A form within me rose, within me wrought   10
With such strong magic, that I cry'd aloud,
Thou ancient SKIDDAW! by thy helm of cloud,
And by thy many-colour'd chasms so deep;
And by their shadows, that for ever sleep;
By yon small flaky mists, that love to creep   15
Along the edges of those spots of light,
Those sunshine islands on thy smooth green height;
 And by yon shepherds with their sheep,
 And dogs and boys, a gladsome crowd,
 That rush even now with clamour loud   20
Sudden from forth thy topmost cloud;
And by this laugh, and by this tear,
I would, old Skiddaw! SHE were here!
A Lady of sweet song is she,
Her soft blue eye was made for thee!   25
O ancient Skiddaw! by this tear,
I would, I would, that she were here!

Then ancient SKIDDAW, stern and proud,
 In sullen majesty replying,
Thus spake from out his helm of cloud,   30
 (His voice was like an echo dying!)
"She dwells, belike, by scenes more fair,
"And scorns a mount so bleak and bare!"
I only sigh'd, when this I heard,
Such mournful thoughts within me stirr'd,   35
That all my heart was faint and weak,
 So sorely was I troubled!
No laughter wrinkled now my cheek,
 But O! the tears were doubled.

But ancient Skiddaw, green and high,   40
Heard and understood my sigh:
And now in tones less stern and rude,
As if he wish'd to end the feud,
Spake he, the proud response renewing:
(His voice was like a monarch wooing!)   45

"Nay, but thou dost not know her might,
 "The pinions of her soul how strong!

"But many a stranger in my height
"Hath sung to me her magic song,
  "Sending forth his extacy   50
"In her divinest melody;
"And hence I know, her soul is free,
"She is, where'er she wills to be,
  "Unfetter'd by mortality!
"Now to the 'haunted beach' can fly,   55
  "Beside the threshold scourg'd with waves,
  "Now to the maniac while he raves,
"*Pale moon! thou spectre of the sky!*"
"No wind that hurries o'er my height
"Can travel with so swift a flight.   60
  "I too, methinks, might merit
  "The presence of her spirit!
  "To me too might belong
"The honour of her song, and witching melody,
  "Which most resembles me,   65
  "Soft, various, and sublime,
  "Exempt from wrongs of Time!"
Thus spake the mighty Mount: and I
Made answer with a deep-drawn sigh,
Thou ancient SKIDDAW! by this tear   70
I would, I would, that she were here!

271.X1. THE TRIUMPH OF LOYALTY

[Dec 1800–Jan 1801]

See vol III.

55. Mary Robinson's *The Haunted Beach* was published in *M Post* (26 Feb 1800), where it greatly pleased C, who recommended it to RS for the *Annual Anthology* (*CL* I 575–6: [postmark 28 Feb 1800]).

58. From Mary Robinson's *Jasper* 12, a poem which C particularly recommended to RS for inclusion in the *Annual Anthology* (*CL* I 562–3: 25 Jan 1800).

272. THE NIGHT-SCENE:
A DRAMATIC FRAGMENT

[Dec 1800–Jan 1801]

C's lines are repeated almost unchanged from the play he wrote, or at least began to write, in Dec 1800–Jan 1801, taking the plot from Lessing's *Hamburgische Dramaturgie* Nos 600–8 (see *CN* I 869, 871). It is a version of the Elizabeth and Essex story, set in Spain, though only the overall plan and the first three scenes of Act I remain. See vol III **271.X1** *The Triumph of Loyalty* for further details.

The present text makes up lines 92–173 of the second scene; it is the only part C published, and not until *SL* (1817) and thereafter. The published texts vary little from the ms draft or from each other. In the very first ms draft Earl Henry's speech was 66 lines long; Sandoval's interjection at line 36 was introduced in ms revision, and lines 52–6 were first given to Sandoval in *SL*. *SL* elsewhere introduces a few improvements of wording, and throughout regularises the light punctuation of the ms. The texts of *PW* (1828, 1829, 1834) change only punctuation, capitals, and spelling. The present text reproduces that of *SL*, incorporating errata in lines 23 and 24. For further textual variants see *The Triumph of Loyalty* I ii 91–172.

SANDOVAL.
You lov'd the daughter of Don Manrique?

Earl HENRY.
Lov'd?

SANDOVAL.
Did you not say you woo'd her?

Earl HENRY.
Once I lov'd
Her whom I dar'd not woo!

SANDOVAL.
And woo'd, perchance,
One whom you lov'd not!

Earl HENRY.
     Oh! I were most base,
Not loving Oropeza. True, I woo'd her,   5
Hoping to heal a deeper wound; but she
Met my advances with empassion'd pride,
That kindled love with love. And when her sire,
Who in his dream of hope already grasp'd
The golden circlet in his hand, rejected   10
My suit with insult, and in memory
Of ancient feuds pour'd curses on my head,
Her blessings overtook and baffled them!
But thou art stern, and with unkindly countenance
Art inly reasoning whilst thou listen'st to me.   15

SANDOVAL.
Anxiously, Henry! reasoning anxiously.
But Oropeza—

Earl HENRY.
    Blessings gather round her!
Within this wood there winds a secret passage,
Beneath the walls, which opens out at length
Into the gloomiest covert of the Garden—   20
The night ere my departure to the army,
She, nothing trembling, led me thro' that gloom,
And to that covert by a silent stream,
Which, with one star reflected near its marge,
Was the sole object visible around me.   25
No leaflet stirr'd; the air was almost sultry;
So deep, so dark, so close, the umbrage o'er us!
No leaflet stirr'd;—yet pleasure hung upon
The gloom and stillness of the balmy night-air.
A little further on an arbor stood,   30
Fragrant with flowering trees—I well remember
What an uncertain glimmer in the darkness
Their snow-white blossoms made—thither she led me,
To that sweet bower—Then Oropeza trembled—
I heard her heart beat—if 'twere not my own.   35

SANDOVAL.
A rude and scaring note, my friend!

Earl HENRY.
                    Oh! no!
I have small memory of aught but pleasure.
The inquietudes of fear, like lesser streams
Still flowing, still were lost in those of love:
So love grew mightier from the fear, and Nature,   40
Fleeing from Pain, shelter'd herself in Joy.
The stars above our heads were dim and steady,
Like eyes suffused with rapture. Life was in us:
We were all life, each atom of our frames
A living soul—I vow'd to die for her: 45
With the faint voice of one who, having spoken,
Relapses into blessedness, I vow'd it:
That solemn vow, a whisper scarcely heard,
A murmur breathed against a lady's ear.
Oh! there is joy above the name of pleasure,   50
Deep self-possession, an intense repose.

    SANDOVAL (*with a sarcastic smile*).
No other than as eastern sages paint,
The God, who floats upon a Lotos leaf,
Dreams for a thousand ages; then awakening,
Creates a world, and smiling at the bubble,   55
Relapses into bliss.

        Earl HENRY.
                    Ah! was that bliss
Fear'd as an alien, and too vast for man?
For suddenly, impatient of its silence,
Did Oropeza, starting, grasp my forehead.
I caught her arms; the veins were swelling on them.   60
Thro' the dark bower she sent a hollow voice,
Oh! what if all betray me? what if thou?
I swore, and with an inward thought that seem'd
The purpose and the substance of my being,
I swore to her, that were she red with guilt,   65
I would exchange my unblench'd state with hers.—
Friend! by that winding passage, to that bower
I now will go—all objects there will teach me
Unwavering love, and singleness of heart.
Go, Sandoval! I am prepar'd to meet her—   70

Say nothing of me—I myself will seek her—
Nay, leave me, friend! I cannot bear the torment
And keen inquiry of that scanning eye.—

               [*Earl* HENRY *retires into the wood.*

      SANDOVAL. (*alone.*)
O Henry! always striv'st thou to be great
By thine own act—yet art thou never great   75
But by the inspiration of great passion.
The whirl-blast comes, the desert-sands rise up
And shape themselves: from Earth to Heaven they stand,
As tho' they were the pillars of a temple,
Built by Omnipotence in its own honor!   80
But the blast pauses, and their shaping spirit
Is fled: the mighty columns were but sand,
And lazy snakes trail o'er the level ruins!

273. TWO LINES ON REMORSE

[Dec 1800–Jan 1801]

The lines are found only in Notebook 21 (*CN* I 877). It is impossible to say whether C wrote them with his play in mind.

     To each reproach that thunders from without
     May Remorse groan an echo.

77–9. For the personal application of this image of the whirl-blast see *CL* II 663: to H. Davy 11 Jan 1801; 664: to TP 19 Jan 1801; and, for the shaping spirit of imagination, see **289** *A Letter to* —— 242; **293** *Dejection: An Ode* 86.

274. TWO LINES ON THE CUR, ARTHRITIS

[May 1801]

C quoted the lines in a letter to TP (*CL* II 732: 17 May 1801), in which he described how his knee was "swoln, & my left ?ancle in flames of fire", and how "last night these pretty companions kept me sleepless the whole night—hour after hour". He was moved to verse by a similar affliction in Oct 1832 (see **679** *Sciatic Rheumatism* and **680** *An Autograph on an Autopergamene*).

> I utter'd, and suppress'd full many a groan,
> The Cur, Arthritis, gnawing my knee-bone—

275. AFTER BATHING IN THE SEA AT SCARBOROUGH IN COMPANY WITH T. HUTCHINSON, AUGUST 1801

[Aug 1801]

C, still suffering the effects of the previous damp Keswick winter and an unhappy household, arrived on 1 Aug to stay at Bishop Middleham with George Hutchinson and SH, and had fallen ill with a swollen, agonising left knee, for which a Dr Fenwick (the "sage Physician" of line 5) had recommended horse-riding and warm sea-baths (*CL* II 748: to RS 1 Aug 1801). He had then moved on, accompanied by SH, to stay for a fortnight at Gallow Hill near Scarborough with Thomas Hutchinson, MH, Joanna Hutchinson, and others. He enclosed the poem in a letter to RS following his return to Bishop Middleham, with the following explanation:

> Dr Fenwick at Durham dissuaded me from bathing in *the open Sea*—he thought it would be fatal to me. I came out all at once on the Beach, and had Faith in the Ocean. I bathed regularly, frolicked in the Billows, and it did me a proper deal of good. . . . On my first emersion I composed a few lines which will please you as a symptom of convalescence—for alas! it

title. The version of the poem sent to RS, given here, bore no title. The present title is taken from an early ms fair copy.

is a long [time] since I have cropt a flowering weed on the sweet Hill of Poesy— (*CL* ɪɪ 751, 752: 11 [=12] Aug [1801])

The recovery of C's health was short-lived (**276** *Verse Letter to Miss Isabella Addison and Miss Joanna Hutchinson* 30–1); but the essence of his lines is their celebration of feelings of happiness and release, in the days spent at Gallow Hill in the company of SH and the others. The lines were published soon afterwards in *M Post*, over a pseudonym, and placed last among the love poems in *SL* (1817) and subsequent collections.

    C tinkered with the text in the versions up to *SL*, after which it was reprinted without change. He later referred to the poem as an ode and a song, although its essence is to state a mood of warming heart's-ease, of physical and emotional relief despite prognostication, of trust in the face of impossible circumstances. The first ms version is given here, omitting the stanza-numbering of the letter, on the grounds that C's revisions are in the direction of depersonalising and conventionalising a spontaneous, private impulse. The *SL* version incorporates his final revisions, but of course they were made after he left the north, never to return.

God be with thee, gladsome Ocean!
How gladly greet I thee once more—
    Ships and Waves and endless Motion
And Life rejoicing on thy Shore.

Gravely said the sage Physician,   5
To bathe me on thy shores were Death;
    But my Soul fulfill'd her Mission,
And lo! I breathe untroubled Breath.

Fashion's pining Sons and Daughters
That love the city's gilded Sty,   10
    Trembling they approach thy Waters
And what cares Nature, if they die?

Me a thousand Loves and Pleasures
A thousand Recollections bland,
    Thoughts sublime and stately Measures   15
Revisit on thy sounding Strand—

Dreams, the soul herself forsaking,
Grieflike Transports, boyish Mirth,

Silent Adorations, making
A blessed Shadow of this Earth!   20

O ye Hopes, that stir within me,
Health comes with you from above:
God is with me, God is in me,
I cannot die, if Life be Love!

276. VERSE LETTER TO MISS ISABELLA ADDISON AND MISS JOANNA HUTCHINSON

[Aug 1801]

C's verse letter was written on 19 Aug 1801, addressed to Gallow Hill (between Wykeham and Brompton, where WW and MH were to be married in 1802, in the Vale of Pickering), which he had left in the company of SH some ten days before. The farm was being worked by Tom Hutchinson (b 1773), one of SH's elder brothers. MH was with him there, along with the two recipients of C's letter. Isabella Addison (b 1784) was later to marry John Monkhouse, one of SH's favourite cousins, and Joanna Hutchinson (b 1780) was SH's younger sister. Antony (line 15) presumably worked for Tom Hutchinson.

The letter was written from Bishop Middleham in Co Durham, where one of SH's younger brothers, George (b 1778), had taken a farm and where SH was acting as his housekeeper. C's health had not been good, and the reference in line 27 is to the sulphur baths at Dinsdale, 12 miles south of Bishop Middleham, which had been his reason for returning from Gallow Hill (*CL* II 751–2: to RS 11 [=12] Aug [1801]). His health improved, as he describes here, and he was able to go home to Keswick about four days later.

The text given here is from the ms, which C never published. A few marks of punctuation have been supplied.

Respected Miss Is'bel,
             Ioanna, my Dear!
This comes to you hoping.—We're happy to hear
By a Pigeon, that early this morn did appear
At our window with two Billet-deux in it's Bill,
The Mare all obedient to Isabel's Will.   5

Two such beautiful Girls in so *knowing* a Pha'ton
(*Mem. A Board nail'd behind with a name and a date on*)
Two such *very* sweet Girls in a Taxer so green,
Miss Addison driving as bright as a Queen
And Joanna so gay—by the ghost of old Jehu,   10
It was well worth a shilling, my Lasses! to see you!
Why, even the Dust fell in love, I'll be bound,
With you both, and for Love could not rest on the ground
And Mary, for gladness & joy did not scant any
When she said Tom & you, with the Horse, Mare, & Antony.   15
But this topic, I fear, I've exhausted.—'twere better
With some news and advice, to enliven my Letter
But enough is as good as a feast—and for More,
Why, you know, it might surfeit—at least, make one snore.
But *one thing* indeed I am *forc'd* to declare—   20
You are both fair as Angels, and good as you're fair,
And I'll purchase a glazier's diamond, my Lasses,
To scribble your names on all windows & glasses.

Now for News.—There is none. My eyes I've not cock'd on
Brother George since last night: for he's gone into Stockton—   25
And on Saturday last, as that wit told you scoffing,
To Dinsdale I rode, & was boil'd in a coffin.
And then I *did* smell—aye, I smelt, by old Davy,
Like a Pole Cat serv'd up in an Addle-egg gravy.
High in health I return'd; but on Sunday grew bad,   30
And on Monday was worse, & a fever I had,
On Tuesday grew better, & on Wednesday, you see,
Am as gay as the Lark that sings high o'er the Lea.

6–8. A phaeton was a fashionable four-wheeled open carriage of light construction, usually drawn by a pair of horses and with one or two seats facing forward. A taxer, on the other hand, was a two-wheeled vehicle drawn by a single horse, used mainly for agricultural or trade purposes. Its name derives from a statute passed in 1795 (35 Geo III c 109 sec 2): "[by bearing the words] 'A taxed Cart', and also the Owner's Name and Place of Abode" it qualified for reduced road tax. The "ghost of old Jehu" (line 10) alludes to the fast and furious driver of 2 Kgs 9.20.

25. A market town on the Tees, 10 miles SE of Bishop Middleham.

28. old Davy] Davy Jones, the sailors' devil.

And next for ADVICE.—Aye, of that I have plenty
If instead of but two you were 20 times 20.   35
There's a Lake by the fir-grove—don't bathe there, I say;
Tis *tempting*, I own; but too much in the way
And it rouges, like Lamp-black—and then it were risible
To paint such fair Maids, as Joanna & Isabel.
A Brunette is a pretty complexion, *as such*—   40
But black & all black—why, tis somewhat too much.—
The sweet Lake hath a Die, that's too deep for a Lady—
So pray, be content with what Nature has made 'e.

But, secondly—Mind !—You'll be going to Scarborough—
I intreat and admonish you tho', not to harbour a   45
Thought of electing from Dukes or from Earls
A Husband to suit you—twon't answer, my Girls.
A Baronet?—Why, if he's eager to wed you,
You may do as you like—*I* shall not forbid you.
But as plain Meat is all that the Healthy desire,   50
Were I you, I'd put up with a simple Esquire.
Such a one now *as me. (Nota bene. I'm married,
And Coals to Newcastle must never be carried!!)*

But thirdly & *lastly*, for Enough, as I tell you,
Is as good as a feast—and More would but swell you.—   55
At present, they are doctoring George's black Mare—
I intreat and admonish you, *do* have a care
(You, Miss Addison, YOU I now am addressing,)
As you love poor Joanna, and hope for my Blessing,
Do keep the Mare's Physic snug out of her way   60
For Enough is as good as a Feast, as I say;
She has taken three ounces of Salts without manner
But she *may* take too much—& then farewell Joanna.

My love to dear Mary—& tell Tom to bear in
Remembrance his promise to come after shearing.   65
He might visit all way from the Thames to the Tyne
And not meet a Welcome more glowing than mine.

44. Scarborough, on the coast to the W of Gallow Hill, was a more exclusively fashionable resort in C's time than it became during the 19th century. Cf R. B. Sheridan *A Trip to Scarborough* (1777).

And if Mary will come, a kind kiss I will gi' her,
And at Grasmere are Folks, will be happy to see her;
At least, they will treat her with all due civility—   70
And Politeness is better than downright Hostility.
Bless my soul! What, turn over!—Why, I've written a whole Ridge—
Enough is a Feast—so adieu from

Your

Coleridge

P.S. Dear Girls! I had almost forgotten to say,
That I think, that you both possess charms in your way.   75

277. INSCRIPTION FOR A FOUNTAIN
ON A HEATH

[Sept 1801?]

Real-life, literary, and imagined elements intermingle in the poem. DC, in his copy of *SL*, cited Virgil *Georgics* 4.146 "Iamque ministrantem platanum potantibus umbras" tr Fairclough (LCL) ɪ 207 "and the plane already yielding to drinkers the service of its shade". Both WW and C were interested in the conventions of inscription-writing at this time. Specifically, C might have had in mind J. H. Voss's *Die Quellnymfe an den Wanderer*, which he could have read in the *Musen Almenach für 1793* ed Voss 98:

> Silberrein, unversiegt, dem vorüberwandelnden Fremdling
> Sprudelt aus wallendem Kies unten am Berge der Quell.
> Ringsumkränzt von Platanen und freundlich-grünenden Lorbern,
> Breit' ich auf kühlem Moos' einen beschattenden Sitz.
> Komm denn getrost in der Schwül', o Wanderer; labe den Durst dir,
> Und das ermattete Herz, lauschend dem stillen Geräusch.

C had translated Matthisson's *Milesisches Märchen* (pp 61–6 at 61–2 of the same issue of the *Musen Almenach*) as part of **186** *English Duodecasyllables*.

The sycamore held a particular place in the affections of the WW's circle— see *WPW* v 251, 465 (quoting lines 1–2 of the present poem); *WL* (*M* rev) ɪ 159; *W Prose* ɪɪ 203, 219—and C also associated the same group of friends with

69. at Grasmere are Folks] WW and DW.   **72.** The line begins a new page.

such a spring as the poem describes (*CN* I 980, 981), even though the real-life spring he had in mind appears to have been St Peter's Well, in the grounds of the Old Rectory at Upper Stowey (see *CN* II 2557 f 76ᵛ; cf *CN* I 980, 981; *CL* II 1000: to Sir George and Lady Beaumont 1 Oct 1803; *CN* II 2495 f 41ʳ). The location is confirmed as an imagined composite if lines 13b–14 below are taken to refer specifically to "Sara's Seat" (for which see also *CM—CC—*III 837), as is likely.

The first surviving version of the poem is the one copied into SH's album. In later years C came to associate it with AG, as a note in Lucy Gillman's copy of *PW* (1828) explains:

> This Fountain is an exact Emblem of what Mʳˢ Gillman was by Nature, and would still be, if the exhaustion by casualties and anxious duties & hope-surviving hopes, had not been too, too disproportionate ⟨to⟩ the "tiny", tho' never-failing, Spring of reproductive life at the bottom of the pure Basin. No Drouth! No impurity from without, no alien ingredient in it's own composition, it was indeed a crystal Fount of Water undefiled—But the Demand ~~was~~ has been beyond the Supply! the Exhaustion in merciless disproportion to the reproduction! But God be praised!—it is *immortal*, & will shoot up it's bright column of living Waters, where it's God will be ⟨the⟩ Sun, whose light it reflects! and it's place in Christ the containing and protecting Basin.
>
> 1832.

The earliest texts of the poem differ only very slightly from that found in *SL* (1817)—the text given here—and after.

> This Sycamore, oft musical with Bees,—
> Such Tents the Patriarchs lov'd! O long unharm'd
> May all its aged Boughs o'er-canopy
> The small round Basin, which this jutting stone
> Keeps pure from falling leaves! Long may the Spring,   5
> Quietly as a sleeping Infant's breath,
> Send up cold waters to the Traveller
> With soft and even Pulse! Nor ever cease
> Yon tiny Cone of Sand its soundless Dance,
> Which at the Bottom, like a Fairy's Page,   10
> As merry and no taller, dances still,
> Nor wrinkles the smooth Surface of the Fount.
> Here Twilight is and Coolness: here is Moss,
> A soft Seat, and a deep and ample Shade.
> Thou may'st toil far and find no second Tree.   15
> Drink, Pilgrim, here! Here rest! and if thy Heart

Be innocent, here too shalt thou refresh
Thy Spirit, list'ning to some gentle Sound,
Or passing Gale or Hum of murmuring Bees!

278. SONG TO BE SUNG BY THE LOVERS OF ALL THE NOBLE LIQUORS COMPRISED UNDER THE NAME OF ALE

[Before Sept 1801]

The only known version of the poem apppeared in *M Post* (18 Sept 1801) over the signature "Εστησε.", with a typographical error in line 2 (here corrected). It is not known whether it was prompted by rumoured changes in the availability or taxation of beers, or is merely a *jeu d'esprit.*

A.

Ye drinkers of Stingo and Nappy so free,
Are the Gods on Olympus so happy as we?

B.

They cannot be so happy!
For why? they drink no Nappy.

A.

But what if Nectar, in their lingo,   5
Is but another name for Stingo?

B.

Why, then we and the Gods are equally blest,
And Olympus an Ale-house, as good as the best!

1. Stingo was slang for strong ale or beer; nappy likewise, especially for a heady, strong, foaming ale.

279. DRINKING VERSUS THINKING
or, A SONG AGAINST THE NEW PHILOSOPHY

[Before Sept 1801]

The poem was published in *M Post* (25 Sept 1801), over the signature "Εστησε.", and is clearly connected with poem **278**.

My Merrymen all, that drink with glee,
This fanciful Philosophy,
Pray, tell me, what good is it?
If *antient Nick* should come and take
The same across the Stygian Lake, 5
I guess we ne'er should miss it.

Away, each pale, self-brooding spark,
That goes truth-hunting in the dark,
Away from our carousing!
To Pallas we resign such fowls— 10
Grave birds of wisdom! ye're but owls,
And all your trade but *mousing!*

My Merrymen all, here's punch and wine,
And spicy bishop, drink divine!
Let's live while we are able. 15
While MIRTH and SENSE sit, hand in glove,
This DON PHILOSOPHY we'll shove
Dead drunk beneath the table!

14. bishop] A kind of mulled or spiced wine or port, popular from the early 18th to the mid-19th century.

280. LINES WRITTEN IN BED AT GRASMERE

[Oct 1801]

The present text follows C's original ms version; the occasion was explained by DW when she copied the lines into WW's Commonplace Book: "Lines written by Coleridge in bed at Grasmere on Thursday night October 1ˢᵗ or rather on the Morning of Friday October 2ⁿᵈ 1801—". C's visit to Dove Cottage appears to have been for one night only, following WW's return from a month-long tour of the Scottish lakes with Basil Montagu and others (Reed ɪɪ 123–4). C had spent the same month at Keswick, suffering from the effects of the wet and the cold, and depressed by his domestic circumstances; while there he was visited by Mrs Southey and later RS himself (*CL* ɪɪ 760: to D. Stuart 19 Sept 1801; 762–3: to W. Godwin 22 Sept 1801; etc). His increasing resolve to leave his wife and live in a drier climate than the Lake District, combined with his appreciation of the understanding and domestic warmth he escaped to at Dove Cottage, whose vicinity he would also be leaving, lies behind the joking tone.

When the poem appeared in *M Post* a year later—three days after publication of **293** *Dejection: An Ode* in the same newspaper and after WW's wedding-day—C rewrote some lines (notably 41–7, 59–66) so as to make it seem that WW and DW had been visiting him at Keswick, and to disguise and dignify the original situation. The untitled *jeu d'esprit* becomes *An Ode to the Rain*; an introductory letter and a long footnote suggest that the poem is about how rain threatened to delay the departure of "a very worthy, but not very pleasant, visitor".

Although the revision incorporates several improvements of phrasing, it appears to have been made hastily. In particular, the transition in the mind of the speaker, as he shifts from the personified rain to the person of the supposed visitor, is incomplete. It is not mended by the long footnote, claiming the parallel authority of Schiller's *Wallenstein* v i 23–38, 48–9, and C soon afterwards described the revision as "feeble" and "unpolished" (*CL* ɪɪ 876: to T. Wedgwood 20 Oct 1802). For this reason, although the *M Post* version was reprinted in *SL* (1817) with a few more minor improvements (the footnote is dropped, a fifth section is begun at line 54, etc), the rougher but more spirited and coherent ms draft is given here. Punctuation is supplied at line 24 only, and for ms deletions see vol ɪɪ.

1

I know, tis dark; & tho' I've lain
Awake, I guess, an hour or twain,
I have not once open'd the Lids of my eyes;
But lie in the Dark, as a blind man lies.

O Rain! that I lie listning to,   5
You're but a doleful Sound at best,
I owe you little thanks, tis true,
For breaking thus my needful Rest,
Yet if as soon as it is light,
Dear Rain! you will but take your flight,   10
I'll neither rail nor malice keep
Though sick & sore with want of sleep.
Only as soon as it is day,
Do go, dear Rain! do go away.

2

O Rain, with your dull twofold sound,   15
The Clash hard by, & the Murmur all round,
You know, if you know aught, that we
Both day & night as ill agree,
As Funeral Hymn with Fal de Ral—
The Lord in Heaven knows, when we shall!   20
For Weeks & months & almost Years
Have limp'd on through the Vale of Tears
Since body of mine & plashy Weather
Have been on easy terms together;
But yet if you'll but go away,   25
Dear Rain! as soon as it is day
Tho' you should come again tomorrow
And bring with you both pain & sorrow,
Tho' Stomach should sicken & knee should swell,
I'll nothing speak of you, but well—   30
But only now—for this one day—
Do go, dear Rain! do go away.

15–16. Adapted in later versions of **107** *Allegoric Vision* 41–2. Cf *LS* (*CC*) 133.

17–22. C's description of the rain and its effect on his health is curiously and significantly close to descriptions of his marriage in e.g. **289** *A Letter to ——* .

29. C's "swoln & troublesome" knee and leg had been followed, during Sept, by "a frightful seizure of the Cholera morbus, or bilious Colic" (*CL* II 757: to TP 7 Sept 1801; 763: to D. Stuart [c 27 Sept 1801]). Indeed, he appears to have been bedridden—writing to friends of "Carcase Coleridge" and about the prospects for his widow—up to the very moment of his sudden overnight visit to the Wordsworths, some 12 miles distant.

3

Dear Rain! I ne'er refuse to say,
You're a good creature in your way,
Nay, I could write a book myself,   35
Would fit a Parson's lower Shelf,
Shewing, how *very* good you are.
What then? *Sometimes* it must be fair—
And if sometimes, why not to day—
Dear worthy Rain! do go away!   40

4

Come, inter nos—(but bye the bye
You *must* not be *hurt* now) I'll whisper why—
You know, who's who! Well, he & I
And she, whom we both call our own,
Dear Rain! we want to be alone—   45
We three, you see—& not one more
We want to be alone *so sore*!
We have so much to talk about,
So many sad things to let out,
So many Tears, in our Eye-corners   50
Sitting like little Jacky Horners—
In short, dear Rain! as soon as day
I trust in God, you'll go away.
And if you will, dear honest Rain!
I swear, when e'er you come again,   55
Return as dull as e'er you wou'd,
And in plain truth, tis understood
You're not so pleasant as you're good,
I swear by my own heart, we three
Will welcome you with hearts of glee—   60
And tho' you should stay twice as long,
And only sing your own old song,
Dear honest Rain! when you had spent
A long week with us, on the score
Of your good heart & kind Intent   65
We'd make you stay a long week more.

41. inter nos] Between ourselves.   section in *SL*.
54. This line (var) begins a fifth

But only now—for this one day—
Dear honest Rain! do go away.

281. THE WILLS OF THE WISP: A SAPPHIC, FROM STOLBERG

[Before Oct 1801]

C copied the lines in a letter to RS of 21 Oct 1801, as follows: "I shall end this Letter with a prayer for your speedy arrival, & a couple of Sapphic Verses translated *in my way* from Stolberg—You may take your Oath for it, it was no admiration of the Thought, or the Poetry that made me translate them—." C continued afterwards: "It is more poetical than the original, of which this is a literal Translation—Still play, juggling Deceiver! still play thy wanton Dances, Fugitive Child of Vapor, that fervently temptest onward the Wanderer's feet, then coyly fleest, at length ~~temptes~~ beguilest into Ruin. These maiden Wiles—I know them—learnt them all out of thy blue eyes, fickle Nais" (PML MA 1848 (42) = *CL* II 769).

The original, in sapphics like C's adaptation, dates from 1772 and is the first poem in most collections of F. L. Stolberg's works. It reads as follows in C. and F. L. Stolberg *Gedichte* 3–4:

Der Irrwisch.

Spiele nur immer, gaukelnder Betrüger!
 Spiele nur immer deine losen Tänze,
  Flüchtiges Dunstkind, das des Wandrers Füße
   Brünstig heranlockt;

Spröde dann fliehet, endlich ins Verderben
 Reißet! Ich kenne diese Mädchenränke,
  Lernte sie all', aus deinen blauen Augen,
   Flatternde Nais!

For other translations by C from Stolberg see poems **212, 257–9.**

When the lines were published in *M Post* (1 Dec 1801), over a pseudonym, C gave no indication of their source and added the motto from Ovid *Metamorphoses* 13.141 (tr "I can hardly call these verses mine"), which he had copied into a notebook from the brief biography prefixed to Sidney's *Arcadia* in 1674 (*CN* I 1011). When C used the same motto with **283** *Ode to Tranquillity*, again in *M Post* (4 Dec 1801), it was with a different meaning.

Vix ea nostra voco

Lunatic Witch-fires! Ghosts of Light and Motion!
Fearless I see you weave your wanton dances
Near me, far off me; you, that tempt the traveller
                    Onward and onward.

Wooing, retreating, till the swamp beneath him   5
Groans—and 'tis dark!—This woman's wile—I know it!
Learnt it from *thee*, from *thy* perfidious glances!
                    Black-ey'd REBECCA!

282. LINES TRANSLATED
FROM BARBAROUS LATIN

[Nov 1801]

C first drafted his lines in Notebook 21 (*CN* I 1003), following a transcription
of Latin lines which are remarkable for—even absurd because of—the number
of elisions in the first line. They scan as follows:

Ēst mĕ(um,) ĕt | ēst tŭ(um;) ălmīc(e!) āt | s(i) āmbōrlūm nĕquĭt | ēssĕ,
Sīt mĕ(um,) ălmīcĕ, prĕlcōr: quĭă | cērtē | sūm măgĕ | pāupĕr.

C inserted the following description into the space above the Latin: "⟨in the
lame & limping metre of a barbarous Latin Poet—⟩".
    The translation was first drafted as a couplet, although C did not aim at the
dactylic hexameters of the original. He may have made the slight alterations in
the notebook text, which convert it into a quatrain, when he decided to use the
lines in the Preface to **176** *Christabel* (lines ⁻1.20–4). The printed texts of 1816
and thereafter introduce the poem as "this doggrel version of two monkish Latin
hexameters" but do not supply the Latin. The version of the Latin given above
is this later, slightly improved, version; for the first draft see **176.**⁻1.19EC.

        'Tis mine and it is likewise your's,
        But an if this will not do;
        Let it be mine, good friend! for I
        Am the poorer of the two.

283. ODE TO TRANQUILLITY

[Aug–Nov 1801]

The first version of the poem began with two stanzas which point up a political theme:

> What Statesmen scheme, and Soldiers work,
> Whether the Pontiff, or the Turk,
> Will e'er renew th' expiring lease
> Of Empire: whether War or Peace
> Will best play off the CONSUL's game;
> What fancy-figures, and what name
> Half-thinking, sensual France, a natural Slave,
> On those ne'er-broken Chains, her self-forg'd Chains, will grave;

> Disturb not me! Some tears I shed,
> When bow'd the Swiss his noble head;
> Since then, with quiet heart have view'd
> Both distant Fights, and Treaties crude,
> Whose heap'd-up terms, which Fear compels,
> (Live Discord's green Combustibles,
> And future Fuel of the funeral Pyre)
> Now hide, and soon, alas! will feed the low-burnt Fire.

When the poem was first published thus in *M Post* (4 Dec 1801), a motto from Ovid *Metamorphoses* 13.141 reinforced the point: "VIX EA NOSTRA VOCO." In the present context the Latin means something like: "The joys of tranquillity are hardly characteristic of Britons at war with Bonaparte" (Woodring 188). C copied the phrase from the 1674 edition of Sidney's *Arcadia*, and had already used it as a motto in *M Post* three days previously: see **281** *The Wills of the Wisp* headnote. On the reference to slavery in line 8 of the stanzas quoted above see *CN* I 206; *TT* 14 Aug 1831 (*CC*) II 142; **174** *France: An Ode* 85–8 and EC.

In so far as the poem was written on the eve of an anticipated separation from his wife and the turmoil of his household, it also anticipates domestic tranquillity, at which point C's feelings for SH make an appearance. The "mossy seat" in line 20 might refer either to the "sofa of sods" or "Windy Brow seat" built by WW, DW, and C the previous summer (13 Aug 1800) on Latrigg, or to "Sara's Seat", begun on 26 Mar and completed on 10 Oct 1801, as the poem was being written, on White Moss Common. See poems **270** and **277,** with headnotes. Each seat focused slightly different feelings concerning SH, and each possibility is supported by a slightly different understanding of the poem. C approached the subject of hope and tranquillity in a different mood some ten years later (*CN* III 3747; **464** *Further Lines on Tranquillity*).

It is just possible, on ms evidence, that the last ten lines were added a month or so after the bulk of the poem was written. Few changes were made, apart from dropping the opening stanzas, in the three ms and six printed texts. Texts were reprinted in several newspapers. That given here is taken from *SL* (1817).

Tranquillity! thou better name
Than all the family of Fame!
Thou ne'er wilt leave my riper age
To low intrigue, or factious rage:
For oh! dear child of thoughtful Truth,   5
To thee I gave my early youth,
And left the bark, and blest the stedfast shore,
Ere yet the Tempest rose and scar'd me with its roar.

Who late and lingering seeks thy shrine,
On him but seldom, power divine,   10
Thy spirit rests! Satiety
And sloth, poor counterfeits of thee,
Mock the tired worldling. Idle Hope
And dire Remembrance interlope,
To vex the feverish slumbers of the mind: 15
The bubble floats before, the spectre stalks behind.

But me thy gentle hand will lead
At morning through the accustom'd mead;
And in the sultry summer's heat
Will build me up a mossy seat!   20
And when the gust of Autumn crowds
And breaks the busy moonlight-clouds,
Thou best the thought canst raise, the heart attune,
Light as the busy clouds, calm as the gliding Moon.

The feeling heart, the searching soul,   25
To thee I dedicate the whole!
And while within myself I trace
The greatness of some future race,
Aloof with hermit-eye I scan

14. interlope] In the version printed in the 1812 *Friend* C wrote alongside in one annotated copy: "O Rhyme! Rhyme! what hast thou not to answer for!"

The present works of present man—   30
A wild and dream-like trade of blood and guile,
Too foolish for a tear, too wicked for a smile!

284. TO A CERTAIN MODERN NARCISSUS, FROM HAGEDORN

[1799–Dec 1801]

The epigram was published in *M Post* (16 Dec 1801), unsigned, along with another demonstrably by C (**235** *Epigram to a Critic*). It was never collected by C, although it was included in *EOT* (1850) III 978. The source is an epigram by Friedrich von Hagedorn, *Hilar an Narciß*, in *Sämmtliche poetische Werke* (3 vols Hamburg 1764) I 109; also in *Blumenlese deutscher Sinngedichte* ed Joerdens 138:

> O stelle dich, Narciß, doch morgen bey mir ein!
> Mein großer Spiegel soll für dich zu Hause seyn.

Carlyon I 29 describes C in Germany "fixing his prominent eyes upon himself (as he was wont to do whenever there was a mirror in the room)". See *CN* I 174 (6) and n for further, similar references.

> Do call, dear Jess! whene'er my way you come!
> My looking-glass will always be at home.

285. PASTORAL FROM GESSNER

[Sept–Dec 1801? 1799?]

C's lines are a literal translation from the prose idyll *Daphnis* (1754) by the Swiss poet Salomon Gessner, where they are sung "tenderly as a young lark" by a young girl. C might have found them in Gessner's *Schriften* II 146, or in some other edition, or in a songbook. He copied out the German original early

31–2. C marked the couplet in an annotated copy of the 1812 *Friend*, adding: "These two lines were composed during Sleep. S. T. Coleridge."

in 1799 as follows, making only minor changes in punctuation while he wrote out Gessner's prose as verse (*CN* I 396):

> Seh ich den Schäfer
> Den braunen Schäfer,
> Dann sag' Ich: Schäfer,
> Ich will nicht lieben.
> Ach! sagt mir, Mädchen,
> Die ihr schon liebet,
> Ich habe, denk' ich,
> Doch nichts zu fürchten;
> Wenn ich gleich seufze
> So oft ich sage,
> Du brauner Schäfer,
> Ich will nicht lieben.

C's translation appeared in *M Post* (21 Dec 1801), unsigned, and was never collected. It might have been made at any time in the interval after his transcription of the German. (KC provides an alternative translation in her note to *CN* I 396.)

C adapted another song from *Daphnis*, likewise turning prose into verse, but did not publish it. See **194** *Metrical Adaptation of Gessner*.

> See I the Shepherd,
> The bold brown Shepherd,
> I tell him, "Shepherd!
> "I will not love thee!"
> Ah tell me, Maidens!　　　　　　　5
> Who've lov'd already,
> There's nothing, think you,
> In this to alarm me,
> That I say it *sighing*,
> Whene'er I tell him,　　　　　　　10
> "Thou bold brown Shepherd,
> "I will not love thee."

286. ADAPTATION OF BEN JONSON'S
THE POETASTER

[Dec 1801]

C's lines derive from *The Poetaster* I iii 67–75, where the character Ovid says:

> O my Tibullus,
> Let us not blame him; for against such chances
> The heartiest strife of virtue is not proof.
> We may read constancy and fortitude
> To other souls; but had ourselves been struck
> With the like planet, had our loves (like his)
> Beene ravish'd from us by injurious death,
> And in the height and heat of our best days,
> It would have crackt our sinnews, shrunk our veins,
> And made our very heart-strings jar, like his.
>> (*The Dramatic Works of Ben Jonson, and Beau-
>> mont and Fletcher* ed J. Stockdale—4 vols 1811—
>> I 151)

C copied out his version in a notebook (*CN* I 1061). The text given here was published as from an "*Old Play*" in *Bl Mag* XI (Jan 1822), where improvements were made in lines 2, 5, and 6.

> Let us not blame him: for against such chances
> The heartiest strife of manhood is scarce proof.
> We may read constancy and fortitude
> To other souls—but had ourselves been struck,
> Even in the height and heat of our keen wishing,   5
> It might have made our heart-strings jar, like his!

287. FRAGMENT ON TIME,
FROM SCHILLER

[Feb–Mar 1802]

C drafted two slightly different versions of the lines in two notebooks at about the same time (*CN* I 1127, 1138). They derive from Schiller's *Spruch des*

Confucius, first printed in his *Musen-Almenach für das Jahr 1796* (Neustrelitz 1795) 39, then together with a second part in *Gedichte* (1800):

Dreyfach ist der Schritt der Zeit.
Zögernd kommt die Zukunft hergezogen,
Pfeilschnell ist das Jetzt entflogen,
Ewig still steht die Vergangenheit.

Keine Ungeduld beflügelt
Ihren Schritt, wenn sie verweilt.
Keine Furcht, kein Zweifeln zügelt
Ihren Lauf, wenn sie enteilt.
Keine Reu, kein Zaubersegen
Kann die stehende bewegen.

Möchtest du beglückt und weise
Endigen des Lebens Reise?
Nimm die Zögernde zum Rath,
Nicht zum Werkzeug deiner That.
Wähle nicht die Fliehende zum Freund,
Nicht die Bleibende zum Feind.

It will be noted that C gives a line-for-line equivalence in Schiller's first stanza, and syncopates pairs of lines in the remainder.

The text given here reproduces the text of *CN* I 1138, dividing it into verses.

Time—3 fold—
Future slow—
Present swift—
Past immoveable—
No impatience will quicken the Loiterer—   5
no Terror, no delight rein in the Flyer—
No Regret set in motion the stationary—
Would'st be happy, take the Delayer for thy counselor,
do not choose the Flyer for thy Friend,
nor the ever-remainer for thy Enemy—   10

288. LINES ON THE BREEZE AND HOPE

[1802?]

The lines are known only from a transcript in SH's hand, where they are untitled and unsigned. The supposition of C's authorship rests on association and internal evidence alone.

> If even the Breeze, that agitates the Air,
> Effect a celebrated *pur*pose there;
> If even the Thistle Down, it wafts away,
> Soft-bearing future Plants but *seem* to stray;
> Surely the Hope, that agitates the Mind,   5
> Is not a Thing without an *end* design'd.

289. A LETTER TO ——

[Apr 1802]

The lines were never intended for publication, even though they appear to have been revised and improved, and their circulation was confined to a few members of the Wordsworth–Coleridge circle before they were "discovered" in 1937. Two very similar ms texts are known, and they appear to derive from a lost original. The version given here is from C's own fair copy, which he perhaps made for WW and DW. The ms was prepared with deliberation but muddled in the execution, and suggests that the title was determined at a later stage.

    The lines draw on observations and feelings that had been gestating for twelve months and more before they were written. C had lamented his marriage, declaring that "the Poet is dead in me" (*CL* II 713–17: to W. Godwin 25 Mar 1801; 715–17: to T. N. Longman 26 [27] Mar 1801; 725: to W. Godwin 28 Apr 1801; 774–5: to RS 9 Nov 1801; etc); indeed, he sketched an outline of the lines back in Dec 1801:

> A lively picture of a man, disappointed in marriage, & endeavoring to make a compensation to himself by virtuous & tender & brotherly friendship with an amiable Woman—the obstacles—the jealousies—the impossibility of it.—Best advice that he should as much as possible withdraw himself from pursuits of morals &c—& devote himself to abstract sciences— (*CN* I 1065)

The incident central to lines 99–110, which C later detached and worked up

10. *A View Taken in the Vale of St John Looking towards Keswick in Cumberland*, pen and watercolour sketch made on 17 Aug 1786 by Francis Towne. Coleridge frequently traversed the valley when he lived at Keswick, writing in Oct 1803: "Sᵗ John's Vale, o the Lights, the watry white Sun-sections, like a moonlight/ indeed the whole walk is enchantment" (Notebook 16 f 18ʳ: *CN* I 1542)

into a separate poem (see **294** *The Day Dream*, **629** *A Day Dream*), took place at Gallow Hill between 2 and 13 Mar 1802; and there is evidence that a number of other features—e.g. the connection with Milton's poems—were in C's mind at about the same time (see *CN* I 1155, and entries 1151–7 as a whole).

In view of the associative and evolving manner of the poem, it is unlikely to have been written precisely in its present form at one sitting. The first definite reference to the lines is an account of C reading them on 21 Apr (*DWJ* I 135–6), and it is not absolutely certain that they were sent to SH. Although one of the two mss is in MH's hand, there are reasons for thinking that this is a copy of a copy, possibly made some months after, and although it is addressed to SH, it may have been shown only to WW and DW.

The ms title continues on a second line "April 4, 1802.—Sunday Evening." The occasion and the unnamed recipient of the "letter" are as much a focus for events extending before and afterwards in C's personal and literary life as they are a record of historical fact. The date was the eve of WW's departure to propose to the sister of the woman C loved, thereby taking a step which involved irrevocable separation from Annette Vallon and their child. C had stayed up all night on 3 Apr to urge on WW this course of action, which his own conscience prevented him from taking himself (*CN* III 3304). And the date also marks the end of a visit from WW and DW, in which C's hopes for WW's future mingled with despondency and apprehension for his own present and future state. The EC notes point to some of the personal and literary connections of the lines.

When C recited the poem on 21 Apr, DW was deeply affected (*DWJ* I 135–6), and their reverberations continue into poems which WW wrote before he left to visit Calais and settle matters with Annette in mid-Jul. The echoes are particularly strong in *Stanzas Written in my Pocket-copy of Thomson's "Castle of Indolence"* and *The Leech Gatherer*, and other connections are described by Newlyn 59–86, etc. WW's response makes up the background against which C constructed **293** *Dejection: An Ode* from the materials of the *Letter*, in which a cry of pain and a plea for sympathy are converted into an affirmation fit to be published on WW's wedding-day. *Dejection: An Ode* is C's own comment, and the most complete, on the values and form of the present lines.

> Well! if the Bard was weatherwise, who made
> The grand old Ballad of Sir Patrick Spence,
> This Night, so tranquil now, will not go hence
> Unrous'd by winds, that ply a busier trade

2. C quoted the relevant stanza of the ballad of Sir Patrick Spens as an epigraph to **293** *Dejection: An Ode*. The rimmed circle of the moon was an image C privately shared with WW and DW before and after his lines were written (see *RX* 173–5).

Than that, which moulds yon clouds in lazy flakes,   5
Or the dull sobbing Draft, that drones & rakes
Upon the Strings of this Eolian Lute,
  Which better far were mute.
For, lo! the New Moon, winter-bright!
And overspread with phantom Light,   10
(With swimming phantom Light o'erspread
But rimm'd & circled with a silver Thread)
I see the Old Moon in her Lap, foretelling
The coming-on of Rain & squally Blast—
O! Sara! that the Gust ev'n now were swelling,   15
And the slant Night-shower driving loud & fast!

A Grief without a pang, void, dark, & drear,
A stifling, drowsy, unimpassion'd Grief
That finds no natural Outlet, no Relief
  In word, or sigh, or tear—   20
This, Sara! well thou know'st,
Is that sore Evil, which I dread the Most,
And oft'nest suffer! In this heartless Mood
To other thoughts by yonder Throstle woo'd,
That pipes within the Larch-tree, not unseen,   25
(The Larch, which pushes out in tassels green
It's bundled Leafits) woo'd to mild Delights
By all the tender Sounds & gentle Sights
Of this sweet Primrose-month—& *vainly* woo'd
O dearest Sara! in this heartless Mood   30
All this long Eve, so balmy & serene,
Have I been gazing on the western Sky
And it's peculiar Tint of Yellow Green—
And still I gaze—& with how blank an eye!
And those thin Clouds above, in flakes & bars,   35
That give away their Motion to the Stars;
Those Stars, that glide behind them, or between,
Now sparkling, now bedimm'd, but always seen;
Yon crescent Moon, as fix'd as if it grew

17. Cf Gen 1.2 "And the earth was without form, and void; and darkness was upon the face of the deep"; and 303–4EC.

26–7. C had observed the larches thus appearing during Mar 1802 (*CN* I 1142).

In it's own cloudless, starless Lake of Blue—   40
A boat becalm'd dear William's Sky Canoe!
—I see them all, so excellently fair!
  I see, not feel, how beautiful they are.

      My genial Spirits fail—
      And what can these avail   45
To lift the smoth'ring Weight from off my Breast?
      It were a vain Endeavor,
      Tho' I should gaze for ever
On that Green Light which lingers in the West!
I may not hope from outward Forms to win   50
The Passion & the Life whose Fountains are within!
These lifeless Shapes, around, below, Above,
      O what can they impart?
When even the gentle Thought, that thou, my Love!
      Art gazing now, like me,   55
      And see'st the Heaven, I see—
Sweet Thought it is—yet feebly stirs my Heart!

      Feebly! O feebly!—Yet
      (I well remember it)
In my first Dawn of Youth that Fancy stole   60
With many secret Yearnings on my Soul.

---

41. dear William's Sky Canoe] An allusion to the Prologue to WW's then unpublished *Peter Bell* (*WPW* II 331–8).

42–3. Cf *King Lear* IV i 70–1 "that will not see ǀ Because he doth not feel".

44. genial Spirits] The phrase comes from *Samson Agonistes* 594, and Milton's blind lonely hero who mourns a gift he had lost through an imprudent marriage offers obvious parallels. The phrase had been used before by WW in *Tintern Abbey* 113 (*WPW* II 262), and C repeats it (var) in **652** *The Garden of Boccaccio* 2.

49. When RS met the line in its later, published version (with "that" for "which"), he told Anna Seward on 25 Jul 1807 that it derived from the part of *Madoc* he had completed by 1799: "The last green light that lingers in the west" (*Madoc*—1805—II xxxvi 260). (RS's letter has not been published: its contents were communicated to me by KC.) At the same time, **116** *Written at Shurton Bars* 5 is evidence that C had previously been awakened to the perception of "green radiance" by WW. (*Shurton Bars* indeed constitutes an earlier "Answer to a Letter", written in the happy, early days of C's marriage.)

At eve, sky-gazing in "ecstatic fit"
(Alas! for cloister'd in a city School
The Sky was all, I knew, of Beautiful)
At the barr'd window often did I sit,   65
And oft upon the leaded School-roof lay,
        And to myself would say—
There does not live the Man so stripp'd of good affections
As not to love to see a Maiden's quiet Eyes
Uprais'd, and linking on sweet Dreams by dim Connections   70
To Moon, or Evening Star, or glorious western Skies—
While yet a Boy, this Thought would so pursue me
That often it became a kind of Vision to me!

        Sweet Thought! and dear of old
        To Hearts of finer Mould!   75
Ten thousand times by Friends & Lovers blest!
        I spake with rash Despair,
        And ere I was aware,
The Weight was somewhat lifted from my Breast!
O Sara! in the weather-fended Wood,   80
Thy lov'd haunt! where the Stock-doves coo at Noon,
        I guess, that thou has stood

62. ecstatic fit] From Milton *The Passion* 42. Milton's stanza describes Ezekiel's vision of the chariot of God—a vision that possessed particular significance for Böhme and other such writers as well as for C. The skygazing scene is also described in **171** *Frost at Midnight* 51–3; cf WW *The Prelude* (1850) VI 266–70. C's sense of loss at having been separated from natural surroundings in childhood was exacerbated as he came to compare WW's experience, and the difference between the childhood experiences of the two poets became a shared myth.

68–73. C described the same early thoughts—which he claimed he had in 1787—in a poem written in the 1820s. See **574** *First Advent of Love* and headnote.

80. "Weather-fends" is a Shakespearean coinage (*The Tempest* V i 10), and the phrase was used again by William Crowe in *Lewesdon Hill* 4—a book C borrowed in Mar 1795 (*Bristol LB* No 38) and later praised highly (*BL* ch 1—*CC*—I 17–18), and a favourite text with WW and DW, who lived near Lewesdon at Racedown before moving to Alfoxden. Cf *Excursion* II 417–20 (*WPW* v 56–7): "a penthouse, framed . . . To weather-fend a little turf-built seat."

81. the Stock-doves] C remembered them at other times also: see e.g. *CN* III 3639. An early sketch of Gallow Hill, now at DCL, shows an unusual and prominent dovecote on the barn adjoining the house.

And watch'd yon Crescent, & it's ghost-like Moon.
And yet, far rather in my present Mood
I would, that thou'dst been sitting all this while   85
Upon the sod-built Seat of Camomile—
And tho' thy Robin may have ceas'd to sing,
Yet needs for *my* sake must thou love to hear
The Bee-hive murmuring near,
That ever-busy & most quiet Thing   90
Which I have heard at Midnight murmuring.

I feel my spirit moved—
And wheresoe'er thou be,
O Sister! O Beloved!
Those dear mild Eyes, that see   95
Even now the Heaven, *I* see—
There is a Prayer in them! It is for *me*—
And I, dear Sara—*I* am blessing *thee*!

It was as calm as this, that happy night
When Mary, thou, & I together were,   100
The low decaying Fire our only Light,
And listen'd to the Stillness of the Air!
O that affectionate & blameless Maid,
Dear Mary! on her Lap my head she lay'd—
Her Hand was on my Brow,   105
Even as my own is now;
And on my Cheek I felt thy eye-lash play.
Such Joy I had, that I may truly say,
My Spirit was awe-stricken with the Excess
And trance-like Depth of it's brief Happiness.   110

Ah fair Remembrances, that so revive
The Heart, & fill it with a living Power,

---

86. the sod-built Seat of Camomile]
Completed by C, WW, and DW on 10
Oct 1801: *DWJ* I 77; *CM* (*CC*) III 837.
91. Cf **629** *A Day Dream* 35.
99–110. The incident described in
this stanza took place at Gallow Hill
on C's visit between 2 and 13 Mar
1802. It formed the focus of a separate poem, written perhaps immediately after the *Letter* and before **293**
Dejection: An Ode, viz **294** *The Day
Dream* (also **629** *A Day Dream*). C recalled it vividly in Mar 1810 (*CN* III
3708 f 11ᵛ).

Where were they, Sara?—or did I not strive
To win them to me?—on the fretting Hour
Then when I wrote thee that complaining Scroll   115
Which even to bodily Sickness bruis'd thy Soul!
And yet thou blam'st thyself alone! And yet
    Forbidd'st me all Regret!

And must I not regret, that I distress'd
Thee, best belov'd! who lovest me the best?   120
My better mind had fled, I know not whither,
For o! was this an Absent Friend's Employ
To send from far both Pain & Sorrow thither
Where still his Blessings should have call'd down Joy!
I read thy guileless Letter o'er again—   125
I hear thee of thy blameless Self complain—
And only this I learn—& this, alas! I know—
That thou art weak & pale with Sickness, Grief, & Pain—
    And *I—I* made thee so!

O for my own sake I regret perforce   130
Whatever turns thee, Sara! from the Course
Of calm Well-being & a Heart at rest!
When thou, & with thee those, whom thou lov'st best,
Shall dwell together in one happy Home,
One House, the dear *abiding* Home of All,   135
I too will crown me with a Coronal—
Nor shall this Heart in idle Wishes roam
    Morbidly soft!
No! let me trust, that I shall wear away
In no inglorious Toils the manly Day,   140
And only now & then, & not too oft,
Some dear & memorable Eve will bless
Dreaming of all your Loves & Quietness.

Be happy, & I need thee not in sight.
Peace in thy Heart, & Quiet in thy Dwelling,   145

136. Cf *Intimations Ode* 40 "My head hath its coronal" (*WPW* IV 280). WW had begun his poem on 27 Mar, and the first four stanzas were per- haps among the verses repeated to C at Greta Bank on 4 Apr (*DWJ* I 129). See line 295 below.

Health in thy Limbs, & in thine Eyes the Light
Of Love, & Hope, & honorable Feeling—
Where e'er I am, I shall be well content!
Not near thee, haply shall be more content!
To all things I prefer the Permanent.   150
And better seems it for a heart, like mine,
Always to *know*, than sometimes to behold,
    Their Happiness & thine—
For Change doth trouble me with pangs untold!
To see thee, hear thee, feel thee—then to part   155
    Oh!—it weighs down the Heart!
To *visit* those, I love, as I love thee,
Mary, & William, & dear Dorothy,
It is but a temptation to repine—
The transientness is Poison in the Wine,   160
Eats out the pith of Joy, makes all Joy hollow,
All Pleasure a dim Dream of Pain to follow!
My own peculiar Lot, my house-hold Life
It is, & will remain, Indifference or Strife—
While *ye* are *well & happy*, twould but wrong you—   165
If I should fondly yearn to be among you—
Wherefore, O wherefore! should I wish to be
A wither'd branch upon a blossoming Tree?

But (let me say it! for I vainly strive
To beat away the Thought) but if thou pin'd,   170
Whate'er the Cause, in body, or in mind,
I were the miserablest Man alive
To know it & be absent! Thy Delights
Far off, or near, alike I may partake—
But o! to mourn for thee, & to forsake   175
All power, all hope of giving comfort to thee—
To know that thou are weak & and worn with pain,
And not to hear thee, Sara! not to view thee—
    Not sit beside thy Bed,
    Not press thy aching Head,   180
    Not bring thee Health again—
    At least to hope, to try—
By this Voice, which thou lov'st, & by this earnest Eye—

Nay, wherefore did I let it haunt my Mind
    The dark distressful Dream!   185
I turn from it, & listen to the Wind
Which long has rav'd unnotic'd! What a Scream
Of agony by Torture lengthen'd out
That Lute sent forth! O thou wild Storm without!
Jagg'd Rock, or mountain Pond, or blasted Tree,   190
Or Pine-grove, Whither Woodman never clomb,
Or lonely House, long held the Witches' Home,
Methinks were fitter Instruments for Thee,
Mad Lutanist! that in this month of Showers,
Of dark brown Gardens, & of peeping Flowers,   195
Mak'st Devil's Yule, with worse than wintry Song
The Blossoms, Buds, and timorous Leaves among!
Thou Actor, perfect in all tragic Sounds!
Thou mighty Poet, even to frenzy bold!
    What tell'st thou now about?   200
'Tis of the Rushing of an Host in Rout—
And many Groans from men with smarting Wounds—
At once they groan with smart, and shudder with the Cold!
Tis hush'd! there is a Trance of deepest Silence,
Again! but all that Sound, as of a rushing Crowd,   205
And Groans & tremulous Shudderings, all are over—
And it has other Sounds, and all less deep, less loud!
    A Tale of less Affright,
    And temper'd with Delight,
As William's Self had made the tender Lay—   210
    Tis of a little Child
    Upon a heathy Wild,
Not far from home—but it has lost it's way—
And now moans low in utter grief & fear—
And now screams loud, & hopes to make it's Mother hear!   215

Tis Midnight! and small Thoughts have I of Sleep—
Full seldom may my Friend such Vigils keep—

191. Cf *Il Penseroso* 135–7.

197–206. The phrasing of the other ms differs at several points.

202–3. A similitude for the wind which C had noted on 21 Oct 1800 (*CN* I 832).

208–15. A reference to WW *Lucy Gray* (*WPW* I 234–6).

215. The same image of the wind occurred to C as early as 1 Feb 1801. See *CL* II 669: to TP.

O breathe She softly in her gentle Sleep!
Cover her, gentle Sleep! with wings of Healing—
And be this Tempest but a Mountain Birth!   220
May all the Stars hang bright above her Dwelling,
Silent, as tho' they *watch'd* the sleeping Earth!
Healthful & light, my Darling! may'st thou rise
    With clear & chearful Eyes—
And of the same good Tidings to me send!   225
    For, oh! beloved Friend!
I am not the buoyant Thing, I was of yore—
When like an own Child, I to JOY belong'd;
For others mourning oft, myself oft sorely wrong'd,
Yet bearing all things then, as if I nothing bore!   230

    Yes, dearest Sara! Yes!
There *was* a time when tho' my path was rough,
The Joy within me dallied with Distress;
And all Misfortunes were but as the Stuff
Whence Fancy made me Dreams of Happiness: 235
For Hope grew round me, like the climbing Vine,
And Leaves & Fruitage, not my own, seem'd mine!
But now Ill Tidings bow me down to earth/
Nor care I, that they rob me of my Mirth/
    But oh! each Visitation   240
Suspends what Nature gave me at my Birth,

---

220. a Mountain Birth] An allusion to Horace *Ars poetica* 139 "Parturient montes, nascetur ridiculus mus" tr Fairclough (LCL) 463 "Mountains will labour, to birth will come a laughter-rousing mouse!" Cf *CM* (*CC*) III 334.

221–2. Quoted (var) at the close of C's letter to SH about Sir Thomas Browne, 10 Mar 1804 (*CL* II 1083).

222⁺. The other ms has an extra line here—"Like elder Sisters, with love-twinkling Eyes!"—and omits line 224. Manuscript evidence suggests that the passage containing lines 222–42 might have been particularly problematic for C up to the time the present transcript was made.

231. Absent from the other ms.

232. In a notebook entry of 1809 C repeated the opening phrase (from the opening line of WW's *Intimations Ode*) in a couplet which jocularly inverts the present mood (*CN* III 3635 = **456** *Couplet Written in November 1809*). Cf **269** *The Mad Monk* 9.

236–7. C quoted the lines when he described how he was "in the first dawn of my literary life" in *BL* ch 22 (*CC*) II 159. Cf Virgil *Georgics* 2.82 "miraturque novas frondes et non sua poma" tr Fairclough (LCL) I 122–3 "and marvels at its strange leafage and fruits not its own".

My shaping Spirit of Imagination!
I speak not now of those habitual Ills
That wear out Life, when two unequal Minds
Meet in one House, & two discordant Wills—   245
   This leaves me, where it finds,
Past cure, & past Complaint—a fate Austere
Too fix'd & hopeless to partake of Fear!

But thou, dear Sara! (dear indeed thou art,
My Comforter! A Heart within my Heart!)   250
Thou, & the Few, we love, tho' few ye be,
Make up a world of Hopes & Fears for me.
And if Affliction, or distemp'ring Pain,
Or wayward Chance befall you, I complain
Not that I mourn—O Friends, most dear! most true!   255
   Methinks to weep with you
Were better far than to rejoice alone—
But that my coarse domestic Life has known
No Habits of heart-nursing Sympathy,
No Griefs, but such as dull and deaden me,   260
No mutual mild Enjoyments of it's own,
No Hopes of it's own Vintage, None, o! none—
Whence when I mourn'd for you, my Heart might borrow
Fair forms & living Motions for it's Sorrow.
For not to think of what I needs must feel,   265
But to be still & patient all I can;
And haply by abstruse Research to steal
From my own Nature all the Natural Man—
This was my sole Resource, my wisest plan!
And that, which suits a part, infects the whole,   270
And now is almost grown the Temper of my Soul.

---

242. shaping Spirit] For other, sig-
nificant contexts of the phrase see
271.X1 *The Triumph of Loyalty* I ii
170, **272** *The Night-scene* 81; cf also
CL II 663: to H. Davy 11 Jan 1801;
664: to TP 19 Jan 1801.
   259–60. Transposed in the other
ms.

267. abstruse Research] The phrase
occurs later in *CN* II 2036, from which
it is quite clear that it refers in the
poem to an antidote of his feelings for
SH, not to the opposite of poetry and
imagination.

My little Children are a Joy, a Love,
   A good Gift from above!
But what is Bliss, that still calls up a Woe,
   And makes it doubly keen   275
Compelling me to *feel*, as well as KNOW,
What a most blessed Lot mine might have been.
Those little Angel Children (woe is me!)
There have been hours, when feeling how they bind
And pluck out the Wing-feathers of my Mind,   280
Turning my Error to Necessity,
I have half-wish'd, they never had been born!
That seldom! But sad Thoughts they always bring,
And like the Poet's Philomel, I sing
My Love-song, with my breast against a Thorn.   285

With no unthankful Spirit I confess,
This clinging Grief too, in it's turn, awakes
That Love, and Father's Joy; but O! it makes
The Love the greater, & the Joy far less,
These Mountains too, these Vales, these Woods, these Lakes,   290
Scenes full of Beauty & of Loftiness
Where all my Life I fondly hop'd to live—
I were sunk low indeed, did they *no* solace give;
But oft I seem to feel, & evermore I fear,
They are not to me now the Things, which once they were.   295

O Sara! we receive but what we give,
And in *our* Life alone does Nature live.
Our's is her Wedding Garment, our's her Shroud—
And would we aught behold of higher Worth
Than that inanimate cold World allow'd   300
To the poor loveless ever-anxious Crowd,
Ah! from the Soul itself must issue forth
A Light, a Glory, and a luminous Cloud
   Enveloping the Earth!

295. Cf *Intimations Ode* 9 "The things which I have seen I now can see no more" (*WPW* iv 279). The previous line in the other ms (reading "I fear") brings the couplet slightly closer to WW. Cf line 136EC.

303–4. Cf Gen 1.3 "And God said, Let there be light: and there was light"; see line 17EC.

And from the Soul itself must there be sent   305
A sweet & potent Voice, of it's own Birth,
Of all sweet Sounds the Life & Element.

O pure of Heart! thou need'st not ask of me
What this strong music in the Soul may be,
    What, & wherein it doth exist,   310
This Light, this Glory, this fair luminous Mist,
This beautiful & beauty-making Power!
JOY, innocent Sara! Joy, that ne'er was given
Save to the Pure, & in their purest Hour,
JOY, Sara! is the Spirit & the Power,   315
That wedding Nature to us gives in Dower
    A new Earth & new Heaven
Undreamt of by the Sensual & the Proud!
Joy is that strong Voice, Joy that luminous Cloud—
    We, we ourselves rejoice!   320
And thence flows all that charms or ear or sight,
All melodies the Echoes of that Voice,
All Colors a Suffusion of that Light.

Sister & Friend of my devoutest Choice!
Thou being innocent & full of love,   325
And nested with the Darlings of thy Love,
And feeling in thy Soul, Heart, Lips, & Arms
Even what the conjugal & mother Dove
That borrows genial Warmth from those, she warms,
Feels in her thrill'd wings, blessedly outspread—   330
Thou free'd awhile from Cares & human Dread
By the Immenseness of the Good & Fair
    Which thou see'st every where—

313, 315, 319. In a later notebook entry C glosses "Joy" as when "the Heart is full as of a deep & quiet fountain overflowing insensibly, or the gladness of Joy, when the fountain overflows ebullient" (*CN* II 2279). The word became an almost technical term in his poetic vocabulary, but always associated with images of the conflict and reconciliation of oppo-sites, in some sort of balanced tension, and with his love for SH—as here.

317. Cf Rev 21.1 "And I saw a new heaven and a new earth: for the first heaven and the first earth were passed away".

325–30. In 1807 C took up the image for the opening lines of **423** *To Two Sisters*.

Thus, thus should'st thou rejoice!
To thee would all Things live from Pole to Pole,   335
Their Life the Eddying of thy living Soul.
O dear! O Innocent! O full of Love!
A very Friend! A Sister of my Choice—
O dear, as Light & Impulse from above,
Thus may'st thou ever, evermore rejoice!   340

290. A SOLILOQUY OF THE FULL MOON, SHE BEING IN A MAD PASSION

[Late Apr 1802]

Although C had noted the sight of a remarkable moon on 15 Sept 1801 (*CN* I 983) and at other times, as had DW, the present soliloquy was probably prompted by the full moon of 16 Apr 1802 and sent to the Wordsworths on 27 Apr (*DWJ* I 139). The poem was therefore probably written at the end of the same month as the verse letter to SH (poem **289**), and it celebrates, from another point of view and in a different spirit, the full moon, as the earlier poem had fixed on the new(ish) moon. Whether C was prompted by any such thoughts is unknown, but the two poems do share a number of motifs besides the central one. The thought might also have been in SH's mind when she chose this as the first of all C's poems to be copied into her album.

There are two ms texts—one in C's hand, sent to WW and DW, another copied later by SH into her album—and the poem was never published. The later version omits thirteen superfluous lines at the end, adds others (lines 16– 21), and makes other revisions; this is the version reproduced here, but the layout of C's holograph is followed, in which all lines are centred on the page-width.

Now as Heaven is my Lot, they're the Pests of the Nation!
Wherever they can come
With clankum and blankum
'Tis all Botheration, & Hell & Damnation,

336. Eddying] No previous examples of the word are recorded by *OED*. C used it again in *BL* ch 22 (*CC*) II 136—"an eddying instead of progression of thought"—to describe a limitation of WW's style.

With fun, jeering   5
Conjuring,
Sky-staring,
Loungering,
And still to the tune of Transmogrification—
Those muttering   10
Spluttering
Ventriloquogusty
Poets
With no Hats
Or Hats that are rusty.   15
They're my Torment and Curse
And harrass me worse
And bait me and bay me, far sorer I vow
Than the screech of the Owl
Or the witch-wolf's long howl,   20
Or sheep-killing Butcher-dog's inward Bow Wow
For me they all spite—an unfortunate Wight.
And the very first moment that I came to Light
A Rascal call'd Voss the more to his scandal,
Turn'd me into a sickle with never a handle.   25
A Night or two after a worse Rogue there came,
The head of the Gang, one Wordsworth by name—
"Ho! What's in the wind?" 'Tis the voice of a Wizzard!
I saw him look at me most terribly blue!
He was hunting for witch-rhymes from great A to Izzard, 30
And soon as he'd found them made no more ado
But chang'd me at once to a little Canoe.

19–21. Perhaps a jocular reference to the opening lines of **176** *Christabel*.

24. Voss] Johann Heinrich Voss (1751–1826), whose *Idylls* C thought of translating in Aug 1802 (*CL* II 856–7: to W. Sotheby 26 Aug 1802; cf 834: to SH [1–5 Aug 1802]; also *CL* III 522: to J. Murray [23 Aug 1814] and **215** *Before Gleim's Cottage*).

30. Izzard] Johnson's *Dictionary* (1765) records that the letter "z" is "more commonly izzard or uzzard". RS used the word as a con-venient comic rhyme in one of his *Nonedescripts* ("Robert the Rhymer's True and Particular Account of Himself"). C himself used the form "zed" in **561** *A Character* 70.2.

32. Canoe] A recollection of WW's *Peter Bell*, a revised form of which DW had transcribed as recently as 20–2 Feb 1802 (*DWJ* I 115), as well as of **289** *Letter to* ——. Voss's *Idyll* 3 *Die Leibeigenen* 2, in *Gedichte* (Hamburg 1785) 11, provides a parallel in "sil-berner Kahn" ("silver boat or canoe").

From this strange Enchantment uncharm'd by degrees
I began to take courage & hop'd for some Ease,
When one Coleridge, a Raff of the self-same Banditti   35
Past by—& intending no doubt to be witty,
Because I'd th' ill-fortune his taste to displease,
He turn'd up his nose,
And in pitiful Prose
Made me into the half of a small Cheshire Cheese.   40
Well, a night or two past—it was wind, rain, & hail—
And I ventur'd abroad in a thick Cloak & veil—
But the very first Evening he saw me again
The last mentioned Ruffian popp'd out of his Den—
I was resting a moment on the bare edge of Naddle   45
I fancy the sight of me turn'd his Brains addle—
For what was I now?
A complete Barley-Mow
And when I climb'd higher he made a long leg,
And chang'd me at once to an Ostrich's Egg—   50
But now Heaven be praised in contempt of the Loon,
I am I myself I, the jolly full Moon.
Yet my heart is still fluttering—
For I heard the Rogue muttering—
He was hulking and skulking at the skirt of a Wood   55
When lightly & brightly on tip-toe I stood
On the long level Line of a motionless Cloud
And ho! what a Skittle-ground! quoth he aloud
And wish'd from his heart nine Nine-pins to see
In brightness & size just proportion'd to me.   60
So I fear'd from my soul,
That he'd make me a Bowl,
But in spite of his spite

35. a Raff] Something of a vogue word at this time for a blackguard or low, worthless fellow—as in **676** *The Three Patriots*. "Botheration" (line 4) and "Loungering" (line 8) were also, at the time, newly coined words with modish dimensions.

45. Naddle] Naddle Fell, $3\frac{1}{2}$ miles SE of Greta Hall, dividing St John's Vale from Naddle Beck.

52. I am I myself I] C made fun of the phrase differently in **525** ΕΓΩΕΝΚΑΙΠΑΝ, after reading Fichte. The phrase also developed meanings which derived from his reading in Schelling (*BL* ch ch 12—*CC*—I 275–6 and nn provides further references). On "I AM" as the name of God (Exod 3.14) cf *CM* (*CC*) I 239, II 726, III 1065, etc.

This was more than his might
And still Heaven be prais'd! in contempt of the Loon   65
I am I myself I, the Jolly full Moon.

291. ANSWER TO A CHILD'S QUESTION

[Early May 1802?]

The poem was originally a sonnet, entitled "The Language of Birds, Lines spoken extempore, to a little child, in early spring." C pruned couplets from the end of the octave and from the end of the sestet when the poem was included in *SL* (1817) and subsequent collections. One ms title—"Extempore to a Child of six years old"—prompted WW to subtitle his poem *To H. C.* in a similar way when he included it in his 1807 collection (see Reed II 180–1n). The texts differ little apart from the omission of the four lines. The present text is from *SL*.

Do you ask what the birds say? The Sparrow, the Dove,
The Linnet and Thrush say, "I love and I love!"
In the winter they're silent—the wind is so strong;
What it says, I don't know, but it sings a loud song.
But green leaves, and blossoms, and sunny warm weather,   5
And singing, and loving—all come back together.
But the Lark is so brimful of gladness and love,
The green fields below him, the blue sky above,
That he sings, and he sings; and for ever sings he—
"I love my Love, and my Love loves me!"   10

6⁺. The first published and early ms versions here include the couplet:

"I love, and I love," almost all the birds say,
From sun-rise, to star-rise, so gladsome are they!

10. Adapted from the refrain "I love my love, because I know my love loves me", from Matthew Prior's song *One Morning Very Early, One Morning in the Spring.*

10⁺. The poem originally concluded with an additional couplet:

'Tis no wonder that he's full of joy to the brim,
When HE loves his LOVE, and his LOVE loves HIM!

292. EPITAPH ON LORD LONSDALE

[1802? 1809?]

C's lines were published in the 1812 *Friend* among other epigrams which were first published in Sept–Oct 1802, and which derive from German sources; no such parallel has been found for the present poem. John Payne Collier also recorded two slightly different versions which he heard from C in 1811 and 1832, and on both occasions C described the lines as referring to the late Lord Lonsdale.

Sir James Lowther, Earl of Lonsdale, died on 24 May 1802. C had been staying with WW and DW at DC, and left that same day for Keswick (Reed II 173). The troubles the Wordsworth family had with the "bad earl", who (in C's words to Collier) "seemed to make himself happy by making everybody else unhappy", are recorded in Moorman *William Wordsworth: The Early Years 1770–1803* 167–9 and, more fully, in Kenneth R. Johnston *The Hidden Wordsworth: Poet, Lover, Rebel, Spy* (New York 1998) 19–31, 452–3, and esp 781–2, and WW was pressing for a settlement of the case throughout Jun 1802. The poem may have been composed on 10–12 Jun, when C returned to Grasmere and discussed various matters relating to Lord Lonsdale. See also **307** *Epigram on the Devil*.

The version given here reproduces the untitled text of the 1812 *Friend* (*CC*) II 170.

An excellent Adage commands that we should
Relate of the Dead, that alone which is good;
But of the great Lord, who here lies in lead,
We know nothing good but that he is dead.

293. DEJECTION: AN ODE

[Jul 1802?]

There are two transcripts of the poem in C's hand, another transcript, perhaps written c 1806, and records of another from 1814. It was published in *M Post* (4 Oct 1802), and was collected in *SL* (1817) and *PW* (1828, 1829, 1834). The various texts incorporate different selections of the text published in *SL* and thereafter, and are divided into parts in different ways, but otherwise they vary relatively little. The origins and such development as the poem underwent are to be seen against the background of **289** *Letter to* ———. The *Letter* forms the matrix and for a long time a kind of shadow alternative, which inhibited C from committing himself to the other version he had extracted.

C wrote the *Letter* between 4 Apr (perhaps in part before) and 21 Apr 1802. He certainly never intended to publish it and he appears not to have shown it to friends as close as RS and CL; it is not even known if he sent it to SH. He was sufficiently detached by 7 May to pretend to TP (and to himself) that he had written it to TP (*CL* II 801), but further work on the poem probably depended on the building confidence of succeeding months. The first version of the *Ode*, sent in Jul to RS, may have been put together not long before—perhaps between 16 and 19 Jul, or actually on the latter date.

C had a clear objective at this first stage of the poem's evolution, but was profoundly uncertain as to whether it would be acceptable. His purpose was to convert a gesture of love and an appeal for sympathy into a poem about imagination. His revision omits about ten stanzas concerning his domestic life, and brings forward the original conclusion to the centre of the new poem, where it becomes a postulate. Specifically, the *Ode* follows the *Letter* closely for stanzas I, II, and III; turns to the end of the *Letter* for stanzas IV and V, which it also follows closely; turns back to the preceding passage for stanza VI, which is constructed by running together several stanzas and omitting the personal material; and turns back to the passage before this again for stanzas VII and VIII. Stanza VIII is completed by using the last few lines of the original poem. The effect of the revision—or, rather, reconstruction—is to ascribe the loss of the shaping spirit of imagination to an infection of the soul caused by abstruse research, with no reference to the trials of C's domestic life and his love for SH, to which the research had been an antidote.

The new poem thereby ceases to trace a circling process of uncertain self-examination and instead makes a general proposition about life. In the new context, the replacing of SH's name with WW's was not opportunistic or evasive, and the first publication on WW's wedding-day was a tribute with no trace of conscious irony. WW's example in *The Leech Gatherer*, the poem he wrote and rewrote between early May and early Jul, was instrumental in buoying up C's confidence, and the two poems were copied out one after another in the second ms in C's hand.

The intimate connection between *The Leech Gatherer* and C's poem may be reflected in the anxiety of WW's commentary on it for SH (*WL—E* rev—366–7), just before he left for France to make a settlement with Annette Vallon and just before C copied out the first version of his own poem. There are a number of thematic and other links between the two poems: for example, the close of the first published version (see VAR lines 133.1.3–4) may be read as a tribute to WW in WW's own language. *Dejection: An Ode* anticipates **300** *The Picture* and **301** *Hymn before Sun-rise* in its attempt to surmount self-concern, to affirm larger principles. The numbering of the stanzas and the new format heighten the sense of formality and control, of resolution and independence, as do the amendments of punctuation in their slowing down of the pace of individual lines.

Whether or not the revision was thoroughgoing enough is another matter, and C remained uncertain until he went to Malta, perhaps until after his return. He continued to quote or paraphrase the unpublished, personal parts of the *Letter* to different correspondents (e.g. *CL* II 875: to Thomas Wedgwood 20 Oct 1802; *CL* II 901: to TP 17 Dec 1802; *CL* II 903–4: to Mary Robinson 27 Dec 1802); and the second ms in his hand, for Sir George and Lady Beaumont in Aug 1803 (*CL* II 970–2), breaks off at a crucial point (line 86).

The problem was partly technical: for instance, how to integrate the storm passage, a difficulty which C met by adding four lines to the end of stanza I. Even more, it was caused by doubts concerning the ability of the new poem to exist apart from its personal background, as is apparent in C's hesitation over the second part of stanza VI.

C continued to think of the poem as private, even unpublished, until at least 1814—as a poem whose parts were not in an inevitable final form—but the text arrived at in *SL* was thereafter reprinted with changes of punctuation only, the first poem in the section "Odes and Miscellaneous Poems". In their new setting, phrases like "abstruse research" and "natural man", "joy" and "lady", have an altered, sufficient new meaning; and the *Letter* and the *Ode*, even while they share many lines and whole groups of lines, make up two poems with separate tendencies and aspirations, in their own right.

The text given here is that of *SL* (1817), taking in the Errata. Annotation of the personal and literary background is given at **289** *Letter to* —— EC.

> Late, late yestreen I saw the new Moon,
> With the old Moon in her arms;
> And I fear, I fear, my Master dear!
> We shall have a deadly storm.
> *Ballad of Sir* PATRICK SPENCE.   ⁻1.5

I.

Well! If the Bard was weather-wise, who made
    The grand old ballad of Sir Patrick Spence,
    This night, so tranquil now, will not go hence
Unrous'd by winds, that ply a busier trade

epigraph. C has modernised and selected from five lines of *Sir Patrick Spens*, in Bishop Percy's version (*Reliques of Ancient English Poetry*— 4th ed 3 vols 1794—I 80). He had read and drawn upon this collection at the time of his most fruitful collaboration with WW (see *RX* 244, 331).

Than those which mould yon clouds in lazy flakes,   5
Or the dull sobbing draft, that moans and rakes
   Upon the strings of this Æolian lute,
   Which better far were mute.
  For lo! the New-moon winter-bright!
  And overspread with phantom-light,   10
  (With swimming phantom-light o'erspread
  But rimm'd and circled by a silver thread)
I see the old Moon in her lap, foretelling
  The coming on of rain and squally blast.
And oh! that even now the gust were swelling,   15
  And the slant night-shower driving loud and fast!
Those sounds which oft have raised me, whilst they awed,
   And sent my soul abroad,
Might now perhaps their wonted impulse give,
Might startle this dull pain, and make it move and live!   20

II.

A grief without a pang, void, dark, and drear,
  A stifled, drowsy, unimpassion'd grief,
  Which finds no natural outlet, no relief,
   In word, or sigh, or tear—
O Lady! in this wan and heartless mood,   25
To other thoughts by yonder throstle woo'd,
  All this long eve, so balmy and serene,
Have I been gazing on the western sky,
  And it's peculiar tint of yellow green:
And still I gaze—and with how blank an eye!   30
And those thin clouds above, in flakes and bars,
That give away their motion to the stars;
Those stars, that glide behind them or between,
Now sparkling, now bedimm'd, but always seen;
Yon crescent Moon, as fix'd as if it grew   35
In its own cloudless, starless lake of blue;

17–20. One of the few instances of a passage added to the *Letter* to make up the *Ode*. See also line 66, which was not added until the proof stage of *SL*.

25. Lady] In earlier versions C here and elsewhere addressed his poem to "Edmund" or "dearest William". In the personal context of the *Letter* he appealed directly to SH.

I see them all so excellently fair,
I see, not feel how beautiful they are!

III.

My genial spirits fail,
And what can these avail, 40
To lift the smoth'ring weight from off my breast?
It were a vain endeavor,
Though I should gaze for ever
On that green light that lingers in the west:
I may not hope from outward forms to win 45
The passion and the life, whose fountains are within.

IV.

O Lady! we receive but what we give,
And in our life alone does nature live:
Ours is her wedding-garment, ours her shroud!
And would we aught behold, of higher worth, 50
Than that inanimate cold world allow'd
To the poor loveless ever-anxious crowd,
Ah! from the soul itself must issue forth,
A light, a glory, a fair luminous cloud
Enveloping the Earth— 55
And from the soul itself must there be sent
A sweet and potent voice, of its own birth,
Of all sweet sounds the life and element!

V.

O pure of heart! thou need'st not ask of me
What this strong music in the soul may be! 60
What, and wherein it doth exist,
This light, this glory, this fair luminous mist,
This beautiful, and beauty-making power.
Joy, virtuous Lady! Joy that ne'er was given,
Save to the pure, and in their purest hour, 65
Life, and Life's Effluence, Cloud at once and Shower,
Joy, Lady! is the spirit and the power,

66. A late addition to the poem (see 17–20EC). This line adds to the Miltonic echoes: cf *PL* III 6 "Bright effluence of bright essence increate". See **289**EC for more examples.

Which wedding Nature to us gives in dow'r
   A new Earth and new Heaven,
Undreamt of by the sensual and the proud—   70
Joy is the sweet voice, Joy the luminous cloud—
   We in ourselves rejoice!
And thence flows all that charms or ear or sight,
   All melodies the echoes of that voice,
All colours a suffusion from that light.   75

VI.

There was a time when, though my path was rough,
   This joy within me dallied with distress,
And all misfortunes were but as the stuff
   Whence Fancy made me dreams of happiness:
For hope grew round me, like the twining vine,   80
And fruits, and foliage, not my own, seem'd mine.
But now afflictions bow me down to earth:
Nor care I that they rob me of my mirth,
   But oh! each visitation
Suspends what nature gave me at my birth,   85
   My shaping spirit of Imagination.
For not to think of what I needs must feel,
   But to be still and patient, all I can;
And haply by abstruse research to steal
   From my own nature all the natural Man—   90
   This was my sole resource, my only plan:
Till that which suits a part infects the whole,
And now is almost grown the habit of my Soul.

VII.

Hence, viper thoughts, that coil around my mind,
   Reality's dark dream!   95

87–93. C was particularly sensitive about these lines, and for a long time uncertain of their place. They appear in the first ms version of the *Ode*, out of sequence, and were quoted separately in letters thereafter (*CL* II 815, 831–2, 875, 1008, 1201); but another ms version breaks off just before them, while a further ms and the first published version omit them. They were not restored to the poem until the proof stage of *SL*. The lines have a different meaning in the other context of the *Letter* (lines 265–71), although clearly C was uncertain how obvious this significance would be.

I turn from you, and listen to the wind,
   Which long has rav'd unnotic'd. What a scream
Of agony by torture lengthen'd out
That lute sent forth! Thou Wind, that rav'st without,
   Bare crag, or mountain-tairn,* or blasted tree,   100
Or pine-grove whither woodman never clomb,
Or lonely house, long held the witches' home,
   Methinks were fitter instruments for thee,
Mad Lutanist! who in this month of show'rs,
Of dark brown gardens, and of peeping flow'rs,   105
Mak'st Devils' yule, with worse than wint'ry song,
The blossoms, buds, and tim'rous leaves among.
   Thou Actor, perfect in all tragic sounds!
Thou mighty Poet, e'en to Frenzy bold!
     What tell'st thou now about?   110
     'Tis of the Rushing of an Host in rout,
With groans of trampled men, with smarting wounds—
At once they groan with pain, and shudder with the cold!
But hush! there is a pause of deepest silence!
   And all that noise, as of a rushing crowd,   115
With groans, and tremulous shudderings—all is over—
   It tells another tale, with sounds less deep and loud!
     A tale of less affright,
     And temper'd with delight,
As Otway's self had fram'd the tender lay—   120
     'Tis of a little child

* Tairn is a small lake, generally if not always applied to the lakes up in the mountains, and which are the feeders of those in the vallies. This address to the Storm-wind will not appear extravagant to those who have heard it at night, and in a mountainous country.

100fn. Tairn] C added a note to the transcript of **176** *Christabel* he made for SH, in which he elucidated the etymology of the word with reference to Edward Lye *Dictionarium Saxonico et Gothico-Latinum* (2 vols 1772).

120. Thomas Otway (1652–85), remembered here as the author of *The Orphan* and other sentimental tragedies. In earlier versions of the poem C instead addressed WW (as "Edmund" or, in the *Letter*, "William"), whose *Lucy Gray* better fits the lines that follow than does Otway's play. Otway was himself an object of pity, as Chatterton became: see e.g. Charlotte Smith's sonnets on him (*Elegiac Sonnets* 26, 30, 32); C drew on this edition for *A Sheet of Sonnets*.

Upon a lonesome wild,
Not far from home, but she hath lost her way:
And now moans low in bitter grief and fear,
And now screams loud, and hopes to make her mother hear.   125

VIII.

'Tis midnight, but small thoughts have I of sleep:
Full seldom may my friend such vigils keep!
Visit her, gentle Sleep! with wings of healing,
   And may this storm be but a mountain-birth,
May all the stars hang bright above her dwelling,   130
   Silent as though they watch'd the sleeping Earth!
     With light heart may she rise,
      Gay fancy, cheerful eyes,
   Joy lift her spirit, joy attune her voice:
To her may all things live, from Pole to Pole,   135
Their life the eddying of her living soul!
   O simple spirit, guided from above,
Dear Lady! friend devoutest of my choice,
Thus may'st thou ever, evermore rejoice.

294. THE DAY DREAM

[Jul–Aug 1802]

The poem centres on an incident which took place between 2 and 13 Mar 1802, when C stayed at Gallow Hill on his way home from London—an incident described at greater length and more directly at **289** *A Letter to* —— 99–110 (4–21 Apr 1802). It is not known whether the present poem preceded the *Letter*, or if it grew out of attempts to find a more public significance and form for the longer poem. The latter possibility is the more likely. The poem might have been one of those C sent to the Wordsworths on 27 Apr or 6 May (*DWJ* ɪ 139, 144); or it might have followed on the extraction of **293** *Dejection: An Ode* from the *Letter*, perhaps in Jul–Aug 1802.

The lines were almost certainly written before **300** *The Picture*—a poem, in C's words, "on the endeavor to emancipate the soul from day-dreams" (*CN* ɪ 1153). MH copied it out, without a title, following on her transcript of the *Letter*, and this is the version given here, with minor corrections. A slightly revised version was published in *M Post* (19 Oct 1802), with the title "The Day Dream, From an Emigrant to his Absent Wife" over the signature "ΕΣΤΗΣΕ."

In fact, as C appears to have realised, the suggested public meaning involves a troubling inconsistency. Instead of republishing the poem, he redrafted it entirely as **629** *A Day Dream*, in a form closer to the *Letter*, perhaps as late as 1826–8.

If Thou wert here, these Tears were "Tears of Light"!
  —But from as sweet a day-dream did I start
As ever made these Eyes grow idly bright;
  And tho' I weep, yet still about the *heart*
A dear & playful Tenderness doth linger   5
Touching my Heart as with a Baby's finger.

My Mouth half-open like a witless Man,
  I saw the Couch, I saw the quiet Room,
  The heaving Shadows, & the fire-light Gloom;
And on my Lips, I know not what there ran—   10
On my unmoving Lips a subtile Feeling—
I know not what—but had the same been stealing

Upon a sleeping Mother's Lips I guess
  It would have made the loving Mother dream
That she was softly stooping down to Kiss   15
  Her Babe, that something more than Babe did seem—
An obscure Presence of it's darling Father,
Yet still it's own sweet Baby self far rather!

Across my chest there liv'd a weight so warm
  As if some bird had taken shelter there;   20
And lo! upon the Couch a Woman's Form!
  Thine, Sara! thine! O Joy, if thine it were!

1. "Tears of Light"] From WW *Matthew* 24 (*WPW* IV 69).

5–6. Anticipated—in a form curiously closer to the printed rather than the ms version—in a notebook entry of early Feb 1802 (*CN* I 1105):

  a playful Tenderness
Touching the Heart, as with an infant's finger

7. Mouth half-open] "I cannot breathe thro' my nose—so my mouth, with sensual thick lips, is almost always open" (*CL* I 260: to John Thelwall 19 Nov [1796]). C's description is confirmed by other reports and by portraits; for a possible bearing on the phonetic patterning of his poetry see **178** *Kubla Khan* 1 EC.

I gaz'd with anxious hope, & fear'd to stir it—
A deeper Trance ne'er wrapt a yearning Spirit.

And now when I seem'd SURE my Love to see,   25
    Her very Self in her own quiet Home,
There came an elfish Laugh, & waken'd me!—
    'Twas Hartley, who behind my Chair had clomb,
And with his bright Eyes at my face was peeping—
I bless'd him—try'd to laugh—& fell a weeping.   30

295. SONNET TO ASRA

[1801–4]

The only known text of the sonnet is in C's holograph, on a piece of paper pasted into the inside cover of the transcript of **176** *Christabel* he made for SH (MS 2), perhaps in Nov 1801. The sonnet is on a different paper from *Christabel*, and there is no way of knowing whether the two texts were brought together in the album by SH or, after her death, by someone else.

Are there two things, of all which Men possess,
That are so like each other and so near
As mutual Love seems like to Happiness?
Dear Asra, Woman beyond utterance dear!
This Love, which ever welling at my heart   5
Now in it's living fount doth heave and fall,
Now overflowing pours thro' every part
Of all my Frame, and fills and changes all,
Like vernal waters springing up thro' Snow—
This Love, that seeming great beyond the power   10

28. Hartley] When the poem was published in *M Post*, the name was changed to "FREDERIC". Readers of the published version were also meant to assume—if they wished to make an identification—that the Sara of line 22 was Mrs C, not SH. They might still have been puzzled by the suggestion that the small child was with the emigrant father rather than the absent wife for whom the husband yearned.

3. Cf Pope *Essay on Man* IV 55 "But mutual wants this happiness increase". The sonnet is otherwise resonant with Shakespearean images of seasonal and organic growth.

Of Growth, yet seemeth evermore to grow—
Could I transmute the whole to the rich dower
Of Happy Life, and give it all to Thee,
Thy Lot, methinks, were Heaven, thy Age Eternity!

296. LINES COMPOSED DURING A NIGHT RAMBLE BEHIND SKIDDAW, AT THE FOOT OF MOUNT BLENCARTHUR, IN 1802

[Jul–Aug 1802? Oct 1800?]

Although the lines were composed in 1802, or even perhaps as early as 1800, they might not have been written down until Mar 1806, and were not printed until 1833. Three ms and two printed versions are extant; they differ in details of phrasing, and the version given here is from the fair copy C made some time after 1820. In an introductory note to one version C describes the lines merely as a "stanza": "It may not arrogate the name of Poem".

The note on Walter Scott appears only in the version given here (in which some typographical details have been regularised). The quotation is (var) from *The Lay of the Last Minstrel* canto II stanza 1 (1805) p 35, and the borrowing might have come through a mutual friend like John Stoddart, from whom Scott heard **176** *Christabel*. C's contention is none the less disputable, and it distracts attention from a conscious borrowing on his own part. The first two lines are taken directly from Isaac Ritson, as quoted by William Hutchinson *History of Cumberland* I 336n. Indeed, the form of C's "stanza" is explained as a rewriting of the Ritson extract:

> The winds upon Blenkarthur's head,
> Are often loud and strong;
> And many a tempest o'er his cliffs
> Careering sweeps along.
> Like him, Helvellyn swells on high
> In sullen misty pride;
> And low'ring o'er his subject hills,
> Surveys the world so wide.

A note in another version emphasises the impromptu, non-literary character of the lines, describing them as having been composed "while the Writer was gazing on three parallel Forces—on a Moonlight Night at the foot of the Saddle-back Fell". A force, as C explains, "is the provincial term in Cumberland for any narrow Fall of Water from the summit of a Mountain Precipice". The forces here would be those that flow into Roughten Gill, some 4–5 miles up behind Greta Hall.

> The Winds on stern Blencarthur's Height
>   Are tyrannous and strong:
> And flashing forth unsteady light
> From stern Blencarthur's skiey Height*
>   As loud the Torrents throng.   5
>
> Beneath the Moon in gentle Weather
> They bind the Earth and Sky together:
> But O! the Sky and all *it's* Forms, how quiet!
> The Things, that seek the *Earth*, how full of noise & riot!

297. SONNET ADAPTED FROM PETRARCH

[1802–4? 1804–6? 1810–15?]

The sonnet exists only in a untitled transcript by Mrs C, endorsed by her "transcribed by S from *S T C*." The circumstances of the transcript might suggest that it was made when she and SC were beginning Italian (1810–15), and the translation might date from then. However, C was reading Petrarch from before the time he went to Malta (*CL* III 431: to Mrs C [27 Jan 1813]; IV 635: to J. Murray [27 Apr 1816]; 655: to J. H. Frere 16 Jul 1816), when his interest was literary-poetic: on his return he was chiefly interested in Petrarch's Latin prose writings (*CN* III 3360, 3467, 3633, etc).

The text is as follows in the edition of Petrarch which C owned (*Opera* [ed J. Herold]—4 vols Basle 1581—III 158A = *Canzoniere* 209 in Gianfranco Contini's now standard numbering):

---

* Imitated by Sir W. Scott, and applied to Melrose Abbey in his couplet:

> The Moon's cold Light's uncertain Shower
> Streams on the ruin'd central Tower.

2. tyrannous and strong] From **161** *The Rime of the Ancient Mariner* 42. The phrase had also been used by   WW in *The Waterfall and the Eglantine* 15 (*WPW* II 129).

SONNETTO CLXXV

I dolci colli; ou'io lasciai me stesso
Partendo, onde partir giamai non posso;
Mi vanno innanzi; & emmi ogni hor adosso
Quel caro peso, ch'amor m'ha commesso.
   Meco di me mi meraviglio spesso;
Ch'i pur vò sempre; e non son ancor mosso
Dal bel giogo più volte indarno scosso:
Ma com'più me n'allungo, e' più m'appresso:
   E qual cervo ferrito di saetta
Col ferro auelenato dentr'al fianco
Fugge, e più duolsi, quantò più s'affretta;
   Tal io con quello stral dal lato manco;
Che mi consuma, e parte mi diletta,
Di duol mi struggo, e di fuggir mi stanco.

If the translation dates from the time before C went to Malta, some features (most obviously, its transposition into Shakespearean sonnet form) might be accidental. Alternatively, if it dates from the time he was teaching his wife and daughter Italian, they might embody some pedagogic purpose. Cf the sonnet C translated from Marino in 1808, poem **440.** Its positioning at this point in the sequence, among poems describing C's feelings for mountains (which he expands on from the original) and for SH (Petrarch's emotions are heightened and deepened), makes it an Asra poem. It is relevant that a motto from Petrarch opens the section of "Love Poems" in *SL*.

The text given here supplies some punctuation at line-endings, and emends ms "huntsmen" to the singular in line 10.

Those pleasant hills high tow'ring into air
Where lingers with delight my captive soul
Are ever in mine eyes: and still I bear
Love's burden e'en to earth's extremest pole.
Oft do I strive to free myself in vain   5
From the sad yoke imposed by despot Love;
Nor time, nor distance can relieve his pain,
Who's doom'd such bitter pangs as mine to prove.
Swift bounding o'er the plain the wretched hart
Whom cruel huntsman, from afar, espies   10
Receives into his side the envenom'd dart
Which galls him all the more, the more he flies.
Thus rankling in my heart love's shaft doth lie:
Tis death to tarry, but what pain to fly!

298. A VERSION OF A NURSERY RHYME

[1801–3]

C must have composed the verses some time before he travelled to Malta, perhaps as a performance for DC, whose interest in food elicited such a kind of affectionate humour. RS is reported to have said that "all Derwent's Brains [are] in his Guts" (*CL* II 1022: to Matthew Coates 5 Dec 1803); it happens that a pig was one of the principal dishes at DC's christening (*WL—E* rev—418). The exaggeratedly accented style at the same time mimics an aspect of Mrs C's *lingo grande*: cf **342** *Hexameter Lines to Mrs Coleridge* for a more sumptuous example which also shares similar imagery.

C's verses build on the words of a child's nursery rhyme, modified only in that it is told in a comic accent, but thereby extended backwards to incorporate the child's mother, the speaker's wife, into the dialogue. The original rhyme was first recorded by J. O. Halliwell some decades afterwards, as follows:

> The pettitoes are little feet,
>   And the little feet not big;
> Great feet belong to the grunting hog,
>   And the pettitoes to the little pig.
>   (*The Nursery Rhymes of England*
>   —1853; rpt 1970—215)

For analogous uses of nursery rhyme see **138.X1** *Nursery Song* and **325** *For a House-dog's Collar* headnote. The present text is taken from a fair copy in the hand of either Mrs C or DW.

C was reminded of the verses when he was in Malta, perhaps by the speech of a Dr Paolo Cesareo, whose name he wrote above them (*CN* II 2178). At the same time, he added two further lines which may be intended to reinterpret the woman as SH:

> Come, Sara dear, carissima anima mia,
> Go, boil the Kettle, make me some green Tea a.

The Italian may be translated as "my dearest soul". Green tea is said to foster dreams (cf *CL* II 1079: to Sir George Beaumont 8 Mar 1804).

> Mon Charmant, prenez gard a
> Mind vat your Signior begs
> Ven you wash, don't scrub so hard a
> You may rub my Shirt to rags.

While you make the water hotter   5
Un solo I compose.
Put in the Pot the nice Sheeps Trotter
And de leetle Petti toes—

De pettitoes and leetle feet
De leetle feet not big   10
  Great Feat belog
    To de grunting Hog
Pettitoes to the leetle Pig.

299. THE KEEPSAKE

[1800–2]

The lines were written during the first years of C's acquaintance with SH, and might be connected with **300** *The Picture* via the larger project of **294.X1** *The Soother of Absence*. They were published over a pseudonym in *M Post* (17 Sept 1802), copied out in *SH's Poets*, and included in *SL* (1817) and C's later collections. The texts do not differ significantly; the *SL* version is given here.

The tedded hay, the first-fruits of the soil,
The tedded hay and corn-sheaves in one field,
Shew summer gone, ere come. The foxglove tall
Sheds its loose purple bells, or in the gust,
Or when it bends beneath the up-springing lark,   5
Or mountain-finch alighting. And the rose
(In vain the darling of successful love)
Stands, like some boasted beauty of past years,
The thorns remaining, and the flowers all gone.
Nor can I find, amid my lonely walk   10
By rivulet, or spring, or wet road-side,
That blue and bright-eyed flowret of the brook,

Hope's gentle gem, the sweet FORGET-ME-NOT!*
So will not fade the flowers which Emmeline
With delicate fingers on the snow-white silk   15
Has work'd, (the flowers which most she knew I lov'd,)
And, more belov'd than they, her auburn hair.

In the cool morning twilight, early waked
By her full bosom's joyless restlessness,
Leaving the soft bed to her sleeping sister,   20
Softly she rose, and lightly stole along,
Down the slope coppice to the woodbine bower,
Whose rich flowers, swinging in the morning breeze,
Over their dim fast-moving shadows hung,
Making a quiet image of disquiet   25
In the smooth, scarcely moving river-pool.
There, in that bower where first she own'd her love,
And let me kiss my own warm tear of joy
From off her glowing cheek, she sate and stretch'd
The silk upon the frame, and work'd her name   30
Between the MOSS-ROSE and FORGET-ME-NOT—
Her own dear name, with her own auburn hair!
That forc'd to wander till sweet spring return,
I yet might ne'er forget her smile, her look,
Her voice, (that even in her mirthful mood   35
Has made me wish to steal away and weep,)

* One of the names (and meriting to be the only one) of the *Myosotis Scorpioides Palustris*; a flower from six to twelve inches high, with blue blossom and bright yellow eye. It has the same name over the whole Empire of Germany (*Vergissmein nicht*), and we believe, in Denmark and Sweden.

13. FORGET-ME-NOT] *OED* cites the present instance as a revival of 16th-century usage, although the word was presumably common in popular speech—perhaps specifically northern in its usage. C associated it with SH after she interpolated it into a list of flower names copied from William Withering's *Arrangement of British Plants* (1796) in Notebook 21. Cf *CN* I 863 f 15ᵛ and n.

14. Emmeline] For another equation of SH with this name see *CN* II 2588. It possibly refers to the virtuously independent heroine of Charlotte Smith's first novel, *Emmeline: The Orphan of the Castle* (1788).

17. her auburn hair] The beauty of SH's hair is confirmed by other sources. See Ernest de Selincourt *Dorothy Wordsworth* (Oxford 1933) 56.

Nor yet th' entrancement of that maiden kiss
With which she promis'd, that when spring return'd,
She would resign one half of that dear name,
And own thenceforth no other name but mine!　　40

300. THE PICTURE
OR, THE LOVER'S RESOLUTION

[Aug 1802?]

The scope of the poem is described in a memorandum: "A Poem on the endeavor to emancipate the soul from day-dreams & note the different attempts & the vain ones" (*CN* I 1153). In the working out of such an idea C is indebted to Gessner's 45-line idyll *Der feste Vorsatz* ("The Fixed Resolution"), as well as to Shakespeare's *Midsummer Night's Dream* and *The Tempest*. There are also echoes of the poem which Mrs Barbauld had addressed to him in Sept 1797 (transcript in Mrs Estlin's hand in BPL B 21076; pub anonymously in *The Poetical Register for 1808–9* VII—1812—420–1), to which C's poem is to some extent an answer. The whole method of handling humorously a solemnly held theory about the healing powers of nature, in choice bombast, is anticipated by Cowper's lines on the cucumber, and was probably abetted by CL, who was staying with C when the poem was written.

The tone of mock recantation and the incongruities of pace are not always under control, however. C admitted as much in a note prefixed to the poem in Francis Wrangham's (?) copy of *SL*:

I do not recollect any Number of Lines under the name of a Poem, that more strikingly illustrates the nature and necessity of some *one Spirit*, a Unity beside and beyond mere connection, a Life in and over all, as the Light at once hidden and revealed in all the Colours that are the Component Integers of the Vision.—In this poem there is no defect of *connection*. The thoughts pass into each other without a saltus, the Imagery is sufficiently homogeneous, and the Feelings harmonize with both, and ~~are~~ plainly produce or modify both. ~~Finally,~~ But there is no under-current, that "moves onward from within"—the *one Spirit* is absent, "*and it is he, That makes the ship to go.*" *S. T. C.*

The poem is one of those copied into SH's album. It was published over the signature "ΕΣΤΗΣΕ." in *M Post* (6 Sept 1802) and underwent considerable additions (lines 17–26, 32–42, 76–7, 127–32) in *SL* (1817); further modifications were made in the collections of 1828 and 1829. The text given here is that of *PW* (1829).

Eric Adams has argued that *The Picture*, along with **148** *To an Unfortunate Woman at the Theatre*, influenced Danby, who was working in Bristol when the poems were republished in *SL* (*Francis Danby: Varieties of Poetic Landscape*—New Haven 1973—22–3). Danby's huge oil-painting of 1821, *Disappointed Love*, became enormously popular after it was acquired by the V&A in 1857, and thereby mediated the influence of C's poem in the later 19th century.

> Through weeds and thorns, and matted underwood
> I force my way; now climb, and now descend
> O'er rocks, or bare or mossy, with wild foot
> Crushing the purple whorts; while oft unseen,
> Hurrying along the drifted forest-leaves,　　　　　　　　5
> The scared snake rustles. Onward still I toil
> I know not, ask not whither! A new joy,
> Lovely as light, sudden as summer gust,
> And gladsome as the first-born of the spring,
> Beckons me on, or follows from behind,　　　　　　　　10
> Playmate, or guide! The master-passion quelled,
> I feel that I am free. With dun-red bark
> The fir-trees, and the unfrequent slender oak,
> Forth from this tangle wild of bush and brake
> Soar up, and form a melancholy vault　　　　　　　　15
> High o'er me, murmuring like a distant sea.
>
> Here Wisdom might resort, and here Remorse;
> Here too the love-lorn Man who, sick in soul,
> And of this busy human heart aweary,
> Worships the spirit of unconscious life　　　　　　　　20

4. purple whorts] C added a note to the *M Post* text, which identified them as "*Vaccinium Myrtillus*, known by the different names of Whorts, Whortle-berries, Bil-berries; and, in the North of England, Blea-berries, and Bloom-berries." He was probably conscious that SH had written both northern and southern names—blea-berries and whortle-berries—into his notebook (*CN* I 863). Myrtle (cf line 27) was sacred to Venus and an emblem of love.

17–25. C quoted the lines to Joseph Cottle in May 1814 (*CL* III 499), introducing them as follows: "And in my early manhood in lines, descriptive of a ~~moody~~ gloomy solitude, I disguised my own sensations in the following words". He quoted lines 20–4 in a letter to EC of Feb 1826 (*CL* VI 555), to illustrate a "sickly" state of mind, "in too close a neighbourhood to the relaxing Malaria of the Mystic Divinity, which affects to languish after an extinction of individual Consciousness."

In tree or wild-flower.—Gentle Lunatic!
If so he might not wholly cease to be,
He would far rather not be that, he is;
But would be something, that he knows not of,
In winds or waters, or among the rocks!   25

    But hence, fond wretch! breathe not contagion here!
No myrtle-walks are these: these are no groves
Where Love dare loiter! If in sullen mood
He should stray hither, the low stumps shall gore
His dainty feet, the briar and the thorn   30
Make his plumes haggard. Like a wounded bird
Easily caught, ensnare him, O ye Nymphs,
Ye Oreads chaste, ye dusky Dryades!
And you, ye EARTH-WINDS! you that make at morn
The dew-drops quiver on the spiders' webs!   35
You, O ye wingless AIRS! that creep between
The rigid stems of heath and bitten furze,
Within whose scanty shade, at summer-noon,
The mother-sheep hath worn a hollow bed—
Ye, that now cool her fleece with dropless Damp,   40
Now pant and murmur with her feeding lamb.
Chase, chase him, all ye Fays, and elfin Gnomes!
With prickles sharper than his darts bemock
His little Godship, making him perforce
Creep through a thorn-bush on yon hedgehog's back.   45

    This is my hour of triumph! I can now
With my own fancies play the merry fool,
And laugh away worse folly, being free.
Here will I seat myself, beside this old,
Hollow, and weedy oak, which ivy-twine   50
Clothes as with net-work: here will I couch my limbs,
Close by this river, in this silent shade,
As safe and sacred from the step of man
As an invisible world—unheard, unseen,

28–30. The lines repeat an experience at Stowey recorded in the Gutch Memorandum Book (*CN* I 230) and again in Germany (*CL* I 504: to Mrs C 17 May [1799]). Cf the stanza dropped at line 44+ of **253** *Love* q **253** headnote.

And listening only to the pebbly brook 55
That murmurs with a dead, yet tinkling sound;
Or to the bees, that in the neighbouring trunk
Make honey-hoards. The breeze, that visits me,
Was never Love's accomplice, never raised
The tendril ringlets from the maiden's brow, 60
And the blue, delicate veins above her cheek;
Ne'er played the wanton—never half disclosed
The maiden's snowy bosom, scattering thence
Eye-poisons for some love-distempered youth,
Who ne'er henceforth may see an aspen-grove 65
Shiver in sunshine, but his feeble heart
Shall flow away like a dissolving thing.

    Sweet breeze! thou only, if I guess aright,
Liftest the feathers of the robin's breast,
That swells its little breast, so full of song, 70
Singing above me, on the mountain-ash.
And thou too, desert Stream! no pool of thine,
Though clear as lake in latest summer-eve,
Did e'er reflect the stately virgin's robe,
The face, the form divine, the downcast look 75
Contemplative! Behold! her open palm
Presses her cheek and brow! her elbow rests
On the bare branch of half-uprooted tree,
That leans towards its mirror! Who erewhile
Had from her countenance turned, or looked by stealth, 80
(For fear is true love's cruel nurse), he now
With steadfast gaze and unoffending eye,
Worships the watery idol, dreaming hopes
Delicious to the soul, but fleeting, vain,
E'en as that phantom-world on which he gazed, 85
But not unheeded gazed: for see, ah! see,
The sportive tyrant with her left hand plucks
The heads of tall flowers that behind her grow,
Lychnis, and willow-herb, and fox-glove bells:
And suddenly, as one that toys with time, 90
Scatters them on the pool! Then all the charm
Is broken—all that phantom-world so fair
Vanishes, and a thousand circlets spread,
And each mis-shape the other. Stay awhile,

Poor youth, who scarcely darest lift up thine eyes!   95
The stream will soon renew its smoothness, soon
The visions will return! And lo! he stays:
And soon the fragments dim of lovely forms
Come trembling back, unite, and now once more
The pool becomes a mirror; and behold   100
Each wildflower on the marge inverted there,
And there the half-uprooted tree—but where,
O where the virgin's snowy arm, that leaned
On its bare branch? He turns, and she is gone!
Homeward she steals through many a woodland maze   105
Which he shall seek in vain. Ill-fated youth!
Go, day by day, and waste thy manly prime
In mad Love-yearning by the vacant brook,
Till sickly thoughts bewitch thine eyes, and thou
Behold'st her shadow still abiding there,   110
The Naiad of the Mirror!

           Not to thee,
O wild and desert Stream! belongs this tale:
Gloomy and dark art thou—the crowded firs
Spire from thy shores, and stretch across thy bed,
Making thee doleful as a cavern-well: 115
Save when the shy king-fishers build their nest
On thy steep banks, no loves hast thou, wild stream!

   This be my chosen haunt—emancipate
From passion's dreams, a freeman, and alone,
I rise and trace its devious course. O lead,   120
Lead me to deeper shades and lonelier glooms.
Lo! stealing through the canopy of firs
How fair the sunshine spots that mossy rock,
Isle of the river, whose disparted waves
Dart off asunder with an angry sound,   125
How soon to re-unite! And see! they meet,
Each in the other lost and found: and see
Placeless, as spirits, one soft water-sun
Throbbing within them, Heart at once and Eye!
With its soft neighbourhood of filmy clouds,   130
The stains and shadings of forgotten tears,
Dimness o'erswum with lustre! Such the hour

Of deep enjoyment, following love's brief feuds;
And hark, the noise of a near waterfall!
I pass forth into light—I find myself   135
Beneath a weeping birch (most beautiful
Of forest-trees, the Lady of the woods,)
Hard by the brink of a tall weedy rock
That overbrows the cataract. How bursts
The landscape on my sight! Two crescent hills   140
Fold in behind each other, and so make
A circular vale, and land-locked, as might seem,
With brook and bridge, and grey stone cottages,
Half hid by rocks and fruit-trees. At my feet,
The whortle-berries are bedewed with spray,   145
Dashed upwards by the furious waterfall.
How solemnly the pendent ivy mass
Swings in its winnow: All the air is calm.
The smoke from cottage-chimneys, tinged with light,
Rises in columns; from this house alone,   150
Close by the waterfall, the column slants,
And feels its ceaseless breeze. But what is THIS?
That cottage, with its slanting chimney-smoke,
And close beside its porch a sleeping child,
His dear head pillowed on a sleeping dog—   155
One arm between its fore legs, and the hand
Holds loosely its small handful of wild-flowers,
Unfilletted, and of unequal lengths.
A curious picture, with a master's haste
Sketched on a strip of pinky-silver skin,   160
Peeled from the birchen bark! Divinest maid!
Yon bark her canvas, and those purple berries
Her pencil! See, the juice is scarcely dried
On the fine skin! She has been newly here;
And lo! yon patch of heath has been her couch—   165
The pressure still remains! O blessed couch!
For this mayst thou flower early, and the Sun,
Slanting at eve, rest bright, and linger long

139. overbrows] Borrowed from
Collins *Ode on the Poetical Charac-
ter* 58.
  140–4. George Whalley speculates

that the scene described is Calder
Abbey, which C visited on 4 Aug
1802 (*C&SH* 15n). Cf *CN* I 1212 f
8^v; *IS* (1979) 229–30.

Upon thy purple bells! O Isabel!
Daughter of genius! stateliest of our maids! 170
More beautiful than whom Alcæus wooed
The Lesbian woman of immortal song!
O child of genius! stately, beautiful,
And full of love to all, save only me,
And not ungentle e'en to me! My heart, 175
Why beats it thus? Through yonder coppice-wood
Needs must the pathway turn, that leads straightway
On to her father's house. She is alone!
The night draws on—such ways are hard to hit—
And fit it is I should restore this sketch, 180
Dropt unawares no doubt. Why should I yearn
To keep the relique? 'twill but idly feed
The passion that consumes me. Let me haste!
The picture in my hand which she has left;
She cannot blame me that I followed her: 185
And I may be her guide the long wood through.

301. HYMN BEFORE SUN-RISE, IN THE VALE OF CHAMOUNY

[Aug–Sept 1802]

The subject of the poem was a favourite of English artists before and after C: see e.g. the paintings by Francis Towne and J.M.W. Turner reproduced by Jonathan Wordsworth, Michael C. Jaye, and Robert Woof *William Wordsworth and the Age of English Romanticism* (New Brunswick 1987) 162, 168. C's dependence on his sources has none the less been argued over since the year of his death, when DeQ took the poem as an instance of unacknowledged borrowing (*DeQ* II 143–4). The description in the Prefatory Note of the gentians, in particular, suggests first-hand experience which C did not have. The argument will continue, because the real-life and literary backgrounds intermingle in ways that make priority incalculable.

C told William Sotheby on 10 Sept 1802 that on Scafell "I involuntarily poured forth a Hymn in the manner of the *Psalms*, tho' afterwards I thought the

171–2. The lyric poet Alcaeus was a contemporary of Sappho of Lesbos. See **81** *With a Poem on the French Revolution* 24.

Ideas &c disproportionate to our humble mountains—& accidentally lighting on a short Note in some swiss Poems, concerning the Vale of Chamouny, & it's Mountain, I transferred myself thither, in the Spirit, & adapted my former feelings to these grander external objects" (*CL* II 864–5).

The "short Note" accompanies the the first poem in Friederike Brun's *Gedichte* (Zurich 1795) 1–3:

Chamonix[1]
beym Sonnenaufgange.
(Im Mai 1791.)

La Terra, il Mare, le Sfere
Parlan del tuo potere.

Metastasio

Aus tiefem Schatten des schweigenden Tannenhains
Erblick' ich bebend dich, Scheitel der Ewigkeit,
Blendender Gipfel, von dessen Höhe
Ahndend mein Geist ins Unendliche schwebet!

Wer senkte den Pfeiler tief in der Erde Schoos,
Der, seit Jahrtausenden, fest deine Masse stützt?
Wer thürmte hoch in des Aethers Wölbung
Mächtig und kühn dein umstrahltes Antlitz?

Wer goß Euch hoch aus des ewigen Winters Reich,
O Zackenströme, mit Donnergetös' herab?
Und wer gebietet laut mit der Allmacht Stimme:
"Hier sollen ruhen die starrenden Wogen!"[2]

Wer zeichnet dort dem Morgensterne Bahn,
Wer kränzt mit Blüthen des ewigen Frostes Saum?[3]
Wem tönt in schrecklichen Harmonieen,
Wilder *Arveiron*, dein Wogentümmel?

Jehovah! Jehovah! kracht's im berstenden Eis;
Lavinendonner rollen's die Kluft hinab:
Jehovah! rauscht's in den hellen Wipfeln,
Flüstert's an rieselnden Silberbächen.

---

1. *Chamonix* ist eins der höchsten Bergthäler der Baronie *Faucigny* in *Savoyen*. Es wird seiner romantischen, im Kontrast der wildesten Naturszenen mit den sanftesten Schönheiten abwechselnden Lage wegen, vorzüglich von Reisenden besucht; und außer der *Arve* wird es von den Gletscherwassern des unaufhaltsam tobenden *Arveiron*, und vier andern, aus den sich ins Thal senkenden Gletschern entstehenden, Schneewassern durchrauscht.
2. Die aus schwindelnder Höhe in den Ungeheuren Felsklüften herabgleitenden

Gletscher gleichen gewaltigen Strömen, die mitten im Tumult der raschesten Bewegung von plötzlichem Froste gefesselt werden.

3. Ich pflückte am Gletscher du *Bosson*, wenige Schritte vom ewigen Eise, die schöne *Gentiana major* in großer Menge.

The account given to Sotheby is complicated by the consideration that C must have known the volume of Brun's poems from at least Aug 1800, when WW took from it the story of *The Seven Sisters*, probably with C's assistance (*WPW* II 492; Reed II 80). Also, there are other less obvious literary sources, such as William Bowles's *Coombe Ellen*, possibly other Alpine poems by Brun, and Stolberg's poem on a cataract (see poem **258**). None the less, the echoes of earlier personal observations (*CN* I 523, 536, 540, 541, 766, etc; *CL* II 853–4: to SH 25 Aug 1802) make it likely that C had already conceived a version of his poem before taking up the Brun volume in the way he describes, and his account is most probably true in substance. His copy of the 1798 edition of Brun's *Gedichte* was sold with Green's library at Sotheby's 28 Jul 1880 lot 466, but has not been traced.

The poem was clearly important to C, who continued to place a high value on it in spite of criticisms made by WW (reported in *CL* IV 974: to an unknown correspondent [Nov 1819] and in *The Prose Works of William Wordsworth* ed Grosart III 442). It was connected in his mind with a sense of exhilaration and a new beginning following the dejection of the previous months, and he positioned it first in the section "Meditative Poems in Blank Verse" in *SL* and after. Its frequent reprinting, especially in America, indicates that it was one of the most popular of his poems during his lifetime. Keats and Byron appear to have had it in mind in several of their comments on the "egotistical sublime" and on the kind of poetry written by their elders; DeQ's attack only participates in the same broad reaction. The most profound engagement with the values of the poem is P. B. Shelley's, in *Mont Blanc* (1816).

There are four ms and seven printed texts. Words, phrases, and lines vary between the earlier texts, but only two passages were actually recast (lines 17–29, 76–9) and one added (lines 70–3) before the text reached substantially its completed form in 1812. The first published versions of lines 17–29 and 76–9, in *M Post* (11 Sept 1802), are as follows:

17–29   Yet thou, meantime, wast working on my soul,
E'en like some deep enchanting melody,
So sweet, we know not, we are list'ning to it.
But I awake, and with a busier mind,
And active will self-conscious, offer now
Not, as before, involuntary pray'r
And passive adoration!—

                        Hand and voice,
Awake, awake! and thou, my heart, awake!
Awake, ye rocks! Ye forest pines, awake!

Green fields, and icy cliffs! All join my hymn!
And thou, O silent mountain, sole and bare,

76–9   In adoration, I again behold,
And to thy summit upward from thy base
Sweep slowly with dim eyes suffus'd by tears,
Awake, thou mountain form! rise, like a cloud!

After 1812 the poem was modified only in details. The present version is
from *SL* (1817), taking in the Errata and introducing line-spaces at lines 35⁺,
57⁺.

Besides the Rivers, Arve and Arveiron, which have their sources
in the foot of Mount Blanc, five conspicuous torrents rush down its
sides; and within a few paces of the Glaciers, the Gentiana Major
grows in immense numbers, with its "flowers of loveliest blue."

Hast thou a charm to stay the Morning-Star
In his steep course? So long he seems to pause
On thy bald awful head, O sovran B L A N C!
The Arve and Arveiron at thy base
Rave ceaselessly; but thou, most awful Form!   5
Risest from forth thy silent Sea of Pines,
How silently! Around thee and above
Deep is the air and dark, substantial, black,
An ebon mass: methinks thou piercest it,
As with a wedge! But when I look again,   10
It is thine own calm home, thy crystal shrine,
Thy habitation from eternity!
O dread and silent Mount! I gaz'd upon thee,
Till thou, still present to the bodily sense,
Did'st vanish from my thought: entranc'd in prayer   15
I worshipped the Invisible alone.

    Yet, like some sweet beguiling melody,
So sweet, we know not we are listening to it,
Thou, the meanwhile, wast blending with my Thought,
Yea, with my Life and Life's own secret Joy: 20

⁻**1.4.** "flowers of loveliest blue."]   also Milton *Comus* 993, *PL* IV 256.
From lines 56–7 of the poem itself. Cf

Till the dilating Soul, enrapt, transfus'd,
Into the mighty Vision passing—there
As in her natural form, swell'd vast to Heaven!

Awake, my soul! not only passive praise
Thou owest! not alone these swelling tears,   25
Mute thanks and secret extacy! Awake,
Voice of sweet song! Awake, my Heart, awake!
Green Vales and icy Cliffs, all join my Hymn.

Thou first and chief, sole Sovran of the Vale!
O struggling with the Darkness all the night,   30
And visited all night by troops of stars,
Or when they climb the sky or when they sink:
Companion of the Morning-Star at Dawn,
Thyself Earth's ROSY STAR, and of the Dawn
Co-herald! wake, O wake, and utter praise!   35

Who sank thy sunless pillars deep in Earth?
Who fill'd thy Countenance with rosy light?
Who made thee Parent of perpetual streams?

And you, ye five wild torrents fiercely glad!
Who call'd you forth from night and utter death,   40
From dark and icy caverns call'd you forth,
Down those precipitous, black, jagged Rocks
For ever shattered and the same for ever?
Who gave you your invulnerable life,
Your strength, your speed, your fury, and your joy,   45
Unceasing thunder and eternal foam?
And who commanded (and the silence came),
Here let the Billows stiffen, and have Rest?

21–2. The meaning is elucidated by C's remarks on Spenser's "effeminacy" and "sweetness" (*CN* III 4501; *BL* ch 2—*CC*—I 36; etc), which involve a degree of identification and should be contrasted with his remarks on WW's "masculinity" and tendency to "*matter-of-fact*" (Allsop II 228; *BL* ch 22—*CC*—II 129 et seq). Altogether, his position is significantly different from the conventional (Burkean and Wordsworthian) notion of the sublime.

48. The phrasing echoes the account of God stilling the sea for Moses in Exod 14.

Ye Ice-falls! ye that from the Mountain's brow
Adown enormous Ravines slope amain—   50
Torrents, methinks, that heard a mighty Voice,
And stopp'd at once amid their maddest plunge!
Motionless Torrents! silent Cataracts!
Who made you glorious as the Gates of Heaven
Beneath the keen full Moon? Who bade the Sun   55
Cloath you with Rainbows? Who, with living flowers
Of loveliest blue, spread garlands at your feet?—

GOD! let the Torrents, like a Shout of Nations
Answer! and let the Ice-plains echo, GOD!
GOD! sing ye meadow-streams with gladsome voice!   60
Ye Pine-groves, with your soft and soul-like sounds!
And they too have a voice, yon piles of Snow,
And in their perilous fall shall thunder, GOD!

Ye living flowers that skirt th' eternal Frost!
Ye wild goats sporting round the Eagle's nest!   65
Ye Eagles, play-mates of the Mountain-Storm!
Ye Lightnings, the dread arrows of the Clouds!
Ye signs and wonders of the element!
Utter forth GOD, and fill the Hills with Praise!

Thou too, hoar Mount! with thy sky-pointing Peaks,   70
Oft from whose feet the Avalanche, unheard,

55–63. CL comments on this passage in a letter of 5 Oct 1802 (*LL*—M—II 72–3, 74–5). It appears that C was in the habit of making the mountains echo the name "Dodd". He demonstrated to CL what he had done alone on the top of Scafell (cf *CL* II 844: to SH 6 Aug [1802]).

Dr Dodd was either the well-known forger or another who later played a part in the origins of RS's *The Doctor* (*RX* 553–4 n 52), and the name is common in the Lake District, meaning "limb of a mountain". Whatever the origins of the private joke, the mss of several of C's poems have the name "Doctor Dodd" jotted down on them: e.g. the first draft ms of **271.X1** *The Triumph of Loyalty* (BM Add MS 34225 f 32ᵛ), and the ms containing **358** *"This yearning Heart"* and other poems (VCL S MS F2.11 f 8ᵛ).

Echoes were a conventional aspect of the sublime, to be evoked by horns or gentler instruments, such as WW records in *Prelude* (1850) II 164–74. They are a reminder that the sublime was, by definition, exclamatory.

70–3. Added (var) in the version published in the 1812 *Friend*.

Shoots downward, glittering thro' the pure Serene,
Into the depth of Clouds that veil thy breast—
Thou too again, stupendous Mountain! thou
That as I raise my head, awhile bow'd low   75
In adoration, upward from thy Base
Slow-travelling with dim eyes suffus'd with tears,
Solemnly seemest, like a vapoury cloud,
To rise before me—Rise, O ever rise,
Rise like a cloud of Incense, from the Earth!   80
Thou kingly Spirit throned among the hills,
Thou dread Ambassador from Earth to Heaven,
Great Hierarch! tell thou the silent Sky,
And tell the Stars, and tell yon rising Sun,
Earth, with her thousand voice, praises GOD.   85

302. DIALOGUE CONCERNING
A GOOD GREAT MAN

[Before Sept 1802]

The dialogue was published in *M Post* (23 Sept 1802) over the signature "ΕΣΤΗΣΕ." When C wrote to Thomas Wedgwood a month later, he dismissed such epigrams as "wretched" and "feeble", "merely the emptying out of my Desk" (*CL* II 876). The dialogue was reprinted in *The Friend*, over C's initials (the version given here), but was never collected by him.

In *The Friend* the poem follows on a discussion of whether fortune favours fools:

Hardihood and Fool-hardiness are indeed as different as green and yellow, yet will appear the same to the jaundiced eye. Courage multiplies the chances of success by sometimes *making* opportunities, and always availing itself of them: and in this sense Fortune may be said to *favour Fools* by those, who however prudent in their own opinion are deficient in valour and enterprize. Again: an eminently good and wise Man, for whom

72. the pure Serene] A substantival use of the adjective which the *OED* suggests was coined by Sir William Jones in his *Palace For-* *tune*: "And twinkling stars emblaz'd the blue serene" (*Poems*—1777—28). C's usage gave the phrase wider currency during the Romantic period.

the praises of the judicious have procured a high reputation even with the
world at large, proposes to himself certain objects, and adapting the right
means to the right end attains them: but his objects not being what the
world calls Fortune, neither money nor artificial rank, his admitted inferi-
ors in moral and intellectual worth, but more prosperous in their worldly
concerns, are said to have been favoured by Fortune and he slighted: al-
though the fools did the same in their line as the wise man in his: they
adapted the appropriate means to the desired end and so succeeded. In this
sense the Proverb is current by a misuse, or a catachresis at least, of both
the words, Fortune and Fools. (*The Friend* XIX 28 Dec 1809 p 292—*CC*—
II 250)

C applied the distinction between a good man and a good great man to Thomas
Clarkson soon afterwards, in Jan 1810 (*CN* III 3671); and subsequently he
appears to have thought of J. H. Frere as the "fair and good" (*CN* IV 5440,
5441).

How seldom Friend! a good great man inherits
Honour or wealth with all his worth and pains!
It sounds, like stories from the land of spirits,
If any man obtain that which he merits,
Or any merit that which he obtains.   5

REPLY

For shame, dear Friend! renounce this canting strain!
What would'st thou have a good great man obtain?
Place? Titles? Salary? a gilded Chain?
Or Throne of Corses which his sword hath slain?
Greatness and goodness are not *means* but *ends*!   10
Hath he not always treasures, always friends,
The good great Man? Three treasures, LOVE, and LIGHT,
And CALM THOUGHTS regular as infant's breath:
And three firm friends, more sure than day and night,
HIMSELF, his MAKER, and the Angel DEATH.   15

303. THE KNIGHT'S TOMB

[1802?]

The stanza is most probably associated with **176** *Christabel*, in metre and in character. Neither the place-name nor the place of Helvellyn have any association with a Sir Arthur O'Relhan or, in another version, O'Kellyn. Indeed, the forms of the names are so unusual, if they exist at all (for O'Reilly? or for O'Kelly, O'Killeen/O'Killen?), that one might suppose they were conjured up by the difficult rhyme. Orellan might have auditory associations with Orellana, the earlier name of the Amazon, so called after a lieutenant of Pizarro, its first explorer in 1541; C would have been familiar with this form from his earlier reading in travel books.

A different background is suggested by a traditional border rhyme which describes "A storm of wind":

> Arthur O'Bower has broken his band,
> He comes roaring up the land;—
> The King of Scots, with all his power,
> Cannot turn Arthur of the Bower!
> (*The Nursery Rhymes of England* ed
> J. O. Halliwell—4th ed 1846—206)

There is some doubt about the date of composition: here SC's suggestion of 1802 is adopted in preference to 1817 (suggested by JDC and EHC). Walter Scott quoted the last three lines in *Ivanhoe* (1820), which, according to C, he got from a mutual friend (John Stoddart or J. H. Frere). The quotation confirmed C's suspicion that Scott was the author of the Waverley novels (*C Life*—G— 277), and prompted him to write out several fair copies of the complete stanza during the 1820s. It was not printed in full until *PW* (1834).

The ms which supplies the text given here is dated 1824. C introduced it with the comment that the stanza was composed "as an experiment in metre that had passed thro' my brain—Suppose it the first Stanza of a Ballad—". He also wrote in the scansion of several lines. The title is taken from the 1834 printing; one fair copy is entitled "The knightly Sword, a Ballad"; the other two fair copies (including the one used here) are untitled.

> Where is the Grave of Sir Arthur O'Relhan?
> Where may the Grave of that good man be?
> By the side of a Spring, on the breast of Helvellan,
> Under the Twigs of a Young Birch Tree!
> The Oak that in summer was sweet to hear   5
> And rustled it's leaves in the Fall o' the Year,

And whistled and roar'd in the Winter, alone—
Is gone! And the Birch in its stead is grown.
The Knight's Bones are Dust:
And his Good Sword Rust: 10
His Soul is with the Saints, I trust.

304. TO MATILDA BETHAM,
FROM A STRANGER

[Sept 1802]

A ms exists in C's hand, initialled and dated Keswick, 9 Sept 1802 (the version given here, except for deletions), from which the lines were printed in a pamphlet devoted to Matilda Betham, in which they may be considered a letter of tribute. Although C quoted a few lines to a correspondent the day afterwards, he seems then to have forgotten the poem.

By the time C's lines were written, Mary Matilda Betham (1776–1852) had published *Elegies, and Other Smaller Poems* (Ipswich [1797]) and had gained some success as a painter of miniatures. C was shown her poems by a mutual friend, Catherine Rose, who, with her husband, Sir Charles William Rose Boughton, visited Greta Hall in Sept 1802 and to whom Betham's next book of verse (*Poems*, 1808) would be dedicated. The company also included Miles Peter Andrews and Captain Topham, in whose newspaper, *The World*, C's first published poem had appeared: see *CL* II 869–70: to W. Sotheby 19 Sept 1802; also *EOT—CC*—III 168 and **20** *The Abode of Love*.

The circumstances bear on the present poem, in which C incorporates a specific allusion to Betham's "Rhapsody" (*Elegies* 79–80) as he offers her advice. See Morton D. Paley "Coleridge's 'To Matilda Betham, from a Stranger'" *TWC* XXVII (Summer 1996) 169–72. It perhaps also looks forward to Betham's *Biographical Dictionary of the Celebrated Women of Every Age and Country*, to be published in 1804, which C could have learned about from her friends. He did not actually make her acquaintance and begin a correspondence with her until 1808, when she painted a miniature of him, from which an engraving was published in *The Cabinet* in Feb 1809 (cf *CN* III 4049n). The original portrait is reproduced as *CN* III frontispiece.

Matilda! I have heard a sweet Tune play'd
On a sweet Instrument—thy Poesy
Sent to my soul by BOUGHTON's pleading Voice,
Where FRIENDSHIP's zealous Wish inspirited,

Deepen'd, and fill'd, the subtle Tones of TASTE— 5
(So have I heard a Nightingale's fine Notes
Blend with the murmur of a hidden Stream!)
And now the fair wild Offspring of thy Genius,
Those Wanderers, whom thy Fancy had sent forth
To seek their fortune in this motley World, 10
Have found a little Home within *my* Heart,
And brought me, as the Quit-rent of their Lodging,
Rose-buds, and Fruit-blossoms, and pretty Weeds,
And timorous Laurel Leaflets half-disclos'd,
Engarlanded with gadding woodbine Tendrils, 15
A coronal, which with undoubting Hand
I twine around the Brows of patriot HOPE!

The Almighty having first compos'd a Man
Set him to Music, framing Woman for him,
And fitted each to each, and made them one! 20
And 'tis my faith, that there's a natural Bond
Between the female Mind, and measur'd Sounds—
Nor do I know a sweeter Hope than this,
Than this sweet Hope, by Judgment unreprov'd,
That our own Britain, our dear Mother Isle, 25
May boast one Maid, a Poetess *indeed*,
Great, as th' impassion'd *Lesbian, in sweet song
And O! of holier Mind and happier Fate.

Matilda! I dare twine *thy* vernal wreath
Around the Brows of patriot Hope! But thou 30
Be wise! be bold! fulfil my Auspices!
Tho' sweet thy Measures, stern must be thy Thought,
Patient thy Study, watchful thy mild Eye!
Poetic Feelings, like the stretching Boughs
Of mighty Oaks, pay homage to the Gales, 35
Toss in the strong winds, drive before the Gust,
Themselves one giddy Storm of fluttering Leaves—
Yet all the while, self-limited, remain
Equally near the fix'd and solid Trunk
Of Truth and Nature, in the howling Storm 40
As in the Calm, that stills the Aspen Grove.

* Sappho.

Be bold, meek Woman! but be wisely bold!
Fly, ostrich-like, firm Land beneath thy Feet,
Yet hurried onward by thy wings of Fancy
Swift as the whirlwind singing in their Quills.   45
Look round thee! Look within thee! Think & feel!
What nobler meed, Matilda! can'st thou win,
Than Tears of Gladness in a BOUGHTON's Eyes,
And Exultation ev'n in STRANGER's Hearts?

305. EPIGRAM ON EPIGRAMS,
FROM WERNICKE

[1799–1802]

The lines were published without a title in *M Post* (23 Sept 1802) and in
The Friend (1812) 192 (*CC*) II 170. They adapt the first two lines of Wer-
nicke *Epigrams* 1.1 *Beschaffenheit der Überschriften*, in *Christian Wernickens
Überschriften, nebst Opitzens, Tschernings, Andreas Gryphius und Adam Ole-
arius epigrammatischen Gedichten* ed Ramler 3; also in Joerdens *Blumenlese
deutscher Sinngedichte* ed Joerdens 109:

> Dann läßt die Überschrift kein Leser aus der Acht,
> Wenn in der Kürz' ihr Leib, die Seel' in Witz besteht,
> Wenn sie nicht allzutief mit ihrem Stachel geht,
> Und einen Abriß nur von einer Wunde macht;
> Vor Lachen nur uns Thränen aus den Augen preßt,
> Und kitzelnd einem, ders bedarf, zur Ader läßt.

> What is an Epigram? a dwarfish whole,
> Its body brevity, and wit its soul.

43. C identified himself with os-
triches, not merely because they could
not fly (*CM—CC* I 482) but also be-
cause of their habit of laying eggs for
others to find (e.g. *CN* I 1248; *CL* III
126: to F. Jeffrey [c 7 Nov 1808]; *BL*
ch 2—*CC*—I 45–6).

306. EPIGRAM ON A CONGENITAL LIAR, FROM WERNICKE

[1799–1802]

The lines were published without a title in *M Post* (23 Sept 1802), and in a newspaper and an album in 1827. They are adapted from Wernicke *Auf den wahrhaftigen Marius*, in *Christian Wernickens Überschriften, nebst Opitzens, Tschernings, Andreas Gryphius und Adam Olearius epigrammatischen Gedichten* ed Ramler 50; also in *Blumenlese deutscher Sinngedichte* ed Joerdens 113:

> Umsonst daß Marius auch einst die Wahrheit spricht,
> Nachdem er mich so oft gesucht hat zu betriegen:
> Ich glaube seine Wahrheit nicht,
> Glaubt er gleich selber seine Lügen.*

> * Dieses begegnet den meisten Lügnern: sie lügen nicht allein so oft, daß man ihnen nicht glaubet, wenn sie auch die Wahrheit sagen; sondern sie lügen auch Ein Ding so oft, daß sie es zuletzt selber für wahr halten.

For C's earlier epigram on a similar theme, from an original by Lessing, see **220** *Epigram on a Notorious Liar*.

> Charles, grave or merry, at no lie would stick,
> And taught at length his mem'ry the same trick.
>   Believing thus, what he so oft repeats,
> He's brought the thing to such a pass, poor youth!
>   That now himself, and no one else, he cheats,   5
> Save when unluckily he tells the truth.

307. EPIGRAM ON THE DEVIL, FROM A GERMAN ORIGINAL?

[1799–1802]

The lines were published without a title in *M Post* (23 Sept 1802) and in *The Friend* (1812) 192 (*CC*) II 170. They are probably an adaptation of, or prompted by, a German original which has not been traced. It is just possible that they relate to Lord Lonsdale, who had long been pictured as the Devil incarnate in political pamphlets and cartoons (Johnston *The Hidden Wordsworth* 30, illustration following 104). Cf **292** *Epitaph on Lord Lonsdale*.

> Here lies the Devil—ask no other name.
> Well—but you mean Lord ——— ? Hush! we mean the same.

308. EPIGRAM ADDRESSED TO ONE WHO PUBLISHED IN PRINT WHAT HAD BEEN ENTRUSTED TO HIM BY MY FIRE-SIDE, FROM WERNICKE

[1799–1802]

The lines were published in *M Post* (23 Sept 1802), without acknowledgment of the German original, and never reprinted. They are adapted from Wernicke *Epigrams* 1.7 *An einen falschen Freund*, in *Christian Wernickens Überschriften, nebst Opitzens, Tschernings, Andreas Gryphius und Adam Olearius epigrammatischen Gedichten* ed Ramler 6:

> Daß ich mich dir vertraut, eh ich dich recht gekennet,
> Und einen Heuchler Freund genennet,
> Das büß' ich zwiefach itzt: du machst der Welt bekannt
> Wie meine Heimlichkeit, so meinen Unverstand.

C might also have known Matthew Prior's epigram, which in turn depends on Gombauld and perhaps Martial:

> To JOHN I ow'd great Obligation;
> But JOHN, unhappily, thought fit
> To publish it to all the Nation:
> Sure JOHN and I are more than Quit.

For Prior and Gombauld see *The Literary Works of Matthew Prior* ed H. B. Wright and M. K. Spears (2nd ed 2 vols Oxford 1971) I 454, II 951–2; for the Latin poem see Martial 5.52. If C had in mind anyone in his own experience, the reference is probably to Charles Lloyd, in his novel *Edmund Oliver* (1798).

> Two things hast thou made known to half the nation,
> My secrets, and my want of penetration:

For O! far more than all, which thou hast penn'd,
It shames me to have call'd a wretch, like thee, my friend!

309. ON THE CURIOUS CIRCUMSTANCE, THAT IN THE GERMAN LANGUAGE THE SUN IS FEMININE, AND THE MOON MASCULINE, AFTER WERNICKE

[1799–1802]

The text given here is from a ms collection of such epigrams, all from German sources, where it is untitled. It was published in *M Post* (11 Oct 1802) as a single unbroken stanza and praised by CL as "admirable" in a letter of the same date (*LL*—M—II 78), but was never reprinted.

The poem is an expansion of Wernicke *Epigrams* 7.15 *Die Sonne und der Mond*, in *Christian Wernickens Überschriften, nebst Opitzens, Tschernings, Andreas Gryphius und Adam Olearius epigrammatischen Gedichten* ed Ramler 181; also in *Blumenlese deutscher Sinngedichte* ed Joerdens 123:

> Die Sonn' in unsrer Sprach' heißt die, der Mond heißt der:
> Weißt du Kornut, sprach Lepidus, woher?
> Die Frauen pflegen so gemein,
> Wie die, die Männer so gehörnt, wie der, zu seyn.

C had made a note of the title of the Wernicke epigram in a list he put together in May 1799 (*CN* I 432 f 51ᵛ).

The "curious circumstance" was a topic of discussion at the time. James Beattie drew attention to it in his *Dissertations Moral and Critical* (1783) 331 and *The Theory of Language* (1788) 138–9; and the anonymous translator of the Edda in *Monthly Magazine* VI (Dec 1798) 454–5n commented further:

> The Goths make the sun feminine, and the moon masculine. This is natural in a cold climate. Among savages every male is a foe, every female a friend. Displeasing and unwelcome objects therefore are in their languages masculine, pleasing and welcome objects feminine. In hot countries where the night is more welcome than the day, an opposite allotment of gender takes place.

John Thelwall made the moon masculine, drawing attention to his innovation and referring to Beattie and the *Monthly Magazine*, in *Poems Chiefly Written in Retirement* 14, 205. Others meanwhile commented on the "inevitability" of the

genders of sun and moon in Greek and Latin—e.g. James Harris *Hermes* (1751)
45–6; [H. J. Pye] *Sketches on Various Subjects* (1796) 83n.

C's interest in the topic continued to the end of his life: *TT* 7 May 1830 (*CC*)
ı 119–20.

Our English Poets, bad & good, agree
To make the Sun a male, the Moon a Shee.
He drives *his* Dazzling Diligence on high,
In verse, as constantly as in the Sky—
And cheap as blackberries our Sonnets show   5
The Moon Heaven's Huntress with *her* silver Bow.
By which they'd teach us, if I guess aright,
Man rules the Day, & Woman rules the Night.

In Germany they just reverse the Thing,
The Sun becomes a Queen, the Moon a King.   10
Now that the Sun should represent the women,
The Moon the men, to me seem'd mighty humming—
And when I first read German made me stare—
Surely, it is not, that the Wives are there
As *common* as the Sun, to Lord & Loon?   15
And all *their* Husbands *horned*, as the Moon?

310. EPIGRAM ON SPOTS IN THE SUN,
FROM WERNICKE

[1799–1802]

The text given here is from a ms collection of such epigrams, all from German
sources, where it is untitled. It was published in *M Post* (11 Oct 1802) and
never reprinted. The lines are a free adaptation of Wernicke *Epigrams* 7.21
Auf den scheinheiligen Phax, in *Christian Wernickens Überschriften, nebst
Opitzens, Tschernings, Andreas Gryphius und Adam Olearius epigrammati-
schen Gedichten* ed Ramler 184; also in *Blumenlese deutscher Sinngedichte* ed
Joerdens 128:

12. humming] A cant word, revived   meaning "an impressive deceit".
in C's time but now obsolete, here

Wenn ich den Phax von ungefähr
Bey einer schönen Thais finde,
Spricht er: Mein Amt bringt mich hieher,
Um sie von ihrer schnöden Sünde
Durch meinen treuen Unterricht
Und ernste Warnung abzuschrecken:
Er wärmt sich an der Sonn', und spricht,
Er schaue nur nach ihren Flecken.

C's substitution of Annette for the name of the courtesan is odd, coming as it does at the end of a summer during which WW had been busy making arrangements with Annette Vallon concerning their child, and being published so soon after WW's wedding (which C had greeted—to some eyes oddly—in the same newspaper, with **293** *Dejection: An Ode*). Some have supposed that WW must have chided C for his love of SH, and is now sarcastically accused of hypocrisy, but there is no knowing whether the allusion was intended or was an unfortunate (perhaps "Freudian") error.

My Father Confessor is strict & holy
Mi Fili, still he cries, peccare noli.
But yet how oft I find the pious man,
At Annette's Door, the lovely Courtesan.
Her soul's deformity the good man wins   5
And not her Charms: he comes to hear her sins.
Good Father, I would fain not do thee wrong;
But O! I fear that they who oft & long
Stand gazing at the Sun to count each spot,
Must sometimes find the Sun itself too hot.   10

311. EPIGRAM ON SURFACE,
FROM WERNICKE

[1799–1802]

The text given here is from a ms collection of such epigrams, all from German sources, where it is untitled. It was published in *M Post* (11 Oct 1802), and never reprinted. The lines adapt Wernicke *Epigrams* 7.29 *Auf den Koridon*,

2. Tr "My son, . . . do not sin."

in *Christian Wernickens Überschriften, nebst Opitzens, Tschernings, Andreas Gryphius und Adam Olearius epigrammatischen Gedichten* ed Ramler 187:

> Wenn Koridon von andern Leuten spricht,
> Dünkt mich daß ihm Verstand gebricht;
> Und wenn er, was er selbst verrichtet hat, erzählet,
> Daß es ihm am Gedächtnis fehlet.

When Surface talks of other people's worth,
He has the Weakest memory on earth.
And when his own good deeds he turns to mention,
His memory still is no whit better grown;
But he makes up for it, as all will own,   5
By a prodigious Talent of Invention.—

312. A DIALOGUE BETWEEN
AN AUTHOR AND HIS FRIEND,
AFTER WERNICKE

[1799–1802]

The text given here is from a ms collection of such epigrams, all from German sources. It was published in *M Post* (11 Oct 1802) and never reprinted. The lines adapt Wernicke *Epigrams* 7.31 *An die Korinna, wegen ihrer Briefe*, in *Christian Wernickens Überschriften, nebst Opitzens, Tschernings, Andreas Gryphius und Adam Olearius epigrammatischen Gedichten* ed Ramler 188:

> Die Briefe, die von dir an mich ergehn,
> Korinna, schildern mir dein ganzes Wesen:
> Was du mir schreibst, kann ich kaum lesen,
> Und was ich lese, kaum verstehn.
> Ich kenne deinen Sinn so wohl als deine Hand,
> Der Buchstab ist so falsch, wie der Verstand.

Author
Come! your opinion of my Manuscript!

Friend
Dear Jo! I would almost as soon be whipt!

Author

But I *will* have it!

Friend (hesitating)
If it *must* be had—
You write so ill, I could not read the hand—

Author

Psha! mere Evasion!

Friend
And you write so bad,   5
That what I read, I did not understand!

313. EPIGRAM ON POSSESSION, FROM A GERMAN ORIGINAL

[1799–1802]

The text given here is from a ms collection of such epigrams, all from German sources, where it is untitled. It was published in *M Post* (23 Sept 1802) and again in *The Friend* (1812) 192 (*CC*) II 170, but never collected. The other epigrams in the ms collection derive from German sources, but in this case it is difficult to be exact. Cf e.g. D. G. Morhof's epigram *Geld*, in *Epigrammatische Anthologie* ed Haug and Weisser II 157:

> Herrsch' über Geld und Gut! denn brauchest du es recht;
> Dann bleibest du sein Herr. Wo nicht, bist du sein Knecht.

Or the lines in Wenzel Scherffer *Eines Geitzigen Grabschrift*, in *Geist: und weltlicher Gedichte erster Teil* (Brzeg 1652) 296:

> . . . habe doch erkennet ich,
> Daß du nicht das Geld gehabt, sonderns Geld, das hatte dich.

An evil Spirit's on thee, Friend, of late,
Even from the hour, thou cam'st to thy estate—
Thy mirth all gone, thy kindness, thy discretion,
The estate has prov'd to thee a most complete *Possession*.

Shame, shame, my friend! would'st thou be truly blest, 5
Be thy Wealth's Lord, not Slave! Possessor, not Possess'd!

314. EPIGRAM ON CASTLES IN THE AIR, FROM WERNICKE

[1799–1802]

The text given here is from a ms collection of such epigrams, all from German sources, where it is untitled. It was published in *M Post* (23 Sept 1802) and never reprinted. The lines are adapted from Wernicke *Epigrams* 7.35, *An einen Geizhals*, in *Christian Wernickens Überschriften, nebst Opitzens, Tschernings, Andreas Gryphius und Adam Olearius epigrammatischen Gedichten* ed Ramler 190:

> Ziemt es dir, Harpagon, zu spotten, daß Neran
> Auf etwas hofft, was nie geschehen kann?
> Gönn' ihm, daß ihn ein Hirngespinst ergetze,
> Und wisse, daß die Welt, die alles wohl erwägt,
> Auf Eine Wageschal die ungebrauchten Schätze
> Der Geizhäls' und der Narren Hoffnung legt.

Old HARPY jeers at Castles in the air,
And thanks his stars, whenever Damon speaks,
That such a fool as that is not his Heir;
But know, old Harpy! that these Fancy-freaks
Though vain & light as floating Gossamer   5
Always amuse, and sometimes mend the Heart!
A young man's idlest Hopes are still his pleasures,
And fetch an higher price in Wisdom's mart,
Than all the unenjoying Miser's Treasures.

315. TO A VAIN LADY,
FROM THE GERMAN AND FROM MARTIAL

[1799–1802]

The text given here is from a ms collection of such epigrams, all from German sources. It was published in *M Post* (23 Sept 1802) and in *The Friend* (1812) 192 (*CC*) II 170, but never collected. The original of C's lines is ultimately Martial 1.65:

> Bella es, novimus, et puella, verum est,
> Et dives, quis enim potest negare?
> Sed cum te nimium, Fabulla, laudas,
> Nec dives neque bella nec puella es.

Tr Ker (LCL) I 68–9 "You are beautiful, we know, and young, that is true, and rich—for who can deny it? But while you praise yourself overmuch, Fabulla, you are neither rich, nor beautiful, nor young." However, the immediate source is more likely to have been German. See *Marcus Valerius Martialis in einem Auszuge, lateinisch und deutsch* ed and trans K. W. Ramler (Leipzig 1787) 29 and *Anhang zum ersten Theile* (Leipzig 1793) 21:

> An die Fabulla.

> Du bist schön, es ist wahr; bist Jungfer niemand
> Kann es läugnen; bist reich: das wissen alle.
> Aber weil du Fabulla, stets dich dessen
> Rühmest, bist du nicht schön, nicht reich, nicht Jungfer.

See also Johann Grob *Der eingebildete Ortlieb*, in *Epigrammatische Anthologie* ed Haug and Weisser II 121:

> Ortlieb wär' ein wackrer Pursche, und berühmt in aller Welt,
> Wenn er andern halb gefiele, wie er selbst sich ganz gefällt.

> Didst thou think less of thy dear self,
>   Far more would others think of thee,
> Sweet Anne! thy knowledge of thy wealth
>   Reduces thee to Poverty.
> Boon Nature gave Wit, Beauty, Health,   5
>   On thee, as on her Darling, pitch'd—
> Could'st thou forget, that thou'rt thus enriched,
>   That moment would'st thou become rich in;

And wert thou not so self-bewitch'd,
Sweet Anne! thou wert indeed bewitching.   10

316. EPIGRAM TO MY CANDLE,
AFTER WERNICKE

[1799–1802]

The text given here is from a ms collection of such epigrams, all from German sources. It was published in *M Post* (11 Oct 1802) and never reprinted. C was moved to write about domestic appurtenances throughout his life—e.g. his kettle and his shaving-pot (poems **21, 675**); but the present lines were probably prompted by Wernicke *Epigrams* 7.59 *Gedanken zur Abendzeit bey Licht*, in *Christian Wernickens Überschriften, nebst Opitzens, Tschernings, Andreas Gryphius und Adam Olearius epigrammatischen Gedichten* ed Ramler 203–4:

> Licht, du erleuchtest nur mein Blatt und meine Sinne:
> Indem du abnimmst, werd' ich, daß ich abnehm' inne,
> So still und unvermerkt, obgleich so sehr geschwinde,
> Daß ich den Abgang nur nach dem Verlust empfinde,
> Ich schreib', indem du brennst, und sorg', indem ich schreibe,
> Daß ich bey deiner Flamm', als meinem Vorbild, bleibe,
> Daß ich durch Sinnlichkeit nicht den Verstand verstelle,
> So schreibe, wie du scheinst, so spitzig, doch so helle:
> O würde mir, wie dir, der Lobspruch noch gewähret,
> Daß ich, wie du, mich selbst in andrer Dienst verzehret!

Good candle, thou that with thy Brother, Fire,
Art my best friend & comforter at night,
Just snuff'd thou look'st as if thou did'st desire
That I on thee an Epigram should write.
Good Candle, brought down to finger joint   5
Thy flame itself an Epigram of Light—
Tis thin, & pointed, and all over Light,
And gives most Light, & burns the keenest at the point.
                      —*Good Night*!

317. FROM AN OLD GERMAN POET
(AFTER WERNICKE)

[1799–1802]

The text given here is from a ms collection of such epigrams, all from German sources. It was published in *M Post* (11 Oct 1802) and never reprinted. The lines derive from Wernicke *Epigrams* 8.4 *Auf die Buhlereyen der Deutschen in Frankreich,* in *Christian Wernickens Überschriften, nebst Opitzens, Tschernings, Andreas Gryphius und Adam Olearius epigrammatischen Gedichten* ed Ramler 209:

> Daß Frankreich uns weiß zu verwunden
> Mit Pulver, welches wir erfunden;
> Daß es in Büchern uns verlacht,
> Die wir zu drucken erst erdacht;
> Daß wir dort unser Geld verschwenden,
> Mit dem es uns hernach besticht;
> Daß es in unsre Länder bricht
> Mit Pferden, die wir ihnen senden:
> Dieß alles fass' ich eh, als daß wir, toll und blind,
> Die Jugendkräfte dort verlieren,
> Und ihre Weiber selbst verführen,
> Und unsrer Feinde Väter sind.

> That France has put us oft to rout
> With Powder which ourselves found out—
> And laughs at us for fools in print
> Of which our Genius was the mint
> All this I easily admit—   5
> For We have Genius, France has Wit.
> But 'tis too bad that blind & mad
> Keen to their Wives the vigorous German goes,
> Expends his manly vigor by *their* sides,
> Becomes the Father of his Country's Foes,   10
> And turns their Warriors oft to Parricides.

6. A common enough notion at the time, which C shared. Cf *Friend (CC)* I 421; *CL* IV 667: to T. Boosey 4 Sept 1816; etc.

318. EPIGRAM ON BOND STREET BUCKS, ADAPTED FROM WERNICKE

[1799–1802]

The text given here is from a ms collection of such epigrams, all from German sources, where it is untitled. It was published in *M Post* (11 Oct 1802) and never reprinted. The lines derive from Wernicke *Epigrams* 8.5 *Auf die Kleidung*, in *Christian Wernickens Überschriften, nebst Opitzens, Tschernings, Andreas Gryphius und Adam Olearius epigrammatischen Gedichten* ed Ramler 210; also in *Blumenlese deutscher Sinngedichte* ed Joerdens 129:

> In deiner Kleidung sey bedacht
> Auf Nothdurft mehr, als Zierd', auf Zierde mehr, als Pracht;
> Und nimm dir dieß zur Richtschnur hin:
> Was deinen Leib bedeckt, das zeiget deinen Sinn.

C might possibly have known Wernicke's own source, and been influenced by it—Friedrich von Logau *Kleider*, in *Sinngedichte: Zwölf Bücher, mit Anmerkungen über die Sprache des Dichters* ed Ramler and Lessing 11.41 p 325:

> Was ist's, was uns bedeckt, und gleichwohl auch entdeckt?
> Das Kleid bedeckt den Mann und weist was in ihm steckt.

> Each Bond street Buck conceits, unhappy Elf,
> He shews his Cloathes! Alas! he shews himself—
> O that they knew, these over dress'd Self-lovers,
> What hides the Body, oft the Mind discovers.

319. EPIGRAM ON VIRGIL'S "OBSCURI SUB LUCE MALIGNA", AFTER WERNICKE

[1799–1802]

The text given here is from a ms collection of such epigrams, all from German sources. It was published in *M Post* (23 Sept 1802), with the title drawn from Virgil, and never reprinted. The quotation runs together phrases from *Aeneid* 6.268, 270 tr Fairclough (LCL) I 525 "dimly . . . under the grudging light [of the moon]"; while the lines themselves freely adapt Wernicke *Epigrams* 8.7 *Auf das gemeine Gerücht*, in *Christian Wernickens Überschriften, nebst Opitzens, Tschernings, Andreas Gryphius und Adam Olearius epigrammatischen Gedichten* ed Ramler 211:

> Der Ruf is selten ohne Grund,
> Vergrößert er gleich alle Sachen;
> Die Wahrheit öffnet ihm den Mund,
> Und lehret ihn die Lügen machen:
> Er setzt, uns besser zu betriegen,
> Zur Finsternis ein wenig Klarheit,
> Spricht keine Wahrheit ohne Lügen,
> Und keine Lügen ohne Wahreit.

> Scarce any Scandal but has a Handle—
> In Truth each Falsehood has its Rise—
> Truth first unlocks Pandora's Box
> And out there fly a Host of Lies.
> Malignant Light by cloudy Night   5
> To precipices it decoys one,
> One Nectar Drop from Jove's own Shop
> Will flavour a whole cup of Poison.

320. ΜΩΡΟΣΟΦΙΑ
or, WISDOM IN FOLLY,
FROM A GERMAN ORIGINAL?

[1799–1802]

The text given here is from a ms collection of such epigrams, all the others being from German sources. It was published in *M Post* (11 Oct 1802) and never reprinted. C's lines are likely to be an adaptation—perhaps a free adaptation—of a German original which has not been traced.

> Tom Slothful talks, as slothful Tom beseems,
> What he shall shortly gain, what he shall soon be doing;
> Then drops asleep, & so prolongs his Dreams—
> And thus enjoys at once what half the world are wooing.

321. WESTPHALIAN SONG

[1799–1802]

The poem appeared untitled and unsigned in *M Post* (27 Sept 1802) and was never claimed by C or reprinted; it was included as his by SC in *EOT* (1850). In the newspaper it was introduced with this explanation: "The following is an almost literal translation of a very old and very favourite song among the Westphalian Boors. The turn at the end is the same with one of Mr. Dibdin's excellent songs, and the air to which it is sung by the Boors, is remarkably sweet and lively."

C described the manner of the dramatist and songwriter Charles Dibdin (1745–1814) in *CN* I 1536 (cf 569). He might have heard the verses sung in Germany, as he implies: the German is very simple, and he departs from it only in line 4. Or he might have used a printed version, one of the earliest of which can be found in *Eyn feyner kleyner Almanach* ed Christoph Friedrich Nicolai (2 vols Berlin 1777–8) 22 *Eyn Lyd an eyn'n Potten* (II 106):

> Wenn du bey meyn Schatzgen kommst,
> Sag: ych lyesz sye gruszen;
> Wenn sye fraget: wye's myr geet?
> Sag: uff beyden Fuszen.
> Wenn sye fraget: ob ych krank?
> Sag: ych sey gestorbenn.
> Wenn sye an tzu weynen fangt,
> Sag: ych keme morgen.

> When thou to my true-love com'st,
>   Greet her from me kindly;
> When she asks thee how I fare?
>   Say, folks in Heav'n fare finely.

> When she asks, "What! Is he sick?"   5
>   Say, dead!—and when for sorrow
> She begins to sob and cry,
>   Say, I come to-morrow.

322. A HINT TO PREMIERS AND FIRST CONSULS

[1799–1802]

The epigram appeared unsigned with a poem of German origin (**321** *Westphalian Song*) in *M Post* (27 Sept 1802), and was attributed to C in *EOT* (1850). The *M Post* title continues: "FROM AN OLD TRAGEDY, VIZ. AGATHA TO KING ARCHELAUS", which is a garbled reference (presumably the printer's error rather than C's) to Agathon, a Greek tragic poet of the 5th century B.C., to whom this advice is attributed. For the prose original see Stobaeus *Anthology* ed C. Wachsmuth and O. Hense (5 vols plus supplement Berlin 1884–1923) IV 203.1–4. The recipient, unnamed in Stobaeus, could be assumed to be Archelaus, king of Macedon, at whose court Agathon spent some years. C's immediate source was probably the metrical version by J. H. Voss in the *Musenalmenach für 1794* ed J. H. Voss (Hamburg n.d.) 72:

> *Fürstenspiegel.*
> (Der Tragiker Agathon an den König Archelaus.)
>
> Drei Lehren fass' ein Herscher wohl ins Herz.
> Die eine: daß er über Menschen herscht;
> Die andre: daß er nach Gesetzen herscht;
> Die dritte: daß er nicht auf immer herscht.

C may also have had in mind the Prologue to *Cambises* (in *Chief Pre-Shakespearean Dramas* ed J. Q. Adams—Cambridge, Mass 1924—640):

> Agathon, he whose counsail wise to princes weale extended,
> By good advice unto a prince three things he hath commended:
> First is, that he hath government and ruleth over men;
> Secondly, to rule with lawes, eke iustice, saith he, then;
> Thirdly, that he must wel conceive he may not alwaies raigne.

Or perhaps the two are named in some other English or German tragedy.

> Three truths should make thee often think and pause;
>   The first is, that thou govern'st over men;
> The second, that thy pow'r is from the laws;
>   And this the third, that thou must die!—and then?—

323. LATIN LINES TO WILLIAM SOTHEBY

[Sept 1802]

The lines appear only in a letter to Sotheby dated 27 [=28] Sept 1802 (*CL* II 872). C has just imagined or remembered himself walking with the Sothebys in summer—as he had at Keswick that summer—and goes on to speak in the poem of a meeting at Sotheby's fireside. A literal translation is as follows:

> But if the cold north wind blow stronger in the woods or if
> Winter showers fall from the rainy clouds,
> Let us stay indoors and let the hearth glow with a great fire.
> My little one, Iulus, shall be before the hearth, and play,
> And give us caresses and not yet certain words:
> While I shall read with you the memorials of great Plato.

It is unclear whether Iulus is one of Sotheby's youngest sons or one of C's. Although the phrasing of the Latin ("mihi . . . erit") strongly suggests personal possession, the rest of the letter dwells on HC and DC equally, and imagines a meeting definitely at Sotheby's fireside.

> Frigidus at sylvis Aquilo si increverit, aut si
> Hyberni pluviis dependent nubibus Imbres,
> Nos habeat domus, et multo Lar luceat igne.
> Ante focum mihi parvus erit, qui ludat, Iulus,
> Blanditias ferat, et nondum constantia verba: 5
> Ipse legam magni tecum monumenta Platonis!

324. EPIGRAM ON AURELIA, FROM GRYPHIUS

[1799–1802]

The epigram is one of three which appeared over a pseudonym in *M Post* (2 Oct 1802), and it was never reprinted. C's source is Andreas Gryphius *An Aurelien*, in *Christian Wernickens Überschriften, nebst Opitzens, Tschernings, Andreas Gryphius und Adam Olearius epigrammatischen Gedichten* ed Ramler 396; also in *Blumenlese deutscher Sinngedichte* ed Joerdens 106:

> Ihr wünschet Euer Lob von meiner Hand zu lesen?
> Ihr seyd die Schönheit selbst, Aurelia,—gewesen.

From me, AURELIA! you desir'd
Your proper praise to know;
Well! you're the FAIR by all admir'd—
Some twenty years ago.

325. FOR A HOUSE-DOG'S COLLAR, FROM OPITZ

[1799–1802]

The epigram was published in *M Post* (2 Oct 1802) and in *The Friend* (1812) 192 (*CC*) II 170, but was never collected. C's immediate source was almost certainly Martin Opitz *Grabshrift eines Hundes*, in *Christian Wernickens Über-schriften, nebst Opitzens, Tschernings, Andreas Gryphius und Adam Olearius epigrammatischen Gedichten* ed Ramler 343; also in *Blumenlese deutscher Sinngedichte* ed Joerdens 71:

> Die Diebe lief ich an, den Buhlern schwieg ich stille:
> So ward vollbracht des Hern und auch der Hausfrau Wille.

Joerdens reads "war" for "schwieg", and adds the subtitle "Nach dem Mar-tial." (meaning "in the manner of Martial", since no such lines appear among Martial's epigrams).

Another English version—preceded by a Latin original, which is not by Martial—was published anonymously in *The Spirit of the Public Journals for 1800* IV (1801) 89:

THE HOUSE-DOG, TO HIS FELLOW-SERVANT, THE VALET.

> "Latratu fures excepi, mutus amantes;
> Sic placui domino, sic placui dominae."

> At the robbers I bark'd, at the lovers was mute;
> So I pleas'd both my Lord and my Lady to boot!

There is a curious analogy between C's lines and the fourth stanza of an English nursery rhyme which circulated widely in his time, *The Little Market Woman*, which he knew: see *CN* I 469, 1235; *SW&F* (*CC*) 322; cf *The Oxford Dictionary of Nursery Rhymes* ed Iona and Peter Opie (Oxford 1951 rpt 1969) 428; also *TLS* (4 Jul 1980) 758.

When thieves come, I bark: when gallants, I am still—
So perform both my Master's and Mistress's will.

326. EPIGRAM ON ZOILUS, FROM OPITZ

[1799–1802]

The lines were published over a pseudonym, with two other epigrams, in *M Post* (2 Oct 1802), and were never republished. Their original is a Latin epigram by George Buchanan, *In Zoilum* (*Opera Omnia*—2 vols Leiden 1725—ii 362). Although C had borrowed Buchanan in 1794 (*Jesus LB* No 31), his source on the later occasion was almost certainly Martin Opitz *Auf den Zoilus*, in one of the collections he drew upon for the other epigrams printed in *M Post*—*Christian Wernickens Überschriften, nebst Opitzens, Tschernings, Andreas Gryphius und Adam Olearius epigrammatischen Gedichten* ed Ramler 343; also in *Blumenlese deutscher Sinngedichte* ed Joerdens 71:

> Vergebens lob' ich dich, vergebens fluchst du mir:
> Es glaubet, o Zoilus, mir keiner, keiner dir.

(Joerdens omits the "o" in the second line, so as to preserve the correct trisyllabic pronunciation of the name.) Zoilus of Amphipolis (4th century B.C.) was a notoriously vituperative literary critic.

> In vain I praise thee, Zoilus!
> In vain thou rail'st at me!
> Me no one credits, Zoilus!
> And no one credits thee!

327. EPITAPH ON A MERCENARY MISER, FROM OPITZ

[1799–1802]

The lines were published over a pseudonym in *M Post* (9 Oct 1802), the version given here, and they also exist in a fair copy with a few revisions and in a more extensively reworked version entitled "On Gripe-all" (for which see *CN* ii 2773). The original sources of C's lines are twofold: an epigram by Lucilius in the *Greek Anthology* 11.264 tr Paton (LCL) iv 194–5, and another by George Buchanan, *Jacobo Silvio*, in *Opera Omnia* ii 379. C's immediate sources were two epigrams by Martin Opitz, printed in two collections he drew upon for other epigrams contributed to *M Post* at this time: *Christian Werni-*

ckens Überschriften, nebst Opitzens, Tschernings, Andreas Gryphius und Adam Olearius epigrammatischen Gedichten ed Ramler 296, 343; and *Blumenlese deutscher Sinngedichte* ed Joerdens 65. The fact that they appear on the same page in Joerdens suggests that this was the anthology C used on this occasion:

Auf den geizigen Hermon.

Dem Hermon träumete, er habe viel verschenket;
Aus Kummer hat er sich, als er erwacht, gehenket.

Grabschrift des Silvius.

Hier ruhet Sylvius, der nichts umsonst gethan:
Es schmerzt ihn, dass man diess umsonst hier lesen kann.

Another translation of the second of these epigrams, explicitly a translation from Opitz, was published anonymously together with other epigrams in *The London Magazine* IX (Mar 1824) 237:

EPITAPH ON A MISER.

Here lies old father Gripe, who never cried, "*Jam satis,*"
'Twould wake him did he know you read his tomb-stone gratis.

Opitz.

A poor, benighted Pedlar, knock'd
 One night at SELL-ALL's door,
The same, who sav'd old SELL-ALL's life—
  'Twas but the year before!
And SELL-ALL rose, and let him in,   5
 Not utterly unwilling,
But first he bargain'd with the man,
  And took his only shilling!
That night he dreamt, he'd giv'n away his pelf,
Walk'd in his sleep, and sleeping hung himself! 10
 And now his soul and body rest below,
And here they say his punishment and fate is,
 To lie awake, and ev'ry hour to know
How many people read his tomb-stone GRATIS.

328. LATIN LINES ON A FORMER FRIENDSHIP

[Nov 1802]

The untitled lines were written in Notebook 8 when C was in Wales with Thomas Wedgwood (*CN* I 1283), and were never published. The hendecasyllables scan perfectly, except that a foot is missing at the beginning of the first line, probably for a personal name. They are followed in the notebook by the remark "Male pereant qui ante nos &c" (cf the saying attributed to Aelius Donatus by St Jerome in his commentary on Ecclesiastes (Migne *PL* XXIII 1019): "Pereant . . . qui ante nos nostra dixerunt" tr "Confound those who have said our remarks before us"). This is treated by KC as part of the following entry, but it may well be a comment on the present lines. Tr: "My steadfast comrade of former times, delightful, charming, agreeable, whose silent absence with unspeaking paper I have sadly endured for so many years, if a spark of the old friendship lingers surviving in the ashes I am not utterly dead and gone."

Although the pencil is faint, there is no doubt as to the accuracy of the text given here, which varies little from that in *CN*. The translation given above does vary at several points, mainly because "integer sodalis" in the first line makes it clear that the poem is addressed to a man, and the language of the rest of the poem could be used by a man without impropriety or erotic connotations.

> O vetus integer sodalis,
> Nostri Deliciæ, Lepor, Venustas,
> Quem tot jam misere tuli per annos
> Absentem tacita silere chartâ,
> Si tibi Igniculus vetusti amoris   5
> Forte inter cineres adhuc superstes
> Manet, nec perii omnis excidique/

329. GREEK LINES ON ACHILLES' MEAL OF YESTERDAY

[Feb 1803]

The origin of the two lines may lie in C's schooldays, but he wrote them out in a letter to RS (*CL* II 924: 15 Feb 1803) after a severe attack of diarrhoea. They are an approximation to Homeric language and metre and are signed "'Oμηρ" (=Homer). C complained of the inadequacy of Greek to convey the sound of English "squt" and "shlishshlosh", and had recourse to the Hebrew alphabet for the *sh* sound when he repeated the lines, in still less orthodox Greek, in Aug 1811 (*CN* III 4103) along with other lavatorial verses (poem **488**). This notebook version might be connected with speculations about primitive man raised in his 1812–13 lectures at the Surrey Institution. Cf **502** *Epitaph on Robert Whitmore*.

Two invented words are possibly but not certainly onomatopoeic, so an ex act translation is impossible: "Striking his extended rear off a hard-(?) rock, Achilles makes a shlish-shlosh to the accompaniment of a roaring (?) phlosh-bosh". The fourth letter of υπεχθεινων is a mistake for κ. φλοισβας is also incorrect, although this feminine ending (for φλοίσβου) gives the required sibilant. It forms part of Homer's epithet for the "much-roaring sea" at *Iliad* 1.34, and appears to have possessed peculiar significance for C in less jocular contexts: see **540** *Fancy in Nubibus* headnote.

In the notebook version C seems to have confused πυγή "rump" with πώγων "beard", which might suggest that there had been another version in which Achilles suffered from seasickness.

Νωτα δ' υπεχθεινων πετρᾶς απο σκληροκιρυγδους
Σλισσλοσιται Αχιλευς φλοισβας* επι ρωαριμοιο.

330. THE KISS AND THE BLUSH

[Apr–May 1803?]

The poem might appear to have something in common with verses written during the summer of 1793, such as **56** *On Presenting a Moss Rose* and **57** *Cupid Turn'd Chymist*; cf also the closing stanza of **64** *Songs of the Pixies*. None the less, the only two known texts date from May 1803 and Apr 1804. In the earlier version, published anonymously in *M Post* (12 May 1803), the poem has an additional couplet following line 6:

> And well you know, we all declare
> That face too delicately fair.

The later text, "*By a* STUDENT *of* JESUS COLLEGE" in *Monthly Magazine*, sacrifices symmetry for economy and coherence, and is the one given here. Other differences are slight.

---

* *phloshbosh*

From off that delicate fair cheek,
Oh Maid, too fair, I did but seek
To steal a kiss, and lo! your face,
   With anger or with shame it glows;
What have I done, my gentle Grace,   5
   But change a lily to a rose?

At once your cheek and brow were flush'd,
Your neck and ev'n your bosom blush'd;
And shame may claim the larger part,
   In that smooth neck, and all above: 10
But the blush so near the heart,
   Oh! let it be a blush of love.
Pygmalion thus lit up with life
The statue that became his wife.

331. GRASMERE IN SUNSHINE

[Jul 1803]

The lines appear in Notebook 4 (*CN* I 1413), untitled and written as continuous prose, but with capital letters to mark the beginnings of lines. C was at Grasmere on 17 Jul for the christening of WW's son John, and the poem appears to describe woods seen on that (sunny) occasion. If this is so—and there is no corroborating evidence—the vale is Grasmere.

And every Leaf of every Tree
Thro' all the woody Vale,
Transparent in the Light, all yellow Green,
Shot thro' with level Sunshine

13–14. Pygmalion, the legendary sculptor and king of Cyprus, fell in love with his own ivory statue of Aphrodite. The goddess gave life to the statue and he married it.

332. FRAGMENTS OF AN UNWRITTEN POEM

[Aug–Nov 1803]

The two fragments are given as they appear on different pages of Notebook 16 (*CN* I 1444, 1697). KC suggests that the first set of lines might have been written on 20 Aug 1803 at Lanark, when C was ill and could not go and see the falls with the Wordsworths, with whom he was touring Scotland. Or they might have been written at Keswick, after C's return in Sept. KC dates the second set of lines to 29 Nov 1803. It was a day when C, "in much pain leaning on my Staff", walked down to Derwent Water with the visiting John Thelwall and afterwards recorded several such observations in the same notebook (*CN* I 1689–91, 1693–4, 1696). The connections between the two fragments could nevertheless be fortuitous, and their ascription to a single poem is entirely conjectural.

(*a*)

A Man
Happily made, but most unhappily thwarted,
And oft there came on him—&c
And sudden Thoughts that riv'd his heart asunder
By the road-side, the while he gaz'd at flowers.   5

(*b*)

Happily disengaged & vacant never
Look'd at the Sky & Clouds in every puddle,
Along the Winter Road.

333. THREE LINES ON LOCH LOMOND

[Aug 1803]

The untitled lines were written in Notebook 7 in pencil, which was later inked over (*CN* I 1467). C visited Loch Lomond with the Wordsworths on their Scottish tour. For other descriptions see *DWJ* I 250–8, *CN* I 1462–6, 1468, *CL* II 977–8: to Mrs C [2] Sept [1803]; also *TT* 26 Sept 1830 (*CC*) I 204–5.

Upon a rock beneath a Tree
It's shadow on the sandy shore
It's Image in the glassy Lake

334. LINES ON "SUCH LOVE AS MOURNING HUSBANDS HAVE"

[Sept 1803]

The lines are written out continuously as prose in Notebook 7 (*CN* I 1506), but with line-division marked at lines 2⁺, 3⁺, and 4⁺. The first line in the notebook is followed by a full point (here replaced by a dash), and might have been intended as the title. The prose comment at 4⁺ has no surrounding parentheses in the ms, and a few other marks of punctuation have been revised in the text given here.

On 29 Aug 1803 C had separated from WW and DW on their Scottish tour, being unwell and afraid of the wet weather in an open carriage. He walked back, was seized for a spy and put in jail at Fort Augustus on 5 Sept, went on to Perth and Edinburgh, and eventually rejoined his family at Keswick on 15 Sept. KC dates the lines between 1 and 11 Sept.

Such love as mourning Husbands have—
To her whose spirit hath been newly given
To be his guardian Saint in Heaven
Whose Beauty lieth in the Grave Unconquered

(as if the Soul could find no *purer* Tabernacle, nor place of Sojourn, than the virgin Body it had before dwelt in, & wished to stay there till the Resurrection)

Far liker to a Flower now than when alive,   5
Cold to the Touch & blooming to the eye—

335. THE PAINS OF SLEEP

[Sept 1803]

The poem was written at the nadir of C's fortunes, at the end of his aborted tour of Scotland with the Wordsworths in 1803, "soon after my eyes had been opened to the true nature of the habit into which I had been ignorantly deluded by the seeming magic effects of opium" (ms note dated Apr 1826, cited in *C Life*—G—246). He had walked 263 miles in eight days, he claimed, "in the hope of forcing the Disease into the extremities":

> while I am in possession of my will & my Reason, I can keep the Fiend at arm's Length; but with the Night my Horrors commence—during the whole of my Journey three nights out of four I have fallen asleep struggling & resolving to lie awake, & awaking have blest the Scream which delivered me from the reluctant Sleep. (*CL* II 993: to Sir George and Lady Beaumont 22 Sept 1803)

The poem thus possessed particular significance for C as a direct record of "Guilt, Falsehood, traced to the Gastric Life" (*CN* III 4409 f 5^r): "Sleep a pandemonium of all the shames & miseries of the past Life from early childhood all huddled together, & bronzed with one stormy Light of Terror & Self-torture" (*CN* II 2091 f 43^{r-v}). It was a poem often on C's mind, and frequently quoted (e.g. *CL* II 991: to T. Wedgwood 16 Sept [1803]; *CN* II 2482; *CL* IV 740: to HCR [15 Jun 1817]; *CL* V 216: to T. Allsop 1 Mar 1822), although for many years it was not intended for publication. The ending was reworked in 1814 to illustrate his state of mind for the physician who was then treating him (*CL* III 495: to H. Daniel 19 May 1814), and the entire original poem was published in 1816, along with **176** *Christabel* and **178** *Kubla Khan*, with slight revisions and rearrangements in the middle stanza. It was included in *PW* (1829, 1829, 1834) with only a few changes of punctuation and capitalisation. The 1816 text is reproduced here.

> Ere on my bed my limbs I lay,
> It hath not been my use to pray
> With moving lips or bended knees;
> But silently, by slow degrees,
> My spirit I to Love compose,   5
> In humble Trust mine eye-lids close,
> With reverential resignation,
> No wish conceived, no thought expressed!
> Only a *sense* of supplication,
> A sense o'er all my soul imprest   10

That I am weak, yet not unblest,
Since in me, round me, every where
Eternal Strength and Wisdom are.

But yester-night I pray'd aloud
In anguish and in agony,   15
Up-starting from the fiendish crowd
Of shapes and thoughts that tortured me:
A lurid light, a trampling throng,
Sense of intolerable wrong,
And whom I scorn'd, those only strong!   20
Thirst of revenge, the powerless will
Still baffled, and yet burning still!
Desire with loathing strangely mixed
On wild or hateful objects fixed.
Fantastic passions! mad'ning brawl!   25
And shame and terror over all!
Deeds to be hid which were not hid,
Which all confused I could not know,
Whether I suffered, or I did:
For all seemed guilt, remorse or woe,   30
My own or others still the same
Life-stifling fear, soul-stifling shame!

So two nights passed: the night's dismay
Sadden'd and stunn'd the coming day.
Sleep, the wide blessing, seemed to me   35
Distemper's worst calamity.
The third night, when my own loud scream
Had waked me from the fiendish dream,
O'ercome with sufferings strange and wild,
I wept as I had been a child;   40
And having thus by tears subdued
My anguish to a milder mood,
Such punishments, I said, were due
To natures deepliest stain'd with sin:
For aye entempesting anew   45
Th' unfathomable hell within
The horror of their deeds to view,
To know and loathe, yet wish and do!
Such griefs with such men well agree,

But wherefore, wherefore fall on me? 50
To be beloved is all I need,
And whom I love, I love indeed.

336. EPITAPH ON POOR COL,
BY HIMSELF

[Sept 1803]

C composed the epitaph in his sleep under the notion he had died, during his tour of Scotland. It was the first and only night he ever passed in Edinburgh, at the Black Bull (*CL* II 992: to T. Wedgwood 16 Sept [1803]), "& where I first had heard the preceding evening the word pronounced *Embro'*" (*CL* VI 754: to F. M. Reynolds [25 Aug 1828]). "I remember, I awoke from the stimulus of pure vanity from the admiration of my own fortitude, coolness, and calmness in bearing my death so heroically—as to be able to compose my own Epitaph" (*CN* IV 5360 f 42ᵛ).

C copied the lines for Thomas Wedgwood in a letter written a few days after he composed them, but the present text is from the slightly improved version copied in Apr 1826 in the notebook entry quoted above. It was never published with his permission or in any of his collections during his lifetime. Cf his later epitaph on himself, **693** *S.T.C.*, written when he was indeed close to death.

Here lies poor Col. at length, and without Screaming,
Who died as he had always liv'd—a dreaming!
Shot thro' with pistol by the Gout within,
Alone and all unknown at Embro' in an Inn.

337. BREVITY OF THE GREEK
AND ENGLISH COMPARED

[1803?]

C copied out the Greek and English together, and claimed that the translation might be considered to be in as few words as the original, in a notebook entry which KC dates to 25 Oct 1803 (*CN* I 1613), but which could have been made several years earlier or later. The lines were printed in *Omniana* (1812) No 205 (*SW&F—CC*—341-2), with a fuller comment describing the occasion when this "mere trial of comparative brevity, wit and poetry quite out of the question" was produced and emphasising that the number of syllables rather than words is more to the point when the nature of the two languages is considered. This section is marked in the table of contents with the asterisk which indicates C's contributions. The present version is taken from *Omniana* with minor corrections.

The original epigram is in the *Greek Anthology* (on the editions of which see **234** *The Lethargist and Madman* headnote). In the Planudean anthology it is 1.84, and attributed to Statyllius Flaccus (*Epigrammatum Graecorum Libri VII*—1600—168). In Brunck *Analecta Poetarum Graecorum* I 172 it is attributed to Plato; in the Palatine anthology it is 9.44 tr Paton (LCL) III 24–5. C could have better brought out the meaning by substituting "noose" for "rope", but WW used the same word in his "instance of very close translation", in two fourteen-syllable lines, reported (Mar 1837) by Thomas Moore *Memoirs, Journals, and Correspondence* ed Lord John Russell (8 vols 1853–6) VII 85 and repeated in *PW* (JDC) 463A. Ausonius *Epigram* 22 produced a more explicit four-line Latin version, which was translated by Opitz as *Änderung des Glücks* in two anthologies C knew well—*Christian Wernickens Überschriften, nebst Opitzens, Tschernings, Andreas Gryphius und Adam Olearius epigrammatischen Gedichten* ed Ramler 317; and *Blumenlese deutscher Sinngedichte* ed Joerdens 73. Wyatt and P. B. Shelley also turned the epigram into English.

Χρυσον ανηρ ευρων ελιπε βροχον· αυταρ ὁ χρυσον
Ον λιπεν, ουκ ευρων, ηψεν ον ευρε βροχον.

Jack finding gold left a rope on the ground;
Bill missing his gold used the rope, which he found.

338. LINES AFTER HEARING WILLIAM WORDSWORTH'S *MICHAEL*

[Dec 1803]

C drafted the lines in Notebook 16 (*CN* I 1779) on 31 Dec 1803. He was staying at Grasmere, and had that day visited Greenhead Ghyll with WW, who read him *Michael*. The surrounding notebook entries (*CN* I 1776–85) consist of prose descriptions of other things seen on the same day.

My Spirit with a fixed yet leisurely gaze
Following it's ever yet quietly changing Clusters of Thoughts,
As the outward Eye of a happy Traveller a flock of Starlings.

339. LINES WRITTEN AT DOVE COTTAGE

[Jan 1804]

The lines were written in a notebook (*CN* I 1837), whose text is reproduced here with the addition of a comma at the end of line 8 (for ms deletions see vol II). KC suggests that the alder in line 2 refers to an alder seen on the Scottish tour (*CN* I 1489 ff 53^v–54^r) and that possibly C was going over the tour notes with DW, who was writing up her journal. Under her influence and that of the whole "dear Room with such dear Friends", he summons up the poet in him to this attempt at detailed description in blank verse. The lines also recall the description of Holford Glen, in the earlier celebration of C's friendship with WW and DW in **156** *This Lime-tree Bower my Prison*; and the trees in C's lines are to be set against the solitary oak which remains at the close of WW's *Michael*, a poem C had recently heard for the first time (*WPW* II 94; Reed II 246). The date suggested is one of his last nights at Dove Cottage; he left Grasmere on 14 Jan, for London and Malta.

Over the broad tho' shallow, rapid Stream,
The Alder, a vast hollow Trunk, & ribb'd
Within/ all mossy green with mosses manifold,
And Ferns still waving in the river breeze,
Sent out, like Fingers, 7 projecting Trunks,   5
The shortest twice 6 of a tall man's Strides,
One curving upward, and in it's middle growth
Rose straight with grove of Twigs, a pollard Tree,
The rest more brookward, gradual in descent,
One on the Brook, & one befoam'd it's waters,   10
One ran along the bank, with elk-like Head
And pomp of Antlers/—but still that one
That lay upon or just above the brook
And straight across it, more than halfway o'er
Ends in a broad broad head, & a white Thorn   15
Thicket of Twigs—& here another Tree
As if the winds & waves had work'd by art

That it, with similar Head, & similar Thicket
Bridging the Stream compleat/ thro' these two Thickets
The Shepherd Lads had cut & plan'd a Path/   20
O sweet in summer/ & in winter Storms
I have cross'd the same unharm'd.

340. PATRIOTIC STANZAS

[Jan 1804]

The stanzas are drafted in a somewhat extravagant hand in Notebook 9 (*CN*
II 1857). As KC remarks, they are much in the manner of many an ephemeral
patriotic poem of the time—see e.g. *The Anti-Gallican* I–XII (1804) for other
examples. It might be doubted that the poem is by C, but no alternative source
has been found, and the appearance of the ms, with its reordering of the stanzas,
"arouses the suspicion of original composition" (KC). Some punctuation has
been supplied in the text given here.

Why rest thy Banners? lo the Eastern blush
Gilts thy ten thousand sails once more in Vain;
Or dost thou tremble at the stormy main,
Or is thy dream of Blood & Conquest past?

Come thou Destroyer! With expecting eye   5
A patriot Band awaits thy murderous host;
The proud Avengers of thy ill timed boast
In awful power resolve on Victory.

Haste thou Usurper! Raise the battle storm.
'Tis Heaven's decree thy Meteor fortunes fade;   10
Inglorious Rout, thy last sad Hour shall shade,
No lingering hope thy dying Heart shall warm—

My Soul prophetic hears the dying groans
Of those thy Victims, thy devoted slaves;
Their blood shall stain the bosom of the Waves,   15
The Shore shall whiten with unhallowed Bones—

341. A TRIPLET ON TRIPLETS

[Feb 1804]

The lines are written into Notebook 9 (*CN* II 1904). KC records "Source not traced", and it is even likely that they were copied. But they are included here as C's since no other source has been found.

> When my Triplets you see
> Think not of my Poesy
> But of the holy Trinity.

342. HEXAMETER LINES
TO MRS COLERIDGE

[Feb 1804]

The lines begin a letter of 19 Feb 1804 from C to his wife, which thereafter continues in prose (*CL* II 1068–9). The scansion is marked in the first line as follows: "Tēn ŏ'Clōck ŏ' thĕ Mōrnīng Fēbruārȳ thĕ 1̄9̄ᵗʰ", and on "ōdŏroŭs" in line 8. Several phrases are the result of reworking, and the sense (nonsense) appears deliberately to eschew punctuation.

The nonsensical and associative humour (see the EC notes) indeed shares the spirit of what became known in the Greta Hall household as Mrs C's *lingo grande* (see *S Letters*—Warter—III 270–3; quotations and further references are given by Molly Lefebure "The Imagination of Mrs Samuel Taylor Coleridge" in *Coleridge's Imagination* ed Richard Gravil, Lucy Newlyn, and Nicholas Roe—Cambridge 1985—79–87); compare the tone and imagery of **298** *Version of a Nursery Rhyme*.

Ten o' Clock o' the Morning February the 19ᵗʰ,
Sunday/
     —To Thee I propos'd to write an hexameter Letter,
Thou of the Anakim fairest, beautiful Andandona!

3. Anakim] The giant children of Anak. See Num 13.28, 33 "we were in our own sight as grasshoppers, and so we were in their sight"; Deut 2.10, 9.2. They were driven from Israel by Joshua (Josh 11.21–2).

Yes! in my Dreams I beheld thee: the Cawl of incarnate Osiris
Turban'd thy Head! thy Knees with profitless fury assailing   5
Curly-tail'd Gruntlets accus'd thee, O false & immane to thy
    Guest-friend!
For lo! to those Knees there depended the Hide of their grunnient Mother
Slain as she swill'd at thy Trough! save only this odorous She-shirt,
Other robe hadst thou none, O beautiful ANDANDONA!
Thus began I in Verse; but thinking that Prose will do better,   10
Fly, ye Hexameters! fly to William Taylor of Norwich
That so he once more may exclaim, O sav'd from Death and the Razor,
Welcome Dear pedlaring Jew, with the long white beard on thy Bosom.

343. CARTWRIGHT MODIFIED

[Feb–Mar 1804]

The two poems were written in different notebooks at about the same time (*CN* II 1935, 1940), and they are given here with minor modifications of punctuation. C was reading William Cartwright's *Comedies, Tragi-Comedies, with other Poems* (1651), and the adaptations are taken from several extracts he copied into the notebooks at this time (see *CN* II 1914–21, 1929–37, 1939–43, 1949). Many entries take across phrases and passages unchanged, others with only minor changes (*CN* II 1915, 1916, 1920, 1931, 1932, 1933, 1937, 1939, 1943, 1949). The two given here include the most significant modifications. See poem **460** for a later modification of a passage from Cartwright copied out on the same occasion, in 1804.

In poem (*a*) the first line is C's and the second and third are Cartwright's, from *The Lady Errant* IV vi, in *Comedies . . . Poems* 63. Charistes says, "Love is not perfect till it begins to fear"; and C grafts on to his own line some lines from the reply of Eumela:

It is not Jealousie
That ruins Love, but we our selves, who will not

4. Osiris] In Egyptian mythology the husband of Isis and the foe of Set, his brother.

6. immane] A 17th-century word, meaning cruel or savage.

7. grunnient] Apparently a coinage for "grunting" or "gruntling".

13. Adapted from William Taylor's "O 'tis a pedlaring jew, by the long white beard on his bosom", in *The Show: An English Eclogue* pub *Annual Anthology* ed RS (2 vols Bristol 1799–1800) II 200 (signed "Ryalto").

> Suffer that fear to strengthen it; Give way
> And let it work, 'twill fix the Love it springs from
> In a staid Center.

Poem (b) is considerably altered from Cartwright's *Sadness* stanza 1, in *Comedies . . . Poems* 220:

> Let Sadness only wake;
> That whiles thick Darkness blots the Light,
> My thoughts may cast another Night:
> In which double Shade,
> By Heav'n, and Me made,
> O let me weep,
> And fall asleep,
> And forgotten fade.

The reading in C's line 4 is uncertain; the second word may be "then".

(a)

> My irritable Fears all sprang from Love—
> Suffer that Fear to strengthen it; give way
> And let it work—'twill fix the Love, it springs from.

(b)

> There in some darksome Shade
> Methinks, I'd weep
> Myself asleep
> And there forgotten fade—

344. EPIGRAM ON "DEAR ANNE"

[Before Mar 1804]

The lines were sent to George Dyer, to be published in his series of "Cantabrigiana" in the *Monthly Magazine*, where they are headed "*By a* STUDENT *of* JESUS COLLEGE". The other poem which appeared on the same occasion (**330** *The Kiss and the Blush*) had been published a year previously and might have been written some years earlier. The present lines might also date from an earlier period (cf e.g. **79** *To Ann Brunton*), and they were never republished by C.

Dear Anne, a wond'rous Trinity
Hath made thee a Divinity,
The being strangely beautiful,
And strangely chaste and dutiful,
And what is more than either,   5
The being each together.

345. BALSAMUM IN VITRO

[Before Mar 1804]

The lines were sent to George Dyer with others (poems **330, 344**), to be in-
cluded in Dyer's series of "Cantabrigiana" (*CL* II 1091–2). They might date
from an earlier time, and might have a German source. They were published
in the *Monthly Magazine*, under the heading "*By a* STUDENT *of* JESUS", but
never collected or republished by C. The title means, literally, "Balsam in a
Glass (Vial)".

Chastity's a balsum—woman's but a glass—
That, alas, how costly!—how fragile, this, alas!

346. TEARS AND SYMPATHY

[Apr 1804]

The untitled lines were written into Notebook 9 as C journeyed to Malta (*CN* II
2018). They are introduced as follows: "Last night Squalls, desperate Rocking,
my Dreams full of Grief & bitter weeping." They are followed by a paragraph
of prose: "This in rhyme, & either greatly compressed or highly touched up.
And now for the Metaphysics/ In cases of violent weeping is there not always
Pity mixed & predominant? . . ." Etc. KC speculates that the dream described
by the lines had to do with C's smarting under the withheld sympathy of friends
like John Rickman and C. V. Le Grice, and was perhaps a Christ's Hospital
dream.

Oft in his sleep he wept, & waking found
His Pillow cold beneath his Cheek with Tears,

And found his Dreams
(So faithful to the Past, or so prophetic)
That when he thought of what had made him weep,   5
He did not recollect it as a Dream,
And spite of open eyes & the broad Sunshine
The feverish Man perforce must weep again.

347. PHANTOM

[Before Apr 1804]

The central image (lines 4–5) is a recollection of the incident at Bagborough
and Sockburn treated also in **253** *Love*, and C's earliest explicit reference to
the poem supplies a gloss: "My Dreams *now* always connected in some way
or other with Isulia, all their forms in a state of fusion with some Feeling or
other, that is the distorted Reflection of my Day-Feelings respecting her/"—
Isulia being SH; again: "in one or two sweet Sleeps the Feeling has grown
distinct & true, & at length has created it's appropriate form, the very Isulia/ or
as I well described it in those Lines, 'All Look' &c." (*CN* II 2055).

C's subsequent notebook transcriptions of his poem are accompanied by fur-
ther commentary, e.g. "This abstract Self is indeed in it's nature a Universal
personified—as Life, Soul, Spirit, &c. Will not this prove it to be a *deeper*
Feeling, & of such intimate affinity with ideas, so to modify them & become
one with them" (*CN* II 2441).

The present text is the second of two which C copied into his notebooks
(without supplying a title), in 1805 and 1808 (*CN* II 2441, III 3291). He copied
the poem into SC's album in 1827, under the title "Fragment from a Dream" and
with a note that set a conventional Gothic scene; it was published as "Phantom"
in *PW* (1834). The texts all differ from one another in details of phrasing and
punctuation.

All Look or Likeness caught from Earth,
All accident of Kin or Birth,
Had pass'd away: there was no trace
Of aught upon her brighten'd face,
Uprais'd beneath that rifted Stone,   5
But of one Image—all *her own!*
She, She alone, and only She
Shone thro' her body visibly.—

348. TO CAPTAIN FINDLAY

[May 1804]

C drafted the lines in Notebook 15 en route to Malta (*CN* II 2071), Captain John Findlay being the master of the *Speedwell*. The name of the ship is the same as that on which the mariner sailed in Shelvocke's *Voyage* when he shot the albatross, and the coincidence undoubtedly reinforced C's sense of identification (see **161** *Rime of the Ancient Mariner* headnote for references). The notebook entry begins with, and the lines grow out of, the following sentence: "~~Thurs~~ Friday Morning, ½ past 8, May 4ᵗʰ, 1804. ~~Bravo Capt Findlay & Capt.~~ ~~ran Headlong when~~ the Squalls were flitting and fleering and the Vessel was tacking & veering." It is possible that lines 6–15 were meant to supersede lines 1–5 rather than being a continuation of the same poem. The poem may be conceived as a charm, to invoke a favourable wind. It is followed by: "Well/ & we have got a wind the right way at last!—"

   The ms text is reproduced here (apart from deletions and insertions), with the addition of a full point in line 11.

              Bravo, Captain Findlay
              Who foretold a fair Wind
              Of a constant mind
              For he knew which way the wind lay,—
              Bravo! Captain Findlay!   5

              ─────────────

              A Health to Captain Findlay!
              Bravo! Captain Findlay!
              When we made but ill Speed with the Speedwell,
              Neither Poet, nor Sheep could feed well
              And Poet & Pig! how grief rotted Liver   10
              And yet Malta, dear Malta as far off as ever.
              Bravo! Captain Findlay—
              Foretold a fair wind
              Of a constant mind,
              For he knew which way the Wind lay.   15

349. MERCURY DESCENDING: A METRICAL EXPERIMENT

[Before Oct 1804]

The experiment forms the beginning of a long entry in Notebook 22, and it appears to have changed direction as it was written. It derives from an attempt to translate Raphael's flight to earth in *PL* v 246–87 into a different, less regular, metre; and the relevant part of the notebook entry begins with a prose memorandum, followed by a first draft of the experiment, which was deleted with a single large cross:

7 ĩ0 7 9 ĩ1. Da Capo. Then an Epod of the metre of Milton's Christmas-day Hymn/ 9 & 11 of S^t. and Antist: first an Amphib: followed by two Dactyls, the 11th a Trochee+amph: &c.

> Dropping Balsams, dropping ~~nectar~~ wine
>   Descends the heavenly Herald, Maia's Son,
> ~~Comes the winged God, the Son of Maia~~
> ~~His feet are winged, the Caduceus~~
>   Flying feet, and charmed Rod
> The Sire of Quiet, wreath'd with Serpents
> ~~Comes wing'd Mercury, the Son of Maia~~
> Mercurius winged Son of Maia.

The lines given here have the scansion-marks written alongside and below in the original, for which see *CN* II 2224 f 24^v. They afterwards develop with no obvious break into a description of the sun setting in a mountainous country, for which see poem **350**.

> Hĕ sōftlў | līghtĭng ŏn | Sēā,
> Hīs mīld | Cădūceŭs | wrēāthĕd wĭth | Sērpĕnt-twīne |
> Yēs! ĭt ĭs | *Hē!* ĭt ĭs | Hē!
> Thĕ Vāllĕys | mūrmŭr nŏt | pleasureless,
> Ānd thĕ jūbĭlātĭng Ōcĕăn's (rĕ)jōĭcĭng ĭs | mēāsŭrelĕss |.　　5

350. DESCRIPTION OF THE SUN SETTING IN A MOUNTAINOUS COUNTRY: A FRAGMENT

[Before Oct 1804]

The fragment was never published in C's lifetime, and the version here is from a fair copy made for an autograph hunter in 1819. In its original form it was part of a sequence of metrical experiments in Notebook 22 (*CN* II 2224 f 25ʳ). On rereading his notebook in 1805, C commented: "These lines I wrote as nonsense verses merely to try a metre; but they are by no means contemptible—at least, on reading them over I am surprised at finding them so good."

In the notebook the lines are preceded by a note concerning metrics, followed by some extensively recast verses which describe Mercury descending to the sea (poem **349**). The relation between this experimental beginning and the fragmentary description of a sunset which it developed into is oblique. One must suppose that C changed direction in mid-course as he turned over a page in the notebook; or that he began with a line (1) which echoes the suspended stresses of poem **349** and then composed two 6-line stanzas to conclude with rhythmically identical lines (8 and 14). It is relevant that the present poem is unaccompanied by metrical analysis, and that it has a different rhyme-scheme from the preceding verses.

*　*　*　*　*　*　*　*　*　*　*　*　*　*　*　*　*　*　*

Upon the Mountain's edge with light touch resting.

There a brief while the Globe of Splendor sits
   And seems a Creature of this Earth; but soon
     More changeful than the Moon
To Wane fantastic his great orb submits,   5
Or Cone or Mow of Fire: till sinking slowly
Even to a Star at length he lessens wholly.

Abrupt, as Spirits vanish, he is sunk!
A soul-like Breeze possesses all the Wood:
   The Boughs, the Sprays have stood   10
As motionless, as stands the ancient Trunk!
But every Leaf thro' all the Forest flutters:
And deep the Cavern of the Fountain mutters.

351. WHAT IS LIFE? A METRICAL EXPERIMENT

[Oct 1804]

The lines were drafted immediately following poems **349** *Mercury Descending* and **350** *Description of the Sun Setting* in Notebook 22. They are headed: "Now will it be a more English Music if the first & fourth are double rhymes; & the 5 & 6th single?—or all single; or the second & 3rd double? Try." C afterwards commented on their relation to poem **350:** "Written in the same manner, and for the same purpose, but of course with more conscious Effort" (*CN* II 2224 f 25ᵛ).

C made a fair copy of the lines in 1819 for an autograph collector, and they were published in an album over his name in 1829 but never collected. When he copied them in 1819, he pretended that they were a juvenile production and emphasised their fragmentary nature, both of which actions suggest that he was somewhat self-conscious about their wisdom. The three texts differ slightly; the one given here is the ms fair copy, with the first part of the title supplied from the printed version.

*   *   * ————————————

Resembles Life what once was held of Light,
Too simple in itself for human sight?

An absolute Self? an Element ungrounded?
All that we see, all colors of all shade
    By "incroach of Darkness" made?   5
Even so, is Life by *conscious* thought unbounded?
And all the Joys and Woes of Mortal Breath
A War-embrace of wrestling Life and Death!

5. The quotation-marks are present only in the fair copy. The substantive derived from the verb (here meaning "encroachment", "gradual approach") is a 17th-century usage rare in C's time. It has Miltonic overtones, but is not from Milton.

352. ADAPTATION OF HAGEDORN

[Oct 1804?]

The lines were written in a notebook which was in use in Malta (*CN* II 2224 f 81ʳ), but they may have been composed before. They are untitled, and were never published by C.

The poem adapts the first stanza of Friedrich von Hagedorn *Die Vögel*, in *Sämmtliche poetische Werke* III 34, which C copied out on another page of the same notebook (*CN* II 2224 f 15ʳ) as follows:

> In diesem Wald, in diesen Gründen
> Herrscht nichts, als Freyheit, Lust, und Ruh.
> Hier sagen wir der Liebe zu,
> Im dicksten Schatten uns zu finden:
> Da find ich dich, da findet mich findest du.

See *CN* for a literal translation by KC.

C's lines link SH with a holly-tree at Alfoxden, described by WW for Lady Beaumont in Dec 1806: "it was attired with woodbine, and upon the very tip of the topmost bough that 'looked out at the sky' was one large honeysuckle flower, like a star, crowning the whole" (*WL—M* rev—I 120; the quotation adapts **176** *Christabel* 52).

> Within these circling Hollies Wood-bine-clad
> Beneath this small blue Roof of vernal Sky
> How warm, how still! tho' Tears should dim mine eye,
> Yet will my Heart for days continue glad—
> For here, my Love! thou art! and here am I!   5

353. METRICAL EXPERIMENTS FROM NOTEBOOK 22

[1801?–Oct 1804–1807?]

The verses given here form part of a series of more than 48 metrical analyses and experiments written into a notebook in ink and pencil and afterwards numbered, involving metres in German, Italian, and other languages as well as English. The parenthetical numbers heading each piece are those of *CN* II 2224, which regularises C's numbering. Nos 29, 43, and 47 were published in C's lifetime, and together with Nos 28 and 42 are given separately as poems **351, 354, 216** (headnote), **349–50,** and **352** respectively. C modified the originals he transcribed in several other instances, but not significantly enough to merit inclusion here.

(4)

C wrote the following metrical analysis on f 15^r, under the same heading "(4)" as his verses—although the scheme has an extra breve in line 1 (on which see C's comment below) and an extra longum at the end of lines 3 and 6:

$$– \cup, \; – \cup \cup, \; –$$
$$–, \; – \cup \cup, \; – \cup,$$
$$– \cup, \; – \cup \cup, \; – \cup \cup, \; –$$
$$–, \; – \cup \cup, \; –$$
$$–, \; – \cup \cup, \; – \cup$$
$$– \cup, \; – \cup \cup, \; – \cup \cup, \; –$$

C afterwards inserted the following comment at the foot of f 13^v: "Where the subject admits a Stress on, and pause *after*, the first monosyllable/ but for other subjects for the first – , put an – $\cup$ ./"

(12)

The lines are preceded, as part of the same item, by C's transcript of their German original, the ninth stanza of Selina's song in J. H. Voss *Der Frülingsmorgen,* in *Gedichte* (Hamburg 1785) 9:

> Kehre wieder, mein Bräutigam,
> Kehre wieder in meinen Arm
> Ach! wie zittr' ich, dich zu küssen!
> Kehre wieder, Selino!

(13)

The lines are preceded, as part of the same item, by C's transcript of the German original, the first stanza of J. H. Voss *Minnelied,* in *Gedichte* II (Königsberg 1795) 151:

> Der Holdseligen
> Sonder Wank
> Sing' ich frö[h]lichen
> Minnesang:
> Denn die Reine
> Die ich meine,
> Winkt mir lieblichen Habedank.

C has adapted the metre and content freely. A literal translation is supplied by KC:

> To the Gracious Lady
> In constancy
> I sing a glad
> Love-song:
> For the Pure One
> Whom I love
> Waves me her lovely thanks.

(38)

C wrote the following metrical scheme at the foot of f 79^v, at the beginning of the section:

1.	∪–∪ . ––∪ . ––∪ . ∪– .	Two Antibacchiuses for Amphibrachs
2.	∪–∪ . ∪–∪ . ∪–∪ . ∪– .	Amphibrachs catalectic
3	–∪∪ . –∪∪ . –∪∪ . –	Dactyls hypercatalectic
4.	–∪∪ . –∪∪ . –∪– .	Two Dactyls with one Amphimacer.
5.	–∪– . –∪– . ∪	⎰ Amphimacer with Ditrochæus
6.	–∪– . –∪– . ∪	⎱
7.	∪∪– . ∪∪– . –∪– . ∪∪–	Two Anapæsts. Amphimacer. Anapæst.

After this analysis, C wrote the following lines at the head of f 80^r:

> I heard a ~~Bird~~ voice pealing in triumph ~~this~~ to Day,
> O Freedom divinest of Ardors twas thine
> Sumptuous Tyranny floating this way
> Drunk with Idolatry, drunk with wine

He then cancelled the four lines with a single cross, and wrote the following line beneath them, which he subsequently deleted:

> Safe on the mountain rock, the storm and the eagle my guardians

The relation between the cancelled lines and the lines given below as the RT (which follow on directly, numbered again "38") is not clear. "Drunk with Idolatry, drunk with wine" is from *Samson Agonistes* 1670. C had quoted it earlier in the same notebook (f 17^r), along with line 1072 (var) "Sumptuous Dalila floating this way" (cf line 3 of the RT). In common with the first part of No 28 on f 24^v (=**349** *Mercury Descending*), the RT lines are full of Miltonic echoes.

Following the RT, at the bottom of f 80^r, C provided a metrical analysis (which seems to come adrift from what he wrote after line 4):

$$––∪\,/\,––∪\,/$$

1. Amphibrach tetrameter catalectic ∪–∪ / ∪–∪ / ∪–∪ / ∪–
2. Ditto
3. Three pseudo ~~dactyls~~ amphimacers (& one long syllable——
4. Two Dactyls, and one perfect Amphimacer

5 =1 & 2
6. $-\cup-/-\cup-\cup$
7. $-\cup-/-\cup-\cup$
8. $-\cup-/-\cup-/-\cup-/-\cup-$.

(41)

C introduces his lines with the comment "Adaptation of M.25—Trochaics." What he had said under the heading "25." (on f 24ʳ) was as follows:

8́ 1́0 1́0 1́0 1́0 8́. In Italian where all are double rhymes this is a pretty measure: in English 3 double rhymes in one stanza if there were more than two stanzas in the poem would never do¢; but the second line might be made rhymeless, tho' isometrical with the 5 & 6ᵗʰ double-rhymed/

> endless, gore, sor . . row, morrow, lore, sore/ *or*
> gore, endless, lore, sore, sorrow, morrow.

(44)

C headed the lines "Nonsense Verses." Vol II records C's revisions; the RT below adds a full point at the end of lines 7 and 11.

(44a)

C inserted the lines into the notebook after the other experiments in the sequence. He headed them "Nonsense Verses for the trial of the Metre/", which points away from their bearing on his feelings for SH. The first word in line 3 has been obliterated in the ms. A word has also been obliterated in line 6, whose second half is interpreted by KC as "and lust as lust".

(45, 46)

C copied out the verses twice, developing them differently after line 10—for which see vol II. The RT follows C's instructions for the second version.

(48)

The lines are headed "Nonsense", but they contain images refracted from **299** *The Keepsake* and **300** *The Picture*, buoyed up by currents of feeling associated with SH.

(4)

> Dance, merrily, dance
> Off, gloomy suspicion
> Here be nothing but amity

(4) *CN* II 2224 f 13ᵛ.

Eyes looking askance
Tongues, courting contrition   5
Flee to, Ocean's extremity

(12)

Hither, hither, Beloved one!
O return to my faithful arms!
Ah! to kiss thee, how I tremble!
Hither, hither, Selino!

(13)

Rhymes Three Syllable,
Tuneful Swan,
I tho' ill able
Murmur on:
For her maiden   5
Lips there play'd on
Smiles that solace the Woebegone.

(38)

I heard a voice pealing loud triumph today,
The Voice & the Triumph, O Freedom were thine,
Sumptuous Tyranny challenged the fray
Drunk with Idolatry, drunk with Wine/
Friend of Mankind! O Freedom, divinest of ardors   5
Whose could the Triumph! O Freedom but thine
    Stars of the Heaven shine to feed thee;
    Hush'd are the Whirlblasts & heed thee,
By her Depths, by her Heights Nature swears Thou art mine!

(41)

Thus she said; and all around
Her diviner spirit 'gan to borrow;
Earthly Hearings hear unearthly sound,
Hearts heroic faint & sink aswound;

(12) *CN* II 2224 f 16^r.   (38) *CN* II 2224 f 80^r.
(13) *CN* II 2224 f 16^v.   (41) *CN* II 2224 ff 80^v–81^r.

Welcome, Welcome, spite of pain & sorrow,   5
    Love today, and Thought tomorrow.

(44)

Go, vanish into Night,
Ye fowls of ill presage!
Let all things sweet and fair
Yield Homage to the Pair—
    From Infancy to Age.   5
Each Brow be smooth, and bright,
As Lake in evening Light.
    Today be Joy! and Sorrow—
    Devoid of Blame
    The widow'd Dame—   10
Shall welcome be tomorrow.
Thou too, dull Night! may'st come unchid
This wall of Flame the Dark hath hid
With turrets, each a Pyramid!
For the Tears, that we shed, are Gladness   15
    A mockery of Sadness.

(44a)

Some sager Words two meanings tell
For instance, Love is such!
[. . .] cannot LOVE *too well*
And yet may *love too much/*
Would we make sense of this, we must   5
First construe Love as Love:/ [. . .] AY⟨ΣT⟩PIA.

(45, 46)

I wish on earth to sing
Of Jove the bounteous store,
That all the Earth may ring
With Tales of Wrong no more.
I fear no Foe in Field or Tent   5
Tho weak our cause, yet strong his Grace,
As polar Roamers clad in Fur

(44) *CN* II 2224 f 83^r.   (45, 46) *CN* II 2224 f 83^r–v.
(44a) *CN* II 2224 f 83^r.

Unweeting whither we were bent,
We found, as twere, a native place,
Where not a Blast could stir. 10
I wish on earth to sing
O then I sing Jove's bounteous Store
On rushing wing while Sea-mews soar,
The raking Tides roll Thunder on the Shore.

(48)

O Sara! never rashly let me go
Beyond the precincts of this holy Place,
Where streams as pure as in Elysium flow
And flowrets view reflected Grace,
What tho in vain the melted Metals glow, 5
We die, and dying own a more than mortal love.

354. RECOLLECTIONS OF LOVE

[Oct 1804? 1806–7?]

An earlier version, comprising the first four stanzas only, follows on and grows out of C's adaptation of Hagedorn, in an entry in Notebook 22 which KC dates to Oct 1804 (*CN* II 2224 ff 81ᵛ–82ᵛ = poem **352**). Stanza 3 became the centre of the new poem, as two trial versions of it show, and C repeated and developed phrases from it in subsequent notebook fragments (*CN* II 3003, III 4036). There are other instances of his associating SH with periods of his life before they met; cf e.g. *CN* II 2998, III 3303n; *C&SH* 135–6; **253** *Love*. The poem developed from its beginnings after C returned from Malta, and might just as well have been positioned in 1806–7, or indeed later.

The germ of line 27 appears to lie in **406** *Fragments Written in February 1807*, but stanzas 5 and 6 might not have been composed until the time C made the poem ready for publication in *SL* (1817), the text reproduced here. Stanzas 1–4 carry over from the final ms draft almost unchanged, their tendency being modified by the added stanzas, as the title advertises. The enlarged poem was included without change in the three subsequent collections.

(48) *CN* II 2224 f 83ᵛ.

I.

How warm this woodland wild Recess!
  LOVE surely hath been breathing here.
  And this sweet bed of heath, my dear!
Swells up, then sinks with faint caress,
  As if to have you yet more near.   5

II.

Eight springs have flown, since last I lay
  On sea-ward Quantock's heathy hills,
  Where quiet sounds from hidden rills
Float here and there, like things astray,
  And high o'er head the sky-lark shrills.   10

III.

No voice as yet had made the air
  Be music with your name: yet why
  That asking look? That yearning sigh?
That sense of promise every where?
  Beloved! flew your spirit by?   15

IV.

As when a mother doth explore
  The rose-mark on her long lost child,
  I met, I lov'd you, maiden mild!
As whom I long had lov'd before—
  So deeply had I been beguil'd.   20

V.

You stood before me like a thought,
  A dream remember'd in a dream.
  But when those meek eyes first did seem
To tell me, Love within you wrought—
  O Greta, dear domestic stream!   25

---

6. Eight springs] If C refers to the spring of 1798, and the stanza was written in Oct 1804, he miscounted. It is less likely that the stanza was written in 1806–7.

25. Greta] The river passing behind Greta Hall, where C moved in Jul 1800. "The river Greta flows behind our house, roaring like an untamed Son of the Hills, then winds round,

VI.

Has not, since then, Love's prompture deep,
Has not Love's whisper evermore,
Been ceaseless, as thy gentle roar?
Sole voice, when other voices sleep,
Dear under-song in Clamor's hour.   30

355. FRAGMENT: "AND LAUREL CROWN . . ."

[Dec 1804]

The lines were written into Notebook 21½ (*CN* II 2386). C expressed similar
views on action and passivity in earlier notes (*CN* I 1072, 1834). KC suggests
that the line and a half may be connected with the revising of **146.X1** *Osorio*.

And laurel Crown, the Enemy of Death,
If Life be action!

356. FRAGMENT: "WHAT NEVER IS, BUT ONLY IS TO BE"

[1804–5]

The fragment is known only from *PW* (EHC) II 999 No 12.

What never is, but only is to be
This is not Life:—
O hopeless Hope, and Death's Hypocrisy!
And with perpetual promise breaks its promises.

& *glides* away in the front—so that   Josiah Wedgwood 1 Nov 1800).
we live in a peninsₗula," (*CL* I 644: to

357. CONSTANCY TO AN IDEAL OBJECT

[1804–7? 1822?]

The date and, therefore, C's exact intention are problematic, as with other poems which explore similar themes. Phrases and images link the poem to his time in Malta, yet the earliest known version dates from the early 1820s, and the poem was not published till 1828. The image to which the poem builds, and which the footnote enlarges on, describes a phenomenon which attracted other writers at the time. A climactic scene of James Hogg's *Private Memoirs and Confessions of a Justified Sinner* (1824), for example, set on Arthur's Seat in Edinburgh, describes the appearance of the fiendish younger brother as a giant apparition in the mist while a "halo of glory" surrounds the elder brother's head. C included the poem in his three late collections, and there are few differences between the versions: in the earliest, a transcript by SC, lines 16–32 are given in quotation-marks, as against lines 16–24 only in *PW* (1828) and just lines 16–18 in *PW* (1829, 1834). There are also a few ms variants in the last half-dozen lines. The version here reproduces *PW* (1829), for reasons described in the Introduction (p lxxxvi).

> Since all, that beat about in Nature's range,
> Or veer or vanish; why should'st thou remain
> The only constant in a world of change,
> O yearning THOUGHT, that liv'st but in the brain?
> Call to the HOURS, that in the distance play,   5
> The faery people of the future day—
> Fond THOUGHT! not one of all that shining swarm
> Will breathe on *thee* with life-enkindling breath,
> Till when, like strangers shelt'ring from a storm,
> Hope and Despair meet in the porch of Death!   10
> Yet still thou haunt'st me; and though well I see,
> She is not thou, and only thou art she,
> Still, still as though some dear *embodied* Good,
> Some *living* Love before my eyes there stood
> With answering look a ready ear to lend,   15
> I mourn to thee and say—"Ah! loveliest Friend!
> "That this the meed of all my toils might be,
> "To have a home, an English home, and thee!"

9–10. The image is the same as one which appeared (only) in the third version of **107** *Allegoric Vision* (see *LS—CC*—133).

Vain repetition! Home and Thou are one.
The peacefull'st cot, the moon shall shine upon,   20
Lulled by the Thrush and wakened by the Lark
Without thee were but a becalmed Bark,
Whose Helmsman on an Ocean waste and wide
Sits mute and pale his mouldering helm beside.

And art thou nothing? Such thou art, as when   25
The woodman winding westward up the glen
At wintry dawn, where o'er the sheep-track's maze
The viewless snow-mist weaves a glist'ning haze,
Sees full before him, gliding without tread,
An image* with a glory round its head;   30
The enamoured rustic worships its fair hues,
Nor knows, he *makes* the shadow, he pursues!

* This phenomenon, which the Author has himself experienced, and of which
the reader may find a description in one of the earlier volumes of the Manchester
Philosophical Transactions, is applied figuratively in the following passage of
the AIDS to REFLECTION:
"Pindar's fine remark respecting the different effects of music, on different 5
characters, holds equally true of Genius: as many as are not delighted by it are
disturbed, perplexed, irritated. The beholder either recognizes it *as a projected
form of his own Being, that moves before him with a Glory round its head*, or
recoils from it as a spectre."—AIDS to REFLECTION, p. 220.

30fn. This appears only in the printed texts. C transcribed the description referred to in the Gutch Notebook (*CN* I 258; cf *Memoirs of the Literary and Philosophical Society of Manchester*—1790—III 463; *Bristol LB* No 104) and alluded to it in **155 Continuation of "The Three Graves"** 291. He noted an experience of the same phenomenon on his voyage to Malta in Apr 1804 (*CN* II 2052), at which time several other images in the poem were remarked (*CN* II 1996, 2001, 2046, 2058); see also *CN* III 3466; *AR* (*CC*) 227–8, 556–7. The Pindar passage he refers to in his extract from *AR* is *Pythian Ode* 1.10–14.

The note modifies C's distance from the lines it is attached to in the same way as his experiments with quotation-marks. It is significant that lines 27–8 repeat and modify WW's image in *Resolution and Independence* 8–14 to describe the delight of their shared Stowey experience (*WPW* II 235); and cf the "glory" that "hath past away" of WW's *Intimations Ode* 18 (*WPW* IV 279). C drew the attention of J. H. Green to the passage on 11 Jun 1825 (*CL* V 467).

358. "THIS YEARNING HEART . . ."

[After 1804]

The lines are written on paper watermarked 1804, along with other notes dating from 1807 and 1810. The beginning of the poem was much reworked; the last three lines seem to have come more easily. The poem was never published by C.

> This yearning Heart (Love! witness what I say)
> Enshrines thy form as purely as it may,
> Round which, as to some spirit uttering Bliss,
> My Thoughts all stand ministrant, night and day,
> Like saintly Priests, that dare not think amiss.—   5

359. LOVE—WHY BLIND?

[Feb 1805]

The lines were drafted in Notebook 21 without a title (*CN* II 2424 var), but then deleted and portions perhaps cut away. They were published over C's initials in *Felix Farley's Bristol Journal* (30 Sept 1815), and reprinted with slight changes in *PW* (1828, 1829, 1834). C might have come to wish the poem read in conjunction with the one which precedes them in the three later printings, **492** *To a Lady, Offended by a Sportive Observation that Women Have No Souls*. The newspaper text is given here.

> I've heard of reasons manifold,
>   Why L O V E must needs be blind;
> But this the best of all I hold—
>   His Eyes are in his mind.
>
> What *outward* form and feature are,   5
>   He guesses but in part;
> But what *within* is good and fair,
>   The heart sees with the heart.

4. ministrant] In his fair copy C added a mark to show that the middle syllable was long.

360. CLOSING LINES IN NOTEBOOK 21

[Feb 1805]

The whole entry (*CN* II 2426), which is signed "S. T. C.", is given here (a word or phrase has been torn away at the beginning of the second line, and an indecipherable word deleted before "So"). The first page of the notebook (excluding the front pastedown, on which the end of this entry appears) bears a dated inscription by Joseph Cottle "to his valued Friend" (*CN* I 306).

From Decemb^r 6th 1797 to Feb.3, 1805, this Pocket-book has been filling—

and now let it end/
[. . .] So begin! so end!
Heart and Breathing no more life shall lend!

361. COUPLET WRITTEN IN FEBRUARY 1805

[Feb 1805]

The couplet is part of a paragraph-long memorandum which questions the value of writing such memoranda (*CN* II 2458). C's authorship is not certain.

Thus ends the Day, so *hopingly* begun,
Much Evil *perpetrated*, nothing *done!*

362. VERSES ON LOVE AND MORAL BEING

[Mar–Apr 1805]

The two sets of verses appear in fragmentary drafts on two different pages of Notebook 17 (*CN* II 2500, 2524). The first set extended further, before it was trimmed with scissors; the second set was considerably reworked. KC speculates that they have to do with a note elsewhere in the same notebook, written at about the same time (*CN* II 2514):

⌐. . .⌐ & overcome by LOVE, by VERY Love! that it has been quenched
utterly in the memory, annihilated in the moral Being. That I may not lose
and forget it, let me remember to write that Poem on this subject at the end
of this Book.—

It is equally possible that the verses were drafted independently of each other
and of any such purpose.

(*a*)

But Love is there—
The Clouds—but when they past,
Did I not dance with all my waves
   hailed the Light renewed

(*b*)

Your Gift seem'd two, 'twas givn so fleetly
Warm Heart made cool Brain bubble
For Gratitude surprized so sweetly
Like Drunkenness, sees double.

363. DOLEFUL DIALOGUE

[Apr 1805]

The lines were drafted in a notebook in Malta (*CN* II 2523). KC speculates that
they might be the product of boredom in the Admiralty Court. A near-illegible
description alongside suggests that they describe a dialogue between a judge
and a Dutchman.

Of the Judge that condemns to the tune of ⌐. . . .⌐,
For "keep all you take?" turns a Punt to a Brig,
While your damn'd further Proofs to be made hugger-mugger
Change a Spanish Galleon to an empty Dutch Lugger

364. CURTAILED LINES IN NOTEBOOK 17

[Apr 1805]

The lines are written in a notebook (*CN* II 2532), with only one word altered. The following five leaves have been cut away, leaving just stubs and the beginnings and ends of lines.

> O! th' oppressive, irksome weight
> Felt in an uncertain State:
> Comfort, peace, and rest adieu,
> Should I prove at last untrue!
> Self-confiding Wretch I thought   5
> I could love thee as I ought,
> Win thee and deserve to feel
> All the love, thou can'st reveal.
> And still I chuse thee, follow still
> Every notice   10

365. A METAPHOR

[May 1805]

The lines are written in Notebook 15 (*CN* II 2582), the title following. KC compares the metre in *CN* II 2806 (=**381** *Lines on a Death*) and 2926 (q **502.X3** *Remorse* (Printed) IV ii 52–65TN). She also suggests that the title is a blind, concealing the fact that the lines have a personal application.

> And as he gazed with his dull serpent eyes,
> The Poison-duct behind the orbit of the eye
> Was working still; and ever as it work'd,
> Created venom from the innocent Blood.—

366. APOSTROPHE TO BEAUTY IN MALTA

[May–Jun 1805]

The lines, untitled and considerably revised, appear in a Malta notebook (*CN* II 2597). The Italian means "in charming (mortal) spoils I a most beautiful soul!"

O Beauty, in a beauteous Body dight!
Body! that veiling Brightness becom'st bright/
Fair Cloud which less we see, than by thee see the Light!
              in avvenenti spoglie
Bellissim' Alma!   5

367. TO GOD

[Jun 1805]

The lines, entitled, initialled, and dated 27 Jun 1805 by C, are written in Notebook 17 (*CN* II 2606). The poem is followed by a paragraph in prose:

—The Fish gasps on the glittering mud, the mud of this once full stream, now only moist enough to be glittering mud/ the tide will flow back, time enough to lift me up with straws & withered sticks and bear me down into the ocean. O me! that being what I have been I should be what I am!—

Thou who the weak and bruised never breakest,
Nor ever triumph in the Yielding seekest/
Pity my weak estate, o now or never/
I ever yet was weak, and now more weak than ever.

368. IRREGULAR LINES ON
THE SICK MAN'S COMFORTER

[Jul 1805]

The untitled lines are written in Notebook 17 (*CN* II 2622). They have the appearance of an adaptation, but no source has been found.

> Or as Lucina, giving *aid*. In birth to women—mild as any *maid*
> Full of sweet Hope her (or *his*) Brow seem'd; & her (*his*) Eyes
>   Like to the morning Skies
> Seem'd more to shed than dart
> Their comfortable Light upon the sick man's heart.   5

369. LINES CONNECTED WITH THE
GRASMERE CIRCLE

[Jul–Oct 1805]

The lines were inserted into a notebook entry comprising, at the time, two sequences of names and initials standing for WW, DW, MH, C, and SH, differently combined (*CN* II 2623). C's attention was caught by the sheep on board the *Speedwell* on his way to Malta (*CN* II 2005, 2016). Cf **372** *On the Names in a Malta Notebook*.

> O blessed Flock! I the sole scabbed Sheep!
> And even me they love, awake, asleep.

370. LINES ON HEARING A TALE

[Aug 1805]

C wrote the lines into Notebook 22 (*CN* II 2644), but it is not certain that he is the author. He added his initials at the end, but might have done so to suggest the application of the verses to himself rather than to signify his authorship. The prose style and other aspects of the footnote recall **160** *The Wanderings of Cain*.

Scarce half the Tale*
Impatiently he heard: then scour'd away
Swift as a famish'd Vulture scenting prey.

371. LINES REWRITTEN FROM SANNAZARO

[Jul 1804–Jun 1806?]

C provided alternative wording for lines 37–8 and 40 of Jacopo Sannazaro *Ad Petrum de Roccha-Forti Maximum Regis Galliarum Cancellarium*, in *Opera Omnia* (Frankfurt 1709) 86 (*CM—CC—*IV 339–40). Sannazaro's lines are as follows:

> Delentur nullos hominum benefacta per annos,
>   Quaque licet faciunt nos ratione Deos.
> At si quis serae spernit praeconia famae,
>   Quercubus Alpinis adnumerare potes.

Tr "The good deeds of mankind are not obliterated by any lapse of years, and so far as is lawful they make us into gods. But if anyone scorns the long-lasting proclamation of his fame, you may count him among the Alpine oaks [for his rarity or imperturbability?]."

C put forward a simple emendation in his second line (Sannazaro's 38)— "suos" ("their own", i.e. "our good deeds benefit us as well") for "Deos" ("gods")—and substituted a less obscure phrase at the beginning of his fourth (Sannazaro's line 40). In a further note at the bottom of the page he paraphrased the first pair of lines, retaining Sannazaro's "Deos": "Beneficence is immortal; & as far as we dare use such an expression, it makes Gods of us." He followed this with an alternative Latin version, the text given here, tr "Divine love of humankind, fairer than any crown, glorifies kings and makes them into gods. But if anyone scorns the long-lasting proclamation of his fame, you may already count him among those who are forgotten." In the concluding words of C's first

---

* The Tidings were ecstacy to his ears; yet he listened to it, as if on the rack/ scarce half the Tale, beating the earth with his right foot, & his staff trembling in his hand, he heard, & even that half seemed rather to mould a dream than to convey the simple Truth, then scourd away/—

line the last three letters of "pulchrior" and the whole of "omni" are supplied
by conjecture.

> Dius Amor hominum diademate pulchrior omni
> Illustrat reges et facit esse deos.
> At si quis seræ spernit praeconia famæ,
> Iam nunc oblitis adnumerare potes.

372. ON THE NAMES IN A MALTA
NOTEBOOK

[Oct 1805]

C wrote the lines in Notebook 18 (*CN* ii 2691) above the name of Tauromina,
Sicily. He wrote a revised version elsewhere in the same notebook at Grasmere
in 1810 (*CN* iii 3865):

> The Lover, the Beloved, the Sister, the Brother!
> (Tis lonely Fancy's Bittersweet)
> Close in, dear Names! upon each other!
> Ah that the names alone can meet!

The names C refers to are those of SH, WW, DW, and MW together with
his own, plus, in the second version, those of the Coleridge and Wordsworth
children. Their initials are inscribed in different combinations, anagrams, etc
throughout the notebook, in the corners of pages before they were written on, as
described in *CN* ii, General Note on N 18. The circumstances of C's separation
in Sicily in 1805 and at Grasmere in 1810 of course imply different thoughts
and intentions. Cf **369** *Lines Connected with the Grasmere Circle*.

> Friend, Lover, Husband, Sister, Brother!
> Dear Names! close in upon each other!
> Alas! poor Fancy's Bitter-sweet!
> Our names, and *but* our names, can meet!

373. PERHAPS A TRANSLATION OF
SOME COMICALLY BAD VERSES

[Oct–Nov 1805]

C wrote the untitled lines into Notebook 16 (*CN* II 2716). They read like a translation, although no source has been found. It is also possible that they are not by C at all.

> There laves upon so white a Breast
> That well a Maiden's it might seem
> (I know not, if by Heaven's Behest
> Or by a longing Mother's Dream)
> A crimson Rose that shed no leaves   5
> A man's large Heart beneath it heaves
> And He with the Rose on his Bosom bereaves &c/

374. LATIN LINES TO WILLIAM
WORDSWORTH AS JUDGE

[Dec 1805? 1807–10?]

The untitled lines were written in Notebook 16 (*CN* II 2750), at an uncertain date. C addresses WW in hendecasyllables; cf **328** *Latin Lines on a Former Friendship* and **430** *Ad Vilmum Axiologum: Latin Version*. The scansion of the first line is shaky, and C has had to provide his own translation of "meumque Regem" (lit "and my king") in line 8. KC provides a free translation. The following version is closer to the Latin at some points:

> Deference? No, indeed, this is tyranny! You will yourself deny that I toady to anyone; moreover, you will not deny that I am sound of mind. Therefore, William, I ask you, is your veto (as long as you yourself live) going to pronounce in one name jointly on Morals, Philosophy, and the sacred Muses, and why and by what right does it constrain *me*? I have come to recognise you, fully and willingly, as poet, sage, and my most honoured Friend, but *not* as Judge.

As to C's footnote, "rex" would appropriately be translated in Martial 5.22 and elsewhere as "patron", hardly consistent with C's attitude of defiance.

The lines attempt to present respect for WW as poet (if not friend) and rejection of him as moral mentor, attitudes which are presented separately in the English and Latin versions of *Ad Vilmum Axiologum* (poems **429** and **430**).

Verecundia? imo, tyrannis hoc est!
Quod cuivis adulor, negabis ipse;
Nec non quod sapiam, haud negabis. Ergo
Mores, et Sophiam, sacrasque Musas
Uno nomine (dumque vivis ipse)   5
Dicturum, Gulielme—quæso, cur me,
Et quo Jure tuum "Veto" coercet?
Te vatem, atque Sophum, meumque Regem*
Agnovi, usque lubens! at haud Tribunum.

375. EPITAPH ON MAJOR DIEMAN,
WITH COMMENT

[c 1805]

C wrote the epitaph in Greek letters in Notebook 22, and on the facing page wrote it again in roman letters, with minor variations in wording and an additional comment "On the above" (*CN* II 2769, 2771). If the lines were written in Malta one might suppose Major Dieman to have been a member of the garrison there.

Know thou who walk'st by, Man! That wrapp'd up in lead, man
What once was a Dieman, Now lies here a Dead man:
Alive a proud MAJOR! but ah me! of o͞ur po̎or ă̋ll
The Soul being gone, he is now merely *Corporal*.

ON THE ABOVE

As long as e'er the Life-blood's running,   5
Say, what can stop a Punster's Punning?
He dares bepun even thee, O Death!
To *pun*ish him stop thou his Breath.

* Rex Meus for the most honored Friend/ Vide Martial, V 22. et passim.

3. o͞ur po̎or ă̋ll] The scansion-marks   *Corporal*.
emphasise the dactylic rhyme with

376. ON THE NAME "CHASTENUT GROVE", DERIVED FROM ARIOSTO

[c 1805?]

The lines were drafted, with many revisions, in Notebook 22 (*CN* II 2770), where they are introduced as follows:

> On a Gentleman's Grove was written Chastenut Grove/ I justified the Spelling by the Latin Castanea, & it reminded me of the whimsical Latin Charade of Ariosto from the original Italian of Florio Angelo Monosinio/
>
> > Arbos inest sylvis, quo scribitur octo figuris
> > Fine tribus deruptis vix unam e mille videbis/
>
> Which I imitated thus paraphrastically . . .

C may have found the charade in Ariosto *Opere in versi* (4 vols Venice 1741) IV 897, where it appears with the solution in the title *Castanea* and with the note "*Ex Italicæ Linguæ Flore Angeli Monosinii, pag.* 402"—meaning that it was taken from A. Monsinius *Flos Italicae Linguae: Libri Novem* (Venice 1604), not that Monsinius was the author. C's spelling "arbos" for "arbor" is very common; but his "quo" for "quae", which is almost certainly the reading in the ms, is ungrammatical. KC supplies the following translation: "There is a tree in the wood which is written in eight letters. Take off the last three, and you will scarcely see one in a thousand."

A few details of capitalisation and punctuation are added in the following text.

Fair Nymph of the Forest, nor fairer than good,
Sweet Wood Nymph, what art thou, I whisper'd & what is thy name,
And the Wood Nymph made answer: Thro' the whole of this wood
We're a Thousand to one all around you the same,
We've a name of eight Letters, ah! cut off the last three,   5
It's but one in a Thousand—if e'en one you should see.

Yet not, O ye nine hundred, ninety nine left
Between us & you is all Likeness bereft;
We are thrown to the Swine, save the best that are *roasted*
You belong to horn'd Cattle, the fairest being *toasted*.   10

377. ON FETID, WHO DIED OF A CATARRH

[c 1805]

The only text is a draft in Notebook 22 (*CN* II 2772), in which the first stanza is written out as here with only a few emendations, while the second is preceded by two drafts. Presumably the poem was never published because of the mild offence it might have caused.

Thee, Fetid, oft did armed Death attack,
As oft thou mad'st thy famin'd Foe draw back.
Thy Breath was dread, as Dragon's in Romance,
And carried farther than Death's missile Lance.
Ah! Whence then hear we now thy Death-bell Knelling?   5
Did Death too catch a Cold, & lose his sense of Smelling!

"Sweet Fetid dead! No!—No!" The Thought so shock'd her
His Widow would not in the House abide,
All grief-bewilder'd still she sought the Doctor—
Ere she return'd, her sweet Love putrefied—   10
And stepping o'er her Thresh-hold, wild of brain,
She sniff'd the air, then scream'd—Joy! Joy! he *breathes* again!

378. ON THE FAMILY VAULT OF THE BURRS

[c 1805?]

The title continues, in the revised version of Notebook 22 (*CN* II 2779) given here: "a notorious Lady of whose Household was the last person attacked by the Pestilence who caught the Gibraltar Fever at New York but recovered." There were severe epidemics of yellow fever in New York in the summer and autumn of 1803, and again in 1805; and in early 1805 there was an epidemic of the plague in Gibraltar, which it was feared would spread to Malta. C might have learned of Jane Burr from an American newspaper, or an American officer at this time, but no trace of her has been found in the available records. The circumstantial title which accompanies the two notebook drafts might suggest that C wrote with a particular tombstone or vault in front of him.

The first version in the notebook reads as follows (omitting revisions and supplying some punctuation):

Of all the Tombs of Victims pack'd
Close in the Church-yard, this (strange fact!)
Much grief must wake, much gladness win.
For after Jane were none attack'd—
But ah! Jane Burr is *not* within.

The yellow Fiend in Lust and Pride
Would clasp a Fury as his Bride,
And met his last Hour clasping H E R—
So of the Plague seven Thousand died,
And the Plague died of fierce Jane Burr.

This version is in some respects more coherent than the second, which is meant to supersede it. C began to rewrite the poem in three stanzas. As it is, for the RT based on the second complete version it has been necessary to borrow line 9 from the first draft, and to supply some punctuation. It is as if C lost interest in the rewriting while it proceeded.

For by that Town by Fever sack'd
Where lie Contagion's Victims pack'd
In all the Yard—This Tomb—strange Fact—
Great Grief must wane, great Joy must win.
O Joy! Jane Burr the last attacked—   5
But O Grief! Jane is *not* within.
The yellow Fiend in Lust & Pride
Would clasp a Fury as his Bride
And met his last Hour clasping H E R,
And the Plague died of fierce Jane Burr.   10

379. LINES WRITTEN IN A DREAM

[Feb–Mar 1806?]

The lines were written in Notebook 16 in 1806 (*CN* II 2799), but it is possible that they are a recollection of lines composed earlier (as is the case with the immediately preceding lines in the notebook, a version of **296** *Lines Composed*

4. C wrote "wake" in the first draft, and the "n" here could be a careless anticipation of the last letter of "win". Both readings make a kind of sense.

during a Night Ramble behind Skiddaw). On the subject of dreams cf **335** *The Pains of Sleep*; *CN* I 848, 1619 f 76ᵛ, 1649; also **160** *The Wanderings of Cain* I 17 "Has he no friend, no loving mother near?"

> I know tis but a Dream, yet feel more anguish
> Than if 'twere Truth. It has been often so,
> Must I die under it? Is no one near?
> Will no one hear these stifled groans, & wake me?

380. A SINGLE LINE ON REVENGE

[Feb–Mar 1806]

The line is written into Notebook 16 (*CN* II 2800). It might have been recollected from an earlier time—also a possibility with the two previous entries on the same page (*CN* II 2798, 2799 = **296** *Lines Composed during a Night Ramble behind Skiddaw* and **379** *Lines Written in a Dream*). It has a dramatic ring, and might perhaps suggest **146.X1** *Osorio*.

> A sumptuous and magnificent revenge.

381. LINES ON A DEATH

[Mar–Apr 1806]

The lines were written into Notebook 15 (*CN* II 2806). KC links them with *CN* II 2582 and 2926 (=**365** *A Metaphor* and **502.X3** *Remorse* (Printed) IV ii 52–65ᵀᴺ), and comments: "Possibly all are related to a germinating poem that was not written." One might also link the lines to other fragments, such as **380** *A Single Line on Revenge*, and thus to **146.X1** *Osorio*.

> He died
> In all the beauty and power of early Manhood—
> Yet with such meek surrender of his Spirit
> As quietly, as when the gliding Moon
> Glides on into a black Cloud in mid Heaven—   5

382. WRITTEN AT OSSAIA

[May 1806]

The lines were written into Notebook 15 (*CN* II 2851), where they are followed by phrases—"Dogana di Ossaia" tr "customs house at Ossaia", a frontier village between the Papal States and Tuscany, and "Una bella ragazza" tr "a pretty girl"—which suggest an occasion on which the lines were composed.

> Where micant Conchs and micanter conchoids
> Do scintillate upon the Shores of Rhodes.

383. ON DEATH AT PISA

[Jun 1806]

The lines were drafted in Notebook 15 (*CN* II 2866), where they follow at the end of a prose note which turns on thoughts of death and suicide. The entry is the last before C sailed from Livorno, towards home, his family, and friends. C's verses echo the third stanza of the Percy ballad "Waly, Waly, Love be bonny" (*Reliques of Ancient English Poetry* III 145):

> Marti'mas wind, when wilt thou blaw
> And shake the green leaves aff the tree?
> O gentle death, whan wilt thou cum?
> For of my life I am wearìe.

> Come, come, thou bleak December Wind,
> And blow the dry Leaves from the Tree!
> Flash, like a Love-thought, thro' me, Death
> And take a Life, that wearies me.

384. THE TASTE OF THE TIMES

[Aug 1806–Apr 1807]

The only known text of the poem is a transcript by JTC in his Commonplace Book, subscribed "S. T. C." It is likely that the poem was copied from a contemporary newspaper which has not been traced, and there is no reason to doubt C's authorship—unless JTC merely guessed at it. The "Ministry of All the Talents"—in which Henry Petty was Chancellor of the Exchequer at the age of 25—had taken office following the death of Pitt in Jan 1806. C arrived back in England on 17 Aug, and, if his authorship is accepted, probably wrote the poem very soon afterwards. The Ministry of All the Talents resigned on 8 Apr 1807.

The furore over the notorious boy actor Betty lasted for two years. His debut on the London stage on 1 Dec 1804 at the age of 13 spawned pamphlets and a fashion for infant wonders, which are described by Allardyce Nicoll *A History of English Drama 1660–1900* IV *Early Nineteenth Century Drama 1800–1850* (1955) 20–2. On Henry Petty, 3rd Marquis of Lansdowne (1780–1863), see *DNB*.

Some whim, or fancy pleases every age,
For talents premature 'tis now the rage.
In Music how great Handel would have smil'd
T' have seen whole crowds enraptur'd with a child.
A Garrick we have had in little Betty   5
And now we're told we have a Pitt in Petty.
All must allow, since thus it is decreed
He is a very *Petty* Pitt indeed.

385. LINES REWRITTEN FROM SPENSER'S *EPITHALAMIUM*

[c 1806–10]

C's rewriting was done in a copy of Anderson's *British Poets* which once belonged to John Wordsworth. *CM* (*CC*) I 76–80 gives details of the provenance of the copy, and prints all of C's marginalia on Spenser.

Apart from correcting a misprint in line 67, all of C's emendations are deletions. These, together with his rewriting, tend in a single direction confirmed by two marginal notes and his other comments on the poem: they all work to dissolve the carnality of Spenser's original.

(*a*) [*Epithalamium* 250–3]

Spenser's text reads as follows:

> Pour out the wine without restraint or stay,
> Pour not by cups, but by the belly-full:
> Pour out to all that wull,
> And sprinkle all the posts and walls with wine,

(*b*) [*Epithalamium* 349–52]

C deleted the following lines, which close a stanza in Spenser's poem, before rewriting them:

> Ne let th' unpleasant quire of frogs still croking
> Make us to wish their choking;
> Let none of these their drery accents sing,
> Ne let the woods them answer, nor their eccho ring.

(*c*) [*Epithalamium* 376–97]

C deleted the lines before and after this passage, and joined them with his substitution, thereby making one stanza out of two. He also rewrote line 400 ("Without blemish or stain,") as "With Bleshmish none or Stain/".

(*a*)

Brim the deep Bowls, the ample Goblets fill!
Fill out to all, that will:—

(*b*)

But only let my Voice mid our caressings
Sometimes sound forth the Blessings,
The thanks, which I from year to year shall sing,
While them my Heart shall answer & their echo ring.

(*c*)

all the night/
Thee oft the fruitful Wife invok'd of yore
To aid her Travail sore
If bless thou can'st, o bless this lovely Band,

And all thy aid for *my* Beloved store!   5
And thou, Glad Genius! &c

386. LINES ON A KING-AND-EMPEROR-MAKING EMPEROR AND KING, ALTERED FROM FULKE GREVILLE

[Aug–Sept 1806]

C's lines were published in *The Courier* (12 Sept 1806), over the signature "Civis." There the second part of the title reads "ALTERED FROM THE 93D SONNET OF FULK GREVILLE, THE FRIEND OF SIR PHILIP SIDNEY." Napoleon had abolished the Holy Roman Empire on 12 Jul, and on 25 Jul had formed the Confederation of the Rhine. Open warfare involving France and Prussia broke out on 6 Sept. Talleyrand, formerly a freethinking bishop, was his foreign minister (see *EOT—CC—*I 65n; **262** *Talleyrand to Lord Grenville*).

On his return from Malta, C had read and annotated CL's copy of *Certaine Learned and Elegant Workes of the Right Honorable Fulke, Lord Brooke* (2 pts 1633) in Aug–Sept 1806. The copy has since been lost, but see *CN* II 2918, 2920, 2921; **387** *Farewell to Love*; etc.

The text of the poem in Greville's 1633 volume (II 240) is as follows:

The *Augurs* were of all the world admir'd,
Flatter'd by Consulls, honour'd by the State,
Because the euent of all that was desir'd,
They seem'd to know, and keepe the books of Fate:
    Yet though abroad they thus did boast their wit,
    Alone among themselues they scorned it.

Mankinde, that with his wit doth gild his heart,
Strong in his Passions, but in Goodnesse weake;
Making great vices o're the lesse an Art,
Breeds wonder, and moues ignorance to speake,
    Yet when his Fame is to the highest borne,
    We know enough to laugh his praise to scorne.

The Augurs were of all the world admir'd,
    Flatter'd by Consuls, honour'd by the State,
Because the event of all that was desir'd
    They seem'd to know, and keep the books of fate;

Abroad they thus did boast each other's wit,   5
   Alone, among *themselves*, they scorned it.

Behold yon Corsican with dropsied heart,
   Strong in his passions, but in goodness weak,
Making great vices o'er the less an art,
   He wonder breeds, moves ignorance to speak.   10
Yet when his fame is to the highest borne,
   TALLEYRAND inly laughs his Creature's praise to scorn.

387. FAREWELL TO LOVE

[Aug–Sept 1806]

C's lines are modelled upon and in part borrowed from sonnet LXXXIV of Greville's *Caelica*, which appears in the 1633 *Workes* as follows (II 234):

> Farewell sweet Boy, complaine not of my truth;
> Thy Mother lou'd thee not with more deuotion;
> For to thy Boyes play I gaue all my youth,
> Yong Master, I did hope for your promotion.
>
> While some sought Honours, Princes thoughts obseruing,
> Many woo'd *Fame, the child of paine and anguish*,
> Others iudg'd inward good a chiefe deseruing,
> I in thy wanton Visions ioy'd to languish.
>
> I bow'd not to thy image for succession,
> Nor bound thy bow to shoot reformed kindnesse,
> Thy playes of hope and feare werc my concession,
> The spectacles to my life was thy blindnesse:
>   But *Cupid* now farewell, I will goe play me,
> With thoughts that please me lesse, & lesse betray me.

   C's lines were written with SH in mind, as well as Greville. And although they do not quite represent his feelings immediately following his return from Malta, the cluster of quotations from Greville in *CN* III 3709–19, at the time when SH withdrew from Allen Bank to Wales (Mar 1810), suggests that their personal applicability was more keenly understood afterwards. Lines 6–7, which C added to Greville, describe how in one mood he felt about WW (cf e.g. **374** *Latin Lines to WW as Judge* and **430** *Ad Vilmum Axiologum: Latin Version*).

   The first version of the lines was written in the margin of CL's copy of

Greville's *Workes*, and was published later in 1806 in *The Courier* and *The Morning Herald*. The text given here is from *Felix Farley's Bristol Journal* (9 Sept 1815), which appears to rest on a fresh appraisal of the ms text. C did not include it in *SL*, however, or in any of his later collections.

> Farewell, sweet LOVE! Yet blame you not my truth!
> More fondly ne'er did mother eye her child,
>   Than I your form: *your's* were my hopes of youth,
> And as *you* shap'd my thoughts, I sigh'd or smil'd.
>
> While most were wooing wealth, or gaily swerving   5
> To Pleasure's secret haunts; and some apart
>   Stood strong in pride, self-conscious of deserving;
> To YOU *I* gave my whole weak wishing heart.
>
> And when I met the maid, that realiz'd
> Your fair creations, and had won her kindness;   10
>   Say, but for her if aught on earth I priz'd!
> *Your* dreams alone I dreamt, and caught your blindness.
>
> O grief!—but farewell LOVE! I will go play me
> With thoughts that please me less, and less betray me!

388. TIME, REAL AND IMAGINARY:
AN ALLEGORY

[1806–7? 1811?]

C consistently claimed that the lines were a juvenile production, a "school-boy poem", although all the extant versions belong to a much later period. The first of these, in *SH's Poets* (written and transcribed in the winter of 1806–7?), opens with a 14-line preamble, subsequently dropped, which repeats the claim in a form close to descriptions of C's time at Christ's Hospital:

> In the great City rear'd, my fancy rude
> By natural Forms unnurs'd & unsubdued,
> An Alien from the Rivers & the Fields
> And all the Charms, that Hill or Woodland yields,
> It was the pride & passion of my Youth

T' impersonate & color moral Truth
Rare Allegories in those Days I spun,
That oft had mystic senses oft'ner none.
Of all Resemblances however faint,
So dear a Lover was I, that with quaint
Figures fantastically grouped I made
Of commonest Thoughts a moving Masquerade.
'Twas then I fram'd this obscure uncouth Rhyme,
A sort of Emblem 'tis of HOPE & TIME.

Cf WW *Prelude* (1805) II 466–79, VI 274–84; CL *Christ's Hospital Five-and-twenty Years Ago*; **171** *Frost at Midnight*; **289** *Letter to* —— ; etc. At the same time, the form of the central emblem in all extant versions of the lines appears to derive from a later period, when "Hope is long dead to me".

A notebook entry of Jan 1811 (*CN* III 4048), which is likely to have prefaced a version of the lines as we now have them, supplies a helpful gloss:

Contrast of troubled manhood, and joyously-active youth, in the sense of Time. To the former ~~it~~ Time, like the Sun in a ~~cloudl~~ empty Sky is never seen to move, but only to *have moved*—there, there it was—& now tis here—now distant—yet all a blank between/ To the latter it is as the full moon in a fine breezy October night—driving on amid Clouds of all shapes & hues & kindling shifting colors, like an Ostrich in its speed—& yet seems not to have moved at all—This I feel to be a just image of time real & time as felt, in two different states of Being—The Title of the Poem therefore (for Poem it ought to be) should be Time real, and Time felt (in the sense of Time) in Active Youth/ or Activity and Hope & fullness of aim in any period/ and in despondent objectless Manhood—Time *objective* & subjective—

C's comment in the Preface to *SL* (p iii) has a slightly different emphasis:

By imaginary Time, I meant the state of a school boy's mind when on his return to school he projects his being in his day dreams, and lives in his next holidays, six months hence: and this I contrasted with real Time.

Analogies to the distinction between two sorts of time extend from the Greek distinction between χρόνος and καιρός to Samuel Beckett's *Whoroscope* and beyond—Renaissance treatments, in particular, assuming such emblematic-allegorical form. There are parallels between C's treatment here and other poems in which he was involved c 1811–12 (see *CN* III 4073 f 146^{r-v}=**478** *Limbo*). At the same time, C's comments in the notebook entry and Preface obscure as much as they illuminate the subject of the poem, by displacing attention on to its figuration.

Besides the 14-line preamble quoted above, there are few differences between the single ms version and the text published in *SL* and C's three subsequent collections. The present text reproduces *SL* (1817).

On the wide level of a mountain's head,
(I knew not where, but 'twas some faery place)
Their pinions, ostrich-like for sails outspread,
Two lovely children run an endless race,
    A sister and a brother!   5
    This far outstript the other;
Yet ever runs she with reverted face,
And looks and listens for the boy behind:
    For he, alas! is blind!
O'er rough and smooth, with even step he pass'd,   10
And knows not whether he be first or last.

389. TWO EPIGRAMS ON PITT AND FOX

[Sept 1806; Mar 1807]

The first epigram was published in *M Post* (26 Sept 1806). The second appears in JTC's Commonplace Book, unsigned, and was published in James Sayers's satirical anthology *All the Talents' Garland* (1807) 52 and *M Post* (31 Mar 1807). It was also republished in *The Oracle* (7 Apr 1807), with two additional lines which it is claimed were "malignantly and unfairly" omitted at the close:

    Yet Mourn not, BRITAIN—JENKY's *left behind*;
    And Old GEORGE ROSE *remains*—to save *Mankind*!

Neither epigram was ever claimed by C, and his authorship is very much open to question.

Charles James Fox died on 13 Sept 1806; William Pitt the Younger had died on 23 Jan of the same year. Poem (*a*) and the shorter forms of (*b*) more carefully praise Pitt at the expense of Fox. The extended form of (*b*) overrides this theme to become a topical comment on the newly formed Portland ministry. George Rose Sr (1744–1818) had been Pitt's manager of the press and of elections; Robert Banks Jenkinson, Lord Hawkesbury and later 2nd Earl of Liverpool (1770–1828), had been home secretary in Pitt's last ministry (1804–6) and occupied the same office again in Mar 1807, under Portland. Old Rose and Jenky had the reputation of being the most astute and powerful managers of the Pittite interest.

The supposition that C was the author of poem (*a*) is prompted by his letter to Daniel Stuart of 15 Sept 1806, in which he says that he intends to answer the *M Chron*'s assertions "that Mr Fox was the greatest & wisest Statesman/ that Mr Pitt was no Statesman—/ I shall endeavor to shew, that both were undeserving of that high character; but that Mr Pitt was the better/ that the evils, which befel him, were undoubtedly produced in great measure, by blunders and wickedness on the continent, which it was almost impossible to foresee/ while the effects of Mr Fox's measures must in and of themselves produce calamity and degradation" (*CL* II 1179). C's authorship of the shorter form of poem (*b*) is also, of course, compatible with the same stated aim, and might appear to be confirmed by JTC's transcription. Poem (*b*) was first published as C's by Bertram Dobell in *The Athenaeum* 6 Jan 1904, and was collected, along with (*a*), in *PW* (EHC) II 970–1 No 63.

But there are also points to be made against C's authorship. With reference to poem (*a*), against the circumstantial evidence of the letter must be set the fact that C was connected at the time not with *M Post* but with *The Courier*. EHC's argument—that the initials STC are concealed in "Sense and Truth unClue" in line 3—is weakened because the *M Post* text does not in fact employ these capitals. With reference to poem (*b*), its presence in JTC's Commonplace Book is inconclusive: if JTC knew that the lines were C's, why did he not initial them so? The coincidences between JTC's transcript and James Sayers's version can be argued either way, to strengthen or to diminish the likelihood of C's authorship. Again, given the anti-*M Post* and pro-Pittite connection of *The Oracle*, the claim that Stuart deliberately omitted lines 5–6 probably represents a mischievous inversion or modification of the original, rather than a restoration of omitted lines.

Even if C wrote one poem, it is open to question whether he also wrote the other. (*a*) was the poem to which Byron wrote a reply, "for insertion in the *Morning Chronicle*": see Lord Byron *The Complete Poetical Works* ed Jerome J. McGann (7 vols Oxford 1980–93) I 42. On internal grounds, this is the more likely to be C's. He might have placed it with the *M Post* because he felt some embarrassment about the judgment it publicly expressed, or again for the very reasons that might make a reader sense that the text does not have the feel of one of C's compositions. Either way, C expressed views on Fox's death in private which were at odds with what he said in public. He wrote on a leaf used in his fragmentary introduction to Greek grammar (*SW&F—CC—*196): "Sheridanus vi[. . .] I Populus A[. . .]us mortuum I Foxium, Sheridanum desiderat" tr (probably) "Long live Sheridan! The English people long for Fox, who has died, and for Sheridan". Compare his embarrassment over his uncharitable portrayal of the recently dead Burke in **145** *The Raven*.

(*a*) *Impromptu on the Different Sensations*
Produced in France, by the Death of
Two Late Public Characters

Our Nation's Foes lament on FOX's death,
But bless the hour when PITT resign'd his breath.
These feelings wide let sense and truth unclue:
We give the palm where Justice points it due.

(*b*) *On Pitt and Fox*

Britannia's boast, her glory and her pride,
Pitt in his Country's Service liv'd and died.
At length resolv'd, what Pitt had done, to do;
For once to serve his Country, Fox died too.

390. ADAPTED FROM FULKE GREVILLE'S *ALAHAM*

[Oct–Nov 1806]

C's lines are given here as they appear in a notebook entry (*CN* II 2921), with the addition of capital letters at the start of some lines, and omitting cancellations. Punctuation and metre have not been regularised.

C's lines follow on a passage of prose in the same notebook entry:

A bodiless Substance, an unborrow'd Self, God in God immanent, the eternal Word, That goes forth yet remains, Crescent and Full, and Wanes. Yet ever ~~one~~ entire and one/—At the same time ⟨it dawns & sets & crowns the Height of Heaven⟩ the dawning, setting Son, at the same time the Tenant of each Sign Thro' all the zodiac/ ~~Yet~~ While each in it's own Hour Boasts & beholds ~~the~~ exclusive Presence, ~~the~~ a Peculiar Orb. Each the great Traveller's Inn/ Yet still the unmoving Sun—Great genial agent on all finite Souls, And by that action ~~cloathes itself with~~ puts on finiteness absolute Infinite whose dazzling robe Flows in rich folds & plays in shooting Hues of infinite Finiteness.

The entry as a whole is one of several which derive from C's reading in *Certaine Learned and Elegant Workes of the Right Honourable Fulke, Lord Brooke* (1633). What C wrote was suggested by the first chorus of spirits in *Alaham*, in *Workes* II 20–2:

And what is that but Man? A crazed soule, vnfix'd;
Made good, yet fall'n, not to extremes; but to a meane betwixt:
Where (like a cloud) with windes he toss'd is here, and there,
We kindling good hope in his flesh; they quenching it with feare.
We with our abstract formes, and substance bodilesse,
Image by glaunces into him our glories, their distresse,
And in prospectiue Maps make ille farre off appeare,
Lest it should worke with too great power, when it approacheth neare.
Beauties againe of *Truth* (which those ill spirits conceale)
With *Optike* glasses we reflect on man to kindle zeale.

But whether idle man, exceeding orders frame,
(As out of heauen justly cast) must *Vulcan*-like goe lame;
Or that those euill spirits so dazle humane eyes,
As they thinke foule forbidden things more beautifull, more wise;
Wee see, though they want power to change our reall frame,
Yet in the world they striue to gaine by changing of our name:
Calling the Goodnesse, weake; . . .
So while the o'reswoll'n pride of this *Mahumetan*,
By wounding of his Princely race, playes false with God and man;
He in it doth disperse those clouds of reuerence,
Which betweene man, and Monarchs Seate keep sweet intelligence;
And while he would be lord of order, nature, right,
Brings in disorder, that deuouring enemy of might,
Which with her many hands unweaues what time had wrought,
And proues, what power obtaines by wrong, is euer dearly bought.

      Bright clouds of reverence sufferably bright
      That intercept the dazzle not the Light
      That veil the finite form, the boundless power reveal
      Itself an earthly sun, of pure intensest White,
      Adorn the sky—and what might be   5
      Disregard by borrowed Beauty swells
      To Honor without form/ & what might be idolatry,
      Makes spiritual worship—
      Satisfies the mind's & eyes' necessity
      With form, a form that all informs against   10
      Itself, grateful proclaims it's limited Honors whence
      As silence too deep disturbs, tumultuates
      Distracts the mind that fain would feed itself
      By awe, Some gentle Sound, Huge forests'
      Whispers voyaging from far or musical   15
      Murmur of the distant ocean Preserves
      The inner silence, makes it fruitful,
      Like prattling rill that trills down to
      The roots, the dark & voiceless Parent
      Of the Tree, Its waving Branches, &   20
      Its fluttering Leaves, Sweet undersong
      And hospitable Bower, and dear Repast
      Of hymning Birds—On ceremonies for Religion—
      Especially, the Cherubim &c of the Jewish Temple—

391. MORE LINES INSPIRED BY FULKE GREVILLE

[Oct–Nov 1806]

The two lines are given here as they appear in Notebook 16 (*CN* II 2924). There they are surrounded by excerpts from Greville's play *Alaham*, which deals with themes compatible with those broached here. KC suggests that they are a reworking in Greville's manner of the feelings contained in a prose note earlier on the same page (*CN* II 2922).

> And sad experience saw your Treachery,
> Yet saw not half for the Tears that bedimmed her eyes//

392. INSPIRED BY FULKE GREVILLE'S *ALAHAM*

[Oct–Nov 1806]

C's lines were drafted in Notebook 15 (*CN* II 2932), and, although he quoted them in a letter to TP, were never published. The idea of spurring his Pegasus to "tortoise Gallop" was an old one (*CN* I 94 etc), but the immediate occasion was his reading of the following in Greville's *Alaham* IV i, in *Certaine Learned and Elegant Workes of the Right Honourable Fulke, Lord Brooke* (1633) II 60:

> *Celica*! Call vp the dead; awake the blinde;
> Turne backe the time; bid windes tell whence they come;
> As vainly strength speakes to a broken minde.
> Fly from me *Celica*! hate all I doe: . . .

In the first version in the notebook C had a different first line: "Bid winds tell whence they come, & turn them back—".

> Let Eagles bid the Tortoise sunward soar—
> As vainly Strength speaks to a broken mind.

393. A GREEK SONG SET TO MUSIC AND SUNG BY HARTLEY COLERIDGE, ESQ^{RE}., GRECOLOGIAN, PHILOMETRIST, AND PHILOMELIST

[Nov 1806]

C rejoined his family at Keswick on 30 Oct (see *CL* II 1199n: to the Wordsworths [c 19 Nov 1806]). He gave HC a "Notebook for his Greek Exercises" on 4 Nov 1806, and HC copied the Greek alphabet on the second page and the present lines on the third. The text of C's "A Greek Grammar" follows on the fourth page (*SW&F—CC*—160). The version of the lines given here is in C's hand, copied in clear, large letters, as if to be framed or pinned on a nursery wall. It is unclear which version has priority, that is, whether HC's was recollected or copied from one by C, or whether C's tidied-up one by HC or was taken down from dictation.

It should be noted that the letters sigma, upsilon, and omega are given places out of their usual sequence, perhaps for the sake of the rhythm and rhyme (Rho~Tau, Phi~Psi). It may be wondered why C should trouble to invent such a mnemonic, since traditional versions were presumably available which maintained the letters in their usual sequence—e.g. *"This is Greek, and how they spelt her"*. The explanation might lie in the title. C may have written down and regularised a version which HC had arrived at for himself in his absence, so that the present song should be considered a "collaboration" and/or a family joke.

DC gave the text of this Greek alphabet in the memoir prefixed to his edition of HC's *Poems* (2 vols 1851) I xxx, suggesting that the "rhythmical enumeration of their names . . . may serve for other very juvenile Grecians, as it served for us". He shows no awareness of an "authorship problem", or of the existence of other mnemonics. Nor, in spite of having been master of Helston Grammar School for sixteen years, is he worried about the disruption to the alphabetic order.

1

Alpha, Beta   A. B.
    Gamma, Delta: Γ. Δ.
Epsilon, Zeta, with Eeta, and Theta,   E. Z. H. Θ.
Iota, and Kappa, and Lamda, and Mu   I. K. Λ. M.

2

Nu, Xi,	N. Ξ.	5
Omicron, Pi.	O. Π.	
Sigma, Rho, Upsilon, Tau—	Σ. P. Y T.	
Omega, and Phi,	Ω. Φ.	
And Chi, and Psi—	X. Ψ.	

I have sung the whole Alphabet, twenty four,   10
And he fibs or he blunders, who says there are more.

394. VERSES TO DERWENT COLERIDGE, ACCOMPANYING GREEK LESSONS

[Dec 1806]

The verses are written at intervals in a brief and fragmentary introduction to Greek grammar, now at VCL (*SW&F—CC*—198). C had begun teaching HC Greek, and in Nov 1806 wrote a grammar for him in the special notebook which opens with **393** *A Greek Song Set to Music*. He was no doubt conscious that the 6-year-old DC might feel left out, and the present lessons and verses should be read in the same way as **395** *A Lesson on Metrical Feet*. DC commented on the way he and his brother learned Greek in the memoir given in *Poems by Hartley Coleridge* (2 vols 1851) I xxix–xxx.

It was at first intended that DC should accompany C and HC to Coleorton (*CL* II 1200: to the Wordsworths [c 19 Nov 1806]; 1203: to the Wordsworths [c 3 Dec 1806]; *WL—M* rev—I 101, 107), although, as it turned out, DC did not do so. It is probable that the ms was left behind at Greta Hall when C left, since C, having arrived at Coleorton on 21 Dec (Reed II 343), makes it clear in a letter dated 7 Feb 1807 (*CL* III 2–3: to DC) that DC already had more material on Greek grammar than this, and promises to send still more. The references to food in both sets of verses reflect another of DC's keen interests at the time.

(*a*)

These 7 or 8 Pages let **Derwent** read over:
He will find it the Gate to a whole Field of Clover:
Where his Soul may feed nicely, till the Table is put on
A Dish for his Body of Beef or of Mutton.—

(*b*)

My fattest Darl, Derwent, whom I almost dote on,
In the morning as soon as the Maid's put your coat on;
Read the pages inclos'd seven times for the Day,
Remember too all that you can; then away
To the Trees or the Woodhouse to see-saw, or sway   5
With Hartley & Sara to talk & to play.
My Son, as your Father, for you I'm concerned:
I TRUST, you'll be *good*; and I *hope*, you'll be *learned!*—

395. TO DERWENT COLERIDGE: THE CHIEF AND MOST COMMON METRICAL FEET EXPRESSED IN CORRESPONDING METRE

[Dec 1806–Mar 1807]

When C sent the lines to DC from Coleorton, he added the date 3 Mar 1807. EHC says none the less: "The metrical lesson was begun for Hartley Coleridge in 1806 and, afterwards, finished or adapted for the use of his brother Derwent" (*PW*—EHC—I 401n). This may be so: C took HC's study of Greek in hand when he arrived back in Keswick at the end of Oct 1806 (see **393** *A Greek Song Set to Music*), and the two of them had been together at Coleorton since 21 Dec 1806 (Reed II 343). C seems to have begun to teach Greek to DC in a similar way at the same time (see **394** *Verses Accompanying Greek Lessons*; *CL* III 1–3: to DC 7 Feb 1807). *SW&F* (*CC*) 201–6 publishes three fragments on English prosody with lists of the feet as exemplified in English words. Probably they are roughly contemporary with this poem, two leaves being watermarked 1804 and 1805, and they have much in common with C's accounts of the relations between English, German, and classical prosody (for which see e.g. the headnotes to **185** *English Hexameters*, **216** *Mahomet*, **257** *Hymn to the Earth*).

The lines are given here with the metrical markings as they appear in the letter, the feet to the left of lines 1–3 and, in part, lines 4–7, 9 being supplied conjecturally (the ms is torn). When the lines were printed in *PW* (1834), there were some slight changes in the display of the scansion, and line 7 "two" was corrected to "one".

– ᴗ   TRŌCHĔE | trīps frŏm | lōng tŏ | short:
ᴗ –   Frŏm lōng | tŏ lōng | ĭn sōllĕmn sōrt

Slōw Spōndĕē stālks—strōng Fŏot! yet ill-able

Ĕvĕr tŏ l cōme ŭp wĭth l Dāctȳl trĭlsyllable.

Ĭāmbĭcs mārch frŏm shōrt tŏ lōng: 5

Wĭth ă Leāp l ănd ă Bōund the swift Anapests throng!

One Syllable long, with two short at each side,

Ămphībrălchȳs hāstes wĭth l ă stātelȳ l Stride.

Fīrst ănd Lāst l bēĭng lōng, l Mīddlĕ shōrt l Āmphĭmācer

Strīkes hĭs thūnldērĭng Hōofs, l līke ă prōud l hīgh-brĕd Rācer.   10

If Derwent be innocent, steady, and wise,

And delight in the Things of Earth, Waters, and Skies;

Tender Warmth at his Heart, with these metres to shew it,

With sound Sense in his Brains, may make Derwent a Poet!

May crown him with Fame, and *must* win him the Love   15

Of his Father on earth, and his Father above.

My dear dear Child!

Could you stand upon Skiddaw, you would not from it's whole
Ridge

See a man who so loves you, as your fond S. T. Coleridge.

396. THE BLOSSOMING OF
THE SOLITARY DATE-TREE

[1807–8? 1802–4?]

The last three stanzas are a loose paraphrase from a collection of medieval German love poetry which C borrowed from the Göttingen library and read with "sedulous accuracy" (*Göttingen LB* No 2; *BL* ch 10—*CC*—I 209; and see *WL—E* rev—235). The imitation was printed in *The New Times* (31 Jan 1818) and there stated to have been introduced into C's lecture on the Middle Ages, the second of the series. Although he did not have time to include all the translations he intended to use, there is no reason to doubt that he used this one. See *Lects 1808–1819 (CC)* II 66–8, 77–8. The original poem by Johans Hadloub reads as follows in *Sammlung von Minnesingern aus dem schwäbischen Zeitpuncte* (2 vols Zurich 1758–9) II 185–97 at 187B–188A:

Ach ich sach si triuten vvol ein kindelin
Davon vvart min Muot liebes irmant
Si umbevieng es unde truchte es nahe an sich
Davon dacht ich Lieblich ze hant

Si nam sin antliute in ir hende vvis
Und truchte es an ir munt
Ir vvengel clar O vve so gar Wol kuste sit

Es tet ouch zvvar als ich hete getan
Ich sach umbvan Es ouch si do
Es tet recht als es enzstuende ir vvunnen sich
Des duchte mich Es vvas so fro
Don mochte ich es nicht ane nit verlan
Ich gidachte o vve vvere ich das kindelin
Unz das si sin vvil minne han

Ich nam vvar do das kindelin erst kam von ir
Ich nams zuo mir Lieblich ouch do
Es duchte mich so guot vvan sis ê druchte an sich
Davon vvart ich Sin gar so fro
Ich umbevieng es vvan si es ê schone umbevie
Und kusts an die stat swa es von ir kiusset ê was
Was mir doch das Ze herzen gie.

C's full five-stanza poem as given here may date from the period 1802–4, the "Sweet Friend" being of course SH, the "Sweet Babes" and "Bookroom Window" at Greta Hall, showing "a Heaven on Earth" that was much on his mind between Apr and Oct 1802 especially. Or it may date from 1807–8, from the time of C's renewed intimacy with WW, who so obviously stood like a god alone, and the Morgans, the "Sweet Friend" in this case merging also with Charlotte Brent.

The poem was never printed in the form given here. Instead it was included in C's last three collections with an apologetic preface and three new stanzas to replace the first two given here, the first two of the new stanzas being in prose summary form and the third in ten verse-lines. These appear in *PW* (1829), the last text to include minor improvements:

I seem to have an indistinct recollection of having read either in one of the ponderous tomes of George of Venice,[1] or in some other compilation from the uninspired Hebrew Writers, an Apologue or Rabbinical Tradition to the following purpose:

While our first parents stood before their offended Maker, and the last words of the sentence were yet sounding in Adam's ear, the guileful false serpent, a counterfeit and a usurper from the beginning, presumptuously took on himself the character of advocate or mediator, and pretending to intercede for Adam, exclaimed: "Nay, Lord, in thy justice, not so! for the Man was the least in fault. Rather let the Woman return at once to the

---

[1] Referring to Franciscus Georgius (1460–1540), "the Hammer of Heretics": see *CN* III 4152. A more likely source is the "inspired Hebrew Writer" T. Tanith, translated by Hyman Hurwitz in *Hebrew Tales* (1826) 93–4. Even so, C's dependence on his source is loose.

dust, and let Adam remain in this thy Paradise." And the word of the Most High answered Satan: *"The tender mercies of the wicked are cruel.* Treacherous Fiend! if with guilt like thine, it had been possible for thee to have the heart of a Man, and to feel the yearning of a human soul for its counterpart, the sentence, which thou now counsellest, should have been inflicted on thyself."

The title of the following poem was suggested by a fact mentioned by Linnæus,[2] of a Date-tree in a nobleman's garden which year after year had put forth a full show of blossoms, but never produced fruit, till a branch from a Date-tree had been conveyed from a distance of some hundred leagues. The first leaf of the MS. from which the poem has been transcribed, and which contained the two or three introductory stanzas, is wanting: and the author has in vain taxed his memory to repair the loss. But a rude draught of the poem contains the substance of the stanzas, and the reader is requested to receive it as the substitute. It is not impossible, that some congenial spirit, whose years do not exceed those of the author, at the time the poem was written, may find a pleasure in restoring the Lament to its original integrity by a reduction of the thoughts to the requisite Metre.

S. T. C.

[2] The ultimate source of the anecdote C refers to is not a work by Linnaeus but a paper by Johann Gottlieb Gleditsch (1714–86), "Essai d'une fécondation artificielle, fait sur l'espèce Palmier, qu'on nomme Palma dactylifera folio flabelliformi", in *Histoire de l'académie royale des sciences et belles lettres de Berlin année 1749* (Berlin 1751) 103–8. Gleditsch, who had charge of the Berlin botanic garden, found that the female plant of the dwarf Mediterranean palm, *Chamaerops humilis*, never produced any fruit during the fifteen years he had observed her there, and the gardener asserted that she had never fruited. There was, however, a male plant in Leipzig in the garden of Caspar Bose. It took nine days in 1749 to bring a pollen-bearing inflorescence from Leipzig, but the scattering of pollen on the Berlin plant ended her eighty years or so of involuntary virginity and she ripened fruit during the winter. Seeds germinated in 1750. The anecdote could have descended to C via Gottlieb Kölreuter (1733–1806), and could have descended to C from him or several other sources—possibly (given the misascription) through the bald account given by James Edward Smith in *A Dissertation on the Sexes of Plants, Translated from the Latin of Linnaeus* (1786) 51 (Smith, an English botanist, is referred to along with other followers of Linnaeus in *Friend—CC—*ı 468–9). If this is the case, the modifications of the anecdote are likely to be C's own, his awareness of the metaphorical implications of Linnaeus having been heightened by his reading of Erasmus Darwin: cf *The Botanic Garden* ıı iv 328fn, on the fig-tree.

THE BLOSSOMING OF THE SOLITARY DATE-TREE

A LAMENT.

1.

Beneath the blaze of a tropical sun the mountain peaks are the Thrones of Frost, through the absence of objects to reflect the rays. "What no one with us shares, seems scarce our own." The presence of a ONE,

> The best belov'd, who loveth me the best,

is for the heart, what the supporting air from within is for the hollow globe with its suspended car. Deprive it of this, and all without, that would have buoyed it aloft even to the seat of the gods, becomes a burthen and crushes it into flatness.

2.

The finer the sense for the beautiful and the lovely, and the fairer and lovelier the object presented to the sense; the more exquisite the individual's capacity of joy, and the more ample his means and opportunities of enjoyment, the more heavily will he feel the ache of solitariness, the more unsubstantial becomes the feast spread around him. What matters it, whether in fact the viands and the ministering graces are shadowy or real, to him who has not hand to grasp nor arms to embrace them?

3.

> Imagination; honourable Aims;
> Free Commune with the choir that cannot die;
> Science and Song; Delight in little things,
> The buoyant child surviving in the man;
> Fields, forests, ancient mountains, ocean, sky,
> With all their voices—O dare I accuse
> My earthly lot as guilty of my spleen,
> Or call my destiny niggard! O no! no!
> It is her largeness, and her overflow,
> Which being incomplete, disquieteth me so!

The five-stanza version given here is from a ms at the Pforzheimer Library. The title was torn away from the ms, and is perhaps unlikely to have been the one given here, which is borrowed from *PW* (1828, 1829, 1834). For a comparable instance where C added an apologetic preface as a means of framing something written a good deal earlier see **178** *Kubla Khan*.

Hard is my Lot, a Life of stifled Pain!
And oft to thee do I bewail my Doom/
Yet think not thou that loving to complain
I nurse sick fancies and distemper'd Gloom,
A man diseas'd in nature! O no! no!   5
It is Joy's greatness and it's overflow
Which, being incompleat, disquieteth me so!

I am not a God, that I should stand alone,
And having all, but Love, I want the Whole;
The Organ, that makes outward Bliss our own,   10
The Door, that lets it in upon the Soul!
Sweet Babes make beautiful my Parlour Hearth,
My Bookroom Windows shew a Heaven on Earth;
And I have a Heart attun'd alike to Joy or Mirth!

But even as the Gladness stirs my Heart,   15
All timorously beginning to rejoice,
Like a blind Arab, that from sleep doth start
In lonesome Tent, I listen for *thy* Voice—
Beloved! 'tis not thine! Thou art not there!
Then melts the Bubble into idle Air,   20
And wishing without Hope I restlessly despair!

A Mother with anticipating Glee
Laughs o'er the Child, that standing at her Chair
And couching his round cheek upon her knee
Looks up, and doth his rosy mouth prepare   25
To ape her coming words: at that sweet sight
She hears her own Voice with a new delight;
And when the Babe at length relisps the Song aright,

15–35. For another, contemporary version of the same German stanzas on which C's are based see *Lays of the Minnesingers or German Troubadours* ed Edgar Taylor (1825) 195 q *Ed Rev* XLIII (Nov 1825) 118.

17. The Arab figure recurs in C's writing: see e.g. *CL* II 810: to W. Sotheby 13 Jul 1802 ; *CN* I 1244; **688** *Love's Apparition and Evanishment*; also **492.X2** *Diadestè*. In 1800 he had inscribed a copy of *Sonnets from Various Authors* to SH as "Asahara, the Moorish Maid" (annex C 4.2).

Then is she tenfold gladder than before!
But should Mischance or Death her Darling take,   30
What then avail those songs, which sweet, of yore,
Were only sweet for their sweet Echo's sake?—
—Sweet Friend! no Prattler at a Mother's Knee
Was e'er so deeply priz'd, as I prize Thee:
Why was I made for Love, yet Love denied to Me!   35

397. LINES WRITTEN IN NOVEMBER–DECEMBER 1806

[Nov–Dec 1806]

The lines are squeezed into a narrow space in Notebook 11 (*CN* II 2951 var), with some cancellation at the beginning and some reworking throughout. They read as if they were part of a larger composition. Perhaps they are connected with **176** *Christabel*, which C took up again at about this time. The central image anticipates *The White Doe of Rylstone* (*WPW* III 281–340), which WW began following in the winter spent with C at Coleorton.

As the shy Hind, the soft-eyed gentle Brute,
Now moves, now stops, approaching by degrees
At length emerges from the sheltring Trees,
Lur'd by her Hunter with the shepherd's Flute
Whose music travelling on the twilight Breeze   5
When all beside was mute,
She oft had heard unharm'd & *ever* loves to hear,
She, fearful Beast! but that no Sound of Fear.

35. C quotes and glosses the line in *CL* IV 907: to an unknown correspondent 8 Jan 1819; v 216: to T. Allsop [1 Mar 1822]; see also *C&SH* 108.

398. WRITTEN AT COLEORTON

[Dec 1806]

C wrote the lines into Notebook 11 (*CN* II 2958). Cf **399** *"Those eyes of deep & most expressive blue"*.

> —To me the opening of thy bright blue eye
> Suffused with Light on every object nigh,
> And shed a kind of Life.—

399. "THOSE EYES OF DEEP & MOST EXPRESSIVE BLUE"

[Before Dec 1806?]

The only known version of the lines appears, unsigned, in the hand of JG's former assistant, J.H.B. Williams, in J.M.?B.'s notebook album. The context in which they were transcribed, as well as their style, suggests that they might be by C. At the same time, an unsigned epigram which immediately precedes them is by Samuel Rogers, and the authorship of the present lines cannot be proved on the available evidence.

While the transcript into the album is likely to have been made c 1832, the lines, if they are by C, might date from any time between 1804 and 1806. Cf **398** *Written at Coleorton*. Such striking blue eyes belonged to the women of C's poetry, like Christabel, rather than of his real-life acquaintance (SH, DW, Mrs C). Cf also **271** *A Stranger Minstrel* 24–5.

> Those eyes of deep & most expressive blue
> Came between him & his midnight dreams
> Oftener than any other eyes he ever knew.

400. A LINE WRITTEN AT COLEORTON

[Dec 1806–Feb 1807]

The line is written into Notebook 11 (*CN* II 2977), and is not certainly by C. He had recorded on the previous leaf a crucial moment in the history of his jealous fears of SH's intimacy with WW, and an unexplained entry intervenes.

And the free Light may triumph in our faces—

401. TO WILLIAM WORDSWORTH, COMPOSED ON THE NIGHT AFTER HIS RECITATION OF A POEM ON THE GROWTH OF AN INDIVIDUAL MIND

[Jan 1807]

The occasion of C's poem was the reading aloud, on a succession of evenings after Christmas 1806 at Coleorton, of the whole of WW's "poem to Coleridge", later named *The Prelude*. C had been familiar with the five-book version since the time he left for Malta in Mar 1804, but had seen nothing of the expanded version before the reading of 1806–7. His tribute lays particular stress on WW's French experiences in 1791–2, introduced into book IX, as well as on his developing sense of estrangement from the others in the circle round the Coleorton fire (DW, MW, SH). His annotations soon afterwards to the duplicate fair copy known as MS B (DCL MS 53) are confined to the second half of book VI—as he said, "for the deadening of a too strong feeling, which the personal Passages, so exquisitely beautiful, had excited" (*Prelude* p 559 (Notes); and see Moorman *William Wordsworth* II 89–92). The personal level of C's response appears to have been different from what WW hoped: C's spirits were not lifted and WW's work on *The Recluse* was not helped forward. When *The Excursion* was published in 1814, along with the prospectus to *The Recluse*, the main philosophical section of the poem had hardly been begun.

C quoted from his tribute in the 1809 *Friend* and in *BL* as part of his argument that WW's greatness could only find expression in a philosophical poem on man, nature, and society. Publication of the whole tribute in *SL* called further attention to something known up until then only to members of the Wordsworth circle, and at the same time put pressure on WW to realise an ambition that was

as much C's as WW's own. WW's resistance to the publication of C's tribute is
therefore understandable. C's poem celebrated a specific, semi-private occasion,
yet it should be compared with other, more private thoughts he entertained about
his friend (e.g. **374** *Latin Lines to WW as Judge* and **430** *Ad Vilmum Axiologum:
Latin Version*), and with other poems which engage in a dialogue with WW less
directly (e.g. **301** *Hymn before Sun-rise*).

One of the two known mss was in WW's possession and the other in Lady
Beaumont's when the poem was published, so that differences between the ms
and printed texts may be due to the vagaries of C's memory. It was included
with successive small revisions in *PW* (1828, 1829), and *PW* (1834) publicly
introduced WW's name into the title (as given here) for the first time. The
version reproduced below is that of *PW* (1829).

       Friend of the Wise! and Teacher of the Good!
       Into my heart have I received that Lay
       More than historic, that prophetic Lay
       Wherein (high theme by thee first sung aright)
       Of the foundations and the building up   5
       Of a Human Spirit thou has dared to tell
       What may be told, to the understanding mind
       Revealable; and what within the mind
       By vital Breathings secret as the soul
       Of vernal growth, oft quickens in the Heart   10
       Thoughts all too deep for words!—

                          Theme hard as high!
       Of smiles spontaneous, and mysterious fears
       (The first-born they of Reason and twin-birth)
       Of tides obedient to external force,
       And currents self-determined, as might seem,   15
       Or by some inner Power; of moments awful,
       Now in thy inner life, and now abroad,
       When Power streamed from thee, and thy soul received
       The light reflected, as a light bestowed—
       Of Fancies fair, and milder hours of youth,   20
       Hyblean murmurs of Poetic Thought
       Industrious in its Joy, in Vales and Glens
       Native or outland, Lakes and famous Hills!

    21. Hyblean] Hybla was a city and
mountain in Sicily, famous for its honey. The allusion is appropriately
conventional.

Or on the lonely High-road, when the Stars
Were rising; or by secret Mountain-streams,   25
The Guides and the Companions of thy way!

   Of more than Fancy, of the Social Sense
Distending wide, and Man beloved as Man,
Where France in all her Towns lay vibrating
Like some becalmed Bark beneath the burst   30
Of Heaven's immediate Thunder, when no cloud
Is visible, or shadow on the Main.
For thou wert there, thine own brows garlanded,
Amid the tremor of a realm aglow,
Amid a mighty nation jubilant,   35
When from the general Heart of Human kind
Hope sprang forth like a full-born Deity!
—Of that dear Hope afflicted and struck down,
So summoned homeward, thenceforth calm and sure
From the dread Watch-Tower of man's absolute Self,   40
With light unwaning on her eyes, to look
Far on—herself a glory to behold,
The Angel of the vision! Then (last strain)
Of Duty, chosen Laws controlling choice,
Action and Joy!—An orphic song indeed,   45
A song divine of high and passionate thoughts,
To their own Music chaunted!

                   O great Bard!
Ere yet that last strain dying awed the air,
With stedfast eye I viewed thee in the choir
Of ever-enduring men. The truly Great   50
Have all one age, and from one visible space
Shed influence! They, both in power and act,
Are permanent, and Time is not with *them*,
Save as it worketh *for* them, not *in* it.
Nor less a sacred Roll, than those of old,   55

43. The Angel of the vision] Possibly an allusion to "the great vision of the guarded mount" in *Lycidas* 161.

50–4. C's phrasing echoes *The Prelude* (1805–6) x 968–70; and the same idea is developed differently in *Sh C* I 126, 137–8, II 229. See also WW's *Convention of Cintra* (1809) (*W Prose* I 339).

And to be placed, as they, with gradual fame
Among the Archives of Mankind, thy work
Makes audible a linked lay of Truth,
Of Truth profound a sweet continuous lay,
Not learnt, but native, her own natural notes!   60
Ah! as I listened with a heart forlorn
The pulses of my Being beat anew:
And even as Life returns upon the Drowned,
Life's joy rekindling roused a throng of Pains—
Keen Pangs of Love, awakening as a babe   65
Turbulent, with an outcry in the heart;
And Fears self-willed, that shunned the eye of Hope;
And Hope that scarce would know itself from Fear;
Sense of past Youth, and Manhood come in vain,
And Genius given, and knowledge won in vain;   70
And all which I had culled in Wood-walks wild,
And all which patient toil had reared, and all,
Commune with *thee* had opened out—but Flowers
Strewed on my corse, and borne upon my Bier,
In the same Coffin, for the self-same Grave!   75

That way no more! and ill beseems it me,
Who came a welcomer in Herald's Guise,
Singing of Glory, and Futurity,
To wander back on such unhealthful road,
Plucking the poisons of self-harm! And ill   80
Such intertwine beseems triumphal wreaths
Strewed before *thy* advancing!

                              Nor do thou,
Sage Bard! impair the memory of that hour
Of thy communion with my nobler mind
By Pity or Grief, already felt too long!   85
Nor let my words import more blame than needs.
The tumult rose and ceased: for Peace is nigh
Where wisdom's voice has found a listening heart.
Amid the howl of more than wintry storms,

The Halcyon hears the voice of vernal Hours   90
Already on the wing.

                    Eve following eve,
Dear tranquil time, when the sweet sense of Home
Is sweetest! moments for their own sake hailed
And more desired, more precious for thy song,
In silence listening, like a devout child,   95
My soul lay passive, by thy various strain
Driven as in surges now beneath the stars,
With momentary Stars of my own birth,
Fair constellated Foam,* still darting off
Into the darkness; now a tranquil sea,   100
Outspread and bright, yet swelling to the Moon.

    And when—O Friend! my comforter and guide!
Strong in thyself, and powerful to give strength!—
Thy long sustained Song finally closed,
And thy deep voice had ceased—yet thou thyself   105
Wert still before my eyes, and round us both
That happy vision of beloved Faces—
Scarce conscious, and yet conscious of its close
I sate, my being blended in one thought
(Thought was it? or Aspiration? or Resolve?)   110
Absorbed, yet hanging still upon the sound—
And when I rose, I found myself in prayer.

---

* "A beautiful white cloud of Foam at momentary intervals coursed by the side of the Vessel with a Roar, and little stars of flame danced and sparkled and went out in it: and every now and then light detachments of this white cloud-like foam darted off from the vessel's side, each with its own small constellation, over the Sea, and scoured out of sight like a Tartar Troop over a Wilderness."— 5
THE FRIEND, p. 220.

90. vernal Hours] The phrase is the first entry in the Gutch notebook (*CN* I 9); it is traceable to Erasmus Darwin and his *Botanic Garden* I i 428 and I ii 45, and connected with Thomson's *Seasons*. See *RX* 13 and 473 n 13.
99fn. The context in *The Friend* XIV (23 Nov 1809) 221 (*CC*) II 193 (var) is a description of C's and the Wordsworths' voyage to Cuxhaven in Sept 1798 (see also *CN* I 335 f 1ᵛ; *CL* I 425: to Mrs C 3 Oct 1798; *BL—CC*—II 168).

402. PSYCHE
OR, THE BUTTERFLY

[1806–7?]

The way the several texts of the poem develop and vary suggests it may have been composed and held in C's head, and was only written down as occasion prompted. The first such occasion was probably on his return, at Coleorton in the winter of 1806–7, significantly enough in SH's album. Four of the five extant ms versions may be considered album inscriptions or for presentation (the fifth being in a notebook discussion of symbolism: *CN* IV 4832 f 62ʳ). The poem was printed in a footnote to *BL* (ch 4—*CC*—I 78fn), and again later, perhaps without C's knowledge or permission. The versions all differ slightly, and not all of the variations are improvements. The text given here is from an album inscription of 1830.

In an earlier album version C introduced the poem as follows: "In the Greek the same word, Psyche, means the Soul and the Butterfly. In the following lines the Verse-man observes, that the Butterfly may be a just emblem of our Soul in it's future state; but that the Caterpillar is the fittest emblem of our Soul in it's present state."

The butterfly does not appear as an emblem of the soul in ancient Greek literature, although it is so described and represented in Greek art. It is therefore relevant that C's transcription of the poem in *CN* IV 4832 was prompted by the discussion of the subject by G. F. Creuzer in *Symbolik und Mythologie der alten Völker* (4 vols Leipzig 1810–12) I 130–1. Cf also **435** *Latin Lines to Accompany a Personal Emblem* headnote for a suggestion that these might derive from a commentary by Alexander von Humboldt published in 1795. The Greek word Psyche ψυχή (*psychē*) is found only twice meaning butterfly, on both occasions in purely etymological contexts in Aristotle and Plutarch. However, Psyche is also the name of the mortal woman loved by Cupid in the myth told by Apuleius, which C so much admired. John Beer (*AR*—*CC*—551–2) points out that C could have read in school about representations of Cupid and Psyche in the form of a butterfly, in Joseph Spence *Polymetis* (3rd ed 1774) 71.

The image in the succeeding lines is used to describe the transition from young folly to mature wisdom in *CL* VI 797: to W. Sotheby [13 Jul 1829]; 850: to J. E. Reade [Dec 1830]. The natural process is inverted in the poem, and the "reptile" caterpillar succeeds the hatched-out butterfly. The last line might be compared with the conclusion of C's prose note made in Malta on 12 Dec 1804, where the butterfly is the soul of the flower, the caterpillar's hunger for plants representing self-love and lust which come to be refined into love (*CN* II 2317).

The Butterfly the Ancient Grecians made
The SOUL's fair emblem, and it's only *name;
But of the Soul escaped the slavish trade
Of earthly life! For in this mortal frame
Our's is the Reptile's lot, much toil, much blame,   5
Manifold motions making little speed,
And to deform and kill the things, whereon we feed!

403. A METRICAL CONCLUSION?

[Feb 1807]

What is given here (and in *PW*—EHC—II 1002 No 27) as a line of verse was inserted at the end of a prose memorandum in Notebook 11 (*CN* II 2990). Whether it was intended as verse, and what relation it bears to the preceding prose memorandum, is an open question. It could plausibly be regarded as a metrical conclusion which at once concludes and steps outside the prose, the whole having all the shapeliness of a poem.

The prose note is as follows:

I languish away my Life in misery, unutterably wretched from the gnaw-ings of the Disease, and almost equally miserable by the Fear of the Remedy.—or—harrassed by the Disease, and miserable from the Fear of the Remedy.—

While by the Delay not only the Remedy becomes more difficult, & the Fear consequently greater, in addition to the growing exacerbation of the Disease, but there is regularly annexed to it the pangs of Self-reproach & blackning Despair from the Delay.

And sapp'd Resolves, the rotten Banks of Fools against the swelling Tide of Habit.

The last paragraph might also be seen as verse, with a line-break after "Fools". The line given below as the RT was inserted immediately following "Habit.", beginning with a lower-case "a."

And my Heart *mantles* in it's own delight.

* PSYCHE means both Butterfly & the Soul.

404. LINES ON THE YELLOWHAMMER

[Feb 1807]

The lines were drafted, without a title, in Notebook 11 (*CN* II 2991). The observation on which they are based was made in Notebook 6 in Apr–May 1802 (*CN* I 1168).

> The spruce and limber Yellow Hammer
> In the dawn of Spring, in the sultry Summer,
> In hedge, or tree his hours beguiling
> With notes, as of one that Brass is filing.

405. PARODY EPITAPH ON TOM NAVEL

[Feb 1807]

C drafted the lines in Notebook 11 (*CN* II 2993). He had copied down real epitaphs at Ashby-de-la-Zouch in the same notebook earlier in the month (*CN* II 2982). Punctuation has here been added at the end of lines 1 and 2.

> With kindred earth-clods on a level,
> No more in lusts to roll and revel,
> Here lies the churl, call'd fat Tom Navel,
> Who was a Beast and is a Devil.

406. FRAGMENTS WRITTEN IN FEBRUARY 1807

[Feb 1807]

The fragments constitute three entries in Notebook 11 (*CN* II 2995–7), separated from each other by a rule, the last two perhaps having been added to the first on a later occasion. It is not clear whether the couplet here labelled (*c*) is to be taken as the conclusion to (*b*). Line (*b*)2 directly echoes **354** *Recollections of*

Love 27, and there are other coincidences of mood and theme which confirm that C had SH in mind. Punctuation has been added in lines (*b*)4 and (*b*)6.

(*a*)

And in Life's noisiest hour,
There whispers still the ceaseless Love of Thee,
The Heart's *Self-commune* & soliloquy.

(*b*)

You mould my Hopes, you fashion me within;
And to the leading Love-throb in the Heart
Thro' all my Being all my pulses beat.
You lie in all my many thoughts, like Light;
Like the fair Light of Dawn, or summer Eve   5
On rippling Stream, or cloud-reflecting Lake.

(*c*)

And looking to the Heaven, that bends above you
How oft I bless the Lot, that made me love you.

407. ALLEGORICAL DESCRIPTION

[Feb 1807]

The lines were written in Notebook 11 (*CN* II 3004), the draft given here superseding another preliminary draft which has been cancelled. C might have in mind an actual description—say, an Indian shrine in a banyan-tree, the idol in the branches, the fakir below—although no source has been found. Even so, the horror remains to be explained, and he evidently intends the many-stemmed tree as an allegory of polytheism. C's awareness of the allegorical aspects of trees was lifelong, from the poison-dropping Upas-tree (*CN* I 37 etc) to the comparison of himself with WW in terms of two trees, one rotten at the core and one robust and sound (*CL* II 959: to RS 1 Aug 1803; *CN* I 926; *BL* ch 22—*CC*—II 155–6). Perhaps **413** *On the Roots of a Tree* describes the roots of the same tree.

As some vast tropic Tree, itself a Wood,
That crests its Head with clouds, beneath the flood

Feeds its deep roots, and with the bulging flank
Of its wide Base controlls the fronting bank,
(By the slant currents pressure scoop'd away   5
The fronting Bank becomes a foam-pil'd Bay).
High in it's Fork the uncouth Idol knits
His channel'd Brows: low murmurs stir by fits:
And dark below the horrid Faquir sits;
An Horror from its broad Head's branchy Wreath   10
Broods o'er the rude Idolatry beneath.—

408. THREE LINES ON PENITENCE

[c May 1807]

The lines appear without a title in Notebook 24 (*CN* ii 3016), between passages
from Italian authors and entries in cipher. They might not be by C, although
they undoubtedly have a personal application.

Drown'd in the Offender's penitence sincere
The offence too dies—
So gracious is a soul-sublimed Tear.

409. FATE AND CONSCIENCE

[Feb–May 1807]

The lines were written into Notebook 11 (*CN* ii 3035), between C's time at
Coleorton and his residence in Bristol. It is not certain that they are by him.

There is a Fate which flies with towering Spirit
Home to the Mark, & never checks at Conscience—

410. BIRDS IN MAY

[May 1807]

C wrote the lines into Notebook 19 (*CN* II 3046).

> Or wren or linnet
> In Bush and Bushet:
> No tree, but in it
> A cooing Cushit.

411. EPIGRAM ON CONFESSIONS AURICULAR

[May 1807]

C drafted the lines in Notebook 19 (*CN* II 3051), incorporating an alternative in line 4—the substitution of "A sly leering" for "Sad slippery". Cf the much later **641** *Verses Trivocular* for a coincidence of rhyme.

> What is fair, good & right Mankind wish in *general*
> And this I have learnt from Confessions *auricular*,
> (Said a shrewd Priest to me) but believe me, Sir! Men are all
> Sad slippery Sinners in wishes *particular*.

412. THE PANG MORE SHARP THAN ALL: AN ALLEGORY

[1807 and later; then 1822–5 and later]

The only known version of C's poem was published in *PW* (1834), the text reproduced here. The time of composition is a mystery, as is its relation to

4. Cushit] I.e. cushat, a North   pigeon or ring-dove.
Country and Borders word for wood

a draft in Notebook 20 of what became lines 9–20, and to an unpublished holograph fragment containing drafts of lines 36–44 followed by further lines which provide a quite different context. Various dates have been suggested: 1807, 1811, 1819, autumn 1822, autumn 1823, 1825–6. The poem would seem to be related to feelings which were strong following C's return from Malta, yet there are also similarities with poems written in the 1820s. If the later date is correct, it is possible to read the poem as a comment by C on his relation with HC, whom he was not to see face to face after Jul 1822.

KC dates the Notebook 20 draft c Sept 1825 (*CN* IV 5245). The paper on which the draft lines 36–44 are written bears an 1819 wm, yet the draft coincides in phrase and mood with notebook entries of 1807 (*CN* II 3056, 3075, 3076; cf 3053). The final version of the holograph fragment draft—which would fit into the RT before line 44—is as follows:

> My stirring thoughts all gone, and Hope is dead.
> Yet the deep Yearning will not die! Yet Love
> Clings on & cloathes the Marrowless Remains,
> Like the fresh Moss that grows on dead Men's Bones,
> Quaint Mockery! and fills it's scarlet Cups
> With the chill dew-damps of the Charnel-House—
> O ask not for my Heart! My Heart is but
> The darksome Vault where Hope lies dead & buried,
> And Love with asbest lamp bewakes the Corse.

The poem is here positioned early in the possible chronological sequence. A later placement would be equally valid, on the grounds that, although its beginnings date from 1807, they were not developed until the 1820s.

I.

> He too has flitted from his secret nest,
> Hope's last and dearest Child without a name!—
> Has flitted from me, like the warmthless flame,
> That makes false promise of a place of rest
> To the tir'd Pilgrim's still believing mind;—   5
> Or like some Elfin Knight in kingly court,
> Who having won all guerdons in his sport,
> Glides out of view, and whither none can find!

5. believing mind] C applied the phrase to Spenser as well as himself.   See *CN* II 2075; *Misc C* 332; **171** *Frost at Midnight* 24EC.

II.

Yes! He hath flitted from me—with what aim,
Or why, I know not! 'Twas a home of bliss,   10
And He was innocent, as the pretty shame
Of babe, that tempts and shuns the menaced kiss,
From its twy-cluster'd hiding place of snow!
Pure as the babe, I ween, and all aglow
As the dear hopes, that swell the mother's breast—   15
Her eyes down gazing o'er her clasped charge;—
Yet gay as that twice happy father's kiss,
That well might glance aside, yet never miss,
Where the sweet mark emboss'd so sweet a targe—
Twice wretched he who hath been doubly blest!   20

III.

Like a loose blossom on a gusty night
He flitted from me—and has left behind
(As if to them his faith he ne'er did plight)
Of either sex and answerable mind
Two playmates, twin-births of his foster-dame:—   25
The one a steady lad (Esteem he hight)
And Kindness is the gentler sister's name.
Dim likeness now, tho' fair she be and good
Of that bright Boy who hath us all forsook;—
But in his full-eyed aspect when she stood,   30
And while her face reflected every look,
And in reflection kindled—she became
So like Him, that almost she seem'd the same!

9–20. There is reason to connect the feelings of this stanza with a meeting between C and SH at Ramsgate in Oct 1823. See *The Letters of Sara Hutchinson* ed Kathleen Coburn (1954) xxxi fn.

13. twy-cluster'd] A Coleridgean coinage. Cf **101** *Religious Musings* 204 "twy-streaming", also a coinage of C's.

21. C compared HC to "a blossom whirling in a May-gale" in a draft letter to the Provost of Oriel (*CL* v 111: to E. Coppleston [c 11 Oct 1820]). Compare also "the magic Child" (37) and "the faery Boy" (56) with the "little Child, a limber Elf" in **176** *Christabel* 656, and "that crystal orb" (39) with the "mirror seeking of itself" in **171** *Frost at Midnight* 22.

IV.

Ah! He is gone, and yet will not depart!—
Is with me still, yet I from Him exil'd!   35
For still there lives within my secret heart
The magic image of the magic Child,
Which there He made up-grow by his strong art,
As in that crystal* orb—wise Merlin's feat,—
The wondrous "World of Glass," wherein inisl'd   40
All long'd for things their beings did repeat;—
And there He left it, like a Sylph beguiled,
To live and yearn and languish incomplete!

V.

Can wit of man a heavier grief reveal?
Can sharper pang from hate or scorn arise?—   45
Yes! one more sharp there is that deeper lies,
Which fond Esteem but mocks when he would heal.
Yet neither scorn nor hate did it devise,
But sad compassion and atoning zeal!
One pang more blighting-keen than hope betray'd!   50
And this it is my woful hap to feel,
When at her Brother's hest, the twin-born Maid
With face averted and unsteady eyes,
Her truant playmate's faded robe puts on;
And inly shrinking from her own disguise   55
Enacts the faery Boy that's lost and gone.
O worse than all! O pang all pangs above
Is Kindness counterfeiting absent Love!

---

* Faerie Queene, B. III. c. 2. s. 19.

39. crystal orb] The wondrous mir-
ror in which Britomart has a vision
of Artegall, with whom she falls in
love. Earlier in *The Faeirie Queene*
it is called "*Venus* looking glas" (III
i 8); here (III ii 21), as "glassie globe"
or orb, it signifies fragile marital har-
mony, in accordance with Renais-
sance iconography.

413. ON THE ROOTS OF A TREE

[1807]

C drafted the untitled lines in Notebook 19 (*CN* II 3074). KC suggests that he might have been influenced by his reading, at about the same time, of an article entitled "Observations on the Subterraneous Trees in Dagenham, and Other Marshes, Bordering on the River Thames, in the County of Essex" by the Rev W. Derham, in *Philosophical Transactions of the Royal Society: Abridgement* ed C. Hutton, G. Shaw, and R. Pearson (18 vols 1792–1809) v 681–4. C might at the same time have been testing an image of the Wordsworthian imagination: cf *CN* I 926; *BL* ch 22 (*CC*) II 155–6; **425** *Lines Prompted by Chapman* headnote. Or the tree might be the same as the one in **407** *Allegorical Description*, a metaphor for polytheism.

> The strong and complex Cordage of it's Roots
> Tying it's almost self-supported Weight
> To the firm earth in countless Intertwine
> Subtly embracing & soliciting,—

414. AN IMAGE COMPRESSED
FROM CRASHAW

[1807]

The image was drafted without a title in Notebook 19 (*CN* II 3100). As KC points out, Crashaw's poem, from Marino *Sospetto d'Herode* 1 (*B Poets* IV 714–19), contains all the elements here in the eight lines of stanza 17 (cf *CN* II 3102–5 and nn). Or perhaps there is also a blending of Crashaw and Ralegh (cf *CN* II 3079).

> Sun-rise
> As all the Trees of Paradise reblossoming in the East.

415. BETWEEN CONCURRENCES OF FATE

[1807]

C wrote the lines, without a title, into Notebook 19 (*CN* II 3101). The entries before and after derive from or are connected with his reading of Crashaw in *B Poets*. This entry is not, and C may not be the author.

> Wedg'd in and utterly crush'd
> Between two dire Concurrences of Fate.

416. IMITATIONS OF DU BARTAS ETC

[1807]

C drafted the lines in Notebook 19 (*CN* II 3107). They are numbered continuously below, but there is a case for considering them as three separate fragments. Lines 31–41 are preceded in the ms by a cancelled earlier version. Following line 41, and before the next entry in the notebook, C squeezed in the comment: "(I wrote these Lines, as an imitation of Du Bartas, as translated by our Sylvester—)". *PW* (EHC) I 486 gave lines 31–41 alone under the expressive title *Coeli ennarant*, "The Heavens are Telling".

The first two sets of lines (1–17, 18–26) appear to be written in a form that only works towards metrical expression. For this reason several lines are left without initial capitals in the RT, as C wrote them. Most obviously through their imagery but equally through their rhythms, they explore intensely personal concerns. KC points out that the third and most regular set of lines (27–41) has connections with Crashaw, whom C had been reading, as well as with the First Day of the First Week in Du Bartas *His Divine Weekes and Workes* tr Josuah Sylvester (1605). It is important that the imitation of Du Bartas was not intended from the outset, and C's sources undergo a change as they are incorporated. The equation or ambiguity between the letter "O" and the numeral "0", though traditional, recasts what has come before in a different, more pessimistic, mould.

> Fire, That slept in it's Intensity, Life
> Wakeful over all knew no gradations,
> And Bliss in it's excess became a Dream,
> And my visual powers involved such Sense,
> all Thought, Sense, Thought, & Feeling,   5

and Time drew out his subtle
Threads so quick, That the long
Summer's Eve was one whole web,
A Space on which I lay commensurate—
For Memory & all undoubting Hope   10
Sang the same note & in the selfsame
Voice, with each sweet *now* of
My Felicity, and blended momently,
Like Milk that coming comes & in it's
easy stream Flows ever in, upon the   15
mingling milk, in the Babe's murmuring
Mouth/ or mirrors each reflecting each/—

Life wakeful over all knew no gradation
That Bliss in it's excess became a Dream;
For every sense, each thought, & each sensation   20
Lived in my eye, transfigured not supprest.
And Time drew out his subtle threads so quick,
And with such Spirit-speed & silentness,
That only in the web, of space like Time,
On the still spreading web I still diffused   25
Lay still commensurate—

What never is but only is to be
This is not Life—
O Hopeless Hope, and Death's Hypocrisy!
And with perpetual Promise, breaks it's Promises.— 30

The Stars that wont to start, as on a chase,
And twinkling insult on Heaven's darkened Face,
Like a conven'd Conspiracy of Spies
Wink at each other with confiding eyes,
Turn from the portent, all is blank on high,   35
No constellations alphabet the Sky—
The Heavens one large black Letter only shew,
And as a Child beneath it's master's Blow
Shrills out at once it's Task and it's Affright,
The groaning world now learns to read aright,   40
And with it's Voice of Voices cries out, O!

417. TRANSLATION OF A DISTICH
BY SCHILLER

[Sept 1807]

C's translation is the ninth in a sequence of 28 distichs and extracts from Schiller's *Musen-Almenach für das Jahr 1797* which he copied out in Note-book 12 (*CN* II 3131). In this case he attempted a translation; all but one of the remainder are copied as they appear in the German. Schiller's original reads (p 279):

Griechheit.

Griechheit was war sie? Verstand und Maaß und Klarheit! drum dächt' ich,
Etwas Geduld noch ihr Herrn, eh ihr von Griechheit uns sprecht.

Tr "Greekness, what was it? Plain sense, measure, clearness! Wherefore I would have thought, a little patience, gentlemen, before you start talking of Greece!" Note that C has added the terms "Dignity" and "Grace"; he particularly admired Schiller's essay *Über Anmut und Würde* ("On Grace and Dignity").

In the RT punctuation has been added at the end of line 1, and line 2 has been given an initial capital letter.

Plain Sense, Measure, Clearness, Dignity, Grace—
Over all, these made the genius of Greece.

418. TRANSLATION OF A DISTICH
BY GOETHE AND SCHILLER

[Sept 1807]

C's translation is the twenty-fourth in a sequence of 28 distichs and extracts from Schiller's *Musen-Almenach für das Jahr 1797* which he copied into Note-book 12 (*CN* II 3131). In this case he attempted a translation: all but one of the remainder were copied as they appear in the German. The original comprises lines 5 and 6 of *Einer* (p 192):

Wie im Winter die Saat nur langsam keimet, im Frühling
Lebhaft treibet und schoßt, so war die Neigung zu dir.

Tr "As in winter the seed germinates but slowly, in spring is busy sending forth shoots, thus was my love for you."

In line 2 capital letters have been introduced at the start and after the dash.

> The seed beneath the snow—lives & shoots—
> But when the Spring comes—O then it appears.

419. ON TOM POOLE'S MEANDERINGS

[Sept 1807]

The holograph is a pretend letter, with a ficitious frank on the reverse side: "Post Mark | From London, viâ Carlisle | and Penzance." A note on *gëorgoepiscopal* has been trimmed away. *OED* does not include the word, presumably a nonce formation referring to the "agricultural-supervisory" aspects of TP's meanderings, with a sideways glance at his pastoral-episcopal or church-dignatory manner.

From Nether Stowey to Enmore is about 6 miles direct; via Perriton (Ferriton) and Combwich (Cummage) the journey is about 26 miles, involving a ferry across the Parrot and taking the traveller a good way towards Bristol.

> Relative to a Friend remarkable for *gëorgoepiscopal* Meanderings,
> and the combination of the *utile dulci* during his walks to and from
> any given place: composed, together with a book & a half of an
> Epic Poem during one of the *Halts*.

> Lest after this Life it should prove my sad story
> That my soul must needs go to the Pope's Purgatory,
> Many prayers have I sigh'd, "May T. P**** be my guide,
> For so often he'll halt, and so lead me about,
> That e'er we get there thro' earth, sea, or air,   5
> The last Day will have come, and the Fires have burnt out."

> Job junior,
circumbendiborum patientissimus.

P.S. Shortly will be published a new road Map of the country be-

---

6⁺. Tr (probably) "Job the Younger, highly tolerant of circuitous paths". *OED* gives many examples of the jocular compound with an ablative end-ing *circumbendibus*, but none of its being treated as a masculine noun and further inflected.

tween N. Stowey & Enmore, comprising many pleasant new roads from the former place to the latter by way of Ferriton, Fairfield, Cummage, &c.

420. LINES ON WORDSWORTH AND COLERIDGE

[Sept 1807]

C wrote the lines in Notebook 12 (*CN* II 3134), without a title but introduced by the following remarks: "But should a friend think foully of that wherein the pride of the Spirit's purity is in shrine—should he—&c— | O the agony! the agony!" The reference to WW's attitude to C's relation to SH is clear (cf *CN* II 3146); and the lines should also be read against an entry dating from 27 Dec 1806 (*CN* II 2975), which records C's shocked delusion that WW and SH were lovers.

> Nor Time, nor varying Fate,
> Nor tender memory old or late,
> Nor all his Virtues, great tho' they be,
> Nor all his Genius can free
> His friend's Soul from this agony!　　　　5

421. VERSIFIED FROM BACON

[Oct 1807]

C wrote the lines without a title in Notebook 12 (*CN* II 3174). They are versified from Bacon's sentence in the essay *Of Revenge*: "A man that studieth revenge, keeps his wounds green, which otherwise would heal and do well" (*Works*—10 vols 1803—II 262). They are accompanied by a number of extracts from and observations prompted by C's reading in the same 1803 edition, which make up the sum of the notebook entry. Perhaps they have something to do with C's brooding over WW's relation to SH. Cf *CN* II 2975 and 3134=**420** *Lines on Wordsworth and Coleridge*.

Keeps his wounds green,
By moody day-dreams of Revenge.

422. ADAPTED FROM A SHAKESPEARE SONNET

[Dec 1807]

The line is written into Notebook 19 (*CN* II 3194), between other entries and without title or explanation. It adapts Shakespeare *Sonnets* 124.5 "No it was builded far from accident".

My Love is built up far from accident.

423. TO TWO SISTERS: A WANDERER'S FAREWELL

[Nov–Dec 1807]

C's departure from Bristol was delayed by illness for three weeks, which he spent with his old friend J. J. Morgan, his young wife, and her sister at St James's Square. A version of the poem in just twelve lines was presented to the sisters when he left on 22 Nov 1807. It was expanded with the comparison between Mary Morgan and Charlotte Brent and MW and SH soon after C arrived in London, and this version, the one given here, was published over a thinly veiled pseudonym in *The Courier* (10 Dec 1807). A slightly revised version of the original shorter poem (which approximates to lines 1–5 and 47–52 here) was included in *PW* (1834).

Mrs C had been irritated by C's malingering in Bristol, and both she and RS thought the poem in *The Courier* "unmanly". "It is a beautiful Poem but it was, in my opinion, a most ungenerous action, the publishing it, it abounds with gratitude to these young Ladies, and bitter complaints and woful murmurings at his own unhappy fate!" (*Minnow* 10). Mrs C must also have been conscious that the allusions which identify MW and SH as the older sisters exclude herself and Mrs RS. Possibly some misgiving on the score she describes prompted the exclusion of the poem from *SL* and the republication of the shorter version in 1834 (incorporating the misleading date 1817 in the title).

C was fond of quoting the opening couplet: see *LS* (*CC*) 238; *CL* ɪv 963: to M. Starke 28 [=30] Oct 1819; vɪ 577: to Mrs D. Stuart 4 May 1826. He made it the text for a paragraph in prose addressed to someone called Margaret, who was apparently about to emigrate:

> To meet, to know, to love—and then to part!
> Is the sad tale of many a feeling heart.

The World, my dear Margaret! is a circle with a thousand circumferences, of which God is the common Center. However widely we may be separated from each other, we have only to tend towards *him*, and to sail on a *strait* line by the compass-needle of Conscience interpreted by the fixed Marks of Scripture, and we shall be sure to meet hereafter whatever was worthy of our Love here. For all good things come from God and to God they all return. Farewell, dear Margaret! Prefer Health to Wealth, Peace of Heart to Splendor of Circumstances, and Innocence to all—remembering that they, who are not actively virtuous in their allotted Sphere, cannot long remain ~~virtuous~~ innocent. You depart with the best good wishes, and shall be remembered in the prayers, of

S. T. Coleridge | 4 October, 1825

(From a photostat—only—of a page, possibly from an album: presented to Yale University Library—Photostat File 6—by Prof Edward B. Reed of New Haven, 6 Aug 1936.)

> To know, to esteem, to love,—and then to part—
> Makes up life's tale to many a feeling heart:
> Alas for some abiding-place of love,
> O'er which my spirit like the mother dove,
> Might brood with warming wings!
>
> O fair! O kind!   5
> Sisters in blood, yet each with each intwin'd,
> More close by sisterhood of heart and mind!
> Me disinherited in form and face
> By nature, and mishap of outward grace;
> Who, soul and body, thro' one guiltless fault,   10
> Waste daily with the poison of sad thought,
> Me did you soothe, when solace hop'd I none!
> And as on unthaw'd ice the Winter sun,
> Tho' stern the frost, tho' brief the genial day,

8–9. C soon afterwards quoted the two lines (var) to SH: *CL* ɪɪɪ 68: to SH   [12 Feb 1808]; *CM* (*CC*) ɪɪ 1120.

You bless my heart with many a cheerful ray;   15
For gratitude suspends the heart's despair,
Reflecting, bright tho' cold, your image there.

Nay more! its music by some sweeter strain,
Makes us live o'er our happiest hours again,
Hope re-appearing dim in mem'ry's guise—   20
Even thus did you call up before mine eyes
Two dear, dear Sisters, prized all price above,
Sisters, like you, with more than Sisters' love;
So like you *they*, and so in *you* were seen
Their relative statures, tempers, looks, and mien,   25
That oft, dear Ladies! you have been to me,
At once a vision and reality.
Sight seem'd a sort of memory, and amaze
Mingled a trouble with affection's gaze.

Oft to my eager soul I whisper blame,   30
A Stranger bid it feel the Stranger's shame—
My eager soul, impatient of the name,
No strangeness owns, no Stranger's form descries:
The chidden heart spreads trembling on the eyes.
First-seen I gaz'd, as I would look you thro'!   35
My best-belov'd regain'd their Youth in you,—
And still I ask, tho' now familiar grown,
Are you for *their* sakes dear, or for your own?

O doubly dear! may Quiet with you dwell!
In Grief I love you, yet I love you well!   40

18 et seq. Cf C to DW, 24 Nov 1807 (*CL* III 37–8): "I never knew two pairs of human beings so alike, as Mrs Morgan & her Sister, Charlotte Brent, and Mary and Sara. I was reminded afresh of the resemblance every hour—& at times felt a self-reproach, that I could not love two such amiable, pure, & affectionate Beings for their own sakes. But there is a time in Life, when the Heart stops growing.—" C's feelings account for the echoes of poems written in 1802, such as **289** *A Letter to* —— and **294** *The Day Dream.* See also *CM* (*CC*) II 1121, *LL* (M) III 162 for CL's opinion.

36. Charlotte Brent celebrated her 24th birthday while C was staying at St James's Square; Mary Morgan was 17 months older—as C noted (*CN* II 3186). At the same time, MW was 37 and SH 32. C is probably also alluding to a difference of spirits as much as of years. John Morgan was himself of C's—and MW's and SH's—generation.

HOPE long is dead to me! an Orphan's Tear
LOVE wept despairing o'er his Nurse's Bier.
Yet still she flutters o'er her Grave's green slope:
For Love's DESPAIR is but the Ghost of HOPE!

Sweet Sisters! were you plac'd around one hearth   45
With those, your other selves in shape and worth,
Far rather would I sit in solitude,
Fond recollections all my fond heart's food,
And dream of *you*, sweet Sisters! (ah not mine!)
And only *dream* of you (ah dream and pine!)   50
Than boast the presence and partake the pride,
And shine in the eye, of all the world beside.

424. THINKING MERRILY ALONE

[1807–8]

The lines are written between two prose entries in Notebook 22 (*CN* II 3208),
untitled and without explanation.

Thinking many a merry thought
All by himself alone.—

425. LINES PROMPTED BY CHAPMAN

[1807–8]

The lines make up a separate entry in Notebook 22 (*CN* II 3211 var). They are
followed immediately by lines and passages copied from Chapman's *Homer*
(1616). KC suggests that C is here adapting and improving on lines from one
of Chapman's dedicatory sonnets prefatory to the *Iliad*, *To . . . the Earle of
Salisbury* (*The Whole Works of Homer*—1616—Gg 4ᵛ):

Wherein as th' Ocean walks not, with such waues,
    The Round of this Realme, as your Wisedomes seas;
Nor, with his great eye, sees; his Marble, saues,

> Our State, like your Vlyssian policies:
> So, none like HOMER hath the World enspher'd;
> Earth, Seas, & heauen, fixt in his verse, and mouing . . .

However, the phrase which C adds to Chapman—"the Flux and Reflux of his Thoughts"—derives from the Preface to the 1800 *LB* (*W Prose* I 126) and was in turn applied to WW's poetry by C (e.g. *BL* ch 22—*CC*—II 147; cf *Friend*—*CC*—II 17; *BL* chs 15, 23—*CC*—II 21, 211). Perhaps Chapman's lines suggested an opportunity to explore an image of WW's genius. Cf **413** *On the Roots of a Tree* headnote; **429** *Ad Vilmum Axiologum*.

> Nor do the Ocean Tides move ceaselessly
> Entring each Bay & voicing on each shore
> Still wake and watch around our British Isle,
> Than did the Flux and Reflux of his Thoughts/

426. A LINE FROM A LOST POEM?

[1807–8]

The line is quoted in a long prose entry in Notebook 22 (*CN* II 3215), to complete the following sentence (which begins with what might be a phrase from a letter from or for WW): "I trust, you are very happy in your domestic being; very—because, alas! I know that to a man of sensibility, & more emphatically, if he be a literary man,—there is ⟨no⟩ medium between that and—".

The suggestion that the line might be from a lost poem of C's was made by KC. Such a poem might never have been composed—perhaps merely glimpsed, the subject possibly akin to that of **423** *To Two Sisters*.

> The secret pang that eats away the Heart.

427. TWO LINES: "OR LIKE
THE SWALLOW ..."

[Early 1808]

C wrote the untitled lines in a copy of his translation of Schiller's *Wallenstein* (1800), where they are followed by an early fragment of **402** *Psyche*. They appear not to have any connection with the Schiller text. C more usually identified with birds which are completely unlike swallows, such as ostriches: see **304** *To Matilda Betham* 43EC.

> Or like the Swallow, I by instinct taught
> Could track the Sun, & still find Summer food!

428. PRAYER FOR NIGHT:
FOR HARTLEY AND DERWENT

[1808?]

The version of the poem given here is from an album which was once the property of Joanna Hutchinson. The prayer appears afterwards to have been revised slightly for use by SC, and a few further modifications were made for its incorporation in *PW* (1834).

> Ere on my Bed my Limbs I lay,
> God! grant me grace my prayers to say.
>
> O God! preserve my Mother Dear
> In strength and health for many a year!
> And O! preserve my Father too,
> And may I give him reverence due—
> And let me my best thoughts employ
> To be my Parents' Hope and Joy.

5

---

1. The same opening line as in published versions of **335** *The Pains of*   *Sleep.*

My Brother and my Sister both
From evil doings keep and sloth! 10
And may we always love each other,
Our Friends, our Father, and our Mother.

But chiefly, Lord! to us impart
An innocent and grateful Heart,
That after Life's last Sleep we may 15
Awake to thy Eternal Day!

Amen!

429. AD VILMUM AXIOLOGUM

[1807–8]

Poem **401** *To WW* is among the most coherent of several private attempts by C in verse to extend his semi-public response to *The Prelude*. Many of these attempts began, as here, in the form of modifications of other texts (cf **413** *On the Roots of a Tree* and **425** *Lines Prompted by Chapman*), which is appropriate given C's understanding of his dependent genius alongside WW's confidently solitary one.

The first version in Notebook 24 lacks the present lines 7–9 (*CN* II 3220). It grew out of C's version of three distichs from the *Tabulae Votivae* of Goethe and Schiller (*Musen-Almenach für das Jahr 1797* 178, 179):

Der berufene Leser

Welchen Leser ich wünsche? den unbefangensten, der mich,
Sich und die Welt vergißt und in dem Buche nur lebt.

Die Unberufenen

Tadeln ist leicht, erschaffen so schwer; ihr Tadler des schwachen,
Habt ihr das trefliche denn auch zu belohnen das Herz?

Die Belohnung

Was belohnet den Meister? der zartantwortende Nachklang,
Und der reine Reflex aus der begegnenden Brust.

C began by translating the first poem fairly closely:

title. WW signed his first published poem "Axiologus", a Greek translation of his name (see *WPW* I 269; *WEPF* 396).

> Whom should I choose for my Judge? the earnest *impersonal* Reader
> Who in the work forgets me and the world and himself.

Then he paraphrased, still quite closely, *Die Unberufenen* and proceeded without a break to give a looser expansion of *Die Belohnung*:

> Ye who have eyes to detect and Gall to chastise the Imperfect,
> Have you the Heart too that loves, feels and rewards the compleat.
> Whenceat is the meed of thy Song? From 'Tis the ceaseless, the thousand-
>   fold Echo
> Which from the welcoming Hearts of the Pure repeats and prolongs it,
> Each with a different Tone, compleat or in musical fragments.

The first version of the present poem then follows, divided from the previous line of C's paraphrase merely by "or".

In a fair copy a few pages later in the same notebook (*CN* II 3231) the lines are set out separately under their present title, where they accompany a draft and a fair copy of Latin hexameters bearing the same title (poem **430**), along with remarks on poetry and other matters in prose. It is the fair copy that is printed here.

This be the meed, that thy Song creates a thousandfold Echo!
Sweet as the warble of woods that awake at the gale of the Morning!
List! the Hearts of the Pure, like Caves in the ancient Mountains
Deep, deep *in* the Bosom, and *from* the Bosom resound it,
Each with a different Tone, complete or in musical fragments,   5
All have welcom'd thy Voice, and receive and retain and prolong it!
This is the word of the Lord!—it is spoken, and Beings Eternal
Live and are born, as an Infant—the Eternal begets the Immortal!
Love is the Spirit of Life, and Music the Life of the Spirit.—

430. AD VILMUM AXIOLOGUM:
LATIN VERSION

[1808?]

C's lines to WW were drafted and then copied out in Notebook 24 (*CN* II 3231), but were never published by him. They describe an important stage in the development of his feelings about WW and SH, and they embrace a quite different subject-matter from the English lines which share the same title (poem **429**). The pair of poems combine the two attitudes expressed in **374** *Latin Lines* *to WW as Judge*: respect for WW as poet (if not friend) and rejection as moral mentor. The following translation varies at several points from that in *CN* II 3231n (the draft is mentioned only where it differs in substance):

> Do you command me to endure Asra's forgetting me? and to be able to look at my Asra's [*draft:* to look calmly at] averted eyes? and to know that she is false and cruel who was and always will be dear to me? And to endure the daylight [*draft:* and you bid me endure this/ to endure day and night] when I love an empty [*draft:* false] woman and the whole of Nature [*or:* my whole being; *draft:* for me] shakes and totters? Why do you not bid me, hiding my pain, to let my guts be pierced with a knife? Rather, tear out my heart or my eyes, or whatever is more precious—if anything *can* be more precious! I shall order my failing spirit to submit to whatever you wish, as long as Asra's faith [*or:* my faith in Asra] may endure, though I may die. But I have seen the last rites of faith and I am dying! Do you think that I shall be overcome by facile reasoning? by *Reason*? The Devil take the man who can apply reasonings in Love! The Devil take him who can love without total abandon! Let those whose hearts are whole see what is right and proper, and what is not. My life is over! Asra lives on, forgetting me.

For C on WW's total incapacity for and understanding of love, as opposed to friendship-plus-lust, see *CL* III 305: to HCR [12 Mar 1811]; *CM* (*CC*) II 197; *TT* 26 Sept 1830 (*CC*) I 206; **665** *Love and Friendship Opposite*.

Me n' Asræ perferre jubes oblivia? et Asræ
Me aversos oculos posse videre meæ?
Scire et eam falsam, crudelem, quæ mihi semper
    Cara fuit, semper cara futura mihi?
Meque pati lucem, cui vanam perdite amanti,   5
    Quicquid Naturæ est, omne tremit, titubat!
Cur non ut patiarque fodi mea viscera ferro,
    Dissimulato etiam, Vilme, dolore jubes?
Quin Cor, quin Oculosque meos, quin erue vel quod
    Carius est, si quid carius esse potest!   10
Deficientem animam, quod vis, tolerare jubebo,
    Asræ dum superet, me moriente, fides,
At Fidis Inferias vidi! et morior! Ratione
    Victum iri facili, me *Ratione*, putas?
Ah pereat, qui in Amore potest rationibus uti!   15
    Ah pereat, qui, ni perdite, amare potest!
Quid deceat, quid non, videant quibus integra mens est:
    Vixi! vivit adhuc immemor Asra mei.

431. AN ANAGRAM OF
MARY MORGAN'S FACE

[Late 1807–early 1808]

The poem is one of several in the same spirit written at about this time, prompted by Mary Morgan and Charlotte Brent (see also poems **432–4** etc). C's relationship with the two sisters, as with John Morgan, appears to have been of a particularly easy and light-hearted kind—different, for instance, from his developed relationship with the Wordsworths, the Hutchinsons, and later with the Gillmans. On Mary Morgan see **423** *To Two Sisters* headnote.

The Blue, the rosy Red, the Black, the White
Are the four Elements that charm our sight
In Woman's Face; and when together met
Form female Beauty's total Alphabet.
All these hast thou! of Teeth what jetty rows!   5
Thy lips, how white! how very blue thy Nose!
Thy Hair so red resembles, charming Friend!
The fibres from a tough old Carrot's End,
Thine Eyes, (the Light how modestly they shun!)
Red as the Gravy from Beef underdone.   10
As wits diversely the same letters place,
And so a God into a Dog disgrace,
Thus laughing Nature in thy Phiz did trace
An *Anagram* of Mary Morgan's Face!

432. TO CHARLOTTE BRENT

[Late 1807–early 1808]

On Charlotte Brent see **423** *To Two Sisters* headnote. The present lines might have been written on the same occasion as **431** *An Anagram of Mary Morgan's Face*. The end of the poem has been torn away in the ms.

Dear Charlotte!
There are, dear Charlotte! who pretend
A love which neither wears the name
Of Son, of Brother, or of Friend,
As chaste as their's, yet not the same: 5
A love, to one fair Form confin'd
Yet dwelling only in the Mind—
A dedication of the Soul
(For Souls, they say, have sexes too)
Like, the bright Star, that guards the Pole,   10

     *   *   *

433. EXTREMES MEET:
A FILL-A-SOPHA-COL NOTE

[Oct 1807–Jan 1808]

On the Morgan household at St James's Square, Bristol—the inhabitants and the spirit which reigned there—see poems **423, 431–3, 435,** etc. C refers to the sofa in the drawing room in a letter of 22 Jan 1808 (*CL* III 46: to Mrs J. J. Morgan [22] Jan 1808). The proverb about extremes meeting held an almost totemic interest for him (cf *Friend*—*CC*—I 110 and n), to the extent that it was quoted against him by his enemies (see *EOT*—*CC*—I cliv).

    Extremes meet. For instance, a person's Absence may be very good Company. Likewise, one added to three, instead of making four, may in certain cases unmake the society of the former Three.

Dialogue

Charlotte.
    At full length on a sofa thee, Coleridge!
                an Oaf I call.

S. T. Coleridge.
    Yet you'll allow, my dear Charlotte! 'Twas quite
                fill-a-sopha-Col.

| Small Charlotte and Mary | Sure, such a society | This paper being small |
| S.T.C. and Vic-Hairy— | Needs no other variety. | Puts an end to this scrawl. |

433A. LINES TO CHARLOTTE BRENT

[Late 1807–early 1808; or any time thereafter up to 1816]

See the Addendum at the end of this volume.

434. ON A HAPPY HOUSEHOLD

[Jan 1808]

C wrote the lines in Notebook 17 (*CN* III 3234) without a title, and never published them. Their ambience resembles his descriptions of the Morgan household at this time in Bristol—see, besides contemporaneous poems, *CN* III 3237; *CL* III 46–8: to Mrs J. J. Morgan [22] Jan 1808; etc—but the Morgans are not known to have had any children and the lines may be make-believe.

> The singing Kettle & the purring Cat,
> The gentle Breathing of the cradled Babe,
> The silence of the Mother's love-bright Eye,
> And tender Smile answ'ring it's smile of Sleep/

435. LATIN LINES TO ACCOMPANY
A PERSONAL EMBLEM

[c Feb 1808]

C drafted the lines in Notebook 21 (*CN* III 3264), the first of three consecutive entries describing alternative pictorial emblems and mottoes. He wrote to Matilda Betham in May 1808 with a request for her to make a seal for him (*CL* III 101). In the notebook the present fair-copy version is followed by an apparently abortive reworking of the same lines, and both are preceded by a prose description of an emblem: "Lily in the garden Pot—a lighted Torch by it—a butterfly flying off from it/ underneath". KC's translation of the fair-copy version is as follows:

> Alas! when my Butterfly is gone,
> Sweet delight of sunny spring,

> Lovely Consort of the Breezes—
> Alas! while my Soul flies from me,
> How can your torch, unloved Juno,
> Delight me, pale and wan as I am?

The emblems of lighted torch and butterfly—representing the life-force and the soul—were central in a celebrated philosophic commentary by Alexander von Humboldt, "Die Lebenskraft oder der rhodische Genius", which appeared in Schiller's *Die Horen* I (5) (1795) 90–6. KC speculates that C might have seen the journal in Germany (*CN* III 4111n), and notes that he met Humboldt in Rome in 1805 (*IS*—1979—417 n 30). On Psyche as butterfly and soul (of flower or man), as well as the beloved of Cupid, see **402** *Psyche*. Juno is here the goddess of marriage; see the Latin lines of uncertain authorship, based on Avogadro, at **475.X1** *Lovers' Quarrels*.

For verses to accompany a public emblem see **513** *Motto for a Transparency*.

> Eheu! dum me mea Psyche,
> Dulce decus veris aprici,
> Pulchra Comes et Zephyrorum,
> Dum Psyche me fugit eheu!
> Pallidulum me tua tæda   5
> Quid juvat, o inamata Juno!—

436. LATIN LINES TO ACCOMPANY A SECOND EMBLEM

[c Feb 1808]

C drafted the lines in Notebook 21 (*CN* III 3265), where they are introduced by the following prose description of a pictorial emblem: "a Peacock holding a hymenæal Torch—a water lily—a Swan with reverted Neck—". They make up the second of three consecutive drafts of alternative personal emblems and mottoes—and in fact appear in the notebook intercalated between the fair copy and the recasting of the first such motto. KC provides the following translation:

> Without sun, without Leda,
> What joy to me is Juno's [marriage] torch?

> Sine sole, absque Ledâ
> Quid juvat nos junonia Tæda?

437. A MOTTO TO ACCOMPANY
A THIRD EMBLEM

[c Feb 1808]

C drafted the motto in Notebook 21 (*CN* III 3266), where it is introduced by the following prose description of a pictorial emblem: "A Cage—in it a Dove & a Crow/ on the top & outside of the Cage a Dove over the Dove/ Motto—". The description and motto make up the third of three consecutive notebook entries in similar vein; the present entry appears in the notebook intercalated (along with the second in the series) between the fair copy and the recasting of the first motto.

The Italian phrase (with accent "sarà") means "What will be will be", although the initial capital "S" gives it a punning twist. It is of course not C's, or even necessarily verse. The Greek is a dactylic pentameter and means "I yearn for her who yearns for me: a loveless man together with a loveless woman." C used the last word transliterated into English, "Aphilos", as a pseudonym in 1811: see **448** *Another Epitaph on an Infant.*

　　　　　　Che Sara sara—or
　　　　　　Ἄ με ποθεῖ, ποθεω· σὺν αφίλᾳ ἀφιλὸς.

438. AN EXEMPLARY DESCRIPTION

[Mar 1808]

The lines were published in *BL* ch 15 (*CC*) II 23, but C appears to have spoken them in his first Shakespeare lectures. In *BL* he quotes two lines as follows:

> Behold yon row of pines, that shorn and bow'd
> Bend from the sea-blast, seen at twilight eve.

He introduces the couplet by saying that "there is nothing objectionable, nothing which would preclude them from forming, in their proper place, part of a descriptive poem".

After the couplet *BL* continues: "But with the small alteration of rhythm, the same words would be equally in their place in a book of topography, or in a descriptive tour. The same image will rise into a semblance of poetry if thus conveyed"; and the lines given below then follow, "as an illustration, by no means as an instance, of that particular excellence which I had in view, and in which Shakspeare even in his earliest, as in his latest works, surpasses all other poets."

> Yon row of bleak and visionary pines,
> By twilight-glimpse discerned, mark! how they flee
> From the fierce sea-blast, all their tresses wild
> Streaming before them.

439. LATIN ELEGIACS ON GUY FAWKES

[May 1808? Nov 1807?]

The Guy Fawkes story is well enough known. C and his circle were probably familiar with the old print, often reproduced, of the scene of the arrest, Guy Fawkes in front of the cellar with the barrels, taper alight, and the Devil behind him, the party, including an angel, arriving to arrest him, and, unhistorically, the king and parliament already present above. The point of the couplet does not rest in the historical matter of Guy Fawkes, however, but in the situation of implied speaker and auditor to which the reader is privy. The footnote about the constable is present in all three mss, and it works to construct a sense of dialogue between a schoolboy who has spoken his own composition and a master who has asked for clarification.

The version given below was written without comment in Notebook 23 (*CN* III 3313), and was probably the earliest. A second version appears in C's revision of a gloss by Dr Johnson quoted in *Stockdale's Edition of Shakespeare* (1784) 392–3 (*King John* II i 183–90; *CM—CC—*IV 757). Here C enlarges on the couplet in a way which recalls his description of **145** *The Raven* as a schoolboy production. "Dr Johnson's ₍e₎xplanation reminds me of the School-boy's Construing ₍o₎f his Guy Vulpes":

> Guy Vulpes, Guy Faux, calidus, a hot-headed Fanatic, frigidus, a cool deliberate villain, postquam ₍o₎mnia cœpit, after he had stowed all the barrels of Gun-powder in the Cellar under the Parliament House, Attamen inventus, Never the less having been found out, ille he recepit eum took him into custody ⌐. . . .¬ ille ?~~boy~~—ille is the Constable.

A third version appears in a letter to John Morgan of 29 Jun 1814 (*CL* III 512). C describes Allston's transparency for the peace celebrations which began on 27 Jun 1814, and continues: "it is a truly Michael Angelesque figure . . . the finest in the City—but the meaning thereof greatly resembled my old story of Guy Vulpes, frigidus, calidus". Such transparencies—emblems or pictures on some translucent substance, made visible by means of a light behind—were increasingly popular in England from the 1780s onwards.

It is clear that C's schoolboy is supposed to have written the lines in the first instance. Translated literally, they mean: "Guy Fawkes, hot, cold, after he began everything, but nevertheless, having been discovered, *he* received him." The emphasis on "*he*" signals that the grammatical subject has changed, the added footnote being a desperate lunge to secure this. While anacoluthon is sometimes an effective rhetorical device, C appears to have thought that Allston's picture was enigmatic in the discontinuous way of the Latin lines. Again, his complaint against Johnson is that he failed to mend the corrupt text he commented upon: the gloss quoted by Stockdale reinforces obscurity like a schoolboy attempting vainly to bolster up a defective composition.

There is a good pun (in the then standard pronunciation) in "cœpit" and "recipit", and the reversal of fortune is further brought out by the emphatic "*ille*" ("*he*") and the more neutral "eum" ("him"). Two metrical faults add to the unserious effect: in the Notebook version C marked the correct prosody "frīgidus", to call attention to the error (a short syllable is needed in this position); and "inventus" ends with a short syllable at a point where a long vowel is required (although this liberty is occasionally taken by good ancient poets at the caesura of the pentameter).

> Guy vulpes, calidus, frīgidus, postquam omnia cœpit,
> Attamen inventus, *ille** recepit eum.

440. SONNET TRANSLATED FROM MARINO

[Sept 1808]

C wrote out the sonnet in Notebook 13 (*CN* III 3377), after returning to Keswick and Grasmere. It translates a sonnet by Giovanni Battista Marino, which goes as follows:

> Donna, siam rei di morte. Errasti, errai;
> > Di perdon non son degni i nostri errori;
> > Tu ch' avventasti in me sì fieri ardori,
> > Io che le fiamme a sì bel sol furai.
>
> Io ch' una fera rigida adorai,
> > Tu che fosti sord' aspe a' miei dolori;

---

* The Constable.

Tu ne l' ire ostinata, io ne gli amori,
Tu pur troppo sdegnasti, io troppo amai.

Or la pena laggiù nel cieco Averno
Pari al fallo n' aspetta. Arderà poi
Chi visse in foco, in vivo foco eterno.

Quivi, s' Amor fia giusto, ambeduo noi
A l' incendio dannati avrem l' inferno;
Tu nel mio core, ed io ne gli occhj tuoi.

The poem comes early in the "Rime amorosi" in pt 3 of Marino's *La lira*, or *Rima*, first published in 1614, but when C transcribed poems by Marino in *CN* II 2625 he appears to have drawn on the 31-page selection in *Lirici misti del secolo xvii* (Venice 1789) 6, 16, 21, 22, where every poem is headed *Sonnetto*. *Lirici misti* comprises vol XLI of *Parnaso italiano* ed A. Rubbi, and was presumably available separately. RS owned a copy of the 1675 Venice edition of *La Lira, rime* (3 vols in 1)—RS Sale Catalogue, Sotheby's, 8–23 May 1844 lot 1803—but the present text is from *Lirici misti* 25.

C became interested in Marino in Malta, partly, as he said, to use "in giving Hartley or Derwent a gode and a guide to the close Hunt of Good Sense" after his return to England (*CN* II 2625 f 100^{r-v}). As it turned out, the translation may also have had something to do with teaching his daughter Sara and her mother a few years later (see *Minnow* 12; *SW&F—CC*—260–6 etc; *CM—CC*—III 930–1). The imagery, carried over in subsequent notebook entries (esp *CN* III 3379), makes it clear that the poem addresses the third Sara he met again in Sept 1808 (SH), and the relationship bears on the burlesque tendency in which C's sonnet departs from its original. His attitude towards Marino was never entirely respectful (*CN* II 2625; *BL* ch 4—*CC*—I 74).

Cf **297** *Sonnet Adapted from Petrarch.*

Lady, to Death we're doom'd, our crime the same!
Thou, that in me thou kindledst such fierce Heat;
I, that my Heart did of a Sun so sweet
The Rays concenter to so hot a flame.
I, fascinated by an Adder's Eye,   5
Deaf as an Adder thou to all my Pain;
Thou obstinate in Scorn, in passion I—
I lov'd too much, too much didst thou disdain,
Hear then our doom, in Hell as just as stern,
Our sentence equal as our crimes conspire   10
Who living basked at Beauty's earthly Fire
In living flames eternal there must burn/—

Hell for us both fit places too supplies—
In *my* Heart thou wilt burn, I roast before thine Eyes—

441. ALTERNATIVE STANZAS
IN THE MANNER OF MARINO

[Sept 1808]

C wrote the two stanzas into Notebook 13 (*CN* III 3379), after the following prose note:

> If love be the genial Sun of human nature, unkindly has he divided his rays in acting on me and [Asra]—on her poured all his Light and Splendor, & permeated my Being with his invisible Rays of Heat alone/ She shines and is *cold*, as the tropic Firefly—I dark and uncomely would better re-semble the Cricket in hot ashes—my Soul at least might be considered as a Cricket eradiating the heat which gradually cinerizing the Heart produced the embery ashes, from among which it chirps, out of it's hiding-place.—
> N.B. This put in simple & elegant verse, as an imitation of Marini—and of too large a part of the Madrigals of Guarini himself.

The name Asra (=SH) is in cipher. The occasion is among the first in which C ascribes to her irreconcilable qualities of coldness and fire (on which see *CN* I 1233, II 2398n, etc). In the poems C identifies his story with that of Pyramus and Thisbe from Ovid's *Metamorphoses* 4.55 et seq.

On C and Marino see **440** *Sonnet Translated from Marino* headnote. **441.X1** *Fragmentary Lines in Pencil* follows on from the present lines in Notebook 13, and may represent a further attempt in the same vein.

(*a*)

Two wedded Hearts, if e'er were such
Imprison'd in adjoining cells
Across whose thin partition wall
The Builder left one narrow rent,
And there most content in discontent   5
A Joy with itself at strife,
Die into an intenser Life/

(*b*)

The Builder left one narrow rent,
Two wedded Hearts, if e'er were such,
Contented most in discontent
There cling, and try in vain to touch!
O Joy with thy own Joy at Strife,   5
That yearning for the Realm above
Would'st die into intenser Life
And union absolute of Love.

442. THE HAPPY HUSBAND: A FRAGMENT

[1808–10? 1802?]

The lines are something of a mystery: as EHC says, "There is no evidence as to the date of composition" (*PW*—EHC—I 388n). Four lines of stanza 3 exist in a slightly different form in a ms letter to an unnamed correspondent written, apparently, some time between 1808 and 1810. On the other hand, the concatenation of themes might be reckoned to have been particularly active in C's mind before he went to Malta. The complete fragment was published in *SL* and thereafter; small improvements were made in 1817 in certain annotated copies of *SL*, but were not carried forward to subsequent printings. C quoted two lines in a letter to Allsop of 16 Mar 1822 (*CL* v 222), but otherwise appears never to refer or allude directly to the fragment or to the poem of which it might have been a part. The *SL* text given here incorporates the listed erratum (only).

Oft, oft methinks, the while with Thee
  I breathe, as from the heart, thy dear
  And dedicated name, I hear
A promise and a mystery,
  A pledge of more than passing life,   5
  Yea, in that very name of Wife!

A pulse of love, that ne'er can sleep!
  A feeling that upbraids the heart
  With happiness beyond desert,

7². Here mingling with the image of a pulsing spring, which contained a great deal of emotional resonance for C. Cf e.g. **277** *Inscription for a Fountain on a Heath* and headnote.

That gladness half requests to weep!   10
   Nor bless I not the keener sense
   And unalarming turbulence

Of transient joys, that ask no sting
   From jealous fears, or coy denying;
   But born beneath Love's brooding wing,   15
And into tenderness soon dying,
   Wheel out their giddy moment, then
Resign the soul to love again.

A more precipitated vein
   Of notes, that eddy in the flow   20
   Of smoothest song, they come, they go,
And leave their sweeter understrain
   Its own sweet self—a love of Thee
   That seems, yet cannot greater be!

443. LINES ON THE MOON

[Sept–Oct 1808]

The lines were written into Notebook 13 (*CN* III 3402 var), but never published by C.

The moon—how definite it's orb!
Yet gaze again & with a steady gaze
Tis there indeed—but where is it not—
It is suffused o'er all the sapphire Heaven,
Trees, herbage, snake-like Stream, unwrinkled Lake   5
Whose very murmur does of it partake/
and low and close the broad smooth mountain
Is more a thing of Heaven, than when
Distinct by one dim shade
& yet undivided from the universal cloud   10
In which it towers, infinite in height/—

22. understrain] A Coleridgean coinage. Cf the similar coinage "un-   derpain" in *BL* ch 24 (*CC*) II 234.

444. COUPLET ON SINGING IN CHURCH

[Dec 1808–Jan 1809]

C wrote the lines into Notebook 14 (*CN* III 3434). The two previous entries in the same notebook, perhaps made on the same occasion, appear to reflect some unhappy experience of church or chapel. C's experience of church music at Christ's Hospital appears to have given him high standards: cf **36** *Ode on the Ottery and Tiverton Church Music*.

If sounds like these thro' Heaven's high Temples swell,
I muse, what sort of Noise Folks make in Hell!

445. TO MR AMPHLETT

[Mar 1809]

C's jocular verse letter was not written for publication. It might have been addressed to James Amphlett, perhaps the author of *Invasion: A Descriptive and Satirical Poem* (Wolverhampton [1804]), whose brother had married a third Brent sister and who frequently met C at the Morgans'; or to the brother himself, "a Unitarian, with literary taste and literary friends" (see James Amphlett *The Newspaper Press, in Part of the Last Century, and up to . . . 1860: Recollections*—London and Shrewsbury 1860—22–3). It would appear that one or other of the Amphlett brothers had written to C at Keswick, introducing Mr Baker and promising a hare and a sucking-pig to help entertain Mr Baker (on whom see **453** *On Mr Baker's Marriage*).

Mumps went through the entire Greta Hall household at this time. C appears to have been among the first to suffer; among the last, a month later, was RS (*S Letters*—Warter—II 135–6).

In reply to your note I must tell you, dear Amphlett,
That Coleridge (S.T.) that notorious Wise-acre,
Who has *let* poems many, and *committed* one pamphlet,
Has the mumps and In grumps, & can't see Mr Baker:
His Tongue is as dumb as a bellowsless Organ: 5
For which Lord be prais'd! cry the Ears of J. Morgan.

P.S. Tho' the Thought of the Hare
Without Mr Baker
Spreads a smile in the care
Of the said Poem-maker;   10
Yet his grief is so big
For the loss of the Pig
(And the babe of a Sow
'S no small dainty, I trow)
That in trying to speak   15
He most surely would squeak.

446. ADELPHAN GREEK RIDDLE

[Mar–Apr 1809]

C drafted the lines into Notebook 62 (*CN* III 3470), and then cancelled all but line 5. The Greek characters spell English words, as follows:

Wife sister husband—husband sister wife
Gynandrian incest's union, nature's strife.
Solution of the riddle tho' to seek
Tri-bad is . . . success. Adelphan Greek.
Tri-bad/ that ne'er/near succeed!

"Gynandrian" in line 2 may bear a different sense from "androgynous". The word (the first and only example in *OED* is dated 1828) is used in the botanical sense of flowers with stamens and pistils united in one column. The two elements can mean female and male, wife and husband. "Tri-bad" is underlined in line 4 possibly to mark a pun: thrice bad, trying to be bad or do a bad thing, and, in Greek-derived English, tribade, a female homosexual, from the verb τρίβειν "to rub" (see *OED*). Adelphan might be expected to mean brotherly or sisterly or sibling, but Adelphan Greek here is provokingly more likely to be "un-Delphic", unoracular, perfectly clear—no doubt again with a pun intended.

C has wrapped up his meaning so successfully that it would be foolhardy to attempt to disentangle it. It is unclear whether the riddle describes incest; or a homosexual relationship, male or female; or a more complex intra- and extra-marital relationship; or even—giving full value to the botanical associations of "gynandrian"—whether it was intended as a skit on the second part of Erasmus Darwin's *Botanic Garden, The Loves of the Plants* (1789).

If it is reckoned that the lines recall other riddling meditations on the WW household (e.g. *CN* III 4243), with which C was so deeply involved emotionally, it should be emphasised that they were not written for other eyes than his own.

The language is ambiguous in the extreme, and may even be meant to suggest emotional rather than physical relationships. It should also be borne in mind that family groupings of wife–sister–husband as in the Morgan household, and husband–sister–wife–sister-in-law as in WW's household, were less exceptional then than now (cf also RS's household) and less liable to such interpretations. C used a phrase from the last line, transliterated into Greek, in *503 Couplet on Lesbian Lovers*, but the meanings of that poem are also less straightforward than this editorial title might suggest.

> Ουῖφ σιστηρ ὕσβανδ—ὕσβανδ σιστηρ ουῖφ
> Γυνανδριαν ἰνσεστς ὕνιον, νατυρς στρεῖφ.
> Σολυτιον ὀφ θέ ριδδελ θοῦ το σηκ
> Τρι· βαδ ἴς . . . συκσες. Αδελφαν γρηκ.
> Τρί· βαδ/ θάτ νῆρ συκσηδ!   5

447. VERSE LETTER TO MRS COLERIDGE

[Apr 1809]

The lines are known only from a Sotheby's catalogue: they are signed "S. T. C." and dated 2 Apr 1809 at the end, presumably after a sequence of c 10 lines. C was recovering from mumps at the time (cf *CL* III 183: to B. Montagu [28 Mar 1809]; 184: to D. Stuart [28 Mar 1809]), and harassed by arrangements for printing *The Friend* at Penrith. In the fourth line "a gay till lock" might be a misreading by the Sotheby cataloguer, or it might be a household joke for "at eight o'clock". A similarly humorous tone informs the verse letter **445** *To Mr Amphlett*, written under the same conditions at about the same time.

> My dearest love! Whom I did whilome wed
> I at an early hour shall move to bed,
> And beg, that you, meek Pigeon most uncruel!
> Will make for me a gay till lock of gruel, &c.
>
>   *   *   *

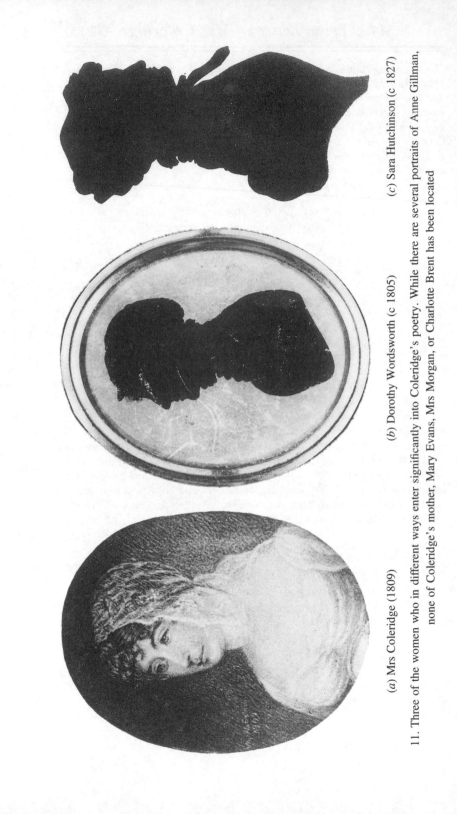

(a) Mrs Coleridge (1809)　　　　(b) Dorothy Wordsworth (c 1805)　　　　(c) Sara Hutchinson (c 1827)

11. Three of the women who in different ways enter significantly into Coleridge's poetry. While there are several portraits of Anne Gillman, none of Coleridge's mother, Mary Evans, Mrs Morgan, or Charlotte Brent has been located

448. ANOTHER EPITAPH ON AN INFANT

[Apr 1809?]

C's lines appear to have been written as a result of his rereading in Apr 1809 of the 1797 *Poems*, containing text (*a*) of **77** *Two Versions of an Epitaph on an Infant*; he was at that time planning another edition with Longman. The present poem was published in a newspaper two years later over the pseudonym Aphilos, "Loveless", "Unloving", or "Friendless"—echoing **437** *A Motto to Accompany a Third Emblem*. It was included in *SL* (1817) and subsequent collections, which differ little from the two earlier versions. The *SL* text is given here, supplying a full point at the end.

> Its balmy lips the Infant blest
> Relaxing from its Mother's breast,
> How sweet it heaves the happy sigh
> Of innocent Satiety!
>
> And such my Infant's latest sigh!   5
> O tell, rude stone! the passer by,
> That here the pretty babe doth lie,
> Death sang to sleep with Lullaby.

449. A MOTTO ADAPTED FROM *LOVE'S LABOUR'S LOST*

[Apr 1809]

The motto is one of several that C copied down after reading Chillingworth's *Religion of Protestants* and Shakespeare's play with mottoes for *The Friend* in mind (*SW&F—CC*—251; cf *CN* III 3812n, 3488). As he remarked while making the transcriptions: "not a line of his silliest character, & poorest play but furnished some profound Truth, or happy illustration of Truth, or (as most frequently) both together".

The present lines develop via an intermediate version (given in vol II) from the King's words to Longaville at *Love's Labour's Lost* IV iii 131–4:

> You do not love Maria? Longaville
> Did never sonnet for her sake compile,

Nor never lay his wreathed arms athwart
His loving bosom, to keep down his heart!

As it turned out, C used other mottoes in the 1809–10 and 1818 *Friend* (see poems **548–54**), and the present one remained unpublished.

How oft I lay'd my wreathed arms athwart
My bosom, to keep down my loving heart!
And then the very pressure seem'd to make
My loving Breast all heart; & heart-like, it would ake!

450. THREE-LINE FRAGMENT

[Apr–Aug 1809]

C drafted the lines in Notebook L (*CN* iii 3506).

Or in vernal or autumnal Nights,
See a black Cloudlet in the middle sky
Make large Oh crescent of the bright full moon.

451. CONTRIBUTION TO
TO MY THRUSHES,
BY THOMAS WILKINSON

[May 1809]

Thomas Wilkinson (1751–1836), a Quaker, was a friend of Charles Lloyd and his family for several years and the Wordsworths from Feb 1801. He was the "friend" of WW's lines *To the Spade of a Friend* (*WPW* iv 75–6) and negotiated the purchase of Broad How. C wrote him a long letter on *The Friend* and Quakerism (*CL* iii 155–7: 31 Dec 1808) and visited him at Yanwath, on his way back to Grasmere from Penrith, where he had been making arrangements for publication; the happy week C spent at Yanwath made Wilkinson, according to DW, "the Father of *The Friend*" (*WL—M* rev—i 356). C added his lines to the fifth of six poems by Wilkinson contained in a small home-made notebook.

The full title of Wilkinson's poem is "To my Thrushes, Blackbirds &c Some Friends having found eight of their Nests in my Garden and looked into the same, to the no small annoyance of the Inhabitants." (He later amended the title to "Birds in Distress" etc.) The poem ends by praising the good conduct of the wild birds in his garden, comparing it jocularly to the behaviour of his hens. Thus, in the original version C first saw:

> But your Cousins, the *Hens*, have insur'd my Displeasure
> In scratching my Borders and stealing their Treasure,
> So I've put their small Ankles in Boots that are sable,
> And perhaps they may travel e're long to the Table.

C placed a cue (†) above the last of these lines, and wrote opposite:

> † Might I venture to suggest these Lines, or rather the *thought* in them far better than these, as the conclusion of this very sweet Poem?

The full text is given by Hilton Kelliher "Thomas Wilkinson of Yanwath, Friend of Wordsworth and Coleridge" *The British Library Journal* VIII (Autumn 1982) 147–67 at 160–2.

Following C's intervention, Wilkinson deleted the last line of the poem as he had written it, and substituted three lines (two of which he had to copy down after C's, and key in) as a transition:

> Yet instead of directing a March to the Table
> Forthwith to the Barnyard I order'd their Route,
> Where their Cockships and Henships might forage about:

———————————————————————— sable.
Would they keep to the Barton, the Barn or the stable,
They might scratch in their mine, and peck at their Table,
Both mouth-free and leg-free, as long as they are able.
But with you, my wild Tenants! I enter no suit—   5
My sweet Fellow-bards, Fellow-gard'ners to boot—
At two thirds of your Meal ye are doing my Work
Then to grudge you the rest asks the heart of a Turk!
O take without Fear your Desèrt for your Wages
And still be my Trees and trim Thick-set your Cages!   10

452. FOR A CLOCK IN A MARKET-PLACE

[Jul–Oct 1809]

C wrote a draft of the lines in Notebook L, and later copied out a revised version, given here, for TP (see *CN* III 3546; *CL* III 236: 9 Oct 1809). Cf the later **673** *Inscription on a Time-piece.*

> What now, O Man! thou dost, or mean'st to do,
> Will help to give thee Peace or make thee rue,
> When hovering o'er the Dot this Hand shall tell
> The moment, that secures thee HEAVEN or HELL!

453. ON MR BAKER'S MARRIAGE:
A FRAGMENT

[1809–11]

C drafted the lines in Notebook 25, the version given here, and later quoted them to Allsop (see *CN* III 3607; Allsop II 21). A Mr Baker—introduced by James Amphlett, whom C had met frequently at the Morgans—had apparently tried to visit C at Greta Hall in Mar 1809: see **445** *To Mr Amphlett.*

> So Mr Baker heart did pluck,
> And did a-courting go!
> And Mr Baker is a Buck
> For why? he needs the Doe.

4. needs the Doe.] In the notebook   the Doe?"
version C wrote underneath: "kneads

454. VERSES BASED ON PARACELSUS

[1809]

C drafted the lines in Notebook 24 (*CN* III 3616), where they are followed by the sentence which appears to have prompted them:

"Philosophiæ etenim meæ ea doctrina est, quod natura ipsa morbus sit"— says Paracelsus in his Prima Medicinæ Basis seu Columna Philosophia.

The Latin is from the *Paragranum* tractatus I "De philosophia" or "Prima medicinae basis, seu Columna. Philosophia", in *Opera Omnia* (3 vols Geneva 1658) I 188B—this being the edition C was using (*CM—CC—*I 296n); tr "For that is the teaching of my philosophy, that nature is itself a disease."

Ills from without extrinsic Balms may heal,
Oft cur'd & wounded by the self-same Steel—
But us what remedy can heal or cure,
Whose very nature is our worst disease.

455. A TOMBLESS EPITAPH

[Oct–Nov 1809]

The lines were first published as an epigraph to C's introduction to "Satyrane's Letters", inserted in the 1809 *Friend* to diversify its tone (*Friend—CC—*II 184). They were included with only minor changes in subsequent collections, and the present text reproduces that of *SL*, incorporating a correction from the Errata.
    C pointed out in a footnote to the untitled *Friend* version that the lines were

Imitated, though in the movements rather than the thoughts, from the VIIth. of Gli Epitafi of *Chiabrera:*

Fu ver, che Ambrosio Salinero a torto
Si pose in pena d' odiose liti, &c.

The reference, in the edition C owned and annotated, is to Gabriello Chiabrera *Opere* (5 vols Venice 1782) II 175–6 (cf J. H. Green sale, Sotheby's 28 Jul 1880 lot 89; *CM—CC—*II 23). C had perhaps been interested in adapting Chiabrera some time before (*CN* III 3318), but it was WW who in the event became enthusiastic and contributed several translations to subsequent issues of *The Friend* (*CC* II 248–9, 269–70, 334–5). WW also translated the same epitaph

C acknowledged in his footnote, and later told HCR that C was at least in part indebted to him (*WL—L* rev—iv 50–1). Although WW's poem was not published until 1836–7 (*WPW* iv 250–1), and although it remains close to the original in a way that C's lines do not, there is little doubt that C's interest was heightened by WW's burst of enthusiasm.

C had been planning and making notes for an attack on various sorts of superstition—"for my Idoloclastes"—since 1802 or so (*CL* ii 893: to J. P. Estlin 7 Dec 1802; *CN* i 1646, 1729). His adoption of the sobriquet Idoloclast, "breaker of idols", owes something to Bacon's attack on idols in the *Novum Organum*, and perhaps something to Luther. The "ancient truths" of "elder times" C held up against his own age were indeed very much those of the 17th century as he understood it, i.e. as Platonic. The "long-neglected holy cave, | The haunt obscure of old Philosophy" deliberately summons up the cave of Plato's *Republic* in this connection.

Satyrane is the "Satyres sonne yborne in forrest wyld" from *The Faerie Queene* i vi. C appears to identify with him as a child of nature, possessed of "child-like simplicity". His suggestion in lines 2–5 (and in the prose text which follows in *The Friend* version) that he was known as Satyrane among his school and college companions is not confirmed by other evidence.

'Tis true, Idoloclastes Satyrane!
(So call him, for so mingling Blame with Praise
And smiles with anxious looks, his earliest friends,
Masking his birth-name, wont to character
His wild-wood fancy and impetuous zeal,)   5
'Tis true that, passionate for ancient truths
And honoring with religious love the Great
Of elder times, he hated to excess,
With an unquiet and intolerant scorn,
The hollow puppets of an hollow Age,   10
Ever idolatrous, and changing ever
Its worthless Idols! Learning, Power, and Time,
(Too much of all) thus wasting in vain war
Of fervid colloquy. Sickness, tis true,
Whole years of weary days, besieged him close,   15
Even to the gates and inlets of his life!
But it is true, no less, that strenuous, firm,
And with a natural gladness, he maintained
The Citadel unconquer'd, and in joy
Was strong to follow the delightful Muse.   20
For not a hidden Path, that to the Shades
Of the belov'd Parnassian forest leads,

Lurk'd undiscover'd by him; not a rill
There issues from the fount of Hippocrene,
But he had trac'd it upward to its source, 25
Thro' open glade, dark glen, and secret dell,
Knew the gay wild flowers on its banks, and cull'd
Its med'cinable herbs. Yea, oft alone,
Piercing the long-neglected holy cave,
The haunt obscure of old Philosophy, 30
He bade with lifted torch its starry walls
Sparkle, as erst they sparkled to the flame
Of od'rous Lamps tended by Saint and Sage.
O fram'd for calmer times and nobler hearts!
O studious Poet, eloquent for truth! 35
Philosopher! contemning wealth and death,
Yet docile, childlike, full of Life and Love!
Here, rather than on monumental stone,
This record of thy worth thy Friend inscribes,
Thoughtful, with quiet tears upon his cheek. 40

456. COUPLET WRITTEN IN AUTUMN 1809

[c Nov 1809]

C wrote the lines into Notebook L (*CN* III 3635). The opening words echo the
beginning of WW's *Intimations Ode* (*WPW* IV 279), **269** *The Mad Monk* 9, **289**
Letter to —— 232, and **293** *Dejection: An Ode* 76. The present couplet could
perhaps be a jocular reworking of the earlier mood.

There was a time when Fortune made me glad/
I was her bright Boy, and her golden Lad!

457. LINES WRITTEN IN LATE AUTUMN 1809

[c Nov–Dec 1809]

C drafted the lines in Notebook 18 (*CN* III 3649), where they are introduced as
follows: "One lifts up one's eyes to Heaven as if to seek there what one had lost

on Earth/". KC suggests that the emphatic word "inward" applied to the dream, and the conjunction of these repressed feelings with the heavenward searching gaze recall other entries such as *CN* II 2346, 2453, 2546, 3159.

Eyes—
Whose Half-beholdings thro' unsteady tears
Gave shape, hue, distance, to the inward Dream/

458. VERSE LINE, LATE AUTUMN 1809

[c Nov–Dec 1809]

C wrote the line into Notebook 18 (*CN* III 3651), where it completes a sentence which begins thus: "He was so ⟨universally & so deeply⟩ beloved that many a man began to affect his bitterest Foe".

For his deep lamentation of their common Love.

459. ADAPTATION OF LINES FROM DANIEL'S *CIVIL WARS*

[Dec 1809]

The lines were printed in *The Courier* (7 Dec 1809), in a postscript to C's "Letters to the Spaniards" (*EOT—CC—*II 42). The postscript begins:

> If you should have no Verses in your Poet's corner for the day, permit me to recommend the following quotations, the latter from an obscure Poet of the reign of CHARLES the First; the former from a Poet of ELIZABETH's days, whose name indeed is better known, but whose works are almost as little read. The excellent good sense of the first, sufficiently atones for the langour of the metre, and the prosaic character of the diction: the application of both is too striking to need any comment.

(C's second "quotation" is from Cartwright; see poem **460.**) C appends the reference "DANIEL's Civil Wars, B. 7. Stan. 14. 15." The original of the verses (in *B Poets* IV 174; cf *Poetical Works*—2 vols 1718—II 220) is as follows:

XIV.

Here Scottish-border broils, and fears of France,
Urg'd with the present time's necessity,
Brought forth a subtle-shadow'd countenance
Of quiet peace, resembling amity;
Wrapt in a strong and curious ordinance
Of many articles, bound solemnly:
As if those gordian knots could be so ty'd,
As no impatient sword could them divide:

XV.

Especially, whereas the self-same ends
Concur not in a point of like respect;
For that each party covertly intends
Thereby their own designments to effect:
Which peace with more endang'ring wounds offends,
Than war can do; that stands upon suspect,
And never can be ty'd with other chain,
Than intermutual benefit and gain.

For a stanza written in the manner of the *Civil Wars*, applied to the condition of Ireland, see poem **514;** cf also later adaptations of other poems by Daniel (poems **548, 550, 552, 601**).

Here Irish discontents and fears of France,
Urged with the present times' necessity,
Brought forth a subtly-shadow'd countenance
Of quiet PEACE, resembling amity;
Wrapt in a strong and curious ordinance   5
Of many articles bound solemnly,
As if those gordian knots could be so tied
That no ambitious sword could them divide!

Especially, whereas the self-same ends
Concur in no one point of like respect,   10
But that each party covertly intends
Thereby its own designment to effect.
Such Peace with more endangering wounds offends
Than War can do, which stands upon suspect;
And never can be tied with other chain   15
Than intermutual benefit and gain.

460. CARTWRIGHT MODIFIED AGAIN

[Dec 1809]

The lines appeared in *The Courier* (7 Dec 1809), in a postscript to the first of C's "Letters on the the Spaniards" (*EOT—CC*—II 43), which is given in **459** *Adaptation of Lines from Daniel's "Civil Wars"* headnote. A reference is appended to the poem: "Love's Convert, by CARTWRIGHT."

C had copied out the original from Cartwright's *The Siedge; or, Love's Convert* I i 86–94 (*Comedies, Tragi-comedies, with Other Poems*—1651—100) in a notebook in 1804 (*CN* II 1943). When he first copied the lines, he changed only "aime" to "name" in the last line (here = "praise"); and he quoted this version, incorporating the same single change, in *The Friend* XXII (31 Jan 1810) 363–4 (*CC*) II 306; cf *The Friend* (1818) II 135 (*CC*) I 272.

The *Courier* version given here changes "yourself" to "yourselves" in line 2; "impious" to "treacherous" in line 8; and "name" (originally "aime") to "praise" in line 9. See poem **343** for an earlier modification of Cartwright.

> Fear never wanted arguments: you do
> Reason yourselves into a careful bondage,
> Circumspect only to your misery.
> I could urge Freedom, Charters, Country, Laws,
> Gods, and Religion, and such precious names,   5
> Nay, what you value higher, WEALTH; but that
> You sue for bondage, yielding to demands
> As treacherous as they are insolent, and have
> Only this sluggish praise—to PERISH FULL!

461. SEPARATION, AFTER CHARLES COTTON

[Early 1810?]

C first drafted his stanzas in Notebook 18 (*CN* III 3653), at a time when SH departed with her cousin John Monkhouse for his new farm at Hindwell, on the banks of the Wye. The visit had been planned at least as early as Aug 1809 (*WL—M* rev—I 366, 370), John Monkhouse had arrived at Allan Bank c 14 Feb 1810, and he and SH left for Hindwell a month or so later (Reed II 448, 450). It is possible that the stanzas were conceived much earlier, in Malta c 1805, but more likely that they grew from the situation in 1809: they display C's consciousness that his feelings of jealousy were exaggerated even as he gave them utterance. The stanzas were arranged in a different order and revised in a more detached, fictional form for *PW* (1834), the version given here.

C is in part indebted to Charles Cotton's *Ode* (to Chlorinda), which he is likely to have read in Chalmer's *English Poets* at the time SH left for Hindwell (*The Works of the English Poets, from Chaucer to Cowper* ed Alexander Chalmers—21 vols 1810—VI 728–9; *CN* III 3653n). An element of self-conscious, humorous exaggeration is a distinguishing element of Cotton's wit at large, and may also have influenced C. The fourth and sixth stanzas in C's revised version adapt the eleventh and twentieth of Cotton, and C's fifth is Cotton's eleventh. The text of Cotton's stanzas 9–12 and final stanza (20) is as follows in Chalmers:

> I first by you was worthy made,
> Next by her choice; let me not prove
> Blasphemous, if I'm not afraid
> To say most worthy by my love.

> And must I then be damn'd from bliss
> For valuing the blessing more,
> Be wretched made through happiness,
> And by once being rich more poor?

> This separation is, alas!
> Too great a punishment to bear,
> Oh! take my life, or let me pass
> That life, that happy life, with her.

> O my Chlorinda! couldst thou see
> Into the bottom of my heart,
> There's such a mine of love for thee,
> The treasure would supply desert.

> *   *   *

> Meanwhile my exit now draws nigh,
> When, sweet Chlorinda, thou shalt see
> That I have heart enough to die,
> Not half enough to part with thee.

> A sworded man whose trade is blood,
>   In grief, in anger, and in fear,
> Thro' jungle, swamp, and torrent flood,
>   I seek the wealth you hold so dear!

> The dazzling charm of outward form,   5
>   The power of gold, the pride of birth,

Have taken Woman's heart by storm—
    Usurp'd the place of inward worth.

Is not true Love of higher price
    Than outward Form, tho' fair to see,   10
Wealth's glittering fairy-dome of ice,
    Or echo of proud ancestry?—

O! Asra, Asra! couldst thou see
    Into the bottom of my heart,
There's such a mine of Love for thee,   15
    As almost might supply desert!

(This separation is, alas!
    Too great a punishment to bear;
O! take my life, or let me pass
    That life, that happy life, with her!)   20

The perils, erst with steadfast eye
    Encounter'd, now I shrink to see—
Oh! I have heart enough to die—
    Not half enough to part from Thee!

462. LINES ALTERED FROM
FULKE GREVILLE'S
A TREATISE OF HUMANE LEARNING

[Mar–Jun 1810]

C wrote out the lines in Notebook 18, the version given here, and again in the margin of a book by James Sedgwick, where he attributes them to "Lord Brook" (*CN* III 3709; *CM—CC*—IV 620). The notebook version constitutes the first in

11. Cf the pleasure-dome of **178** *Kubla Khan*, which C associated with the ice-palace of Catherine of Russia, pride and property. Orangeries, conservatories, greenhouses, and domed skylights were popular forms of conspicuous consumption at the time; cast iron made it possible for rich men to emulate great potentates, substituting glass for ice.

a series of 11 consecutive entries which derive from Fulke Greville's *Certain Learned and Elegant Workes* (see *CN* III 3717=poem **463**). The original lines make up stanza 140 of *A Treatise of Humane Learning* (*Workes* 49):

> For onely that man understands indeed,
> And well remembers, which he well can doe,
> The *Laws liue, onely where the Law doth breed*
> *Obedience to the workes it bindes us to:*
>> And as the life of Wisedome hath exprest,
>> If this you know, then doe it, and be blest.

> For only that man understands indeed
> Who well remembers what he well can do:
> The Faith lives only where the Faith doth breed
> Obedience to the Works, it binds us to,
> And as the Life of Wisdom hath exprest—   5
> If this you know, then do it and be blest.

463. FULKE GREVILLE MODIFIED

[Mar 1810]

C drafted the lines in Notebook 18, and used a revised version in *A Lay Sermon* and *Aids to Reflection* (*CN* III 3717; *LS—CC—*120; *AR—CC—*100). The present text is from *AR*.

The lines in the notebook constitute one of a series of 11 consecutive entries which derive from Fulke Greville's *Certaine Learned and Elegant Workes*. Four of these (*CN* III 3709, 3715, 3716, 3717) involve the transcription of verses, and *CN* III 3709 is given separately as poem **462**. *CN* III 3717 combines and adapts stanzas 66–7 of Greville's *A Treatie of Warres* (*Workes* 82), which read as follows:

> 66.
>
> God and the World they worship still together,
> Draw not their lawes to him, but his to theirs,
> Vntrue to both, so prosperous in neither,
> Amid their owne desires still raising feares:
>> "Vnwise, as all distracted Powers be.
>> "Strangers to God, fooles in humanitie.

67.

Too good for great things, and too great for good;
Their Princes serue their Priest, yet that Priest is
Growne King, euen by the arts of flesh and bloud;
Blind *Superstition* having built vp this,
    "As knowing no more than it selfe can doe,
    "Which shop (for words) sells God & Empire too

The verses are preceded in the notebook by the comment: "The Christians as contrasted with the first Mohametans,=the English to the French Government—". When they were printed in *LS*, it was as an epigraph between the title-page and the Introduction. In J. G. Lockhart's copy C wrote:

From the publication of Pope's Essay on Man or rather from Blackmore's Creation, our English Poetry has been crowded with didactic and sentimentaliary poems, those ⟨found among the minor poems⟩ of Wordsworth and of our Laureate appearing to me the best, among many good. But I challenge the admirers of modern Verse to produce eight lines, in the same kind of writing, equal to the motto wr above—and I leave to them to hunt out the Author: informing them only, that he wrote before the Restoration.

In *AR* the verses were used to illustrate Aphorism xvii, "Inconsistency".
    The last of the eight lines, added in the two printed texts, is from *Macbeth* I vii 44.

God and the World we worship both together,
    Draw not our Laws to Him, but His to ours;
Untrue to both, so prosperous in neither,
    The imperfect Will brings forth but barren Flowers!
Unwise as all distracted Interests be,   5
Strangers to God, Fools in Humanity:
Too good for great things, and too great for good,
While still "I dare not" waits upon "I wou'd."

464. FURTHER LINES ON TRANQUILLITY

[Mar 1810]

C drafted the lines in Notebook 18 (*CN* iii 3747), where it is not clear whether the first line is to be taken as an epigraph (as given here) or as continuous with the four lines that follow. It is also unclear whether C wrote "*Hope*" or "*Hopes*".

Poem **283** *Ode to Tranquillity*, belonging to the close of 1801, was reprinted in the first number of *The Friend* on 1 Jun 1809 (*CC*) II 14. The present fragment reflects the altered mood of nearly a decade later. The image here of bird-flight, the "wheeling . . . Coil", is elsewhere associated by C with disappointment in himself: cf *CL* II 814: to W. Sotheby 19 Jul [1802]; *CN* II 2531. On "the Bird Hope" cf *CN* III 3314 and n.

> *When Hope* but *made* Tranquillity be felt—

> A Flight of Hopes for ever on the wing
> But made Tranquillity a conscious Thing—
> And wheeling round and round in sportive Coil
> Fann'd the calm Air upon the brow of Toil—

465. LINES ON THE BODY AND THE SOUL

[Apr–Jun 1810]

C drafted the lines in Notebook 17 (*CN* III 3764). They may be connected with a reading of K. E. Schelling or some writer of the same school. KC compares and quotes his marginal note on *Jahrbücher der Medicin als Wissenschaft* ed A. F. Marcus and F.W.J. Schelling (3 vols Tübingen 1805–8) II (2) 200–1 No 25 (*CM—CC—*III 119–20).

> The body—
> Eternal Shadow of the finite Soul/
> The Soul's self-symbol/ it's image of itself,
> It's own yet not itself—

466. WRITTEN IN DEJECTION, MAY 1810

[May 1810]

C drafted the lines in Notebook 18 (*CN* III 3795), where they grow out of an entry which begins in prose:

?When I was white [. . . .] care had I To feel and know. That all my body

high and low Even parts that never met men's Eye, were pure of stain
as new-fallen Snow/—When absent soon to meet again That morning &
that last Employ Had only so much Pain, As the fears of Hope detract
from certain Joy—And now—O then I am least opprest When with the
cleansing Stream I mix my tears—and oft I'd fain neglect myself—Such
anguish & such sinking down of Heart comes o'er me—yet never can I—

Although it is clear from the initial capitals of some words and from the rhymes
that C was in part thinking of verse-lines here, it is often not clear where the
lines are meant to begin and end. KC suggests that C might have **293** *Dejection:
An Ode* in mind. As in 1802, he here takes refuge in the "abstruse research" of
the notebook entries that follow.

> For neither death, nor absence, nor demerit
> Can free the love-enchanted spirit—
> And I seem always in her eye,
> And she will never more appear to mine.

467. THE VISIONARY HOPE

[1810?]

The lines are something of a mystery. In *PW* (JDC) 171B JDC suggests that they
might have been written in 1807 or 1810; in *PW* (EHC) I 416 EHC suggests
1810. In fact, they could have been written on several occasions between 1802
and 1815: e.g. at about the time of **335** *The Pains of Sleep* (Sept 1803), during
the revision of *Remorse* or after it was staged, or even at the time when *BL*
was dictated (for these last two suggestions see the references in *PW*—JDC—
632A). C referred to the poem directly just once, when he quoted two lines in
a letter to Daniel Stuart of 14 Oct 1828 (*CL* VI 765). Poem **482** *Human Life*
presents a similar situation.

The lines were first published in *SL* (1817), and later included in the three
major collections. Although there is no ms, and the printed texts do not vary
except in punctuation and spelling, the *SL* printing is peculiar in that it is not
as well prepared as most other texts in the same volume, and several slovenly
mistakes remain uncorrected. The version given here is from *PW* (1829).

> Sad lot, to have no Hope! Though lowly kneeling
> He fain would frame a prayer within his breast,
> Would fain entreat for some sweet breath of healing,

That his sick body might have ease and rest;
He strove in vain! the dull sighs from his chest   5
Against his will the stifling load revealing,
Though Nature forced; though like some captive guest,
Some royal prisoner at his conqueror's feast,
An alien's restless mood but half concealing,
The sternness on his gentle brow confessed,   10
Sickness within and miserable feeling:
Though obscure pangs made curses of his dreams,
And dreaded sleep, each night repelled in vain,
Each night was scattered by its own loud screams:
Yet never could his heart command, though fain,   15
One deep full wish to be no more in pain.

That HOPE, which was his inward bliss and boast,
Which waned and died, yet ever near him stood,
Though changed in nature, wander where he would—
For Love's Despair is but Hope's pining Ghost!   20
For this one hope he makes his hourly moan,
He wishes and *can* wish for this alone!
Pierced, as with light from Heaven, before its gleams
(So the love-stricken visionary deems)
Disease would vanish, like a summer shower,   25
Whose dews fling sunshine from the noon-tide bower!
Or let it stay! yet this one Hope should give
Such strength that he would bless his pains and live.

468. FRAGMENT IN BLANK VERSE

[May 1810]

C drafted the lines in Notebook 18 (*CN* III 3796), and they read like a fragment
from a drama. The word "disrent" (line 7), for "split in two directions", is not
in the *OED*. On the inner and outer margins of the page are C's anagrams, in
Greek capitals, for SH: "ΣΑΡΑ" and "ΑΣΡΑ ѱΟΝΘΙΝΥ". At the four corners
of the page are written (clockwise) "W+M+D=W", "Coleridge", "Mary", and
"William".

                    I have experienc'd
The worst, the World can wreak on me; the worst
That can make Life indifferent, yet disturb
With whisper'd Discontents the dying prayer.
I have beheld the whole of all, wherein   5
My Heart had any interest in this Life,
To be disrent and torn from off my Hopes,
That nothing now is left. Why then live on?
That Hostage, which the world had in it's keeping
Given by me as a Pledge that I would live,   10
That Hope of Her, say rather, that pure Faith
In her fix'd Love, which held me to keep truce
With the Tyranny of Life—is gone ah whither?
What boots it to reply?—"tis gone! and now
Well may I break this Pact, this League, of Blood   15
That ties me to myself—and break I shall"—

469. HUMOROUS LINES, SPRING 1810

[c May 1810]

C drafted the lines in Notebook 18 (*CN* iii 3831); their purpose is unclear. KC
suggests that he wrote them for a song in some projected dramatic entertain-
ment, as he was in the habit of doing in his notebooks (cf *CN* iii 4254; also ii
2692); they might have been even less premeditated than that. Oxymel is liter-
ally "sour honey", and C's was evidently made with lemon. The poem suggests
that it was not necessarily a medicinal drink, in spite of the *OED* entry (which
mentions vinegar).

The little Birds shoot out their *gushes* round
Mellow tho' shrill, an Oxymel of Sound:
As if with sweet confusion sway'd,
The thirsty Ear drank Lemonade.

11. Faith] Cf the play on *fides*   *Ad Vilmum Axiologum: Latin Version.*
"faith" in association with SH in **430**

470. VOLTAIRE VERSIFIED

[Jun–Jul 1810]

C drafted the lines in Notebook 18 (*CN* III 3928). They are an attempt to versify Voltaire's prose: "Men seem all to be employed at present in mutual destruction, and, from the empire of the Mogul to the straits of Gibraltar, all is war. It is supposed that France also will foot it in this vile Pyrrhic dance." (letter CII—Paris Sept 1739—in Voltaire's correspondence with Frederick the Great: *Posthumous Works of Frederick II, King of Prussia* tr Thomas Holcroft—13 vols 1789—VII 14). The next two entries in Notebook 18 are connected with C's reading of this work.

A *pyrrhichē* is literally a dance in armour or war-dance, but Voltaire and C undoubtedly intend to suggest a victory won at too great a cost, like that of Pyrrhus at the battle of Asculum (279 B.C.). C might also intend a further suggestion of double-short pyrrhic rhythm in the middle of his second line.

Nations mad with France
All foot it in the Pyrrhic Dance.

471. GILBERT WHITE VERSIFIED, ON THE OWL

[Jul 1810]

C drafted the lines in Notebook 18 (*CN* III 3959), in the course of a long note in which he quoted, condensed, and remarked on Gilbert White's *Natural History of Selborne* in *Works* ed J. Aikin (2 vols 1802), which he was reading and annotating at the time. The facts versified by C come from White's letter XV to Barrington (I 260–1):

> The plumage of the remiges of the wings of every species of owl that I have yet examined is remarkably soft and pliant. Perhaps it may be necessary that the wings of these birds should not make much resistance or rushing, that they may be enabled to steal through the air unheard upon a nimble and watchful quarry.

Lines 2, 3, and 4 appear to be alternatives, although none of them is cancelled.

The owl with pliant, downy, unresisting wings
Steals thro' the cheated air,
Deludes the unbetraying air—
deepens the still sleep of the breathless air—

472. OBSERVATION ON COLOUR AND LIGHT

[Jul 1810]

C drafted the lines in Notebook 18 (*CN* III 3967), with no apparent connection
to the adjacent entries.

The sparkling Color moats upon the Brook,
And glorious dust of Light that interweaves
It's restless Dance above/

473. BURLESQUE IN THE MANNER OF WALTER SCOTT

[Oct 1810]

C quoted his lines in a letter to WW (*CL* III 295) comprising a long examination
of Scott's *Lady of the Lake*, which had been published in May 1810 and which
C had before him as he wrote. He makes the point that Scott introduces

a vast string of patronymics, and names of Mountains, Rivers, &c—the
most commonplace imagery the Bard gars look almaist as well as new, by
the introduction of Benvoirlich, Uam Var,

on copse-wood gray
That *waved & wept* on *Loch Achray*,
And mingled with the pine trees *blue*
On the bold Cliffs of Benvenue—

The quoted lines (written continuously as prose in the ms) are from *The Lady
of the Lake* I v 9–12. C's own lines follow after a gap, and are made up from
and mimic I v and vi of Scott's poem. His italicisation of certain phrases is
explained by his criticisms of Scott's repetitive language and ambling rhythms
elsewhere in the letter (cf also *CN* III 3970).

How should the Poet e'er give o'er,
With his eye fix'd on Cambus-More—
Need reins be tighten'd in Despair,
When rose Benledi's ridge *in air*—
Tho' not one image grace the Heath,   5
It gain such charm from flooded Teith—
Besides, you need not travel far,
To reach the Lake of Vennachar—
Or *ponder refuge* from your Toil
By far Lochard or Aberfoil!—   10

474. TRANSLATION OF A GOETHE EPIGRAM

[1810–11]

C drafted the lines in Notebook 18 (*CN* III 4045). As KC explains, they are a
translation of No 65 of Goethe's *Venezianische Epigramme*, although it is un-
certain which version C had in front of him. In its first, anonymous publication
in Schiller's *Musen-Almenach für das Jahr 1796* 241 (epigram 65), it read:

> Ist's denn so großes Geheimniß, was Gott und der Mensch und die Welt sei?
> Nein! Doch niemand mags gern hören, da bleibt es geheim.

This version appears in at least two reprintings from the *Musen-Almenach*.
Revising the epigrams, Goethe printed No 65 thus:

> Ist's denn so großes Geheimniß, was Gott und der Mensch und die Welt sey?
> Nein! Doch niemand hört's gerne; da bleibt es geheim.

First published in this form in *Neue Schriften* ed J. F. Unger (7 vols Berlin
1792–1800) VII.

A third and later variant ("Ist denn so groß das Geheimnis") is found in
several collected editions, only two of which (Tübingen 1806–10 in 13 vols and
Vienna 1808–11 in 15 vols) were early enough to have been a possible source
for this entry. In any case, as KC also explains, a nuance of C's translation
perhaps excludes this last version. "*Is't* then *a* Myst'ry so great" would suggest
either the *Musen-Almenach* or *Neue Schriften* version ("*Ist's* denn *so großes*
Geheimniß") rather than one of the later editions, whose text C would more
probably have rendered "Is then *the* Myst'ry".

Is't then a Myst'ry so great, what God and the Man and the World is?
No!—but we hate to hear! Hence it a Myst'ry remains.

475. THE MOON ON THE PACIFIC MAIN

[Mar 1811]

C drafted the lines in Notebook 18 (*CN* III 4052), without explanation.

As when the new or full moon urges
The high, long, large, unbreaking surges
Of the pacific Main.

476. ON THE FIRST POEM IN DONNE'S BOOK

[Apr–May 1811]

Donne's first poem is *The Flea*, and C inscribed his lines, in the version given below, alongside it in CL's copy of Donne's 1669 *Poems* (*CM—CC*—II 217; cf vol II lines 8–15.1.4). His lines were originally part of a long, loosely evolving sequence written in a notebook a little earlier, which began in a prose meditation on wit and wound compulsively and ominously into other topics, such as limbo and the paradoxical polarity of the godhead (*CN* III 4073, 4074). A reference to Crathmocraulo in the notebook might associate the beginning of the lines with a satire on an Irish literary adventurer recently arrived in London, George Croly (for whom see **703** *Lines on George Croly's "Apocalypse"*). See also **477** *Moles*; **478** *Limbo*; **479** *Ne Plus Ultra*. The continuous sequence is given in vol II **476**.

C wrote other lines on Donne in a copy of Chalmers's *English Poets*, which he incorporated into **120** *Fragments of an Epistle to Thomas Poole*, begun much earlier.

Be proud, as Spaniards. Leap for Pride, ye Fleas!
In Nature's *minim* Realm ye're now Grandees.
Skip-jacks no more, nor civiller Skip-Johns,
Thrice-honor'd Fleas! I greet you all, as *Dons*.
In Phœbus' Archives register'd are ye,   5
And this your Patent of Nobility!

477. MOLES

[Apr–May 1811]

The poem is extracted from the longer and not wholly satisfactory sequence from which **476** *On the First Poem in Donne's Book*, **478** *Limbo*, and **479** *Ne Plus Ultra* were also extracted. The five lines were printed with slight modification in the 1818 *Friend*, to describe the reaction of "the partizans of a crass and sensual materialism, the advocates of the Nihil nisi ab extra" (tr "Nothing except what has evidence from outside") (*CC* I 494fn). A draft development of them is also to be found in the ms that subsequently developed into *Confessions of an Inquiring Spirit* (*SW&F—CC*—1111–71). They were reprinted in the form in which they appear here, again with modifications of punctuation and capitalisation, in *PW* (1834).

In their original context (VAR **476**.29–33) the lines describe the fate of the souls annihilated by the pulverised flea of Donne's poem. They concentrate a metaphysical paradox to be found in Pope:

> Most souls, 'tis true, but peep out once an age,
> Dull sullen pris'ners in the body's cage:
> Dim lights of life, that burn a length of years
> Useless, unseen, as lamps in sepulchres;
> Like Eastern Kings a lazy state they keep,
> And close confin'd to their own palace, sleep.
> (*Elegy to the Memory of an Unfortunate Lady* 17–22)

>   —They shrink in, as Moles
> (Nature's mute monks, live mandrakes of the ground)
> Creep back from Light—then listen for its sound;—
> See but to dread, and dread they know not why—
> The natural alien of their negative eye.   5

478. LIMBO: A FRAGMENT

[Apr–May 1811]

The fragment is from a longer sequence of lines written in Notebook 18 in Apr–May 1811, which began with an elaborate conceit on the varieties of wit to be seen among C's friends and acquaintances, in turn developed into a celebration of the fertile wit of Donne as seen in *The Flea*, and then imagining the journey of Donne's pulverised flea to Limbo (*CN* III 4073). The sequence is consistent in its development away from its witty onset towards a penumbral zone of nightmare and horror, but compulsively so, and the present fragment is one of several autonomous portions which C published in his lifetime under separate titles.

The text given here is from the ms of the notebook version, passing over the deletions (cf VAR **476**.34–61). It appears thus in *PW* (1834), with only minor variations, under the title *Limbo*. C had previously copied it, under the heading "a Dream of Purgatory, alias Limbo", into SC's album in Oct 1827, where it has a different ending:

> No such sweet Sights does Limbo Den immure,
> Wall'd round and made a Spirit-goal secure.
> In one sole Outlet yawns the Phantom Wall:
> And thorough this, grim road to worser thrall,
> Oft homeward scouring from a Sick Child's Dream
> Old **Mother Brownrigg**[1] shoots upon a Scream;
> And turning back her Face with hideous Leer
> Leaves Sentry there INTOLERABLE FEAR!

> A lurid thought is growthless dull Negation:
> Yet that is but a Purgatory Curse.
> SHE knows a fear far worse—
> Flee, lest thou hear it's Name! Flee, rash Imagination!

In 1828 C claimed to have revised and expanded the whole of which the present poem is a part as "a pretended Fragment of Lee, the Tragic Poet", "written by Lee while in Bedlam" (*CL* VI 758: to A. A. Watts 14 Sept 1828; 779: to A. A. Watts [Dec 1828]); but he was able to quote only the first 20 lines of the present text for his publishers.

The backgrounds to the longer poem are various. This fragment seems closely related to J. Böhme *Works* ed G. Ward and T. Langcake (10 pts in 4 vols 1764–81) II (1) *Forty Questions concerning the Soul*, esp question 34, and also to *The Threefold Life of Man* (in the same vol) 4.32. Again, the echoing of the lines in the last chapter of *BL*, particularly the first and last paragraphs (ch 24—*CC*—II 234–5, 247), points up their intimate connection with C's concepts and feelings. Cf also *CN* IV 4692, in which a variant form of the opening lines is discussed in a prose context.

---

[1] Mother Brownrigg, a midwife, was hanged in 1767 for beating her female apprentices to death and hiding their bodies in a coal hole—as related in a parody of RS in the first number of *The Anti-Jacobin*, 20 Nov 1797; see also *CN* I 1183.

Tis a strange Place, this Limbo! not a Place,
Yet name it so—where Time & weary Space
Fetter'd from flight, with night-mair sense of Fleeing
Strive for their last crepuscular Half-being—
Lank Space, and scytheless Time with branny Hands   5
Barren and soundless as the measuring Sands,
Mark'd but by Flit of Shades—unmeaning they
As Moonlight on the Dial of the Day—
But that is lovely, looks like Human Time,
An Old Man with a steady Look sublime   10
That stops his earthly Task to watch the Skies—
But he is blind—a statue hath such Eyes—
Yet having moon-ward turn'd his face by chance—
Gazes the orb with moon-like Countenance
With scant white hairs, with fore-top bald & high   15
He gazes still, his eyeless Face all Eye—
As twere an Organ full of silent Sight
His whole Face seemeth to rejoice in Light/
Lip touching Lip, all moveless, Bust and Limb,
He seems to gaze at that which seems to gaze on Him!   20

No such sweet Sights doth Limbo Den immure,
Wall'd round and made a Spirit-jail secure
By the mere Horror of blank Naught at all—
Whose circumambience doth these Ghosts enthrall.
A lurid thought is growthless dull Privation   25
Yet that is but a Purgatory Curse

7–8. C likens reading the Scriptures while setting at nought "those inward means of grace" to reading in "a dead language: a sun-dial by moonlight" (*SM*—*CC*—57).

16. eyeless Face all Eye] Cf C on John Gough of Kendal, who was the model for WW's blind man in *The Excursion*: "Why, his face sees all over! It is all one eye! . . . it is the mere stamp, the undisturbed *ectypon*, of his own soul!" (*Omniana*—1812— "The Soul and its Organs of Sense": *SW&F*—*CC*—335–6); also WW on

Newton's statue seen in moonlight (*Prelude*—1805—III 56–9).

25–8. Privation . . . *Negation*] In C's first draft the sequence of terms is reversed. A later notebook entry (*CN* III 4213) makes the distinction between "a negation of Life, instead of the mere privation—it's ~~opposi~~ positive and real Opposite, not the vaccuum of its cessation".

26. Purgatory] C is usually rather nice about a theological distinction which his poem obscures. Limbo and Purgatory are strictly separate,

Hell knows a fear far worse,
A fear, a future fate. Tis *positive Negation!*

479. NE PLUS ULTRA

[Apr–May 1811, or later]

The lines occur at the end of the long and not wholly satisfactory sequence in Notebook 18 which includes **476** *On the First Poem in Donne's Book*, **477** *Moles*, and **478** *Limbo* (*CN* III 4073, 4074; VAR **476**.62–82). It is not certain whether they are meant to be taken with the preceding lines or not, although the balance of evidence is slightly in favour of doing so. At the same time, it is likely that they were drafted elsewhere, and copied into Notebook 18 in their present form so as to complement the lines that precede them. The negative light or timelessness of Limbo is matched by positive darkness or Hell, and the sense of privation and horror has its counterpart in the paradoxical, exhilarating polarity of the godhead. C came explicitly to repudiate the ideas his poem celebrates by 1818 (*CL* IV 873–6: to J. H. Green 30 Sept 1818; 883: to C. A. Tulk [24 Nov 1818]; *CN* III 4445; etc), but the poem was printed with changes only of punctuation and capitalisation in *PW* (1834).

Sole Positive of Night!
Antipathist of Light!
Fate's only Essence! Primal Scorpion Rod!
The one permitted Opposite of God!
Condensed Blackness, and Abysmal Storm   5
Compacted to one Sceptre
Arms the Grasp enorm,
The Intercepter!
The Substance, that still casts the Shadow, Death!

Limbo being that region on the border of Hell where the souls of the just— the saints of the Old Covenant and of unbaptised infants—await the Last Judgement, while Purgatory is where the souls of the redeemable undergo punishment for their venial sins while they await the same. The souls in Limbo are deprived of the blessedness of the Beatific Vision, but beyond that privation they suffer no punishment.

title. In the notebook the lines follow on the last (unrevised) line of **478** *Limbo*, almost as if that last line was their title: "Of aye-unepithetable P̶r̶i̶v̶ Negation". The present title was given when the lines were first published, separately but immediately following *Limbo*, in *PW* (1834).

The Dragon foul and fell!   10
   The unrevealable
And hidden one, whose Breath
Gives Wind and Fuel to the fires of Hell!
   Ah sole Despair
Of both th' Eternities in Heaven!   15
Sole Interdict of all-bedewing Prayer,
   The All-compassionate!
   Save to the Lampads seven
Revealed to none of all th' Angelic State,
   Save to the Lampads seven   20
   That watch the Throne of Heaven!

480. ADAPTATION OF MILTON'S LINES ON SHAKESPEARE

[Apr–May 1811]

C wrote the lines in the margin of a copy of Donne's 1669 *Poems* which belonged to CL (*CM—CC*—II 234). They combine Milton *On Shakespear. 1630* 7–8, 15–16 (var). The last couplet reads in the original:

> And so Sepulcher'd in such pomp dost lie,
> That Kings for such a Tomb would wish to die.

C quoted lines 1–8, 15–16 of Milton's poem, run together but without other variation, in *The Friend* XXV (22 Feb 1810) (*CC*) II 346.

Thou in our wonder & astonishment
Hast built thyself a live-long Monument;
And there sepulchred in such state dost lie
That Kings for such a Tomb might wish to die.

20. Lampads seven] Also referred to in lines inserted into **142** *Ode on the Departing Year* (see 89⁺EC), they derive from Rev 4.5 and Cabbalistic tradition. C himself provides a gloss in *P Lects* lect 10 (1949) 299. He appears to have been the first to use the word in English (as is apparently the case with line 2 "Antipathist").

481. LINES INSCRIBED IN
BENEDETTO MENZINI

[1804–12]

C wrote the lines on a front flyleaf of Menzini's *Poesie* (2 vols Nice 1782) (*CM—CC*—III 863). The construction "nor . . . Have I, to whom" might suggest that they have an Italian original ("non ho cui"), but no model, Italian or otherwise, has been traced; nor is the occasion of composition known. Although they might have been written when C acquired the book in the Mediterranean (presumably), and although he wrote poems on flyleaves and title-pages before he began the practice of annotating systematically, the mood and manner of the lines suggests that they might have been written later, following the break with WW and SH (*C&SH* 101, 173).

> I stand alone, nor tho' my Heart should break
> Have I, to whom I may complain or speak.
> Here I stand, a hopeless man and sad
> Who hoped to have seen my Love, my Life.
> And strange it were indeed, could I be glad   5
> Remembring her, my Soul's betrothed Wife/
> For in this World no creature, that has life,
> Was e'er to me so gracious & so good/
> Her Love was to my Heart, like the Heart-blood.

482. HUMAN LIFE,
ON THE DENIAL OF IMMORTALITY

[1811–15?]

There are no mss. The lines were first published in *SL* (1817), and were reprinted with changes only of punctuation in the three later collections.

In two copies of *SL* C claimed that the poem was written in proposed imitation of Donne. He made another attempt at such an imitation at the time he was reading and annotating Donne in Chalmers's *English Poets*, and the present attempt is possibly connected with this (see *CN* III 4073; **476** *On the First Poem in Donne's Book*). C reports in one of the same annotated copies of *SL* that CL saw "no other resemblance but that more thought is *packed* together than is compatible with poetry". He was himself inclined to accept that the thought was condensed "beyond what is consistent with the nature and purposes of poetry". At the same time, in an answering marginal note, J. H. Frere reports C's very successful and fluent reading of the same lines. Poem **700** *"E Cælo Descendit"* might be seen as a companion to or development from the same argument.

The text given here is that of *PW* (1828), embodying a minor correction.

> If dead, we cease to be; if total gloom
>   Swallow up life's brief flash for aye, we fare
> As summer-gusts, of sudden birth and doom,
>   Whose sound and motion not alone declare,
> But *are* their *whole* of being! If the Breath   5
>   Be Life itself, and not its Task and Tent,
> If even a soul like Milton's can know death;
>   O Man! thou vessel purposeless, unmeant,
> Yet drone-hive strange of phantom purposes!
>   Surplus of nature's dread activity,   10
> Which, as she gazed on some nigh-finished vase,
> Retreating slow, with meditative pause,
>   She formed with restless hands unconsciously!
> Blank accident! nothing's anomaly!
>   If rootless thus, thus substanceless thy state,   15
> Go, weigh thy dreams, and be thy Hopes, thy Fears,
> The counter-weights!—Thy Laughter and thy Tears
>   Mean but themselves, each fittest to create,
> And to repay the other! Why rejoices
>   Thy heart with hollow joy for hollow good?   20
>   Why cowl thy face beneath the Mourner's hood,
> Why waste thy sighs, and thy lamenting voices,
>   Image of Image, Ghost of Ghostly Elf,
> That such a thing as thou feel'st warm or cold?
> Yet what and whence thy gain, if thou withhold   25
>   These costless shadows of thy shadowy self?
> Be sad! be glad! be neither! seek, or shun!
> Thou hast no reason why! Thou can'st have none!
> Thy being's being is contradiction.

5–6. C wrote alongside in Francis Wrangham's (?) copy of *SL*: "Halitus = Anima/Animæ tabernaculum" tr "Breath equals soul/the dwelling-place of the soul". DC copied the phrase into his own copy of the same.

483. PHLEGETHON, COCYTUS, AND EUTERPE: ABANDONED STANZAS

[1811?]

The lines are preserved, in heavily revised form as if C were starting from scratch, on a fragmentary ms now in the BM. There is no real clue as to the date, although the wm points to 1807 or later; nor to the connection between the stanzas and the rest of C's poetry, nor to his intentions—unless they are somehow connected with **478** *Limbo*. The pattern of revision shows C feeling his way into the subject as he writes, but not to the extent of becoming deeply engaged.

O'er hung with Yew, midway the Muses' Mount,
From thy sweet murmur far, O Hippocrene,
Turbid and black upboils an angry fount
Tossing it's shatter'd foam in vengeful spleen:
Phlegethon's Rage, Cocytus' wailings hoarse   5
Alternate now, now mixt, make known it's headlong course.

Thither with terror stricken and surprize
(For sure such Haunts were ne'er the Muses' Choice)
Euterpe led me; mute with asking eyes
I stood expectant of her heavenly race—   10
Her Voice entranc'd my terror and made flow
In a rude Understrain the maniac fount below.

Whene'er (the Goddess said) abhorr'd of Jove
Usurping Power his hands in blood imbues,
And   15

9. Euterpe] Her sphere was usually music. For what follows, see Pindar *Pythian Ode* 1, to which C referred in *AR* and in **357** *Constancy to an Ideal Object* 30fn.

484. FRAGMENTARY LINES ON CHANGE

[c Mar–Jul 1811]

C wrote the lines into Notebook 18 (*CN* III 4095). The top of the page has been cut off, and it is possible that the preserved lines were the conclusion of a longer poem.

> O mercy! O me miserable man!
> Slowly my Wisdom, & how slowly comes
> My Virtue! and how rapidly pass off
> My Joys, my Hopes, my Friendships, & my Love!

485. LINES INSPIRED BY JEAN PAUL

[c May–Jul 1811]

The fragments labelled (*a*)–(*c*) below comprise three separate entries in Notebook 18 (*CN* III 4092, 4093, 4097). They are part of a sequence which derives from C's reading of Johann Paul Friedrich Richter [Jean Paul] *Geist, oder Chrestomathie* (2 vols Weimar & Leipzig 1801) and *Das Kampaner Thal* (2 vols Erfurt 1797), both of which he annotated (*CM—CC—*IV 261–80).

(*a*) versifies a sentence in *Geist* No 9 I 37–8 = *Das Kampaner Thal* I 30: "Durch die ganze Nacht ging ein halb verlorner Donner, gleichsam als zürnte er im Schlafe" tr "Throughout the entire night, there passed a half-lost [half-audible] thunder, as if he were angry in his sleep". C used the lines when he rewrote *Osorio* as *Remorse* (**502.X3** *Remorse* (Printed) IV ii 96–7).

(*b*) is written out in the notebook continuously, like prose. The imagery of (*c*) again perhaps derives from Jean Paul: Geist No 22 I 58 "Sieh, da entfiel droben dem nachtblauen Himmel ein heller Tropfen, so groß wie eine Thräne, und sank wachsend neben einer Welt nach der andern vorbei—als er groß, und mit tausend Farbenblitzen durch den schwarzen Bogen drang; so grünte und blühte dieser wie ein Regenbogen und unter ihm waren keine Gestalten mehr— und als der Tropfen, großglimmend wie eine Sonne, auf einer Blume lag" tr "Behold, there fell from the night-blue sky a bright drop, as big as a tear, and as it grew, it fell past one world after the other—when, great and with a thousand flashing colours, it penetrated the black arc; the arc grew green and blossomed like a rainbow, and beneath it, there were no more forms and figures—and as the drop, glistening great as a sun, lay on a flower".

(*a*)

A low dead Thunder muttered thro' the Night,
As twere a Giant angry in his Sleep—

(*b*)

Nature! sweet Nurse! O take me in thy Lap—
And tell me of my Father yet unseen
Sweet Tales & True, that lull me into Sleep,
& leave me dreaming.—

(*c*)

The Day of our dire Fate as yet but dawns,
These Tears the bright Drops of the morning Rainbow
Foretelling Tempest!—

486. ADAPTATION OF BEN JONSON'S
A NYMPH'S PASSION

[Aug 1811?]

The lines were printed in *The Courier* (21 Sept 1811), and were included almost unchanged, at the last moment, in *SL* (1817). Both printings have the title "Mutual Passion. Altered and Modernized from an Old Poet." The poem was not included in any collections thereafter, although in one copy of *SL* C made alterations of phrasing to stanza 4 and in another copy he deleted the second stanza. The *Courier* version is given here.

C found the original in Ben Jonson's *Underwoods* v (*B Poets* IV 565):

A Nymph's Passion

I love, and he loves me again,
    Yet dare I not to tell who;
For if the nymphs should know my swain,
    I fear they'd love him too;
        Yet if he be not known,
        The pleasure is as good as none,
For that's a narrow joy is but our own.

I'll tell, that if they be not glad,
    They yet may envy me:
But then if I grow jealous mad,

And of them pitied be,
   It were a plague 'bove scorn,
And yet it cannot be forborn,
Unless my heart would as my thought be torn.

He is, if they can find him, fair,
   And fresh and fragrant too,
As summer's sky, or purged air,
   And looks as lilies do
     That are this morning blown;
   Yet, yet I doubt he is not known,
And fear much more, that more of him be shown.

But he hath eyes so round, and bright,
   As make away my doubt,
Where Love may all his torches light,
   Though Hate had put them out:
     But then t' increase my fears,
   What nymph soe'er his voice but hears,
Will be my rival, though she have but ears.

I'll tell no more, and yet I love,
   And he loves me; yet no
One unbecoming thought doth move
   From either heart I know;
     But so exempt from blame,
   As it would be to each a fame,
If love or fear would let me tell his name.

I love, and he loves me again,
   Yet dare I not tell who:
For if the nymphs should know my swain,
   I fear they'd love him too.
     Yet while my joy's unknown,   5
   It's rosy buds are but half-blown:
What no one with me shares, seems scarce my own.

I'll tell, that if they be not glad,
   They yet may envy me:
But then if I grow jealous mad,   10
   And of them pitied be,
     'Twould vex me worse than scorn!
   And yet it cannot be forborn,
Unless my heart would, like my thoughts, be torn.

He is, if they can find him, fair   15
    And fresh, and fragrant too;
As after rain the Summer air,
    And looks as Lilies do,
        That are this morning blown!
        Yet, yet I doubt, he is not known,   20
Yet, yet I fear to have him fully shewn.

But he hath eyes so large, and bright,
    Which none can see, and doubt
That love might thence his torches light
    Tho' hate had put them out!   25
        But then to raise my fears,
        His voice—what maid so ever hears
Will be my rival, tho' she have but ears.

I'll tell no more! yet I love him,
    And he loves me; yet so,   30
That never one low wish did dim
    Our love's pure light, I know—
        In each so free from blame,
        That both of us would gain new fame,
If love's strong fears would let me tell his name!   35

487. ADAPTATION OF BEN JONSON'S
THE HOUR-GLASS

[Aug 1811?]

The lines appeared in *The Courier* (30 Aug 1811), along with **199** *The Virgin's Cradle-hymn*. Both poems were unsigned, and the dependence on Jonson was not acknowledged.

C found the original in Ben Jonson's *Underwoods* VI (*B Poets* IV 565):

On a Lover's Dust, made Sand for an Hour-glass.

Do but consider this small dust,
    Here running in the glass,
        By atoms mov'd:
        Could you believe that this

The body was
  Of one that lov'd?
And in his mistress' flame, playing like a fly,
  Turn'd to cinders by her eye?
Yes, and in death, as life unblest,
    To have 't exprest,
Ev'n ashes of lovers find no rest.

A footnote in *B Poets* gives the alternative 1640 version (as well as the Latin original by Jerome Amalthcus), which might also lie behind C's adaptation:

On a Gentlewoman working by an Hour-glass.

Do but consider this small dust,
  Here running in the glass;
Would you believe that it the body was
  Of one that lov'd?
And in his mistress' flames playing like a fly,
Was turned into cinders by her eye?
Yes; as in life, so in their deaths unblest,
A lovers ashes never can find rest.

O think, fair Maid! these sands, that pass
In slender threads adown this glass,
Were once the Body of some swain,
Who lov'd too well and lov'd in vain.
And let one soft sigh heave thy breast,   5
That not in life alone unblest,
E'en Lover's ASHES find no rest.

488. LAVATORIAL LINES

[Aug 1811]

C preceded the verses in Notebook 18 (*CN* III 4103) with a reference (in Latin) for the lines from Moschion, titulus XI.33 in the Stobaeus selection *Dicta Poetarum* ed Hugo Grotius (2 pts Paris 1623) I 145 = Stobaeus *Anthologium* ed C. Wachsmuth and O. Hense (5 vols Leipzig 1884–1923) I 8.38, which he gives as μηδ' ἐν ὀφλαλμοῖς [*sic*] ἐὰν | Τῆς προσθε θοίνης μνημόνευμα δυσσεβές tr "and do not leave in view any unholy testimony to your previous meal". He adds a reference to Deut 23.12–13 (". . . when thou wilt ease thyself abroad . . . turn back and cover that which cometh from thee") and quotes Hesiod *Works and Days* 759, which he gives as Ουτ' αρ αποψυχειν· το γαρ εστιν λωϊον ουδεν tr H. G. Evelyn-White (LCL rev 1936) "And do not ease yourself in them [sc rivers]; it is not well to do this". C's first couplet translates Moschion fairly closely. The notebook entry concludes with a second version of **329** *Greek Lines on Achilles' Meal of Yesterday*. There is a remote possibility that the entry could have been prompted by C's recent reading in Ben Jonson, e.g. *The Famous Voyage*.

> Alike, my friends! from eyes & nose conceal
> The irreverent record of your yester's Meal
> And if you yearn to hear, who taught me *that*,
> 'Twas Hesiod, Moschio, Moses, and my Cat!

489. LATIN LINES PERHAPS
CONNECTED WITH JOHN MORGAN

[1811–16]

C drafted the lines in Notebook 3½ (*CN* III 4108), writing them at right angles to the normal orientation of the page and signing them with a combination of his own initials and a cipher name for Morgan. The following translation varies at one point from KC's: "Hapless and suffering the worst kind of haplessness is he who, half a man, has taken to his bed a woman half as much again, and with the tearful dew from his small rigid tube scarcely strikes the silent thirsty orifice and the gulf of that great aperture."

Cf **423** *The Two Sisters* 36EC on the difference in age between John and Mary Morgan, although the lines suggest inadequacy on the man's part rather than over-enthusiasm on the woman's, and are not necessarily personal. Cf also *CM* (*CC*) III 681 for a note about painful private matters which were perhaps confided by Morgan. On the other hand, the lines could merely versify a morsel of after-dinner conversation.

> Infelix, ah plusquam infelicissimus Ille,
> Semivir in thalamum qui duxit Sesqui-puellam;
> Mutumque os sitiens, tantique voraginem hiatûs
> Vix rigidi tubuli lacrymoso róre lacessit!

490. THE SUICIDE'S ARGUMENT, WITH NATURE'S ANSWER

[1811]

C drafted the lines in Notebook 18 (*CN* III 4106), as he looked back over his relationship with SH during the preceding years. This first draft was untitled, and continued for a further line: "Be thy own heart our common arbiter." The poem was first published in *Felix Farley's Bristol Journal* (14 Oct 1815), over C's initials, with the title "*ARGUMENT for Suicide, in the character of CHAT-TERTON.*" (C identified with Chatterton from his schooldays onwards, and continued to do so during the first years he spent in Bristol: cf e.g. **82** *Monody on the Death of Chatterton.*) The *Felix Farley* version had a further three lines:

> But none e'er rushed to death, whose Life dar'd send
> A courteous Invitation to Life's End.
> And when Death came, could say: Welcome in *God's name*, FRIEND!

The version given here is from a fair copy subscribed "Grove, Highgate", which was collected in *PW* (1828, 1829, 1834) without further revision.

The lines appear to be unrelated to the projected—and perhaps partly written—poem on suicide which C refers to in Mar 1805 (*CN* II 2510), although suicidal thoughts were frequent in Malta (see *CN* II 2100 f 3^r, 2527, 2557, etc).

THE SUICIDE'S ARGUMENT.

Ere the birth of my Life, if I wish'd it or no
No question was ask'd me—it could not be so!
If Life itself be the Question—a thing sent to try,
And to live on be YES: what can No be? To die.

NATURE'S ANSWER.

Is't return'd as 'twas sent? Is't no worse for the Wear?   5
Think first, what You *are*! Recollect what You *were*!
I gave you innocence, I gave you hope,
Gave health and genius and an ample scope!
Return you me Guilt, Lethargy, Despair?
Make out th' Invent'ry! Inspect, Compare!   10
  Then die—if die you dare!

491. SIR JOHN DAVIES ON THE SOUL,
ADAPTED TO THE IMAGINATION

[Oct–Nov 1811]

C drafted the adaptation in his lecture notes in Notebook M (*CN* III 4112; cf
Lects 1808–1819—CC—I 246, 255–6), and it was printed in *BL*, the version
given here. The original stanzas occur in *Nosce Teipsum: Of the Soule of Man
and the Immortalitie Thereof* IV 11–13 (*B Poets* II 689):

> Doubtless, this could not be, but that she turns
> 　Bodies to Spirits, by sublimation strange;
> As fire converts to fire the things it burns;
> 　As we our meats into our nature change.
>
> From their gross matter she abstracts the forms,
> 　And draws a kind of quintessence from things;
> Which to her proper nature she transforms,
> 　To bear them light on her celestial wings.
>
> This doth she, when, from things particular,
> 　She doth abstract the universal kinds,
> Which bodyless and immaterial are,
> 　And can be only lodg'd within our minds.

Doubtless this could not be, but that she turns
Bodies to spirit by sublimation strange,
As fire converts to fire the things it burns,
As we our food into our nature change.

From their gross matter she abstracts their forms,　　　　　　　5
And draws a kind of quintessence from things;
Which to her proper nature she transforms
To bear them light, on her celestial wings.

Thus does she, when from individual states
She doth abstract the universal kinds;　　　　　　　　　　　　10
Which then re-clothed in divers names and fates
Steal access through our senses to our minds.

492. TO A LADY, OFFENDED
BY A SPORTIVE OBSERVATION
THAT WOMEN HAVE NO SOULS

[1811–12?]

The origins of C's lines lie in a distich by Schiller, *Das Werthe und Würdige* ("Value and Worth"), which C transcribed along with three others in Dec 1801:

> *Hast* du etwas, so theile mir's mit und ich Zahle was recht ist;
> *Bist* du etwas, o dann tauschen die Seelen wir aus.
>
> (*CN* I 1063; cf Schiller *Gedichte* I 305)

C translated the distich in *Omniana* (1812) No 124 (*SW&F—CC*—315–16) under the heading "*To* HAVE *and to* BE", the poem following the translation by way of "a mere playful illustration":

> *Hast* thou any thing? Share it with me and I will pay thee the worth of it.
> *Art* thou any thing? O then let us exchange souls."

He quoted his trans (var) in a letter to Thomas Allsop dated 15 Sept 1821 (*CL* v 164).

The earliest notebook draft of the poem (*CN* III 4119) has Sara (deleted) for Anna in the first line. This suggests that it might date from a time "when playfulness with either Mrs C or SH in verse was still possible" (KC), or the deletion might suggest a date after the estrangement from WW in Oct 1810. A later holograph version, perhaps intended for an album, has the name Eliza. The notebook draft contains a cancelled, slightly different version of the lines, and also a succeeding set of four:

> There's a difference, I wis
> Betwixt "Has" and "Is":
> And this chop-logic Quiz
> Has inform'd you, what 'tis.

In *Omniana* C replaced these with his direct translation from Schiller. The poem was first collected in *PW* (1828) and appeared in both subsequent collections. The four printed texts differ only in punctuation; the version reproduced here is from *PW* (1828).

title. C's title for the lines in *Omniana* was "Women have no souls, says Prophet Mahomet."

Nay, dearest Anna! why so grave?
I said, you had no soul, 'tis true!
For what you *are*, you cannot *have:*
'Tis I, that *have* one since I first had *you!*

492.X2. DIADESTÈ

[1811–12]

See vol III.

493. LATIN DISTICH ON
GIVING AND RECEIVING

[Late 1811–Jan 1812?]

C copied the epigram into Notebook 29 (*CN* III 4122), the version given here, and later into a letter of Nov 1819 to Charles Abbott, Lord Chief Justice, begging his acceptance of a copy of *LS* (*CL* IV 964). He also copied them on to a slip of paper which he signed with his initials and which is now tipped in to a copy of *LB* (1800) (annex C 8.2).

The attribution to C is made with considerable reservations. The vocabulary and sentiment have something in common with Ovid *Amores* 1.10.53–4, 63–4, Horace *Odes* 3.16.42–3, and Martial 5.59.3. C's initials might signify only that these were his sentiments in making a presentation of the book rather than that he was the author of the lines, and when he wrote down the couplet in Notebook 29 it was in a context of collecting scraps. Other Latin lines, appearing in a similar context and more obviously modern, might be thought to have as strong a claim—e.g. *CN* III 3667 in Notebook 16.

The present lines may be translated "He will give much who can give much; for me, who can give little, and ask little, it is enough to have given little." In the letter to Abbott, C appropriately substituted "Nullaque" for "Parvaque": "I ask nothing" rather than "I ask little".

Magna dabit qui magna potest: mihi parva potenti,
    Parvaque poscenti, parva dedisse sat est.

494. A HALF-ATTEMPT AT VERSE

[1811–12]

The draft of the lines in Notebook M (*CN* iii 4135) contains several deletions (and it is here assumed that C inadvertently left "and" undeleted after "of" in line 3). They are untitled and followed by the comment "Yet even this is accepted as a hymn of Thanksgiving."

> The wild Colt in the Meadow—venting
> & flinging up against the Sky—in
> rampancy of Self-assenting,
> Life & Freedom's rapture high/—/

495. A DROLL FORMULARY
TO RAISE DEVILS

[1811–12?]

C drafted the lines in Notebook M (*CN* iii 4138), where there is a good deal of deletion and reworking, leaving the text defective at lines 15, 25, 28, and 39 (supplemented in the RT below, where the erratic indentation has also been regularised). The poem recalls earlier ones in which C touched on the Devil (**214** *The Devil's Thoughts* and **267** *The Two Round Spaces on the Tombstone*); HCR described him reciting it in 1812 and considered it "very droll" (*CRB* i 108–9). The title given here also comes from HCR, who describes the poem as being "founded on a saying that whoever should repeat a certain formulary of Hebrew words would cause a number of devils to rise". In *PW* (EHC) i 399n EHC notes that the invocation in lines 4, 9, etc is "a cabbalistic invocation of Jehovah, obscure in the original Hebrew". He compares the poem as a whole with RS's *Ballad of a Young Man that Would Read Unlawful Books, and How he was Punished* in *Annual Anthology* ed RS (2 vols Bristol 1799–1800) i 198–200. References to C's serious interest in whether devils could be said to exist are given in *CM* (*CC*) iii 305n.

> Strong spirit bidding Sounds!
> Twixt Hope and Dread
> With a deep & hollow voice I said/

Seven Times Johva Mitzoveh Vohæen,
And up came an Imp in the Shape of a Pea-hen!   5
    I saw, I doubted,
    And 7 times shouted
    And 7 times
Johva, Mitzoveh Yahó Evohäen—
When Antichrist started up, butting and bāing   10
In the shape of a mischievous curly black Lamb—
With a vast Flock of Devils behind and beside,
And before 'em their Shepherdess, Lucifer's Dam
    Riding astride
    On an old black Ram.   15
With Tartary Stirrups, Knees up to her Chin,
And a sleek chrysom Imp to her Dugs nuzzled in.
Gee-up! My old Belzy! (she cried,
As she sung to her suckling Cub)
Trot, a trot, trot! We'll go far & wide—   20
Trot, Ram-devil! Trot! Belzebub!
Her petticoat fine was of Scarlet Brocade
And soft in her Lap her Baby she lay'd
With his pretty Nubs of Horns a Sprouting,
And his pretty *little Tail* all Curly twirly—   25
Sᵗ Dunstan—and this comes of spouting—
Of Devils what a Hurly-Burly!
"Behold! we are up! What wantst thou then?"
Sirs! only, that—"Say, where, and what!"
You'd be so good—"Say, what! & when!"   30
This moment to get down again!—
We do it! we do it! we all get down!
But we take you with us to swim or drown!
Down a down to the grim Engulpher!
O me! I am floundring in Fire & Sulphur!   35
That the Dragon had scrounched you, squeal & squall
Cabbalists! Conjurers! great & small
Johva Mitzoveh Evohäen & all!—
Had *I* never utter'd your Jaw-breaking Words
I might now have been sloshing down Junket & Curds   40
    Like a Devonshire Christian:

26. Sᵗ Dunstan] For Dunstan and   *Rhapsody* 28–30ᴇᴄ.
the Devil see **11** *The Nose: An Odaic*

But now a Philistine!
Ye Earthsmen! be warn'd by a Judgement so tragic,
And wipe yourselves cleanly with all books of Magic.
Hark! Hark! it is Dives!—Hold your Bother You Booby!   45
"I am burnt ashy white, and you yet are but ruby."

EPILOGUE

We ask and urge (here ends this Story)
All Christian Papishes to pray
That this unhappy Conjurer may
Instead of Hell be but in Purgatory,   50
For then there's Hope—
Long live the Pope!

CATHOLICUS.

496. VERSIFIED NOTE TO J. J. MORGAN

[Jan 1812]

C wrote the note on the back of the address sheet of an old letter, in letter format
(*CL* III 363–4).

My Dear Morgan
I wish you would be my Organ
And when you pass down Picadilly
To call in at Escher's, who sells books wise and silly
But chiefly in a Lingo by the Learned called German,   5
And who himself looks less like a Man than a Mer-man/
And ask him if he still has a work called Ardinghello,

4. Escher's] Henry Escher was a bookseller at 201 Piccadilly from 1807 to midsummer 1812.

7. Ardinghello] J.J.W. Heinse *Ardinghello und die glückseeligen Inseln* (2 vols Lemgo 1787–94). C had known Heinse's romance for some years (cf *CN* II 3155), and apparently wanted the book in 1812 for his lectures. Morgan failed to obtain it, so that C had to write and ask Mrs C to send it from Keswick (*CL* III 387; see also *WL—M* rev—II 13).

It was in his Catalogue, I am sure, and of course to sell o/
And if it is, to buy it for me. Don't forget it, my dear Fellow!

S. T. C.

497. EPIGRAM ON MAULE AND MATHER

[Feb 1812?]

C wrote the lines, signing them "S. T. C.", near the end of RS's copy of Cotton Mather's *Magnalia Christi Americana* (1702), apparently before he left Greta Hall for the last time. His annotations for the most part reflect his distaste for the aggressive orthodoxy of the New England Church. Thomas Maule (1645–1724) is among several Quakers whose persecution Mather describes and to which C responded; Maule, a resident of Salem, was imprisoned for his pamphlet *Truth Held Forth and Maintained* in 1695. C also read Mather's *The Wonders of the Invisible World* (Boston 1693) (*CN* III 4394; IV 5403; etc). C addresses Mather with a disconcerting switch to Maule and back again in line 3 (Maule the victim creates his own mauler).

Why at Tom Maule dost fret & foam?
Thy own Book's but a mauling Tome.
Add to thy name an R: for rather,
A Mauler art thou than a Mather!

498. ON THE NAMING OF BOMBAY

[Feb–Mar 1812]

C wrote the lines to gloss a passage in RS's copy of Abraham Parsons *Travels in Asia and Africa* (1808), which he read while he was staying at Greta Hall (*CM—CC—*IV 30):

Bombay, was first called so by the Portuguese, literally in English, Good-bay, which it is in all respects; being so very capacious, as to be capable of receiving any number of ships of any size or draft of water, with room sufficient to moor clear of each other in safety.

Harbour'd from Toil *here* did th' Adventurers Gay
Squat down at ease, and nam'd it hence *Bum*-Bay.

499. FAITH, HOPE, CHARITY, TRANSLATED FROM GUARINI

[1812? 1815?]

C made memoranda on Battista Guarini in Sept 1806 (*CN* ɪɪ 2871, 2872) and Apr 1817 (*CN* ɪɪɪ 4354). He asked Mrs C to send his copy of *Il pastor fido*— "for the sake of the minor Poems"—on 24 Apr 1812 (*CL* ɪɪɪ 393)—this after Mrs C had been teaching Italian to SC, apparently to C's satisfaction (*Minnow* 20). The present translation is written in the margins of a fair copy by HC, and might have been made during the summer months of 1815, which HC spent with C at Calne. It breaks off incomplete.

The original is from Guarini *Il pastor fido, con le rime* (2 pts Amsterdam 1663) ɪɪ 138–9:

DIALOGO.

FEDE, SPERANZA, CARITA.

FEDE.

Canti terreni amori,
    Chi terreno hà il pensier, terreno il zelo;
    Noi Celesti Virtù cantiam del Cielo.

CARITA.

Mà chi fia, che n'ascolti?
    Fuggirà i nostri accenti orecchia piena
    De le lusinghc di mortal Sirena.

SPERANZA.

Cantiam pur, che raccolti
    Saran ben in virtù di chi li move;
    E suoneran nel Ciel, se non altrove.

FE. SP. CA.

Spirane dunque, eterno Padre, il canto,
    Che già festi al gran Cantor Ebreo,
    Che poi tant' alto feo
Suonar la gloria del tuo nome Santo.

CA. FE.
Noi siam' al Ciel rapite,
  E pur lo star in terra è nostra cura,
  A ricondur à Dio l'alme smarrite.

FE. SP.
Così facciamo, e'n questa valle oscura
  L'una sia scorta al Sol de l'intelletto,
  L'altra sostegno al vacillante affetto.

CA.
E com' è senz' amor l'anima viva?

SP. FE.
Come stemprata cetra,
  Che suona sì, mà di concento priva.

CA. SP.
Amor' è quel, ch'ogni gran dono impetra.

FE.
Mà tempo è, che le genti
  Odan l'alta virtù de' nostri accenti.

FE. SP. CA.
O mondo—ecco la via;
  Chi vuol salir' al Ciel, creda, ami, e speri.
  O felici pensieri
  Di chi per far in Dio santa armonia,
  E per ogn' altro suon l'anima hà sorda,
FEDE, SPERANZA, e CARITA, accorda.

C wrote down his translation of about half the poem in the margin of HC's complete translation, which reads as follows:

From the Italian of Guarini.
Faith, Hope, Charity.

Faith.
Let those whose hearts to earth are given
  Sing of their earthly loves, but we
  Will make diviner minstrelsy
Hymning bright virtue, eldest born of Heaven

Charity.
Alas, we shall but lose our pains:
  Such music none is fain to hear
  Unheeded falls it on the ear
That glutted is with this world's Syren strains.

Hope.
Yet let us sing of virtue's praise
  The mortals all despise our voice
  For Angels there at will rejoice
And tune their harps responsive to our lays.

Faith. Hope. Charity
Then, Heavenly Father, us inspire
  As erst the Bard of Israel,
  The glories of thy name to tell,
Give us the Prophets light, the Psalmist's fire.

Charity. Faith.
Yet tho' towards Heaven we turn our eyes
  Our feet must still on earth remain,
  That through us Adam's sons may gain
Than that he lost, a brighter Paradise.

Faith. Hope.
So let us do; and in this vale
  Of darkness; guide and stay mankind
  Lead back to light the erring mind,
Or timely aid the soul that's like to fail.

Charity
What is man's soul, of love deprived?

Hope. Faith.
It like a harp untuned is
That sounds indeed, but sounds amiss

Charity. Hope
From holy love, all good gifts are derived.

Faith.
But 'tis time, that every nation
  Should hear how loftily we sing

Faith, Hope, Charity.
See, O World, see thy salvation
  Let the Heavens with praises ring.
    Who would have a Throne above
    Let him hope, believe, and love.
      And whoso loves no earthly song,
      But does for heavenly music long,
        Faith, Hope, and Charity to him
        Shall sing like winged Cherubim.

Faith

Let those whose low Delights to Earth are given
  Chaunt forth their earthly Loves! But we
  Must make an holier minstrelsy
And heavenly born will sing the Things of Heaven!

Charity

But who for us the listning heart shall gain?   5
  Inaudible as of the Sphere
  Our music dies upon the ear
Inchanted with the mortal Syren's Strain.

Hope.—

Yet let our choral songs abound!
  The inspiring Power, it's living Source,   10
  May flow with them and give them force—
If elsewhere all unheard, in Heaven they sound.

All.

Aid then our voice, great Spirit, thou whose flame
  Kindled the Songster sweet of Israel
  Who made so high to swell   15
Beyond a mortal strain thy glorious Name.

Charity & Faith

Tho' rapt to Heaven, our mission, and our care
  Is still to sojourn on the earth,
  To shape, to soothe, Man's second Birth,
And reconduct to Heaven/ Heaven's prodigal Heir!   20

Faith and Hope
*   *   *

500. METRICAL EXPERIMENT IN MAY 1812

[May 1812]

C copied the lines into Notebook 61 (*CN* III 4149). He followed them with a metrical analysis:

1. Four Trochees/
2. 1 Spondee, 1 Iambic
3. Four Trochees/
4. Repeated from 2.
5. 6. 7.   a Triplet of 4 Troch. 8 repeated

He then cancelled the whole entry with a single line.

  If the lines are by C, they involve an element of pastiche. His authorship has not been confirmed.

> Once again, sweet Willow, wave thee!
>   Why stays my Love?
> Bend & in yon Streamlet lave thee
>   Why stays my Love?
> Oft have I at evening straying   5
> Stood thy Branches long surveying
> Graceful in the light Breeze playing,
>   Why stays my Love?

501. THE KING OF THE NORTH COUNTRIE

[1812?]

The only known version of the lines is a transcript in AG's (late?) hand. There is no evidence that would help to date them; if they were written for the young SC (b 1802), they might have been written earlier than is suggested here; and they could have been composed at Highgate.

> There was a king in the *North Countrie*
> And he had daughters *one two three*,
> The *Eldest* daughter to him came,
> But he loved best the *youngest* dame.
> He bought the *youngest* a beaver hat,   5
> The Eldest she thought much of *that*
> And when they came to Sillymouse brim,
> The Eldest she pushed the youngest in,
> She swum up, & she swum down
> Until they came to Sittymouse Town   10

The Shepherd came out with his long Crook
And pulled her out by the *petticoat*.

Take warning from this all ye young women
That ye do learn the art of swimming

502. EPITAPH ON THE LEARNED ROBERT WHITMORE, E^SQRE, WHO DIED OF A DIARRHŒA, 4 AUGUST 1812, ÆTATIS SUÆ 57

[Aug 1812]

C's lines are written on a page which continues with material connected (digressively) with the 1812–13 lectures he was then planning and soon afterwards gave at the Surrey Institution (cf *CL* III 418–19: to R. Saumarez 12 Aug [1812]; *Lects 1808–1819—CC*—I 480–1). There might be a connection, via the topic of primitive man and defecation, with **329** *Greek Lines on Achilles' Meal of Yesterday* (see VAR TEXT MS 2).

C may well have written this irreverent epitaph while its subject was still alive, the death being demanded by the rhyme (cf e.g. **579** *Mock Epitaph on Sir William Curtis*). No Robert Whitmore has been traced, but the bookselling firm of Whitmore and Fenn is recorded as functioning at the Homer's Head, 6 Charing Cross, from 1809 to 1831. This Whitmore, whose first name has not been traced, seems a likely possibility. Alternatively, if C did not know anyone of that name in person, he might have heard of the case from Robert Gooch, who was attending him for "Indigestion, & Erysypelatous Inflamation" at the time (*CL* III 414: to D. Stuart 7 Aug 1812). The original reading is given in line 2 (subsequently altered to "spit", possibly in a hand other than C's).

Here lies learned Whitmore!
He'll never shit more,
No, not a bit more:
Learned Bob Whitmore!

502.X2. REMORSE (STAGE VERSION)

[Dec 1812–Feb 1813]

See vol III.

502.X3. REMORSE (PRINTED VERSION)

[Dec 1812–Feb 1813]

See vol III.

503. COUPLET ON LESBIAN LOVERS

[1813–15?]

C wrote the couplet into Notebook M (*CN* III 4187). The Greek letters translit-
erated read "succeed", given as two words to point up the pun. "Ne'er succeed"
appears in another poem which mentions female homosexuality, written entirely
in transliterated Greek, **446** *Adelphan Greek Riddle*. For C's views on male ho-
mosexuality see Notebook 42 [=BM Add MS 47537] ff 42ʳ–43ʳ (*CN* v); **619**
Virgil Applied to the Hon Mr B and Richard Heber.

> Alternate agents, tho' of passive Breed,
> Successful Lovers both, yet neër συκ σηδ!

504. ON THE SECRECY OF A CERTAIN LADY

[Before Jan 1814]

The epigram appeared unsigned in *The Courier* (3 Jan 1814). It was collected
and attributed to C in *EOT* (1850), and there is no confirmatory proof of his
authorship.

"She's secret as the grave! allow."
I do; I cannot doubt it;
But 'tis a grave with tombstone on,
That tells you all about it.

505. MAEVIUS–BAVIUS EXEMPLUM

[Early 1814]

C wrote the lines in pencil in a copy of the folio *Travels of Monsieur de Thevenot into the Levant* (1687) while he was staying with Josiah Wade in Bristol. Maevius and Bavius were minor poets pilloried by Virgil *Eclogues* 3.90, and their names became synonymous with inferior poetry. Thus, Horace made Maevius the satirised protagonist of his tenth *Epode* and William Gifford entitled his satires of Della-Cruscanism *The Baviad* (1791) and *The Maeviad* (1795).

C was no admirer of Gifford (the distaste was mutual), but the present lines may be connected with Gifford's assault. C's first published poem appeared in the Della-Cruscan journal *The World* (**20** *The Abode of Love*), and later in the 1790s he had sought out members of the circle like Mary Robinson and Ann Brunton (Mrs Merry). His phrasing here recalls his earlier style: cf **115** *The Eolian Harp* 4 "white-flowered Jasmin". In short, he appears to have begun to write with less parodic intent than when he ended. His tone is certainly more complicated than Gifford's, which is crude and aggressive (and also uses footnotes to frame the points he makes).

The copy of Thevenot's *Travels* in which C wrote his lines is inscribed "E Libris ?Cowper". C may have been prompted to write his Della-Cruscan lines by a memory of the scandalous affair between Robert Merry and Lady Cowper, wife of the chief figure in the English colony in Florence, in the early 1780s.

Her forehead whiter than the Jasmin Flower,
That play'd a sunny shadow, half-love, half-envy,
To deck or dim that forehead's Whiterness.*

                                        Maevius

* N.B. A compleat NEW word = superior Whiteness. *Bavius.*

506. LINES ON LOOKING SEAWARD

[May 1814?]

C drafted the lines in Notebook 24, without a title (*CN* III 4194). They may be recalled from an earlier occasion: they echo an entry in the Gutch Notebook (*CN* I 213 = **122** *From the Gutch Notebook* (*n*)) and, differently, a letter to TP of 24 Mar 1801 (*CL* II 710).

> Seaward, white-gleaming thro' the busy Scud
> With arching Wings the Sea-mew o'er my head
> Posts on, as bent on speed; now passaging
> Edges the stiffer Breeze, now yielding *drifts*,
> Now floats upon the Air, and sends from far   5
> A wildly-wailing Note.

507. LINES ON ZEPHYRS

[May 1814]

C drafted the lines in Notebook 24, without a title (*CN* III 4200).

> Zephyrs, that captive roam among these Boughs,
> Strive ye in vain to thread the leafy maze,
> Or have ye lim'd your wings with honey-dew?
> Unfelt, ye murmur restless o'er my head,
> And rock the feeding Drone, or bustling Bees   5
> That blend their eager, earnest, happy Hum!

508. NATIONAL INDEPENDENCE:
A LATIN FRAGMENT

[c Jun 1814]

C wrote two sets of five lines, apparently of his own composition, each followed by three lines from Claudian, in Notebook 29 (*CN* III 4202). The first group of 8 lines is deleted with several diagonal strokes; only the second group is given here. Its full title in the ms is "National Independence, or the Vision of the Maid of Orleans. A Poem." "The Vision of the Maid of Orleans" is the title under which C revised his contribution to *Joan of Arc* (poem **110**) before he settled on "The Destiny of Nations" (see vol II **139** *The Destiny of Nations* PR *1* title and n). It is not clear what connection the Latin lines were intended to have with *Joan of Arc* or *The Destiny of Nations*. Although they might appear in the notebook to have the function of an epigraph or opening, the first, cancelled effort reads more like a conclusion; and the second reads well as an independent poem.

In the cancelled group of lines, lines 1–5 were ascribed to an "anonymous poet in the chains of hell"; lines 6–8 were offset to the right and attributed to Claudian (see *Panegyric on the Fourth Consulship of the Emperor Honorius* 98–100). The second, uncancelled group may be translated: "Has any work of feminine valour ever more deservedly exercised other bards? O Maid, powerful in arms, Posterity of both lands honours you, beloved of your country and of God, and rejoices that before your victorious banners the Britons, now better for their defeat, once yielded to the Gauls. They have confirmed the justice of your triumph, they have proved that the gods were present. From this let the ages learn that by the righteous nothing is unconquerable, for the guilty nothing is safe." It will be noted that, although the words from Claudian remain the same, "Illi" in line 6 can be taken to refer (as here) to the Britons; the meaning changes from a series of victories in the first effort to a single victory in the second.

Dignius an vates alios exercuit ullum
Fæmineæ Virtutis opus? Tibi mutua laudes,
Armipotens Virgo, patriæ dilecta Deoque,
Tradit Posteritas, semel et succumbere Gallis,
Te victrice, juvat meliores clade Britannos.   5
Illi justitiam confirmavere triumphi,
Præsentes docuere Deos. Hinc Sæcula discant,
Indomitum nihil esse pio, tutumve nocenti.

509. TO A LADY, WITH FALCONER'S *SHIPWRECK*

[Jun 1814]

C's poem was written on behalf of his friend William Hood, who inscribed it in a copy of William Falconer's *The Shipwreck* (1804) for a Miss Kay who lived at Aldersgate Street, London. Hood sent her C's holograph as well as the inscribed copy, and she and C subsequently corresponded, although the letters have not survived.

It appears that Miss Kay was unknown to C when he wrote his poem, which parodies elements in the Falconer original and also in Bowles's 1803 sonnet on Falconer, *The Dirge of Poor Arion*, included on the very last page of the prefatory memoir included in the 1804 edition. The poem was published in its original form in *Felix Farley's Bristol Journal* in 1818, but the version included in *SL* (1817) and subsequent collections had previously been revised. The text printed here is that of *SL*.

Ah! not by Cam or Isis, famous streams,
 In arched groves, the youthful poet's choice;
Nor while half-list'ning, mid delicious dreams,
 To harp and song from lady's hand and voice;

Nor yet while gazing in sublimer mood 5
 On cliff, or cataract, in alpine dell;
Nor in dim cave with bladdery sea-weed strew'd,
 Framing wild fancies to the ocean's swell;

Our sea-bard sang this song! which still he sings,
 And sings for thee, sweet friend! Hark, Pity, hark! 10
Now mounts, now totters on the Tempest's wings,
 Now groans, and shivers, the replunging Bark!

"Cling to the shrowds!" In vain! The breakers roar—
 Death shrieks! With two alone of all his clan,
Forlorn the poet paced the Grecian shore, 15
 No classic roamer, but a ship-wreck'd man!

Say then, what muse inspir'd these genial strains,
 And lit his spirit to so bright a flame?

The elevating thought of suffer'd pains,
   Which gentle hearts shall mourn; but chief, the name   20

Of Gratitude! Remembrances of Friend,
   Or absent or no more! Shades of the Past,
Which Love makes Substance! Hence to thee I send,
   O dear as long as life and memory last!

I send with deep regards of heart and head,   25
   Sweet maid, for friendship form'd! this work to thee:
And thou, the while thou can'st not choose but shed
   A tear for FALKNER, wilt remember ME!

510. GOD'S OMNIPRESENCE: A HYMN

[Jun 1814]

The poem exists in two versions. The first, given here, is dated Sunday 19 Jun 1814, and was apparently addressed to Mrs Hood at Brunswick Square, Bristol. The second version bears the same date, but was probably copied out for Thomas Pringle more than ten years later. It was published in *The Cape of Good Hope Literary Gazette* (1 Oct 1832), where lines 7–16 read as follows:

    Thou mad'st, then fillest, Earth and Air,
    Yet didst the lisper, Man, declare
       The whole Earth's voice and mind!
    O! let us still with heedful heart,
    Lord! even as Thou all-present art,
       Thy presence know and find!

    My Maker! of thy Power the Trace
    In every Creature's Form and Face
       The wond'ring Soul surveys:
    Thy Wisdom, infinite above
    Seraphic Thought, a Father's Love   5
       As infinite displays!

    From all that meets or Eye or Ear,
    There falls a genial holy Fear

Which, like the heavy Dew of Morn,
Refreshes while it bows the Heart forlorn!   10

Great God! thy Works how wond'rous fair!
Yet sinful man didst thou declare
    The whole Earth's Voice & Mind!
Lord! ev'n as Thou all-present art,
O may we still with heedful Heart   15
    Thy Presence know & find!

Then come, what will, of Weal or Woe,
Joy's Bosom-spring shall steady flow:
For tho' 'tis *Heaven* thy SELF to see,
Where but thy **Shadow** falls, Grief cannot be!   20

511. A COUPLET TO ILLUSTRATE
PAEON AND EPITRITE

[1814?]

C drafted the lines in Notebook 29 (*CN* III 4214), at the end of a list of examples of feet of three and four syllables, taken from the preliminary pages of the *Gradus ad Parnassum* (see **27** *Ardua Prima Via Est* 9–10EC). The examples of the paeon are: –∪∪∪ Lætitia, ∪–∪∪ Potentia, ∪∪–∪ Alienus, ∪∪∪– Celeritas. The examples of epitrite are: ∪––– Sacerdotes, –∪–– Permanebant, ––∪– Discordiæ, –––∪ Adventare. Of the latter, only words scanning as "first epitrite" (∪–––) can be fitted into the dactylic hexameter, the conventional metre of Roman epic (see *SW&F—CC—*1216–51 on Latin metre).

Short Pæon, tripping, slurring, to delight us—
Grave Roman Epic *craves* long Epitritus.

512. A PLAINTIVE MOVEMENT,
AFTER PHINEAS FLETCHER

[1814]

C drafted the lines in Notebook L (*CN* III 4234). Following the heading or title, he wrote the scheme for the metre thus:

$$11.4 \quad 11 \; 4/ \quad 10 \; 6 \quad 4 \qquad 10/$$
$$6?$$
$$10?$$

After the lines themselves, he wrote:

It would be better to alter this metre—

$$10 \; 6 \quad 6 \; 10/ \quad 11 \; 4 \quad 11 \; 4.$$

—and still more plaintive, if the 1st & 4th were 11 11, as well as the 5th & 7th.

The page is torn off beneath the entry, and there may been more lines.

Lines 1 and 3 are borrowed from the last stanza of Phineas Fletcher *To Mr. Jo. Tomkins* (*B Poets* IV 465).

Go, little Pipe! for ever I must leave thee,
  Ah vainly true!
Never ah never must I more receive thee
  Adieu! adieu!
Well, thou art gone! and what remains behind   5
  Soothing the soul to hope?
  The moving wind
Hide with sear leaves my grave's undaisied Slope!

513. MOTTO FOR A TRANSPARENCY

[Jun 1814]

C's lines were written for a transparency (a picture or device on some transparent substance, made visible by means of a light behind), designed by Washington Allston and exhibited at Josiah Wade's in Queen's Square, Bristol, on Proclamation of Peace Day (29 Jun 1814). They were reported in the *Bristol*

Gazette on 30 Jun, and in other Bristol papers on subsequent days. When C copied out the original version for Lady Beaumont on 3 Apr 1815 (*CL* IV 565), i.e. during the Hundred Days, he changed "seems" in the second line to "is".

The *Gazette* describes the transparency as measuring 14×12 feet, in terms so similar to the description C gave Lady Beaumont that one wonders if C supplied it: "a vulture with human head, chained to a rock (Elba) Britannia clipping its wing with a shears, on one blade of which was Nelson, the other Wellington." Washington Allston also designed a transparency for the occasion (presumably one of the many others described in the newspaper reports, although Allston is not named). C found its appearance magnificent but its meaning banal (*CL* III 512: to J. J. Morgan [29 Jun 1814]), which is presumably why he did not recall it for Lady Beaumont, who was acquainted with Allston.

Cottle *E Rec* II 145 reports that C offered Wade the following alternative caption:

> We've conquer'd us a PEACE, like lads true metalled:
> And bankrupt NAP.'s accompts seem all now settled.

For other mottoes to accompany (personal) emblems see poems **435–7**.

We've fought for Peace and conquer'd it at last,
The rav'ning *Vulture's* leg seems fettered fast,
Britons rejoice! and yet be wary too,
The chain may break, the clipt wing sprout anew.

514. ON THE CONDITION OF IRELAND, IN THE MANNER OF DANIEL'S *CIVIL WARS*

[Aug–Sept 1814]

C quoted the lines towards the end of his first letter to Mr Justice Fletcher, in *The Courier* (20 Sept 1814) (*EOT—CC*—II 378). They are attributed to "DANIEL'S CIVIL WARS" and the letter as a whole is signed "AN IRISH PROTESTANT". They complete a sentence which begins: "Your Lordship might have learnt from one of our wisest Poets and Historians, how unphilosophic it is to transfer the whole blame of disquiet or rebellion from a country to its governors:".

David V. Erdman comments that "C was steeped in Daniel, and he seems to have created this stanza for the occasion; it is not in the *Civil Wars*; some of the words and phrases are, though not the obtrusive (and Coleridgean) pun in the last line." The false attribution clearly adds a historical perspective to the lines, and affects the way they are made to apply. For an earlier adaptation of Daniel's *Civil Wars* see poem **459;** for adaptations from other poems see e.g. poems **548, 550, 552, 601.** C's understanding of Ireland and things Irish is of course entirely English: cf e.g. **207** *On the United Irishmen,* **677** *The Irish Orator's Booze,* **678** *Cholera Cured Beforehand.*

> For never are the people wholly free
> From guilt of wounds, they suffer in the war:
> Never did any public misery
> Rise of itself! God's plagues still grounded are
> On common stains of our humanity: 5
> And to the flame which ruineth mankind,
> Man gives the fuel or at least gives wind.

515. WRITTEN IN RICHARD FIELD'S
OF THE CHURCH

[Nov 1814]

C's lines were written on a front flyleaf of Richard Field's *Of the Church* (3rd ed Oxford 1635). They follow on a careful, even laboured, inscription by a previous owner: "Hannah Scoltock | Her Book February 10 | 1787"; and they are dated "15 Nov.ʳ 1814. Ashley, Box, Bath." The same volume also contains a letter from C to DC on the reverse of the title-page, dated 28 Mar 1819, and numerous annotations on the text, for which see *CM* (*CC*) II 649–86. The flyleaf containing C's lines is reproduced as pl 1 (frontispiece) in *CM* (*CC*) II.

> This, Hannah Scollock! may have been the case:
> Your writing therefore I will not erase.
> But now this Book, once your's, belongs to me,
> The Morning Post's & Courier's **S. T. C.**
> Elsewhere in College, Knowlege, Wit and Scholerage   5
> To Friends & Public known, as S. T. Coleridge.

6. Coleridge] For other examples of a trisyllabic pronunciation see *CL* III 518fn: to J. J. Morgan 7 Jul 1814; **637** *Written in William Upcott's Album;* **697** *Other Lines on Lady Mary Shepherd; RX* 583–4 n 35, 604s; etc. Bristol and Nether Stowey spellings suggest that he earlier pronounced it as a

Witness hereto my Hand, on Ashley Green,
One thousand, twice four Hundred, & fourteen
Year of our Lord—and of the Month November,
The fifteenth Day, if right I do remember.   10

516. REVISIONS OF THE OPENING
OF SOUTHEY'S *RODERICK*

[1814?]

The drafts are written in C's hand on a single leaf. They bear no title but appear
to be suggestions for the opening of RS's *Roderick, the Last of the Goths*. RS
had planned the poem as early as 1805 (*S Letters*—Curry—I 386, 479, 486,
etc), and began to write it in Dec 1809 (*Poetical Works*—10 vols 1837–8—IX
p ix). He discussed its progress in a series of letters to Landor, but there is no
record of his involving C.

Asterisks have been inserted at the two points where the text breaks off. At
line 18⁺ the text continues in prose, as follows:

—*blasphemy*!—There is one God & Mahomet is his Prophet—does not de-
serve so harsh a name—I should prefer "The blazoned Scrolls of their false
faith."—The gales of Shame from *that* unhappy Land" is to me obscure—
if I understand it right, I should ~~suggest~~ better like—

"Too soon the Gales did from the unhappy Land
Watfft, as from out an open charnel house &c

And "atmosphere" is not only ~~too se~~ at once too bookish & yet too col-
loquial but even as to the metre falls flat, for the final word of a §§—
?"Corruption thro' the infected air of Spain.—

In the ms line 1 is preceded by a reference to page 1, line 8 by a reference
to page 2, and line 18 by a reference to page 3. C appears to be working
with RS's text prior to publication, probably a proof since the page-numbers
he cites correspond to the first printed edition (1814). He quotes lines which
differ from the published version, and some of his suggestions appear to have
been adopted, in whole or in part. Others were apparently ignored, perhaps
because they would have involved resetting, or in some cases purely because

---

disyllable. The question of pronunci-
ation led to extended controversy in
N&Q during the 19th century; it is
worth noting that a deliberately tri-
syllabic pronunciation would still be
quite natural in rural Devonshire.

RS preferred his original version. An alternative possibility is that C was simply amusing himself by rewriting passages from the printed version, primarily for his own edification. He did not think highly of RS's poem—although he was shocked by the "fiendish disposition" of the review in *Ed Rev* xxv (49) (Jun 1815) 1–31 (*CL* IV 578: to Dr Sainsbury [Jul 1815])—and he is unlikely to have gone very far into the text rewriting and revising in such detail.

RS's poem went through six editions by 1826 without change. To enable comparision with C's drafts, the text of the opening of the poem in the 1814 edition is given here:

p 1   Long had the crimes of Spain cried out to Heaven;
       At length the measure of offence was full.
       Count Julian call'd the invaders: not because
       Inhuman Priests with unoffending blood
       Had stain'd their country; not because a yoke
       Of iron servitude oppress'd and gall'd
       The children of the soil; a private wrong
       Rous'd the remorseless Baron. Mad to wreak
       His vengeance for his violated child
       On Roderick's head, in evil hour for Spain,
       For that unhappy daughter and himself,
       Desperate apostate, . . on the Moors he call'd;
p 2   And like a cloud of locusts, whom the South
       Wafts from the plains of wasted Africa,
       The Musslemen upon Iberia's shore
       Descend. A countless multitude they came;
       Syrian, Moor, Saracen, Greek renegade,
       Persian and Copt and Tatar, in one bond
       Of erring faith conjoin'd, . . strong in the youth
       And heat of zeal, . . a dreadful brotherhood,
       In whom all turbulent vices were let loose;
       While Conscience, with their impious creed accurst,
       Drunk, as with wine, had sanctified to them
       All bloody, all abominable things.

       Thou, Calpe, saw'st their coming: ancient Rock
       Renown'd, no longer now shalt thou be call'd
       From Gods and Heroes of the years of yore,
       Kronos, or hundred-handed Briareus,
       Bacchus or Hercules; but doom'd to bear
       The name of thy new conqueror, and thenceforth
       To stand his everlasting monument.
       Thou saw'st the dark-blue waters flash before
       Their ominous way, and whiten round their keels;
       Their swarthy myriads darkening o'er thy sands.

p 3   There on the beach the misbelievers spread
      Their banners, flaunting to the sun and breeze:
      Fair shone the sun upon their proud array,
      White turbans, glittering armour, shields engrail'd
      With gold, and scymitars of Syrian steel;
      And gently did the breezes, as in sport,
      Curl their long flags outrolling, and display
      The blazon'd scrolls of blasphemy. Too soon
      The gales of Spain from that unhappy land
      Wafted, as from an open charnel-house,
      The taint of death; and that bright Sun, from fields
      Of slaughter, with the morning dew drew up
      Corruption through the infected atmosphere.

      Then fell the kingdom of the Goths; their hour
      Was come, and Vengeance, long withheld, went loose.
      Famine and Pestilence had wasted them,
      And Treason, like an old and eating sore,
      Consumed the bones and sinews of their strength;
      And, worst of enemies, their Sins were arm'd
      Against them. Yet the sceptre from their hands
      Past not away inglorious; nor was shame
      Left for their children's lasting heritage.

Of Spain the crimes, and (their large measure full)
Thro' one man's guilt the Fall and how restor'd
By one man's Virtue after dolorous Years
Of Expiation, Faith and pious Love,
Remorseful Anguish and thro' strength from Heaven   5
Pelayo Victor crown'd—I sing!

                   In wrath
Count Julian &c

          *   *   *

And Calpe saw their coming: ancient Rock
Henceforth, tho' famous still, no more to bear
Name or from Gods derived, or godlike men   10
Kronos or 100 handed Briareus,
Iacchus or Alcides—but the Hill
Of the obscure barbarous victor doom'd to stand
His sole and everlasting monument—

Thou, Calpe! sawst the blue waves flash before   15
Their ominous way, and whiten round their keels—
Thou saw'st their myriads darkening o'er thy sands.—
There on the beach the swarthy Miscreants spread &c

*   *   *

517. GLYCINE'S SONG FROM *ZAPOLYA*

[Apr 1815–Feb 1816? Jan–Mar 1806?]

C's poem grew from a translation of Ludwig Tieck's *Herbstlied*, which he
might have read in Schiller's *Musen-Almenach für das Jahr 1799* (Tübingen
1798) 26–7; or he may have obtained it from Tieck himself when they met in
Rome in Jan–Mar 1806. The *Musen-Almenach* text is as follows:

Feldeinwärts flog ein Vögelein
Und sang im muntern Sonnenschein
Mit süßen wunderbaren Ton:
Ade! ich fliege nun davon,
    Weit, weit,
    Reis' ich noch heut.

Ich horchte auf den Feldgesang,
Mir ward so wohl und doch so bang,
Mit frohem Schmerz, mit trüber Lust
Stieg wechselnd bald und sank die Brust,
    Herz, Herz,
    Brichst du vor Wonn' oder Schmerz?

Doch als ich Blätter fallen sah,
Da sagt' ich: ach! der Herbst ist da,
Der Sommergast, die Schwalbe zieht,
Vielleicht so Lieb' und Sehnsucht flieht
    Weit, weit,
    Rasch mit der Zeit.

Doch rückwärts kam der Sonnenschein,
Dicht zu mir drauf das Vögelein,
Es sah mein thränend Angesicht
Und sang: die Liebe wintert nicht,
    Nein! nein!
    Ist und bleibt Frühlingsschein!

C's rough draft translation in prose (given in vol II) appears to date from Jan–

Mar 1806 (*CN* II 2791), although he made notes on "slanting pillars of misty light" some six years earlier (*CN* I 713, 781), and there are haunting echoes of **178** *Kubla Khan*. It is not known whether C worked on the verse translation at the same time or later, in Apr 1815–Feb 1816. *Zapolya* is filled with echoes of Shakespeare, Drayton, and other Elizabethan writers, who combine with Tieck as a literary background in the present instance. In the play the lines are sung by Glycine, whose name C appears to have invented, deriving it from γλυκύς "sweet"; or he may be using the feminine form of Glycinus, a philosopher mentioned by Iamblichus (*Life of Pythagoras* 36). Most of the other names in *Zapolya*, like the central episodes, are drawn from Hungarian history.

Besides the early drafts of the Tieck original in prose and verse, the poem exists in three separate fair copies (plus another known only by report). It was printed only as part of *Zapolya*—first in the separate edition of 1817, thereafter in *PW* (1828, 1829, 1834); see **517.X1** *Zapolya* II i 66–79. The version given here reproduces the fair copy which C made for John Murray when he gave him the ms of *Zapolya*. In the late 1820s he inserted further lines into the last stanza after line 10:

> The Blossoms—they
> Make no delay,
> The sparkling Dew-drops will not stay!

At the same time he revised line 5 to read: "He rose, he sunk, he rustled, he troll'd" and divided line 11 into two short lines. The changes modify the tone by accentuating the diminuendo effect.

> A sunny Shaft did I behold—
>   From sky to earth it slanted:
> And pois'd therein a Bird so bold—
>   Sweet Bird! thou wert enchanted!
>
> He sank, he rose, he twinkled, he troll'd,   5
>   Within that Shaft of sunny Mist:
> His Eyes of Fire, his Beak of Gold,
>   All else of Amethyst!
>
> And thus he sang: Adieu! Adieu!
>   Love's dreams prove seldom true.   10
> Sweet Month of May! We must away!
>   Far, far away!
>   To day! to day!

517.X1. ZAPOLYA

[Apr 1815–Feb 1816]

See vol III.

518. A METRICAL LINE IN NOTEBOOK 22

[Aug–Sept 1815]

C drafted the line in Notebook 22 (*CN* III 4254), without comment.

Thicker than rain-drops on November Thorn.—

519. METRICAL VERSION OF JOB, FROM JACOBI

[1815?]

The lines were printed in *BL* ch 10 (1817) I 197 (*CC*) I 202; C refers to Job 28, and the poem specifically renders verses 1–3, 12, 14, and 20–8. The lines are in fact a literal translation of the German paraphrase in F. H. Jacobi *Über die Lehre des Spinoza* (enlarged ed Breslau 1789) 248–9, where they are quoted in the course of a prose argument upon which C is also dependent:

> Silber und Gold erspäht der Mensch
> bringt Erz aus der Erden und die Nacht ans Licht,
> aber wo findet er Weisheit?
> wo ist Verstandes Ort?
> Im Lande der Lebenden ist sie nicht;
> der Abgrund spricht: sie ist nicht in mir!
> und das Meer schallt wieder: ist nicht in mir!—
> Woher kommt Weisheit dann?
> wo wohnt der Verstand?
> verholen den Augen der Lebenden
> verborgen den Vögeln des Himmels!
> Höll' und der Tod antworten:

wir hörten von fern ihr Gerücht.
Gott weist den Weg ihr und weiß wo sie wohnt.
Er schaut die Enden der Erden
Er schaut, was unter dem Himmel—
Und als er den Wind wog
und als er das Meer maß
und gab Gesetze dem Regen
und Donner und Blitzen den Weg;
da sah er sie und zählte sie
und forschte sie tief und bestimmte sie,
und sprach zum Menschen: dir ist die Furcht des Herrn Weisheit
und meiden das Böse, das ist Verstand.

Silver and gold man searcheth out:
Bringeth the ore out of the earth, and darkness into light.

But where findeth he wisdom?
Where is the place of understanding?

The abyss crieth; it is not in me!   5
Ocean echoeth back; not in me!

Whence then cometh wisdom?
Where dwelleth understanding?

Hidden from the eyes of the living:
Kept secret from the fowls of heaven!   10

Hell and death answer;
We have heard the rumour thereof from afar!

GOD marketh out the road to it;
GOD knoweth its abiding place!

He beholdeth the ends of the earth;   15
He surveyeth what is beneath the heavens!

And as he weighed out the winds, and measured the sea,
And appointed laws to the rain,
And a path to the thunder,
A path to the flashes of the lightning!   20

Then did he see it,
And he counted it;
He searched into the depth thereof,
And with a line did he compass it round!

But to man he said,   25
The fear of the Lord is wisdom for THEE!
And to avoid evil,
That is *thy* understanding.

520. SPECIMEN TRANSLATION
OF PINDAR, "WORD FOR WORD"

[Jul–Sept 1815?]

C quoted the lines in *BL* ch 18 (1817) II 90 (*CC*) II 87 as an impromptu translation "as nearly as possible, word for word" of the first strophe of Pindar's *Olympian Ode* 2: it was, he suggested, a more rational alternative to Cowley's version of 1656. He might have added that his translation is also as near as possible line for line; editions of C's day gave the strophe in fourteen lines, whereas modern editions have only seven (cf **258** *To a Cataract*). Apart from this, the only significant variation in the LCL text is in lines 10–11, where ὅτι δίκαιον ξένων is translated "just in his regard for guests".

C's translation keeps fairly close to the Latin versions contained in the three editions of Pindar he is known to have used (and which exhibit only insignificant variations in the Greek at this point), although in two places he typically expands to bring out the full meaning of compound adjectives: "That bore victory" rather than simply "victorious" (Lat "victrices") and "even him . . . safe" rather than "ruler of cities" (Lat "rectorem urbium") or "protector of the state" (Lat "civitatis tutelam").

The Greek text as C knew it reads as follows:

Αναξιφόρμιγγες ὕμνοι
Τίνα θεὸν, τὶν' ἥρωα,
Τίνα δ' ἄνδρα κελαδήσομεν;
Ητοι Πίσα μὲν Διος·
Ολυμπιάδα δ' ἔστα-
σεν Ἡρακλέης,
Ακρόθινα πολέμου.
Θήρωνα δὲ τετραορίας
Ενεκα νικαφόρου

Γεγωνητέον ὀπὶ,
Δίκαιον ξένον,
Ερεισμ' Ακράγαντος,
Εὐωνύμων τε πατέρων
Αωτον ὀρθόπολιν.

This version is from *Poetae Graeci Veteres Tragici, Comici, Lyrici, Epigrammatarii* ed de La Rovière, the source of most of C's Greek quotations in *BL*. He had left this and its companion volume behind at Keswick, and sent for them from London on 27 Jan 1813 (*CL* III 431: to Mrs C; see also *BL—CC—*I 58n and *CN* III 4189). For his notebook entries on Erasmus Schmied's edition of Pindar (Wittenberg 1616) see *CN* II index I (his annotations on his copy appear in *CM—CC—*IV 118–21); for his transcriptions from and comments on C. G. Heyne's edition (4 vols Göttingen 1798–9) see *CN* III index I.

Ye harp-controuling hymns! (or) ye hymns the sovereigns of harps!
What God? what Hero?
What Man shall we celebrate?
Truly Pisa indeed is of Jove,
But the Olympiad (or the Olympic games) did Hercules establish,   5
The first-fruits of the spoils of war.
But Theron for the four-horsed car,
That bore victory to him,
It behoves us now to voice aloud:
The Just, the Hospitable,   10
The Bulwark of Agrigentum,
Of renowned fathers
The Flower, even him
Who preserves his native city erect and safe.

521. CONTEMPORARY CRITICS

[Mar–Sept 1815?]

The lines were printed over C's initials in *BL* ch 21 (1817) II 118 (*CC*) II 109, following his comment on the "*habit* of malignity in the form of mere wantonness" in contemporary reviewers. The whole chapter is given over to "Remarks on the present mode of conducting critical journals", and the prominence given to *Ed Rev* may make it more likely that C's lines owe something to Burns's *To*

Robert Graham of Fintry, Esq. (*Poems, Chiefly in the Scottish Dialect*—2 vols Edinburgh 1793—II 184):

> Critics—appall'd, I venture on the name,
> Those cut-throat bandits in the paths of fame:
> Bloody dissectors, worse than ten Monroes;
> He hacks to teach, they mangle to expose.

C had drawn on the same poem by Burns in a letter to Josiah Wade of c 10 Feb 1796 (*CL* I 185 = **122.X1** *Habent sua Fata—Poetae*). At the same time, his lines might also owe something to Schiller's *Xenien* No 178, *Sections Wut* (first printed in *Musen-Almenach für das Jahr 1797* 243):

> Lebend noch exenterieren sie euch und seid ihr gestorben,
> Passet im Nekrolog noch ein Prosector euch auf.

For another poem on the same theme see **235** *Epigram to a Critic*.

> No private grudge they need, no personal spite;
> The *viva sectio* is its own delight!
> All enmity, all envy, they disclaim,
> Disinterested thieves of our good name:
> Cool, sober murderers of their neighbour's fame!   5

522. TRANSLATION OF DANTE

[Mar–Sept 1815?]

The translation appears in *BL* ch 22 (*CC*) II 147, following on the original ("which Dante addresses to one of his own Canzoni"), given by C as follows:

> Canzon, io credo, che sarranno radi
> Che tua ragione intendan bene:
> Tanto lor sei faticoso ed alto.

In 1807–8 C had copied the Italian into Notebook 22 (*CN* II 3219), with "Color," at the beginning of line 2, and "parli" for "sei" and "e forte" for "ed alto" in line 3. The lines derive from *Convivio* 2.1.53–5. In a copy of *BL* given to DC C altered "intendan bene" to "bene intenderrano", as he did when he quoted the Italian again in the 1818 *Friend* (*CC*) I 511fn.

2. *viva sectio*] In surgery or anatomical operations, a cutting into or division of living substance.

In both *BL* and *The Friend* C quotes Dante's lines in connection with WW's
Intimations Ode. He had gone back to Notebook 22, when composing *BL* ch 5
in particular, for material connected with Aquinas, Hobbes, and others (cf *CN* I
973A, 1000C, 1000I).

> O lyric song, there will be few, think I,
> Who may thy import understand aright:
> Thou art for *them* so arduous and so high!

523. LINES ON AURELIA COATES

[1815?]

The only text is an untitled, unsigned ms in C's hand, which looks like a first
draft. The text given here omits C's deletions, and incorporates a few minor
corrections to make it comprehensible.

It can be assumed that the poem was written while C was living at Calne.
The evidence provided by parish registers and county records is incomplete, but
sufficient to suggest that the lines are based on a local incident. Robert Davis,
a butcher, did marry Elizabeth Wedding at Calne on 18 Sept 1791, and had
at least nine children by her. At the same time, a labourer's family—that of
William and Ann Coates (spelt variously Coat, Coats, Coatts)—lived in Calne;
their daughter Frances Coates, b 17 Feb 1776, might have been the mother of
Aurelia Coates. The matter is difficult to decide since Aurelia appears not to
have been baptised in the parish.

One might have expected such a story to have provided material for the wife
of W. L. Bowles, in her *Characters and Incidents of Village Life* (1831), which
draws on such episodes from recent Bremhill history, but it is not mentioned
there.

> The Butcher Davis, then a lusty Gallant,
> Lived as an House-mate with two gentle Damsels,
> Both their fair forms pleas'd *him*—and his fair form
> Both *them* did please! Ah then! had swell'd their Hearts!
> Their waists too swell'd. What could the Lover do?   5
> One only could he wed, and one did wed,
> His present Spouse—and time enough to save
> If not her Honor, yet the Child's. The other
> Condemn'd to stain the pale puerperal Cheek

With the deep Blushes of discover'd Frailty   10
Brought forth a Girl—since nam'd Aurelia Cotes—
She grew, & not untrain'd in virtuous Lore,
But plied the needle—& so shone her Beauty
That no eye saw it save a youthful Tradesman's
Of Marlborough—Him Love had smitten—he   15
Woo'd and woo'd her oft—as oft repell'd.
He follow'd her to Calne, & there receiving
Bitter Repulse & scornful, he went home
And hung himself. Too soon was he aveng'd—
Alas! thought she, I am worse than Barbara Allen—   20
Not to hope kill'd him, but my cruel Scorn.
Thick Melancholy then became her Meat,
And for her Drink it was chiefly British Gin,
She pin'd, and pin'd, and so she died—
They buried her $^\lceil$...$^\rceil$ I $^\lceil$...$^\rceil$ & heard this Evening   25
As the B$^\lceil$....$^\rceil$

524. LINES IN PRAISE OF RABELAIS

[Aug–Sept 1815? 1815–16?]

The verses are the conclusion of seven successive drafts in Notebook $3\frac{1}{2}$ (*CN*
III 4264). KC compares the spirit of C's 1818 lectures on Rabelais (*L Lects—
CC*—II 171–82) and also *TT* 15 Jun 1830, 1 May 1833 (*CC*) I 165–7, II 220–1.
C's earliest known discussion of the Gothic and the mixed descent of the Celts
from Shem and Ham—to which he often reverted—appears in lecture 1 of the
1818 series (*L Lects—CC*—II 47–63). KC suggests 1816–17 as an alternative
to 1815, which would bring the present lines up to the time of preparation for
the lectures.

C continued after line 5 with a note for the continuation of the poem: "Then
Pascal—& Moliere, the Gothics/". What he had in mind is explained by a note
of 1825 on Pepys's *Memoirs*. Having said he could not conceive of Rabelais
as French, C went on, "except on my hypothesis of a continued dilution of the

20. Barbara Allen] The ballad *Bar-
bara Allen's Cruelty* describes how
her indifference and scorn bring about
the death of her lover. The version C
knew, in *Reliques of Ancient English*
Poetry [ed Percy] III 124–7, differs
from that most widely known today
as "Bonny Barbara Allen" (Child *The
English and Scottish Popular Ballads*
No 84).

Gothic blood from the reign of Henry IV; Descartes, Malebranche, Pascal, and Molière being the *ultimi Gothorum*, the last in whom the Gothic predominated over the Celtic" (*Misc C* 286). Presumably the poem was to be continued along these lines, in praise of Pascal and Molière, perhaps to close with a lament for "the last of the Goths" and an attack on the Celtic spirit.

> And wisest Rabelais! wise, humane & good,
> He would have given as far as man can give,
> Manifold Thought & pity's gentle pangs
> Hid in a laugh of pious *resignation*
> And truest Tolerance—   5

525. ΕΓΩΕΝΚΑΙΠΑΝ: A DITHYRAMBIC ODE

[Jul–Sept 1815?]

The only text is that published in *BL* ch 9 (1817) I 148–9fn (*CC*) I 159–60fn. The lines are introduced as follows:

> The following burlesque on the Fichtean Egoismus may, perhaps, be amusing to the few who have studied the system, and to those who are unacquainted with it, may convey as tolerable a likeness of Fichte's idealism as can be expected from an avowed caricature.

For another relevant passage, out of many, see *CN* IV 5377 (11 May 1826), especially f 43ᵛ. Another, more serious, gloss may be provided by a note now at the University of Waterloo, Ontario (CoS 1094.7), pub *SW&F* (*CC*) 829–30. When the note was acquired as part of the Bertram Davis Collection, it was contained in an envelope endorsed by Edward Dowden, who wrote: "Now placed in vol ii of S. T. Coleridge's Poet & Dramatic Works—page 86. ~~with the~~ side by side with the poem it glosses in MS. I E. Dowden July 30 83". It seems likely that Dowden connected the prose note with the present lines, which were first collected by RHS in *P&DW* (1877–80) (although Dowden gets the page-reference wrong: it is II 370–1). However, the connection between the note and the lines cannot be proved.

title. The pantheistic phrase ἓν καὶ πᾶν ("one and all") is preceded by the word for "I" (ἐγώ): "I—the (true) One and All". Querkopf ("wrong-head") Von Klubstick burlesques the odes of F. G. Klopstock. The Gymnasium is a traditional German secondary school. *BL* ch 9 (*CC*) I 159n annotates the more serious allusions to philosophical (pantheistic) themes.

C converted a favourite nursery rhyme into a similar parody of German Idealist logic when he annotated *Omniana* for JG in late 1819 (*CM—CC—*III 1071; cf *CN* I 469, 1235; *SW&F—CC—*322).

The categorical imperative, or the annunciation of the new Teutonic god, ΕΓΩΕΝΚΑΙΠΑΝ: a dithyrambic Ode, by QUER-KOPF VON KLUBSTICK, Grammarian, and Subrector in Gymnasio ****.

Eu! Dei vices gerens, ipse Divus,
(*Speak English, Friend!*) the God Imperativus,
Here on this market-cross aloud I cry:
I, I, I! I itself I!
The form and the substance, the what and the why,   5
The when and the where, and the low and the high,
The inside and outside, the earth and the sky,
I, you, and he, and he, you and I,
All souls and all bodies are I itself I!
    All I itself I!   10
   (Fools! a truce with this starting!)
    All my I! all my I!
He's a heretic dog who but adds Betty Martin!
Thus cried the God with high imperial tone:

1. Tr "Hurrah! God's vicegerent, myself God".

12–13. C enjoyed playing with the vulgar expression of disbelief, "That's all my eye and Betty Martin": see **605** *Lines on J. F. Meckel's "System der vergleichenden Anatomie"*; *CN* III 3335, IV 4809 f 65^r, 5206 f 17^v, 5377 f 43^v; *CL* VI 564: to EC [8 Feb 1826]. The editors' notes in the latter two places quote *CRB* I 114 for C's implausible, surely jocular, and possibly original explanation of it as a Protestant corruption of a Roman Catholic address, "O mihi, Beate Martine". The earliest published occurrences of such an explanation appear unattributed in the dictionaries of slang compiled by Francis Grose (1823) and John Bee (1823).

The speaker's pantheistic views are heretical in C's eyes, so the appeal is ironic. It is also possible—but not likely—that C wanted to incorporate some reference to the Catholic tendency of post-Kantian philosophy. He nowhere else takes notice of Fichte's Catholicism (only Schelling's), and the present instance is the only one where the religious explanation of the phrase could be relevant. Moreover, if such an explanation had been an invention of his own (or of CL?), it could not have been understood by most readers.

In robe of stiffest state, that scoff'd at beauty,   15
A pronoun-verb imperative he shone—
Then substantive and plural-singular grown
He thus spake on! Behold in I alone
(For ethics boast a syntax of their own)
Or if in ye, yet as I doth depute ye,   20
In O! I, you, the vocative of duty!
I of the world's whole Lexicon the root!
Of the whole universe of touch, sound, sight
The genitive and ablative to boot:
The accusative of wrong, the nom'native of right,   25
And in all cases the case absolute!
Self-construed, I all other moods decline:
Imperative, from nothing we derive us;
Yet as a super-postulate of mine,
Unconstrued antecedence I assign   30
To X, Y, X, the God infinitivus!

526. TO THE MORGANS

[Aug–Sept 1815?]

C wrote the lines on a front flyleaf of F.W.J. Schelling *Philosophische Schriften* I (Landshut 1809) (*CM—CC—*IV 404). They are preceded by a prose memorandum and a first version of the couplet:

Το ασκ ἐμεμσῆ, ει θε μεανς καν βε ραισδ, οὐεθερ θαῖ οοδ σπενδ α ενιαυτον συν εμοι εν Γερμανια ἡ Σουιτσερλαντ.

Δῆρ Φρενζ, Jαjά—Εμ-Εμ́—Σιβῆ!
Λυφ, ασ ηυ'ρ λυφτ βεῖ, Εϛ-Τι-Σῆ.

21. An early illustration of C's interest in the verb substantive as corresponding in grammar to the "Absolute I AM", from which all grammatical forms derive. Cf e.g. *CN* IV 4644 and *AR* (1831) 170fn (*CC*) 180fn, i.e. the expansion of the fn in *AR* (1825) 171 et seq—the note so much admired by William Rowan Hamilton (*TT—CC—*I 69n).
31. For C's objection to calling God infinite see *CM* (*CC*) I 585, II 596; *C&S* (*CC*) 168; *CN* IV 5087.

The prose combines phonetic transliteration of English words with some Greek ones; and there are typographical differences between the first and second (RT) versions of the couplet, affecting nearly every word. The meaning is:

> To ask MMC, if the means can be raised, whether they would spend a year with me in Germany or Switzerland.

> Dear Friends, J.J., M.M., C.B.,
> Love, as you're loved by, S.T.C.

(MMC = Morgan, Mary and Charlotte; J.J. = John Morgan; M.M. = Mary Morgan; C.B. = Charlotte Brent, Mary Morgan's unmarried sister.)

C's interest in German philosophy revived as he turned to Schelling and others for help with the philosophical chapters of *BL*, and his spirits lifted as he contemplated the completion of the publishing project represented by *SL* and *BL*. He might have wondered about a trip to Germany at any time during his intimacy with the Morgans, but Aug–Sept 1815 would seem to have been a most opportune moment. Cf **372** *On the Names in a Malta Notebook* for a play on the initials of other friends; and e.g. **433** *Extremes Meet* for his sense of ease in the Morgan household.

Δῆρ Φρενδς, Ια-Ια, Εμ-Εμ; Ση Βῆ!
Λυφ, ας ηυ'ρ λυφδ βει, Ες Τι Σῆ.

527. LINES ON SUPERSTITION

[1815–16]

C drafted the untitled lines in Notebook 22 (*CN* III 4283). They recall in particular a Brocken phenomenon (*CN* I 430, 431; see also *CN* III 4158; **357** *Constancy to an Ideal Object* 25–32). He wrote down an almost exact prose version of the poem in another notebook in 1819: "Superstition the Giant Shadow of Humanity with it's back to the setting Sun of true Religion" (*CN* III 4491). On the sun image see *SM* (*CC*) 10 and n, etc.

> O! Superstition is the Giant Shadow
> Which the Solicitude of weak Mortality
> It's Back toward Religion's rising Sun,
> Casts on the thin mist of the uncertain Future.

528. LINES HEADED "ORPHEUS"

[1815–16?]

C drafted the lines, under the title "Orpheus", in Notebook 22 (*CN* III 4286). Their texture might suggest a dramatic context, but they are unexplained.

Tho' with the Vulgar
Strange Customs lead to blind Conjectures, what
The curious Wench discusses with the Laundress
And then takes council of the key-hole, that
The Man, whose Science Practice still impregnates,   5
Sees at one glance. *He's Nature's Confessor!*
To *him* she opens out her tale of Wrongs,
And in the sequels (Eye, Look, Gestures, Moods)
Engraves the history of the causing Acts.
Lock'd doors & curtain'd Windows prove vain safe-guards.   10
The sole sure plan the Theban Women taught,
Who tore wise Orpheus piece-meal. Tho' no Tell-tale,
He had pierc'd backwards into Deeds unseen:
And woe to Him, who being guiltless knows,
Or is thought to know, a lurking Guilt! For Shame,   15
That leads not to Amendment, wakes Revenge.

529. LINES ADAPTED FROM JEAN PAUL

[1815–16]

C drafted the lines in Notebook 22 (*CN* III 4298). They represent an attempt to paraphrase, condense, and versify a passage in Jean Paul's *Geist*:

Die ehemaligen Darstellungen hoher Menschen sind durchlebte warme Blütenzeiten der Seele, ach die niemals wiederkommen, so wenig wie die erste Liebe, oder der Jugend Silberblick, oder irgend eine Begeisterung. Denn der Mensch läuft in keiner runden Mondsbahn, ja in keiner langen Kometenbahn, um irgend eine Sonne, und treibt sich in keinem wiederkehrenden Tausche von Neu- und Volllicht, von Haar- und Schwanzstern um; sondern er zieht gerade und kühn, wie ein fliegender Engel, durch die Schöpfung und durch die Systeme, immer von dem Morgen neuer Sonnen bestralt, und von dem Erdschatten neuer Erdkörper verdunkelt, und *niemals tritt er einen Lauf von neuem an.* (*Geist, oder Chrestomathie* No 462 ɪɪ 78)

KC's translation is as follows:

The old representations of noble men are the warm and deeply experienced blossom times of the soul, which will, alas, never come again, irrevocable as first love, or the bright eye of youth, or any enthusiasm. For man's life does not move in a circular course like the moon, nor even in the long path of the comet around some sun, nor does it move in any recurrent cycle from new to full, from coma to tail; no, like a flying angel, his path is straight and bold, through creation and the stellar systems, always illuminated by the morning of new suns, and darkened by the shadows of new earths, and *he never starts his course anew*.

> Let klumps of Earth however glorified
> Roll round & round & still renew their cycle/
> Man rushes like a winged Cherub thro'
> The infinite Space, and that which has been
> Can therefore never be again—　　　　　　　　　　5

530. FURTHER LINES ADAPTED FROM JEAN PAUL

[1815–16]

C drafted the lines in Notebook 22 (*CN* ɪɪɪ 4299), immediately following poem **529.** They pluck one sentence, from a long paragraph on man's uncertain view into the future, from Jean Paul's *Geist, oder Chrestomathie* No 467 ɪɪ 84: "Die *Blüte* trägt und gibt nicht nur künftige *Früchte*, sondern auch gegenwärtigen *Honigsaft*, und man darf ihr diesen nehmen und schadet jenen nicht" tr "The *blossom* bears and produces not only future *fruits*, but also present *honey*, and you can take the latter from it without harming the former."

> The Blossom gives not only future fruits
> But present Honey. We may take the one,
> The other nothing injured.

1. klumps] A contamination from Ger *Klumpen* "lumps, clods".

531. EPIGRAM ON MONEY

[1815]

PW (JDC) 451A supplies the only known text, from ms. The occasion of the lines is not known—perhaps conversation with the impecunious Morgans.

> Money, I've heard a wise man say,
> Makes herself wings and flies away—
> Ah! would she take it in her head
> To make a pair for me instead.

532. LINES ON CRIMES AND VIRTUES

[1815–16]

C drafted the lines, without title or explanation, in Notebook 22 (*CN* III 4303).

> Each Crime, that once estranges one from the Virtues
> Doth make the memory of their features daily
> More dim and vague, till each coarse Counterfeit
> Can have it's passport to our Confidence
> Sign'd by ourselves—And fitly are they punish'd   5
> Who prize and seek the Honest man, but as
> A safer Lock to guard dishonest treasures.

533. ELEVATED DIARRHOEA

[c 1815–18]

C wrote the lines in his copy of Mesmer's *Mesmerismus* (*CM*—*CC*—III 870). Mesmer's editor, Wolfart, had written of "das Element, in welchem der reine urthätige Ausfluß des Unerschaffenen und Ewigen als möglichst freithätiges Leben erwacht" tr "the element in which the pure, primarily active outflowing of the uncreated and eternal awakens as the most freely active life possible".

C's comment was no doubt inspired by the basic meaning of "Ausfluß"—the Germanic equivalent of "emanation". He added an asterisk and, in the margin, "Q? *Urfläthige?*"—that is, changing the meaning of the word to "primally dirty". He then answered his own query at the foot of the page, adding: "Why, it is as plain as a Pike-staff!" and continuing with the verse-lines.

C enjoyed composing lavatorial verses which drew on this kind of linguistic inventiveness: cf **329** *Greek Lines on Achilles' Meal of Yesterday.* Elsewhere in the same Mesmer volume he calls Wolfart wool- or fizzle-fart and describes him "distill[ing] the ~~crude~~ dreggy Materialism of Mesmer into the hyper-alcoholic Spirit of Schellingianism", writing "a child's *Picture-book* to the System der Natur-philosophie" (*CM—CC—*III 867).

Inner and Inner,
Thinner and thinner.
Our Thoughts are the *volatile* T—ds of our Dinner
And sententiâ meâ
The Soul's but a thin sort of Diupsorrhea!   5

534. VERSE LINES FROM *A LAY SERMON*

[1816]

(*a*) is quoted in *A Lay Sermon* (1817) to complete the sentence describing those who, "more attentive to the prudential advantages of a decorous character, yield the customary evidence of their church-membership; but, this performed, are at peace with themselves, and" (*LS—CC—*185). (*b*) is quoted later in the same book to continue a sentence "on the revolution in the *mode* of preaching as well as in the matter, since the fresh morning and fervent noon of the Reformation, when there was no need to visit the conventicles of fanaticism in order to" (*LS—CC—*198–9).

The two sets of lines may be unrelated, and even if they are from the same work, they may not have occurred there in their present order. Nor is it certain that they are by C at all: the phrase "God's ambassador" in line 3 is from Cowper *The Task* (1785) II 464.

3. T—ds] Turds.
4. sententiâ meâ] "in my opinion".
5. Diupsorrhea] A coinage based on Gk ὕψος "height", meaning "Elevated Diarrhoea" or "Diarrhoea of Sublimities".

(*a*)

—think their Sunday's task
As much as God or Man can fairly ask;

(*b*)

See God's ambassador in the pulpit stand,
Where they could take notes from his Look and Hand;
And from his speaking *action* bear away
More sermon than our preachers use to *say*;

535. ALTERNATIVE TRANSLATION OF VIRGIL'S *BUCOLICS*

[Dec 1816–early 1817]

C wrote his translation in the margin of a presentation copy of Francis Wrangham's *Scraps* (1816) (*CM—CC—*vi), pt 8 of which comprises Virgil's *Bucolics* (i.e. *Eclogues*) with Wrangham's facing translation. The Latin text (*Eclogue* 1.1–2) is given there as follows:

> *Mel.* Tityre, tu patulae recubans sub tegmine fagi
> Sylvestrem tenui Musam meditaris avenâ:

Wrangham's translation runs:

> *Meliboeus.* Beneath this beech you, Tityrus, thrown at ease
> Pour through the reed your sylvan melodies:

The Latin literally means: "Tityrus, you, lying under the cover of a spreading beech, meditate on the woodland Muse upon a slender oaten pipe." C's version is evidently closer to the original than Wrangham's—given that the rhyming couplets break the continuity, and are more appropriate to elegiacs than to Virgil's hexameters.

> Beneath the spreading Beech you, Tityrus! note
> The Sylvan Muse upon the slender Oat.

536. MOTTO FOR MEMORANDA IN NOTEBOOK 25

[Jan 1817]

C drafted the lines in Notebook 25, and signed them "S. T. C.—" (*CN* III 4327). In their context they make up an epigraph, following the heading in the half-filled notebook:

Referentiary
(from p. 49 (E)—1817, 1 Jan.ʸ)
to the Book
&
Page
of the Facts, Thoughts, & Cetera
that had impressed
me for good or evil, during
my Reading.

One book at a time
Read steadily thro
Makes one's Thoughts chime
And's the quickest way too!

537. LINES AFTER PUNCH

[Mar 1817]

C drafted the lines in Notebook 22 (*CN* III 4344). KC points out that the *OED* attributes *punched*, the verb meaning "drank punch", to C (cf *CM*—*CC*—I 760), and that *Pudel* is the German spelling of poodle (see also *CN* II 2754 and n)—a word which the *OED* records as entering English in 1825.

The morning after Punch-inebriation
To spit Dogs' faces in the Chamber-pot
White curly Pudel's of Froth with bladder-eyes/

538. LINES FOR AN AUTOGRAPH HUNTER

[1817? 1827–32?]

C inscribed the present version on the front wrapper of a copy of *A Lay Sermon* (1817) which he is said to have given to Mrs Aders. He wrote out another version in 1832 and 1834, which includes a few variations and two further lines:

> Author of Works, whereof, tho' not in Dutch
> The Public little knows, the Publisher too much.

C was fond of quoting the extra couplet in later years: cf e.g. *CL* VI 873: to R. Fieldier 10 Nov 1831; Folio Notebook [=HEHL HM 17299] f 69ᵛ, dated 24 May 1828 (*CN* V); also **637** *Written in William Upcott's Album*. It is possible that both versions date from this later time, when C was much pursued by autograph hunters and while his friendship with the Aderses deepened. The present version is known only from a sale catalogue; the original has not been located.

> A haughty Graff: Graff? That's what Germans call
> Their Counts. Haughty enough most of them are, Lord knows.
> What can a Lady want one for, I wonder!
> "Nonsense! she means your name." Ho! is that all?
> Bear witness then my Hand, that here I underwrite,   5
> S. T. Coleridge, Scribe in verse & prose.

539. TO A YOUNG LADY
COMPLAINING OF A CORN

[Jun–Jul 1817?]

The only ms is a fair copy in the hand of JG's assistant J.H.B. Williams. The evidence of other material in the same ms suggests that it might date from early in C's sojourn at Highgate, although a slightly different two-stanza version in *LR* is dated 1825.

> The rose that blushes like the Morn,
> Bedecks the vallies low;

And so dost thou, sweet infant Corn!
My Angelina's toe.
But on the rose there grows a thorn,   5
That breeds disastrous woe:
Ah! so wilt thou remorseless Corn!
To Angelina's toe.—

540. FANCY IN NUBIBUS

[Oct 1817]

The sonnet was written on 29 Oct 1817, after C had spent a month at Littlehampton in Sussex. It was sent back to JG at Highgate with the following explanation: "As I came in this evening after a glorious Sunset a sort of lazy poetic mood came on me and almost without knowing it I composed the following Sonnet, which merely because it is the first Resumption of the rhyming Idleness Mrs G will have me send you—It has the character of a Sonnet—that it is like a something that we let escape from us—a Sigh, for instance" (*CL* IV 779–80).

The last five lines consciously or unconsciously owe something to two stanzas of Stolberg's *An das Meer* (C. and F. L. Stolberg *Gedichte* 210):

> Der blinde Sänger stand am Meer;
> Die Wogen rauschten um ihn her,
> Und Riesenthaten goldner Zeit
> Umrauschten ihn im Feierkleid.

> Es kam zu ihm auf Schwanenschwung
> Melodisch die Begeisterung,
> Und Ilias und Odüssee
> Entstiegen mit Gesang der See.

The phrase "the voiceful sea" in C's last line was C's translation of the Homeric formula πολυφλοίσβοιο θαλάσσης (*Iliad* 1.34, and often) in *CN* II 2777, which he also translated (not very seriously) as "the Sea of much roar" in **118** *Translations of Homer "Iliad" 1.34, 49*. Note also his comparison of the onomatopoeic effect of the Greek epithet with English "brisk" to describe the sound of the sea on the voyage to Malta (*CN* II 2004); his use of it to describe a church congregation in *CN* III 4021 f 30^v; and his jocular reference to "phloshbosh" in **329** *Greek Lines on Achilles' Meal of Yesterday*. The etymology of φλοῖσβος is obscure. Modern reference works connect it with a root meaning "swell", while lexicons of C's day describe it as denoting the sound of water; πολυ- can imply either that the sound is loud or that it is multitudinous.

C made transcripts of the poem for JG and, apparently, for H. F. Cary, the translator of Dante, whose acquaintance he made when he heard him and his son reading Homer, the "blind bard" of line 11, on the strand at Littlehampton (Henry Cary *Memoir of the Rev. Henry Francis Cary*—2 vols 1847—II 18); and the meeting forms a significant background to the sense of renewal and reviving confidence which the poem celebrates. The following year (1818) C made a transcript for CL apparently on dried seaweed, which CL carried across into gift copies of *SL*, thereby confusing book collectors after his death. The poem was published in *The Courier* (30 Jan 1818), the text given here, and afterwards included without change in the three late collections. Two of C's transcripts were published without his knowledge in 1819 and 1829.

A Sonnet, Composed by the Sea Side, October 1817

O! it is pleasant, with a heart at ease,
   Just after sunset, or by moonlight skies,
To make the shifting clouds be what you please,
   Or let the easily persuaded eyes
Own each quaint likeness issuing from the mould   5
   Of a friend's fancy; or with head bent low
And cheek aslant, see Rivers flow of gold
   'Twixt crimson banks; and then, a traveller, go
From mount to mount, thro' CLOUDLAND, gorgeous land!
   Or list'ning to the tide, with closed sight,   10
Be that blind bard, who, on the Chian strand,
   By those deep sounds possessed with inward light,
Beheld the ILIAD and the ODYSSEE
   Rise to the swelling of the voiceful sea.

541. IMITATED FROM ARISTOPHANES

[Aug–Nov 1817]

C used the lines in "General Introduction; or, A Preliminary Treatise on Method" *Encyclopaedia Metropolitana* (29 vols 1817–45) I 23 (*SW&F*—*CC*—659); vol I came out in Jan 1818. In Nov 1818 they appeared again in the same context in *The Friend* sec 2 essay 6 (1818) III 178–9; in *Friend* (*CC*) I 473 this has become essay 7, following C's instructions in the list of Errata in vol I

9. CLOUDLAND] This appears to be C's coinage.

(*Friend*—*CC*—I 464n). There are obvious errors in the *Encyclopaedia*'s Greek, and the present text is taken from *The Friend*. C describes the "glittering VA- PORS, that (as the comic poet tells us) fed a host of sophists", and then quotes Aristophanes *Clouds* 316–18 (Socrates speaking), followed by his own imitation:

> μεγάλαι θέαι ἀνδράσιν ἀργοῖς
> Αἵπερ γνώμην καὶ διάλεξιν καὶ νοῦν ἡμῖν παρέχουσιν,
> Καὶ τερατείαν καὶ περίλεξιν καὶ κρόυσιν καὶ κατάληψιν
> ΑΡΙΣΤΟΦ. Νεφ. Σκ. δ.

C translates the first line literally. What follows may be rendered: "who give us judgment and debating skills and intelligence, and marvel-mongering, circumlocution, browbeating, and quick apprehension". The appended reference means "[Act I] sc 4".

C's interest in Aristophanes was reinforced in 1816, when he read J. H. Frere's translations/imitations (which he quoted in an earlier essay in the 1818 *Friend*: *CC* I 18). Cf also **560** *To a Comic Author* headnote.

> Great goddesses are they to lazy folks,
> Who pour down on us gifts of fluent speech,
> Sense most sententious, wonderful fine *effect*,
> And how to talk about it and about it,
> Thoughts brisk as bees, and pathos soft and thawy.　　　5

542. PART OF A SONNET TO MISS BULLOCK

[Nov 1817]

The lines are known only from a Sotheby's catalogue description in 1913, where they are quoted as part of an autograph ms sonnet to Miss E. Bullock, signed and dated Nov 1817, on a quarto page. Betsy Bullock was the sister of Mrs Milne, a Highgate neighbour, whose family was especially friendly with the Gillmans. KC (*CN* IV 4878n) describes the movements of the Bullock–Milne and Gillman households around Highgate during C's lifetime. C was sending her remembrances as early as Sept 1816 (*CL* IV 684: to J.H.B. Williams), and the letter to an unknown correspondent in Apr 1819 appears also to be to her (*CL* IV 935–6; cf *CL* V 42n: to an unknown correspondent [May 1820?]). In *CN* IV 4606 C records receiving a birthday present of flowers from her on 20 Oct 1819; cf IV 4878 (23 Mar 1822).

5. thawy] C appears to have been the first to use the word in print.

C was at Littlehampton in early Nov 1817, and arrived back at Highgate on 13 Nov. On his return he was busy with the *Preliminary Treatise on Method* for the *Encyclopaedia Metropolitana* (*SW&F—CC*—625–87) and with **543** *Israel's Lament* (see *CL* IV 784: to H. Hurwitz [23 Nov 1817]).

> 'Twas dull November: dim the Moon: each Flower
> That in it's beams erewhile had gleam'd or glitter'd,
> Had left our Garden, ... etc.

543. ISRAEL'S LAMENT ON THE DEATH OF THE PRINCESS CHARLOTTE OF WALES, TRANSLATED FROM THE HEBREW OF HYMAN HURWITZ

[Nov 1817]

C's poem is based on a Hebrew dirge chanted in St James's Place Synagogue on the day of Princess Charlotte's funeral, 19 Nov 1817. The princess was the only child of the Prince Regent and Princess Caroline. She had married in 1816, soon after her twentieth birthday, and she died after a long labour, giving birth to a stillborn son. The details were reported in *The Times* (6 Nov 1817) and explain the allusions in the poem. She went into labour at about noon on 5 Nov; the child was perfectly formed and alive up to a few moments before its birth at 9.00 P.M. She herself was apparently well, and her husband, the Prince Leopold of Saxe-Cobourg, is reported to have said, "Thank GOD! thank GOD! the Princess is safe." He and the doctors had retired when, after midnight, she went into spasms and died at 2.30 A.M. on 6 Nov. The poem is sometimes cited as a contribution to Tory propaganda, but it is not likely that much party-political meaning was intended by the author or translator. Even allowing for the exaggeration customary on such occasions, the princess does appear to have been universally liked. Cf *EOT* (*CC*) II 478–9 for an obituary in *The Courier* (7 Nov 1817) conjecturally attributed to C.

CM (*CC*) II 1188–9 provides a full note on C's acquaintance with Hyman Hurwitz. Hurwitz's Hebrew echoes, in both form and structure, a lament over the destruction of Jerusalem which continues to be sung to the present day after the reading of Lamentations on the 9th of Ab (the anniversary of the destruction of the first and second Temples in Jerusalem). It reads as follows:

קִינַת יְשֻׁרוּן

אֱלִי יְשֻׁרוּן וּבְנֶיהָ!
כְּמוֹ אִשָּׁה בְּחֶבְלֶיהָ;
וְכִבְתוּלָה, חֲגוּרַת־שַׂק
עֲלֵי בַעַל נְעוּרֶיהָ.

אלי וכ״ו

עֲלֵי גְבִירָה, אֲשֶׁר נִפְטָרָה
בְּעוֹדָהּ בִּנְעוּרֶיהָ.—
וְעַל בֵּן רַךְ, אֲשֶׁר נִלְקַח,
וְהִרְבָּה מַכְאֹבֶיהָ.

אלי וכ״ו

עֲלֵי שׁוֹשַׁנָּה, אֲשֶׁר נִקְטָפָה
בְּטֶרֶם צֵאת פְּרָחֶיהָ!
וְעַל הַצִּיץ, אֲשֶׁר קָצַץ,
וְשָׁת מָוֶת בְּקִרְבֶּיהָ.

אלי וכ״ו

עֲלֵי עֶלְטָה, אֲשֶׁר עָטָה
פְּנֵי תֵבֵל וְיֹשְׁבֶיהָ;
בְּמוֹת פְּרִינְצֶעס שַׁארְלָטֶה,
בְּטֶרֶם מְלֹאת יָמֶיהָ.

אלי וכ״ו

עֲלֵי שָׂרָה מְאַשְׁרָה[1]
אֲשֶׁר[2] עָזְבָה עֲפָרֶיהָ;
לְהִתְעַדֵּן ,בְּגַן־עֵדֶן;
וְלֶאֱכוֹל פְּרִי דְרָכֶיהָ.

אלי וכ״ו

עֲלֵי הַשֹּׁד, אֲשֶׁר שֻׁדַּד
פְּאֵר לְעִפְאָלְךְ אֲדֹנֶיהָ!
אֲשֶׁר בְּמַר נַפְשׁוֹ, יְמָאֵן
לְהִתְנַחֵם עָלֶיהָ.

אלי וכ״ו

עֲלֵי שֶׁבֶר, אֲשֶׁר שֻׁבַּר
לְבַב נְסִיכָךְ! וְהוֹרֶיהָ!
בְּחָטְפוֹ הַחֲבַצֶּלֶת,—
וְשָׁם חֹחַ תַּחְתֶּיהָ.—

אלי וכ״ו

---

[1] An error for מְאֻשָּׁרָה.   [2] An error for אֲשֶׁר.

חֲבִי רֶגַע!—רְשׁוּר נֶגַע!—
אֲשֶׁר³ פָּשָׂה בְּבֵית אָבִיהָ!
לָשַׁמָּה⁴ שָׂם אֶת גַּפְנוֹ,—
וְהִשְׁחִית שָׂרִיגֶיהָ.—

אֵלִי וכ״ו

עֲלֵי צָרוֹת, וְרֹב מַחֲלַת
בְּרִטַאנְיָא וּבְנוֹתֶיהָ;
אֲשֶׁר אָבְדָה מַחֲמַדָּהּ,
כְּלִיל יָפְיָהּ,—וְשָׂרֶיהָ.—

אֵלִי וכ״ו

בְּכָל שָׁנָה, נִשָּׂא קִינָה,
וּבְלֵב דַּוָּי, נִצְעַק הוֹי,
עֲלֵי שׁוֹשַׁנָּה, אֲשֶׁר נִקְטְפָה
בְּטֶרֶם צֵאת פְּרָחֶיהָ.—

אֵלִי וכ״ו

וְאָהִימָה, יָמִים יְמִימָה,
בְּרוּחַ צַר, וּמִסְפַּד מַר,
עַל הַצִּיץ, אֲשֶׁר קָצַץ,
וְשָׁת מָוֶת בְּקִרְבֶּיהָ.

אֵלִי וכ״ו

בְּמוֹת רְשָׁעִים, יֹאבַד שְׁמָם:
וְאַתְּ צְבִיָּה! תְּחִי חֲרוּתָה
בְּלֵב יְשָׁרִים: וּבַשְּׁעָרִים
יְהַלְלוּ תֹם מַעֲשֶׂיהָ.

אֵלִי וכ״ו

רְאֵה אֵלִי! יְגוֹן עַמִּי,
וּרְפָא נָא תַחֲלֻאֶיהָ:
עֲוֹנָהּ סְלַח, מְנַחֵם שְׁלַח,
אֱלֵי יְשֻׁרוּן וּבָנֶיהָ.

אֵלִי וכ״ו

חֲרֹנְךָ⁵ אֵל! מְאֹד הֶאֱבִיל
בְּרִטַאנְיָא וְשָׂרֶיהָ.
תְּחִנָּה שְׁמַע, וְתֵן יֶשַׁע,
לְמַלְכָּהּ, וּלְיֹשְׁבֶיהָ.

תם

---

³ An error for אֲשֶׁר.
⁴ An error for לְשַׁמָּה.
⁵ An error for חֲרֹנְךָ.

C described the character of the original as:

> in the simplicity of the Thoughts, well suiting a dirge and still more a Hebrew Dirge; but for that reason hard to be translated into our compressed & monosyllabic Language without one or other of two evils—either, the Translator must add thoughts & images, & of course cease to be a Translator; or he must repeat the same thought in other words and become tautological—the more so, as some of the Thoughts can from our habits of Thinking and feeling only be *hinted*—compressed instead of expanded (*CL* IV 784: to H. Hurwitz [23 Nov 1817]).

His version in fact changes the character of the original considerably. Shorter rhyming lines make it less antiphonal and public, and specific biblical allusions are generalised. C's version retrieves for English poetry a poem whose achievement, such as it is, assimilated the death of Princess Charlotte to a different, older tradition. It is therefore a back translation as much as a translation, and a comparison with the following literal rendering of Hurwitz's Hebrew (which retains the punctuation of the original) makes this clear:

THE LAMENT OF JESHURUN[6]

Lament Jeshurun and her sons!
Like a woman in her birth-pangs;[7]
and like a virgin, girded in sackcloth
for the husband of her youth.[8]

Lament etc[9]
Over the young woman, who has departed [this world]
while still in her youth.—
And over [her] infant son, who was taken away,
and increased her pains greatly.

Lament etc
Over the rose, which was plucked
before the emergence of its blooms!
and over the blossom, which was cut off,
and placed death within her.

Lament etc
Over the darkness, which has wrapped
the face of the earth and its inhabitants;

---

[6] A title for Israel which appears only in Deut 32.15; 33.5, 26; Isa 44.2, probably related to *yashar* "upright". (Scriptural references are to the Hebrew Bible in the notes to this poem.)

[7] The image of a woman in the pain of birth-pangs occurs in Isa 26.17; Jer 22.23; 49.24.

[8] The Hebrew is an exact quotation of Joel 1.8 "Lament like a virgin girded in sackcloth for the husband of her youth."

[9] The imperative "Lament" governs the syntax of the verses which follow.

on the death of Princess Charlotte,
before her days reached fulfilment.

Lament etc
Over a princess who was blessed,
who has left her dust[10] behind;
to be rejuvenated,[11] in the garden of Eden;
and to eat the fruit of her ways.[12]

Lament etc
Over the violence, which was perpetrated against
the glory of Leopold her lord!
who in his bitterness of soul, refuses
to be consoled on her account.

Lament etc
Over the fracture, which has broken
the heart of your prince! and her parents!
when it snatched away the young lily,—
and placed a thorn in its stead.—

Lament etc
Wait a moment!—and the [umbilical] cord has struck her down!—[13]
which was broken in the house of her father!
unto desolation did it render his vine,—
and destroyed her tendrils.—

Lament etc
Over the tribulations, and abundance of sickness
of Britannia and her daughters;
because her beloved one has been lost,
the crown of her beauty,—and her princesses.—

Lament etc
Throughout the year, a lament will be taken up,
and with a mournful heart, will woe be cried forth,
over the rose, which was plucked
before its blooms had emerged.—

And I will mourn, on the anniversary,
with an anguished spirit, and bitter mourning,
over the blossom, which was cut off,
and placed death within her.

---

[10] The word is in the plural and may refer to the more abstract concept of "mortality".

[11] There is a play on words between the verb and the substantive "Eden".

[12] Probably in the sense of "her just reward".

[13] Difficult to render; the Hebrew of this line is obscure.

At the death of the wicked, their name shall perish:
but thee, O gazelle![14] may thou be engraven
in the heart of the upright: and in the gates
may they praise the perfection of her deeds.

———————

See my God! the grief of my people,
and heal her diseases;
pardon her iniquity, send forth consolation,
lament Jeshurun and her sons.

Your anger O God! greatly indeed do mourn
Britannia and her princes.
Be gracious, listen, and give deliverance,
to her king, and to her inhabitants.

 END

C's translation faced the Hebrew in the original published pamphlet, and C later copied out the whole of his version almost unchanged in a lady's album. For *PW* (1834) he none the less abridged the text according to the principles enunciated in his letter, even though in the event it was one of seven poems "accidentally omitted". This abridged version, given here, omits a stanza at lines 20[+] and 24[+], and three stanzas at line 28[+]; the rule marking off the last two stanzas was also omitted, and there are a few minor improvements. The omitted stanzas are as follows:

20[+]   Mourn for the widow'd Lord in chief,
                    Who wails and will not solaced be!
               Mourn for the childless Father's grief,
                    The wedded Lover's Agony!

24[+]   O press again that murmuring string!
                    Again bewail that princely Sire!
               A destin'd Queen, a future King
                    He mourns on one funereal pyre.

28[+]   While Grief in song shall seek repose,
                    We will take up a Mourning yearly:
               To wail the Blow that crush'd the Rose
                    So dearly priz'd and lov'd so dearly.

               Long as the Fount of Song o'erflows,
                    Will I the yearly dirge renew;
               Mourn for the firstling of the Rose,
                    That snapt the stem on which it grew.

[14] By extension, a graceful thing or person.

The proud shall pass, forgot; the chill,
    Damp, trickling Vault their only mourner!
Not so the regal Rose, that still
    Clung to the Breast which first had worn her!

Mourn, Israel! Sons of Israel, mourn!
    Give utterance to the inward throe,
As wails of her first love forlorn
    The virgin clad in robes of woe!

Mourn the young Mother snatch'd away   5
    From light and life's ascending sun!
Mourn for the Babe, Death's voiceless prey,
    Earn'd by long pangs, and lost ere won!

Mourn the bright Rose that bloom'd, and went
    Ere half disclosed its vernal hue!   10
Mourn the green Bud, so rudely rent,
    It brake the stem on which it grew!

Mourn for the universal woe
    With solemn dirge and falt'ring tongue;
For England's Lady is laid low,   15
    So dear, so lovely, and so young!

The blossoms on her tree of life
    Shone with the dews of recent bliss;—
Translated in that deadly strife
    She plucks its fruit in Paradise.   20

Mourn for the Prince, who rose at morn
    To seek and bless the firstling Bud
Of his own Rose, and found the thorn,
    Its point bedew'd with tears of blood.

Mourn for Britannia's hopes decay'd;   25
    Her daughters wail their dear defence,
Their fair example prostrate laid,
    Chaste love, and fervid innocence!

O Thou! who mark'st the monarch's path,
　　To sad Jeshurun's sons attend!　　　　　　　　　　30
Amid the lightnings of thy wrath
　　The showers of consolation send!

Jehovah frowns!—The Islands bow,
　　And Prince and People kiss the rod!
Their dread chastising Judge wert Thou—　　　　　　35
　　Be Thou their Comforter, O God!

544. REWRITING OF LINES BY
BEAUMONT AND FLETCHER

[1817–19]

C drafted the lines in the margins of a copy of *The Dramatic Works of Ben Jonson, and Beaumont and Fletcher (CM—CC—*I 404). His marginalia in the copy—the "Stockdale Edition" of 1811—is extensive and fills *CM (CC)* I 373–408 (see also 362–72). C is throughout particularly concerned with the corrupt state of the text, which he emends, rearranges, and rewrites. The present passage is characteristic of his interventions in their kind, although others are more brief.

The original passage is a speech by Oldcraft in *Wit at Several Weapons* I i 74–83:

I'm arm'd at all points against treachery,
I hold my humour firm; if I can see thee thrive by
Thy wits while I live, I shall have the more courage
To trust thee with my lands when I die; if not,
The next best wit I can hear of, carries 'em:
For since in my time and knowledge so many rich children
Of the city conclude in beggery, I'd rather
Make a wise stranger my executor
Than a foolish son my heir, and have my lands call'd after
My wit than after my name; and that's my nature.

C has marked the passage and added the following comment, which leads to his own alternative version: "It would be easy to restore this passage to metre, by supplying a sentence of four syllables, which the Reasoning almost demands,

---

30. Jeshurun] In *CN* IV 5193 C re-
marked on the literal meaning of the
word—"Strait forward" in the sense
of "upright".

and correcting the grammar—'next' is a mere interpolation, otherwise '*can*' might be struck out."

> Arm'd at all points gainst treachery, I hold
> My humour firm. If living I can see thee
> Thrive by thy wits, I shall have the more courage,
> Dying, to trust thee with my Lands. If not,
> The best Wit, I can hear of, carries them.   5
> For since so many in my time & knowledge,
> Rich Children of the City, have concluded
> *For lack of Wit* in beggary, I'd rather
> Make a wise Stranger my Executor
> Than a fool Son my Heir, and have my lands calld   10
> After my Wit than name—And that's my Nature.

545. A DESCRIPTION OF A NIGHTINGALE

[1817–18]

C drafted the untitled lines in Notebook 61 (*CN* III 4365), where they are written continuously as prose. They may be based upon recollections from Stowey days: cf **156** *This Lime-tree Bower my Prison* 13–16; **180** *The Nightingale*; also **112** *To the Nightingale*.

> On the weak Spray of a Slim Ash,
> Whose few poor yearly Leaves
> Shook in the Gale and glitterd in the Spray
> Of a nigh Waterfall, I saw a Nightingale.
> And by the heaving plumage of her Throat and busy Bill   5
> That seemed to cut the Air,
> I saw he sang—
> And sure he heard not his own song or did but inly hear—
> With such a loud confused sound
> The Cataract spread wide around—   10

546. LINES SUGGESTED BY
SIR THOMAS BROWNE

[1817–18]

C drafted the untitled lines in Notebook 61 (*CN* III 4370), where they are much revised. They were suggested by a sentence near the beginning of Browne's *Hydriotaphia* ch 5: "What Song the *Syrens* sang, or what name *Achilles* assumed when he hid himself among women, though puzzling Questions are not beyond all conjecture." C had begun to copy out the previous paragraph (from his copy of the 1659 folio of Browne's *Pseudodoxia Epidemica*—2 pts in 1—II 45) on the previous page of the notebook. He continued to transcribe and make notes on Browne's writing in subsequent notebook entries.

C's lines appear to draw on recollections of Statius *Achilleis* bk 2, although they are combined in compressed and allusive fashion. In *Achilleis* 2.93–5 Deidamia clasps the disguised Achilles to her bosom to hide his chest, which had caught the attention of Ulysses because of his open (C's "unslit") robe. Previously, at 2.90, Achilles' gaze had appeared different from that of the surrounding maidens in not being downcast (that is, by implication, appearing assertive or martial: C's "arm-enamoured"). Achilles does not actually hold a lance until he receives it, along with a shield, from Ulysses at 2.201–11, when at the same time he abandons his female covering (the lance "protrudes" from his robe only in a proleptic sense as Ulysses begins to discover him). Ulysses is eveywhere described as "sly".

> What Song the Syrens sang?
> What names, perchance
> The unslit Girl with robe-protruding Lance,
> Achilles bore, whose arm-enamoured Eye
> Betrayed the Hero to Ulysses sly?—   5

547. COUPLET ON THE HEART
DEAF AND BLIND

[May 1818]

C quoted the lines in a letter to J. H. Green (*CL* IV 854: 2 May 1818). They could be a fragment from a larger enterprise, but it is also possible that he is not the author. In the letter C was commenting on the earl of Lauderdale's motives for speaking on the bill, then before the House of Lords, to alleviate the condition of children working in cotton factories. "In short, he wants to make a speech almost as much as I do to have a release ~~from~~ signed by Conscience from the duty of making or anticipating answers to such speeches." Cf *SW&F* (*CC*) 714–51; also *EOT* (*CC*) III 155–8 for C's contribution to the same debate. Then, after quoting the two lines, C continues: "Verily, the *World* is mighty: and for all but the Few the orb of Truth labors under eclipse from the Shadow of the World!"

O when the *Heart* is deaf and blind, how blear
The Lynx's Eye! how dull the Mould-warp's Ear!

548. ADAPTATION OF DANIEL'S
EPISTLE TO SIR THOMAS EGERTON

[1818]

The lines are quoted as the epigraph to essay 13 of *The Friend* (*CC*) I 91, with the description "*Adapted from an elder Poet.*" The subject of the essay—continued from essay 11 in the introductory section—is libel and tolerance. The source of the lines is the *Epistle to Sir Thomas Egerton* stanzas 5, 14, and 15, in Samuel Daniel *Poetical Works* (2 vols 1718) II 343, 345:

Must there be still some Discord mix'd among
The Harmony of Men; whose Mood accords
Best with Contention, tun'd t' a Note of Wrong?
That when War fails, Peace must make War with Words,
And b' arm'd unto Destruction ev'n as strong,
As were in Ages past our Civil Swords:
Making as deep, altho' unbleeding Wounds;
That when as Fury fails, Wisdom confounds.

        *   *   *

See'ng ev'n Injustice may be regulate;
And no Proportion can there be betwixt
Our Actions, which in endless Motion are,
And th' Ordinances, which are always fixt:

2. Mould-warp] A mole (lit "earth-thrower"), a word mainly preserved in northern dialect from the 18th century onwards.

Ten Thousand Laws more cannot reach so far,
But *Malice* goes beyond, or lives immixt
So close with Goodness, as it ever will
Corrupt, disguize, or counterfeit it still.

And therefore did those Glorious Monarchs (who
Divide with God the Stile of Majesty,
For being Good; and had a Care to do
The World Right, and succour Honesty)
Ordain this Sanctuary, whereunto
Th' Oppress'd might fly; this Seat of Equity,
Whereon thy Virtues fit with fair Renown,
The greatest Grace and Glory of the Gown.

For an earlier, different use of Daniel see **514** *On the Condition of Ireland*; for other similar adaptations see poems **459, 550, 552, 601.**

Must there be still some discord mixt among
The harmony of men, whose mood accords
Best with contention tun'd to notes of wrong?
That when War fails, Peace must make war with words,
With words unto destruction arm'd more strong   5
Than ever were our foreign Foemans' swords:
Making as deep, tho' not yet bleeding wounds?
What War left scarless, Calumny confounds.

Truth lies entrapp'd where Cunning finds no bar:
Since no proportion can there be betwixt   10
Our actions which in endless motions are,
And ordinances which are always fixt.
Ten thousand Laws more cannot reach so far,
But Malice goes beyond, or lives commixt
So close with Goodness, that it ever will   15
Corrupt, disguise, or counterfeit it still.

And therefore would our glorious Alfred, who
Join'd with the King's the good man's Majesty,
Not leave Law's labyrinth without a clue—
Gave to deep Skill its just authority,—   20
* * * * * * * * * * * * * * * * * *
But the last Judgement (this his Jury's plan)
Left to the natural sense of Work-day Man.

549. ADAPTATION OF DONNE'S
TO SIR HENRY GOODYERE

[1818]

The lines were published as the epigraph to essay 15 of *The Friend* (*CC*) I 107, where they are ascribed to Donne. Essay 15 is the penultimate of the sixteen which make up the introductory section, and is concerned with genius, novelty, and conscience.

C read CL's copy of Donne's *Poems* (1669) in May 1811. The adaptation is from *To Sir Henry Goodyere* 5–17, in Donne *Poems* 150–1 (here completing the last stanza, not rendered by C):

> A Palace when 'tis that, which it should be,
> Leaves growing, and stands such, or else decays:
> But he which dwells there is not so; for he
> Strives to urge upward, and his fortune raise.
>
> So had your body her morning, hath her noon,
> And shall not better; her next change is night:
> But her fair larger guest, to whom Sun and Moon
> Are sparks, and short liv'd, claims another right.
>
> The noble Soul by age grows lustier,
> Her appetite, and her digestion mend;
> We must not sterve, nor hope to pamper her
> With womans milk, and pappe, unto the end.
>
> Provide you manlier diet, You have seen
> All Libraries, which are Schools, Camps, and Courts;
> But ask your Garners if you have not been
> In harvest, too indulgent to your sports.

For later examples of C rewriting Donne see poems **551, 663.**

A palace when 'tis that which it should be
Leaves growing, and stands such, or else decays;
With him who dwells there, 'tis not so: for he
Should still urge upward, and his fortune raise.

Our bodies had their morning, have their noon,   5
And shall not better—the next change is night;
But their fair larger guest, t' whom sun and moon
Are sparks and short-lived, claims another right.

The noble soul by age grows lustier,
Her appetite and her digestion mend;   10
We must not starve nor hope to pamper her
With woman's milk and pap unto the end.

Provide you manlier diet!

550. ADAPTATION OF DANIEL'S
MUSOPHILUS

[1818]

The lines were published as the epigraph to essay 16 of *The Friend*, (*CC*)
I 114, where they are ascribed to Daniel. Essay 16 is concerned with self-
knowledge, principles, and actions, and concludes the sequence which makes
up the introductory section.

C's original is *Musophilus* st 147 (lines 110–15) in Daniel *Poetical Works* II
392:

> Who will not grant, and therefore this observe,
> No State stands sure, but on the Grounds of Right,
> Of Virtue, Knowledge; Judgment to preserve,
> And all the Pow'rs of Learning requisite?
> Tho' other Shifts a present Turn may serve,
> Yet in the Tryal they will weigh too light.

See poem **552** for another adaptation of *Musophilus*.

Blind is that soul which from this truth can swerve,
No state stands sure, but on the grounds of right,
Of virtue, knowledge; judgment to preserve,
And all the pow'rs of learning requisite?
Though other shifts a present turn may serve,   5
Yet in the trial they will weigh too light.

551. ADAPTATION OF DONNE'S
ECLOGUE 1613, DECEMBER 26

[1818]

The lines were quoted in the sixteenth and last of the opening set of essays of the 1818 *Friend*, where they are ascribed to Donne, to point the truth that "The first step to knowledge, or rather the previous condition of all insight into truth, is to dare commune with our very and permanent self" (*Friend—CC*—I 115). They are adapted from lines 49–53 of *Eclogue 1613, December 26*, in Donne *Poems* 106–7:

> So reclus'd Hermits oftentimes do know
> More of heavens glory, then a worldling can.
> As man is of the world, the heart of man,
> Is an epitome of Gods great book
> Of creatures, and man need no farther look . . .

See poems **549, 663** for adaptations of other poems by Donne.

> The recluse Hermit oft' times more doth know
> Of the world's inmost wheels, than worldlings can.
> As Man is of the World, the Heart of Man
> Is an Epitome of God's great Book
> Of Creatures, and Men need no further look.   5

552. A FURTHER ADAPTATION
OF DANIEL'S *MUSOPHILUS*

[1818]

The lines were published as the epigraph to essay 1 of the First Landing Place of *The Friend*, where they are ascribed to "DANIEL'S MUSOPHILUS" (*Friend—CC*—I 129). They bring together and adapt *Musophilus* 181–6, 175–80, 163–4 (stanzas 30, 29, 27). The proper sequence of stanzas 27–30 reads as follows in Daniel *Poetical Works* II 372–73:

> Altho' the stronger Constitutions shall
> Wear out th' Infection of distemper'd Days,
> And come with Glory to out-live this Fall,

Recov'ring of another springing of Praise;
Clear'd from th' oppressing Humours wherewithal
The idle Multitude surcharge their Lays.

When as (perhaps) the Words thou scornest now
May live, the speaking Picture of the Mind;
The Extract of the Soul, that labour'd how
To leave the Image of her self behind;
Wherein Posterity, that love to know,
The just Proportion of our Spir'ts may find.

For these Lines are the Veins, the Arteries,
And undecaying Life-strings of those Hearts,
That still shall pant, and still shall exercise
The Motion, Spir't and Nature both imparts,
And shall with those alive so sympathize,
As nourish'd with their Pow'rs, enjoy their Parts.

O blessed Letters! that combine in one
All Ages past, and make one live with all.
By you we do confer with who are gone,
And the Dead-living unto Council call:
By you th' unborn shall have Communion
Of what we feel, and what doth us befal.

See poem **550** for another adaptation of *Musophilus*.

O blessed Letters! that combine in one
All ages past, and make one live with all:
By you we do confer with who are gone
And the Dead-living unto Council call!
By you the Unborn shall have communion   5
Of what we feel and what doth us befall.

Since Writings are the Veins, the Arteries,
And undecaying Life-strings of those Hearts,
That still shall pant and still shall exercise
Their mightiest powers when Nature none imparts: 10
And the strong constitution of their Praise
Wear out the infection of distemper'd days.

553. EPIGRAPH VERSES FOR *THE FRIEND*

[1818?]

The lines are quoted in *The Friend* (*CC*) I 223 as the epigraph to essay 6, Section the First, which begins: "I was never myself, at any period of my life, a convert to the system", and goes on to discuss enthusiasm for an ideal world. C wrote after the verses "MSS."

> Truth I pursued, as Fancy sketch'd the way,
> And wiser men than I went worse astray.

554. ADAPTATION OF LINES FROM DODSLEY'S *SELECT COLLECTION OF OLD PLAYS*

[1818]

The lines are quoted as the epigraph to essay 10, Section the First, of *The Friend*, where they are described as having been "*Adapted from an old Play*" (*Friend—CC—*I 263). C's essay is concerned with the war with France and international law, via "a review of the circumstances that led to the Treaty of Amiens, and the recommencement of the war". The treaty of Amiens—"this calm" of line 9—was signed in Mar 1802, and lasted just fourteen months.

C's lines adapt a passage in the anonymous play *Fuimus Troes: The True Trojans*, in *A Select Collection of Old Plays* ed Robert Dodsley (12 vols 1744) III 245. The passage ends Act I sc i:

> Think ye the smoaky mist
> Of sun-boil'd seas can stop the eagle's eye?
> Or can our watry walls keep dangers out,
> Which fly aloft, that thus we snorting ly,
> Feeding impostum'd humours, to be launch'd
> By some outlandish surgeon;
> As they are now, whose flaming towns, like beacons,
> Give us fair warning, and even gild our spires,
> Whilst merrily we warm us at their fires?
> Yet we are next: who charm'd with peace and sloth,
> Dream golden dreams. Go, warlike Britain, go,

For olive-bough exchange thy hazel-bow:
Hang up thy rusty helmet, that the bee
May have a hive, or spider find a loom:
Instead of soldiers fare, and lodging hard,
(The bare ground being their bed and table) ly
Smother'd in down, melting in luxury:
Instead of bellowing drum, and chearful flute,
Be lull'd in lady's lap with amorous lute.
But as for Nennius, know, I scorn this calm:
The ruddy planet at my birth bore sway,
Sanguine, adust my humour; and wild fire
My ruling element. Blood, and rage, and choler,
Make up the temper of a captain's valour.

C borrowed CL's copy of Dodsley's anthology on his return from Malta in 1806 (*CN* II 2961, 2962, 2964; cf *LL*—M—III 13). He used the collection in his Shakespeare lectures of 1811–12, and perhaps read it again for his Shakespeare lectures of 1818 (see *CN* III 4486 and n). He drew on vol III again for **554.X1** *Notes for Revising "The Honest Whore"*.

              Then we may thank ourselves,
Who spell-bound by the magic name of Peace
Dream golden dreams. Go, warlike Britain, go,
For the grey olive-branch change thy green laurels:
Hang up thy rusty helmet, that the bee   5
May have a hive, or spider find a loom!
Instead of doubling drum and thrilling fife
Be lull'd in lady's lap with amorous flutes.
But for Napoleon, know, he'll scorn this calm:
The ruddy planet at *his* birth bore sway,   10
Sanguine, adust his humour, and wild fire
His ruling element. Rage, revenge, and cunning
Make up the temper of this captain's valor.

11. adust his humour] A specific supposed state of body or mind in early medicine, its "burning" symptoms causative of gloom.

554.X1. NOTES FOR REVISING DEKKER'S *THE HONEST WHORE*

[Oct 1818? 1804? 1807?]

See vol III.

555. DRAFT FRAGMENT, PERHAPS DESCRIBING SARA COLERIDGE

[Nov 1818?]

The ms is a much-revised, untitled holograph in C's hand. In several instances C has made a fresh start without cancelling the superseded lines, so that there is some ambiguity as to what he intended to preserve. The lines describe accomplishments for which the young SC was frequently praised—her beauty, her piano-playing, her gift for French and Italian. If she is indeed the subject, the poem is most likely to have been written after C saw William Collins's portrait of SC in Nov 1818 (see *CL* IV 878: to C. Brent [4 Nov 1818]; J. B. Flagg *The Life and Letters of Washington Allston*—1893—142–3; E. L. Griggs *Coleridge Fille*—1940—facing p 32, 38). If the poem was not written then, but SC is nevertheless the subject, it must have been after 1812 (cf C's description of SC for J. J. Morgan, *CL* III 375) and before Christmas 1822, when C saw her again in person.

> Can gracious Nurture lessen Nature's Graces?
> If taught by both She betters both and honours
> Fair Gifts with fair Adornings— ...
> Or gliding with smooth step,
> Mock gliding make admired Silence live,   5
> Music's meek Sister, or her gentler Self,
> Another an' the same—

4, 5. gliding] SC is reclining in the Collins portrait, but the reference may be to fingers gliding across the piano keyboard (cf lines 11–12, where moving fingers convert sound into a quality of living stillness).

Can she give
His native accents to the Stranger's ear.
Skill'd in the tongues of France & Italy—
Or while she warbles with bright eyes uprais'd   10
Her fingers short like to streams of Silver Light
Mid the golden haze of thrilling Strings

556. LINES ON THE USURY OF PAIN

[Jan 1819, or earlier]

Two versions of the lines are known: in a footnote to a letter to a young man on the brink of a hasty marriage, in which C adverts to his own experience (*CL* IV 905fn: 8 Jan 1819), and in a separate memorandum attached to the description of a singular thorn-plant (*SW&F—CC*—1038–9). The second version is given here.

C's memorandum adverts to a description in William John Burchell *Travels in the Interior of Southern Africa* (2 vols 1822–4), which he had seen in a review or journal. It may be of the hookthorn (I 309–10), or perhaps of the karo thorn (I 196), and is continuous with his earlier interest in the upas-tree as described by Erasmus Darwin and others (*CN* I 37; *RX* 14, 18, 464 n 78; etc). C's memorandum suggests that the extract from Burchell should be glossed as follows, the gloss leading into the lines of verse:

> Surely the wit of man could not present a livelýier emblem of a Sinner entangled in the snares of a sinful Habit, without love to the Sin, nay with unutterable dread and condemnation of the same, tempted by no ?hope expectation, impelled by no desire, but goaded on by the inexorable WANT ?that ?the ~~rendered desperate by the one only thought/permitting Restless stung and chased~~ onward by uncontrollable Restlessness, & cowed by the Pain that ~~owes it's desperate~~ subsists in the bewildering Dread of Pain

Lured by no vain Belief
No Hope that flatters Grief
To lawless Spells they flee

1. vain] The earlier version has "fond".

2. flatters] The earlier version has "flatter'd".

3. The earlier version reads "But blank Despair my Plea,".

And borrow short Relief
At frightful Usury.   5

557. DISTICH, WRITTEN IN FEBRUARY 1819

[Feb 1819]

C drafted the lines in Notebook 24 (*CN* III 4480), where they are introduced as follows: "25 Feb! 1819. Five years since the preceding lines were written on this Leaf!! Ah how yet more intrusively has the Hornet, Scandal, ⟨since then⟩ scared away the Bee of poetic Thought and silenced its eager, earnest, happy Hum!!" KC glosses "the Hornet, Scandal" as referring to Hazlitt's gossip about Geraldine in **176** *Christabel* being a man in disguise (cf *CL* IV 917–18: to RS [31 Jan 1819]). See **606** *Work without Hope* headnote for another comment on the way Hazlitt's malice stifled bee-like productivity.

The lines are followed by the comment "Answer to this Distich, or Reasons why I notwithstanding all this, am not a Misanthrope."

> Robb'd, jilted, slander'd, poor, without a hope,
> How can I chuse but be a Misanthrope?

558. THE PROPER UNMODIFIED DOCHMIUS, I.E., ANTISPASTUS HYPERCATALECTICUS

[1819?]

C wrote the lines on the pastedown of Notebook 28 (*CN* IV 4588). An unmodified dochmius is ∪ − − ∪ −, an antispastus ∪ − − ∪; "hypercatalecticus" means "with an additional syllable".

4. And borrow] The earlier version has "I borrowed".

1. Robb'd] This refers to C's dealings with Thomas Curtis and Rest Fenner (see *CL* IV 947n; V 163: to DeQ [8 Aug 1821]).

jilted] I.e. in his relationship with SH.

slander'd] Referring not only to Hazlitt's attacks on C's personal life but also to his savage reviews of *SM*, *BL*, etc.

poor] Not a new complaint, but the concurrent literary and philosophical lectures had not been profitable (cf e.g. *CL* IV 921: to W. Mudford [23 Feb 1819]; 922: to J. H. Bohte 27 Feb 1819).

Bĕnīgn shōotīng Stārs/ ĕcstātīcst dĕlīght

or   The Lord thron'd in heav'n, ămīd āngĕl troops

"   Amid troops of angels God thron'd on high.

559. "BEARETH ALL THINGS"

[Oct 1819? 1832?]

The lines were published in *PW* (1834), and there are no mss. C quoted the first
line—itself a variation on line 22 of Spenser's *February Eclogue*—in a letter
written in Oct 1819 (*CL* IV 961: to J.H.B. Williams 20 Oct 1819). The title, as
PW (1834) made clear, is from 1 Cor 13.7.

Gently I took that which ungently came,
And without scorn forgave:—Do thou the same.
A wrong done to thee think a cat's eye spark
Thou wouldst not see, were not thine own heart dark.
Thine own keen sense of wrong that thirsts for sin,   5
Fear that—the spark self-kindled from within,
Which blown upon will blind thee with its glare,
Or smother'd stifle thee with noisome air.
Clap on the extinguisher, pull up the blinds,
And soon the ventilated spirit finds   10
Its natural daylight. If a foe have kenn'd,
Or worse than foe, an alienated friend,
A rib of dry rot in thy ship's stout side,
Think it God's message, and in humble pride
With heart of oak replace it;—thine the gains—   15
Give him the rotten timber for his pains!

560. TO A COMIC AUTHOR,
ON AN ABUSIVE REVIEW

[Nov 1819?]

C's poem exists in several slightly different ms versions: an untitled draft immediately preceding the first draft of **561** *A Character*; a fair copy apparently made on the same occasion, the version reproduced here; and a fair copy made in 1829. It was published in *Friendship's Offering* and *PW* (1834). The earliest ms version was entitled "To a Comic Author, on an Abusive Review of his Aristophanes", and is addressed to "Peter" (line 3, here "Neighbour"), evidently under the mistaken belief that J. H. Frere, the translator of Aristophanes and C's patron, was Peter Morris, who had come to C's defence against Jeffrey and the *Ed Rev*. Although Thomas Mitchell (1783–1845), a classical scholar from Christ's Hospital, published translations of four plays of Aristophanes in 1820–2 (favourably reviewed by Frere in *Quarterly Review* xxiii—Jul 1820—474–505), there seems no reason to doubt that it was Frere whom C had in mind.

The anonymous author of *Peter's Letters to his Kinsfolk*, published in three volumes in Jul 1819, was in fact J. G. Lockhart. He protested against Hazlitt's *Ed Rev* reviews of *SM* and *BL* and analysed C's work in laudatory terms (ii 218–21). A second edition in the same year (named the third, but the first had been named the second) included an appendix addressed directly to C (iii 355 76). C replied to Peter in terms which echo the cancelled opening of his poem, addressing him as an "unknown and nameless but not quite unconjectured friend" and as "Brother Bard" (*CL* iv 968: to the Author of "Peter's Letters to his Kinsfolk" [Nov 1819]; the second phrase appears in the original letter, but was omitted from the printed version which ELG reproduces). The original letter is among the Blackwood papers at the National Library of Scotland (MS 4937 f 26), on two small leaves (approx 18.2×22.3 cm; wm RUSE & TURNER I 1818; no chain-lines), the paper originating from the same manufacturer as the paper on which C drafted the first version of the poem.

Several other details reinforce the suggestion that C thought that Peter was J. H. Frere. To begin with, C's allusion to the first entry of the chorus, as frogs, in Aristophanes' *Frogs* (lines 209–68 in modern editions) is even more evident in the earliest version. In *BL* he had quoted from the frog chorus in Greek, in a part printed as early as 1815 (*BL* ch 4—*CC*—i 76; cf i 75fn), before he saw Frere's work. He then read Frere's translation of the opening scenes of the play in 1816, in proof-sheets or in a ms lent to him by Murray; transcribed lines 1–180, 184, 372–85, 460–2 of Frere's version in his notebooks (*CN* iii 4331, 4332); and quoted lines 939–43 in the 1818 *Friend* (*Friend—CC*—i 18). He could meanwhile have read Peacock's *Melincourt* (ch 31 "Cimmerian Lodge"), where, as Mr Mystic, he is parodied in terms of Aristophanes' chorus—this prompted, some have argued, by references to *Frogs* in **161** *The Rime of the Ancient Mariner*. Frere published his translation of lines 675–991 in *Bl Mag* IV (Jan 1819) 421–9, although there is no evidence of his having translated the frog chorus by this date. In the event, he did not work methodically through any one play, did not finish *Frogs* until 1829, and did not publish it in full until 1839.

The earliest version of C's poem also refers to Frere's encounter with Jeffrey in 1817 (vol II line 11.1.3), an encounter which might have led Frere to anticipate an abusive review (Lord Cockburn *Life of Lord Jeffrey*—2 vols Edinburgh 1852—II 165). However, things again turned out differently: Jeffrey liked Frere's translations, his praise of them is mentioned in the editorial introduction in *Bl Mag* (p 421), and C found it necessary to generalise him into "the skulking crew". The only two direct references to *Frogs* (vol II lines 2, 11.1.3: see commentary there) were also removed, and the revisions suggest a distancing from Frere as well as from Jeffrey. Frere was not C's "Neighbour" (line 3), unless remotely and temporarily when staying with his brother George at Hampstead. The origins of the poem appear to rest on a number of hasty suppositions which subsequently had to be revised but which left their mark. Frere's presence continues into **561** *A Character*, which follows directly in the earliest version.

The tone of the poem was complicated from the beginning because C couched his sense of private injury as an address to another injured author. The form contaminates epistle with satire; C's uncertainty as to whom he was addressing and how far their circumstances were shared led his own self-vindication to drown out commiseration. The poem should be construed as an appeal which developed into the more straightforward protest and self-justification of **561** *A Character*. The same tone is shared by the curious, bantering denunciation of the age which C contributed to *Bl Mag* in Jan 1822, *The Historie and Gests of Maxilian* (*SW&F—CC—963–85*).

What tho' the chilly wide-mouth'd quacking Chorus
From the rank swamps of murk Review-land croak:
So was it, Neighbour in the times before us,
When Momus throwing on his Attic Cloak
Romp'd with the Graces: and each tickl'd Muse 5
(That Turk, Dan Phoebus, whom Bards call divine
Was married to—at least he *kept*—all nine.)
All fled; but with averted faces ran!

4, 12. Momus was expelled from heaven for his criticism of the other gods. He was the chief speaker in Lucian's dialogue, *Zeus Rants* (Lucian tr A. M. Harmon et al—8 vols LCL 1913–67—II 89–169). He is usually mentioned as the typical carping critic; here he is the representative of the right kind of satire.

Yet somewhat the broad freedoms to excuse,
They had allow'd the Audacious Greek to use,   10
Swore, they mistook him for their own Good Man.
This Momus—Aristophanes on earth
Men call'd him—maugre all his Wit and Worth
Was croak'd and gabbled at: How then should you,
Or I, Friend! hope to 'scape the skulking crew.—   15
No, laugh! and say aloud, in tones of glee
"I hate the quacking Tribe, & they hate me."

561. A CHARACTER

[Nov 1819?]

C had for some time been meditating satirical verses entitled *Puff and Slander* (poem **515.X1**), but the present poem was prompted by a specific occasion— Hazlitt's charge of political apostasy in his reviews of *SM* and *BL*, and Peter Morris's defence. The first draft immediately follows **560** *To a Comic Author*, addressed to Peter Morris—whom C appears momentarily and mistakenly to have taken to be J. H. Frere—in which C dismisses the reviewers as if they were Aristophanes' chorus of frogs.

C's belief that a powerful friend had come to his defence against Hazlitt's condemnation probably helped to rally his spirits and convert plaintiveness into counter-attack. And to the extent that he believed that Peter was Frere, there was added encouragement for him to argue that his earlier political position had been misrepresented: Frere, along with Canning and Gifford, had been prominent among the conservative writers of *The Anti-Jacobin*.

Although C frequently described himself in terms of a bird, as in the opening lines (see the EC), it is likely that in this instance he was prompted to use the bird allegory by thoughts of Frere as translator of Aristophanes. Frere was working on *Birds* "at Tunbridge" (he moved there in late 1818), well before he left for Malta in late 1820 (Frere *Works*—2 vols 1872—I clxxv), and about the time that C mentioned *Birds* and *Frogs* (though without approbation) in the fifth philosophical lecture on 18 Jan 1819 (*P Lects*—1949—181–2).

C's argument did not persuade John Payne Collier, for one, who called it "poor stuff". "One almost pities the great poet while thus condescending, instead of speaking out boldly in his own person, and fairly confessing that he

15. skulking] Cf C's early description of Hazlitt as "brow-hanging, shoe-contemplative, *strange*" (*CL* II 990: to T. Wedgwood 16 Sept [1803]).

and his Bristol friends had been utterly disappointed by the result of the French Revolution. Thousands of other sanguine men (my own father among them) had been disappointed also" ([John Payne Collier] *An Old Man's Diary, Forty Years Ago . . . 1832–1833*—2 vols in 4 pts 1871-2—II (4) 57). C's own confidence in the poem seems not to have held up; when it circulated among his friends it was under the heading "A Trifle".

The poem was incorporated into C's last collection, but in a form demonstrably corrupt in several instances. The RT follows the order of lines in the published version, but for the wording reverts to the (not quite complete) holograph draft—accepting some of the later variations from it but not others. The poem thus constitutes an exception to the principle of unmixed versions employed in the present edition; the text should be treated as unrevised and uncertain in details.

> A Bird, who mongst his other sins
> Had liv'd among the Jacobins,
> Tho' like a kitten amid Rats
> Or callow Tit in Nest of Bats
> He much abhorr'd all Democrats,   5
> Yet natheless stood in ill report
> Of wishing ill to Church and Court—
> Tho' he'd nor claw nor tooth nor sting—
> And learnt to pipe, God Save the King;
> Tho' each day did new feathers bring,   10
> All swore, he had but a leathern Wing—
> Nor polish'd wing nor feathered Tail
> Nor down-clad Thigh would aught avail—
> And tho', being tame, devoid of gall
> He civilly assur'd them all,   15
> "A Bird am I of Phoebus' Breed,
> And on the Sunflower cling and feed.
> My name, good Sirs! is Thomas Tit!"
> The Bats would have hail'd him Brother Cit,
> Or, at the farthest, Cousin German.   20

1 et seq. C frequently described himself in terms of a restricted, caged, or even comic bird (see *CN* II 2531, III 3266, 3314, IV 4613, etc), but bird analogies enter his letter to Peter Morris—to the wren, the nightingale, the sparrow, the eagle, the ostrich— and it seems more likely that Frere's translation of Aristophanes' *Birds* was foremost in his mind. The allusion adds to the political point, as a comment on the unruly confusions of Jacobinism, as well as bearing on the irony and zest with which the fable is pursued.

At length the matter to determine
He publicly disowned the vermin,
He spared the Mouse, he praised the Owl;
But Bats were neither Flesh nor Fowl.
Blood-sucking Vampires, Harpy, Gouls,   25
Came in full clatter from his throat,—
Till his old Nest-mates chang'd their Note
To Hireling, Traitor, and Turn-Coat—
A base Apostate that had sold
His very teeth and claws for Gold—   30
And then his feathers! smokes the jest.
No doubt, he feather'd well his nest!
A Tit indeed! Aye, Tit for Tat
With Places and Title, Brother Bat,
We soon shall see how well he'll play   35
Count Goldfinch or Sir Judas Jay!

Alas poor Bird! and ill-bestarr'd.
Or rather let us say, poor Bard!
And henceforth quit the Allegoric
With Metaphor and Simile   40
For simple facts and style historic—
Alas, poor Bard! no gold had he.
Behind another's team he stept
And plough'd and sowed, while others reapt;
The work was his, but theirs the play.   45
Sic vos non vobis, his whole story.
Besides, whate'er he writ or said
Came from his heart as well as head,
And tho' he never left in lurch
His King, his Country, or his Church,   50
Twas but to humour his own cynical
Contempt of doctrines Jacobinical,

43–6. The echoes of *The Leech Gatherer* st 7, re-entitled *Resolution and Independence* on its publication in 1807 (*WPW* II 236), have more meaning if the lines are read alongside C's complaint against WW's "comfortless discretion", in his letter to Peter Morris (*CL* IV 966–8: to the Author of "Peter's Letters to his Kinsfolk" [Nov 1819]). Both poem and letter counter WW's charge that C was feckless with the suggestion that WW was self-centred.

46. *Sic vos non vobis*] See **214** *The Devil's Thoughts* 28fn19–20 VAR commentary.

To his own Conscience only hearty
Twas but by chance he served the *party*,
The self-same things had said and writ,   55
Had Pitt been Fox and Fox been Pitt,
Content his own applause to win
Would never dash thro' thick and thin
And he can make, so say the wise,
No claim who makes no sacrifice—   60
And bard still less: what claim had he
Who swore, it vex'd his soul to see
So grand a Cause, so proud a realm
With Goose and Goody at the Helm.
Who long ago had fall'n asunder   65
But for their Rival's baser blunders,
The Coward Whine and Frenchified
Slaver and Slang of th' other side—

Thus, his own whim his only bribe,
Our bard pursued his old A B C;   70
Contented if he could subscribe
In fullest sense his name, Ἔστησε
(Tis Punic Greek, for *He hath stood*)
—Whate'er the men, the cause was good—
And therefore with a right good will   75
Poor fool! he fought their battles still.
Tush! squeak'd the Bats;—a mere bravado
To whitewash that base renegado;
Tis plain unless you're blind or mad,
His conscience for the bays he barters;   80
And true it is—as true as said—

64. Goose and Goody] Fox and Pitt, for reasons C gives in *TT* 28 Apr 1832 (*CC*) I 293–4. Other identifications—such as the radical MP Sir Francis Burdett (caricatured by James Gillray as a goose) and the reactionary Lord Chancellor Lord Eldon (described e.g. by Hazlitt as "an exceedingly good-natured man")—have also been suggested.

69–end. The ms shows that these last two stanzas gave C most trouble, and the lines originally stood in a different sequence. Lines 77–83 are not present in the original holograph draft, and may have been added later.

71–3. C glosses the phonetic approximation of his initials to the Greek word ἔστησε in *CL* II 867: to W. Sotheby 10 Sept 1802; IV 902: to W. Godwin 30 Dec 1818, and he used the pseudonym in many newspaper contributions. The Greek actually means "he has made to stand".

These circlets of green baize he had—
But then, alas! they were his garters!

Ah silly Bard! unfed, untended,
His Lamp but glimmer'd in its socket: 85
He liv'd, unhonour'd and unfriended
With scarce a penny in his pocket:
Nay, tho' he hid it from the Many,
With scarce a pocket for his penny.

562. EXTEMPORE SPECIMEN
OF THE PUN POLYSYLLABIC

[Late 1819]

C wrote the lines into the margin of JG's copy of *Omniana*. His annotations
appear to have been written at a single sitting, specifically for JG; cf *CM* (*CC*)
III 1064, 1065; also **37** *Epigram on my Godmother's Beard*; **201** *Epigram on
Goslar Ale*; **227** *Epitaph on an Insignificant*. A parallelepipedon (line 4) is
a geometrical solid whose six faces are parallelograms, opposite pairs being
identical and parallel. A less exactly geometrical, solely etymological, sense
would convey, simply, parallel plain surfaces.

Two Nobles in *Madrid* were straddling side by side,
Both shamefully diseased: espying which, I cried—
What *figures* these men make! The Wight, that Euclid cons,
Sees plainly that they are—Parallel o' *pippy*-Dons!

563. RIDDLE FOR MATERIALISTS

[Jan 1820]

The lines are part of a draft of a long philosophical letter to Hyman Hurwitz of
4 Jan 1820 (*CL* v 8), where they are introduced as follows in the ms:

Permit me to imagine a case, which medical records have proved to be within the limits of possibility: viz. that a series of words could be so ~~printed~~ written, and ~~that~~ the nerves of the Skin be so sensitive, as that two individuals, both of them blind and deaf, could ~~converse with~~ have intelligible communion, ~~with each other,~~ each reading with his finger-ends what the other had placed before him, as if he were playing off a piece of Music on the keys of a Piano Forte. Suppose further, that one of them had been arguing against the asserted power of perceiving Objects at a distance as utterly irrational and consequently false, ⟨grounding his arguments⟩ on the assumption⟨,⟩ that the Touch was the one and only sense. You will readily conceive the rabble of impossibilities and self-contradictions, which ~~thise~~ triumphant ~~Unitarian~~-?~~eum~~ Solitactian would ~~believe himself to~~ detect in this mysterious Tenet, and it's accompaniments. That one and the same Object, and without undergoing any change, should be perceived at one time as angular, and at another time as round/! ~~n~~Nay in one and the same moment, as flat and as projecting ~~/ or-?~~*~~the same repeat~~* ~~convert a very old Riddle into an imagined possible.~~! ~~With what seeming certainty, that no solution was~~ Confident in the impossibility ~~of any solution,~~ ~~w~~With what exulting Irony would he ~~propose the old Riddle~~ describe the supposition ~~in the form of an insoluble~~ repeat the old Riddle—

> What thing is that (tell me without delay)
> That's nothing of itself, yet every way
> As like a man as a thing like can be
> And yet so unlike as clear Contrary.
> For in one point it every way doth miss,   5
> The right side of it a Man's left side is.
> Tis lighter than a feather, and withal
> It fills no place, no room, it is so small!

564. EXTEMPORE, TO CHARLES MATHEWS

[Jan 1820]

Charles Mathews (1776–1835), the comic actor, was a frequent host to C at Ivy Cottage, Kentish Town, after his removal there in 1819. The full title of the lines is "Extempore, on rising from my seat at the close of 'At Home' I on Saturday Night." "At Home" imitations were staged at the Lyceum, under the title *Country Cousins*.

The affectionate friendship between the two men did not prevent Mathews from doing amusing imitations of C: see *The Reminiscences of Alexander Dyce* ed R. J. Schrader (Columbus, Oh 1972) 178–9; *The Journal of Thomas Moore* ed Wilfred S. Dowden (6 vols Newark, NJ 1983–92) II 833. Compare the account by Mathews' widow in her *Memoirs of of Charles Mathews, Comedian* (4 vols 1838) III 188–98.

> If in whatever decks this earthly Ball
> 'Tis still great Mother Nature, *one in all*;
> Thou, Matthews! needs must be her genuine Son,
> A Second Nature that art ALL IN ONE!

565. THE TEARS OF A GRATEFUL PEOPLE

[Feb 1820]

C's lines appeared in a pamphlet entitled *The Tears of a Grateful People: A Hebrew Dirge & Hymn, Chaunted in the Great Synagogue, St. James's Place, Algate, on the Day of the Funeral of His Late Most Sacred Majesty King George III. of Blessed Memory.* By Hyman Hurwitz, of Highgate. Translated into English Verse, by a Friend. The Hebrew text appears on the right-hand pages, with C's English translation opposite. The pamphlet was not printed for publication and perhaps not even for distribution, except to the audience at the synagogue. The English text appears to have been hastily set, or else set by a compositor less familiar with English than with Hebrew. Some copies were printed on white satin, interleaved and specially bound, apparently for presentation. The Hebrew is as follows:

קוֹל נְהִי

א

חזן   נִלְחָץ מִתּוּגָה, יָגוֹן וְצָרָה,
לְבִּי יָחִיל, עַצְמוֹתַי רָעָדוּ.
מוֹרָשֵׁי נִתְּקוּ וַיִּתְפָּרָדוּ;
וְרוּחִי בְּקִרְבִּי תֶּהֱמֶה בִּסְעָרָה.

ב

כִּי קוֹל חוֹלָה, קוֹל זַעַם וְעֶבְרָה,
קוֹל מְפָרֵק וּמְשַׁבֵּר הַלְּבָבוֹת,
קוֹל יְלָלָה מֵבָּנִים וּמֵאָבוֹת,
שָׁמַעְתִּי, יָרֵאתִי, וְנַפְשִׁי נֶעֱכָרָה.

ג

הַמֶּלֶךְ גָּוַע! הוֹדֵנוּ סָרָה.
נָפְלָה נָפְלָה! עֲטֶרֶת רֹאשֵׁנוּ.
סָרָה סָרָה! חֶמְדַּת לִבֵּנוּ.
לָכֵן הָמוּ מֵעַי, וְרוּחִי נִשְׁבָּרָה.

ד

קהל   *נָפְלָה נָפְלָה! עֲטֶרֶת רֹאשֵׁנוּ;
סָרָה סָרָה! חֶמְדַּת לִבֵּנוּ;
לָכֵן שַׂקִּים נָשִׂים בְּמָתְנֵינוּ
וּנְקוֹנֵן וְנִבְכֶּה עַל מוֹת מַלְכֵּנוּ.

ה

חזן   הַשֶּׁמֶשׁ בָּא! חָשַׁךְ אוֹר עֵינָיִם.
כְּסוּת קַדְרוּת לָבְשָׁה הַיָּרֵחַ.
כּוֹכָבִים אָסְפוּ נָגְהָם מִזְרוֹחַ.
וְכָל לֵב דַּוָּי, וְכָל עַיִן מָיִם.
נפלה נפלה וכו'

ו

בַּמְּלָכִים לֹא הָיָה כָמוֹהוּ
מוֹשֵׁל אַדִּיר, רַב חֶסֶד, אִישׁ תָּמִים.
הִרְבָּה צְדָקָה, הֶאֱרִיךְ יָמִים.
אָהַב אֱלֹהִים, בֶּאֱמוּנָה מַעֲשֵׂהוּ.
נפלה נפלה וכו'

ז

וַיֵּרְדְּ מִיָּם עַד יָם, בְּהַרְרֵי קֶדֶם.
עַל עַמִּים רַבִּים, שׁוֹנִים בְּדָתֵיהֶם.
אֲשֶׁרָם דָּרַשׁ, כְּאָב מָלַךְ עֲלֵיהֶם.
אָמַר, אַל בּוֹחֵן לֵב—לֹא אָדָם.—
נפלה נפלה וכו'

ח

עָרִיצִים שָׁמְעוּ—וַיֶּחְפָּרוּ:
עֶלְתָה קָפְצָה פֶּה, זֵדִים סָרוּ;
מִרְמָה וָתוֹךְ כַּמֹּץ נִפְזָרוּ.
וּבְרֵי לֵב אֵזוֹר אֱמוּנָה חָגָרוּ:
נפלה נפלה וכו'

* This Stanza is intended for the Congregation, and is to be repeated by them after each succeeding Stanza, as noted in Hebrew.

ט

תִּקְוָה לַדָּךְ הָיָה, עֹז לְלֹא־כֹחַ:
לְרוֹדְפֵי נָקִי חִנָּם, אָמַר הֶרֶף:
מִמְּתַלְּעוֹת עַוָּל הִצִּיל הַטֶּרֶף:
וְשָׁם אַרְצוֹ מִפְּלָט לְנָכֵי רוּחַ.
נפלה נפלה וכו״

י

גַּם בַּת יְשֻׁרוּן, שְׁכוּלָה נִדָּחָה,
בְּפִי אַכְזָרִים מָשָׁל וּשְׁנִינָה,
תַּחַת מֶמְשַׁלְתּוֹ מָצְאָה חֲנִינָה:
וַתְּבָרְכֵהוּ בְּלֵב וּבְנֶפֶשׁ שְׂמֵחָה.
נפלה נפלה וכו״

יא

לָכֵן עַמִּים אֲהֵבוּהוּ וַיְחִילוּ.
וְגַם עֵת כִּסָּה אֵיד הוֹד הָעֲטָרָה,
לַהֶבֶת הָאַהֲבָה בְּלִבָּם בָּעֲרָה;
סָרוּ לְמִשְׁמַעְתּוֹ, קִוּוּ וַיְחִלוּ.
נפלה נפלה וכו״

יב

וְעַתָּה הָלַךְ, עָזַב הָאָרֶץ,
וַיָּעָף כְּמוֹ כְרוּב לַשָּׁמָיִם,
לְהִתְהַלֵּךְ בְּגַן אֱלֹהִים חַיִּים.
וּבָנוּ חָרָה אֵל, וַיִּפְרָץ פָּרֶץ.
נפלה נפלה וכו״

יג

הָאֲדָמָה תֶּאֱבַל וְגַם יוֹשְׁבֶיהָ,
רַבָּתִי עָם, מִסְפַּד מַר עוֹרֶרֶת:
וּבַת יְהוּדָה תִּבְכֶּה, וְשַׂק חֹגָרֶת;
אַךְ אוֹי יִשָּׁמַע בְּקָהֳלוֹתֶיהָ.
נפלה נפלה וכו״

יד

וּבְרִיטַאנְיָה, כְּאַלְמָנָה יוֹשֶׁבֶת,
שׁוֹמֵמָה, נֶאֱלָמֶת, כְּיוֹרְדֵי קָבֶר:
כִּי גָדוֹל הַכְּאֵב, עָצוּם הַשֶּׁבֶר;
וְהַיָּגוֹן עָצוּר בָּהּ כְּאֵשׁ צָרֶבֶת.
נפלה נפלה וכו״

טו

צַר לִי עָלַיִךְ בְּרִיטַעֲנְיָה אֲהֹתִי.
מִי יִתֵּן וַאֲנַהֲמֵךְ הָאֻמְלָלָה!
רְאִיךְ אֲנַחֲמֵךְ?—וַאֲנִי חֹלָה
כָּמוֹכִי. וְגַם רַבּוֹת אֲנָחָתִי.
נפלה נפלה וכו״

יו

אֲחוּזֵי יָד נֵלֵכָה, וְנַקְרִיבָה
דְּמָעוֹת אַהֲבָה עֲלֵי קֶבֶר מַלְכֵּנוּ.
שָׁמָּה נִשְׁתַּפֵּךְ כְּמַיִם לִבֵּנוּ,
בַּתְּפִלָּה, בִּצְדָקָה, וּבִתְשׁוּבָה.

יז

עַד יַשְׁקִיף אֵל מִמְּרוֹמֵי אֶרֶץ[1]
וְיִרְאֶה עָנְיֵנוּ וְדַאֲבוֹן נַפְשֵׁנוּ:
יִשְׁלַח תְּרוּפָה לְכָל מַכּוֹתֵינוּ,
וּמָחָה דִּמְעָה מֵעַל הָאָרֶץ

יח

חזן וקהל

וְעַתָּה נְבָרֵךְ אֶת אֱלֹהֵינוּ
אֲשֶׁר רָאָה דַּאֲבוֹן נַפְשֵׁנוּ;
וְשָׁלַח מֶלֶךְ צֶדֶק לְרַפְּאֵנוּ,
וְלִמְחוֹת דִּמְעָה מֵאַרְצֵנוּ.

תפלה:

אֲדוֹן אֲדוֹנִים! שׁוֹכֵן מְרוֹמִים
הַסְכֵּת תְּפִלַּת בָּנֶיךָ.
רוֹפֵא שְׁבוּרֵי לֵב! וְכָל מַכְאוֹב!
רְפָא נָא חֲלִי עַמֶּךָ.
רַחֲמֶיךָ אֵל! נָעֵמוּ.
חַסְדְּךָ וְטוּבְךָ עָצֵמוּ.
אָנָּא אֵל! שְׁמַע קוֹלֵנוּ
וּרְצֵה אֶת תְּפִלָּתֵנוּ:

גַּם בְּיִסְּרֶךָ, אֶת־עֲבָדֶיךָ,
תֵּרָאֵם רֹב רַחֲמֶיךָ:
וּבְטֶרֶם תַּכֶּה, תְּרוּפָה לְמַכָּה
תָּכִין כֹּחַ יָדֶיךָ.
רַחֲמֶיךָ אֵל! נָעֵמוּ.
חַסְדְּךָ וְטוּבְךָ עָצֵמוּ.

---

[1] An error for אֶרֶץ.

אָנָּא אֵל! שְׁמַע קוֹלֵנוּ
וּרְצֵה אֶת תְּפִלָּתֵנוּ:

רֶגַע אָנַפְתָּ, עֵץ קְטַפְתָּ,
עוֹד הִשְׁאַרְתָּ פְּרִיֵּהוּ:
אָבִינוּ הָלַךְ, וּבְנוֹ מָלַךְ,
לִגְדֹר פִּרְצַת עַמֵּהוּ.
רַחֲמֶיךָ אֵל! נָעֵמוּ.
חַסְדְּךָ וְטוּבְךָ עָצֵמוּ.
אָנָּא אֵל! שְׁמַע קוֹלֵנוּ
וּרְצֵה אֶת תְּפִלָּתֵנוּ:

מַטַּע נֶאֱמָן, מֵעֵץ רַעֲנָן,
הִצְמַחְתָּ לְמֶלֶךְ עָלֵינוּ,
אֵל! שָׁמְרֵהוּ! בְּהוֹד עַטְּרֵהוּ!
לָעַד יִמְלוֹךְ עָלֵינוּ.
רַחֲמֶיךָ אֵל! נָעֵמוּ.
חַסְדְּךָ וְטוּבְךָ עָצֵמוּ.
אָנָּא אֵל! שְׁמַע קוֹלֵנוּ
וּרְצֵה אֶת תְּפִלָּתֵנוּ:

שְׁלַח אֲרוּכָה, לִבְנֵי הַמְּלוּכָה:
לְאַרְצֵנוּ שָׁלוֹם וּמְנוּחָה.
נַחֵם שָׂרֶיהָ, וְגַם יוֹשְׁבֶיהָ,
וְנָסוּ יָגוֹן וַאֲנָחָה.
רַחֲמֶיךָ אֵל! נָעֵמוּ.
חַסְדְּךָ וְטוּבְךָ עָצֵמוּ.
אָנָּא אֵל! שְׁמַע קוֹלֵנוּ
וּרְצֵה אֶת תְּפִלָּתֵנוּ:

George III died on 29 Jan 1820 and was buried on 16 Feb. In lines 45–8 C's translation makes use of phrases from a prose note written in Sept 1808 (*CN* III 3387). The translation shares the same characteristics as his earlier rendering of Hurwitz's Hebrew, **543** *Israel's Lament*. It again translates an antiphonal structure into something more continuous and lyrical, and converts back into English terms allusions which in Hurwitz's text assimilated English events to Hebrew tradition. A literal translation of the original Hebrew, retaining the original punctuation, is as follows:

A CRY OF LAMENTATION

1

Leader[2]
Oppressed with grief, sorrow, and distress,
my heart is in anguish,[3] my bones shudder.
My desires are broken off[4] and scattered;
and my spirit within me is in turmoil like a tempest.

2

For the cry of a woman in labour,[5] the cry of anger and disturbance,
the cry of the rending and breaking of hearts,
the cry of wailing from sons and fathers,
I have heard, I am afraid, and my soul is disturbed.

3

The king has expired! our majesty has passed away.
Fallen fallen! has the crown of our head.
Passed away passed away! has the beloved of our heart.
Therefore my inwards are in turmoil, and my spirit is broken.[6]

4

Congregation
Fallen fallen! has the crown of our head;
passed away passed away! has the beloved of our heart;
therefore let us put sackcloth on our loins[7]
and let us lament and weep over the death of our king.

5

Leader
The sun has set! the light of eyes is darkened.
A cloak of darkness clothes the moon.
The stars have withdrawn their brightness[8] from shining.
And every heart is sick,[9] and every eye has water.
        Fallen fallen etc.

---

[2] Superintendent or officer, the technical term for the official who led the prayers in the synagogue. Cf stanzas 4 et seq, where the congregation takes up the refrain.

[3] Ps 55.5 "My heart is in anguish." (Scriptural references are to the Hebrew Bible in the notes to this poem.)

[4] The words echo Job 17.11 "My plans are broken off, the desires of my heart."

[5] Cf Jer 4.31 "for I heard a cry as of a woman in labour".

[6] Cf Ps 51.19 "a broken spirit".

[7] A frequently used biblical image. Cf Jer 4.8; Ezek 7.18; 27.31; Amos 8.10; Joel 1.8, 13; Jonah 3.5–8; Ps 35.13.

[8] Joel 2.10; 4.15 "The sun and moon are darkened, and the stars withdraw their shining."

[9] Cf Jer 8.18 "My heart is sick."

6

Among kings there was none like him
a strong ruler, full of steadfast love, a perfect man.
Abundant in righteousness, he prolonged days.
He loved God, through the fidelity of his deeds.

7

He ruled from sea to sea,[10] in the mountains of the East.[11]
Over many peoples, differing in their laws.[12]
Their well-being he sought, he ruled over them like a father.
He said, God tests the heart—not man.—
    Fallen fallen etc.

8

The tyrants heard—and they were put to shame;
injustice shut its mouth,[13] the haughty turned away;
fraud and oppression[14] like chaff were scattered.
And the pure of heart girded themselves with the cincture of faithfulness.
    Fallen fallen etc.

9

He was hope to the crushed, strength to the powerless.
To those persecuting the innocent without cause, he said leave off.
From the fangs of the iniquitous one he delivered the prey.
And he established his land as a shelter[15] for the injured of spirit.
    Fallen fallen etc.

10

Even the daughter of Jeshurun, the bereaved one was banished,
in the mouth of cruel men a proverb and a byword,[16]
but instead of his power she found mercy.
And she blessed him with a joyful heart and spirit.
    Fallen fallen etc.

11

Therefore nations loved him and rejoiced.
And there was also a time when the splendour of the crown protected against
    calamity,[17]

---

[10] Cf Ps 72.8 "May he rule from sea to sea."

[11] The "mountains of the East" occur in Num 23.7 and Deut 33.15.

[12] Cf Esther 3.8 "their laws are different".

[13] Job 5.16 "Injustice shuts its mouth."

[14] Cf Ps 55.12 "oppression and fraud".

[15] Cf Ps 55.9.

[16] Deut 28.37 "a proverb and a byword".

[17] A difficult line to render. The Hebrew is obscure.

the flame of love in their heart was burning;
they turned aside to obey him, they hoped and waited.
    Fallen fallen etc.

12

But now he has passed on, he has left the earth,
and has flown like a cherub to the heavens,
to walk in the garden of the living God.
And with us is God angry, and he has breached the opening.[18]
    Fallen fallen etc.

13

The land is in mourning and also its inhabitants,
full of people,[19]
And the daughter of Judah will weep, and be girded with sackcloth;
even woe will be heard in her assemblies.
    Fallen fallen etc.

14

And Britannia, sitting like a widow,[20]
desolate, widowed, like those going down to the grave:
for great is the pain, strong the wound;
and grief is closed up in her like a smelting fire.
    Fallen fallen etc.

15

I am in distress for you Britannia my sister.
Would that I could comfort you O forlorn one!
And how could I comfort you? and I sick
as you are. For indeed many are my sighs.
    Fallen fallen etc.

16

Hand in hand let us go, and let us bring
tears of love unto the grave of our king.
There let our heart be poured out like water,[21]
in prayer, in righteousness, and in repentance.

---

[18] Presumably in taking away the king.

[19] Cf Lam 1.1 "full of people".

[20] Cf Lam 1.1 "How lonely sits the city that was once full of people! How like a widow she has become."

[21] Cf Deut 12.16, 24; 15.23.

17

While God looks down from the high places of the earth[22]
let him see our distress and our languishing spirit.[23]
May he send healing upon all our afflictions,
and wipe away tears from upon the land.

18

Leader and Congregation
And now let us bless our God
who has seen our languishing spirit;
and let him send an upright king to heal us,
and wipe away tears from our land.

PRAYER

Lord of Lords! dweller in the heights
hear the prayer of your sons.
Healer of the broken-hearted! and every grief!
heal the ills of your people.
> *Your mercy O God! is pleasing.*
> *Your faithful love and your goodness are strong.*
> *Wherefore O God! hear our cry*
> *and grant our prayer.*

Moreover when you chastise, your servants,
you show them the abundance of your mercy.
For before you smite, there is healing for the wound
you hold in readiness the strength of your hands.
> *Your mercy O God! is pleasing.*
> *Your faithful love and your goodness are strong.*
> *Wherefore O God! hear our cry*
> *and grant our prayer.*

For an instant you were angry, the tree you cut down,
still you have allowed its fruit to remain.
Our father has passed on, and his son has become king,
to fence in the breach of his people.
> *Your mercy O God! is pleasing.*
> *Your faithful love and your goodness are strong.*
> *Wherefore O God! hear our cry*
> *and grant our prayer.*

---

[22] Cf Lam 3.50 "while the Lord from heaven looks down". The same words are repeated in the following stanza.

[23] Deut 28.65: "a languishing spirit".

Trustworthy planting, from a verdant tree,
you blossomed forth to rule over us,
O God! keep watch over him! in the glory of his crown!
For ever may he rule over us.

> *Your mercy O God! is pleasing.*
> *Your faithful love and your goodness are strong.*
> *Wherefore O God! hear our cry*
> *and grant our prayer.*

Send long life, to the royal sons.
For our land let there be peace and rest.
Console its princes, and also its inhabitants,
and let grief and sighing be put to flight.

> *Your mercy O God! is pleasing.*
> *Your faithful love and your goodness are strong.*
> *Wherefore O God! hear our cry*
> *and grant our prayer.*

For another translation see Rev William Smith, AM, Minister of Bower, Thurso *The Knell: An Elegy on George III* (printed and published for the translator by William Judd 1827).

DIRGE.

I.

Oppress'd, confused with grief and pain,
    And inly shrinking from the blow,
In vain I seek the dirgeful strain:
    The wonted words refuse to flow.

II.

A fear in every face I find,   5
    Each voice is that of one who grieves;
And all my Soul, to grief resigned,
    Reflects the sorrow, it receives.

III.

The Day-Star of our glory sets!
    Our King has breathed his latest breath!   10
Each heart its wonted pulse forgets,
    As if it own'd the pow'r of death.

IV.

Our Crown, our heart's Desire is fled!
 Britannia's glory moults its wing!
Let us, with ashes on our head,   15
 Raise up a mourning for our King.

V.

Lo! of his beams the Day-Star shorn,*
 Sad gleams the Moon through cloudy veil!
The Stars are dim! Our Nobles mourn,
 The Matrons weep, their Children wail. 20

VI.

No age records a King so just,
 His virtues numerous as his days;
The Lord Jehovah was his trust,
 And truth with mercy ruled his ways.

VII.

His Love was bounded by no Clime: 25
 Each diverse Race, each distant Clan
He govern'd by this truth sublime,
 "God only knows the heart—not man."

VIII.

His word appall'd the sons of pride,
 Iniquity far wing'd her way;   30
Deceit and fraud were scatter'd wide,
 And truth resum'd her sacred sway.

IX.

He sooth'd the wretched, and the prey
 From impious tyranny he tore;
He stay'd th' Usurper's iron sway,   35
 And bade the Spoiler waste no more.

 * The Author, in the spirit of Hebrew Poetry here represents, the Crown, the Peerage, and the Commonalty, in the figurative expression of the Sun, Moon, and Stars.

X.

Thou too, Jeshurun's Daughter! thou,
    Th' oppress'd of nations and the scorn!
Didst hail on his benignant brow
    That safety dawning like the morn.   40

XI.

The scoff of each unfeeling mind,
    Thy doom was hard, and keen thy grief:
Beneath his throne, peace thou didst find,
    And blest the hand that gave relief.

XII.

E'en when a fatal cloud o'erspread   45
    The moonlight splendour of his sway,
Yet still the light remain'd, and shed
    Mild radiance on the traveller's way.

XIII.

But he is gone—the Just! the Good!
    Nor could a Nation's pray'r delay   50
The heavenly meed, that long had stood
    His portion in the realms of day.

XIV.

Beyond the mighty Isle's extent
    The mightier Nation mourns her Chief:
Him Judah's Daughter shall lament,   55
    In tears of fervour, love and grief.

XV.

Britannia mourns in silent grief;
    Her heart a prey to inward woe.
In vain she strives to find relief,
    Her pang so great, so great the blow.   60

XVI.

Britannia! Sister! woe is me!
    Full fain would I console thy woe.

But, ah! how shall I comfort thee,
    Who need the balm, I would bestow?

XVII.

United then let us repair,   65
    As round our common Parent's grave;
And pouring out our heart in prayer,
    Our heav'nly Father's mercy crave.

XVIII.

Until Jehovah from his throne
    Shall heed his suffering people's fears;   70
Shall turn to song the Mourner's groan,
    To smiles of joy the Nation's tears.

XIX.

Praise to the Lord! Loud praises sing!
    And bless Jehovah's righteous hand!
Again he bids a GEORGE, our King,   75
    Dispense his blessings to the Land.

HYMN.

I.

O thron'd in Heav'n! Sole King of kings,
Jehovah! hear thy Children's prayers and sighs!
Thou Binder of the broken heart! with wings
    Of healing on thy people rise!   80
        Thy mercies, Lord, are sweet;
        And Peace and Mercy meet,
        Before thy Judgment seat:
        Lord, hear us! we entreat!

II.

When angry clouds thy throne surround,   85
E'en from the cloud thou bid'st thy mercy shine:
And ere thy righteous vengeance strikes the wound,
    Thy grace prepares the balm divine!

Thy mercies, Lord, are sweet;
And Peace and Mercy meet,   90
Before thy Judgment seat:
Lord, hear us! we entreat!

III.

The Parent tree thy hand did spare—
It fell not till the ripen'd fruit was won:
Beneath its shade the Scion flourish'd fair,   95
    And for the Sire thou gav'st the Son.

Thy mercies, Lord, are sweet;
And Peace and Mercy meet,
Before thy Judgment seat:
Lord, hear us! we entreat!   10(

IV.

This thy own Vine, which thou didst rear,
And train up for us from the royal root,
Protect, O Lord! and to the Nations near
    Long let it shelter yield, and fruit.

Thy mercies, Lord, are sweet;   10:
And Peace and Mercy meet,
Before thy Judgment seat:
Lord, hear us! we entreat!

V.

Lord, comfort thou the royal line:
Let Peace and Joy watch round us hand and hand!   11(
Our Nobles visit with thy grace divine,
    And banish sorrow from the land!

Thy mercies, Lord, are sweet;
And Peace and Mercy meet,
Before thy Judgment seat: 11
Lord, hear us! we entreat!

FINES.

566. COUPLET ON ANTICIPATION AND THEORY, GENIUS AND CLEVERNESS

[Early 1820]

C inserted the metrical lines as a whimsical afterthought to a prose equation in Notebook 28 (*CN* IV 4649), in which, among other relations, Anticipation is opposed to Theory as Genius to Cleverness. Similar conjunctions of the same terms are to be found in *The Friend* (*CC*) I 419–23; cf *TT* (*CC*) I 250–1n. The letters "CL" seem also to be a whimsical reference to Charles Lamb, and perhaps "G" to James Gillman, making line 2 refer, in turn, to postal franking arrangements devolved upon employers like Lamb's East India Company.

As A to THe, so G. to CL:
Pay the Post and go to Hell.

567. COUPLET ON MAN AS SOLAR ANIMAL

[Early 1820]

The lines conclude an entry in Notebook 28 (*CN* IV 4650), comprising what appears to be a series of reflections on the adaptation of animals to their environment. They follow a Latin quotation which ends with the sentence "Homo in fine vere ANIMAL SOLARE EST" tr "Finally, Man truly is A SOLAR ANIMAL."

With feet adhesive to the earth, we shun,
Headward we gravitate toward the Sun.

568. GREEK COUPLET ON LAUDERDALE

[Feb–Oct 1820?]

C wrote the lines in the margin of George Frere's copy of *Reliquiae Baxteri-anae*, and again at the head of the page (*CM—CC—*I 351). Tr "I say this in great anger: for I hold for Lauderdale the same hatred as for tail-horn-hoofed

Satan" (a second version in the same copy alters to ταῦτ᾽ ἔλεγον "I said"). Lauderdale in Baxter's text is John Maitland, the 2nd earl and 1st duke (1616–82), whose actions against Covenanters as secretary for Scottish affairs were cruelly repressive. It is very likely that C was also thinking of James Maitland, the 8th earl (1759–1839). The latter, "that *Scotch* Coxcomb, the plebeian Earl of Lauderdale" (*CL* IV 854: to J. H. Green 2 May 1818), began as a supporter of the French Revolution (see **50.X2** *To the Earl of Lauderdale*) and ended as a Tory. He was a strident opponent of Sir Robert Peel's Cotton Factory legislation on behalf of children, which C actively supported in 1818 (*SW&F—CC*—714–51; *EOT—CC*—III 155–8).

The germ of the lines is likely to be the striking compound in line 2: C first used it with reference to English oppression of the Irish in 1807–8 (*CN* II 3205), although it should be noted that the actual Greek is an afterthought there, written with a different pen. He claimed in *Omniana* I 197 (*SW&F—CC*—301) that the compound derived from "some Greek Hexameters (MSS)", and repeated it by itself in marginalia on John Smith's *Select Discourses* (1660) and in letters (*CM—CC*—V; *CL* IV 823: to H. F. Cary 30 Jan 1818; VI 915: to Baldwin and Cradock 29 Jun 1832). However, whether or not the compound was coined or borrowed, the prosodic shape of the word (–∪∪–∪∪) cried out for inclusion in a dactylic line.

If the present lines had been available when *Omniana* was published, they would surely have been included; RS might even have helped concoct or provide the compound phrase. C copied them out twice in the margins of Baxter, in a way which suggests that he arrived at them here for the first time. Only three accents are omitted in the Greek (and there is one wrong accent), an indication that he was trying to produce a finished text. The adverb περιθύμως comes in the passage of Aeschylus' *Libation-bearers* (38–41) adapted by C in **48** *Sors Misera Servorum* 55–6.

Ταυτα λέγω περίθυμος: εγω γαρ μισεῖ ἐν ἴσῳ
Λαυδερδαῖλον ἔχω καὶ κερκοκερώνυχα Σᾶταν.

569. ON FOOTNOTES, IN A LETTER

[Aug 1820?]

The parody of Hamlet's soliloquy is part of a memorandum addressed to HC, which ELG prints as a letter (*CL* V 97–100: [Aug 1820?]). It concludes the following aside:

A blessing, I say, on the Inventors of Notes! You have only to imagine the lines between the (   ) to be printed in smaller type at the bottom of the page—& the Writer may digress, like Harris, the Historian, from Dan to Barsheba & from Barsheba in hunt after the last Comet, without any breach of continuity.

Harris is probably Walter Harris (1686–1761), the Irish historiographer.

> Digress? Or not digress? That's now no question.
> Do it! Yet do it *not*! See Note I below.

570. A PRACTICAL PROBLEM CONCERNING FLIES

[Early Sept 1820]

The lines conclude an entry in Notebook 29 (*CN* IV 4710), describing "A grave Problem"—whether the advantage of the transmutation of waste matter into flies is equalled by the excretions and extrusions of the same flies. This leads to "A practical Problem, suggested by the Grave Problem—Whether it be practicable by to breed or education to rear a race of House flies having the ⟨cancrine⟩ *felisity* of *going* backwards and performing burial-service." "Cancrine" means "crab-like", hence able to go backwards; "felisity" is a pun alluding to the feline habit of burying excrement.

KC translates the poem as follows:

> Be it white, or be it black
> (Unless it's absurd)
> What was dung in the fly
> Lies as turd *on turd*.

> Sit alba, sit fusca
> (Ni res est absurda)
> Quod fuit Merda in Muscâ
> Jacet Merda *in Merdâ*.

571. MUSIC

[c Oct 1820]

C wrote the lines under the present title in Notebook 60 (*CN* IV 4736). The version given here forms the alternative to a draft which began as follows:

> Sweet discontent
> Of a Contentment overflowing,
> Jet of a Pleasure striving with it's fullness
>   a joy that strives with it's own fullness—

Two pages earlier in the notebook C had begun an attempt to match his under-standing of music with philosophical concepts (*CN* IV 4734), and he may have broken this off in order to continue in verse. For other comments on music see e.g. *IS* (1979) 211–15; *CN* III 4115 f 26ʳ; IV 5458. The movement of the lines here recalls the description in **115** *The Eolian Harp* and related fragments (see lines 19–25EC).

> Sweet Overswell and mimic Discontent
> Of a too full Contentment.

572. SONNET: TO NATURE

[1820? 1797–8?]

The only known version of the poem is recorded in Allsop I 144, where it is printed after a sequence of letters by C dating from 1820, and before letters written during 1821. Allsop prefaces the poem with the explanation that he found it "on a detached piece of paper, without note or observation. How it came into my possession I have now forgotten, though I have some faint impression that I wrote it down from dictation, and that it was the transcript of an early, a *very early* sonnet, written probably at the time when the author's heart, as well as his head, was with Spinoza" (142–3).

It is impossible on present evidence to decide whether the poem was actually written during Nether Stowey days. Its inspiration and form date from this early time, but it is just as likely to have been composed on the spur of the moment in 1820.

It may indeed be phantasy, when I
Essay to draw from all created things
Deep, heartfelt, inward joy that closely clings;
And trace in leaves and flowers that round me lie
Lessons of love and earnest piety.   5
So let it be; and if the wide world rings
In mock of this belief, it brings
Nor fear, nor grief, nor vain perplexity.
So will I build my altar in the fields,
And the blue sky my fretted dome shall be,   10
And the sweet fragrance that the wild flower yields,
Shall be the incense I will yield to Thee,
Thee only God! and thou shalt not despise
Even me, the priest of this poor sacrifice.

573. A COUPLET ADDRESSED TO
THE MIND'S EAR

[Jan 1821]

C's lines are given in parentheses in a letter to H. F. Cary of 8 Jan 1821 (*CL* v 133). The parenthesis follows the comment "This uncouth rise of the Thermometer, f 22 Degrees in scarcely more than the same number of Hours, with the dense Fog, a descendant of the Egyptian, and which I would fain conjure home again, with it's Cousin-germans, the Ghosts & such like Southeïo-Wesleyan burglarious Gentry, to the Red Sea". The parenthesis is completed by the remark, following the lines: "which couplet you should *have* recited to you, it being addressed to the Mind's *Ear* exclusively)". C also wrote at the end of the first line "*punicè sea*"; and beneath this, at the end of the second line, "dº read."

That the Fog we never might *see*
And the Ghosts might cease to be *red*.

574. FIRST ADVENT OF LOVE

[1821–7]

C claimed that the lines were written before or when he was 15, but no early version has been preserved, and the third and fourth lines in fact follow the phrasing of a "pretty unintended Couplet in the Prose of Sidney's Arcadia" which he noticed in 1821 (*CN* IV 4810):

> And sweeter than a gentle South-west wind
> O'er flowry fields and shadow'd Waters creeping
> In Summer's extreme heat.—

The opening line also seems certainly to be a reminiscence of the start of Guinizelli's famous canzone *"Al cor gentil ripara sempre Amore"*, although it is possible that C derived his version from one of Guinizelli's imitators. While it is true, then, that the feeling in the lines corresponds to certain Christ's Hospital experiences (cf esp **289** *A Letter to* —— 68–73), the present form and phrasing are relatively late.

The lines were published in *PW* (1834), but the version given here, with slightly different punctuation, appears to derive from a ms dating from Sept 1827.

> O fair is love's first hope to gentle mind,
> As Eve's first star thro' fleecy cloudlet peeping;
> And sweeter than the gentle south-west wind
> O'er willowy meads and shadow'd waters creeping,
> And Ceres' golden fields! the sultry hind   5
> Meets it with brow uplift, and stays his reaping.

575. WHERE IS REASON?

[1821–2?]

The lines are given here in the form in which they appear in Notebook 29 (*CN* IV 4844). They are a reworked example of "graduated Emphasis"—i.e. some notes on a metrical design—and are headed "Answer" to the supposed question "Where is Reason?" They are partly anticipated in a notebook entry of 1804 (*CN* II 2026 f 7ʳ).

The poem was reprinted in a slightly revised form in the Author's Appendix to *Church and State* (*C&S—CC—*184–5), where they are introduced as follows: "Finally, what is Reason? You have often asked me; and this is my answer;" and they are followed by:

But, alas!

> —————— tu stesso ti fai grosso
> Col falso immaginar, si che non vedi
> Cio che vedresti, se l'avessi scosso.
> DANTE; *Paradiso, Canto 1*

The quotation is from *Paradiso* I 88–90 in *The Vision; or, Hell, Purgatory, and Paradise of Dante Alighieri* tr H. F. Cary (2nd ed 3 vols 1819) III 9:

> "With false imagination thou thyself
> Mak'st dull; so that thou seest not the thing,
> Which thou hadst seen, had that been shaken off.

Thus, C invites the reader, puzzled like Dante at the beginning of *Paradiso*, to abandon his "false imagination" if he wants to enter a different reality. The same lines from Dante are quoted elsewhere in Notebook 29 (*CN* IV 4786 f 125^r) and in *Opus Maximum* II f 80^r.

> Whene'er the Self, that stands twixt God and Thee,
> Defecates to a pure Transparency
> That intercepts no light and adds no stain—
> There Reason is; and then begins *her* reign!

576. ADAPTED FROM HÖLTY

[Aug–Sept 1821?]

The stanzas exist in a fair copy in C's hand, lines 21–2 perhaps being added later. The poem was never published in his lifetime.

The lines derive from L.H.C. Hölty's poem *Adelstan und Röschen*, in *Gedichte* ed A. F. Geisler (Halle 1792) 33 et seq, dated 1771 and first published in the *Musenalmenach* (Göttingen 1774) 178 et seq:

> Der schöne Maienmond begann,
>   Und alles wurde froh;
> Als Ritter Veit von Adelstan
>   Der Königstadt entfloh.
>
> Von Geigern und Kastraten fern,
>   Und vom Redoutentanz,

Vertauscht' er seinen goldnen Stern
　　Mit einem Schäferkranz.

Der Schooß der Au, der Wiesenklee,
　　Verlieh ihm süß're Rast,
Als Himmelbett' und Kanapee
　　Im fürstlichen Pallast.

Er irrte täglich durch den Hain,
　　Mit einer Brust voll Ruh,
Und sah dem Spiel, und sah dem Reihn
　　Der Dörferinnen zu.

Sah' unter niederm Hüttendach,
　　Der Schäfermädchen Preis; . . .

C proposed "The Life of Hölty, with specimens of his poems, translated into English Verse" to William Blackwood on 19 Sept 1821 (*CL* v 166); and a "Life of Holty with specimens of his poetry—First, the Ballad" appears in a list of literary projects drawn up in Oct 1821 (*SW&F—CC*—955). C's attention had perhaps been directed to Hölty during Aug, when he was visited by John Anster (see the inscription recorded in *LS—CC*—235), who was presumably the Dublin author of the "Life of Hölty" which appeared in *The London Magazine* iv (Nov 1821) 518–26.

Alternatively, the stanzas might have been written long before. DeQ records how C gave young ladies copies of verses headed "Lines on ——— , from the German of Hölty", which, he says, they transcribed, omitting the reference to Hölty (*DeQ Works* ii 228). The present adaptation in ballad form does not suit DeQ's description, but it might have been made at the same time (1807–12?). C's annotated copy of Hölty's *Gedichte* (Frankfurt [=Halle?] 1792) was sold in the J. H. Green Sale (Sotheby's 28 Jul 1880 lot 326), but has not been traced: cf *CM* (*CC*) ii 1116.

For ever in the World of Fame
　　We live and yet abide the same,
Clouds may intercept our Rays,
　　Or Desert Lands reflect our Blaze.

The beauteous Month of May began,　　　　　　　5
　　And all was Mirth and Sport—
When Baron Guelph of Adelstan
　　Took leave and left the Court—

From Fete and Rout and Opera far
　　The full Town he forsook;　　　　　　　　　　10

And changd his Wand and golden Star
  For Shepherd's Crown and Crook.

The knotted Net of Light and Shade
  Beneath the budding Tree
A sweeter Day-bed for him made   15
  Than Couch and Canopy.

In Copse or Lane, as Choice or Chance
  Might lead him, was he seen:
And join'd at eve the village Dance
  Upon the village Green.   20

A tradesman He, and well to do,
  Nor endless

577. LINES FROM THE *BHAGAVAD-GITA*, FROM CREUZER

[1821]

C drafted the translation in Notebook 29 (*CN* IV 4832 f 61ᵛ), as an instance of "*poetic* Symbol" (as distinct from "a real Symbol"), drawn from the eighth incarnation of Krishna or Vishnu, as Man. His original is the German version by Friedrich Schlegel *Über die Sprache und Weisheit der Indier* (Heidelberg 1808) 303, as quoted by G. F. Creuzer *Symbolik und Mythologie der alten Völker* (6 vols Leipzig & Darmstadt 1810–23) I 117–18:

"Doch ein andres als dies, höh'res Wesen an mir erkenne Du,
"Was die ird'schen belebt, Orjun! auch die Welt hier erhält und trägt,
"Dies ist die Mutter der Dinge, aller zusammt, das glaube, Freund!
"Ich bin des ganzen Weltenalls Ursprung, so wie Vernichtung auch.
"Außer mir gibt es ein anderes höheres nirgends mehr, o Freund!
"An mir hängt dieses All vereint, wie an der Schnur der Perlen Zahl.

C has rearranged the order of the fourth and fifth lines and exercised poetic licence in other ways. For his earlier condemnation of the *Bhagavad-Gita* as polytheistic, as a result of reading the translation by Charles Wilkins, see *P Lects* lect 3 (1949) 127–9.

"Yet an other in me, a higher Essence acknowledge then,
"That which gives life to the Earthly, that which the World preserves,
   and bears.
"This is the Mother of Things, of all things the Mother, believe me,
   Friend!
"Is there besides Me an Other and Higher?—O never, O no where,
   Friend!
"I am the Universe' Well-spring, I the Destruction too!   5
"I am the String of the Pearls. I, God-man, am Center and Circle too!

578. FIRESIDE ANACREONTIC

[1820–3?]

The lines exist in transcripts by RS, EC, and SC, the first two of which date
from 1820–3 and are connected with Rydal Mount, where SC was a frequent
visitor at this time. The identification of the "old Aunts" and the "girls" partly
depends on the date of the poem, partly, and on whether C would even jokingly
so address and refer to his own family. It seems most likely that he would,
and that, although he did not visit the Lake District after 1812, the aunts are
Edith, RS's wife, and Mary, widow of Robert Lovell, who both lived at Greta
Hall; also DW and SH at Rydal Mount. It is also possible that the lines date
from a considerably earlier time, and were put back into circulation by RS. The
version given here is from RS's transcript, adding punctuation and expanding
some contractions. The title comes from SC's transcript.

[J. H. Reynolds] "A Chit Chat Letter on Men and Other Things from Ned
Ward, jun. a fellow in London, to Anthony Wood, Jun. a Fellow at Oxford"
London Magazine VIII (Oct 1823) 361–4 recommends brandy and water in a
similar metre.

Come damn it girls—don't let's be sad,
The bottle stands so handy,
Drink gin if brandy can't be had,
But if it can drink brandy.
   And if old Aunts—oh damn their chops—   5
   In scolding vent their phthisick,
   Drop in of Laudanum thirty drops,
   And call it opening physick:
For it opens the heart, & it opens the brain,
And if you once take you'll take it again.   10

Oh! Jacky, Jacky, Jacky, Jacky Dandy,
Laudanum's a great improver of Brandy.

579. MOCK EPITAPH ON
SIR WILLIAM CURTIS

[1821–2]

C drafted the lines in Notebook 22 (*CN* IV 4837). Sir William Curtis (1752–1829) was a prosperous city politician and Tory MP, whose vain pretensions were the butt of many contemporary jokes. The lines commemorate an episode in 1821 when, upon becoming the Senior Alderman of London, he took the opportunity to exchange his long-standing representation of Tower Ward for that of Bridge Without. C met him at Ramsgate in 1822 (*CL* v 257: to JG [10 Nov 1822]). KC also mentions the broader implications for C, which are expanded on in *CN* IV 4707, 5278 and nn.

Here lies Sir Willy Curtis, our worthy Lord Mayor
Who has left this here ward & is gone to that there.

580. LINES RECORDED BY THOMAS ALLSOP

[Dec 1821?]

When Allsop recorded the lines in a sequence of extracts from and anecdotes of C (II 75), he did not say that they had been composed (dictated?) by C, but there is an implication that they were. Allsop introduced them as follows: "I find the following lines amongst my papers, in my own writing, but whether an unfinished fragment, or a contribution to some friend's production I know not." Allsop provides no date, but he places the poem between letters of late 1821 and early 1822.

7. Laudanum is the reverse of an opening medicine, as C knew to his cost (cf e.g. *CN* II 2091). Thirty drops, little more than half a teaspoonful, is a small amount: Cottle *E Rec* II 169 claims that at one time C was consuming up to two pints a day.

What boots to tell how o'er his grave
She wept, that would have died to save;
Little they know the heart, who deem
Her sorrow but an infant's dream
    Of transient love begotten;   5
A passing gale, that as it blows
Just shakes the ripe drop from the rose—
    That dies, and is forgotten.

Oh woman! nurse of hopes and fears,
All lovely in thy spring of years,   10
    Thy soul in blameless mirth possessing;
Most lovely in affliction's tears,
    More lovely still those tears suppressing.

581. FICKLE FLOWERS: A MADRIGAL

[Jan 1822]

The only known version of the lines is a fair copy in C's hand, apparently for an album, dated Highgate 20 Jan 1822. C took a particular interest and pleasure in the flowers at Highgate: cf *CL* IV 867: to AG [17 Jun 1818]; L. E. Watson *Coleridge at Highgate* (1925) 52–3; **585** *The Reproof and Reply*, written on another Sunday morning in other circumstances over a year later. Drawings of the back garden of 3 The Grove are included in *Coleridge at Highgate* facing p 52 and *CN* IV facing No 5147.

Some dear loved Flowers were given into my Hand:
I bound them round, yea, fondly I did tie
    My **Heart** within the Band
    With them to live and die!

New Hours come on: away the Old Loves pass!   5
My Flowers were fain to charm a brighter Eye,
        To woo a warmer Hand!
They dropt out one by one—but left, alas!
        My **Heart** within the Band!

582. TO A LADY: A POEM UPON NOTHING

[Before Feb 1822]

The lines were printed, as an impromptu, above C's name in *The Gazette of Fashion* ed C. M. Westmacott I (2 Feb 1822) 14. They bear a resemblance to several earlier poems, and there is no reason to doubt their authenticity.

> On Nothing, Fanny, shall I write?
> Shall not one charm of thine indite?
>   The muse is most unruly;
> And vows to sing of what's more free,
> More soft, more beautiful, than thee,   5
>   And that is NOTHING, truly.

583. THE GOOD, THE TRUE, THE FAIR

[1822 or later]

The lines were written at the close of a discussion of William of Occam's nominalism and its relevance to the subsequent progress of philosophy and the end now to be aimed at (*SW&F—CC*—1003). They are preceded by a cancelled first draft, the first two lines of which are much rewritten in a way which leaves it unclear where prose ends and verse begins (as in **596** *Heraclitus on the Sybil's Utterance*). The cancelled beginning (replaced here by lines 1–3) might have emerged as:

> Where'er I find the Three yet One
> Whate'er unites them is Religion.

There are also indications that the poem was meant to be continued after line 5. The text below supplies the apostrophe in the first word, omits C's comma after "Man" in line 5, and adds a final full point.

> Where'er I find the Good, the True, the Fair,
> I ask no names. God's Spirit dwelleth there!
> The unconfounded, undivided Three,
> Each for itself, and all in each, to see
> In Man and Nature is Philosophy.   5

584. NONSENSE SAPPHICS,
WRITTEN FOR JAMES GILLMAN Jr

[1822–3?]

The only known source for the lines is a transcript in the hand of Henry Langley Porter, JG's assistant, given below with some added punctuation. The poem was later printed by HNC and SC, who supply the date. The full title (which does not have the abbreviation "Jr") adds "as school exercise for Merchant Taylors'?"; but the poem seems in fact to be intended only to congratulate him on his proficiency. James Gillman (1808–77), elder son of C's physician and friend, continued at Merchant Taylors' School from May 1818 until he became Head Boy in 1826–7. C wrote him several letters from 1819 onwards (*CL* VI 1047–8 etc) and several study aids for him and his brother Henry. James would probably have begun writing Latin sapphics in late 1819–20. Cf *SW&F* (*CC*) 809–15, esp 812–14 for two lessons on sapphics, the first of which includes **584.X1** *Virgil's Hexameters Converted to Sapphics.*

Here is Jem's first copy of nonsense verses
All in the antique style of Mistress Sappho
Latin just like Horace the tuneful Roman
    Sapph's imitator.

But we Bards, we classical Lyric Poets,   5
Know a thing or two in a scurvy planet,
Don't we now? Eh? Brother Horatius Flaccus
    Tip us your paw, lad—

Here's to Mæcenas and the other worthies!
Rich men of England would ye be immortal?   10
Patronise Genius, giving Cash & praise to
    Gillman Jacobus!

Gillman Jacobus, he of Merchant Taylors'
Minor ætate, ingenio at stupendus,
Sapphic, Heroic, Elegæic, what a   15
    Versificator!

14. Tr "Younger in age, but stupendous in genius."

585. THE REPROOF AND REPLY
OR, THE FLOWER-THIEF'S APOLOGY

[May 1823]

In the first printed version the subtitle continues: "for a Robbery Committed in Mr and Mrs Chisholm's Garden, on Sunday Morning, 25th of May, 1823, between the Hours of Eleven and Twelve". C was particularly struck and delighted by the flower gardens of Highgate (*CL* IV 867: to AG [17 Jun 1818]; Watson *Coleridge at Highgate* 52–3), and in another Sunday poem written only a year before he had already celebrated his appreciation of them (**581** *Fickle Flowers*). The interest of the present poem is none the less different, and lies in its particular tone of elaborated embarrassment.

The lines imagine a dialogue between DC and Mrs Chisholm, a Highgate neighbour, whom C had met along with her husband early in 1820 and whom he had taken DC to visit that same summer (*CL* V 12: to J. H. Green 14 Jan 1820; 44–5: to Mr Chisholm [May 1820]; 55–6: to Mr Chisholm 16 Jun 1820). The Chisholms had a Miss Hall living with them, perhaps a relative of Mrs Chisholm (*CL* V 209: to Mrs C [9 Feb 1822]), with whom DC fell in love or who became infatuated with DC (*The Hartley Coleridge Letters* ed Stephens 38, 39, 41–2). It may be assumed that she is the Mary H—— of line 31.

The episode is obscure, but seems to have continued into 1821, and its memory was fresh enough in Feb 1822 for C to report the matter to Mrs C. C later referred to it as a "Scrape", and to Mrs Chisholm as "a vulgar tattling Woman" (*CL* V 209; 193: to DC 11 Jan 1822). HC also held Mrs Chisholm culpable for what had happened (*Hartley Coleridge Letters* 73–4), although DC wrote to Mrs Chisholm in a way that wounded C, apparently laying the blame for his conduct on his father's impoverished circumstances (*CL* V 193 "should a Son have placed his Father in so degrading a point of view"?). C's dialogue is thus a retrospective apology on behalf of DC, disguised as an apology for himself.

C wrote a version of lines 36–46 in the margins of Steffens's *Caricaturen* (*CM—CC—*v), which may represent either the beginnings of the poem or a recollection of it. No holograph ms of the poem has been recovered. There are two almost identical printed texts, in *Friendship's Offering* and *PW* (1834). The present text reproduces the first of these, deleting a comma at the end of line 26 in accordance with C's correction on the loose pages at PML.

"Fie, Mr. Coleridge!—and can this be you?
Break two commandments?—and in church-time too!
Have you not heard, or have you heard in vain,
The birth-and-parentage-recording strain?—
Confessions shrill, that out-shrill'd mack'rel drown—   5

Fresh from the drop—the youth not yet cut down—
Letter to sweet-heart—the last dying speech—
And didn't all this begin in Sabbath-breach?
You, that knew better! In broad open day
Steal in, steal out, and steal our flowers away?   10
What could possess you? Ah! sweet youth, I fear,
The chap with Horns and Tail was at your ear!"

Such sounds, of late, accusing fancy brought
From fair C——— to the Poet's thought.
Now hear the meek Parnassian youth's reply:—   15
A bow—a pleading look—a downcast eye—
And then:

                "Fair dame! a visionary wight,
Hard by your hill-side mansion sparkling white,
His thoughts all hovering round the Muses' home,
Long hath it been your Poet's wont to roam.   20
And many a morn, on his becharmed sense,
So rich a stream of music issued thence,
He deem'd himself, as it flowed warbling on,
Beside the vocal fount of Helicon!
But when, as if to settle the concern,   25
A nymph too he beheld, in many a turn
Guiding the sweet rill from its fontal urn;
Say, can you blame?—No! none, that saw and heard,
Could blame a bard, that he, thus inly stirr'd,
A muse beholding in each fervent trait,   30
Took Mary H——— for Polly Hymnia!
Or, haply as there stood beside the maid
One loftier form in sable stole arrayed,
If with regretful thought he hail'd in *thee*,
C——— m, his long lost friend Mol Pomenè?   35
But most of *you*, soft warblings, I complain!

31. Polly Hymnia] Polyhymnia, the
Muse who came to be associated with
mimic art.

35. Mol Pomenè] Melpomene, the
Muse associated with tragedy.

36. C wrote lines 36–46 into Stef-
fens's *Caricaturen*, after the follow-
ing note: "May & June 1823 ⌜...⌝er-
ably s⌜...⌝ing as far as the Eye could
reach either high up in the air & thro'
the air far round about—and then ed-
dying in the whirl-breeze with the
noise of Chaff."

'Twas ye, that from the bee-hive of my brain
Did lure the fancies forth, a freakish rout,
And witched the air with dreams turn'd inside out.

Thus all conspir'd—each power of eye and ear,   40
And this gay month, th' enchantress of the year,
To cheat poor me (no conjurer, God wot!)
And C——m's self accomplice in the plot.
Can you then wonder if I went astray?
Not bards alone, nor lovers made as they—   45
All Nature *day-dreams* in the month of May.
And if I pluck'd "each flower that *sweetest* blows"—
Who walks in sleep, needs follow must his *nose*.

Thus, long accustomed on the twy-fork'd hill,*
To pluck both flower and floweret at my will;   50
The garden's maze, like No-man's land, I tread,
Nor common law, nor statute in my head;
For my own proper smell, sight, fancy, feeling,
With autocratic hand at once repealing
Five Acts of Parliament 'gainst private stealing!   55
But yet from C——m, who despairs of grace?
There's no spring-gun nor man-trap in *that* face!
Let Moses then look black, and Aaron blue,
That look as if they had little else to do:
For C——m speaks. "Poor youth! he's but a waif!   60

---

* The English Parnassus is remarkable for its two summits of unequal height, the lower denominated Hampstead, the higher Highgate.

47. "each flower that *sweetest* blows"] Perhaps a variation on the penultimate line of WW's *Imitations Ode* 203, "the meanest flower that blows" (*WPW* IV 285).

49fn. The "lower" literary circle at Hampstead included Leigh Hunt and John Keats (d 1821).

57. The line echoes a phrase no doubt to be seen on many a notice-board, and reported in *Boswell's Life of Johnson* (ed G. B. Hill rev L. F. Powell—6 vols Oxford 1934–50—II 447–8): "We talked of a work . . . written in a very mellifluous style, but which . . . contained much artful infidelity. I said it was not fair to attack us thus unexpectedly; he should have warned us of our danger, before we entered his garden of flowery eloquence, by advertising, 'Spring-guns and man-traps set here.'" C alludes to the phrase again in *CN* I 457, 1582; *CL* III 280: to TP 28 Jan 1810.

The spoons all right? The hen and chickens safe?
Well, well, he shall not forfeit our regards—
The Eighth Commandment was not made for Bards!"

586. *THE BATTLE OF THE BRIDGE*
REWRITTEN

[1823?]

C's rewriting is of a stanza in S. Maxwell's *The Battle of the Bridge; or, Pisa Defended* (2nd ed Edinburgh 1823), which had first appeared in 1822 as *Chinzica; or, The Battle of the Bridge* by Henry Stobert (*CM—CC*—III 839–40). No record has been found of either Maxwell or Stobert, and it possible that both are pseudonyms. The book is inscribed "To S. T. Coleridge Esqre | From the Author", and the pages are uncut after p 37.

The stanza as originally printed reads as follows:

> How long her thoughts in one dark maze,
> Held her in wild and vacant gaze
> How long, with clasp'd hands, and rais'd eyes,
> She seem'd to supplicate the skies;
> How long, with fervency she pray'd;
> I know not; yet I mark'd the maid.
> Her tall form, in the midnight wind,
> Which toss'd her flowing hair behind,
> I mark'd; and as the increasing blast
> Drove the thick rain unheeded past;
> And as the frequent lightning stream'd,
> She like a marble statue gleam'd.
> I mark'd again: with calm, still air,
> She's like an angel watching there.

The fact that C wrote out the last five lines afresh explains the different capitalisation of the text given below. The original appears to have attracted his attention as an opportunity to develop the same kind of image as is found in **347** *Phantom* or **667** *Phantom or Fact?*

63. C's last line perhaps deliberately recalls Abel Shuffelbottom's first elegy, on how he stole Delia's pocket handkerchief: "*The Eighth Commandment* WAS NOT MADE FOR LOVE!" (*The Minor Poems of Robert Southey*—3 vols 1815— I 138). Cf **590** *Parody Couplet on Wordsworth* for another humorous use of RS at this time.

How long her thoughts in one dark maze,
Fix'd her wild eye in vacant gaze
With clasped hands, and raised eyes,
How long she commun'd with the skies;
How long, how fervently she pray'd;   5
I know: for I behold the maid.
Her tall form in the midnight wind,
Which toss'd her flowing hair behind,
I mark; and as the increasing blast
Drove the thick rain unheeded past;   10
A marble Statue she might seem,
And as the frequent Lightnings stream
Gives a new terror to the gleam.
Again I mark: with calm, still air
I see an Angel watching there.   15

587. LATIN COUPLET ADAPTED FROM
JOHN SWAN

[Jul–Sept 1823]

C's one-and-a-half lines appear in Notebook $3\frac{1}{2}$ (*CN* IV 4970), and are an attempt to improve on a single line from *Schola Salerni*, q John Swan *Speculum Mundi; or, A Glasse Representing the Face of the World* (4th ed 1670) 207–8: "*Ruta viris coitum minuit, mulieribus auget*" tr "Rue detracts from sexual intercourse in men, enhances it in women." The version given below is preceded by a first attempt:

—L̶i̶b̶i̶ Cupidinis Oestumrum
Ruta Viris ⟨   ⟩ minuit, mulieribus auget

The gap in line 2 of this draft may indicate that C's particular objection was to the word "coitum", for which he failed to find a suitable metrical equivalent. The RT version may be translated "Rue diminishes the burning frenzy of carnal desire in men, increases it in women."

Cupidinis Œstrum
Ruta Viris flagrans minuit, mulieribus auget—

588. LINES ON MOONWORT,
WITH DU BARTAS

[Jul–Sept 1823]

C drafted the lines in Notebook 3½ (*CN* IV 4972). Lines 1–4 are a condensation and paraphrase of Du Bartas, as quoted by John Swan *Speculum Mundi; or, A Glasse Representing the Face of the World* 216–17; lines 5–6 are taken over unchanged from the original, which reads as follows:

> *O Moon-wort tell us where thou bidd'st the smith,*
> *Hammer and pincers thou unshoo'st them with.*
> *Alass! what lock or iron engine is't*
> *That can thy subtil secret strength resist,*
> *Sith the best Farrier cannot set a shoe*
> *So sure, but thou with speed canst it undo?*

Who to Du Bartas dare his faith refuse,
That Steeds, that tread on Moonwort, lose their Shoes.
Whence gets't thou, Moonwort? tell us—from what Smith
Hammer and Pincers to unshoe them with.
Sith the best Farrier cannot set a shoe   5
So sure, but thou with speed cans't it undo—

589. THE BRIDGE STREET COMMITTEE

[Jul–Sept 1823]

C drafted the lines in Notebook 25 (*CN* IV 4986), the version given here, and spoke them impromptu in the company of Allsop, who wrote them down or perhaps copied them later (I 90–1fn). In the notebook the poem follows a hostile discussion of "E. Hugh Hussee"'s review of *The Progress of Infidelity* "in the last Quarterly"—i.e. RS's unsigned review of M. Grégoire's *Histoire de la théophilantropie* in *Quarterly Review* XXVIII (Jan 1823) (see *CN* IV 4985n). The discussion makes clear C's profound disagreement with the reactionary conservatism of RS and others like him; and the verses extend the disagreement to a defence of the freedom of the press, which was threatened.

The Constitutional Association for Opposing the Progress of Disloyal and Seditious Principles had been founded in Dec 1820, and was installed in its

Bridge Street headquarters in May 1821. Jack Snipe was another name for John Stoddart, editor of the *New Times*, of whom C had formed adverse opinions in Malta and who was a founder member of the Bridge Street Committee. The Committee in particular opposed the printer William Hone—for his radical broadsides, his blasphemous attacks on established religion and, after Aug 1820, his leading role in the defence of Queen Caroline. Richard Carlile (1790–1843) was a radical printer who had been harried for several years and spent 1819–25 in Dorchester jail. Sir Robert Gifford (1779–1826), the attorney general since 1819, had uncharacteristically exonerated Hone in the several proceedings against him.

C's lines parody the circular, accelerating argument used on behalf of "Association". Jack Snipe eats tripe, therefore tripe must be considered edible, and all who do not eat tripe will go to the Devil. Since the Devil appears not to be in a hurry, and since Gifford will not hasten the process, loyal men must associate for the purpose. C's poem protests against stupidity and against minds which swallow what they cannot digest, more than it supports a particular political cause. C focuses on principle, not on persons. The Committee included, besides obvious reactionaries and Tories, friends and acquaintances of C's such as Sir George Beaumont and C's nephew William Hart Coleridge. C's aim is to show up the hysteria that motivated the defence of conformity, not to defend freethinking and blasphemy. As Allsop reported him saying: "Carlile *may be wrong; his persecutors undoubtedly are so*" (I 91).

> Jack Snipe
> Eats Tripe:
> 'Tis therefore credible,
> That Tripe is edible.
> And therefore, perforce,   5
> It follows of course
> That the Devil will gripe
> All who do not eat Tripe.
>
> And as Nic is too slow
> To fetch 'em below;   10
> And Gifford, th' Attorney
> Won't quicken their journey.
> The Bridge-street Committee
> That colleague without Pity
> To imprison or hange   15
> Carlisle and his gang
> Is the Pride of the City,
> And tis Association

That alone saves the Nation
From Death and Damnation.   20

590. PARODY COUPLET ON WORDSWORTH

[Aug–Sept 1823]

C inserted the lines in his ms commentary on books of church history (*SW&F—CC*—1055), in a paragraph which is critical of the assumptions and pretensions of both his friends. They gloss one of a number of imaginary titles by WW: "Song of Thanksgiving ⟨on the Surrender of Corunna⟩ an irradical Ode, by W. W. To which is added, Anticipation, or my Brother the Bishop a sonnet ⟨and Son John, the Divine—an Apocalyptic Vision⟩ to the French Troops under the command of R. H. the Duke D'Angouleme."

All the titles mock what C took to be WW's self-centredness and betrayal of social and political principle. WW's brother Christopher had become Master of Trinity College Cambridge in 1820, and might have been expected to become a bishop, although he did not. WW's son John entered New College Oxford in 1823 as a gentleman commoner, and was to be ordained in 1828; he had previously hoped to enter WW's old college, St John's Cambridge (*WL—L* rev—I 174–5). The egotistical boast "I and my Brother, the Dean" had previously come to mind when C wrote critically about WW to Allsop three years before (*CL* v 95: to T. Allsop [8 Aug] 1820), and might ultimately derive from John Kestell of Ottery, who boasted of "I and my son-in-law sister's husband" back in 1792 (*CL* I 40–1: to GC 24 Aug 1792; cf *CN* I 484, 1540; **50** *Latin Lines on Ottery's Inhabitants*).

C's awareness of serious differences from WW was longstanding—cf e.g. **374** *Latin Lines to WW as Judge* and **430** *Ad Vilmum Axiologum: Latin Version*—and WW was equally conscious of C's deficiencies. It did not prevent them travelling together to the Continent in 1828.

My Brother the Bishop, Son John the Divine,
Now at Oxford a Gentleman-Commoner fine—

591. LINES ON THE TIME, 10 SEPTEMBER 1823

[Sept 1823]

C drafted the lines in Notebook $3\frac{1}{2}$ (*CN* IV 4993), under the heading "10 Septr 1823. Wednesday Morning, 10 °clock." They are followed by a cancelled line: "The Watch & Clock do both agree". C was in Highgate on 10 Sept.

> On the tenth day of September
> Eighteen Hundred Twenty Three,
> Wednesday Morn, as I remember,
> Ten on the Clock the Hour to be.

592. YOUTH AND AGE

[Sept–Oct 1823]

Lines 18 et seq of the poem were written first, drafted under the heading "*Aria Spontanea*" in a notebook in Sept 1823 (*CN* IV 4994). Shortly afterwards C drafted the first part, perhaps drawing on images and phrases from a much earlier time, and attempted to continue the poem with a third part (*CN* IV 4996). The deeply personal application of the lines is evident in such notebook entries as *CN* IV 5184. C's attempt to continue the poem was subsequently dropped, and the first two parts were copied and published, in annuals and the late collections, with only minor revisions. The version given here is from *PW* (1828).

C provided a metrical analysis of lines 1–17 in the RH margin of MS 3, omitting line 5 (perhaps because the line was omitted when this version was first copied out):

$$
\begin{array}{l}
\overset{-\,\cup}{\underset{-\,\cup\cup}{}}\left\{ -\cup \mid -\cup \mid -\cup \right. \\
\cup - \mid - - \mid \cup - \mid \cup - \\
- \cup \mid - - \mid -\cup \mid -\cup \\
\cup - \mid \cup - \mid \cup - \mid \cup - \\
- \acute{\cup} \mid \cup - \mid - - \mid \cup - \\
- \cup\cup \mid - - \mid -\cup \mid - \\
\cup - \mid \cup - \mid \cup - \mid \cup - \\
\cup\cup\cup \mid \cup - \mid \cup - \mid \cup -
\end{array}
$$

˘ – | ˘ – | ˘ – | ˘ –
˘ – | ˘ – | ˘ – | ˘ –
˘ – | – – | ˘ – ˘ –
˘ – ˘ – ˘ – ˘ –
˘ – ˘ – ˘ – ˘ –
˘ – ˘ – ˘ – ˘ –
– – | ˘ ˘ ˘ | ˘ – ˘ | – ˘
˘ – | ˘ – | – – | ˘ – ˘

VERSE, a Breeze mid blossoms straying,
Where HOPE clung feeding, like a bee—
Both were mine! Life went a maying
     With NATURE, HOPE, and POESY,
        When I was young!   5
When I was young?—Ah, woful WHEN!
Ah for the Change 'twixt Now and Then!
This breathing House not built with hands,
This body that does me grievous wrong,
O'er aery Cliffs and glittering Sands,   10
How lightly *then* it flashed along:—
Like those trim skiffs, unknown of yore,
On winding Lakes and Rivers wide,
That ask no aid of Sail or Oar,
That fear no spite of Wind or Tide!   15
Nought cared this Body for wind or weather
When YOUTH and I liv'd in't together.

FLOWERS are lovely; LOVE is flower-like;
FRIENDSHIP is a sheltering tree;
O the Joys, that came down shower-like,   20
Of FRIENDSHIP, LOVE, and LIBERTY,
        Ere I was old!
Ere I was old?—Ah, woful ERE!
Which tells me, YOUTH's no longer here!

---

1. In MS 3, before writing out his complete metrical analysis, C inserted a stress-mark: "Vérse"; he also added above the line: "? Vērse, ă breeze".

8. The source is St Paul in 2 Cor 5.1: "For we know that if our earthly house of this tabernacle were dissolved, we have a building of God, an house not made with hands, eternal in the heavens."

12–14. Steamships became increasingly common in the 1820s, for pleasure-cruising on the Thames estuary and for cross-channel packets.

O YOUTH! for years so many and sweet,   25
'Tis known, that Thou and I were one,
I'll think it but a fond conceit—
It cannot be, that Thou are gone!
Thy Vesper-bell hath not yet toll'd:—
And thou wert aye a Masker bold!   30
What strange Disguise hast now put on,
To *make believe*, that thou art gone?
I see these Locks in silvery slips,
This drooping Gait, this altered Size:
But SPRINGTIDE blossoms on thy Lips,   35
And Tears take sunshine from thine eyes!
Life is but Thought: so think I will
That YOUTH and I are House-mates still.

593. ALBUM VERSES: "DEWDROPS
ARE THE GEMS OF MORNING"

[1823/Nov 1825–May 1829–Apr 1832]

The lines were first drafted as a continuation beyond the first two parts of **592** *Youth and Age* (cf *CN* IV 4996). But, as C said later, "the poem formed a whole without it: and I must have either made a cheerless conclusion, or a religious one too elevated for the character of the Ode" (see vol II poem **592** TEXT MS 11). He therefore circulated copies of *Youth and Age*, and published it, in two parts only. At the same time, loath to abandon the four or more additional lines he had drafted, he used them as album verses.

The earliest separate form of the verses is the shortest: (*a*) 4–5 lines copied into a notebook, into an album, and as part of a memorandum (vol II poem **592** MSS 2–4 7). (*b*) A second form of the verses, dating from 1828–9, expands them to two quatrains, in one version under the title "Youth and Age". Again they are for album use, although they are oddly gloomy (vol II poem **592** MSS 8–11). (*c*) The third and longest form dates from 1832–3, and comprises 11– 14 lines. C developed the original 4–5 lines to 13, under the title "An Old

37–8. In a ms note on the HRC transcript of MS 3 JDC states: "from the German of Gleim", a source which remains untraced.
38⁺. C's attempt to continue the poem is given below as **593** *"Dewdrops are the Gems of Morning"*. The continuation was published as part of the present poem in *PW* (1834), but probably at HNC's instigation.

Man's Sigh", on one occasion expanding them to 14 lines as a "sonnet" and on another contracting them to 11 (vol II poem **592** TEXTS 12 13 *5* 14 *6*). The 11-line version was printed as a conclusion to *Youth and Age* in *PW* (1834); but in view of C's earlier remarks, it appears likely that this was at HNC's instigation.

All three versions are given below, reproducing poem **592** MSS 4 9 12 respectively.

(*a*) [1823/Nov 1825]

Dewdrops are the Gems of Morning,
But the Tears of mournful Eve:
Where no Hope is, Life's a Warning
That only serves to make us grieve.

(*b*) [May 1829]

Dew-drops are the Gems of Morning,
But the Tears of mournful Eve!
Where no HOPE is, Life's a Warning
That only serves to make us grieve
 When we go tottering down Life's Slope!   5
 And yet, fair Maid! accept this truth,
 Hope leaves not us but we leave Hope,
 And quench the light of inward Youth.

(*c*) [Apr 1832]

Dew-drops are the Gems of Morning,
But the Tears of mournful Eve:
Where no Hope is, Life's a Warning
That only serves to make us grieve,
  In our Old Age!   5
That only serves to make us grieve
With oft and tedious *taking-leave—*
Like a poor related Guest,

1–2. The conceit, though not the movement of the lines, is curiously reminiscent of *Advice to a Lady in Autumn*, ascribed to Lord Chesterfield and quoted by WW in his 1815 Preface (*W Prose* III 37; *The Life of the Late Earl of Chesterfield: or, The Man of the World*—2 vols 1774—II 248–9 var):

The dews of the evening most carefully shun,
They are the tears of the sky for the loss of the sun.

(*c*) **8, 13.** C subsequently amended the phrasing to read "nigh-related" and "total *being*", thereby suggesting an opposition which makes for a more emphatic conclusion.

Who may not rudely be dismiss'd;
Yet hath outstay'd his welcome while,   10
And tells the jest without the smile!
O! might Life *cease*, and selfless *Mind*,
Whose Being is *Act*, alone remain behind!

594. TRANSLATION OF GOETHE: "ONE FRIENDLY WORD . . ."

[Aug 1823–Sept 1824]

The translation was first printed by Thomas Medwin *Journal of the Conversations of Lord Byron . . . in the Years 1821 and 1822* (1824) 282—the text given here. The translation is unsigned, but in his copy of the "New Edition" (also 1824), now at HUL, where the translation appears unchanged on pp 348–9, Medwin noted that it was "by Coleridge". Medwin's editor, Ernest J. Lovell, says "It may be significant that although Goethe's prose [i.e. the letter he wrote following Byron's death, dated Weimar 16 Jul 1824, in which he quotes the poem] was retranslated between the first edition and the New Edition of 1824, his poem was not" (Medwin *Conversations of Lord Byron* ed Lovell 275n). "Although Medwin himself had some German, the lines seem to be of a higher quality than he normally wrote at this time, and he was not, I believe, the kind of man who would attribute to another a translation of his own" (E. J. Lovell to KC 24 Feb 1965).

The translation could well be by C, but the attribution must remain uncertain. If it is correct, C could have acquired the German original from friends of Medwin such as Washington Irving or Thomas Colley Grattan, who saw Medwin's ms before publication; or, more probably, at a later stage in the production of the book, from John Murray.

Goethe originally enclosed his poem in a letter to Byron at Genoa from Weimar, dated 22 Jun 1823. Its background and circumstances are described by E. M. Butler *Byron and Goethe: Analysis of a Passion* (1956) 86–92. Medwin

(c) **12–13.** The last two lines were dropped to make the 11-line version in *PW* (1834). The line added to make the *Bl Mag* "sonnet" was inserted after line 5 of the version given here: "Whose bruised wings quarrel with the bars of the still narrowing cage—". It would be appropriate if the version which W. R. Hamilton heard in Mar 1832 (see poem **592** TEXT MS 11) had the religious conclusion (=lines 12–13?) missing from earlier versions, in view of his admiration for C as a philosopher.

included the German original, with numerous misprints, in an appendix (294; New Edition xiv–xv). The following is a corrected version, together with Miss Butler's translation:

> Ein freundlich Wort kommt eines nach dem andern,
>> Von Süden her und bringt uns frohe Stunden;
> Es ruft uns auf zum Edelsten zu wandern,
>> Nicht ist der Geist, doch ist der Fuß gebunden.

> Wie soll ich dem, den ich so lang begleitet,
>> Nun etwas Traulichs in die Ferne sagen?
> Ihm, der sich selbst im Innersten bestreitet,
>> Stark angewohnt, das tiefste Weh zu tragen.

> Wohl sey ihm doch wenn er sich selbst empfindet!
>> Er wage selbst sich hochbeglückt zu nennen,
> Wenn Musenkraft die Schmerzen überwindet;
>> Und wie ich ihn erkannt mög' er sich kennen.

> One friendly word pursues another hither,
>> Sent from the South, bringing us hours most sweet;
> Noblest of men, his presence lures us hither:
>> Fain is the spirit, fettered are the feet.

> What words of cheer can reach him in the distance,
>> Whom for so long I've watched, nor e'er forgot?
> Who, striving with his inmost self's resistance,
>> Strongly inured, has borne the saddest lot.

> Himself esteeming, may he find relief,
>> And dare to call himself most blest of men,
> When poetry's power conquers his heart's deep grief,
>> And may he know himself (as I do) then!

The English Goethe scholar J. G. Robertson calls the Medwin/?Coleridge translation "hardly a translation at all" (*Goethe and Byron—PEGS* NS 2 1925—70n), but given the essential freedoms of a rhyming verse translation, such as Butler also takes, this seems too hard. Without knowledge of the precise circumstances, "zum Edelsten" does seem obviously to mean to rise to the greatest sublimity rather than to travel to the noblest person, and there is also a case to be made for "etwas Traulichs" meaning "words of love" rather than "words of contempt". When Thomas Moore reprinted yet another translation of Goethe's letter in 1830 (*Letters and Journals of Lord Byron—*2 vols 1830—II 676), he gave the German lines in the original, "as an English version gives but a very imperfect notion of their meaning".

One friendly word comes fast upon another
   From the warm South, bringing communion sweet,—
Calling us amid noblest thoughts to wander
   Free in our souls, though fetter'd in our feet.

How shall I, who so long his bright path traced,   5
   Say to him words of love sent from afar?—
To him who with his inmost heart hath struggled,
   Long wont with fate and deepest woes to war?

May he be happy!—*thus* himself esteeming,
   He well might count himself a favour'd one!   10
By his loved Muses all his sorrows banish'd,
   And he *self-known*,—e'en as to *me* he's known!

595. "KNOW'ST THOU THE LAND . . .?",
FROM GOETHE

[1823–4?]

C's translation of Mignon's song exists in three versions: a ms fair copy, which is reproduced here; a text printed in *Bl Mag* (Sept 1829), which follows the ms version; and a slightly different version of the first stanza only, in *PW* (1834).

The translation might have been made at any time up to late Oct 1824, when C told JG that he had been asked to transcribe it for Sir Alexander Johnston (*CL* v 389). HCR recorded that C was "in raptures" with *Wilhelm Meisters Lehrjahre* in Mar 1813, and that he "repeated *Kennst du das Land* with tears in his eyes" (*CRB* I 124). The apparent echo by Byron in the opening of *The Bride of Abydos* ("Know ye the land where the cypress and myrtle" etc), pub Dec 1813, has no bearing: Byron did not know German and his source was probably ch 28 of Madame de Stael's *L'Allemagne* ("Connais-tu cette terre où les citroniers fleurissent?"). An essay by C's new acquaintance John Anster ("The Faustus of Goethe" *Bl Mag* VII (39)—Jun 1820—235–58) included the first rendering into English of any part of Goethe's poem and in its opening pages made comparisons with **176** *Christabel*, **178** *Kubla Khan*, and **502.X3** *Remorse* (Printed)—perhaps prompting C to turn again to Goethe's poetry; **595.X1** *Verses Sent to John Anster* could in fact be the present poem. "Goethe's Wilhelm Meister" appears in a ms list of literary projects in Oct 1821 (*SW&F— CC*—955). Carlyle presented C with his English translation, *Wilhelm Meister's Apprenticeship*, in Jun 1824; it was reviewed and Mignon's song quoted in *Ed*

Rev XLII (Aug 1825) 409–49 at 428; and C referred to it in *Confessions of an Inquiring Spirit* (*SW&F—CC—*1117).

The original, in J. W. von Goethe *Wilhelm Meisters Lehrjahre* bk 3 ch 1 (4 vols Berlin 1795–6) II 7–8, reads as follows:

> Kennst du das Land? wo die Citronen blühn,
> Im dunkeln Laub die Gold-Orangen glühn,
> Ein sanfter Wind vom blauen Himmel weht,
> Die Myrthe still und hoch der Lorbeer steht.
> Kennst du es wohl?
> > Dahin! Dahin!
> Mögt ich mit dir, o mein Geliebter, ziehn.
>
> Kennst du das Haus? auf Säulen ruht sein Dach,
> Es glänzt der Saal, es schimmert das Gemach,
> Und Marmorbilder stehn und sehn mich an:
> Was hat man dir, du armes Kind, gethan?
> Kennst du es wohl?
> > Dahin! Dahin!
> Mögt ich mit dir, o mein Beschützer, ziehn.
>
> Kennst du den Berg und seinen Wolkensteg?
> Das Maulthier sucht im Nebel seinen Weg,
> In Hölen wohnt der Drachen alte Brut,
> Es stürzt der Fels und über ihn die Fluth.
> Kennst du ihn wohl?
> > Dahin! Dahin!
> Geht unser Weg! o Vater, laß uns ziehn!

Know'st thou the Land where the pale Citrons blow,
And Golden Fruits thro' dark-green foliage glow?
O soft the Gale that breathes from that blue Sky!
Still stand the Myrtles and the Laurels high.
    Know'st thou it well? O thither, Friend!   5
Thither with thee, Beloved! would I wend.

Know'st thou the House? On Columns rests it's Height:
Shines the Saloon: the Chambers glisten bright:
And Marble Figures stand and look at *me*—
Ah thou poor Child! what have they done to thee!   10
    Know'st thou it well? O thither, Friend!
Thither with thee, Protector! would I wend!

Know'st thou the road?—&c—

596. HERACLITUS ON
THE SIBYL'S UTTERANCE

[Mar 1824]

The only known text of the lines is in a marginal note on John Smith *Select Discourses* (1660), in a copy belonging to C. A. Tulk (*CM—CC—*v). C slips from prose to verse, producing a poem without a beginning; the lineation given in the RT below is suggested by the use of capitals in the ms at the beginning of lines 2 and 3 (which do not coincide with C's line-starts). Smith had written: "So the *Sibyll* was noted by Heraclitus ὡς μαινομένῳ στόματι γελαστὰ καὶ ἀκαλλώπιστα φθεγγομένη, *as one speaking ridiculous and unseemly speeches with her furious mouth.*" C commented:

> This fragment misquoted—for γελαστὰ it should be
> αμυριστα, unperfumed—inornate Lays not redolent
> of Art, To win the sense . . .

Lines 4–7 are set out as verse in the ms, and C concludes with the comment "στοματι μαινομένῳ =with ecstatic mouth./"

Smith had, apart from the false reading γελαστὰ "laughable" for ἀγέλαστα "unlaughable", defied the original context in giving this as an example of the pseudo-prophetical spirit combined with mental alienation. For C's own correct and fuller quotation of the Greek from Plutarch *Moralia* 397A, by way of Schleiermacher's *Herakleitos: Museum der Alterthums-Wissenschaft* (2 vols Berlin 1807–10) I 332, see *SM* (*CC*) 26 and fn. He there prefixed another passage from Heraclitus, and translated the one discussed, not over-freely, as "But the SIBYLL with wild enthusiastic mouth shrilling forth unmirthful, inornate, and unperfumed truths reaches to a thousand years with her voice through the power of God." Here C seems to have forgotten that ἀγέλαστα was among the epithets used by Heraclitus.

unperfumed—inornate

Lays not redolent of Art,
To win the sense with flowers of Rhetoric,
Lip-blossoms breathing perishable Sweets—
Yet by the power of the informing WORD   5

4. Lip-blossoms] Not in *OED*. A coinage by C? It is reminiscent of notes addressed to James Gillman the younger, where C refers to Euripides *Orestes* 383 and Isa 57.19 (*CN* IV 5136 f 135ᵛ).

5. informing WORD] C's frequent term for divine revelation, e.g. in *Confessions of an Inquiring Spirit* letter 6 (*SW&F—CC—*1158). The pagans shared its truths to a lesser extent, C maintained.

Roll sounding onward thro' a thousand years
Their deep prophetic Bodements.

597. EXTEMPORE LINES IN NOTEBOOK 28

[Apr 1824]

In the notebook the lines carry the inserted heading "composed extempore, without taking my pen off the paper. Q? Will they stand a second Reading?"; they are dated 24 Apr 1824 (*CN* IV 5146). Lines 1–6 were written on one page, lines 7–10 on the page opposite. The second set of four lines is headed "Item"—in the adverbial Latin meaning, "just so" or "likewise"—and is much revised. The text given here is derived from the notebook.

Whether lines 7–10 are meant to continue lines 1–6 or to replace them, C afterwards appears to have thought of the two sections as separate. He quoted lines 1–6 in a letter, and lines 1–4 were also transcribed by himself and different amanuenses in different revised versions. He recast lines 7–10 for James Keymer's album in Sept 1827, under the heading "The Love that maketh not ashamed", as follows, and they were published in *PW* (1834) under the heading "DESIRE":

> Where true love burns, Desire is Love's pure Flame.
> It is the REFLEX of our earthly Frame.
> That takes it's meaning from the nobler part,
> And but translates the language of the Heart.

It is therefore possible to argue that on reflection C judged the two sets of lines not to cohere at all, and that they amount to two fragments, made up of six and four lines respectively.

An accidental rereading of the lines in 1833 may have prompted C to write **688** *Love's Apparition and Evanishment*, with which they are associated in some early mss (see vol II sec C on that poem).

> Idly we supplicate the Powers above!
> There is no Resurrection for a Love
> That unperturb'd, unshadowed, wanes away
> In the chill'd heart by inward self-decay.
> Poor Mimic of the Past! the Love is o'er,   5
> That must *resolve* to do what did itself of yore.

Desire, of pure Love born, itself's the same:
A Pulse, that animates the outer frame,
It but repeats the life-throb of the Heart—
And takes the impress of the nobler part.   10

598. ALTERNATIVE LINES FOR
CHRISTOPHER HARVEY'S *THE SYNAGOGUE*

[Jun 1824? Feb–Jun 1825?]

Harvey's poem is contained in the 1673 edition bound up with Herbert's *The Temple* (1674) in the copy which C used. C marked lines 5–9 (presumably intending 5–8) of *The Nativity; or, Christmas-day* and wrote his alternative eight lines beside them. The original reads:

> Unfold thy face, unmask thy ray,
> Shine forth, bright sun, double the day.
> Let no malignant misty fume,
> Nor foggy vapour, once presume
> To interpose thy perfect sight
> This day, which makes us love thy light
> For ever better, that we could
> That blessed object once behold.
> Which is both the circumference,
> And centre of all excellence . . .

C also wrote a footnote, keyed by an asterisk to the title of the poem: "The only Poem in this Synagogue which possesses *poetic* merit. With a few changes & additions this would be a striking Poem" (*CM—CC*—II 1044–5).

> To sheath or blunt one happy Ray
> That wins new splendor from the Day.
> This Day that gives thee power to rise
> And shine on Hearts as well as Eyes,
> This Birth-day of all Souls when first   5
> On Eyes of Flesh & Blood did burst—

9–10. First drafted in reverse order, and then marked by C for transposition.

1. Harvey's lines 3–4 must be supposed to precede C's fragmentary first sentence.

That primal, great lucific Light
That Rays to thee, to us gave Sight.

599. THE DELINQUENT TRAVELLERS

[Oct–Nov 1824?]

The only known text is provided by *PW* (EHC) I 443–7, from a ms formerly in the possession of J. H. Green. EHC supplies the date 1824, but does not say whether this information is present in the ms. The allusions in lines 3 and 105 et seq might confirm such a date and suggest that the poem was written late that year, while C was at Ramsgate. The allusions to Ramsgate on their own do not date the poem exactly, since C was there so often, first in 1819 and last in 1833.

Some are home-sick—some two or three,
Their third year on the Arctic Sea—
Brave Captain Lyon tells us so—
Spite of those charming Esquimaux.
But O, what scores are sick of Home,   5
Agog for Paris or for Rome!
Nay! tho' contented to abide,
You should prefer your own fireside;
Yet since grim War has ceas'd its madding,
And Peace has set John Bull agadding,   10
'Twould such a vulgar taste betray,
For very shame you must away!
"What? not yet seen the coast of France!
The folks will swear, for lack of bail,
You've spent your last five years in jail!"   15

title. Complaints against the hectic fashion for travel once Europe opened up following the Napoleonic Wars were common at the time; cf e.g. Mary Shelley in *Westminster Review* VI (Oct 1826) 325–41.

3. Captain Lyon] *The Private Journal of Captain G. F. Lyon of the H.M.S. Hecla, during the Recent Voyage of Discovery under Captain Parry* (1824) 440–1. C was evidently struck by Lyon's frank enjoyment of the manners and conduct of Eskimo women, and he refers again to the "charms" of the most prominent among them in **609** *Captain Parry* 12.

Keep moving! Steam, or Gas, or Stage,
Hold, cabin, steerage, hencoop's cage—
Tour, Journey, Voyage, Lounge, Ride, Walk,
Skim, Sketch, Excursion, Travel-talk—
For move you must! 'Tis now the rage,   20
The law and fashion of the Age.
If you but perch, where Dover tallies,
So strangely with the coast of Calais,
With a good glass and knowing look,
You'll soon get matter for a book!   25
Or else, in Gas-car, take your chance
Like that adventurous king of France,
Who, once, with twenty thousand men
Went up—and then came down again;
At least, he moved if nothing more: 30
And if there's nought left to explore,
Yet while your well-greased wheels keep spinning,
The traveller's honoured name you're winning,
And, snug as Jonas in the Whale,
You may loll back and dream a tale.   35
Move, or be moved—there's no protection,
Our Mother Earth has ta'en the infection—
(That rogue Copernicus, 'tis said
First put the whirring in her head,)
A planet She, and can't endure   40
T'exist without her annual Tour:
The *name* were else a mere misnomer,
Since Planet is but Greek for *Roamer*.
The atmosphere, too, can do no less
Than ventilate her emptiness,   45
Bilks turn-pike gates, for no one cares,
And gives herself a thousand airs—
While streams and shopkeepers, we see,
Will have their run toward the sea—
And if, meantime, like old King Log,   50
Or ass with tether and a clog,

---

26. Gas-car] The hydrogen balloon, which quickly became a fad after it first flew in France in 1783, takes on board the Grand Old Duke of York and his 20,000 men from the nursery-rhyme.

50. King Log rules in peace and quietness, without making his power felt, as in Aesop's fable of the frogs.

Must graze at home! to yawn and bray
"I guess we shall have rain to-day!"
Nor clog nor tether can be worse
Than the dead palsy of the purse.   55
Money, I've heard a wise man say,
Makes herself wings and flys away:
Ah! would She take it in her head
To make a pair for me instead!
At all events, the Fancy's free,   60
No traveller so bold as she.
From Fear and Poverty released
I'll saddle Pegasus, at least,
And when she's seated to her mind,
I within I can mount behind: 65
And since this outward I, you know,
Must stay because he cannot go,
My fellow-travellers shall be they
Who go because they cannot stay—
Rogues, rascals, sharpers, blanks and prizes,   70
Delinquents of all sorts and sizes,
Fraudulent bankrupts, Knights burglarious,
And demireps of means precarious—
All whom Law thwarted, Arms or Arts,
Compel to visit foreign parts,   75
All hail! No compliments, I pray,
I'll follow where you lead the way!
But ere we cross the main once more,
Methinks, along my native shore,
Dismounting from my steed I'll stray   80
Beneath the cliffs of Dumpton Bay,
Where, Ramsgate and Broadstairs between,
Rude caves and grated doors are seen:
And here I'll watch till break of day,
(For Fancy in her magic might   85
Can turn broad noon to starless night!)
When lo! methinks a sudden band

81 Dumpton Bay] The village of Dumpton, near Ramsgate, is set back from the sea, which is accessible at Dumpton Gap. The caves on this stretch of coast and the tracks leading by way of grated doors to the beaches at gaps in the cliffs were notoriously used by smugglers as well as for more legitimate purposes.

Of smock-clad smugglers round me stand.
Denials, oaths, in vain I try,
At once they gag me for a spy,   90
And stow me in the boat hard by.
Suppose us fairly now afloat,
Till Boulogne mouth receives our Boat.
But, bless us! what a numerous band
Of cockneys anglicise the strand!   95
Delinquent bankrupts, leg-bail'd debtors,
Some for the news, and some for letters—
With hungry look and tarnished dress,
French shrugs and British surliness.
Sick of the country for their sake   100
Of them and France *French leave* I take—
And lo! a transport comes in view
I hear the merry motley crew,
Well skill'd in pocket to make entry,
Of Dieman's Land the elected Gentry,   105
And founders of Australian Races.—
The Rogues! I see it in their faces!
Receive me, Lads! I'll go with you,
Hunt the black swan and kangaroo,
And that New Holland we'll presume   110
Old England with some elbow-room.
Across the mountains we will roam,
And each man make himself a home:
Or, if old habits ne'er forsaking,
Like clock-work of the Devil's making,   115
Ourselves inveterate rogues should be,
We'll have a virtuous progeny;
And on the dunghill of our vices
Raise human pine-apples and spices.

102. This shows that C's proposed companions are transported criminals, although Edward Eager made the economic viability of settling Van Diemen's Land and New South Wales a topical issue in 1824. His arguments were presented by W. C. Wentworth *A Statistical Account of the British Settlements in Australasia* II (1824) and, separately, as *Letters to the Rt. Hon. Robert Peel* (1824); they were discussed extensively over the next few years in parliamentary committees on emigration. In Oct 1824 J. H. Frere, then in Malta, seriously proposed that the majority of his family should emigrate with him to Van Diemen's Land (*Works* I clxxxv).

Of all the children of John Bull   12(
With empty heads and bellies full,
Who ramble East, West, North and South,
With leaky purse and open mouth,
In search of varieties exotic
The usefullest and most patriotic,   12⁵
And merriest, too, believe me, Sirs!
Are your Delinquent Travellers!

600. TO MISS JONES (OR MISS A—— T.)

[1824? 1830?]

These album verses exist in three slightly different versions. The version repro-
duced here was copied out for a Miss Jones—probably the daughter of a family
C met frequently at Ramsgate in the 1820s—on 1 Sept 1830. The other two ver-
sions are transcripts, both connected with Highgate circles and both later than
the version to Miss Jones. One of them is addressed to "Miss A—— T."—who
might be the daughter of Sir Coutts Trotter, whom C also met at Ramsgate, or
perhaps a daughter of C. A. Tulk, or else the sister of JG's assistant Mr Taylor.
See further vol II sec A.

Verse, Picture, Music, Thoughts both grave and gay,
Remembrances of dear Friends far away,
On a pure ground of virgin White display'd—
Such should thy ALBUM be: for such art thou, fair Maid!

4. art] C mistakenly wrote "are";   transcripts.
the correct form is given in the two

601. ADAPTATION OF DANIEL'S
TO THE LADY MARGARET,
COUNTESS OF CUMBERLAND

[1824?]

The three lines serve as an epigraph to *Aids to Reflection*, where they are ascribed to "DANIEL." The first two adapt the opening of stanza 10 of Samuel Daniel's poem to the countess of Cumberland (*Poetical Works* II 355), a composition whose rhymes and metre had attracted C during 1807–8 (*CN* II 2224 f 85ᵛ, 3210); C substitutes "This" for Daniel's "Which". The third line derives from a couplet which C copied from Crashaw c 1807 (*CN* II 3103; cf *An Apology for the Precedent Hymn* in *B Poets* IV 722), and which, substituting "his" for Crashaw's "hers", he first considered might constitute an epigraph by itself (BM MS Egerton 2801 f 262ᵛ):

> What Soul so e'er in any language can
> Speak Heaven like his, is my Soul's Countryman.

John Beer suggests that the third line might also have been influenced by a sentence from Böhme (*AR—CC*—2n).

C previously adapted Daniel for epigraphs in the 1818 *Friend*: see poems **548, 550, 552.** He also used stanza 12 of the same poem to the countess of Cumberland, without modification, as an epigraph to essay 14 of *The Friend* (*CC* I 100).

> This makes, that whatsoever here befalls,
> You in the region of yourself remain,
> Neighb'ring on Heaven: and that no foreign land.

602. LINES ON EDWARD IRVING

[1824?]

C's lines conclude a footnote in *AR* (1825) (*CC*) 378fn, in which he opposes Mant and D'Oyly on Infant Baptism. "But *you*, honored IRVING, are as little disposed, as myself, to favor *such* doctrine!"

Edward Irving (1792–1834), Carlyle's friend and a brilliant preacher, met C shortly after his arrival in London in 1822. C went to hear him preach in Jul 1823 (*CL* V 280: to C. Brent 7 Jul 1823; 286–7: to EC 23 Jul 1823), and they were meeting regularly by Jun 1824 (*CL* v 368: to Mrs C. Aders 3 Jun 1824; 369: to B. Montagu 8 Jun [1824]; to H. Taylor 8 Jun 1824; etc). Irving dedicated *For Missionaries after the Apostolical School* to C in 1825, where he expressed deep obligations: "you have been more profitable to my faith in the orthodox doctrine, to my spiritual understanding of the Word of God, and to my right conception of the Christian Church, than any or all of the men with whom I have entertained friendship and conversation". KC reviews C's relations with Irving during the period 1822–6 in *CN* IV 4963n; and C's later, changing attitude towards his "zealous but sadly mistaken friend" (Notebook 48 = BM Add MS 47543 f 42ᵛ; *CN* v) can be traced in his annotations (*CM—CC*—III 3–74; 415–82).

The echo of **289** *A Letter to* —— 308–12 and **293** *Dejection: An Ode* 59–63 is significant. Substituting Irving for SH, C also substitutes an idea of God for what he earlier called Joy. Cf his use of **180** *The Nightingale* 40–1, a passage which is similarly turned in a different direction.

> Friend pure of heart and fervent! we have learnt
> A different lore! We may not thus profane
> The Idea and Name of Him whose absolute Will
> *Is* Reason—Truth Supreme!—Essential Order!

603. EPIGRAM: "SUCH AS IT IS"

[1824–34?]

The only known version of the epigram is a printed fragment preserved at VCL, subscribed "S. T. C." The only clue to the identity of the journal or album in which the epigram was printed is a 23-line fragment of blank verse printed on the reverse:

> "Listen with patience to the poor man's story:
> 'Tis true that war has seen their thousands bleed,
> That one might triumph by the glorious deed;
> And thousands now in pain resign their health,
> That one may wallow in enormous wealth:
> The sallow spinner, amid ceaseless noise,
> Day after day, a chronic life employs;
> Grown old at forty, quick his temples beat
> With fever raging from excess of heat:
> The faithful wife his degradation shares,
> Lighten'd, forsooth, of her domestic cares—

For all her children now the fact'ries claim,
Not e'en excepting those of tender frame.
What cause remains of animating joy,
To bless the spirits of the blooming boy?
He blooms no longer—see his pallid cheek
And meagre form the cruel change bespeak!
His auburn locks with flakes of cotton mix'd,
And the dull eye in vacant ignorance fix'd.
In fields once clothed with nature's favourite green,
Luxuriant verdure now is seldom seen:
Black clouds of smoke in thickest volumes fly,
Darken the scene and shade yon azure sky.["]

The fragment ends thus at the bottom of a page. It might be thought to echo *The Excursion* VIII 306–32 (*WPW* v 275–6).

A preaches,
"'Tis right to try to fill your place,
Whate'er your station be, or age."

B responds,
"*This* verse is right, if that's the case,
For it exactly fills the page."

604. ALBUM VERSES ON ORIGINAL SIN

[1824–34?]

The only known text is a newspaper or magazine cutting pasted into AG's copy of *SL*, which is now at Stanford. The only clue as to the origin of the scrap is that it is formatted in columns some 6.5 cm wide; it might well date from several decades after C's death. The lines are introduced as follows: "The following was written by Coleridge, on a lady asking him for something original:—"

You ask me for something that's novel,
And I scarcely know how to begin;
For I've nothing original in me,
Excepting original sin.

605. LINES ON J. F. MECKEL'S
SYSTEM DER VERGLEICHENDEN ANATOMIE

[Jan 1825]

The lines are written on what must be a detached flyleaf of vol I of the book by Meckel published at Halle in 1821. It is now in NYPL, although the whereabouts of the book itself and of the following volumes is not known (cf *CM—CC*—III 841–2). C's lines conclude a paragraph in which he expresses his surprise at finding, "in the work of a *German* Physiologist to the Fact, which was to be referred, laid down as the Principle, from which it is to be *deduced:* and thus the Problem itself metaphrased into it's own Solution". The note refers in particular to the second and third pages of Meckel's preface (pp vi–vii of the book).

O these facts! these facts!
Of *such* facts I'm aweary
Light I can get none—
For all my eye is mere eye!
My Eye and Betty Martin!   5
And that's a fact for sartain!

606. WORK WITHOUT HOPE

[Feb 1825]

C drafted the poem in a notebook entry, with the following introduction couched in the form of a letter (*CN* IV 5192 var; cf *CL* V 414–16: to an unknown correspondent 21 Feb 1825):

21 Feb. 1825.—My dear Friend
I have often amused my ~~fancy~~ self with the thought of a self-conscious Looking-glass, and the various metaphorical applications of such a fancy— and this morning ~~I~~it struck across ~~my~~ the Eolian Harp of my Brain that there was something pleasing and emblematic (of what I did not distinctly

---

5. For references to C's use of this oath, and a fallacious interpretation of it in Protestant terms, see **525** ΕΓΩΕΝΚΑΙΠΑΝ 12–13EC.

6. C used the same rhyme in May 1808: "Martin | ~~Has~~ Is *sense* for sartain" (*CN* III 3335).

make out) in two ⟨such⟩ Looking-glasses fronting, each seeing the other in itself, and itself in the other.—Have you ever noticed the Vault or snug little Apartment which the Spider spins and weaves for itself, by spiral threads round and round, and sometimes with strait lines, in so that it's Lurking-parlour or Withdrawing-room is an oblong square? This too connected itself in my mind with the melancholy truth, that as we grow older, the World (alas! how often it happens, that the less we love it, the more we care for it; the less reason we have to value it's Shews, the more anxious ⟨are⟩ we about them!—and ⟨alas! how often do⟩ we become more and more loveless, the more this as Love, which can outlive all change save a change with regard to itself, and all loss save the loss of it's *Reflex*, is more needed to sooth us & alone ⟨is⟩ able so to do!)

What was I saying:—O—I was adverting ⟨to⟩ the fact, that ⟨as⟩ we advance in years, the World, that *spidery* Witch, spins it's threads closing narrower and narrower, still closing in on us, till at last it shuts us up within four walls, walls of flues and films, and windowless—and well if there be sky-lights, and a small opening left for the Light from above. I do not know that I have anything to add, except perhaps to remind you, that *pheer* or *phere* for *Mate, Companion, Counterpart,* is a word frequently used by Spencer, G. Herbert, and the Poets generally, who wrote before the Restoration (1660)—before I say, that this premature warm and sunny day, antedating Spring, called forth the following

Strain in the manner of G. HERBERT—: which might be entitled, THE ALONE MOST DEAR: a Complaint of Jacob to Rachel as in the tenth year of his Service he saw in her and or *fancied* that he saw Symptoms of Alienation. N.B. The Thoughts and Images being modernized and turned into *English.*

In the notebook draft version the poem is twice as long as the text given below. Disregarding the abortive drafts and cancellations, it continues and concludes (albeit in unfinished form) as follows:

> I speak in figures, inward thoughts and woes
> Interpreting by Shapes and Outward Shews.
> Where daily nearer me, with magic Ties,
> What time and where (Wove close with
> Line over line & thickning as they rise)
> The World her spidery thread on all sides spun
> Side answ'ring Side with narrow interspace,
> My Faith (say, I: I and my Faith are one)
> Hung, as a Mirror there! And face to face
> (For nothing else there was, between or near)
> One Sister Mirror hid the dreary Wall.
> But *That* is broke! And with that bright Compeer

I lost my Object and my inmost All—
Faith *in* the Faith of THE ALONE MOST DEAR!
                                    JACOB HODIERNUS

The poem was published in its 14-line form in *The Bijou for 1828*, without
C's permission, and thereafter in the three editions of *PW*. The differences
between the texts are few but significant. In particular, the footnote was dropped
from the printed texts, and the three collected editions incorporate the date 1827
into the title. These two changes are connected, as line 7EC explains. The present
text is from the notebook.

The prose introduction and the unfinished continuation provide a context
which give the 14-line published poem a different meaning. AG identified her-
self with Rachel to C's Jacob, which throws light on the poem as a "Complaint"
(see *CN* IV 5184n for further references to C as a "Jacob of Today"): having
resided at Highgate for almost nine years, C saw or fancied he saw "Symptoms
of Alienation". He had come to connect the image of the nourishing fountain
with her, as he had previously with SH and the Wordsworths; cf **277** *Inscription
for a Fountain on a Heath* headnote. It may be no accident that 21 Feb is the
anniversary of a "heart-wringing Letter" from SH, received over twenty years
before, "that put Despair into my Heart, and not merely as a Lodger, I fear, but
as a Tenant for Life" (*CN* II 1912). The word *pheer* does not appear in the draft
verses, despite C's careful explanation, although he previously used it at **161**
The Rime of the Ancient Mariner (1798) 189 (probably deriving it from WW's
beginning of *The Three Graves*: cf *WEPF* 861.57; also *RX* 577–8 n 106).

The curtailed 14-line version has the form of a sonnet in which octet and
sestet have been reversed and the rhyme-scheme loosened, but its transitions
are sudden without an explanatory context. The theme of Work without Hope,
separated from The Alone Most Dear, is more resonant and general; but the
feeling left to hold it together is more generalised and obscure. Poem **289** *A
Letter to* —— is revised into **293** *Dejection: An Ode* in a similar way. C's
footnote emphasises a literary dimension and thereby disguises further aspects
of the personal; that is, it makes "work" central at the expense of disappointed
"hope". He leaves us to recall that the English name for the common garden-
plant *Amaranthus caudatus* is "love-lies-(a)-bleeding". The 14-line version pro-
voked answers from HC and SC: see HC *Poems* (Leeds 1833) 118 and Griggs
Coleridge Fille 166; also Bradford Keyes Mudge *Sara Coleridge, A Victorian
Daughter: Her Life and Essays* (New Haven 1989) 176–7.

All Nature seems at work. Slugs leave their lair;
The Bees are stirring; Birds are on the wing;

2. Cf the last stanza of George Her-
bert's *Praise I* and stanza 5 of his *Em-
ployment I*. C was reading Herbert in
Jun 1824 and Feb–Jun 1826 (*CM*—

CC—II 1032–3). Among other influ-
ences on the poem, Quarles's Emblem
No 12 ("What, never fill'd? Be thy
lips skrew'd so fast") is important.

And 𝔚𝔦𝔫𝔱𝔢𝔯 slumb'ring in the open air
Wears on his smiling face a dream of Spring.
And I, the while, the sole unbusy Thing, 5
Nor honey make, nor pair, nor build, nor sing.

Yet well I ken the banks, where *Amaranths blow,
Have traced the fount whence streams of Nectar flow.
Bloom, O ye Amaranths! bloom for whom ye may—
For Mc ye bloom not! Glide, rich Streams! away! 10
With lips unbrighten'd, wreathless Brow, I stroll:
And would you learn the Spells, that drowse my Soul?
WORK without Hope draws nectar in a sieve;
And HOPE without an Object cannot live.

* *Literally* rendered is Flower Fadeless, or never-fading—from the Greek—*a*
not and *mMaraino* to wither.

Curiously, C expressed the same feelings in the same images, citing Herbert and Quarles, in a letter to Lady Beaumont written on 18 Apr [Mar] 1826 (*CL* VI 571–3).

7fn. The footnote is addressed to a person who may be unaware of the derivation of amaranth (a poetic commonplace: see e.g. **623** *The Improvisatore* 56), although C may well have had in mind Hazlitt's lament on his literary achievement in *The Spirit of the Age*: "Instead of gathering fruits and flowers, immortal fruits and amaranthine flowers" (*H Works* XI 37). Hazlitt's book was published in 1825, but had in fact been available since Nov 1824 (see Herschel Baker *William Hazlitt*—Cambridge, Mass 1962—433n); indeed, the essays were written by Apr 1824 (Geof-frey Keynes *Bibliography of William Hazlitt*—2nd ed 1981—89).

Cf **557** *Distich, Written in February 1819* headnote for suggestions of another context in which Hazlitt's animosity, expressed in similar images of bees and honey, is linked to C's own creative failure.

11. unbrighten'd, wreathless] Both words are characteristic Coleridgean coinages, those ending in -*less* being particularly common in his verse. Cf **84** *To a Young Ass* 30 "ribless"; **85** *Lines on a Friend Who Died of a Frenzy Fever* 43 "graspless"; **139** *The Destiny of Nations* 237 "provisionless"; **262.X1** *CPic* IV iv 40 "planless"; **300** *The Picture* 40 "dropless"; **412** *The Pang More Sharp than All* 3 "warmthless"; **478** *Limbo* 5 "scytheless".

607. THE THREE SORTS OF FRIENDS

[1825?]

The only surviving text, a holograph fair copy, is accompanied by a note from C to JG:

> My dear Gillman,
>   The ground and "Materiel" of this division of one's friends into *Ac-Con-* and *In*-quaintance was given by Hartley Coleridge, when he was scarcely five years old. On some one asking him, if Anny Sealy (a little girl, he went to school with) was an Acquaintance of his, he replied very fervently, pressing his right hand on his heart—No! She is an Å *In*quaintance."—Well! tis a Father's Ttale!"—& the recollection soothes your old Friend & *In*quaintance
>
> S. T. Coleridge

If the event celebrated in the verses took place when HC was 5, that was in late 1801–early 1802. C recalled HC's distinction for Mrs Morgan in 1813 (*CL* III 456; cf *CN* III 4237 f 39ᵛ). The present ms must date from after C's meeting with JG in 1816, perhaps several years after, since C describes himself as "your old Friend". ELG suggests May 1825 (*CL* v 466n), on the basis of a transcript to be found in a copy of *AR* (1825), but the connection between the transcript and the book appears to be fortuitous.

Tho' Friendships differ endless *in degree*,
The *Sorts*, methinks, may be reduced to Three:
*Ac*quaintance many; and *Con*quaintance few;
But for *In*quaintance I know only two,
The Friend, I've mourn'd with, and the Maid, I woo!   5

608. LINES ON THE MOSS BEE, BOMBYX MUSCORUM

[May 1825]

C drafted the lines in Notebook 29 (*CN* IV 5220), the "glossy Scales" being the chaff from the base of the leaves of the beech-tree, "on the ⟨rich dark⟩ green Moss-carpet—". The entry continues in prose on the subject of bees. *CN* IV 4879 reflects a similar interest.

The glossy Scales that gay as living Things
Dance in the Winnow of the Moss-bees' wings
That hovers o'er the Moss beneath the Beech
Then renews his *routing* toil
Delving & tearing up
With head & *sturdy* thighs—.

5

609. CAPTAIN PARRY

[Oct 1825]

The poem was published in *The News of Literature and Fashion* over the initials "S. T. C." Another poem was published over the same initials in the same magazine (**611** *The Booksellers*), which EHC accepted (*PW*—EHC—II 973 No 74), and C wrote other verses which draw on the travel journals of Captains Parry and Lyon (**599** *The Delinquent Travellers* 3). Nevertheless, an element of doubt remains concerning C's authorship, and the notes in particular read as if they might have come from a different pen. Parry was a common subject of mock humour: cf *Ode to Captain Parry* in [Thomas Hood] *Odes and Addresses to Great People* (1825) 91–102, which shares several features of style with the present poem.

William Parry (1790–1855) was the brother of Charles and Frederick Parry, C's companions at Göttingen. An Arctic explorer, who rose eventually to the rank of rear-admiral, he sailed on his third expedition to discover the North-west Passage on 8 May 1824, in the *Hecla* accompanied by the *Fury*. The *Fury* had to be abandoned in Jul–Aug 1825, and Parry returned to England on the *Hecla*. His appointment as acting hydrographer on 1 Dec 1823 was confirmed after his return to England, on 22 Nov 1825. In Oct 1826 he married Isabella Louisa, a daughter of Lord Stanley of Alderley (the Stanley family name was Smith Stanley: the Miss Brown of line 4 is a deliberate mistake). For further evidence of C's interest in William Parry see also *CM* (*CC*) I 204, III 989. He makes an appearance in **637** *Written in William Upcott's Album* 1 and **697** *Other Lines on Lady Mary Shepherd* 7.

All but the first of Parry's books were published in an identical handsome format by John Murray, who was especially keen to publish voyages and travels. He paid Parry 1,000 guineas for an account of the first voyage, published in 1821 (Samuel Smiles *A Publisher and his Friends*—2 vols 1891—II 99), and he published an Appendix to it and a *Second Voyage*, as well as G. F. Lyon's *Private Journal . . . during the Recent Voyage of Discovery under Captain Parry*, all in 1824. The publisher of *The News of Literature and Fashion* was

Archibald Constable, who was in competition with Murray. C appears to have been in his company in late 1825.

> "The *basin* and the *pole*."
> LESLEIUS apud. *Crit. Edin.*

Captain Parry! (*a*) Captain Parry!
    Welcome from the Polar Sea:
Now, I hope, thou'rt come to marry
    Miss Brown (*b*)—if she'll marry thee.

Captain Parry! Captain Parry!   5
    For a husband now thou'lt do;
In the ice thou'st left thy *Fury* (*c*),
    But thy *Fire* (*d*) came safely through.

Captain Parry! Captain Parry!
    Thou hast had the devil's luck,   10
Spite the gifted Secretary (*e*),
    And the charms of Eligluck (*f*).

(*a*) He has returned.
(*b*) Flirtations last year.
(*c*) Fury lost in the ice.
(*d*) Hecla come home.
(*e*) Barrow?
(*f*) The Esquimaux witch and hydrographess.

epigraph. The epigraph apparently refers to John Leslie's anonymous article "Polar Ice, and a North-west Passage" *Ed Rev* xxx (Jun 1818) 1–59; Leslie describes the background to what Parry was attempting. On p 39 he refers to the "basin" of the ice-covered higher latitudes.

11fn. Sir John Barrow (1764–1848) was Secretary of the Admiralty, and a prolific writer on multifarious subjects. The reference in a later stanza (lines 25–8) is explained by the fact that all of Parry's books were published by authority of the Admiralty.

Barrow was of lowly Yorkshire origins, and his ram's horn might refer to sheep and shepherding.

12 and fn. The name is misspelt and two persons are conflated. Iligliak (Lyon) or Iligliuk (Parry) evidently impressed both English captains by her superior intelligence, her vivacity, and her candour, although they eventually became disenchanted. Both describe her skill at drawing accurate charts: Lyon 160 describes her as "hydrographer", and Parry gives examples facing pp 197 and 198. The accuracy of her charts was confirmed

Captain Parry! Captain Parry!
    Thou hast proved an honest man:
Found a passage for thy wherry—   15
    Just a passage—home again (*g*).

Captain Parry! Captain Parry!
    Thy vocation stops not here:
Thou must dine with Mr. Murray,
    And a quarto (*h*) must appear.   20

Mr. Murray! Mr. Murray!
    Order beef and order wine:
Croc. (*i*) and Par. (*k*) and Secretary,
    Inter alios, ask to dine.

Secretary! Secretary!   25
    Through St. Giles' thy ram's-horn blow:
"Quick! a book for Mr. Murray,
    At a crown (*l*) a page, or so!"

Starving Paddies! Craving Paddies!
    Bustle, bustle every rump;   30
To the work at once, my laddies,
    Ne'er a pen, and ne'er a stump.

(*g*) "An honest man returns by the same road."—*Aph. Vet.*
(*h*) Grand object of these expeditions.
(*i*) ?   (*k*) ?
(*l*) This comes of the division of labour.

---

by the chief sorcerer of the same Eskimo tribe, Eewerat (Lyon) or Ewerat (Parry). Lyon 160 describes him as their other hydrographer, and Parry gives a sample of his work facing p 252.

16fn. The proverb (*Aph. Vet.* = "Ancient Aphorism") appears to have been invented; though cf the superstition whereby one has to leave a house by the entrance one has used to come in.

20fn. It might be noted that the epigram by C later in the same journal (poem **611**) is on the same theme of authors and publishers.

23fnn. Croc. is probably Crofton Croker, Secretary to the Lords of the Admiralty. Murray was in touch with him concerning the publication of Parry (Par.)'s voyages (Smiles *A Publisher and his Friends* II 99–100).

Hatching Paddies, Patching Paddies!
Bustle, bustle every one:
Papers, paste, and scissors, laddies:—   35
Paddies, cease,—the book is done.

610. LINES ON RAMSGATE WEATHER

[Nov 1825]

C quoted the lines near the beginning of a letter to JG of 13 Nov 1825 (*CL* v 511), introducing them with: "This most unramsgatish, this obdurate Weather *ipso Novembre Novembrius*[1]—thank God! it is no longer *this*!" He continues after the poem by anticipating a change for the better, "and that we shall have a Spell of the *right Ramsgate*—dry, bracing, cheerful." In fact, at the same time the previous year the weather was even more stormy at Ramsgate (see *CL* v 396–402: to JG 23 Nov 1824 and [26 Nov 1824]).

The ms contains cancellations and insertions, as if the lines were improvised. The allusion in line 4 and fn is to Juvenal *Satires* 6.246–7 "Endromidas Tyrias . . . Quis Nescit?" tr "Who does not know of [women's] Tyrian cloaks?" The endromis was a coarse woollen cloak in which athletes wrapped themselves, and Juvenal was attacking unfeminine women.

Old Mother Damnable on the Sky-Top
Wringing her Dish-clouts or twirling her Mop/
Or astride on her Broom-stick, a notable Roarer
    With her grim duffel Cloak (*vide* Juvenal's Satires)*
Be-trimmd and be-flounced with it's own Rags & Tatters   5
Blown over her head and streaming before her
She gallop'd away, on the scent of the Booty,
    Right over the Deck
        Of a Goodwin sands Wreck
To stop the poor Soul that had not paid the Duty.   10

* Q[y] Why?

1. C's line mingles echoes of the nursery rhymes *Old Mother Hubbard* and *Bye Baby Bunting* ("in the tree-top").

[1] Tr "more Novembrish than November itself".

611. THE BOOKSELLERS

[Late 1825]

The lines, subscribed "S. T. C.", are quoted as the epigraph to an unsigned essay entitled "The Booksellers", in *The News of Literature and Fashion* (10 Dec 1825). C appears to have been in the company of the publisher of the magazine, Archibald Constable, in late 1825, and the doggerel stanzas on Captain Parry were published in the same magazine on 22 Oct, also over his initials (poem **609**). The lines are included in *PW* (EHC) II 973 No 74, but conclusive proof of C's authorship is none the less lacking.

> "A heavy wit shall hang at every lord:"
> So sung Dan Pope; but 'pon my word,
> He was a story teller,
> Or else the times have altered quite,
> For wits, or heavy now, or light,   5
> Hang each by a bookseller.

612. "HE GAVE THEM BUT ONE HEART BETWEEN THEM"

[1825–8]

The lines are drafted in C's hand on the reverse of a scrap of paper which appears to date from 1825 or after (see *SW&F—CC—*1409–10). The opening gave him particular trouble, and the poem appears never to have been copied again or published.

> Tis passing strange—And stranger still
> That use your very best endeavor
> And watch as closely as you will
> Or him or her, you never ever

1[1]. Pope *The Dunciad* (1742) IV   Wit".
132 "A heavy Lord shall hang at ev'ry

Can hit by chance or by surprize   5
A time when either is without it—
So pleasing seen thro' face & eyes,
No soul, that has a heart, can doubt it—

Yet never the less, that so it is
You easily may learn—   10
Ask either for it, you'll strait be told
The other has it in his keeping.

613. LINES TO ELIZA

[Jan–Mar 1826? 1827?]

When C drafted a version of the first poem on the reverse of a leaf containing a
meditation "Of States in which the Will is the predominant Factor" (*SW&F—
CC*—1207–9), he wrote at the head of the page "To Eliza Nixon coming with
a gift of Celandines for me." The poem was given its own heading "Imitation",
and was preceded by the following lines:

Dulcia dona, mihi tu mittis semper, Elisa!
Sweet gifts to me thou sendest always Eliza!
    Et quicquid mittis THURA putare decet
And whatever thou sendest, Sabean odour to think it-behoves-me

The above adapted from an Epigram of Claudians, by substituting THURA
for Mella: the original Distich being in return for a Present of Honey.

The couplet, written in the same ms, is preceded by another Latin distich com-
posed by C himself and a literal translation:

Semper, Elisa! mihi tu suaveolentia donas:
    Nam quicquid donas, te redolere puto.

Always, Eliza! to me things-of-sweet-odor thou presentest:
    For whatever thou presentest, I fancy redolent of thyself.

The second ms of the two poems, given below, is a fair copy on a leaf containing
other verses, and is entitled "To E. A. in return for a present of Eau de Cologne."
    Eliza Nixon in the title of the first ms lived with her father at No 3 The
Grove, and C had been on friendly terms with them since at least 1821 (*CL*
v 186: to JG 31 Oct 1821). They became next-door neighbours in 1823 when
the Gillmans moved to The Grove, and their gardens were contiguous, as C
describes in *CN* IV 5428. She took C a more elaborate bouquet during his last

illness, but he had lost his sense of smell (*CL* VI 984: 14 Jun 1834). The original epigram to which C refers is No 32 of Claudian's shorter poems, *Ad Maximum qui ei mel misit* (tr Platnauer—LCL—II 187). C made a literal version of the same epigram for Henry Gillman to translate back into Latin during the period May–Sept 1825: see **607.X1** *Latin Elegiac Verse Lessons*; *SW&F* (*CC*) 1237–8. Here he has substituted "mittis semper, Eliza" for "mittis, Maxime, semper" as well as "THURA" for "mella". The hyphens used to link the English words translating one Latin word suggest that this too may have begun as a draft for a lesson.

E. A. in the title of the second ms is Mrs Elizabeth Aders, who married Charles Aders in Jul 1820 (*CL* V 129–30n) and was a frequent recipient and subject of poems. She was the daughter of the engraver Raphael Smith. Alexander Gilchrist describes her as "a beautiful and accomplished lady, of much conversational power, able to hold her own with the gifted men who were in the habit of frequenting her house" (*Life of William Blake*—2 vols 1863—I 337). Further references to her and her husband are given in *CL* V 129–30n and *CM* (*CC*) II 179–80. She visited Highgate, and C visited the Aderses, on many occasions; and the friendship evidently continued to the end of his life (cf *CL* VI 955–7: to C. Aders 18 Aug 1833 and 968–71: to Mrs C. Aders [Nov 1833?] with **688** *Love's Apparition and Evanishment*, **693** *S.T.C.*, and **694** *S. T. Coleridge, Ætat Suae 63*). Particularly significant, perhaps, are her visits to Highgate in Jan 1826, at a time when C had promised to work especially hard with Henry Gillman, or those in Jan and May 1827, in view of the ms association with poems published in 1828.

As far as either version refers to an actual event, one might note that celandines flower in Mar–May and are unscented, and that in 1824 the Aderses acquired a German home at the resort of Bad Godesberg, not far from Cologne (*CL* V 367: to Mrs C. Aders 1 Jun 1824). C is unlikely to have used the verses twice, since the two ladies must have been acquainted.

(*a*) IN RETURN FOR A GIFT

Sweet Gift! and always doth Eliza send
Sweet Gifts and full of fragrance to her Friend!
Enough for *him* to know, they come from Her:
Whate'er *She* sends is Frankincense and Myrrh.—

(*b*) ON THE SAME

Whate'er thou giv'st, must still prove sweet to me:
For still I find it redolent of thee.

614. ADAPTATION OF HERBERT'S
THE DIALOGUE

[Feb 1826]

C wrote the lines in the course of an entry in the Folio Notebook (*CN* IV 5327). They are an adaptation of stanza 2 of Herbert's *Dialogue*, and are introduced by the comment that the poem "supplies a thought of support and inward strength to me—". The original in the edition which C owned reads as follows (*The Temple* 10th ed—1674—107):

> *What (Child) is the ballance thine?*
> *Thine the poize and measure?*
> *If I say, thou shalt be mine,*
> *Finger not my treasure.*
> *What the gains in having thee*
> *Do amount to, onely he,*
> *Who for man was sold, can see*
> *That transferr'd th' accounts to me.*

Sweetest Saviour! if my Soul were but *worth* the Saving—It were worth
    the Having!
Quietly then should I control any thought of *waving*—i.e. of giving it
    up—
What, Child! is the Balance thine? Thine the Poize & Measure?
If I say, Thou shalt be mine—Finger not *my* treasure!
What the gains in having thee Do amount to, only He   5
Who bought thee by the Cross can see.

615. VERSES IN THE MARGIN OF
MARTIN LUTHER

[Feb–Aug 1826?]

C wrote the verses in a copy of Luther's *Colloquia Mensalia* belonging to CL (*CM—CC*—III 769), and they appear to reflect a private joke. In an earlier annotation C had written "I like him & love him all the better *therefore!*" (*CM—CC*—III 724); and in 1808 he wrote in CL's copy of Samuel Daniel: "Have I injured thy Book—? or wilt thou 'like it the better there*fore*?'" (*CM—*

CC—II 118). George Whalley speculates that there might be a connection with *The Merry Wives of Windsor* II i 186 "I like it never the better for that"; cf *CM* (*CC*) I 723; *CL* IV 868: to AG [17 Jun 1818]; VI 739: to J. H. Green 5 May 1828.

> "The Angel's like a Flea,
> The Divels are a Bore"—
> No matter for that! quoth S.T.C.
> I love him the better *therefore*!

616. ADAPTATION OF LINES FROM *PARADISE LOST* BOOK X

[Mar 1826]

C drafted the lines in the course of a notebook meditation concerning the personality of God and the personëity of Good and Evil (*CN* IV 5339). Milton's lines (*PL* X 565–70) describe the actions of the serpent devils following the Fall, who

> instead of Fruit
> Chewd bitter Ashes, which th' offended taste
> With spattering noise rejected: oft they assayd,
> Hunger and thirst constraining, drugd as oft,
> With hatefullest disrelish writh'd thir jaws
> With soot and cinders fill'd . . .

> with spattering noise
> And hatefullest disrelish writhe his jaws
> With soot and cinder filled!

617. ADAPTATION OF MARSTON

[Apr 1826]

C drafted his lines in the Folio Notebook (*CN* IV 5349). They are an adaptation of John Marston *The Parasitaster; or, The Fawn* I ii, in *Old English Plays* [ed C. W. Dilke] (6 vols 1814–15) II 311:

> We have been a philosopher, and spoke
> With much applause; but now age makes us wise,
> And draws our Eyes to search the heart of things,
> And leave vain seemings . . .

The notebook entry, in prose and verse, is made up of extracts from and notes on two plays by Marston and one by Chapman.

> I too have been a Disputant & wrangled
> With much applause; but age & home-felt weakness
> Have drawn our eyes to search the heart of things
> And leave vain seemings—

618. THE TWO FOUNTS: STANZAS ADDRESSED TO A LADY ON HER RECOVERY WITH UNBLEMISHED LOOKS, FROM A SEVERE ATTACK OF PAIN

[May–Jun 1826]

The seeds of C's poem lie in eight lines which he drafted in Notebook 26, and which he originally headed "A.G." (*CN* IV 5368). The idea of a "twy-streaming fount, | Whence Vice and Virtue flow, honey and gall", goes back to **101** *Religious Musings* 204–5, and is important in the two voices of secs V and VI of **161** *The Rime of the Ancient Mariner* and the contrasting replies of Skiddaw in **271** *A Stranger Minstrel*. Notwithstanding, the image of a fountain was one which C associated particularly with AG in later years. See e.g. the passage quoted in **277** *Inscription for a Fountain on a Heath* headnote.

The eight lines soon developed into a longer poem, "To Eliza in pain", addressed to Mrs Aders, for whom see **613** *To Eliza* headnote. C explained the immediate background to the poem when he sent it to her on 3 Jun 1826 (*CL* VI 582; cf 663: to Mrs C. Aders [Jan 1827?])—an explanation he repeated when he copied it into her album:

> A few days ago Mrs Gillman was expressing her wonder—I might have said her admiration that with all the intense Suffering, you had undergone, you *looked* just the same; and that neither Pain nor Anxiety seemed to have any power over that beautiful Face of Your's. With this remark in my Head, as I layed it on my pillow, I fell asleep: and out of the gay

weeds that spring up in the garden of Morpheus, I wove next morning the
accompanying wreath—

The poem was included in *PW* (1828, 1829, 1834), but not before it had
been published—without C's permission and to his annoyance—in *The Bijou*.
See *CL* vi 710–11: to A. A. Watts 24 Nov 1827. The differences between the
two ms and four printed texts are small; the text reproduced here is from *PW*
(1828).

In *PW* (JDC) 642A–B JDC records a copy of *PW* (1828), now unlocated,
in which C marked the following stanza, from the draft in Notebook 26, for
insertion at line 16⁺:

> Was ne'er on earth seen beauty like to this,
>   A concentrated satisfying sight!
> In its deep quiet, ask no further bliss—
>   At once the form and substance of delight.

The same copy included an alternative version of lines 19–20, again deriving
from Notebook 26:

> Looks forth upon the troubled air below,
> Unmoved, entire, inviolably bright.

'Twas my last waking thought, how it could be,
That thou, sweet friend, such anguish should'st endure:
When straight from Dreamland came a Dwarf, and he
Could tell the cause, forsooth, and knew the cure.

Methought he fronted me with peering look   5
Fix'd on my heart; and read aloud in game
The loves and griefs therein, as from a book;
And uttered praise like one who wished to blame.

In every heart (quoth he) since Adam's sin
TWO FOUNTS there are, of SUFFERING and of CHEER!   10
That to let forth, and *this* to keep within!
But she, whose aspect I find imaged here,

Of PLEASURE only will to all dispense,
That Fount alone unlock, by no distress

3–4. The lines in their present form
might derive from an occasion some
ten years before the larger part of
the poem was written. See vol II
commentary.

Choked or turned inward; but still issue thence   15
Unconquered cheer, persistent loveliness.

As on the driving cloud the shiny Bow,
That gracious thing made up of tears and light,
Mid the wild rack and rain that slants below
Stands smiling forth, unmoved and freshly bright: 20

As though the spirits of all lovely flowers,
Inweaving each its wreath and dewy crown,
Or ere they sank to earth in vernal showers,
Had built a bridge to tempt the angels down.

Ev'n so, Eliza! on that face of thine,   25
On that benignant face, whose look alone
(The soul's translucence through her chrystal shrine!)
Has power to soothe all anguish but thine own

A Beauty hovers still, and ne'er takes wing,
But with a silent charm compels the stern   30
And tort'ring Genius of the BITTER SPRING,
To shrink aback, and cower upon his urn.

Who then needs wonder, if (no outlet found
In passion, spleen, or strife,) the FOUNT OF PAIN
O'erflowing beats against its lovely mound,   35
And in wild flashes shoots from heart to brain?

Sleep, and the Dwarf with that unsteady gleam
On his raised lip, that aped a critic smile,
Had passed: yet I, my sad thoughts to beguile,
Lay weaving on the tissue of my dream: 40

Till audibly at length I cried, as though
Thou had'st indeed been present to my eyes,
O sweet, sweet sufferer! if the case be so,
I pray thee, be *less* good, *less* sweet, *less* wise!

In every look a barbed arrow send,   45
On those soft lips let scorn and anger live!

Do *any* thing, rather than thus, sweet friend!
Hoard for thyself the pain, thou wilt not give!

619. VIRGIL APPLIED TO THE HON MR B
AND RICHARD HEBER

[May–Jun 1826?]

C wrote the lines in the margin of Milton's *Lycidas*, against Thomas Warton's note on line 63, "Down the swift Hebrus to the Lesbian shore" (*CM—CC—* III 893). Warton suggests that in calling Hebrus "swift", Milton was indebted to Virgil's "volucremque fuga praevertitur Hebrum" (*Aeneid* 1.317 tr Fairclough—LCL—"and outstrips winged Hebrus in flight"). C suggests that "smooth" would have suited Milton's purpose better than "swift", so as to provide a contrast with the vehemence and turbulence of the preceding lines. He adds: "The Virgilian Line might not unhappily be applied to the Hon. Mr B****, who has made a more hasty 'Cut and run' than his *fast* friend, H—r—"; and the couplet follows in explanation. C had pondered the translation of the same Virgilian line a few years earlier, in **596.X1** *Corrections to WW's Virgil*.

The book collector Richard Heber (1773–1833) had been elected MP for the University of Oxford in 1821, but after accusations of pederasty in the early months of 1826 had been given two days' notice to flee the country. (The occasion of his removal is not described in *DNB*; but see *Scott L* X 68, 73, 100–1 and n; *The Journal of Sir Walter Scott* ed W.E.K. Anderson—Oxford 1972—162, 170–1, 236–7; *SL*—Curry—II 402n.) C met him at a dinner party in 1808 (*CL* III 80: to RS [24 Mar 1808]; *WL—M* rev—I 238), and referred to him as an acqaintance in 1817 (*CL* IV 746: to J. H. Frere 27 Jun 1817); he was well known to Scott and RS. Heber acquired a copy of *The Piccolomini* and *The Death of Wallenstein* which C had inscribed to John Anastasius Russell in 1808 (annex C 11.10), although he appears not to have owned any other book by C, and the acquisition could have been part of a larger parcel of books. He was the half-brother of the bishop of Calcutta, with whom C also had a slight acquaintance (see **267** *The Two Round Spaces on the Tombstone* VAR TEXT MS 5).

The bawdy double meaning of C's words does not need to be glossed, and might be compared with Scott's and RS's more proper reactions. It was obscure enough to be passed over by AG, after she received the Milton volume as a present. Cf poems **446** and **503** for C on lesbian lovers; and Notebook 42=BM Add MS 47537 ff 42ʳ–43ʳ and the references collected in *CM* (*CC*) I 42–3n (to which add *CM—CC—*II 926–7, 929) for more considered and generally more censorious statements by C on male homosexuality.

The identity of the Hon Mr B is debatable. C's memorandum is prompted by a distinction between the swift/smooth departure of Mr B on the one hand and the fast/precipitate departure of Heber on the other. Mr B appears to have departed after Heber and to have overtaken him. The most likely candidate is Henry Grey Bennet (1777–1836), the Whig MP for Shrewsbury. Bennet took an active interest in radical causes up until the mid-1820s, when he disappears from the pages of Hansard. His departure was not as turbulent as Heber's, and did not, like Heber's, occasion public comment; but he is referred to as homosexual in the anonymous contemporary poem *Don Leon*, and the cause of his removal is most likely to have been fear of prosecution.

Public and popular attitudes towards homosexuality put particular pressure on MPs at the time, even while reform of the law was being contemplated. Those who did not simply remove themselves, like Heber and Bennet, either had to face a burden of concealment or had to bluff out the consequences. A few years earlier, in 1822, it had been rumoured that Castlereagh's suicide had been caused by fear that he was about to be publicly denounced for a homosexual offence, and this may indeed have been its cause (H. Montgomery Hyde *The Strange Death of Lord Castlereagh*—1959—182–90). The suicide in 1825 of another MP, James Stanhope, is attributed by the author of *Don Leon* to similar fears. Afterwards, in 1833, two MPs, Baring Wall and William Bankes, were arrested and brought to trial on separate charges of homosexual misconduct. Louis Crompton "*Don Leon*, Byron, and Homosexual Law Reform" *Journal of Homosexuality* (New York) VIII (1983) 53–71 provides references and further details.

Prick'd from behind by Fear, his Legs his Bail,
Outruns Swift HEBER following at his *Tail*.

620. SANCTI DOMINICI PALLIUM:
A DIALOGUE BETWEEN POET AND FRIEND

[Jun 1826? Before Apr 1826?]

C's poem is rooted in the controversy surrounding Catholic Emancipation in the mid-1820s (the Catholic Relief Bill was not introduced into Parliament, and passed, until 1829). RS had published his *Book of the Church* in 1824, to which Charles Butler (*The Book of the Roman Catholic Church*—1825) and Bishop John Milner ("John Merlin" *Strictures on the Poet Laureate's "Book of the Church"*—1825) independently replied. RS's *Vindiciae Ecclesiae Anglicanae*, in which Butler's urbanity is contrasted with Milner's scurrility, appeared in Feb 1826, closely followed in Apr by Butler's *Vindication of "The Book of the Roman Catholic Church"*. However, although this controversy supplies the background, the poem does not bear a clear or exact relation to it, and may have been prompted by one of several books or persons. There are internal inconsistencies within the poem in its attitude to the persons and issues it refers to.

C was meditating the work which became *On the Constitution of Church and State* as early as 1825 (see *C&S—CC*—lii), and the feelings embodied in his poem have even earlier antecedents. However, he claims to have involved himself in the controversy at the present juncture through his urge to support Blanco White (rather than RS). White (1775–1841; see *DNB*) had been born in Spain of Catholic Irish parentage, studied with the Dominicans on his way to the priesthood, and took orders in the established Church when he came to England in 1810. He soon made the acquaintance of RS, and joined in the controversy on RS's side in May 1825, with *Practical and Internal Evidence against Catholicism*. He brought out *The Poor Man's Preservative against Popery* later in 1825; and his *Letter to Charles Butler* appeared in Jun 1826. The attitudes he expressed coincided with and reinforced C's long-standing detestation of the Inquisition and monastic asceticism, and the theory of Papal infallibility which furthered them both.

C read and annotated all three of White's books, and claimed in a letter to White of 28 Nov 1827 that his poem was written as a direct response to reading letter 10 in the last (*CL* VI 713). The title of an autograph transcript of the poem appears to corroborate this: "Poet and Friend: a Dialogue occasioned by the Report of Mr Eneas M'Donnell's Speech at the British Catholic Association, Charles Butler Esqre being present.—See the Revd Blanco White's Letter to C. B. Esqre, *p. 80 usque ad finem*. Facit IN DIGNA TIO Versus.";[1] and the copy of White's *Letter to Charles Butler* which he inscribed and presented to C is now in the BM (c 126 h 12). However, his place in C's poem is not as straightforward as C's belated letter of thanks for the book suggests.

C claimed in his letter that he wrote the poem in or after Jun 1826, but he states in a footnote to line 7 of the then recently published version that it had been written before Milner's death, i.e. before 19 Apr 1826. The contradiction is all the more striking because C expected White to have seen the version which maintains the opposite of what he claims in his letter. It seems unlikely that C was referring to two or more stages in the writing of his poem, one from before

---

[1] Tr "*p 80 to the end.* IN DIG NA TION inspires my Verses." The motto is from Juvenal *Satires* 1.79, altering the original "versum" (singular) to the plural.

Milner's death and another after White's *Letter to Charles Butler*. The poem itself also bears an odd relation to the background C suggested for it. White was hardly the moderate churchman C pretends to address, nor likely to be meeting Butler's hand "half-way" (line 20); the moderate Friend expresses a position closer to C's own in *C&S* and the vituperative Poet a position closer to White's. It is odd for C to claim that the poem was inspired by Butler's "Calumnious Abuse" of White (*CL* VI 980: to HNC [Mar 1834]) when it lays so much stress on Butler's smoothness. It is odd to pretend to write a poem in White's defence and not to have sent him a copy at the time (*CL* VI 713–14: to J. B. White 28 Nov 1827); instead to have written it carefully into a copy of a book by Butler himself.

The circumstances surrounding the poem do not fit it comfortably, and it is unclear whether this is due to duplicity, carelessness, or forgetfulness on C's part. Are the roles of Poet and Friend, himself and White, reversed so as to gain distance from his indignation? If he speaks in his own voice as Poet, did some other friend act the soothing part? Were the claims of C's letter to White in 1827 made on the spur of the moment to cover his embarrassment at having delayed acknowledging the gift of the *Letter to Charles Butler* for over a year? Was the poem originally prompted by some other occasion—for instance, might some insult by McDonnell have caused the indignation in the first place? Did C attribute an influence to White's gift only in retrospect, reaching for his recently published poem to bolster his profession of gratitude and overlooking the contradictions in his haste?

RS is reported to have liked the poem very much (*Minnow* 136), but there is evidence that C had misgivings about its questionable taste. He added the note on Milner, which also affirmed that he wrote of Milner's publications, not the man. He deplored the unauthorised publication of the poem in the reactionary ultra-Protestant *Standard*, even though he had previously sent it to Alaric Watts for *The Literary Souvenir*. He removed Milner's and Butler's names altogether from the version which was slipped into *PW* (1834) at the very last moment— thereby bringing it close to the verge of incomprehensibility.

The subtitle C added to two versions and used as the only title of a third— "found written on the blank leaf at the beginning of Butler's Book of the Church"—may be a further attempt to suggest that the poem was written before Milner's death, or it may be the truth. It may also be read as a modest and self-conscious disclaimer of authorship, teasingly cancelled by his well-known Greek signature "ΕΣΤΗΣΕ". Which of Butler's two books he intended to refer to is uncertain, and there seems no reason why he should not, at whatever date, really have written the poem in one of them (although it is not in the surviving annotated *Book of the Roman Catholic Church*, nor, apparently, in the recorded annotated copy of *Vindication of the Book of the Roman Catholic Church*): it was certainly possible for him, in his neatest hand, to fit the verses on to one "blank leaf". The poem does indeed refer to material in both of Butler's books, but it does not suit the first of them particularly.

There are two transcripts in C's hand: the first, said to have been prompted by Blanco White's book in Jun 1826 and still in C's possession in Nov 1827. A second, later transcript lacks the last two stanzas. There are also two printed versions: the one that appeared without C's permission in *The Standard*, which was twice reprinted, and the one included in *PW* (1834). The four texts differ little, apart from the title of the first transcript (and possibly the unrecovered lines) and the blanks for names in 1834, although there are variants in the *Standard* text which may either be printer's errors or deliberate alterations. The present text follows C's second, recovered ms up to the last two stanzas, which are taken from the text of *PW* (1834) and whose capitals and punctuation have been adjusted to the pattern established by the ms. (A metrical footnote by C is given at line 11EC.)

POET

I note the moods and feelings, Men betray
And heed them more than aught they do or say:
The lingering Ghosts of many a secret Deed
Still-born or haply strangled in it's birth
These best reveal the smooth Man's inward Creed!   5
These mark the Spot where lies the treasure, Worth!

MILNER,* made up of impudence and trick,
With cloven tongue prepared to hiss and lick,
ROME's Brazen Serpent! boldly dares discuss
The Roasting of thy Heart, O brave JOHN HUSS!   10

* The notorious Vicar-general—*since* deceased.

7. MILNER] John Milner (1752–1826), Bishop of Castabala and Vicar-Apostolic of the Western District of England, had a reputation from the early 1790s for being a champion of Catholic orthodoxy and of the prerogatives of the Hierarchy. His refusal to compromise earned him the confidence and support of the Irish prelates even as it estranged educated English opinion.
10. JOHN HUSS] Bohemian reformer and follower of John Wycliffe, he was persecuted and finally burned at the stake on 6 Jul 1415. C undoubtedly recalled Fuller's account, "The Life and Death of John Huss", *Abel Redevivus* (1651) 19–20: Fuller tells how he was stifled by the smoke rather than burned by the flames, and "His heart . . . was afterwards pricked upon a sharpe sticke, and rosted at the fire apart untill it was consumed". For "the repulsive effect" of Butler's and Milner's "Apologies for the St Dunstan Treachery to Huss & Jerome of Prague, Massacre of Paris, Queen Mary the Bloody &c/" see *CN* IV 5366, dated 5 May 1826.

And with grim triumph and a truculent glee
Absolves anew the pope-wrought Perfidy
That made an Empire's plighted faith a Lie,
And fix'd a broad Stare on the Devil's Eye—
(Pleas'd with the guilt, yet envy-stung at heart   15
To stand outmaster'd in his own black art!)

Yet Miln—

FRIEND

Enough of MILNER! We're agreed,
Who now defends, would then have done, the deed.
But who not feels Persuasion's gentle Sway?
Who but must meet the proffer'd hand half-way,   20
When courteous BUTLER—

POET (aside)
Rome's smooth Go-between!

FRIEND

Laments the Advice that sour'd a *Milky* Queen—
(For "*Bloody*" all enlighten'd men confess
An antiquated Error of the Press)
Who rapt by Zeal beyond her Sex's Bounds   25
With actual Cautery staunch'd the Church's Wounds!
And tho' he deems, that with *too* broad a Blur
We damn the French and Irish Massacre,
Yet *blames* them both—and thinks, the Pope *might* err!

11. C added a metrical footnote to this line in MS 2: "Trŭcŭlĕnt, a tribrach as ⟨the⟩ isochronous Substitute for the Trochee – ◡. N.B. *If* our Accent, a *quality* of sound, were actually equivalent to the *Quantity* in the Greek and Latin Prosody, *then* "trúculént" would doubtless answer to an Amphimacer – ◡ –, or dactyl ⟨– ◡ ◡⟩ at least. But it is not so. Accent shortens syllables: thus Spĭrĭt. = Sprite, Hŏnĕy, Mŏnĕy, nŏbŏdў &c."

21. BUTLER] Charles Butler (1750–1832), lawyer and Catholic apologist, though he entered into the controversy inaugurated by RS's *Book of the Church*, was in fact as often in conflict with Milner, who resented lay interference in ecclesiatical affairs. Butler was for compromise, e.g. supporting a government right of veto on the appointment of Roman Catholic bishops. C quoted the description of him in lines 39–40 to conclude a roll-call of "Romanish Rabbis" (*CM— CC*—III 459).

What think you *now*? Boots it with Spear and Shield   30
Against such gentle foes to take the field,
Whose beck'ning Hands the mild Caduceous wield?

POET

What think I *now*? Ev'n what I thought before.
What MILNER boasts, tho' BUTLER may deplore,
Still I repeat, *Words* lead me not astray   35
When the shewn *Feeling* points a different way.

Smooth BUTLER* can say Grace at Slander's feast
And bless each Haut-gaut cook'd by Monk or Priest;
Leaves the full lie on Milner's Gong to swell,
Content with half-truths, that do just as well;   40
But duly decks his mitred Comrade's Flanks,
And with him shares th' O'GORMAN Nation's Thanks!

So much for you, my Friend! who own a Church,
And would not leave your Mother in the lurch!
But when a Liberal asks me what I think—   45
Scar'd by the blood and soot of COBBETT's ink,
And JEFFREY's glairy phlegm and CONNOR's foam,
In search of some safe Parable I roam—
An Emblem sometimes may comprize a Tome!

* See the Revd Blanco White's "Letter to C. Butler, Esqre."

38. Haut-gaut] C's use of the then old-fashioned word (meaning highly flavoured or seasoned dish) is the last cited in *OED*.

42. O'GORMAN Nation's] i.e. Ireland's. Nicholas Purcell O'Gorman was for many years Secretary to the Catholic Association. C is less likely to have meant the O'Gorman Mahon, i.e. Charles James Patrick Mahon (1800–91), who did not become well known until after his part in the Clare election of 1828.

46–7. COBBETT . . . JEFFREY . . . CONNOR] William Cobbett (1762–1835), pugnacious and virulent journalist in favour of parliamentary reform, was often attacked by C for demagogy. Francis Jeffrey (1773–1850), lawyer and editor of *Ed Rev* 1802–29, was a strong supporter of the Whig party. Connor is probably Roger O'Connor (1762–1834), a flamboyant Irish nationalist, sometimes known as Captain Rock and a friend of English radicals like Sir Francis Burdett. C is less likely to have meant Charles O'Connor, DD, a supporter of Milner; even less likely is Daniel O'Connell (1775–1847), the Liberator. O'Connell was known habitually as O'Connell, while the O'Connors were each frequently referred to as Connor.

Disclaimant of his uncaught Grandsire's mood,   50
I see a Tyger lapping kitten's food:
And who shall blame him that he purrs applause,
When Brother Brindle pleads the Good Old Cause;
And frisks his pretty tail, and half unsheathes his claws!
Yet not the less, for modern lights unapt,   55
I trust the bolts and cross-bars of the laws
More than the Protestant milk all newly lapt,
Impearling a tame wild-cat's whisker'd jaws!

621. METRE AND RHYME IN
THE LIFE OF JEROME OF PRAGUE

[Jul 1826]

C copied out the lines in the Folio Notebook (*CN* IV 5407), introducing them
with the comment: "Curious instance of casual metre and rhyme in a prose
narrative (The Life of Jerome of Prague)—The metre is Amphibrach Dimeter
Catalectic, i.e. ∪ – ∪ / ∪ – : and the rhymes antistrophic". He wrote the rhyme-
scheme "abcde abcde" against the RH end of the lines. Almost the exact words
of the second stanza appear in Thomas Fuller *Abel Redevivus* (1651) 30, as KC
points out (cf also **625** *The Last Words of Berengarius*), but no source for the
first stanza has been traced.

Then Jerom did call
From his flame-pointed Fence
Which under he trod
As upward to mount
From the fiery flood.   5

I summon you all
A hundred years hence
To appear before God
To give an account
Of my innocent blood!   10

53. A line which merges sug-
gestions of fraternal Jacobinism and
the Good Old Cause of Jacobitism
("Brindle" recalling "Thrice the brin-
ded cat hath mew'd" of the Scottish
play *Macbeth* IV i 1).

622. THE ALTERNATIVE

[1826]

The only known text is *LR*, where it is dated 1826. The title may be C's or HNC's.

> This way or that, ye Powers above me!
> I of my grief were rid—
> Did Enna either really love me,
> Or cease to think she did.

623. THE IMPROVISATORE
OR, "JOHN ANDERSON, MY JO, JOHN"

[Summer 1826?]

The poem was first published in S. C. Hall's *Amulet for 1828* with a prose preamble (as well as the prose introduction given below), which introduced it as the first of a number of "New Thoughts on Old Subjects; or Conversational Dialogues on Interests and Events of Common Life. By S. T. Coleridge Esq.": see vol II for the text of the preamble. Its quotations from Milton (*To Mr Cyriack Skinner upon his Blindness* 5–6) and Burns (*Tam O'Shanter* 61–2) register its closeness in argument and phrasing to C's praise of WW's special originality in *The Friend* and *BL: The Friend* v (14 Sept 1809) (*CC*) II 73–4; *BL* ch 4 (*CC*) I 80–1.

Indeed, the similarities probably account for John Wilson's erroneous suggestion that the poem itself describes C's feelings about WW (see Viscount Cranbrook "Christopher North" *National Review* III—Apr 1884—156–7), and the preamble was dropped when C included the poem in *PW* (1829, 1834). Part of the ms submitted to Hall, which includes a few revisions, is extant. It suggests that the poem might originally have ended at line 48. The three published versions differ only in details. The one given below is from *PW* (1829), incorporating four corrections (at lines INT 41, INT 120, 14, 42).

3. An unusual name for a woman; it is the name of the town in Sicily where Proserpine was carried away by Pluto.

title. The ballad *"John Anderson my Jo, John"* is by Burns.

At the time C wrote the poem, and soon afterwards, he thought it "in sentiment and music of verse . . . equal to anything I ever wrote" (*CL* VI 699: to A. A. Watts [Aug 1827]; see also 801: to F. M. Reynolds [late Jul 1829]; 805: to F. M. Reynolds [6 Aug 1829]). He maintained that the introductory dialogue had cost him much labour. The title might have been suggested by Letitia Landon's *Improvisatore*, published in 1824 and reprinted at least six times in the interval before C's poem was written.

SCENE: *A spacious drawing-room, with music-room adjoining.*

CATHERINE. What are the words?

ELIZA. Ask our friend, the Improvisatore; here he comes: Kate has a favor to ask of you, Sir; it is that you will repeat the ballad that Mr. —— sung so sweetly.

FRIEND. It is in Moore's Irish Melodies; but I do not recollect the INT 5 words distinctly. The moral of them, however, I take to be this:—

> Love would remain the same if true,
> When we were neither young nor new:
> Yea, and in all within the will that came,
> By the same proofs would shew itself the same. INT 10

ELIZA. What are the lines you repeated from Beaumont and Fletcher, which my mother admired so much? It begins with something about two vines so close that their tendrils intermingle.

FRIEND. You mean Charles' speech to Angelina, in "the Elder Brother." INT 15

> We'll live together, like two neighbour vines,
> Circling our souls and loves in one another!
> We'll spring together, and we'll bear one fruit;
> One joy shall make us smile, and one grief mourn;
> One age go with us, and one hour of death INT 20
> Shall close our eyes, and one grave make us happy.

INT 7–10. C's lines paraphrase *Believe me, if all those endearing young charms* (*Irish Melodies*—Dublin 1820—51–2).

INT 16–21. From Beaumont and Fletcher *The Elder Brother* III v, vol II p 203 in the 1811 ed C annotated (now at the BM: c 126 i 1). (C also annotated the 1679 second folio—BM c 45 i 7—but that edition gives the whole play in prose). C substitutes "neighbour" for Beaumont and Fletcher's "wanton", and differs in some details of punctuation.

CATHERINE. A precious boon, that would go far to reconcile one to old age—this love *if* true! But is there any such true love?

FRIEND. I hope so.

CATHERINE. But do you believe it?   INT 25

ELIZA. (*eagerly*). I am sure he does.

FRIEND. From a man turned of fifty, Catherine, I imagine, expects a less confident answer.

CATHERINE. A more sincere one, perhaps.

FRIEND. Even though he should have obtained the nick-name INT 30 of Improvisatore, by perpetrating charades and extempore verses at Christmas times?

ELIZA. Nay, but be serious.

FRIEND. Serious? Doubtless. A grave personage of my years giving a Love-lecture to two young ladies, cannot well be otherwise. INT 35 The difficulty, I suspect, would be for them to remain so. It will be asked whether I am not the "elderly gentleman" who sate "despairing beside a clear stream," with a willow for his wig-block.

ELIZA. Say another word, and we will call it downright affectation.   INT 40

CATHERINE. No! we will be affronted, drop a curtsy, and ask pardon for our presumption in expecting that Mr. —— would waste his sense on two insignificant girls.

FRIEND. Well, well, I will be serious. Hem! Now then commences the discourse; Mr. Moore's song being the text. Love, as INT 45

INT 37–8. The quotations derive in part from the opening stanza of Nicholas Rowe's *Colin's Complaint*:

> Despairing beside a clear stream,
>   A shepherd forsaken was laid;
> And while a false nymph was his theme,
>   A willow supported his head.
>   (*B Poets* VII 143)

They also derive from a parody of Rowe sometimes attributed to George Canning (1770–1827)—e.g. in *A Nonsense Anthology* ed Carolyn Wells (New York 1930) 134–5 at 134—but in fact contemporary with the original (cf *English Verse 1701–1750* ed D. F. Foxon—2 vols Cambridge 1975—I 187B) and for which C was perhaps obligated to RS (see *S Letters*—Curry—I 96):

> By the side of a murmuring stream
>   An elderly gentleman sat,
> On the top of his head was a wig,
>   And a-top of his wig was his hat.

INT 45 et seq. C's comments on love—how it is distinguished from friendship and lust—are anticipated in his comments on Anton Wall's fairy tale *Amatonda* (*CL* III 302–7: to HCR [12 Mar 1811]); also **430** *Ad Vilmum Axiologum: Latin Version* headnote and **665** *Love and Friendship Opposite.*

distinguished from Friendship, on the one hand, and from the passion that too often usurps its name, on the other—

LUCIUS. (*Eliza's brother, who had just joined the trio, in a whisper to the Friend*). But is not Love the union of both?

FRIEND. (*aside to Lucius*). He never loved who thinks so.   INT 50

ELIZA. Brother, we don't want *you*. There! Mrs. H. cannot arrange the flower-vase without you. Thank you, Mrs. Hartman.

LUCIUS. I'll have my revenge! I know what I will say!

ELIZA. Off! off! Now, dear sir,—Love, you were saying—

FRIEND. Hush! *Preaching*, you mean, Eliza.   INT 55

ELIZA. (*impatiently*). Pshaw!

FRIEND. Well then, I was *saying* that Love, truly such, is itself not the most common thing in the world: and mutual love still less so. But that enduring personal attachment, so beautifully delineated by Erin's sweet melodist, and still more touchingly, perhaps, in the   INT 60 well-known ballad, "John Anderson my Jo, John," in addition to a depth and constancy of character of no every-day occurrence, supposes a peculiar sensibility and tenderness of nature; a constitutional communicativeness and *utterancy* of heart and soul; a delight in the detail of sympathy, in the outward and visible signs of the sacrament   INT 65 within—to count, as it were, the pulses of the life of love. But above all, it supposes a soul which, even in the pride and summer-tide of life—even in the lustihood of health and strength, had felt oftenest and prized highest that which age cannot take away, and which, in all our lovings, is *the* Love;—   INT 70

ELIZA. There is something *here* (*pointing to her heart*) that *seems* to understand you, but wants the *word* that would make it understand itself.

CATHERINE. I, too, seem to *feel* what you mean. Interpret the feeling for us.   INT 75

FRIEND.—I mean that *willing* sense of the insufficingness of the *self* for itself, which predisposes a generous nature to see, in the total being of another, the supplement and completion of its own— that quiet perpetual *seeking* which the presence of the beloved object modulates, not suspends, where the heart momently finds, and, find-   INT 80 ing, again seeks on—lastly, when "life's changeful orb has pass'd the full," a confirmed faith in the nobleness of humanity, thus brought home and pressed, as it were, to the very bosom of hourly

---

INT 64. *utterancy*] A Coleridgean coinage.

INT 81–2. "life's . . . full,"] Source untraced.

experience: it supposes, I say, a heart-felt reverence for worth, not
the less deep because divested of its solemnity by habit, by familiar- INT 85
ity, by mutual infirmities, and even by a feeling of modesty which
will arise in delicate minds, when they are conscious of possessing
the same or the correspondent excellence in their own characters.
In short, there must be a mind, which, while it feels the beautiful
and the excellent in the beloved as its own, and by right of love INT 90
appropriates it, can call Goodness its Playfellow; and dares make
sport of time and infirmity, while, in the person of a thousand-foldly
endeared partner, we feel for aged VIRTUE the caressing fondness
that belongs to the INNOCENCE of childhood, and repeat the same
attentions and tender courtesies as had been dictated by the same INT 95
affection to the same object when attired in feminine loveliness or
in manly beauty.

ELIZA. What a soothing—what an elevating idea!

CATHERINE. If it be not only an *idea*.

FRIEND. At all events, these qualities which I have enumerated, INT 100
are rarely found united in a single individual. How much more rare
must it be, that two such individuals should meet together in this
wide world under circumstances that admit of their union as Hus-
band and Wife. A person may be highly estimable on the whole,
nay, amiable as neighbour, friend, housemate—in short, in all the INT 105
concentric circles of attachment save only the last and inmost; and
yet from how many causes be estranged from the highest perfection
in this? Pride, coldness or fastidiousness of nature, worldly cares,
an anxious or ambitious disposition, a passion for display, a sullen
temper—one or the other—too often proves "the dead fly in the INT 110
compost of spices," and any one is enough to unfit it for the pre-
cious balm of unction. For some mighty good sort of people, too,
there is not seldom a sort of solemn saturnine, or, if you will, *ursine*
vanity, that keeps itself alive by sucking the paws of its own self-
importance. And as this high sense, or rather sensation of their own INT 115
value is, for the most part, grounded on negative qualities, so they
have no better means of preserving the same but by *negatives*—that
is, by *not* doing or saying any thing, that might be put down for fond,
silly, or nonsensical.—or (to use their own phrase) by *never forget-
ting themselves*, which some of their acquaintance are uncharitable INT 120
enough to think the most worthless object they could be employed
in remembering.

INT **110–11.** "the dead . . . spices,"] Source untraced.

ELIZA (*in answer to a whisper from Catherine*). To a hair! He must have sate for it himself. Save me from such folks! But they are out of the question.   INT 125

FRIEND. True! but the same effect is produced in thousands by the too general insensibility to a very important truth; this, namely, that the MISERY of human life is made up of large masses, each separated from the other by certain intervals. One year, the death of a child; years after, a failure in trade; after another longer or shorter   INT 130 interval, a daughter may have married unhappily;—in all but the singularly unfortunate, the integral parts that compose the sum total of the unhappiness of a man's life, are easily counted, and distinctly remembered. The HAPPINESS of life, on the contrary, is made up of minute fractions—the little, soon-forgotten charities of a kiss, a   INT 135 smile, a kind look, a heartfelt compliment in the disguise of playful raillery, and the countless other infinitesimals of pleasureable thought and genial feeling.

CATHERINE. Well, Sir; you have said quite enough to make me despair of finding a "John Anderson, my Jo, John," to totter down   INT 140 the hill of life with.

FRIEND. Not so! Good men are not, I trust, so much scarcer than good women, but that what another would find in you, you may hope to find in another. But well, however, may that boon be rare, the possession of which would be more than an adequate reward for   INT 145 the rarest virtue.

ELIZA. Surely, he, who has described it so beautifully, must have possessed it?

FRIEND. If he were worthy to have possessed it, and had believingly anticipated and not found it, how bitter the disappointment!   INT 150

(*Then, after a pause of a few minutes*)

ANSWER, *ex improviso.*

Yes, yes! that boon, life's richest treat,
He had, or fancied that he had;
Say, 'twas but in his own conceit—
    The fancy made him glad!
Crown of his cup, and garnish of his dish!   5
The boon, prefigured in his earliest wish!
The fair fulfilment of his poesy,
When his young heart first yearn'd for sympathy!

But e'en the meteor offspring of the brain
        Unnourished wane!   10
FAITH asks her daily bread,
And FANCY must be fed!
Now so it chanced—from wet or dry,
It boots not how—I know not why—
She missed her wonted food: and quickly   15
Poor FANCY stagger'd and grew sickly.
Then came a restless state, 'twixt yea and nay,
His faith was fix'd, his heart all ebb and flow;
Or like a bark, in some half-shelter'd bay,
Above its anchor driving to and fro.   20

That boon, which but to have possess'd
In a *belief*, gave life a zest—
Uncertain both what it *had* been,
And if by error lost, or luck;
And what it *was*:—an evergreen   25
Which some insidious blight had struck,
Or annual flower, which, past its blow,
No vernal spell shall e'er revive;
Uncertain, and afraid to know,
    Doubt toss'd him to and fro: 30
HOPE keeping LOVE, LOVE HOPE alive,
Like babes bewildered in a snow,
That cling and huddle from the cold
In hollow tree or ruin'd fold.

Those sparkling colors, once his boast,   35
    Fading, one by one away,
Thin and hueless as a ghost,
    Poor Fancy on her sick bed lay;
Ill at distance, worse when near,
Telling her dreams to jealous Fear!   40
Where was it then, the sociable sprite
That crown'd the Poet's cup and deck'd his dish?
Poor shadow cast from an unsteady wish,
Itself a substance by no other right
But that it intercepted Reason's light;   45
It dimm'd his eye, it darken'd on his brow,

A peevish mood, a tedious time, I trow!
Thank Heaven! 'tis not so now.

O bliss of blissful hours!
The boon of Heaven's decreeing, 50
While yet in Eden's bowers
Dwelt the First Husband and his sinless Mate!
The one sweet plant, which, piteous Heaven agreeing,
They bore with them thro' Eden's closing gate!
Of life's gay summer-tide the sovran ROSE! 55
Late autumn's AMARANTH, that more fragrant blows
When Passion's flowers all fall or fade;
If this were ever his, in outward being,
Or but his own true love's projected shade,
Now that at length by certain proof he knows, 60
That whether real or a magic shew,
Whate'er it *was*, it is no longer so;
Though heart be lonesome, Hope laid low,
Yet, Lady! deem him not unblest:
The certainty that struck HOPE dead, 65
Hath left CONTENTMENT in her stead:
And that is next to Best!

624. THE ALIENATED MISTRESS
(LOVE'S BURIAL PLACE)

[1826?]

The poem is one of a number submitted to S. C. Hall for publication in 1826. C
and Hall fell out over money and other matters, and the poem was not published
in Hall's *Amulet* until 1833, where it was the first of "Three Scraps". In the
meantime, SC copied a slightly different version into a friend's album, and this
was published in *PW* (1828) (only).

The version submitted to and eventually printed by Hall is called *Love's
Burial Place* (above which C inserted "Alienation" in the ms). It might be seen
as connected to **623** *The Improvisatore*, which it accompanied, as a kind of
counter-attacking coda. The quite separate version copied by SC and printed in
PW (1828) is called "The Alienated Mistress: A Madrigal from an Unfinished
Melodrama."

The versions differ in the division of the first two lines between the speakers and in a few phrases. The text given here follows SC's transcript, which differs from *PW* (1828) only in capitalisation and punctuation.

LADY

If Love be dead, and you aver it,
Tell me Bard where Love lies buried!

POET

Love lies buried where 'twas born.
Ah faithless Nymph! think it no scorn
If in my fancy I presume   5
To name thy Bosom poor Love's Tomb;
And on that Tomb to read the Line—
Here lies a Love that once was mine,
But took a Chill, as I divine,
And died at length of a Decline.   10

625. THE LAST WORDS OF BERENGARIUS AND RELATED POEMS

[1826?]

The only surviving ms is a fair copy on one leaf, where the poems are written out, regularly spaced and with few alterations, and numbered I–III. They are given below in that form, the connection being that C's own last words in poem I are followed by those of Berengarius in poem II, and poem III contains reflections relevant to both. C's editors were concerned from the beginning about an apparent lack of relation between the first poem and the other two, and it could indeed be that C's numbering of the separate items and the lack of a general title imply disjunction rather than connection. Alaric Watts treated I as a footnote to II, and unnecessarily expanded the title of II, when he published all three in *The Literary Souvenir*. Poem I was dropped altogether in *PW* (1828, 1829, 1834), and HNC brought it back as a separate title in *LR* I 60.

The title of poem I may be translated "The testamentary epitaph of STC [=he stood][1] written with his own hand at the approach of death". There is no doubt

---

[1] Actually "he set up", but C understood this form of the aorist tense of ἴστημι in the sense of the second aorist ἔστη "he stood". Cf **561** *A Character* 71–3EC.

about the ms reading ἐπιθανοῦς, given as επιδανοῦς in *The Literary Souvenir*; the supposed meaning of the latter non-existent word, connected with debt, might have led to an interpretation of the first line of the epitaph as alluding chiefly to C's lack of worldly possessions. The Latin elegiac couplet may be translated: "What I shall leave behind is nothing, or of no value, or scarce my own. My corruption I give to DEATH, the rest I return to thee, O Christ." It is possible that it was C's suggestion to omit the epitaph from *PW* (1828, 1829, 1834). But if he meant it to connect with the other poems in 1826, he presumably intended to point to a contrast. He approached death as a typical protestant, independent and constant (ΕΣΤΗΣΕ) in his faith in Christ the saviour, and despising and rejecting his own achievements in this world. Berengarius contemplated his failure, compelled by authority to deny the truth he saw and to believe in the fires of hell.

Berengarius of Tours (c 999–1088), archdeacon of Angers, professed agreement with the heretical opinions of Scotus Erigena concerning transubstantiation, and argued that Christ is really present in the bread and wine, not physically as bread and wine but ideally. Cf C's summary in *CM* (*CC*) III 439–40. C's source here appears to be Thomas Fuller "The Life and Death of Berengarius" *Abel Redevivus* 6–7. After mentioning Berengarius' two successive recantations on the orders of Popes Leo IX and Gregory VII, Fuller comments: "Remarkable are his words wherewith he breathed out his last gaspe, which *Illyricus* reporteth to this Effect: *now am I to goe, and appeare before God, either to be acquitted by him as I hope, or condemned by him as I feare.*" Besides poem III below, **620** *Sancti Dominici Pallium* and **621** *Metre and Rhyme in "The Life of Jerome of Prague"* also derive in part from *Abel Redevivus*.

C's interest in Berengarius first became apparent in Feb 1819; he was then reading about him in W. G. Tennemann *Geschichte der Philosophie* (11 vols Leipzig 1798–1819) VIII 98–100, with (VIII 106) the lines from Hildebert's epitaph on Berengarius which he intended to quote in his ninth lecture on the history of philosophy, given on 22 Feb 1819 (*P Lects*—1949—272, 275n); he later copied the lines into Notebook 30 (*CN* IV 5062) and quoted them in a footnote to *AR* (1825) 205 (*CC*) 212fn (see also *CN* IV 4831 f 58ᵛ and n). But the second and the last stanzas of poem III, like poem II, evidently owe much to Fuller, who points out in his first paragraph the darkness of the age in which Berengarius lived, and later, before setting out the details of his inexcusable inconstancy: "this I dare bouldly affirme, that if the morning grow so proud as to scorne the dawning of the day, because mixed with darkenesse, Middle day will revenge her *Quarrell*, and may justly take occasion to conteme the Morning, as in lustre infiriour to her selfe" (*Abel Redevivus* 1, 5). Fuller, however, does not mention the "threaten'd death" (line 5), as Tennemann does. (Tennemann here refers to Berengarius' own words, which were first published by Lessing from an incomplete ms in *Berengarius Turonensis*—Brunswick 1770—163. Lessing's *Sämmtliche Schriften*, which C owned, had included Lessing's editorial comments in vol XIII but to C's annoyance—*CM* (*CC*) III 706—not the text.)

KC remarks on C's emotional identification with the loneliness of such early thinkers, which goes well beyond Tennemann's range (*CN* iv 5062n).

I. ΤΟ ΤΟΥ ΕΣΤΗΣΕ ΤΟΥ ΕΠΙΘΑΝΟΥΣ

EPITAPHIUM TESTAMENTARIUM ΑΥΤΟΓΡΑΦΟΝ

Quæ linquam, aut nihil, aut nihili, aut vix sunt mea. Sordes
   Do MORTI: reddo cætera, Christe! tibi.

II. THE LAST WORDS OF BERENGARIUS

(OB. ANNO DOM. 1088)

No more twixt Conscience staggering and the Pope,
Soon shall I now before my God appear
By him to be acquitted, as I hope:
By him to be condemned, as I fear.

III. REFLECTION ON THE ABOVE

Lynx amid Moles! had I stood by thy Bed,
Be of good cheer, meek Soul! I would have said:
I see a Hope spring from that humble Fear.
All are not strong alike thro' storms to steer
Right onward. What? tho' dread of threaten'd death   5
And dungeon torture made thy Hand and Breath
Inconstant to the truth within thy Heart?
That truth, from which thro' Fear thou twice didst start,
FEAR haply told thee, was a *learned* strife,
Or not so vital as to claim thy life: 10
And Myriads had reach'd Heaven, who never knew
Where lay the difference 'twixt the false and true!

Ye, who secure mid trophies not your own
Judge Him who won them when he stood alone,
And proudly talk of *recreant* BERENGARE—   15
O first the Age, and then the Man compare!
That Age how dark! Congenial Minds how rare!
No Host of Friends with kindred zeal did burn!
No throbbing Hearts awaited *his* Return!

Prostrate alike when Prince and Peasant fell,   20
He only disenchanted from the Spell,
Like the weak Worm, that gems the starless night,
Mov'd in the scanty circlet of his Light:
And was it strange if he withdrew the ray
That did but guide the Night-birds to their Prey?   25

The' ascending Day-star with a bolder eye
Hath lit each Dew-drop on our trimmer Lawn!
Yet not for this, if wise, will we decry
The Spots and Struggles of the timid DAWN:
Lest we so tempt the coming NOON to scorn   30
The Mists and painted Vapours of our MORN.

626. THOU AND I

[1820s]

Only one version of the poem is known: it is in an unidentified 19th-century hand, and appears to have been preserved in an album belonging to the 19th-century collector John Keymer. The attribution to C is made on the backing page of the album, and has not been confirmed from other sources. If the poem is his, it was probably written on some social occasion, like the album verses and charades of poem **625.X2.** The other poems in John Keymer's album prove that he inherited some verses by C from his father James, and that he was himself in touch with several mid-19th-century literary figures.

Neither Keymer is listed in standard biographical sources, but it is possible that they descend from John Keymer, a well-known printer, publisher, and bookseller active in Great Yarmouth until his death in 1817. It may also be noted that JG's mother was Frances Keymer, daughter of a Norwich surgeon, and the Yarmouth and Norwich families might be connected. CL wrote a memorial of C in the album of a Mr Keymer in Nov 1834, at the request of John Forster, who quoted it in the memorial article on CL in the *New Monthly Magazine* (Feb 1835); it is collected in *L Works* I 406–7. E. V. Lucas identifies this Keymer as James, a London bookseller of 142 Cheapside to whom Bernard Barton, after CL's death, sent a character sketch of CL. The later John Keymer records that a version of **597** *Extempore Lines in Notebook 28* which C wrote in Sept 1827 was preserved in his father's album, and it is reasonable to assume that this James Keymer is to be identified with the collector of CL.

What am I to thee?
What my lips are to this wine,
What a chain is to the free,
What a pilgrim to the Shrine.
   What the taper to the flame,   5
   What the poet is to fame!
What the Sea-cave to the spar,
What the tempest to repose,
What a cloud is to the star,
What the breeze is to the rose.   10
   Wing to air, or baigne to Sea,
   This—no more—am I to thee!

What art thou to me?
What the wine is to my brain,
What the moonlight to the Sea,   15
What a rainbow is to rain.
   What a bright wave to the beach,
   What the thought is unto Speech.
What the Summer noon to fruit,
What a forest-bough to birds,   20
What thy fingers to thy lute,
What thy breath is to thy words,
   Dew to flow'r, or sap to tree,
   This, and more, art thou to me!

627. DUTY, SURVIVING SELF-LOVE, THE ONLY SURE FRIEND OF DECLINING LIFE: A SOLILOQUY

[Sept 1826]

The poem was written on 2 Sept 1826, at a time when C was ill and weak and on a day when he felt he had many reasons to regret his circumstances (cf *CL* VI 607–8: to T. J. Ouseley 2 Sept 1826). The ms draft begins with a dialogue in prose between Alia and Constantius, out of which the verse soliloquy

11. baigne] Viz the act of bathing   later than 1652.
(Fr *baigner*). *OED* gives no examples

grows. Alia asks Constantius, "Are *you* the happier for your Philosophy?"; to which Constantius replies, "The calmer at least, and less *un*happy . . . for it has enabled me to find, that selfless Reason is the best Comforter and only sure Friend, of declining Life." The verse soliloquy is described as being composed immediately after such an imagined conversation, as perhaps indeed it was:

> Meantime, the grey-hair'd Philosopher, left to his own Musings, continued playing with the thoughts, that ALIA and ALIA's question had excited, till he murmured them to himself in half-audible words, which, at first casually and then for the amusement of his ear, he *punctuated* with rhymes, without however conceiting that he had by these means changed them into poetry.

The draft poem thus introduced is heavily reworked in all but the first three and last three lines of the ms, and lines 4–6 have no ms equivalent. The poem (only) was included in C's last three collections, with variations of capitalisation and punctuation and with the present title. In *PW* (1828, 1829) it was placed first in the section "Prose in Rhyme", whose epigraph is the four lines beginning "In many ways does the full heart reveal" (**631** Ἔρως ἄει λάληθρος ἔταιρος)—which is possibly significant; the poem might qualify as a sonnet in C's loose categorisation. The present text and title are from a fair copy forwarded by JG to an unnamed person, perhaps as part of the preparation of *PW* (1828).

> Unchanged within to see all changed without,
> Is a blank Lot and hard to bear, no doubt:
> Yet why at others' Wanings should'st thou fret?
> Then only might'st thou feel a just regret,
> Hadst thou withheld thy love or hid thy light   5
> In selfish fore-thought of Neglect and Slight.
> O wiselier then from feeble Yearnings free'd,
> *While*, and *on whom*, thou may'st—shine on! nor heed,
> Whether the Object by reflected light
> Return thy radiance, or absorb it quite: 10
> And tho' thou notest from thy safe recess
> Old Friends burn dim, like Lamps in noisome Air,
> Love them for what they *are:* nor love them less,
> Because to *thee* they are not what they *were*.

628. AN IMPROMPTU ON CHRISTMAS-DAY

[Dec 1826?]

AG copied the lines, without a title and perhaps from dictation, into C's copy of William Bartram *Travels through North and South Carolina* (London 1794). C's choice of Bartram, perhaps as a Christmas present for AG, is not accidental: he had earlier given his copy of the 1791 Philadelphia edition to SH (now at DCL: *CM—CC*—I 226–7). Holidays had not been happy times for C from Christ's Hospital days onwards, because they had made him feel alone (see *CN* I 1176, II 2647; **5** *Easter Holidays*). The lines set happy Christmases spent with the Gillmans against C's remembrance of previous, remembered unhappy ones.

The version given here was published over the initials "S. T. C." in *The Literary Magnet* (1827), but the lines were not included in any of C's collections. If the conjecture that the ms was dictated is correct, the lines were conceived (and published and forgotten) in a passing mood; or else they were not written at Christmas, but instead on a day when C's mind returned to thoughts of SH and of a family life he had not known.

> O, Christmas Day! O, happy day!
> A foretaste from above,
> To him who hath a happy home,
> And love returned for love!
>
> O, Christmas Day! O, gloomy day!   5
> The barb in Memory's dart,
> To him who walks alone through life,
> The desolate in heart!

629. A DAY DREAM

[1826–8? Mar 1802?]

The date remains conjectural, depending on the relation of the poem both to **289** *Letter to* —— and to **294** *The Day Dream*. Both *Day Dream* poems are reworkings of that part of the *Letter* which was not included in **293** *Dejection: An Ode*—a part which might even precede the composition of the *Letter* as a whole. It might seem natural to assume that *A Day Dream* precedes *The Day Dream* in the way the *Letter* precedes the *Ode*, and that it dates from c Mar

1802. In support of this, it has been claimed that C did not elsewhere commit the name Asra to writing (as here in line 20) after the break with SH and the Wordsworths in 1810. The evidence for a later date is slight, and rests partly on internal grounds, partly on the negative evidence that no early mss have been traced.

The Day Dream could just as well have been fashioned from the *Letter* at the same time as the *Ode*, and the present poem could represent a refashioning of *The Day Dream*, in a style which returns to that of the *Letter*, dating from as late as 1826–8. It mingles memories of several occasions—conversations around the fire at Gallow Hill, stock-doves in the grove—and transmutes others, so that the initials carved on Sara's Gate (*WL—E* rev—332–3) become carved on a tree (in line 10). The first line recalls two lines from **502.X3** *Remorse* (Printed II ii 48fn, end), while the mood of the summer setting and the admixture of conventional poetic elements is like **652** *The Garden of Boccaccio*.

The poem might have been prompted by a rereading or remembrance of the *Letter*, or by rereading the retrospective prose account of the incident at Gallow Hill in Notebook 18 (*CN* III 3708 f 11ᵛ), or by memories of the original experiences merging in the perspective of time. It was published contrary to C's wishes in *The Bijou*, and collected in *PW* (1828, 1829, 1834), in a section predominantly made up of later poems. The *Bijou* text was set from an unrecovered ms copy; the *PW* (1828) text given here incorporates a few, minor verbal improvements; the two subsequent printings differ only in unimportant details of capitalisation and punctuation.

> My eyes make pictures, when they are shut:—
> I see a Fountain, large and fair,
> A Willow and a ruined Hut,
> And thee, and me and Mary there.
> O Mary! make thy gentle lap our pillow!   5
> Bend o'er us, like a bower, my beautiful green Willow!
>
> A wild-rose roofs the ruined shed,
> And that and summer well agree:
> And, lo! where Mary leans her head,
> Two dear names carved upon the tree!   10
> And Mary's tears, they are not tears of sorrow:
> Our sister and our friend will both be here to-morrow.
>
> 'Twas Day! But now few, large, and bright
> The stars are round the crescent moon!
> And now it is a dark warm Night,   15
> The balmiest of the month of June!

A glow-worm fallen, and on the marge remounting
Shines and its shadow shines, fit stars for our sweet fountain.

    O ever—ever be thou blest!
       For dearly, ASRA! love I thee!   20
    This brooding warmth across my breast,
       This depth of tranquil bliss—ah me!
Fount, Tree and Shed are gone, I know not whither,
But in one quiet room we three are still together.

    The shadows dance upon the wall,   25
       By the still dancing fire-flames made;
    And now they slumber, moveless all!
       And now they melt to one deep shade!
But not from me shall this mild darkness steal thee:
I dream thee with mine eyes, and at my heart I feel thee!   30

    Thine eyelash on my cheek doth play—
       'Tis Mary's hand upon my brow!
    But let me check this tender lay
       Which none may hear but she and thou!
Like the still hive at quiet midnight humming,   35
Murmur it to yourselves, ye two beloved women!

630. EPIGRAM ON A BITCH AND A MARE

[Apr–May 1827? Earlier?]

Two versions of the epigram are known, in a letter to HNC (the text given here) and in a private album, apparently from dictation; the poem was never published. When C sent the present version to HNC, he said it applied to Lady Lyndhurst: "Lady L. (if she had in her Bosom what she ought to have & has not) is under obligations to Mr & Mrs Gillman, which she would thank no one for reminding her of—But she is what Helen was, beauty out of the question" (*CL* VI 681–2: 8 May 1827).

    Lyndhurst had become lord chancellor in Apr 1827. As John Singleton Copley, he had been at Trinity College Cambridge while C was at Jesus (second wrangler 1794). C said he had no recollection of him, but may have written about the £200 sinecure promised by Lord Liverpool (*CL* VI 681), and he later presented him with a copy of *On the Constitution of Church and State* (*CC* 237).

Lyndhurst was later opposed to parliamentary reform, although he was known as a moderate. He married the widowed Sarah Garay Thomas, née Brunsden, a celebrated beauty, in Mar 1819, and, according to *DNB*, was devoted to her until her death in Jan 1834,

The phrase with which C introduced the epigram to HNC—"& as I once pithily observed"—may suggest a date some time earlier than the letter, before Lady Lyndhurst was elevated to her present respectable position. The point may be the witticism that *two* animals caused the fall of Troy: Lady Lyttleton is (or was) a mare of wood, devoid of life and feeling, treacherous, as well as being like the beautiful and promiscuous Helen. No more is known about the cause of C's animus against her than appears in the letter to HNC, and it is possible that he meant only to imply that she resembles Helen in an epigram he wrote (long ago?) on another occasion.

> A bitch and a Mare set Old Troy Bells a knelling:
> The Mare was of Wood and the Bitch was call'd Helen!

631. ΕΡΩΣ ΑΕΙ ΛΑΛΗΘΡΟΣ ΕΤΑΙΡΟΣ

[Before May 1827]

C jotted down the lines in Notebook 26 (*CN* v), the first of a set of four headed "For *Autographs*", although they may date from much earlier. He appears then to have copied them into an album, with the present title (tr "Love is always a talkative companion"), and they were included in his last three collections as an epigraph to the section "Prose in Rhyme: or, Epigrams, Moralities, and Things without a Name", renamed "Miscellaneous Poems" in *PW* (1834). The text of the two ms versions differs slightly from the improved printed version given here (although all printed texts misspell the third word of the title).

> In many ways does the full heart reveal
> The presence of the love it would conceal;
> But in far more th' estranged heart lets know,
> The absence of the love, which yet it fain would shew.

632. BO-PEEP AND I SPY

[Before May 1827]

The poem is the second of four which C copied out in Notebook 26, under the heading "For *Autographs*" (*CN* v). The other three are signed "S. T. C.", but this one is not. No other version, autograph or printed, is known.

"In the corner *one*—
I Spy, Love!
"In the corner *none*—
I spy, Love.

633. SONG:
"THO' HID IN SPIRAL MYRTLE WREATH"

[Before May 1827]

C copied out the verses, without a title, as the third of four short poems headed "For *Autographs*" in Notebook 26 (*CN* v), the version given here, adding a full point at the end. For the source of the figure of the sword hidden in a myrtle wreath see **169** *Modification of "Translation of a Celebrated Greek Song"*. Both poems were included in *PW* (1828), with extensive minor revisions which soften their effect. Thus, lines 6–7 became:

We likewise see Love's flashing blade
By rust consumed or snapt in twain . . .

They were dropped from *PW* (1829, 1834).

Tho' hid in spiral myrtle Wreath,
Love is a sword that cuts its Sheath:
And thro' the Slits, itself has made,
We spy the Glitter of the Blade.

But thro' the Slits, itself had made,   5
We spy no less too, that the Blade
Is eat away or snapt atwain,
And nought but Hilt and Stump remain.

634. LINES FOR MRS SMUDGER'S ALBUM;
AND SEQUEL

[May 1827]

C copied out the lines at the end of a letter to J. H. Green (*CL* VI 686–7: [30 May 1827]), introducing them as follows: "A portly Dame, whose good man has done well for himself in the Carcase-Butcher Line, would fain have something, in the Ottigraph way, from *me* in the splendid Book which by aǹ somewhat *italianized* mode of pronunciation she calls her *Ol*bum or *Awl*bum/—Would this do?" He then quoted the version of **637** *Written in William Upcott's Album* which ends: "Fit for Mrs Smudger's *Ol*bum | Or to wipe her Baby's small bum" (VAR TEXT MS 1). The present set of lines follows, headed "Another". Mrs Smudger is unknown to fame, and the name might be C's invention. Cf **538** *Lines for an Autograph Hunter*, **672** *In a Lady's Album* for similar comments by C on autograph hunters.

The Sequel is reworked, and C has noted that it "*wants polishing*". Some punctuation is supplied in the text given here.

A Dame of Fashion ask'd Sir Toby Jewett,
What *Album* meant. Hem! quoth the Learned Knight:
"Clean Sheets—or your Chemise—or what's next to it—
"In fine, my Lady! *any thing that's white*."

SEQUEL TO THE ABOVE

"Yes, yes! I see it now! rejoin'd the Dame—   5
Last night when we were talking of the Name
Of the Turk's Bible, and you said to me—
You said, as I remember—that *Al* meant *the*.
Me, I confess, it ne'er before did strike,
English and Latin were so near alike.—"   10

635. SONG: "'TIS NOT THE LILY BROW I PRIZE"

[1820s]

The poem was written extempore on hearing a song which contained the words "lilied Brow", as the first title explained (see vol II). It exists in two ms versions (a third has dubious authority) and was printed in *The Keepsake for 1830*; it was not included in any of C's collections. Apart from punctuation and capitalisation, C changed only the words he took from from the song and the phrasing of the last two lines. The present version follows *The Keepsake*.

In one ms the lines accompany **592** *Youth and Age*, the expansion of which they recall in some aspects of versification. Cf also **593** *"Dewdrops are the Gems of Morning"*.

> 'Tis not the lily brow I prize,
> Nor roseate cheeks, nor sunny eyes,
> Enough of lilies and of roses!
> A thousand-fold more dear to me
> The gentle look that love discloses,   5
> The look that love alone can see.

636. PROFUSE KINDNESS

[Before Sept 1827]

SC copied the lines into the album of a friend in 1827 (over C's initials), and they were published with a proverbial saying of Hesiod as an epigraph in *PW* (1834): Νήπιοι, οὐκ ἴσασιν ὅσῳ πλέον ἥμισυ παντός (*Works and Days* 40 tr Evelyn-White—LCL—5 "Fools! They know not how much more the half is than the whole"). C applied it aptly in a nautical context on the way to Malta, and in 1828 in an assessment of James Fennimore Cooper as a writer (*CN* II 2003; *CL* VI 736: to W. Sotheby [28 Apr 1828]).

> What a Spring-tide of Love to *dear Friends* in a Shoal!
> Half of it to *one* were worth double the whole!

637. WRITTEN IN WILLIAM UPCOTT'S ALBUM

[Sept 1827]

C's lines combine elements which appear in other album verses written before and afterwards: cf **538** *Lines for an Autograph Hunter* VAR TEXT MS 2; **697** *Other Lines on Lady Mary Shepherd* 4–5; VAR TEXT MS 1 of the present poem. The lines were put together for the antiquary and autograph collector William Upcott (1779–1845), whose activities are described by A.N.L. Munby *The Cult of the Autograph Letter in England* (1962) 13–32. The poem was printed in *PW* (1834), but is here given from the ms.

The metrical joke of the first couplet was explained by C in a couplet attaching to another version:

> The name will sound less grimmish Sir,
> If you make it an Amphimacer.
> ‾ ᵕ ‾.

On the trisyllabic pronunciation see **515** *Written in Richard Field's "Of the Church"* 6EC.

> PARRY seeks the Polar Ridge:
> Rhymes seeks S. T. COLERIDGE

> Author of Works, whereof, tho' not in Dutch,
> The Public little knows, the Publisher too much.

638. TO MARY S. PRIDHAM

[Oct 1827]

C gave the poem its present title, adding at the end his signature and the date "16 Octr 1827", when he wrote it out as the first entry in an album given to Mary Pridham on the occasion of her marriage to DC (which took place on 6

1. PARRY] See **609** *Captain Parry* for other lines by C on William Edward Parry (1790–1855), brother of Charles and Frederick Parry, C's com- panions in Göttingen. He was at this time engaged in an attempt to reach the North Pole from Spitzbergen.

Dec). JDC reported another version written a day earlier, with variant readings in the first four lines. Lines 7–10 are borrowed from **623** *The Improvisatore* 5–8 (transposed). The poem was not published in C's lifetime.

> Dear tho' unseen! tho' I have left behind
> Life's gayer Views and all that stir the Mind,
> Now I revive, Hope making a new Start,
> Since I have heard with most believing heart,
> That all, my glad eyes would grow bright to see,　　　　5
> My Derwent hath found realiz'd in Thee!
> The Boon pre-figur'd in His earliest Wish;
> Crown of his Cup, and Garnish of his Dish;
> The fair Fulfilment of his Poesy,
> When his young Heart first yearn'd for Sympathy!　　　　10
> Dear tho' unseen! Unseen yet long portray'd!
> A Father's Blessings on thee, gentle Maid!

639. LINES ON TEARS, AS THE LANGUAGE OF THE EYE

[1825–34?]

The lines are written in C's hand, without a title, at the top of a leaf containing **639.X1** *Primitive Christian's Zeal for the Cross* (from Crashaw). They were first attributed to C in *PW* (EHC) II 975 No 79, but doubt about his authorship remains.

> Nothing speaks our mind so well
> As to speak Nothing. Come then, tell
> Thy Mind in Tears, whoe'er thou be
> That ow'st a name to Misery.
> None can *fluency* deny　　　　5
> To Tears, the Language of the Eye.

4¹. most believing heart] Cf e.g. the "most believing mind" of **171** *Frost at Midnight* 24.

640. ROMANCE
OR, TALE OF THE DARK AGE

[Before Feb 1828]

When C drafted two stanzas of his poem on a leaf which is now part of Note-book 37 (*CN* v), he gave them the title "Olim—once on a Time. ~~In good King Olim's golden reign~~". The present text reproduces a signed fair copy, dated 4 Feb 1828.

C wrote other lines set in "old King Olim's reign" in 1799. It is just possible that the present nonsense verses might originally have been composed for one of C's children.

Hear, what befell a gallant Prince
　　All on a day:
Whether before the Flood or since,
　　I cannot say.

But twas in good King OLIM's reign,　　　　　　5
　　I'm quite secure:
And that it happ'd on Salisbury Plain,
　　I'm almost sure.

For by this token he was brought
　　Before the Mayor:　　　　　　　　　　　10
The Horse, on which he rode, was bought
　　At Barnet Fair.

Nay, Sirs! but listen! why so fast?
　　The Table's spread.
Well! so this Prince—he died at last　　　　　15
　　All in his bed.

5. For Olim's reign = "a long time ago" see **234** *The Lethargist and Madman* 1EC.
12. Barnet Fair] The suggestion is that the horse was stolen. The annual horse fair still takes place at Barnet, and has a somewhat doubtful reputation.

641. VERSES TRIVOCULAR

[Jan 1828]

C drafted the lines on a leaf which is now part of the inside back cover of Notebook 37 (*CN* v). They are not headed, and appear to be independent of the other draft poems on the same page (**640** *Romance* and **640.X1** *Overscored Lines in Notebook 37*). The coincidence of rhyme with the **411** *Epigram on Confessions Auricular* appears to be fortuitous.

Of one scrap of Science I've evidence ocular—
A heart of one chamber they call unilocular
And in a sharp frost or when Snow-flakes fell floccular,
Your Wise Man of old wrapp'd himself in a Roquelaire,
Which was call'd a Wrap-rascal, when folks would be jocular.   5
And Shell-fish, tho' small, Periwinkle and Cockle are,
So with them will I finish these verses trivocular.

642. COUPLET ON JOSEPH COTTLE

[Mar 1828?]

C quoted the couplet in Notebook 37 = BM Add MS 47532 f 86^r and then again, about five years later, in Notebook Q = NYPL (Berg Collection) f 69^v (both *CN* v). The two versions differ in the first line, and the earlier is given here. It is not known whether the couplet was composed in 1828, or was recollected at that time from an occasion perhaps c 1814–15. The context in both versions is that Joseph Cottle is alleged to have thought that Malebranche was Moll Branche, a Frenchwoman.

Amos Cottle (? 1768–1800) received his BA from Magdalene College Cambridge, where he translated *Icelandic Poetry; or, The Edda of Sæmund*, and he wrote occasional verse, which Joseph included in his own *Malvern Hills* (1798)

4. Roquelaire] An enveloping long cloak, named after the duke of Roquelaure (1656–1738) and still fashionable in the early 19th century. The first occurrence of the word recorded by *OED* is John Gay *Trivia* (1716) I 51 (*B Poets* VIII 285).

5. Wrap-rascal] The first occurrence of the word recorded by *OED* is in Gay's same description of "a proper coat for winter's wear", at line 57n on the same page of *B Poets*. It continued in use to the end of the 19th century.

and RS in vol I of his *Annual Anthology* (1799). Joseph Cottle (1770–1853) published *Alfred: An Epic Poem, in Twenty-four Books* in 1800, *The Fall of Cambria, in Twenty-four Books* in 1808, and *The Messiah: A Poem in Twenty-eight Books* in 1815 (which C helped him revise: *CL* III 502: to J. J. Morgan 2 [=1] Jun 1814).

Despite C's indebtedness to Joseph Cottle's liberality, his attitude from the first appears to have been humorous and somewhat condescending. Compare **110.X2** *Report on Mr Cottel*, which, though C's authorship remains unconfirmed, represents his attitude. C ignored Cottle's poetry in *The Watchman*; he was privately critical of Cottle's philistinism, obtuseness, and vanity (*CN* I 503, 566, 571); and his attitude was shared by his friends in a way which must have been obvious (cf *LL*—M—I 236, 239–40; *S Letters*—Curry—I 267). He omitted **117** *Lines to Joseph Cottle* from later collections. Cottle took his revenge when he came to write *Early Recollections* (1837).

THE COTTLE of Bristol for Epics so famous—
Not Amos, but Joseph, the Brother of Amos.

643. EXTEMPORE ON THREE SURGEONS

[May 1828]

The untitled lines form part of a jocular passage in a letter to J. H. Green (*CL* VI 738–9: 5 May 1828), in which C digresses on the skill of Green's friend, the sculptor F. L. Chantrey (1781–1841). The references are to Sir Astley Cooper (1768–1841), Sir Anthony Carlisle (1768–1840), and Sir William Blizard (1743–1835). All three were well-known surgeons. It might be noted that the last—perhaps the least famous of the three in 1828—had been surgeon at the London Hospital during 1784–5, when Luke Coleridge studied there and C visited as often as he could, hoping one day also to be a surgeon (*C Life*—G—22–3). J. H. Green, C's correspondent, was of course a surgeon; he was Cooper's godson and succeeded him as President of the Royal College of Surgeons.

Sir Ass. and Sir Ant. and Sir Double you be—
Old Nic may turn Chiss'ler and chip 'em *for me*,

2². Chiss'ler] This occurrence of the noun, for one who cuts or shapes with a chisel, antedates the first use recorded by *OED* (1883). The formation is unremarkable enough, except that in the present context it

While Orpheus's Dancing-kit plays Gramachree
To the crawl of a Louse and the skip of a Flea!

644. ON THE MOST VERACIOUS ANECDOTIST, AND SMALL-TALK MAN, THOMAS HILL, ESQ.

[Jun 1828?]

C drafted the lines in Notebook F° (*CN* v); they were not published in his lifetime. He added the following note to the title: "Extempore in reply to a question of Mr Theodore [?Hook] 'Look at him, and say what you think. Is not he like a Rose?[']'" *LL* (M) III 257 provides a helpful note on the dry-salter and book collector Thomas Hill (1760–1840), a busybody who sought the company of theatrical and literary celebrities. He was a patron of the poets Robert Bloomfield and Henry Kirk White, and a friend of Theodore Edward Hook. He was the model for the character Hull in Hook's novel *Gilbert Gurney* (1836), and E. V. Lucas suggests that he was the original of CL's "Tom Pry" (*L Works* I 324–6; cf 516). C had known him since at least 1795, and the acquaintance was renewed in the 1820s: cf *CL* v 12: to J. H. Green 14 Jan 1820.

> Tom Hill, who laughs at cares and woes,
>   As nauci—nili—pili—
> What is *he* like, do I suppose?

---

might possess a nonsensical Irish flavour. Presumably associated with older words like "childer", it still has widespread currency in Dublin in the sense of boy, child, "nipper", and is quite separate from the emerging 19th-century English slang-word, with no suggestion of cheating. Cf line 3 "Gramachree", conventional in Irish ballads for "love of my heart", and perhaps even the lilting, anapaestic metre. Things Irish were current in England at the time, owing to Daniel O'Connell and the Catholic Associa-tion, and C complained of "the deluge of Paddyism" (*TT* 14 Aug 1831—*CC*—I 246).

2. nauci—nili—pili] "worth a nut—nothing—a hair", extracted from the Latin grammars' list of nouns used to express value with the ending -*i*. Cf *OED* s.v. *floccinaucinihilipilification*. CL and C both used variations on this word, undoubtedly as a shared school-boy joke. The full list of seven nouns appears in *An Introduction to Latin Grammar for the Use of Christ's Hospital* (1785) 120.

Why, to be sure, a Rose—a Rose;
At least, no soul that Tom Hill knows,   5
Could e'er recall a *Li-ly*.

645. LINES BASED ON EXODUS 17

[1828?]

C wrote twelve lines in a copy of N. Brady and N. Tate *A New Version of the Psalms of David, Fitted to the Tunes Used in Churches* (1805 ed), the first four of which are given below. The copy has not been located, and the lines are known only from a Sotheby's catalogue (which gives "Amalet" in line 4): *CM (CC)* I 475.

It is not certain that the lines are by C, although they are said to be in his handwriting. They form the beginning of a verse rendering of Exod 17.8–14: "Then came Amalek, and fought with Israel in Rephidim . . ."

When Moses stood with arms outspread
Success was found on Israel's side,
But when through weariness they failed,
That moment Amalek prevailed,

*   *   *

646. IMPROMPTU LINES AT NAMUR

[Jun 1828]

C repeated the lines to Thomas Colley Grattan, who describes a walk through Namur by the light of a full moon with WW and C, and how a remark of Grattan's concerning the effect of moonlight caused C to pause

till I rejoined him, when he took me by the arm, and in his low recitative

---

6. *Li-ly*] William Lily (?1468–1522), author of a brief Latin grammar which with various additions and revisions became the standard in English schools. The Christ's Hospital grammar and the more generally used Etonian *Introduction to the Latin Tongue* both followed it fairly closely.

way he rehearsed two or three times, and finally recited, some lines which he said I had recalled to his mind, and which formed part of something never published. He repeated the lines at my request, and as well as I could catch the broken sentences I wrote them down immediately afterwards with my pencil as follows.

Cf C's memo in Notebook 40, dated 26 Jun 1828: "Went down to the River Meuse and saw the Castle by Moonlight—Grattan with us—Bridge—Arches— 'apparitions of Moons'—" (Notebook 40=BM Add MS 47535 f 4^r; *CN* v). C had plucked flowers in the inn garden at Waterloo earlier that day.

The lines contain partial repetitions and echoes of **248** *Lines Composed in a Concert-room*, **299** *The Keepsake*, and **300** *The Picture*, composed between 1799 and 1802. The first of these seems never to have pleased C as a poem, and it continued in a fluid state before and after the date 1799. C may well have incorporated parts of it in further plans for "something never published".

The earlier plans and present lines might also have some connection with **294.X1** *The Soother of Absence*, which may indeed be the "something" which C referred to. Alternatively, and perhaps more probably, the lines might date from the occasion at Namur in 1828, as an impromptu inspired by the revival of an earlier impulse.

>   —and oft I saw him stray,
> The bells of fox-glove on his hand—and ever
> And anon he to his ear would hold a blade
> Of that stiff grass that 'mid the heath-flower grows,
> Which made a subtle kind of melody,   5
> Most like the apparition of a breeze,
> Singing with its thin voice in shadowy worlds.

647. WATER BALLAD, FROM PLANARD

[Jun–Jul 1828]

The lines appeared in *The Athenaeum* (29 Oct 1831), over C's signature. No ms is known, and the poem was never collected by C; it is not known who sent it to *The Athenaeum*.

When the lines were published, they carried the title *Water Ballad*, with no indication that they are a modified translation from Eugène de Planard's *opéra comique Marie*. The first and second stanzas are sung by Suzette from a boat

2. on] Perhaps an error for "in".

as Georges and Lubin board it, the last is sung by Lubin and Suzette together (François Antoine Eugène de Planard *Marie: Opéra-comique en trois actes*— 1826—I sc iv):

> SUZETTE, *assise dans la barque.*
> Batelier, dit Lisette,
> Je voudrais passer l'eau,
> Mais je suis bien pauvrette
> Pour payer le bateau.
> Colin dit à la belle:
> Venez, venez toujours . . .
> Et vogue la nacelle
> Qui porte mes amours!

> (Ils abordent. Lubin reste sur la rive à attacher sa barque.)

> SUZETTE, *s'avançant en scène.*
> Je m'en vais chez mon père,
> Dit Lisette à Colin:
> —Eh bien! crois-tu, ma chère,
> Qu'il m'accorde ta main?
> —Ah! répondit la belle,
> Osez, osez toujours . . .
> —Et vogue la nacelle
> Qui porte mes amours!

> LUBIN ET SUZETTE.
> Après le mariage,
> Toujours dans son bateau,
> Colin fut le plus sage
> Des maris du hameau.
> A sa chanson fidèle,
> Il répéta toujours:
> Et vogue la nacelle
> Qui porte mes amours!

The opera was first produced in Paris on 12 Aug 1826 at the Opéra-Comique, and in various European cities (as well as New York) during the years following, but it was not produced in England in an English translation until 1849 (Alfred Loewenberg *Annals of the Opera 1597–1940*—2nd ed Geneva 1955—704–5).

The French edition of the opera was published in 1826, and the song might have been repeated to C on his tour of Belgium, the Rhineland, and Holland in 1828—either in French (the opera had been produced on 18 Jan 1827 in Brussels) or in I. F. Castelli's German translation, perhaps by one of the German literati he met at Mrs Aders's or by Thomas Colley Grattan, who presented C with a book in French—Maxime Odin *Smarra; ou Les Démons de la nuit.*

Songes romantiques (Paris 1821) (cf J. H. Green Sale, Sotheby's 28 Jul 1880 lot 506; W.E.A. Axon "Coleridge Marginalia" *N&Q* 9th ser xii—25 Jul 1903—61–2). A memorandum C made on 30 Jun 1828 in Notebook 40 might bear on the matter: "arrived at Aachen about 5 in the evening Theatre, & untranslatable Inscription Musagetæ—choro" (Notebook 40 = BM Add MS 47535 f 5ʳ—*CN* v; also the account in C's hand at DCL MS "Coleridge Letter Book" No 9 q vol ii poem **650.X1**); but no performance is mentioned. It may also be significant that Jane Reynolds Hood (?) copied on to the same page of the Reynolds–Hood Commonplace Book the version of **673** *Inscription on a Time-piece* found only in Dora Wordsworth's Album, where it is dated 24 Dec 1830 (VAR TEXT MS 3).

"Come hither, gently rowing,
   Come, bear me quickly o'er
This stream so brightly flowing,
   To yonder woodland shore.
But vain were my endeavour   5
   To pay thee, courteous guide;
Row on, row on, for ever
   I'd have thee by my side.

"Good boatman, prithee haste thee,
   I seek my father-land."—   10
"Say, when I there have placed thee,
   Dare I demand thy hand?"—
"A maiden's head can never
   So hard a point decide;
Row on, row on, for ever   15
   I'd have thee by my side."

The happy bridal over,
   The wanderer ceased to roam,
For, seated by her lover,
   The boat became her home.   20
And still they sang together,
   As steering o'er the tide,
"Row on through wind and weather,
   For ever by my side."

648. TWO EXPECTORATIONS FROM COLOGNE

[Jul 1828]

C stayed overnight at Cologne on his way to Mrs Aders at Bad Godesberg, and suffered "Noise, Heat, ~~all~~ Stench—all intolerable—driving Rain". He recorded his visit to Mum's Wine Cathedral and St Gereon's (Notebook 40=BM Add MS 47535 f 5^v; *CN* v). The verses were probably composed at the time, or on the dull journey onwards from Cologne towards Bonn. HNC copied down a version in his *Table Talk* workbook, and they were published in 1834 in *Friendship's Offering* and *PW*. The text given here is from *Friendship's Offering*, incorporating an emendation C made in the first line. The other printed text reverses the order of the two poems and gives them blander titles; neither it nor the ms version has the footnotes.

(*a*) AN EXPECTORATION, OR SPLENETIC EXTEMPORE ON MY JOYFUL DEPARTURE FROM THE CITY OF COLOGNE

As I am a Rhymer,
And now at least a merry one,
Mr. MUM's Rudesheimer*
And the church of St. Geryon
Are the two things alone   5
That deserve to be known
In the body-and-soul-stinking town of Cologne.

(*b*) EXPECTORATION THE SECOND

In COLN,† a town of monks and bones,‡
And pavements fang'd with murderous stones;

* The *apotheosis* of Rhenish wine.
† The German name of Cologne.
‡ Of the eleven thousand virgin martyrs.

(*b*)**1fn^2.** The 11,000 virgin martyrs were the attendants of a British princess, Ursula, murdered for their Christian faith by the heathen inhabitants of Cologne. In Notebook 37 = BM Add MS 47532 f 63^v (*CN* v) C alludes to a theory that the legend was founded on a misunderstanding of the inscription on a Roman milestone, "undecim Mill. a Colon" tr "eleven Miles from Cologne".

And rags, and hags, and hideous wenches;
I counted two-and-seventy stenches,
All well-defined and several stinks!   5
Ye nymphs that reign o'er sewers and sinks,
The river Rhine, it is well known,
Doth wash your city of Cologne;
But tell me, nymphs! what power divine
Shall henceforth wash the river Rhine?*   10

649. IMPROMPTU ON HOCK HEIMAR

[Jul 1828]

The occasion of C's lines is reported in Julian Charles Young *A Memoir of Charles Mayne Young "Tragedian," with Extracts from his Son's Journal* (2 vols 1871) I 182:

> he, Wordsworth, and I, were floating down the Rhine together in a boat we had hired conjointly. The day was remarkably sultry; we had all three taken a considerable walk before our dinner; and what with fatigue, heat, and the exhaustion consequent on garrulity, Coleridge complained grievously of thirst. When he heard there was no house near at hand, and saw a leathern flask slung over my shoulder, he asked me what it contained. On my telling him it was Hock Heimar, he shook his head, and swore he would as soon take vinegar. After a while, however, finding his thirst increasing, he exclaimed, "I find I must conquer my dislike—eat humble pie, and beg for a draught." He had no sooner rinsed his mouth with the obnoxious fluid, than he spat it out, and vented his disgust in the following impromptu . . .

Cf *TT* (*CC*) II 422–3. C found the weather during his continental tour oppressively hot, and his notebooks record his reaction to different kinds of wine, none of which lived up to Mum's Rudesheimer (Notebook 40 = BM Add MS 47535 f 6ᵛ; *CN* v). He, the Wordsworths, and Young were all staying with Mrs Aders at Bad Godesberg.

---

* As Necessity is the mother of Invention, and extremes beget each other, the fact above recorded may explain how this *ancient* town (which, alas! as sometimes happens with venison, *has been kept too long,*) came to be the birthplace of the most fragrant of spirituous fluids, the *Eau de Cologne.*

In Spain, that land of monks and apes,
The thing called wine doth come from *grapes:*
But, on the noble river Rhine,
The thing called *gripes* doth come from wine.

650. ABSURD GERMAN RHYMES

[Jul 1828]

C wrote the lines in Notebook 40 = BM Add MS 47535 f 7ʳ (*CN* v), under the heading "N.B. Haunted by my own absurd German rhymes—", on 13 or 14 Jul. Tr "The Devil and I | Both of us were poorly: | I got better, thanks be to God, | But he remained ill."

    C and his party had left Mrs Aders at Bad Godesberg the previous Wednesday (9 Jul), and were sightseeing on their own. The notebooks record his feeling of ill health at this time.

Der Teufel und Ich
Alle beide war'n siech:
Ich genäs, gott sey dank,
Er aber blieb krank.

651. THE NETHERLANDS

[Aug 1828]

C drafted the lines in Notebook 40 (*CN* v), where they follow an observation in prose: "Assuredly, I have been seldom more agreeably disappointed than in the voyage per Steam-boat from Rotterdam to Antwerp—for the first two or three hours on the Maas." They might have found a place in the long poem on the Rhine which he projected on his return (poem **652.X1**). C was on his way home from Bad Godesberg, where he and the Wordsworths had been staying with Mrs Aders. The weather was close and hot.

Water and Windmills, Greenness, Islets Green,
Willows whose trunks beside the Shadows stood

Of their own higher half, and willowy Swamps,
Farm-houses that at anchor seemed & on the inland sky
The fly-transfixing Spires—   5
Water, wide water, greenness & green banks
And water seen

652. THE GARDEN OF BOCCACCIO

[Jun–Aug 1828?]

The poem draws on early feelings associated with SH (*CN* I 1105; cf lines 25–6) and on C's memories of the Tuscan landscape in 1806. It alludes to and summarises themes from poems written even earlier—e.g. **171** *Frost at Midnight* and **178** *Kubla Khan*. Lines 35–42 enlarge on a connection between Boccaccio and Italy and the Scalds and Scandinavia which C had noted as early, perhaps, as 1797. The poem as a whole also draws on C's interest in Boccaccio, as he had expressed it in his reading and in his lectures (*CM*—*CC*—I 542–4), and makes use of lines on philosophy and poetry he drafted in Oct 1819 (*CN* IV 4623; cf lines 49–56).

The poem was selected by F. M. Reynolds for publication in the *Keepsake* annual before C left for his continental tour in summer 1828; and C afterwards described it as "written for one of the Engravings" (*CL* VI 778: to A. A. Watts [Dec 1828]; cf VI 757: to C. Aders [Sept 1828]). The engraving in *The Keepsake* (=Fig 12) is by Francis Englehart or Engleheart. It represents a scene depicted by Thomas Stothard in a watercolour painted in 1825 different from any of those used in the ten engraved by Augustus Fox from drawings by Stothard and published by William Pickering in *Il decamerone* ed Ugo Foscolo (3 vols 1825) and in a separate folio. It shows the narrators of the *Decameron* stories engaged in the occupations mentioned by Boccaccio in his description of their proceedings on the third day, in the garden by the fountain where they continued to assemble daily. Englehart shows two "serviceable nymphs" with the ten narrators, and his engraving is a more pleasing and interesting composition than Fox's, which includes few of the details described or interpreted by C in lines 61–70. The Friend ("sweet" in the ms) whose quiet hand placed the design on C's desk was surely AG, but it is not known whether she was herself the first to draw his attention to it, as ELG implied (*CL* VI 757n), or whether she simply brought upstairs to him what had been sent to him by Charles Heath, the engraver and proprietor of *The Keepsake*, or Reynolds, the editor.

Whichever was the case, the relevant part of the poem may well have been in progress of composition while the engraving was being made. C had a long-standing interest in Stothard's work. He had met him while the *Decameron* series was in the making, Stothard made a drawing of Christabel which was pub-

12. Thomas Stothard's *Garden of Boccaccio*, as engraved by
Francis Englehart for *The Keepsake for 1829* ed F. M. Reynolds,
facing p 282. Adjustments were evidently made to fit the engraving to
the poem, which modified the original illustration (see the headnote)

lished in *The Bijou* in the same year as the present poem appeared in *The Keepsake*, and C later expressed admiration for Stothard's illustrations to Paltock's *Peter Wilkins* (see *TT* 5 Jul 1834—*CC*—I 494). It is not impossible, therefore, that the present poem is based on a recollection of Stothard's original, or a fresh acquaintance with a version of it. The watercolour of 1825 is reproduced in Shelley M. Bennett *Thomas Stothard* (Columbia, Mo 1988) fig 50, and may be that referred to by Thomas Hood in May 1825 (*Letters* ed P. F. Morgan—Toronto 1973—64–5; the Pickering engravings were not published until Aug).

Hood's interest in Boccaccio's setting surfaced in *The Plea of the Midsummer Faires* (1827) sts 3–6; and for further literary interest of the same kind cf Winthrop Mackworth Praed's *Stanzas Written in Lady Myrtle's Boccaccio*, which was published in *The Literary Souvenir for 1832* (Praed, a friend of DC at Cambridge, dined with C and WW at Antwerp on their tour).

There is only one ms, a hastily written and incompletely revised fair copy submitted to the printer. C made further revisions in proof, and, after the poem had been published in *The Keepsake*, it was included in *PW* (1829, 1834). However, while the poem called on experiences in C's background which were important to him, it appears to have been put together to meet a particular commitment and not to have engaged much more of his attention. The ms given to the printer contains patent errors, owing to its hasty composition, it is incomplete, and it is unrevised. At the proof stage C failed to add a passage he had intended to incorporate; he did not keep a copy of what he had submitted, so that some misreadings of his ms by the printer went uncorrected; and he made no further corrections to the text after it had been printed—indeed, a few additional errors of paragraphing crept in.

No single text of the poem can be printed as it stands: the ms was submitted in the expectation that corrections and additions would be made; the printed texts contain errors of their own, as described. The *Keepsake* text is given here, correcting the errors it obviously introduced and with C's capitalisation preserved.

> Of late, in one of those most weary Hours,
> When Life seems emptied of all genial Powers,
> A dreary Mood, which he who ne'er has known
> May bless his happy lot, I sate alone;
> And, from the numbing Spell to win relief,   5
> Call'd on the PAST for thought of Glee or Grief.
> In vain! bereft alike of Grief and Glee,
> I sate and cow'r'd o'er my own Vacancy!
> And as I watch'd the dull continuous Ache,
> Which, all else slumb'ring, seem'd alone to wake; 10
> O Friend! long wont to notice yet conceal,
> And soothe by silence what words cannot heal,
> I but half saw that quiet hand of thine

Place on my desk this exquisite Design,
Boccaccio's Garden and its Faery,   15
The Love, the Joyaunce and the Gallantry!
An IDYLL, with Boccaccio's Spirit warm,
Fram'd in the silent Poesy of Form.

Like Flocks adown a newly-bathed Steep
Emerging from a mist; or like a Stream   20
Of Music soft that not dispels the Sleep,
But casts in happier moulds the Slumberer's Dream,
Gaz'd by an idle Eye with silent might
The Picture stole upon my inward Sight.
A tremulous Warmth crept gradual o'er my Chest,   25
As though an Infant's Finger touch'd my Breast.
And one by one (I know not whence) were brought
All Spirits of Power, that most had stirr'd my Thought
In selfless Boyhood, on a new world tost
Of wonder, and in its own fancies lost;   30
Or charmed my Youth, that, kindled from above,
Loved ere it loved, and sought a form for Love;
Or lent a lustre to the earnest Scan
Of Manhood, musing what and whence is Man!

Wild Strain of Scalds, that in the sea-worn Caves   35
Rehears'd their war-spell to the winds and waves;

32. C quoted the line in a discussion of love and beauty, which mingled **108** *Composed while Climbing Brockley Coomb* with memories of SH, dated 31 Oct 1830 (Notebook 47=BM Add MS 47542 f 38ᵛ; *CN* v): see poem **108** headnote.

35–42. The progress from the Scandinavian or Icelandic bards (Scalds) to Boccaccio's Italy may owe something to C's use in 1818 of F. Schlegel, who in lecture 6 of his *Geschichte der alten und neuen Litteratur* (2 vols Vienna 1815) derived the spirit of modern European poetry from northern origins. Schlegel also referred to Hertha (line 38), the German and Scandina-

vian goddess of fertility. See *Lects 1808–1819 (CC)* II 54, 74.

C's description also recalls the substance and phrasing of a note (of 1797?) given in *SW&F (CC)* 68; and lines 37–8 include and conflate information he could have found in P. H. Mallet *Northern Antiquities* (2 vols 1770), translated by Thomas Percy from *Introduction à l'histoire de Dannemarc*. C used Mallet in 1796 for his "Historical Sketch of the Manners and Religion of the ancient Germans" (*Watchman—CC—* 89–92). Mallet mentions the warlike songs of the scalds and gives references to Tacitus for two aspects of

Or fateful Hymn of those prophetic Maids,
That call'd on Hertha in deep Forest Glades;
Or minstrel Lay, that cheer'd the Baron's Feast;
Or Rhyme of City pomp, of Monk and Priest,   40
Judge, Mayor, and many a Guild in long Array,
To high Church pacing on the Great Saint's Day.
And many a Verse which to myself I sang,
That woke the Tear yet stole away the Pang,
Of Hopes which in lamenting I renew'd.   45
And last, a Matron now, of sober mien
Yet radiant still and with no Earthly sheen,
Whom as a faery child my Childhood woo'd
Even in my Dawn of Thought—PHILOSOPHY.
Though then unconscious of herself, pardie,   50
She bore no other name than POESY;
And, like a Gift from Heaven, in lifeful Glee,
That had but newly left a Mother's knee,
Prattled and play'd with Bird and Flower, and Stone,
As if with elfin Playfellows well known,   55
And Life revealed to Innocence alone.

Thanks, gentle Artist! now I can descry
Thy fair Creation with a waking Eye,
And *all* awake! And now in fix'd Gaze stand,
Now wander through the Eden of thy Hand;   60
Praise the green Arches, in the Fountain clear
See fragment Shadows of the crossing deer;
And with that serviceable Nymph I stoop

German religion, respect for women and their prophetic gifts (Tacitus *Germania* 8; *Histories* 4.61, 65; Mallet I 141, 316–17), and also for their worship of Hertha in a forest glade (Tacitus *Germania* 40; Mallet I 93). Cf Tacitus *Germania* 9 and Mallet I 78–9 for their belief in a single creator god, not to be worshipped within walls or represented in human form.

43–4. Borrowed from **120** *Fragments of an Epistle to Thomas Poole* 12–13. This part of the *Epistle* was in existence as early as 31 Dec 1796.

49–56. See vol II commentary for the notebook entry of Oct 1819 from which this passage derives (*CN* IV 4623).

62. The two deer in Englehart's engraving are grazing, not crossing (as Fox's four deer are, accompanied by more obvious shadows). C is perhaps imagining the shapes of the deer as they would be seen through the fountain by the company seated on the grass. Cf line 109EC.

63–70. The "serviceable Nymph", the banquet on the grass, and the

The Crystal from its restless Pool to scoop.
I see no longer! I myself am there,   65
Sit on the Ground-sward, and the banquet share.
'Tis I, that sweep that Lute's love-echoing Strings,
And gaze upon the Maid who gazing Sings:
Or pause and listen to the tinkling Bells
From the nigh Tower, and think that there she dwells.   70
With old Boccaccio's Soul I stand possest,
And breathe an Air like life, that swells my Chest.

The Brightness of the World, O thou once free,
And always fair, rare Land of Courtesy!
O FLORENCE! with the Tuscan Fields and Hills,   75
And famous Arno fed with all their Rills;
Thou brightest Star of Star-bright Italy!
Rich, ornate, populous, all treasures thine,
The golden Corn, the Olive, and the Vine.
Fair Cities, gallant Mansions, Castles old,   80
And Forests, where beside his leafy Hold
The sullen Boar hath heard the distant Horn,
And whets his Tusks against the gnarled Thorn;
Palladian Palace with its storied Halls;
Fountains, where LOVE lies listening to their Falls;   85
Gardens, where flings the Bridge its airy Span,
And Nature makes her happy Home with Man;
Where many a gorgeous Flower is duly fed
With its own Rill, in its own spangled Bed,
And wreathes the marble Urn, or leans its Head,   90
A mimic Mourner, that with Veil withdrawn
Weeps liquid Gems, the Presents of the Dawn.

Thine all Delights, and every Muse is thine;
And more than all, the Embrace and Intertwine
Of All with All in gay and twinkling Dance!   95
Mid Gods of Greece and Warriors of Romance,

"nigh Tower" are all missing from the scene depicted in Fox's engraving.

65. The echo of **156** *This Lime-tree Bower my Prison* 46 is significant because C's reverie recovers similar details from other poems written at an earlier time: cf 67–8 below and **115** *The Eolian Harp* 12–25; 69–70 below and **171** *Frost at Midnight* 26–33.

92⁺. C intended to add six lines here (MS 1, used as printer's copy, has six rows of crosses), but never did so.

See! BOCCACE sits, unfolding on his Knees
The new-found Roll of Old Mæonides;*
But from his Mantle's Fold, and near the Heart,
Peers Ovid's *Holy Book of Love's sweet Smart!†*   100

O all-enjoying and all-blending Sage,
Long be it mine to con thy mazy page,
Where, half-conceal'd, the eye of Fancy views
Fauns, Nymphs, and winged Saints, all gracious to thy Muse!

Still in thy Garden let me watch thy pranks,   105
And see in Dian's Vest, between the Ranks
Of the trim Vines, some Maid that half-believes
The *vestal* fires, of which her Lover grieves,
With that sly Satyr peeping through the leaves!

* Boccaccio claimed for himself the Glory of having first introduced the
Works of Homer to his Countrymen.

   † I know few more striking or more interesting proofs of the overwhelm-
ing influence which the Study of the Greek and Roman Classics exercised on
the Judgments, Feelings, and Imaginations of the Literati of Europe at the com-
mencement of the Restoration of Literature, than in the passage in the Filocopo
of Boccaccio: where the sage instructor, Racheo, as soon as the young prince and   5
the beautiful girl Biancofiore had learned their letters, set them to study the *Holy
Book*, Ovid's A R T   O F   L O V E. "Incominciò Racheo a mettere il suo officio in
esecuzione con intera sollecitudine. E loro, in breve tempo, insegnato a conoscer
le lettere, *fece leggere il santo libro d'Ovvidio, nel quale il sommo poeta mostra,
come i santi fuochi di Venere si debbano ne freddi cuori accendere.*"   10

98. Old Mæonides] Homer.
   100fn. For the passage C quotes
here see also *CM* (*CC*) I 543–4, where
he is annotating *Il filocopo* in Boc-
caccio *Opere* ed Lorenzo Ciccarelli (6
vols Naples 1723–4) I 63. Tr "Racheo
began to carry out his duty with com-
plete solicitude. And, having taught
them to recognise the letters, within a
short space of time *he had them read
the holy book of Ovid, in which the
supreme poet demonstrates how the
holy fires of Venus must be kindled in
cold hearts.*
   109. sly Satyr] C's addition, it
seems. It is not present in the Stothard
original or in the engravings by Fox
and Englehart.

653. TO BABY BATES

[1828–9]

The verses are known only from a transcript in a contemporary album and a transcript of a transcript reported in 1888. The album version is addressed to an acquaintance of the Miss Barbour of poem **658,** "who was not satisfied with some very fine verses of the Author's because no mention was made of America, Composed while nodding after dinner." It is this version that is given here, adding some punctuation (the title is JDC's).

Baby Bates was the daughter of Joshua Bates (1788–1864), the American financier and subsequently senior partner in Baring Brothers and Co. In 1828–9 the Bates family were neighbours of the Gillmans at Highgate. For letters of C to Mrs Bates (d 1863) see *CL* vi 774: 28/9 Nov 1828; 792: 23 Jun 1829; and Sotheby's Catalogue 14 Mar 1979 lot 323. P.A.L. "The Drama at Hereford: Dramatic Costumes" *N&Q* 4th ser i (16 May 1868) 464–5 records a dinner at which both C and Joshua Bates were present in 1828; and the American John Wheeler recorded a visit to C in the company of Joshua Bates and Miss Barbour on 28 Jul 1829 (*TT—CC*—ii 429). The collections of Joshua Bates and his wife made up the basis of the Boston Public Library.

You come from o'er the waters,
　　From famed Columbia's land,
And you have sons & daughters,
　　And money at Command.

While I live in an island,　　　　　　　　　　　　5
　　Great Britain is its name,
With money none to buy land,
　　The more it is the shame.

But we are all the Children
　　Of one great Lord of Love,　　　　　　　　　10
Whose mercy, like a mill drain
　　Runs over from above.

Lullaby, Lullaby,
　　Sugar plums & Cates,
Close your lids & peeping eye,　　　　　　　　15
　　Bonny Baby B——s.

654. EXEMPLARY EPITAPH
ON A BLACK CAT

[1828?]

The only known text of the poem is a holograph ms whose wm is dated 1828. The lines are written on the verso, under the title "Epigraph." They are introduced by a prose preamble on the recto:

NOTA BENE!
   The following Epitaph comprizes all the points of perfection, which Dr Johnson—for I scorn such vulgar Authorities as those of Harry Stottle, Long High-Nose, and Squint-ill Young, commonly called Squintillion— requires in this lapidary department of the Muses—ex. gr. the Name of the Defunct, in the Epitaph itself, and not fobbed up in the prose Hic Jacet,[1] at the top; the character, and characteristic events of ~~his~~ the Life, & why and how Hic, haec or hoc[2] died. But to do full justice to all the ~~perfections~~ Beauties of this charming epicedion(, or "Melodious Tear." (mem. MIL-TON)—Tears such

   As eyeless Marbles weep! tho' niggard Doom
   [??]Denied to this ~~Dead~~ceased a Marble Tomb—)

would require a commentary of more pages than the Epitaph itself has words—nay, syllables. P. S. To preclude all suspicion of any exaggeration in this prefatory encomium, it is right to inform the Reader that it was composed and prefixed by the Poet himself—in modest imitation of sundry illustrious Contemporaries who review their own Works—which, however, is seldom done where the Editor of the Review happens to be a Son or Son-in-law.—

   —Now—pause—prepare yourself and
   turn over.

C alludes to Dr Johnson's *Essay on Epitaphs* (1740), which was frequently reprinted during the 18th century, often as an introduction to collections of epitaphs. The allusions to Aristotle, Longinus, and Edward Young (1683–1765)/ Quintilian are deliberately to great authorities in general: none of them is remembered for what he said about the form. "Melodious Tear" is from *Lycidas* 14; the verse quotation is untraced, and may be a generic parody. The allusion to a son or son-in-law is similarly nonsensical: JTC was editor of the *Quarterly Review* for three or four months in 1824, but he was not C's son-in-law; HNC did not become C's son-in-law until 1829, and was not editor of a journal; HC

---

[1] Tr "He lies dead."   [2] Tr "He, she, or it".

and DC do not fit the bill either. It is possible that the Gillmans had a black cat, and that the lines were written for someone like Henry Gillman (1813–58).

In more serious vein, it might be noted that C was a long- time connoisseur of epitaphs: see e.g. *CN* I 418, 450, 494–6, 548, 1267. He discussed the subject with WW in 1799 (*CN* I 1588; cf 494), and the first of WW's three essays on epitaphs was included in *The Friend* xxv (22 Feb 1809) (*CC*) II 334–46 (= *W Prose* II 43–119).

Here lies our Black Cat!—
Caught many a Rat:
Till—sad Exchange!
He caught the Mange:
    And, no Cure found,   5
    In a Water-Tub
We drown'd, drown'd, drown'd,
    Drown'd, drown'd, drown'd,
        Drown'd, drown'd —— drown'd
        DON BELZEBUB!!   10

655. ALICE DU CLÓS
OR, THE FORKED TONGUE: A BALLAD

[1828–9?]

Parts of the poem appear to have been a long time in suspension, and it was never properly concluded. Thus, lines 111–12 appear (var) in a notebook entry which KC dates Dec 1801 (*CN* I 1066; cf *CL* v 249: to T. Allsop 8 Oct 1822); the pun on "Page" (line 169) is anticipated in a line copied out of Cartwright in Feb 1804 (*CN* II 1915); the first four lines were written in a notebook between May and Sept 1812 (*CN* III 4163). It is just possible that this is the ballad C told JG he would finish while he was at Ramsgate on 6 Oct 1824 (*CL* v 375; poem **598.X1**), and fragmentary drafts of lines 9–14 and 15–34 might represent this stage. C had met SH at Ramsgate a year before (*The Letters of Sara Hutchinson* ed K. Coburn—1954—262–7), and the present poem contains significant echoes of writing and situations connected with SH and WW (see lines 91EC, 111-12EC). It indeed turns on an event similar to C's own self-induced misapprehension of a sexual relationship between SH and WW (*CN* II 2975; cf II 3148; III 3328; IV 4537), and might be read as an attempt to expiate C's long-standing sense of betrayal. The present version appears to date from between mid-1828 and mid-1829.

C promised the poem to F. M. Reynolds for *The Keepsake* before he went on holiday with WW and DW in Jun 1828, and gave him the first instalment in Sept (*CL* VI 749n, 752: to C. Aders 14 Aug 1828; 756: to F. M. Reynolds [Sept 1828]). In late Jul 1829 he sent Reynolds the remainder of what he had written—all but the six or eight concluding stanzas, and with a note of some stanzas to be inserted into what he had sent before (*CL* VI 800, 803: [late Jul 1829]; 808: [6 Aug 1829]). There are parallels with other poems written in 1828–9, e.g. **652** *The Garden of Boccaccio*. Owing to some misunderstanding about payment, which might also have had to do with the incomplete state of C's ms, the poem was not included in *The Keepsake* but returned to C. He offered it to *Bl Mag* later in 1829 (*CL* VI 821: to W. Blackwood 20 Oct 1829), but it was not published until 1834, in *PW*.

The only near-complete ms known to exist is the one sent to Reynolds in two instalments in 1828–9. The first batch extended to some point between the present lines 90 and 129, and the second was a revision of the linking passage (including the insertion of lines 97–112) to line 186. C appears never to have written the "sort of Post-script Super-conclusion" of "six to eight stanzas in the legendary, supernatural, imaginative style of popular superstition" (*CL* VI 800; see also 914: to HNC [endorsed 10 Jun 1832]). As he explained again to Reynolds, they would have formed "a highly lyrical & imprcssive conclusion— intimating the fate & punishment of Julian & the Traitor" (*CL* VI 808: [6 Aug 1829]):

> and tho' every thought & image is present to my mind, I have not, in the existing state of my feelings,[1] the power of bringing them forth in the requisite force & fire of diction & metre. For Poetry (if any thing, I write, can deserve that name) is not a matter of will or choice with me. The *sickish* Feel, that is sure to accompany the attempt to compose verses mechanically, by dint of the head alone, acts like a poison on my health.

When C offered the poem to *Bl Mag* two months later, it was as "A Lyrical Tale, 250 lines"—as if he had indeed written the intended sixty or so extra lines—but the version published in 1834 adds only a single stanza to the ms. The text given here is a corrected transcription from the ms, ignoring the several drafts and cancellations, and adding the final stanza from *PW* (1834).

"One Word with two Meanings is the Traitor's Shield and Shaft: and a slit tongue be his Blazon!"

Caucasian Proverb.

"The Sun is not yet risen
But the Dawn lies red on the dew:

---

[1] I.e. C's vexation arising from his sense of Reynolds's unbusinesslike dealings.

Lord Julian has stolen from the Hunter's away,
Is seeking, Lady! for You.

    "Put on your Dress of Green,   5
    Your Buskins and your Quiver!
    Lord Julian is a hasty Man,
      Long waiting brook'd he never.

    I dare not doubt him, that he means
      To wed you on a day   10
    Your Lord and Master for to be
      And you his Lady gay—
    O Lady! throw your Book aside!
    I would not, that my Lord should chide."

Thus spake Sir Hugh, the Vassal Knight   15
    To Alice, Child of old Du Clos,
As spotless fair, as airy light
    As that moon-shiny Doe,
The gold Star on its Brow, her Sire's Ancestral Crest!
For ere the Lark had left his nest,   20
    She in the Garden Bower below
Sate, loosely wrapt in Maiden White,
Her face half-drooping from the sight,
    A Snow-drop in a tuft of Snow!

O close your eyes, and strive to see   25
The studious Maid, with book on knee,
    Ah! earliest-open'd Flower;
While yet with keen unblunted light
The Morning Star shone opposite
    The Lattice of her Bower—   30
Alone of all the starry Host
    As if in prideful scorn
Of flight and fear he stay'd behind
    To brave the' advancing Morn.

O! Alice could read passing well,   35
    And she was conning then

Dan Ovid's mazy tale of Loves,
   And Gods and Beasts and Men.

The Vassal's Speech, his taunting Vein,
It thrill'd like venom thro' her Brain;   40
   Yet never from the Book
She rais'd her head, nor did she deign
   The Knight a single Look.

"Off, Traitor-Friend! how dar'st thou fix
   Thy wanton Gaze on Me?   45
And why, against my earnest suit
   Does Julian send by thee?

"Go, tell thy Lord, that slow is sure:
   Fair speed his shafts to-day!
I follow here a stronger Lure,   50
   And chace a gentler prey."

She said: and with a baleful Smile
   The Vassal Knight reel'd off—
Like a huge billow from a Bark
   Toil'd in the deep Sea-trough   55

That shouldering sideways in mid plunge
   Is travers'd by a Flash:
And staggering onward leaves the Ear
   With dull and distant Crash.

And Alice sate with troubled mien   60
A moment—for the Scoff was keen
   And thro' her veins did shiver!
Then rose and donn'd her Dress of Green,
   Her Buskins and her Quiver.

There stands the flowring May-thorn Tree!   65
From thro' the veiling mist you see

---

37. Cf **652** *The Garden of Boccaccio* 100 "Peers Ovid's *Holy Book of Love's sweet Smart!*" It should also be noted that the word "mazy" had particular connotations for C—with processes such as association and amoral attractiveness.

The black and shadowy Stem,—
Smit by the Sun the Mist in glee
Dissolves to lightsome Jewelry—
   Each Blossom hath its Gem!   70

The tear-drop glittering to a smile,
The gay Maid on the Garden Stile
   Mimics the Hunter's Shout—
"Hip! Florian, hip! To horse! to horse!
   Go, bring the Palfreys out.   75

"My Julian's out with all his clan,
   And, bonny Boy! you wiss,
Lord Julian is a hasty Man—
   Who comes late, comes amiss."

Now Florian was a stripling Squire,   80
   A gallant Boy of Spain
That toss'd his head in joy and pride
Behind his Lady fair to ride,
   But blush'd to hold her train.

The Huntress is in her Dress of Green—   85
And forth they go; she with her Bow,
   Her buskins and her quiver—!
The Squire—no younger e'er was seen—
With restless arm and laughing e'en—
   He makes his Javelin quiver—   90

And had not Alice stay'd the race,
And stopt to see, a moment's space,
   The whole great Globe of Light
Give the last parting kiss-like Touch
To the Eastern Ridge, it lack'd not much,   95
   They had o'er-ta'en the Knight.—

91. Alice] The ms and printed versions give Ellen. C's mistaken substitution of the name of the sisterly friend of the protagonist of **155** *Continuation of "The Three Graves"* is a reminder of how close the emotional concerns of the two unfinished poems are.

It chanced that up the Covert Lane
   Where Julian waiting stood
A neighbor Knight prick'd on to join
   The Huntsmen in the Wood.   100

And with him must Lord Julian go,
   Tho' with an anger'd Mind:
Betroth'd not wedded to his Bride
In vain he sought, twixt shame and pride,
   Excuse to stay behind.   105

He bit his lip, he wrung his Glove,
He look'd around, he look'd above;
But pretext none could find or frame!
Alas! alas! and weladay!
It grieves me sore to think, to say,   110
That Names so seldom meet with Love,
   Yet Love wants courage without a Name!

Strait from the forest's skirt the Trees
   O'er-branching made an Aisle,
Where Hermit old might pace and chaunt   115
   As in a Minster's Pile—

From underneath its leafy screen
   And from the twilight Shade
You pass at once into a green,
   A green and lightsome Glade.   120

And there Lord Julian sate on steed
   Behind him in a round
Stood Knight and Squire and menial train—
Against the leash the Grey-hounds strain;
   The Horses paw'd the Ground.   125

When up the Alley Green Sir Hugh
   Spurr'd in upon the Sward—

111–12. The lines were originally drafted in Dec 1801 (*CN* I 1066), at a time when C was preoccupied with thoughts of SH.

And mute, without a word, did he
    Fall in behind his Lord.

Lord Julian turn'd his steed half round—   130
    "What? doth not Alice deign
To accept your loving Convoy, Knight?
Or doth she fear our woodland sleight,
    And join us on the plain?"

With stifled tones the Knight reply'd,   135
And Look askance on either side—
    "Nay—let the Hunt proceed!
The Lady's Message that I bear,
I guess, would scantly please your ear,
    And less deserves your Heed.   140

"You sent betimes—Not yet unbarr'd
    I found the middle door.
Two Stirrers only met my eyes,
    Fair Alice and one more.—

"I came unlook'd for: and, it seem'd,   145
    In an unwelcome hour:
And found the Daughter of Du Clós
    Within the lattic'd Bower.

"But hush! the rest may wait. If lost,
    No great Loss, I divine—   150
And idle words will better suit
    A fair Maid's Lips than mine."

"God's Wrath! Speak out, Man!" Julian cried,
    O'ermaster'd by the sudden Smart:
And feigning wrath, sharp, blunt and rude   155
The Knight his subtle Shift pursued—
"Scowl not at me. Command my Skill
To lure your Hawk back, if you will—
    But not a Woman's Heart.

" 'Go! (said she) tell him. Slow is sure!—   160
    Fair speed his shafts to day!

I follow here a stronger Lure,
  And chace a gentler Prey.'

"The Game, pardie, was full in sight,
That then did, if I saw aright, 165
  The fair Dame's Eyes engage;
For turning, as I took my ways,
I saw them fix'd with stedfast gaze
  Full on her wanton Page."

The last word of the Traitor Knight 170
It had but enter'd Julian's Ear—-
From two o'er-arching Oaks between
With glistning helm-like Cap is seen
  Borne on in giddy Cheer—

A Youth, that ill his Steed can guide; 175
Yet with reverted Face doth ride
  As answering to a Voice
That seems at once to laugh and chide—
"Not mine, dear Mistress!" still he cryd,
  Tis this mad Filly's Choice." 180

With sudden Bound beyond the Boy
See! see!—that Face of Hope and Joy,
  That regal Front! those Cheeks aglow!
Thou needed'st but the Crescent Sheen
A quiver'd Dian to have been, 185
  Thou lovely Child of old Du Clos!

Dark as a dream Lord Julian stood,
Swift as a dream, from forth the wood,
  Sprang on the plighted Maid!
With fatal aim, and frantic force, 190
The shaft was hurl'd—a lifeless corse,

175–80. The odd, even awkward, position of the rider is determined by the allegorical meaning of moving forward with reverted face: cf **388** *Time, Real and Imaginary* 7–8 (also **560** *To a Comic Author* 8).

187–93. As indicated in the headnote, this stanza is a nominal conclusion used for the poem's publication in *PW* (1834) in lieu of the six or eight stanzas which C intended to write but could not achieve.

Fair Alice from her vaulting horse,
Lies bleeding on the glade.

656. REPLY TO A LADY'S QUESTION RESPECTING THE ACCOMPLISHMENTS MOST DESIRABLE IN AN INSTRUCTRESS

[Jun 1829?]

The poem appears to have been written in the summer of 1829, specifically for Emily Trevenen, a middle-aged spinster and "instructress" who became a friend of C's family after DC moved to Helston in Cornwall. The version given here is the one C transcribed for her, and the admixture of capitalised and bold words, and the metrical markings, are calculated in their effect. An earlier draft differs in some details of punctuation and orthography, and records a prior alternative version of the last stanza:

> Then like a Statue, with a Statue's Strength,
> And with a **Smile**, the Sister-Fay of those   = Fairy
> Who at meek Evening's Close
> To teach our Grief repose
> Their freshly-gather'd Store of Moonbeams wreathe
> On Marble Lips, a CHANTRY has made breathe,
> Stands the mute &c—

The draft might suggest that the germ of the poem lay in a recollection of Viola's description, "She sat like patience on a monument, | Smiling at grief" (*Twelfth Night* II iv 115–16; cf *Pericles* v i 137–8). F. L. Chantrey (1781–1841) was the leading portrait sculptor of the day and a friend of J. H. Green: cf *CL* VI 738: to J. H. Green 5 May 1828 and **643** *Extempore on Three Surgeons* headnote.

A few minor changes were made in the version which was published in *The Keepsake for 1830* and, at the last moment, in *PW* (1834). The *PW* version is entitled *Love, Hope, and Patience in Education*.

O'er wayward Childhood would'st thou hold firm rule,
Yet sun thee in the light of Happy Faces,
LOVE, HOPE and PATIENCE—these must be *thy* GRACES,
And in thy own heart let them first keep school!

For as old Atlas on his broad neck places 5
Heaven's starry Globe and there sustains ìt: so
Do these bear up the little World below
Of **Education**—**Patience, Love** and **Hope**.

Methinks, I see them group'd in seemly shew,
The straiten'd Arms uprais'd, the Palms aslope, 10
And Robes that touching as adown they flow
Distinctly blend, like snow emboss'd on snow.

O part them never! If HOPE prostrate lie,
        LOVE too will sink and die.

But **Love** is subtle and will proof derive 15
From her own life, that **Hope** is yet alive:
And bending o'er, with soul-transfusing eyes
And the low murmurs of the Mother Dove,
Wooes back the fleeting spírít and half-supplies:
Thus **Love** repays to **Hope** what **Hope** first gave to **Love**! 20

Yet haply there will come a weary day,
        When overtask'd at length
Both **Love** and **Hope** beneath the load give way.
Then with a Statue's smile, a Statue's strength
Stands the mute Sister, **Patience**, nothing loth, 25
And both supporting does the work of both.

657. THE TEACHER'S OFFICE

[1829?]

The only known text is a small broadside or handout, subscribed "S. T. COLE-
RIDGE", printed for the Home and Colonial School Society, Gray's Inn Road.

15–20. On Love and Hope keeping each other alive cf **623** *The Impro-visatore* 31–4.
20. On Youth and Hope as "the two realities of this Phantom World", and the relation they bear to Love, cf *CL* VI 705: to DC [Oct 1827]; also *TT* 10 Aug 1833 (*CC*) II 247.
25. nothing loth] The recollection of Milton's famous phrase, describing the newly fallen Eve (*PL* IX 1039), is presumably adventitious.

The Society was founded in 1836 as the Home and Colonial Infant School Society, and took the name The Home and Colonial School Society in 1848. It moved to the Gray's Inn Road address in 1838, and remained there until 1903. It is now defunct.

There are no references to the poem among C's papers or by his contemporaries. Nor is it clear how the Society could have obtained it after his death. DC might have given it to the institution—he was certainly sympathetic to its stated aims—but there is no evidence of his having done so in his extant correspondence, at HRC or elsewhere.

The only clues as to the possible date, if C is indeed the author, are the resemblances to **656** *The Accomplishments Most Desirable in an Instructress*. The internal evidence for C's authorship is weak: the poem could easily have been written by a later author—even by DC himself—in imitation of the poem published in *PW* (1834), and attributed to C by mistake.

"Take heed that ye despise not one of these little ones."—MATT. xviii. 10.

Desirest thou a Teacher's work? Ask wisdom from above:
It is a work of toil and care, of patience and of love.
Ask for an understanding heart, to rule in godly fear
The feeble flock of which the Lord hath made thee overseer,

Alas! thou surely may'st expect some evils to endure— 5
E'en children's faults are hard to bear, and harder still to cure;
They may be wilful, proud, perverse, in temper unsubdued,
In mind obtuse and ignorant, in manners coarse and rude;
Thou may'st contend with sluggish minds, till weary and depress'd,
And trace the windings of deceit in many a youthful breast; 10
Yet scorn them not: remember Him who loved His lambs to feed,
Who never quench'd the smoking flax, nor broke the bruised reed;
Who for the thankless and the vile poured out His precious blood;
Who makes His sun to rise upon the evil and the good.
The love of God extends to all the works His hand has framed; 15
He would not that the meanest child should perish unreclaim'd.
Pray that His Holy Spirit may thy selfish heart incline
To bear with all their waywardness as He has borne with thine.

If by example, or by word, thou leadest them to sin,
Thou perillest the precious souls that Jesus died to win; 20
If thou from indolent neglect shouldst leave their minds unsown,
Or shouldst their evil passions rouse, by yielding to thine own;

Shouldst thou intimidate the weak, and thus destroy their peace,
Or drive the stubborn to rebel, by harshness or caprice;
Shouldst thou their kindlier feelings chill by apathy or scorn,   25
'Twere good for them, and for thyself, that thou hadst ne'er been born.

But oh! what blessings may be thine, when thou hast daily striven
To guide them in the narrow path that leadeth up to heaven;—
What joy to see their youthful feet in wisdom's way remain;
To know that, by the grace of God, thy labour is not vain;—   30
To watch the dawn of perfect day in many a hopeful child;
To see the crooked mind grow straight, the rugged temper mild;—
To mark the sinful habit check'd, the stubborn will subdued;
The cold and selfish spirit warm'd by love and gratitude;—
To read in every sparkling eye a depth of love unknown;   35
To hear the voice of joy and health in every silver tone!

If such the joys that now repay the Teacher's work of love,
If such thy recompence on earth, what must it be above!
Oh! blessed are the faithful dead who die unto the Lord;
Sweet is the rest they find in heaven, and great is their reward;   40
Their works perform'd in humble faith are all recorded there;
They see the travail of their soul, the answer to their prayer:
There may the Teacher and the Taught one glorious anthem raise;
And they who sow, and they who reap, unite in endless praise!

658. LINES WRITTEN IN THE COMMONPLACE BOOK OF MISS BARBOUR, DAUGHTER OF THE UNITED STATES MINISTER TO ENGLAND

[Aug 1829]

James Barbour (1775–1842) had served as US Secretary of War from 1825 to 1828, when he was appointed Minister to Great Britain by President John Quincy Adams. He was accompanied by his daughter, Frances Amelia Barbour, and C's poem is one of about forty entries in an album purchased soon after her arrival. It contains contributions by Thomas Moore, Frederick Marryat ("Peter Simple"), Robert Montgomery, Winthrop Mackworth Praed, Laetitia Landon,

Alan Cunningham, and others. From a version of the title of **653** *To Baby Bates* (given in the headnote to that poem), it seems likely that Miss Barbour presented the album to C on the strength of her friendship with C's American neighbours at Highgate, the Bateses. The American John Wheeler recorded a visit to C in the company of Mr Bates and Miss Barbour on 28 July 1829 (*TT—CC—*II 429). There is also a record of C at a dinner in honour of the American minister, at which he "proposed a very appropriate toast—'To the continued good-understanding between England and America,' which he called 'Great Britain with elbow room'" (P.A.L. "The Drama at Hereford" 464–5).

The poem was written on the eve of Miss Barbour's return to America with her father, and the sentiments include several that C often expressed: cf *The Friend* VI (21 Sept 1809) (*CC*) II 83fn; *The Courier* (29 Jul 1811)=*EOT* (*CC*) II 235; **517.X1** *Zapolya* Prelude i 303–6; *TT* 8 Apr 1833 (*CC*) I 360–1. "That fratricidal war" in line 10 was presumably the war of 1812–14 rather than the War of Independence (1775–83). The poem was contributed to the *New-York Mirror* (19 Dec 1829) by an American acquaintance of Miss Barbour, Daniel Bryan of Alexandria DC, and the text was corroborated by Miss Barbour, then Mrs Collins, when Lord Coleridge visited New York in 1883–4. A transcript in another contemporary album changes line 12 "dove" to "branch" and line 13 "thee" to "them". The present title is from the *New-York Mirror*.

> Child of my Muse! in Barbour's gentle hand
> Go, cross the Main: thou seek'st no foreign land.
> 'Tis not the Clod beneath our feet, we name
> Our Country. Each heaven-sanctiond tie the same,
> Laws, Manners, Language, Faith, Ancestral Blood,   5
> Domestic Honor, Awe of Womanhood,
> With kindling pride thou wilt rejoice to see
> BRITAIN with elbow-room and doubly free!
> Go seek thy Countrymen! And if one Scar
> Still linger of that fratricidal War,   10
> Look to the Maid who brings thee from afar!
> Be thou the Olive Leaf and She the Dove,
> And say, I greet thee with a Brother's Love!

659. DOGGEREL ON
SIR CHARLES SCUDAMORE

[Oct 1829–Jul 1831]

The only known text is a transcript by JG's former assistant, J.H.B. Williams, in a contemporary album above the initials "S. T. C." There is no need to doubt its authenticity or accuracy, but some apostrophes and other punctuation are added in the text given here.

Charles Scudamore (1779–1849) was a fashionable contemporary physician (*DNB*). C's lines allude to his humble origins, and were perhaps prompted by the fact that Scudamore had practised as an apothecary at Highgate for ten years before he began to study medicine at Edinburgh in 1813. C might also have had a special interest because of Scudamore's widely known *Treatise on the Nature and Cure of Gout* (1816) and *Treatise on Rheumatism* (1827), neither of which answered C's medical problems. He annotated JG's copy of Scudamore's pamphlet on *Properties of Mineral Waters* (1820) with tersely critical comments (*CM—CC—*IV 617–18). C wrote several sets of doggerel verses about physicians while he was at Highgate, perhaps encouraged by his friendship with JG and J. H. Green, and indeed with J.H.B. Williams himself. Cf e.g. **643** *Extempore on Three Surgeons*.

> Sciental ogle! Medicine's Sqew D'amour!
> O Squint oblique that from the frontal skull
> The seat of science traverses the heart
> In slanting line that finds its extreme point
> I' the breeches pocket, in that mystic cell 5
> Where the meek patient's purse resides, Oh!
> Great Skew D'Amour! M.D. & F.R.S.
> Glow worm of Doctors tho' with head not tail
> Radiant, yet natheless like that crawling gem
> Thou first must be beknighted then thou shin'st— 10
> And creep'st along all light, Oh Great Sir Charles
> Phȳsīcĭăn ēxtrăōrdĭnărȳ tō
> His Excellency, Ireland's L^d. Lieutenant
> To Great Saxe Cobourg's Prince, Prince Leopold,
> Physician ordinary woundrous Phys— 15
> Or, & Extra, or, both, Oh! if instead

13. The lord lieutenant of Ireland was, at the time, the duke of Northumberland.

Of Iodine, Conium, Aconite,
Thou could'st & would'st but leave me to inhale—
The shifting fragrance of thy vaporing self—
Drink deep of thee: then like a pious Duck   20
That having drunk lifts up his bill to heaven
I'll glorify thee crying Quack! quack! quack!

660. EXTEMPORE ON GEORGE DAWE

[Oct 1829]

C wrote the lines on the verso of a card for Dawe's funeral, which took place
on 27 Oct 1829, the procession travelling from his residence in Kentish Town
to St Paul's Cathedral. Dawe (1781–1829) had enjoyed a fashionable success
as a portrait painter and mezzotint engraver, first in England and later in St
Petersburg, where he became very rich. He had exhibited a bust of C and an
illustration of **253** *Love*, at the Royal Academy in 1812; his crayon sketch of
C is reproduced in *CL* III facing 351. C's earlier opinion of him had soured
quickly (cf *CL* III 386: to Mrs C 21 Apr 1812; IV 576: to WW 30 May 1815).
C introduced his lines with the following explanation:

> I really would have attended the Grub's Canonization in St Paul's, under
> the impression that would gratify his Sister, Mrs Wright; but Mr G. inter-
> posed a ? ꞑꝋ conditional but sufficiently decisive Negative—No! unless you
> want to follow his Grubship still further *down*—So I pleaded ill-health—
> But the very Tuesday Morning I went to Town, to see my daughter for
> the first time as *Mrs Henry* Coleridge, on Gower Street—& odd enough—
> the Stage was stopped by the Pompous Funeral of the Unchangeable and
> predestinated Grub—& I extemporized—

As Grub Daws pass'd beneath his Hearse's Lid,
On which a large RESURGAM met the eye,
COL. who well knew the Grub, cried—Lord forbid!
I trust, he's only telling us a *Lie*!

17. The use of iodine can lead
to a morbid condition (iodism); co-
nium is the poison hemlock; aconite
has poisonous as well as medicinal
properties.
  22. Cf the triple allusion to quacks
which concludes C's peroration on RS

in *BL* ch 3 (*CC*) I 67.
  1. Daws] The name was so misspelt
on the face of the funeral card by the
undertakers.
  2. RESURGAM] Tr "I shall rise
again".

661. TO SUSAN STEELE, ON RECEIVING THE PURSE: EXTRUMPERY LINES

[Dec 1829]

The only known version of the lines is a draft preserved in Notebook 41 (*CN* v): C presumably wrote them just after receiving the purse which had been knitted for him. Susanna Steele was the daughter and only child of an old schoolfriend of C's at Christ's Hospital. The family lived at Highgate and was frequently in the company of the Gillmans, with whom they spent holidays at Ramsgate (*CL* v 498: to JG 9 Oct 1825; 501: to EC 18 Oct 1825). C describes Miss Steele in a letter to John Anster, who wanted to marry her (*CL* vi 793–5: [Jul 1829]), as did the younger James Gillman (*CL* vi 795–6: to JG Jr [Jul 1829?]; 878–9: to JG Jr and S. Steel 10 Jan 1832). C afterwards wrote "Lesson for Susan Steel" for her (BM MS Egerton 2801 ff 108–9; *SW&F—CC—*1508–10).

> My dearest Dawtie!
> That's never naughty—
> When the Mare was stoln & not before
> The wise man got a stable door.
> And as sure as it's wet when it from above rains,   5
> The Man's Brains & mine both alike had thick Cov'rings—
> For if he lost one Mare, poor I lost two Sovereigns.
> I have got a Cash-pouch, but no Cash to put in it—
> Tho' there's Gold in the World & Sir Walter can win it.
> But empty or full, till I ride in my Hearse,   10
> For your sake I'll keep it for better and worse
> So here is a dear loving Kiss for your Purse.

5–7. Added as an afterthought in the ms, replacing the following couplet:

And He & I are Brother Ninnnies
One Beast he lost and I two
Guineas.

9. Sir Walter] Presumably Sir Walter Ralegh (1552–1618), who won gold by privateering against Spain and famously searched for the wealth of El Dorado in expeditions to the Orinoco.

662. EPIGRAPH DERIVED FROM
TROILUS AND CRESSIDA

[Dec 1829–Jan 1830]

C added the epigraph to the second edition of *Church and State*, above the signature "*Shakespear*" (*CC* 10). The lines adapt *Troilus and Cressida* III iii 201–4:

> There is a mystery—with whom relation
> Durst never meddle—in the soul of State,
> Which hath an operation more divine
> Than breath or pen can give expressure to.

C's introduction of the phrase "mere chroniclers" embodies his contempt for history read simply for the facts, not for general principles: cf e.g. *BL* ch 10 (*CC*) I 217–19; *SM* (*CC*) 11; *C&S* ch 3 (*CC*) 32; *TT* 7 Jul 1832 (*CC*) I 304.

THERE IS A MYSTERY IN THE SOUL OF STATE,
WHICH HATH AN OPERATION MORE DIVINE
THAN OUR MERE CHRONICLERS DARE MEDDLE WITH.

663. DONNE BY THE FILTER

[1830]

The programmatic heading and the examples are written into the back of Notebook 43 (*CN* v). After the heading C wrote, "The 3rd—perhaps the 2nd—the 4th, and the 7th—are wholes and need not the Filter. The sixteenth supplies the Stuff for A SONG". In the volume of Donne he was reading—CL's copy of *Poems* (1669), now at Yale—the third, second, fourth, and seventh poems are respectively *Song: "Goe, and catch a falling starre"*, *The Good-morrow*, *Womans Constancy*, and *The Indifferent*.

The first "filtered" poem (*a*) is derived from the sixteenth in Donne's collection, *Breake of Day*. The original is in four numbered stanzas: C omits stanza 3, omits the last two lines of each of the remaining stanzas, rewrites lines 3 and 11 (originally "The day breaks not, it is my heart," and "The poor, the the foul . . ."), and makes numerous changes in punctuation and capitalisation. The second example (*b*) is applied to Donne's twentieth poem, *A Valediction: Of the Booke*: C quotes lines 28–9 of the 45-line original, changing only capitals and punctuation. (*c*) is from Donne's twenty-second poem, *Love's Growth*: C has rewritten lines 19–20 of the 28-line original so as to reverse the sense. The lines read in Donne:

> Gentle love deeds, are blossoms on a bough,
> From loves awakened root doe bud out now.

(*d*) is from Donne's twenty-third poem, *Love's Exchange*, reducing stanza 5 of the 6-stanza original from seven to five lines. (*e*) is from Donne's *A Valediction: Forbidding Mourning*: C suggests that the first six stanzas should be rewritten as one, thereby reducing the original poem from nine stanzas to four.

For earlier adaptations of Donne see poems **549, 551,** also **476.** The "filter" principle is glossed—without reference to Donne—in *TT* 23 Oct 1833 (*CC*) I 446 (see the n there for further references); for an analysis of kinds of readers as filters, possibly deriving from Donne himself, see *CN* III 3242.

The Filter

By successive Chipping the rude Block becomes an Apollo or a Venus. By leaving behind I transmute a turbid Drench into a chrystalline Draught, the Nectar of the Muses. The parts are another's: the Whole is mine. To eject is as much a living Power, as to assimilate: to excrete as to absorb. *Give* therefore honor due, to the Filter-poet, ΈΣΤΗΣΈ. ‾1.5

(*a*) *A Song: Break of Day*

Stay, O sweet! and do not rise.
The Light, that shines, comes from thine eyes.
Tis not the Day breaks but my heart,
Because that you and I must part.

Tis true, tis day. What tho' it be, 5
O wilt thou therefore rise from me?
Why should we rise, because tis Light?
Did we lie down because 'twas Night?

Must Business thee from hence remove?
O that's the worst disease of Love! 10
The poor, the plain, the false Love can
Admit but not the busied Man!

(b)

Here Love's Divines (since all Divinity
Is Love or Wonder) may find all they seek.

(c) Influence of Spring in Love

Gentle Love, dead as Blossoms on the Bough,
From Love's awaken'd Root do bud not now.

(d) Extravaganza truly Donnesque

This Face by which Love could command
And change th' Idolatry of any Land—
This face which wheresoe'er it comes
Can call vow'd men from Cloisters, dead from Tombs
And melt both Poles at once—   5

(e) On Parting

requires an introductory stanza, easily supplied—then

2

Our Souls are two indeed, but so
As stiff twin Compasses are two, . . .

664. "KING SOLOMON KNEW ALL THINGS"

[1827–33?]

The lines are transcribed in an unknown hand, in pencil and as if from dictation, in J.M.?B.'s notebook album. They are not signed, but the context and their manner suggests that C might be the author. However, this cannot be proved in the absence of further evidence. In the text given here some punctuation has been supplied.

King Solomon knew all things
Beginning End & middle;
Tis said he played the Jews harp
But could not play a fiddle.

He was very witty— 5
None like him in the City—

The Royal Abyssinian
Had ingress & egress;
She wore a pearl necklace
And was a loving negress. 10

She trotted on a Camel
From Sheba to Jerusalem;
She stalked into the presence room
And gave the door a due slam.

Oh King Solomon—Hi diddle dum— 15
I know you play the Jews harp
But you cannot play the fiddle.

665. LOVE AND FRIENDSHIP OPPOSITE

[1830?]

The lines were first published in *Friendship's Offering for 1833* under the title *In Answer to a Friend's Question*. They were reprinted with the present title and with minor changes of punctuation in *PW* (1834). The thought is one which C had dwelt on for perhaps some twenty years: cf *CN* III 3370; *CM* (*CC*) II 197, III 265–6; *TT* 26 Sept 1830 (*CC*) I 206–7. It is involved with his disagreement with WW over inclination and duty, and with the several critical issues connected to this.

Her attachment may differ from your's *in degree*,
Provided they are both of one *kind*;
But friendship, how tender so ever it be,
Gives no accord to love, however refin'd.

Love, that meets not with love, its true nature revealing, 5
Grows asham'd of itself, and demurs:
If you cannot lift her's up to your state of feeling,
You must lower down your state to her's.

666. NOT AT HOME

[1830?]

The only known text was published in *PW* (1834). The suggested date comes from *PW* (EHC) I 484. The fact that no mss have been discovered for this and subsequent poems might suggest that they were contributed to albums belonging to persons outside the Coleridge family (cf e.g. **669** *Humility the Mother of Charity*).

That Jealousy may rule a mind
Where Love could never be
I know; but ne'er expect to find
Love without Jealousy.

She has a strange cast in her ee,   5
A swart sour-visaged maid—
But yet Love's own twin-sister she
His house-mate and his shade.

Ask for her and she'll be denied:—
What then? they only mean   10
Their mistress has lain down to sleep,
And can't just then be seen.

667. PHANTOM OR FACT?
A DIALOGUE IN VERSE

[1830?]

The only known text was published in *PW* (1834). The suggested date comes from *PW* (EHC) I 485.

A rather self-conscious archaism inflects the lines with the quality of an

---

5. ee] The archaic form (for "eye") is repeated from **155** *Continuation of "The Three Graves"* 289 and derives from WW and C's reading in 18th-century ballads (cf e.g. "Sir Cauline" I 177 in *Reliques of Ancient English Poetry* ed Percy I 49). Cf also the language of poem **667.**

exercise. "Sate" (line 1) often recurs in contexts like the present one: cf **155** *Continuation of "The Three Graves"* VAR 284, 299, 311, 317; **253** *Love* VAR ⁻1.1.28/7.1, 7; **299** *The Keepsake* 29; **652** *The Garden of Boccaccio* 4, 8; **655** *Alice du Clós* 60, 121; **688** *Love's Apparition and Evanishment* 12. "Unnethe" (line 4), meaning "not easily, scarcely", is recorded in common use by *OED* from c 1300 to c 1600. Walter Scott used it in *The Lay of the Last Minstrel* canto 6 st 30 (1805) 190 (later editions supply an explanatory note). "Fain" (line 8) is a word also connected with the late 18th-century ballad revival.

AUTHOR.

A lovely form there sate beside my bed,
And such a feeding calm its presence shed,
A tender love so pure from earthly leaven
That I unnethe the fancy might control,
'Twas my own spirit newly come from heaven,   5
Wooing its gentle way into my soul!
But ah! the change—It had not stirr'd, and yet—
Alas! that change how fain would I forget!
That shrinking back, like one that had mistook!
That weary, wandering, disavowing look!   10
'Twas all another, feature, look, and frame,
And still, methought, I knew, it was the same!

FRIEND.

This riddling tale, to what does it belong?
Is' t history? vision? or an idle song?
Or rather say at once, within what space   15
Of time this wild disastrous change took place?

AUTHOR.

Call it a moment's work (and such it seems)
This tale's a fragment from the life of dreams;
But say, that years matur'd the silent strife,
And 'tis a record from the dream of life.   20

668. CHARITY IN THOUGHT

[1830?]

The only known text was published in *PW* (1834). The suggested date comes from *PW* (EHC) I 486.

> To praise men as good, and to take them for such,
>   Is a grace, which no soul can mete out to a tittle;—
> Of which he who has not a little too much,
>   Will by Charity's gage surely have much too little.

669. HUMILITY THE MOTHER OF CHARITY

[1830?]

The lines exist in two versions: in an unknown person's album (the version given here) and in *PW* (1834). The published version adds the title and, for metrical and/or theological reasons, inserts the words "God, thy" before "Conscience" in the last line.

> Frail Creatures are we all! To be the Best
>   Is but the fewest faults to have.
> Look thou then to thyself: & leave the rest
>   To Conscience & the Grave.

670. ASSOCIATION OF IDEAS

[1830?]

The verses were included in the article "Coleridgeiana" in *Fraser's Magazine* XI (61) (Jan 1835) 54, "here printed for the first time. They were written in pencil on the blank leaf of a book of lectures delivered at the London University, in which the Hartleyan doctrine of association was assumed as a true basis."

The first Professor of Philosophy at the University of London (later University College), Rev John Hoppus, took up his appointment in 1830, and published his introductory lecture on 8 Nov 1830 as a pamphlet entitled *On the*

Study of the Philosophy of Mind and Logic, which contains a reference to Hartley. Hoppus also published another pamphlet in 1830, *An Essay on the Nature and Objects of the Course of Study in the Class of the Philosophy of the Human Mind and Logic, in the University of London*, but he appears not to have published a book of lectures. The reference might equally well be to the collection of *Ten Introductory Lectures* given in the session 1828–9 and published in 1829, although none of these was specifically on philosophy.

C distrusted the idea of a secular university (e.g. *CL* v 445–7: to T. Allsop 10 May 1825; *C&S—CC*—69) and was influential in the setting up of King's College. His distrust has a broader basis than Hartleian association might suggest, and has to do with his objection to materialism and Benthamite utilitarianism. His analysis of the association of ideas in *BL* chs 5–8 involves more categories and is far more elaborate, but rests on the same grounds.

(*a*) BY LIKENESS

"Fond, peevish, wedded pair! why all this rant?
O guard your tempers! hedge your tongues about!
This empty head should warn you on that point—
The teeth were quarrelsome, and so fell out.—

(*b*) ASSOCIATION BY CONTRAST

"Phidias changed marble into feet and legs.
Disease! vile anti-Phidias! thou, i' fegs!
Hast turned my live limbs into marble pegs.

(*c*) ASSOCIATION BY TIME

SIMPLICIUS SNIPKIN *loquitur.*
"I touch this scar upon my skull behind,
And instantly there rises in my mind
Napoleon's mighty hosts, from Moscow lost,
Driven forth to perish in the fangs of Frost.
For on that self-same month, and self-same day,   5
Down Skinner Street I took my hasty way—
Mischief and Frost had set the boys at play;
I stept upon a slide—oh, treacherous tread!—

(*b*)1. Phidias] c 490–432 B.C. One of the greatest of Athenian artists, famous especially as a sculptor.
(*b*)2. i' fegs!] A conflation of the oath "in faith" with the archaic use of "fig" (fiddlesticks), modified to rhyme with legs/pegs?

Fell smash, with bottom bruised, and brake my head!
Thus Time's co-presence links the great and small,   10
Napoleon's overthrow, and Snipkin's fall."

671. THE TOOTH IN A WINE-GLASS:
A SUDDEN EXCLAMATION

[Sept 1830]

C wrote the lines in Notebook 46 (*CN* v), introducing them as follows: "Monday Night, 20 Sept^r, S̶e̶p̶t̶^f 1830—Mr G. extracted without pain & scarce any hæmorrhage my loose tooth, which Mr Parkinson is to try to replace." C's teeth were in a sorry state at this time, being loose because of receding gums. He had spent a long day in London on 29 Aug, to consult Mr Parkinson about this same front tooth (N 46 f 8^v; *CN* v), and he went to see Parkinson on 5 Oct to have a plate made (N 47 f 12^r; *CN* v). Harriet Macklin was the Gillmans' servant who looked after C's needs. His last letter (*CL* vi 990: to J. H. Green and AG 24 Jul 1834) asks for her to be rewarded after his death.

O Harriet! beware!
Tis my Tooth! have a care!
Tis my Tooth, my front Tooth,
The Friend of my Youth*
Which tho' now tis check-mated   5
Is to be re-instated.

672. IN A LADY'S ALBUM

[Sept 1830]

C wrote the lines on a flyleaf of Scott's *Kenilworth* in *Historical Romances of the Author of Waverley* (Edinburgh 1824), dating them 20 Sept 1830 and describing them as "A thought, (which something better than a thought forbad

---

* Not *expell'd*, but rusticated.

to be realized) for a Lady's AL BUM" (*CM—CC—*IV 602). In Oct 1832 he copied them out in an improved version with a title, along with five other items for autographs (see poems **637, 679, 679.X1, 680, 681**). The later version is given here, with a comma supplied after "opine".

> If without *Head* or brains, and all-bum, be the same
> This Book, I opine, well merits its Name.

673. INSCRIPTION ON A TIME-PIECE

[Nov 1830]

C drafted the lines in Notebook 48 (*CN* v) at a time of particularly poor health, and afterwards used them as autograph verses. Six fair copies in his own hand are known, as well as transcripts in other contemporary hands, and HNC published the latest version in *Table Talk* as one of the poems "accidentally omitted" from *PW* (1834). The versions differ from one another in details but not significantly, and the version given here was copied into Dora Wordsworth's album when she visited C on Christmas Eve 1830. Cf **452** *For a Clock in a Market-place.*

> Now! It is gone.—Our Moments travel post,
> Each with it's deed or thought, it's *what*? and how?
> But, know! each parting Hour gives up a Ghost,
> May live within thee, an Eternal Now.

674. AN EXTEMPORE COUPLET
IN *TABLE TALK*

[Aug 1831]

HNC recorded the couplet on 14 Aug 1831, and it was published (with a change from "swim" to "sink" in the second line) in *TT* (1835) for 20 Mar 1831 (*CC*) I 241 (14 Aug 1831). In a note on the published text HNC suggested that C must have been thinking of some lines by RS. But Carl Woodring points out that Goethe's *Der Zauberlehrling* is closer (*CC* I 241–2n), and, if this is C's source, the translation is likely to have been improvised.

Yes! Yes! we'll go down, we'll go down!
But we'll take you with us to swim or to drown!

675. AN ELEGIAC PLUSQUAM-SESQUI-SONNET TO MY TIN SHAVING-POT

[Jan 1832]

C had been confined to his room for some months with various severe and depresssing illnesses, and he described the occasion of the poem to J. H. Green when he sent a copy in a letter postmarked 12 Jan 1832 (*CL* VI 880):

> You remember the little black Shaving-Pot, that used to stand on the Hob in my Room—? While I was riding on the Chamber-horse, Harriet brought in a new Concern from the Tinman's, & took away my faithful old Mungo, assigning the causes—which satisfied my reason but not my feelings— These I got rid of, on the spur of the moment, and to the rise and fall, the sea-like hexameter & pentameter Rhythm, of my Pegasus in the following Elegy or hypertrophied Sonnet—.

C celebrated his battered tea kettle at Christ's Hospital with similar affection: see poem **21**. Cf also the solicitude expressed in **316** *To My Candle*.

There are six ms texts, all dating from the earlier months of 1832 and differing in particulars. The three earliest texts are transcripts in the hands of medical attendants, perhaps taken from dictation at a time when C was too unwell to write. The present version reproduces a fair copy in his own hand, made in his "Bed, book-room & sick-cage, | Grove | Highgate". In the title, a "sesqui-sonnet" would be $1\frac{1}{2}$ times a sonnet, i.e. 21 lines, and this "more than" ("plusquam") sesqui-sonnet comes to 22 lines. The poem was not published in C's lifetime, nor by JDC or EHC.

My tiny Tin! my omnium usuum Scout!
My Blackie, fair tho' black! the Wanton Fire

---

1. omnium usuum] Tr "for all uses, all-purpose". It is unclear why C calls the tin a scout or spy, unless he intends the sense of servant, as at Oxford. This piece of Oxford slang might derive from the younger James Gillman, who had graduated from St John's the year before and with whom C enjoyed a jocular relation in his sick-room (cf **685** *Specimen of Pure Latinity*).

2. Blackie] First used in the sense of a black or negro person by Thomas Moore in 1815 (*OED*)—which reinforces the case for "scout" in the sense of servant for the soot-covered tin.

Hath long bit off thy pert one-nostril'd Snout;
Unhinged thy lid; and wrought luxation dire,
Where of thy arching Arm the handless Wrist   5
Press'd on thy side! Mid treacherous Coal and Grate
Twice hast thou stumbled, and in rebel Mist,
With smoke and sooty films confederate,
Flown in my face. Yet did I not upbraid
Thy crazy Cranks—yea, held thee the more dear: 10
And morning after morning with thee play'd,
At Rouge et Noir, a game of hope and fear.
And must we part?—Thy Tears on the hot Hob
Say, Iss! Iss! Iss! hard by the Top-bar reeks,
And to each tear makes answer with a Sob!   15
The Cambrian's Broth is none the worse for *Leeks*;
Rents are the landed Noble's pride and glee;
Holes, side or bottom, both to Man and Gun
Are apt and seemly.—Would, twere so with *thee*!
But 'tis not so! and lct Timc's will be done.   20
BLACKIE, adieu!—Ah!—Blackie! blame not *me*!
I turn'd not *you* away! Twas You, that *run*.

676. THE THREE PATRIOTS:
COCKNEY SNIP, IRISH BLARNEY, AND ME

[Feb 1832]

C drafted the lines in the course of a letter to Charles Aders (*CL* vi 883: 11 Feb 1832). The letter is mainly taken up with the description of a caricature of the Reform Bill, to be engraved by Ackerman. "Let these blundering Catalines commit what blunders they may—and however palpable to the Common sense of the H. of C. they may be rendered—No matter!—Swear black is white—or else you will endanger the Reform Bill!" Among the pamphlets on the Reform

4. luxation] An anatomical term for putting out of joint.

8. confederate,] C wrote in the margin, as an alternative: "?colleagued in fate,". A later version adopts this reading.

12. Rouge et Noir] A card game introduced in the 1790s, played on a red and black diamond-patterned table, with a reputation for high risk and connotations of fast living.

Bill which C read is a dialogue which he annotated some time in 1831 (*CM—CC*—II 210–11).

> *Cockney Snip.*
> I'se a *Riff*orman!

> *Irish Blarney.*
> A *Raff*ormer I!

> *Me.*
> And I write them both, a loud cry,
> And for this Riff-raff-form will live and die!

677. THE IRISH ORATOR'S BOOZE:
A SONNET

[May 1832]

The sonnet was published, with a separately entitled prose introduction as here, in *Fraser's Magazine* (Jul 1832), over C's name and dated "18*th May*, 1832—*Grove, Highgate*". It was not republished or collected, and C's authorship cannot be conclusively proved, largely because of the dimension of parody—of himself in the verses and of the "*Fraserian*" manner in the prose introduction.

The background is the Beer Act of 1830, which had repealed the tax on beer in England and Wales while leaving in place the tax on malt (spirits). Thus, it favoured the English national drink at the expense of the Scottish and Irish. The act was put through by Wellington's administration with a good deal of argument, supported by Whigs and opposed by Tories. The issue was still live in 1832 and afterwards, and involved disputes about whether drunkenness was to be blamed more on spirit-drinking or beer-drinking, evangelical opposition to drinking (yet support for the Beer Act), the prominence of Scots in the temperance cause in England, and the Irish reputation for drunkenness. C's introduction mingles details of this background in a deliberately allusive, fast-moving way, such as he had used in his earlier celebrations of drinking vs thinking in *M Post* (Sept 1801): see **278** *Song to be Sung by the Lovers of Ale*; **279** *Drinking versus Thinking*. The details, as an argument, do not quite cohere.

The other immediate background is the debate which accompanied the passage of the Reform Bill: C's contribution was composed at the end of a fortnight of intense political excitement. Lord Lyndhurst's motion in the committee on the Reform Bill was defeated on Monday 7 May; Grey and his colleagues tendered their resignations, which were accepted; but by Monday and Tuesday of the following week it became clear that Wellington could not form an alternative administration. By Friday 18 May the cause of reform appeared to have been sensationally confirmed. The papers were full of petitions in its support and of news of meetings and celebrations all over the country.

The entire piece is closely related, in format and metrically, to C's contribution to *Bl Mag* XXXI (Jun 1832) 956, sent from Highgate on the same day. This was a prose piece couched in much the same tone, *What is an English Sonnet?*, followed by *The Old Man's Sigh: A Sonnet*. See **592** *Youth and Age* VAR TEXTS 5 14. Miriam Thrall *Rebellious Fraser's* (New York 1934) 281, followed by *The Wellesley Index to Victorian Periodicals, 1824–1900* ed Walter E. Houghton and Jean Harris Slingerland (5 vols Toronto 1966–89) II 333, tentatively attributes the present poem to William Maginn, but only by way of "educated guesses" (*Index* II 317). Maginn evidently submitted texts of **267** *The Two Round Spaces on the Tombstone* and **336** *Epitaph on Poor Col* to *Fraser's Magazine* in Feb 1833 (*Index* II 336), but if he is taken to be the author of the present poem, the relation to *What is an English Sonnet?* requires the poem to have been written and inserted into the later periodical in remarkably quick time. On the other hand, C had been mentioned and praised several times in *Fraser's* earlier in 1832 (by J. A. Heraud, anonymously). He had to decline an invitation to write for the magazine in Feb because he was already committed to *Bl Mag* (*CL* VI 884: to C. Aders 11 Feb 1832). The two related pieces, dispatched from Highgate on the same day to two rival magazines, may be seen as C's attempt to preserve a balance.

WHAT IS AN IRISH ORATOR?

What is an Irish Orator? Down with Theory—Facts, facts, facts
must decide. And some myriads of these, with deliberate blarney,
if not fume or fury, perpetrated *fudge*, have established that a man
born in Hibernia, with a touch of the brogue, is an Irish Orator.
What have our *Temperance Societies*, what has our enlightened ⁻1.5
Premier, to do with the Literature of the NATION? With such
a consummate jollifier as O'DOHERTY, who contradistinguished
the Saints, the Tea-drinkers, from the SINNERS, as the Varmint,

⁻**1.5–6.** our enlightened *Premier*] Earl Grey, Whig prime minister 1830–4.

⁻**1.7.** O'DOHERTY] The pseudonymous Morgan O'Doherty, who, writing in *Bl Mag*, had parodied **176** *Christabel* and **161** *The Rime of the Ancient Mariner* in 1819 and **178** *Kubla Khan* in 1822, and had made further contributions to *Bl Mag* in 1824–5. O'Doherty was long thought to be William Maginn, but it has since been discovered that the parodies were written by D. M. Moir, and that J. G. Lockhart and others collaborated in the later contributions.

⁻**1.8.** Saints] Members of the evangelical "Clapham Sect", which in-the Ascarides, and Lumbrici, from the skin and bowels of the Man—though numerous in proportion to the abstinence and ina-nition of the hanimal so tenanted; and who regarded the SAINTS themselves, though contradistinguished from the *Sinners* (Sanc-tos à Peccatoribus), but as the still and punch-bowl for the pro-duction of the Tippler—a JOLLIFICATION.—And as to Hogg—otherwise called the Shepherd—the MORNING POST would soon dish up his business with Ebony, and finish him in the Blackwood style.—Ergo—it is demonstrated that a man born in Hibernia, with a touch of the brogue, neither more nor less, gives the Coleridgean Definition of an Irish Orator—nonsense being the ordinary, but not necessary accompaniment. From all which it is demonstrable, that the following onslaught, or hyperbolical Stanza, of a certain poem, called "Farce and Flummery," having by a suicidal Ligature of the Verse-maker's own tying, detached itself, and bolted away from the rhymes aforesaid, assumes the name and rank of an intolerable Hanimal, and standing the test of reading the rhymes twice seven times exactly, is a descriptive Irish oratorical Sonnet,—according to the convivial Rules established since the happy and glorious reduction of the *Beer*-tax (four-fifths English) from the favourite beverage of England—and the virtual extinction of sobriety in the noon-day blaze of drunkenness.

‾1.
‾1.
‾1.2
‾1.2
‾1.3

THE IRISH ORATOR'S BOOZE. A SONNET

Whisky is the drink of Erin,
But of England foaming Ale:
Where good Drink is, Life is cheering
That only serves to make us brave
　　In our old age,
Whose glad voice chanteth with delight full many a glorious stave—
That only serves to make us gay
With oft and pleasant tol-lol-lay,
Like a poor nigh-drunken guest,

5

---

cluded William Wilberforce, Henry Thornton, and others, and had been so named in e.g. *The Christian Observer* (1813) 617; *John Bull* (10 Nov 1823) 356.

‾**1.14.** Hogg] James Hogg, 1770–1835, the Scottish poet known as the Ettrick Shepherd. He contributed to *Bl Mag* and collaborated with Lock-hart, Maginn, John Wilson, and others in the series "Noctes Ambrosianae", where C was frequently mentioned, mocked, or parodied. (Indeed, in vol XII—1822—79–83 "Paddy" had hailed C satirically in a drinking song.)

‾**1.16.** Ebony] William Blackwood, who had founded his magazine in 1817 in opposition to *Ed Rev*.

That may not rudely be dismiss'd;   10
Yet hath not paid a single rap,
And tells his silly jest mayhap.
O! might Life cease! and folk be blind,
Whose total *Tipple* is *Tea*, their thirsty souls to bind!

678. CHOLERA CURED BEFOREHAND

[Jul 1832]

A violent epidemic of Asiatic cholera occurred at Jessore in Bengal in 1817, and was followed by the gradual spread of the disease to Europe. When it first appeared in England in Oct 1831, in the aftermath of the Bristol riots, it exacerbated the scared and apprehensive tone of politics and became associated with the disorders connected with the Reform Bill. The mortality caused during the epidemic has been estimated at over 31,000 in England, Scotland, and Wales.[1] The epidemic reached London in Jan 1832, and the Reform Bill received royal assent on 7 Jun. Carl Woodring annotates C's views on the spread of contagious disease in *TT* (*CC*) I 282–4nn.

C's poem is, as he explained to those correspondents he sent it to, political as well as philanthropic—"enragé, as the French say, at the presumptuous folly of sundry Cholerophobists, who would fain set up his Blueness, the travelling Nabob, against Lords Gray, Durham and the Reform Bill. Fools! as if filling the Church-yard could be deemed an equal service in Hell with emptying the Church!" (als to J.H.B. Williams, 5 Sept 1832, HRC MS Coleridge S T Letters—not in *CL*; cf *CL* VI 916: to J. H. Green 26 Jul 1832; 923: to HNC [28 Aug 1832]). The distinctions on which C's poem rests might be compared with WW's more straightforward attitude, that the cholera outbreak was an agent of Providence to bring the nation to its senses (*WL—L* rev—II 449–50).

The poem exists in three ms versions sent to correspondents in Jul, Aug, and Sept 1832. *PW* (1834) prints the second of these, sent to HNC, which improves and expands on the first, sent to J. H. Green. The present text prints the further-improved version sent to J.H.B. Williams in Sept, with a few minor editorial corrections.

---

[1] E. A. Underwood "The History of Cholera in Great Britain" *Proceedings of the Royal Society of Medicine* XLI (1948) 165–73 at 168.

CHOLERA CURED BEFOREHAND:

or PREMONITORIES promulgated *gratis* for the Use of the useful
Classes, specially those resident in St Giles's, Saffron Hill, White
Chapel and Bethnal Green: and inasmuch as the good man is mer-
ciful even to the Beasts, likewise for the Bulls and Bears of the
Stock Exchange.   ⁻1.5

Pains ventral, subventral,
In stomach or entrail
Think no longer mere prefaces
For Damns, Grins and Wry faces;
But off to the Doctor, fast as ye can crawl!   5
Yet far better it were, not to have them at all.

Now to scape inward aches
Eat no Plums, nor Plum-cakes;
Cry, Avaunt, New Potatoe!
And don't drink, like Old Cato.   10
Ah beware of DIS* PIPSY:
And therefòre don't get tipsy.
For tho' Gin and Whisky
May make you feel frisky,
They're but Crimps to Dis Pipsy.   15
And nose to tail with the Gypsy
Comes, black as a Porpus,
The DIABOLUS ipse
Call'd CHOLERY MORPUS:
Who with horns, hoof and tail croaks for Carrion to feed him,   20
Tho' being a Devil, nobody never has see'd him.

Ah *then*, my dear Honeys!
There's no Cure for *You*.
For loves or for moneys—

* Sometimes written Dyspepsia; but it is more probable, that Dis is the ab-
breviation of a Christian Name, Dyonisia for instance—and Pipsy a fondling
Diminutive of some young Lady of the PIP Family.

10. Old Cato] Cato the Censor
(234–149 B.C.), proverbial for his
stern morality.

22. Honeys] An Irish term of en-

dearment applied at the time to Irish
people (cf **207** *On the United Irish-
men* 12). Other Scots-Irish expres-
sions (e.g. line 26 "Hallabaloo"; line

You'll find it too true.   25
Och! the Hallabaloo!
Och! och! how ye'll wail,
When the Offal-fed Vagrant
Shall turn you as blue
As the gas-light unfragrant,   30
That gushes in jets from beneath his own Tail!
Till, swift as the Mail,
He at last brings the cramps on,
That will twist you like Sampson!

So without further Blethring,   35
Dear Mud-larks! my Brethren!
Of all Scents and Degrees
(Yourselves with your Shes)
Forswear all Cabal, Lads!
Wakes, Unions and Rows;   40
Hot Drams and cold Sallads;
And don't pig in styes that would suffocate Sows!
Quit Cobbett's, O'Connell's and Belzebub's banners,
And white-wash at once your Guts, Rooms, and Manners.
                                        Philodemus Coprophilus,
                        Physician extraordinary to their sovereign
                                    Majesties, the People.

---

35 "Blethring") link the poem with the Irish involvement in Reform politics, and with **677** *The Irish Orator's Booze*.

43. Cobbett heads the list of demagogues in **620** *Sancti Dominici Pallium* 46–7. He aligned himself with O'Connell's cause in the years following 1832, despite earlier sharp differences. For C on Daniel O'Connell (1775–1847) see e.g. *TT* 5 Feb 1833, 14 Jun 1834, 5 Jul 1834 (*CC*) I 336, 484–6, 497–8.

44⁺. Tr "Lover of People, Lover of Excrement". Earlier signatures (to perhaps more conservative correspondents) interpret people as the rabble, the mob.

13. George Scharf "View looking towards Hampstead from Mr Coleridge's Room, Highgate", signed pencil drawing dated Aug 1834. For Scharf's depiction of the room inside on the same occasion see *CM* (*CC*) I facing p cxv; *TT* (*CC*) I frontispiece

679. SCIATIC RHEUMATISM

[Oct 1832]

The verses exist in only one ms and were never published. They make up the first of six items copied out in C's hand, where their title is "Substitute for swearing under the torture of Sciatic Rheumatism and of equal virtue as a Charm", dated 13 Oct 1832.

C wrote a letter to JG on the same day describing the rheumatism "which is at this very moment playing the Devil with me, and the Devil playing his Grandam in it" (*CL* VI 927), which suggests that the poem was composed on the day it was transcribed (some of the others were composed earlier). J.H.B. Williams's treatment of C's rheumatism occasioned two other poems on the same topic among the six items collected in the ms, **680** *An Autograph on an Autopergamene* and **681** *Dialogue between a Nimble Doctor and a Crippled Patient.* Cf **274** *Two Lines on the Cur, Arthritis.*

O Screams of Scotch Bagpipes! O Rub a Dub Dub!
O Satan! O Moloch! O Bëelzebub!
O Gripes Grapes and Barberries, acrid and crabby!
Diabole diabolissime, abi! abi! abi!

680. AN AUTOGRAPH ON
AN AUTOPERGAMENE

[Oct 1832]

C copied out the lines among other autographs on 13 Oct 1832, and on the same day enclosed them in a letter to JG (*CL* VI 927). His skin was peeling presumably as a result of the treatment he was receiving from J.H.B. Williams for sciatic rheumatism (autopergamene means self-parchment), the complaint described in two other epigrams he copied on the same day (**679** *Sciatic Rheumatism* and **681** *Dialogue between a Nimble Doctor and a Crippled Patient*). C's own copy introduces the lines by way of reference to the sulphurated hot-air baths he had been prescribed. His letter introduces the poem as follows: "By the bye, in proof of commencing Desquamation[1] I wrote the following Lines,

4. Tr "Most devilish Devil! Avaunt! Avaunt! Avaunt!"

[1] Coming off in scales, peeling.

and regret that I cannot at present peel off a strip large enough to make a real Fac Simile for you.—"

C's copy differs in phrasing in lines 1–4, and thereafter continues:

> With clean Slit and Point, to Perryscan akin
> The Pen was a Nail-paring: on his Great Toe't had been.
> The Ink his own Blood and the Parchment his Skin—
> *Thīs* frŏm 's *Lēg*; ănd thĕ ōthĕr frŏm 's rāzŏr-slāsh'd Chīn.
> But the Name? But the Name?—The Name, an it please 'e,
> S. T. COLERIDGE is; but he still signs, **S. T. C.**

"Perryscan" is not in the dictionary, but C appears to intend an allusion to the near-sighted methods of the engraver Francis Perry (d 1765): because he had the use of only one eye, he etched on a white ground and resorted to other such expedients. The allusion is obscure, which is presumably why C dropped it. In his own copy the lines are also followed by a postscript:

> P.S. These melodious Lines should be recited by a Cumbrian of Borrodale, to do them justice & give them the requisite ⟨smoothness and⟩ facility to the abbreviations. Who but a Man of Cumberland can say with unstammering rapidity—"Put t' kettle on 's fire for him and t' tea-things on 's table,⟩and hand me t' knife."

The letter—which contains the version given here—begins and ends with verses, each of which are signed "COLERIDGE." It begins by adjuring JG to prolong his holiday in France—

> And free from Sick-rooms, free from midnight Calls.
> To sojourn yet awhile among the Gauls.

At the end C makes a further reference to the "sciatic paroxism" which the letter has described—

> For with grunts I indite,
> And grin while I write.

Why, sure, such a wonder was never yet seen!
An Autograph on an Autōpergamene!
A Poet's own Name, and own Hand-writing both,
And the Ink and the Parchment all of his own growth—
The Ink his own Blood and the Parchment his Skin—   5
This from 's Leg, and the other from 's razor-snipt Chin—

681. DIALOGUE BETWEEN A NIMBLE DOCTOR AND A CRIPPLED PATIENT

[Oct 1832]

The lines, with the title given here, appear among a group of six items for autographs copied by C on 13 Oct 1832. They might even have been improvised on that occasion. The rheumatism for which C was receiving treatment from J.H.B. Williams is the subject of two of the other epigrams—**679** *Sciatic Rheumatism* and **680** *An Autograph on an Autopergamene*.

> Dr Hop-o-my-thumb! my right Thigh's rheumatic.
> Yes, Sir, a plain case! tis a dolour Sciatic.
> Dr Hop-o'my-thumb, that frisk on so skittish,
> *Sigh Attic* d'ye call it? No, by Jove! 'tis Grunt British.

682. MY BAPTISMAL BIRTH-DAY

[Oct 1832?]

Carl Woodring (*TT—CC*—I 317n) gives references to C's varying opinions concerning infant baptism; but the poem has less to do with C's doctrinal views and more with the sort of distinction Thomas Browne made between the "double Horoscope" of man—"one of his humanity, his birth; another of his Christianity, his baptisme" (*Religio Medici* 1.45). C's feelings are likely to have been prompted by the baptism of his granddaughter, Edith Coleridge, which he attended from his sickbed in Aug 1832 (*Minnow* 164–5; cf *TT* 9 Aug 1832— *CC*—I 317–18). The lines are suffused by the baptism service in the Book of Common Prayer, and C's own gloss emphasises their personal rather than their theological connection:

> There are permitted moments of exultation through faith, when we cease to feel our own emptiness save as a capacity of our Redeemer's fulness! Take such a sabbath moment as the date of this meditation on my Spiritual Birthday, when my Christian name, the name of Christian was made over me. (From a transcript by AG q Watson *Coleridge at Highgate* 151; cf e.g. *TT—CC*—I 414n)

4. Grunt] See C's description of himself writing "with grunts" q **680** *An Autograph on an Autopergamene* headnote.

The subtitle names 28 Oct as the day C took to be the anniversary of his baptism: in fact, he was baptised at Ottery on 30 Dec 1772, and 28 Oct is probably the date in 1832 when the poem was written, one week after his birthday. The poem came to mind again the following summer as C was considering how to meet his commitments to Thomas Pringle, editor of *Friendship's Offering*, when it underwent slight revisions. The earlier version is preserved in transcripts by J. H. Green and JG, and C (or HNC) returned to it for the text included in *PW* (1834). The text given here is the slightly improved version sent to Pringle, which was subsequently published in *Friendship's Offering*. It is one of two ms versions in C's hand (other recorded versions remain untraced).

On my Spiritual Birth-day, October 28—
Lines composed on a Sick-bed under severe
bodily Suffering, by S. T. Coleridge

Born unto God in CHRIST—in Christ, my ALL!
What, that Earth boasts, were not lost cheaply, rather
Than forfeit that blest Name, by which we call
The HOLY ONE, the Almighty God, OUR FATHER?
FATHER! in Christ we live: and Christ in Thee.　　　　　5
Eternal Thou, and everlasting We!

The Heir of Heaven, henceforth I dread not Death.
In Christ I live, in Christ I draw the Breath
Of the true Life. Let Sea, and Earth, and Sky
Wage war against me: on my front I shew　　　　　10
Their mighty Master's Seal! In vain *they* try
To end my Life, who can but end it's Woe.

Is that a Death-bed, where the CHRISTIAN lies?
Yes!—But not *his*: 'tis DEATH itself, *there* dies.

10–11. Alluding to the seven seals of the closing chapters of Rev.

14. Cf the close of Donne's Holy Sonnet No 6, which opens "Death be not proud": "And death shall be no more, Death thou shalt die"; also 1 Cor 15.26, 54.

683. EPIGRAM: A GUILTY SCEPTIC'S DEATH BED

[Before Nov 1832]

When C copied out the epigram on 11 Nov 1832, following **221** *Epitaph on a Bad Man*, which had been published many years earlier in *M Post* (22 Sept 1801), he introduced it as follows: "This reminds me, however, of another thing of the kind, that I—wrote? no—but composed, and now for the first time write down." The title originally continued with "or the Echo, Conscience", which C then bracketed, possibly to indicate deletion. The epigram was never published.

> Rack not my death-bed!—Silence! No replying!
> Ah stern Alternative—Nothing or Hell!
> Of this poor hope would'st rob me, that in dying
> I became nothing! Hark! that distant Yell!
> No! twas the Echo, that repeated—HELL. 5

684. KIND ADVICE AND INVITATION

[Nov 1832]

The epigram is the penultimate of five poems which C copied out in Nov 1832. It was originally entitled "Advice and Invitation", and consisted of only two lines:

> Said the Devil to Jack (What the devil? said he?/
> Cut your throat, my brave fellow! and come to me.

C then wrote the following two lines, and keyed them in before the other two:

> Jack sotted, Jack gamed, Jack was beggar'd & sick—
> When who should step in, but his sworn Friend, Old Nick.

He then wrote out the revised fair copy, given here, but the poem seems never to have been published.

> Jack sotted, Jack gam'd, Jack was beggar'd and sick:
> When who should step in but his sworn Friend, Old Nick.

And Old Nick said to Jack—What, the devil! said he?
Cut your throat, my brave fellow! and come to me.

685. SPECIMEN OF PURE LATINITY,
EX TEMPORE

[Nov 1832]

The lines are copied out in C's hand, dated Nov 1832 and signed, but appear never to have been published. An entirely literal translation runs: (*a*) "I beg, dear James, I who do everything right, I you will put upon this fire I a few coals"; (*b*) "My dear James, I you do everything right: I therefore you will put on the fire I a few coals."

The lines were probably addressed to James Gillman Jr, by now ordained to the priesthood, whom C had helped with his Greek and Latin in his schooldays (**584** *Nonsense Sapphics for James Gillman Jr*; **607.X1** *Latin Elegiac Verse Lessons*). The title is tongue-in-cheek. The rhymes and the scansion by stress are not to be found in "pure" classical Latin; version (*b*) scans reasonably well by stress, while (*a*) is difficult to scan systematically at all. "Superimpones" ("you will put upon") in line (*a*)3 is future indicative where a present subjunctive would be expected, "Erge" in line (*b*)3 is probably a simple miswriting of "Ergo" ("Therefore"), and the climax of the jest, in each version, comes in the final line, with the word-for-word and very un-Latin equivalent of the English idiom "a few coals", (mis)using "Unum" to give full value to the singular "*a few*": normal Latin would be "paucos carbones".

(*a*)

Precor, Care Jacobe,
Qui cuncta facis probe,
Igni huic superimpones
Unum paucum carbones.

(*b*) OR THE SAME MORE LOGICALLY

Mi care Jacobe!
Facis omnia probè:
Erge, igni impones
Unum paucum carbones.

686. TWO LINES IN SPRING

[Apr 1833]

C quoted the lines in a letter to John Sterling (*CL* VI 935: [11 Apr 1833]), introducing them as follows: "I am more than grieved by the contents of your Note, and earnestly adjure you—now especially when . . ." It is not at all certain whether they are quoted from an unpublished (even unwritten) poem by C or from another poet.

> The March Wolf romping with the April Kid
> Mangles his quiv'ring play-mate—

687. THE HUNGER OF LIARS

[Jun–Jul? 1833]

C drafted the lines in Notebook 51 (*CN* V), at the end of a three-page discussion of the craving for permanence. Specifically, the lines complete a sentence which begins: "The Liar is ever deluding & ever in his deluding deluded—he *feeds on Lies*, . . . and sustaining the *Hunger*, which he strove to allay—."

> Feeds but his Hunger, waxing with the food—
> And what he fain would quench
> Lips up the thirsty fire inflaming Thirst—

688. LOVE'S APPARITION AND EVANISHMENT: AN ALLEGORIC ROMANCE

[Aug 1833]

C told Charles Aders on 18 Aug 1833 that the poem was "composed from a rude conception which I accidentally found in one of my many old 'Fly-catchers' . . .

688 title. The first version C submitted to Pringle was subtitled "a Madrigal".

some three or four mornings ago" (*CL* VI 956). He is probably referring to the lines composed extempore on 24 Apr 1824 (*CN* IV 5146), viz poem **597**. The first four of these six lines appear (var) at the beginning of the first draft of the present poem; and they appear with the heading "L'Envoy to 'Like a lone Arab'" in a ms in the hand of JG's assistant H. L. Porter. For this reason, SC printed them as the *envoi* to the present poem in *The Poems of Samuel Taylor Coleridge* ed DC and SC (1852) 374.

Alternatively, it is just possible that the reference in C's letter to Aders was to a much earlier note of Sept 1802 (*CN* I 1244), an image of a blind Arab. Whatever the case, he sent a draft immediately to Thomas Pringle, to whom he had already sent several poems for *Friendship's Offering*. Within a few days, he sent Pringle another revised, expanded version, which Pringle published soon afterwards. C's mind continued to work on the poem, and over the next few months he sent slightly improved versions to Aders and to J. G. Lockhart, and made corrections in the printed text of *Friendship's Offering*. The present text is from *PW* (1834), which incorporates nearly all of C's improvements—although C's capitals and punctuation may well have been emended by HNC and the printer.

Like a lone Arab, old and blind
Some caravan had left behind
Who sits beside a ruin'd well,
Where the shy sand-asps bask and swell;
And now he hangs his aged head aslant,   5
And listens for a human sound—in vain!
And now the aid, which Heaven alone can grant,
Upturns his eyeless face from Heaven to gain;—
Even thus, in vacant mood, one sultry hour,
Resting my eye upon a drooping plant,   10
With brow low bent, within my garden bower,
I sate upon the couch of camomile;
And—whether 'twas a transient sleep, perchance,
Flitted across the idle brain, the while
I watch'd the sickly calm with aimless scope,   15
In my own heart; or that, indeed a trance,
Turn'd my eye inward—thee, O genial Hope,
Love's elder sister! thee did I behold,

12. the couch of camomile] Perhaps C is recalling the "sod-built Seat of Camomile" which C built with the Wordsworths on 10 Oct 1801, an image associated with SH. Cf **289** *Letter to* —— 86 and EC. Or perhaps there was a camomile seat or bank at 3 The Grove (to please C?).

Drest as a bridesmaid, but all pale and cold,
With roseless cheek, all pale and cold and dim   20
    Lie lifeless at my feet!
And then came Love, a sylph in bridal trim,
    And stood beside my seat;
She bent, and kissed her sister's lips,
    As she was wont to do;—   25
Alas! 'twas but a chilling breath
Woke just enough of life in death
    To make Hope die anew.

689. "OH! MIGHT I BUT MY PATRICK *LOVE*"

[Aug 1833]

The poem was transcribed into a contemporary notebook album by JG's former
assistant J.H.B. Williams. It is unsigned but dated 23 Aug 1833, and appears
among poems indubitably by C on pages set aside for transcribing them. C's
authorship must still remain in doubt in the absence of corroborative evidence.
The lack of punctuation in the ms (supplemented in the text given here) suggests
that it was taken down from dictation.

    Oh! might I but my Patrick *love*—
    My mother chides severely
    And says that I must wretched prove
    Because I love him dearly.

    And when she rates me o'er & o'er   5
    With lessons cold & endless,
    It only makes me love him more
    To find him, poor & friendless—

    Oh! Patrick! fly from me
    Or we are lost for ever—   10
    Oh! Fortune kinder be
    Nor thus two lovers sever.

    And then to me my Patrick says
    Tho' true we have not riches

But that we love too little prize   15
Whom gold so much bewitches.

He tells me he enough can earn
And bids me never fear it—
That scanty store will serve his turn
If I will only share it.   20

Oh! Patrick! fly from me
Or we are lost for ever—
Oh! Fortune kinder be
Nor thus two lovers sever.

He tells me when the bosom's warm   25
We mock the storm that's blowing,
That honest hearts can know no harm
Tho' hard the World is going—

He tells me, But alas! I fear
Lest I from duty falter—   30
I wish he could as soon persuade
The Mother as the Daughter.

Oh Patrick—fly from me—
Or we are lost for ever—
Oh—Fortune—kinder be   35
Nor thus two lovers sever—

690. "O SING AND BE GLAD"

[Sept 1833]

C drafted the lines in dialogue form in Notebook 51 (*CN* v), where they carry
the title "A SOLILOQUY-DIALOGUE | ~~Dialogue~~ between my Soul and my
Understanding—i.e. the Subjective ⟨I⟩ and the Objective *I* Myself." He made
two fair copies of the poem at about the same time, differing very slightly, ap-
parently for presentation. The first appears to have been copied for Mrs Aders;
the second, given here, is dated from Highgate 23 Sept 1833. Neither version
was ever published.

O sing and be glad, sing with Heart and Voice!
But who gave me the power to sing and rejoice?
'Twas my Father! my God!
And to whom shall I sing, if not to the Giver,
Whom alone I can sing to, for ever and ever?   5
I will sing to my God.

691. TO THE YOUNG ARTIST, KAYSER OF KAYSERWERTH

[Aug–Oct 1833]

J. Kayser (c 1813–53) painted numerous portraits in the course of his wandering career, on which see *Allgemeines Lexikon der bildenden Künstler* ed Ulrich Thieme and Felix Becker (37 vols Leipzig [1907]) xx 43–4. It is not known who or what led him to C, but a muddled detail suggests that the acquaintance was slight. Kayser was Belgian and Kaiswerweth is in Germany, 5 miles north of Düsseldorf. (A contemporaneous J. P. Kaiser of Kaiserwerth appears in Thieme–Becker as the father of the better-known Engelbert and Heinrich, but he was a tin-moulder.)

C described the sketch to the engraver Edward Finden as "a Likeness, certainly; but with such unhappy Density of the Nose & ideotic Drooping of the Lip, with a certain pervading *Woodeness* of the whole Countenance, that it has not been thought guilty of any great Flattery by Mr Coleridge's Friends" (*CL* vi 974: 6 Nov 1833). The original was in the possession of the late A.H.B. Coleridge, and is reproduced in *CL* vi facing p 974.

One of the two ms versions is in C's hand, and the poem was included in *PW* (1834). The holograph, which differs from the printed version only in capitalisation, spelling, and punctuation, is reproduced here.

KAYSER! to whom, as to a Second Self,
NATURE, or Nature's next-of-kin, the Elf
Hight, GENIUS, hath dispens'd the happy skill
To cheer or sooth the parting Friend's, Alas!
Turning the blank Scroll to a magic Glass,   5
That makes the Absent present at our will;

**5–6². Cf the "magic image" which appears in the "World of Glass" in **412 *The Pang More Sharp than All* 36–41.

And to the Shadowing of thy Pencil gives
Such seeming substance, that it almost lives—

Well hast thou given the *thoughtful* Poet's face!
Yet hast thou on the tablet of his Mind   10
A more delightful Portrait left behind—
Ev'n thy own youthful beauty, and artless grace,
Thy natural Gladness and eyes bright with Glee!
KAYSER! farewell!
Be wise! be happy! and forget not Me.   15

692. FROM A MANUSCRIPT
POEM OF ATHANASIUS SPHINX

[Oct–Nov 1833]

C drafted the lines on an endpaper of Nehemiah Grew's *Cosmologia Sacra* (*CM—CC*—II 888). A lengthy marginal note consists of whimsical punning variations on Grew's "there is no *Minimum*, but a Point, which hath no Dimensions, but only a Whereness, and is next to Nothing" (ch 3 sec 1). C summed it up as "WHERE-ONLY is *Nothing's* Landlord—inasmuch as He *is* at once his own, & his ~~nei~~ Neighbour's, house—Tenementum *merum, quod nihil tenet*" (tr "A *mere* tenement, that contains nothing"). The improvised untitled verses follow on immediately.

The title given here is borrowed from C's concluding ascription. He had in mind Athanasius Kircher's *Oedipus Aegypticus* (3 vols Rome 1652), which he drew on in **168** *Kubla Khan* (see e.g. *RX* 389–91) but which, by Jan 1822 (Notebook 21½—*CN* IV 4854 f 53ʳ), he had come to take as typifying the interpretation of religious symbols by far-fetched etymological associations. The substitution of Sphinx for Oedipus here gives Athanasius a surname which signifies a poser rather than a solver of riddles.

The lines have imagery in common with **478** *Limbo*, but the playful mood is closer to **582** *A Poem upon Nothing* and **639** *Tears as the Language of the Eye*.

Mere WHERENESS! NOTHING'S Landlord & next Neighbor,
Who *art* thy own and NOTHING'S empty house—
Tenentless Tenement!—pinch-gut *only* WHERE!
Would, thou wert No Where! & that thy neighbor, Nothing,
Were any Thing but what He is and is not!—   5

693. S.T.C.

[Oct–Nov 1833; 1807?]

The first version of C's epitaph appears to have consisted of lines 3–6 only, beginning "Here lies a Poet—", written in the spirit of the epitaph he wrote for himself in 1803 at Edinburgh (**336** *Epitaph on Poor Col*), when he was visiting TP in summer–autumn 1807. It was a time following the publication of WW's *Poems, in Two Volumes* in May, when C was looking over his own poems for publication by Longman and was very much aware of the demise of his poetic ambitions. Thereafter, eight later ms versions, in which couplets were added at the beginning and the end, and minor improvements introduced, may be dated from 27–8 Oct to 9 Nov 1833. The poem was included in *PW* (1834) as the last poem in the sequence, a position it occupies in many subsequent editions of C's poems. C made it clear to friends to whom he gave the later version that it was intended for his tombstone, real or pictured or both, and the four added lines change the meaning considerably. The version given here was sent to J. G. Lockhart on 5 Nov 1833 (*CL* vi 973), and has been used because it is the last holograph text.

> Stop, Christian Passer-by! stop, Child of God!
> And read with gentle heart. Beneath this Sod
> A Poet lies: or that which once seem'd He.
> O lift one thought in prayer for S. T. C.
> That he who many a year with toil of Breath   5
> Found Death in Life, may here find Life in Death.

title. In an earlier version sent to J. H. Green on 28 Oct 1833 (*CL* vi 963) C glosses the title as concerning "an Author . . . better known by the initials of his Name than by the Name itself—which he fondly Graecized—ἔστησε. ἔστησε: κεῖται· ἀναστήσει---. Hic Jacet, qui stetit, restat, resurget.—" tr "He hath stood, he hath stood, he lies at rest, he will rise again. Here Lies one who hath stood, awaits, will rise again."

It is unclear whether C actually intended the present version to be inscribed on his tombstone. From a version sent to Mrs Aders (*CL* vi 969–70: [Nov 1833?]), it appears he did not; he instead imagined it appearing on a vignette of a tombstone on the last page of his *PW*. One version does, however, connect it with his own grave, which he expected to be at Hornsey churchyard, on the easterly slope of Highgate Hill (see *CM—CC*—ii 904–5n). As it turned out, he was buried in an extension to the old cemetery at the top of Highgate Hill; but in Mar 1961 his remains were transferred to the nave of St Michael's Church, Highgate, beneath a slab engraved with the *PW* (1834) text of the present poem by Reynolds Stone.

Mercy for Praise, to be forgiven for Fame,
He ask'd, and hoped thro' Christ. Do Thou the Same.

694. S. T. COLERIDGE, ÆTAT. SUÆ 63

[Oct–Nov 1833]

C quoted the lines in a letter to Mrs Aders of Nov? 1833, which has since been
lost and is now known only in transcripts (*Arthur Coleridge: Reminiscences* ed
J. A. Fuller-Maitland—1921—43; *CL* VI 969); the text below reproduces the
surviving transcript in Mrs Aders's hand (omitting deletions and false starts).
C's letter accompanied what he calls a "proof" of the half-length portrait by
Abraham Wivell, by which he possibly means one of the engravings by T. B.
Welch. He says that he wrote the lines under the proof he sent to HNC.

At the probable time of writing C was just beginning his 62nd year, not his
63rd. The letter also contained a version of **693** *S.T.C.*.

| not | handsome | was | but | was | eloquent |
Non formosus erat, sed erat facundus Ulysses

Translation

"In truth he's no beauty!" cry'd Moll, Poll, and Tab,
But they all of them own'd He'd the gift of the Gab.

7. Mercy for Praise] C explains
in a ms note that "for" is meant in
the sense "instead of". He copied the
equivalent Latin words from Erasmus
Parabolae (in *Opera Omnia* [ed J.
Le Clerc]—10 vols Leiden 1703–6—
I 603) in 1811–12 (*CN* III 4121 "ve-
niam pro laude peto"), supporting this
meaning.

title. The full formula is "anno ae-
tatis suae", "in the –th year of his/her
age".

2. Ovid *Ars Amatoria* 2.123 tr J. H.
Mozley (LCL rev G. P. Goold 1979)
75 "Ulysses was not comely, but he
was eloquent."

695. ADAPTATION OF ISAIAH 2.7

[Nov 1833]

C drafted the adaptation in Notebook 52 (*CN* v). The entry consists of a prose paraphrase of Isa 2.6, interpreting it in contemporary terms (imports from the east, the French as Philistines, the Whigs, etc), followed by the rewriting of verse 7 as a quatrain. In the AV verse 7 reads: "Their land also is full of silver and gold, neither is there any end of their treasures: their land is also full of horses, neither is there any end of their chariots." C continues, after his adaptation: "8. Full is the Land of *Idols*."

For C's long-standing, more purely literary, interest in Isaiah see **256** *Hexametrical Version of Isaiah* headnote.

> Full is the Land of Silver & Gold,
> And no end of it's Treasures;
> Full is the Land of Horses*
> And no end of it's Coaches, & Waggons,—

696. LINES ON LADY MARY SHEPHERD

[Jun–Nov 1833]

C wrote the lines in Notebook Q (*CN* v), following the heading given here as an epigraph to the poem. It seems likely that they grew out of Murray's letter; if it was a letter of introduction, this might have taken place at Cambridge (Jun), Ramsgate (Jul or Sept), Highgate (Aug, Oct–Nov), or elsewhere. Poem **697** *Other Lines on Lady Mary Shepherd* may or may not have preceded the present poem.

Lady Mary Shepherd (1777–1847) was the second daughter of Neil Primrose, 3rd earl of Rosebery; she married Sir Samuel Shepherd (1760–1840), a lawyer, in Apr 1808. She was the author of *Enquiry respecting the Relation of Cause and Effect* (1819), *An Essay upon the Relation of Cause and Effect* (1824), and *Essays on the Perceptions of an External Universe* (1827), and of periodical essays such as "Lady Mary Shepherd's Metaphysics" *Fraser's Magazine* v (Jul 1832) 697–708. With respect to her particular interest in causation, she wrote in opposition to Hume and John Fearn.

---

* Still fuller of biped asses.

"Lady Mary Shepheard, Lord Roseberry's Sister, a Lady imbued
with a Taste for Metaphysics."

Mr John Murray's Letter to S. T. C.—

With Sal Atticum corn'd,
With Paper-Spice pepper'd,
With Book-Garnish adorn'd—
Enter Lady Mary Shepheard—
Imbued with a Taste—   5
Imblued with a Colour—
Of or For,
And or Or,
Prose, Poesy, Paste,
& Metaphysics, to lull her—*   10

* Φωνᾶντα συνέτοισι· ες δε το παν
  Ερμηνέως χατιζει.
The following Lines, faithfully *transpoetried* from her Ladyship's own *Prosing*,
may serve as the *Interpretation*—

Or say, to give the Word it's true Tick,   5
Perform the office hermeneutic.

"Before you close your outward Eyes,
Your inward Eye anoint!
This is a Maxim good and wise:
And so, **I** make a point.   10
Each Night, before I go to Sleep,
(For each Day has it's bleeding wound to staunch)
Always to read *something deep*,
Locke, Mol Thus, or Mol Flanders, or Mol Branche."

1. Sal Atticum] Tr "Attic salt", a
common phrase for refined wit.
corn'd] Cured or preserved.
7–10. A version of line 9 origin-
ally followed line 6, and reads in the
ms "~~For~~ Poesy, Paste, ~~for~~". C subse-
quently added lines 7–9 at the foot of
the page and looped them into their
correct position, inserting at the same
time "&" at the beginning of line 10.
10fn. Written on a different page of
the notebook and keyed in afterwards.
The Greek is from Pindar *Olympian
Odes* 2.85–6 (var) tr "Speaking to
those who understand it; but for the

crowd [*or* in general] they need an
interpreter" ("interpreters" in the ori-
ginal). Cf **133** *To a Friend Who had
Declared his Intention of Writing No
More Poetry* 16fn and EC. Here, the
Greek word ἑρμηνεύς "interpreter"
gives C the cue for a facetious rhyme
before his paraphrase of Lady Mary's
words.
    The entry continues in prose, at-
tributing the notion of Moll Branche
as a female philosopher to Joseph Cot-
tle (cf **642** *To Joseph Cottle*, which
appears as a couplet earlier in the
same notebook). John Locke (1632–

Polemics too gull her;
But what's that to You?
She is a desperate Scholar,
Like the Heavens, DEEP BLUE!

697. OTHER LINES ON
LADY MARY SHEPHERD

[Nov 1833]

C drafted the lines in Notebook Q (*CN* v), beneath the date 23 Nov 1833, with the two footnotes on the facing page. He subsequently inserted the following introduction between the date and the first line:

> For I was introduced to Lady Herschell at Cambridge, during the assemblage of the British Philosophers—and she and Professor Airy's wife were confessedly the twin stars of the first magnitude in the Constellation of Beauties.

Lady Mary Shepherd appears to have been introduced by a letter from John Murray (see poem **696**). The present lines suggest that she waited on C at Highgate in Nov, but they could have met at Ramsgate in Jul or Sept.

C added after the closing line: "Mem. The Poet is not an F. R. S., but his best Friend, Dr Green *is*: and *he* is glorified by *reflection*." He attended the meeting of the British Association at Cambridge with JG and J. H. Green in late Jun 1833, and described his experiences in *TT* 29 Jun 1833 (*CC*) I 391–7. Part of what he said there was recorded by [R. A. Willmott] "S. T. Coleridge at Trinity; with Specimens of his *Table-Talk*" *Conversations at Cambridge* (1836) 1–36 (=*TT—CC*—II 449–68).

Lady Mary Shepheard,
As restless as a Leopard
  Tho' not so lithe and starry,
Did wait on S. T. Cōlĕrĭdge

1704), Thomas Malthus (1766–1834), and Nicolas Malebranche (1638–1715) are philosophers of whom C did not much approve; Moll Flanders is the eponymous low-life heroine of Daniel Defoe's novel (1722).

14. DEEP BLUE] I.e. a blue-stocking—a quality which apparently made C somewhat apprehensive (cf **697** *Other Lines to Lady Mary Shepherd* 20).

4–6. For other uses of this rhyme

To learn the extreme polar ridge   5
Of Metaphysic Scholarship
        Unreach'd by Ross or Parry
Ne'er found in Brain or Bottle
By the Stagger-wit, old Stotle,*
        Whose Christian Name was Harry;   10
Nor in Professor Airy's
        Deep Works, nor Bohn's Vagaries
In Tom Aquinas, Duns, Suares,
And Herschel (John) Kn^t Guelph—F. R. S.—

---

* Beyond all doubt the right, now first-recovered Reading of the so strange
Erratum of Pen and Press, Stagyrite:—renitentibus, fateor codicibus, omnibus et
singulis. Nec mirum: commune opprobrium erat. O vos Copistæ! verbicida natio
transmogrificatorum. Oscitantia et Lippitudo sunt Nomen vestrum.

---

by C and the trisyllabic pronuncia-
tion of his name see **515** *Written in
Richard Field's "Of the Church"* 6EC.

7. Ross or Parry] Sir James Clark
Ross (1800–62) sailed in expeditions
with Parry, in the *Hecla* and the
Fury, in 1819–20, 1821–3, 1824–5,
and 1827. In the Felix Booth expe-
dition of 1829–33 he discovered the
magnetic pole, on 1 Jun 1831.

William Edward Parry (1790–
1855) led a number of well-publicised
scientific expeditions to the North-
west Passage and the Arctic during
the first two decades of the 19th cen-
tury, and was knighted in 1829. See
609 *Captain Parry*.

9–10. I.e. Aristotle, whose birth-
place was Stagirus in Chalcidice.

9fn. Tr "admittedly in defiance of
each and every manuscript. Nor is that
surprising: it was a common source
of reproach [viz levelled against mss
that they were full of false readings].
O you copyists! word-butchering tribe
of transmogrifiers. Negligence and
blurred vision are your name."

11–12. George Biddell Airy (1801–
92), Fellow of Trinity since 1824 and
Plumian Professor of Astronomy and

Experimental Philosophy and Director
of the Cambridge Observatory since
1828. He introduced an improved sys-
tem of meridian observations, and
supervised and devised the installa-
tion of several important new instru-
ments. He married Richarda Smith in
1830, and became Astronomer Royal
in 1835.

The enjambment (cf lines 18–19) is
characteristically Pindaric.

12. Bohn's Vagaries] H. M. Bohn
and by 1819, when C was dealing
with the firm, his son H. G. Bohn
(1796–1884) were important figures
in 19th-century bookselling and pub-
lishing. They supplied C with many
of his German books, by sale or loan.

13. Philosophers C had read at
Durham Cathedral Library in 1801, in
the course of his critique of materialist
epistemology, and all of whose works
he subsequently sought to purchase.

14. Sir John Frederick Herschel
(1792–1871) was the son of the
astronomer Sir William Herschel
(1738–1822) and nephew of the as-
tronomer Caroline Herschel (1750–
1848). In 1831 he had been made a
knight of the Guelphian order founded

> Marry, Guelph! Guelph, Marry!*   15
> Deep Wits, tis true, live yet in Paris!
> But Highgate Hill not near so far is.
> There your night owl of Wisdom tarries
> less, wind your way, blue Lady Maries,
> And pounce upon your Quarry.   20

698. EPITAPH OF THE PRESENT YEAR
OR, A MONUMENT TO THE MEMORY
OF DR THOMAS FULLER

[Nov 1833]

C's interest in the 17th-century historian and theological writer Thomas Fuller (1608–61) is documented from 1801 onwards. His annotation of five works by

* The burthens common in our old Songs, as Highrix, Hotrix, under the Greenwood Tree &c &c, I would define as snatches of recollections of past enjoyment, jovial & musical, having no connection with the *thought* but for the purpose of recalling the same or similar sensation and mood in the singer's mind, and of reproducing it in the minds of his Companions. But of the Marry 5 Guelph! Guelph, Marry, I can only say, that being a Burthen in itself, it has no need to an additional burthen of Sense or Meaning—that the phrase, Marry Guelph—occurs in Shakespear—that the Guelphian Knight took the hint, and a very charming woman he married, if my eyes have not declined into a Lippitude for the Lovely.   10

in 1813 (the name goes back to the origins of the Hanoverian kings). He had been a scientific prodigy, and was elected FRS in the year he graduated as senior wrangler (1813). He married Margaret Brodie Stewart in 1829, and went on to become one of the great figures in 19th-century science.

15 and fn. The line is C's third alternative, the earlier versions being: "All, all alike miscarry!" and "Such art they none can carry!" The footnote is wrong to suggest that "Marry Guelph" occurs in Shakespeare. C probably intended "Marry Guep", a

remonstrance which occurs in contemporaries of Shakespeare such as Dekker and Fletcher (see *OED* s.v. "gup"). Lippitude is "blear-eyedness, dimness of vision" (cf the Latin "Lippitudo" in line 9fn).

18–19. Presumably "tarries less" means "presents itself more readily to the hunter". C's "less", with initial lower-case letter, may be another joke, deliberately calling attention to the enjambment typical of the older editions of Pindar which C grew up with.

Fuller bears dates from 1823 to 1829 (*CM—CC*—II 804–39); and he drew on this reading in **620** *Sancti Dominici Pallium*, **621** *Metre and Rhyme in "The Life of Jerome of Prague"*, and **625** *The Last Words of Berengarius*. The present lines appear in a sequence of notes in Notebook Q ff 35ᵛ–45ᵛ, 51ᵛ–52ʳ, and 71ᵛ, relating to Fuller's *A Triple Reconciler* (1654), which C annotated either concurrently or subsequently (*CM—CC*—II 837–9). He described it in the notebook (f 36ʳ) as "a prized addition to my assemblage of Fuller's Works".

The present lines follow a quotation from Fuller: "p. 11. When God, thrifty of his Miracles, was pleased now to drop one down from Heaven", to which C responded in words he afterwards obliterated: "O dear Bishop Fuller if ⌈. . . .⌉ as a ⌈. . . .⌉ for the ⌈. . . .⌉'". In an undated note on Fuller's *Church-history* he commented defensively on Fuller's wit, as the "Stuff and Substance of [his] Intellect", and reckoned that he was in Heaven, not Purgatory (*CM—CC*—II 808–9). Cf *CM* (*CC*) II 834–5, and, on "the witty-wise, tho' not always wisely witty, Fuller", *CN* IV 4963.

> A Lutheran stout, I hold for *Goose* and *Gandry*
> Both the Pope's Limbo, and his fiery Laundry.
> No wit e'er saw I in Original Sin,
> And no Sin find I in Original Wit;
> But if I'm all in the wrong; and Grin for Grin,   5
> Scorch'd Souls must pay for each too lucky Hit—
> Fuller! must I fear—so vast thy Debt,
> Thou art not out of Purgatory yet!
> Tho' One, Eight, Three & Three this year is reckon'd,
> And thou, I think, didst die sub Charles the Second.   10

699. ON AN ELLIPSIS OF JOHN KENYON'S

[Jan 1834?]

C wrote the lines in an inscribed copy of John Kenyon's *Rhymed Plea for Tolerance* (1833), in response to the second pair of the following couplets in the Prefatory Dialogue (*CM—CC*—III 370):

1. *Gandry*] "Goosery", meaning nonsense, is found in Milton (*OED*), but "Gand(e)ry" may well be C's coinage.

2. Laundry] Presumably Purgatory.

5. C added metrical markings: "ĭn thĕ". The syllables need to be given an extra-short value.

9–10. The lines were keyed in afterwards.

A.—'Tis true, of all that ink satiric page
Few dip the pen from purely virtuous rage.
'Tis true, each stroke erased not honest quite,
And blackened leaves, not few, must turn to white . . .

C had known Kenyon since 1814–15; their relationship is reviewed in *TT* (*CC*) I 454n. Most of C's annotation to *Rhymed Plea* is written on the preliminary pages, on the subject of toleration in general; cf *TT* 3 Jan 1834 (*CC*) I 454–6.

Is't true, your pen here wrote not *English quite*?
Th' Ellipsis flickers like a Farthing Light!—

700. "E CŒLO DESCENDIT, ΓΝΩΘΙ ΣΕΑΥΤΟΝ!"

[Jan 1834?]

The immediate source of the title (really an epigraph) is Juvenal *Satires* 11.27 tr "It came from heaven, 'Know thyself.'" The heaven-sprung adage was inscribed on the temple of Apollo at Delphi, was attributed to Thales, traditionally the earliest of Greek philosophers (Diogenes Laertius 1.39), and was discussed by Socrates (Xenophon *Memorabilia* 4.2.24 et seq; cf Plato *Charmides* 47D et seq and *Alcibiades I* 129–35). It is important that in his lines C is disagreeing with more ancient and more philosophical writers than Juvenal.

It might seem that C is rejecting totally the maxim he so often cited as the basis of all philosophy and knowledge (e.g. *SM—CC—*79; *BL* ch 12—*CC—* I 252, 291; *Logic—CC—*116, 143, 205—here referring to Pope, who is also mentioned as favoured by "Antinous" in *CN* IV 4931 f 94ʳ) and more specifically in regard to the attainment of knowledge of God: "We begin with the I KNOW MY SELF, in order to end with the absolute I AM. We proceed from the SELF, in order to lose and find all self in GOD" (*BL* ch 12—*CC—*I 283). But his interest in completing and publishing his whole philosophical system persisted almost to the last; cf *CL* VI 946–7: to J. H. Green [26 Jul 1833]; 977: to J. H. Green [17] Mar 1834). His latest surviving notebook, for Mar 1834 (Notebook 55, in VCL), begins with 23 pages of a treatise on the political measures he would recommend, and at the other end of the notebook he wrote ten pages on the nature of God.

Perhaps the present lines are an injunction to himself, personally, at the approach of death; or, if of more general application, they might be taken as an attempt to convey the uselessness of pursuing human knowledge without at the same time aiming at the divine, the latter achievable only with the help of the

Christian tradition and with an emphasis on the act rather than the impossible total achievement, as in *BL* ch 24 (*CC*) II 240fn: "Know thyself: and so shalt thou know God, as far as is permitted to a creature, and in God all things." The poem can be read as a companion to or development from **482** *Human Life*.

The 10-line version of the poem given here was printed in *PW* (1834). The 6-line holograph version (=lines 1–4, 9–10), dating from Jan of the same year, differs in capitalisation and punctuation. There are only these two texts.

Γνῶθι σεαυτὸν!—and is this the prime
And heaven-sprung adage of the olden time!—
Say, canst thou make thyself?—Learn first that trade;—
Haply thou mayst know what thyself had made.
What hast thou, Man, that thou dar'st call thine own?—   5
What is there in thee, Man, that can be known?—
Dark fluxion, all unfixable by thought,
A phantom dim of past and future wrought,
Vain sister of the worm,—life, death, soul, clod—
Ignore thyself, and strive to know thy God!   10

701. SPLENDIDA BILIS

[Feb 1834]

C drafted the lines in Notebook 54 (*CN* v), where the title is attributed to Horace and followed by a short explanation: "Hexametrized Gobbets, expectorated 3 Feb? 1833, at the 10th Hour A.M. by me, poor body-crazed Sinner." For 1833 read 1834 (see vol II sec A). For the title see Horace *Satires* 2.3.141, where the allusion is to "shining bile", also called "black bile", a diseased condition ("melancholia" in Greek) thought to be a cause of madness. "Pituita" (catarrh) similarly clouded the intellect, as Horace implies in *Epistles* 1.1.108: "sanus nisi cum pituita molesta est" tr "sane, except when his catarrh is troublesome". C would have had this stock of medical terms ready to his mind from his copious reading on the subject, beginning with his schoolboy ambition to follow his brother Luke into medicine, as well as from his companions at Highgate. In the last line "hic et hæc" repeats the formula then used in Latin grammars for indicating masculine/feminine—i.e. common—gender.

After the first two lines, the dactylic hexameter metre is sacrificed to the puns, of which only two come out in a literal translation:

Rumbling in the bowels, laborious Breathing, Bile, troublesome catarrh;
Hand on hand pressed hard across the Duodenum;

Gall, unhappy Cat whose name is purulent *Pus*,
Mucus, when we Sing—i.e. Miew! curse! with Wheezing;
And this common Cough = Hecking, Tuzzle and Tearing.

C wrote "(We sing!)" immediately below "Wheezing" in the ms, to make the pun evident.

Borborygmos, Dyspnoia, χόλη, pituita molesta;
Palma super palmam pressa ægrè trans Duodenum;
Fel, Felis infelix cui nomen *Pus* purulentum,
Mucus, cum Canimus—i.e. Miew! curse! with Wheezing;
Ac hic et hæc Tussis = Hecking, Tuzzle and Tearing.   5

702. LATIN ADDRESS TO CHRISTOPHER MORGAN

[Feb 1834]

The lines as given here constitute a prose epitaph on a certain Christopher Morgan, which serves as a preamble, to four dactylic hexameters, regular in all but the uncertainly read final line. They constitute the arguably most finished portions of a sequence of five loosely related drafts in Notebook 54 (*CN* v). Tr:

The Counsellor concerning Secrets both abdominal and venereal (in English, *Privy* Counsellor) to his sacred Majesty, G. IV, lies here.

Thou happy Morgan! For in thy care are Palate,
Spleen, Teeth, Bowels, Chin, Mind, Knob of the King.

Barber, Surgeon, Parasite and in charge of his food,
And in his Privy affairs ? almost ? sole Factotum.[1]

Christopher Morgan has not been traced, and it is uncertain whether he was dead or alive when C wrote his epitaphic address. The absence of his name from medical and other reference sources suggests that if he practised at all he did not possess formal qualifications.

Draft (*c*) in vol II names Morgan as "Pimp, and Apothecary" to the duke of "Queensborough" as well as George IV. The reference is presumably to the 4th duke of Queensberry, William Douglas (1724–1810), who was a notorious rake and hypochondriac to the end of his life. The dissipations of George IV (1762–1830) continued long after he became Regent in 1811, but he led a more

---

[1] Alternatively "Factotum of the innermost shrine".

sober life after his accession to the throne in 1820; he is known to have taken large quantities of laudanum.

> Consiliarius de Secretis et gastricis et aphrodisiacis (anglicè *Privy Counselor*) sacræ suæ Majestati, G. IV hic jacet.

> Tu felix Morgan! tibi Curæ quippe Palatum
> Splen, Dens, Omentum, Mentum, Mens, Mentula Regis.

> Tonsor, Chirurgus, Παρασιτὴς, και περι σῖτου
> Et de Secretis ?suis, ?fani/?fore/?fere Factotum ?solus.

703. LINES ON GEORGE CROLY'S *APOCALYPSE*

[Feb–Mar 1834? Nov 1833?]

George Croly (1780–1860) had resigned his curacy in Ireland in 1810 to pursue a literary career in London, while still hoping for a living in the Church of England. C might have made his acquaintance at the time of his arrival in England or soon after, before he left for a while to become a European correspondent of *The Times* (cf *CRB* I 121–2, II 745). He was an early contributor to *Bl Mag*, from 1820 at least, and to *The Literary Gazette* (founded 1817). See the obituary in *The Gentleman's Magazine* ser 3 x (Jan–Jun 1861) 104–7; A. L. Strout *A Bibliography of Articles in Blackwood's Magazine* (Lubbock, Tex 1959).

C describes himself in a letter to H. F. Cary of [25–6] May 1827 as looking— "rectius[1] staring"—at George Croly's *The Apocalypse of St John . . . a New Interpretation* (1827) (*CL* VI 683). The present lines were drafted in Notebook 54 (*CN* v), at the conclusion of an entry which runs as follows:

Ab Ireneo usque ad Crathmum Craulum.

> Parson Croley, Crathmo-Crawlo,

to be pardoned if in his ⱥApocalyptica his imagination communed less with the Muses' mystic Choir, than with that of the Cathedral with prebendary Stalls/ and turned ?ἀπὸ Φοιβουῳ Απολλωνοϛι ?τῳ μεσουρανιῳ αρχιεπισκοπῳ, και ταις τηϛῶν εκκλησίαϛῶν αυτου Πρεσβυτεραις και αγγελϕαις (the old maid angels of Apollyon's Church) to meditate on Dean and Chapter/

---

[1] "More correctly."

The Latin phrase, "from Irenaeus to Crathmo-Crawlo", may be connected with a statement in Notebook 54 f 3ᵛ, between entries dated 19 and 22 Nov 1833, referring to Irenaeus and Croly as the first and last of the commentators on Rev, all "gifted" with "a superabundant Lack" of "poetic Light or philosophic Insight". The character Crathmo-Crawlo appears in MS 1 of **476** *On the First Poem in Donne's Book*, although the name comes from Ossian and the identification with Croly might not have been in C's mind in 1811. The Greek, which C partially paraphrases, may be translated: "~~from~~ to Phoebus Apollo, to the mid-heavenly archbishop, and the female Elders and angels of his ~~Church~~ Churches." C's alterations in the manuscript (not all of which can be transcribed) show him struggling over the uneasy transition from Greek to Hebrew mythology, with Apollo first as leader of the Muses, then as Apollyon, king of the locusts in the bottomless pit (Rev 9).

> The Keeper of the Seals inscribes my name—
> What? in the Book of Life? O better far—
> In the Book of LIVINGS! *This* now I call Fame
> O Croley! born beneath auspicious Star!

704. A MOTTO FOR REED'S SHAKESPEARE

[Feb–Mar 1834]

C drafted the lines in Notebook 55, at the end of a prose note on the proliferation of editions of Shakepeare (*CN* v). "They would [sc let] neither Shakespear, nor Malone alone—and out comes Reid's Edition in Twenty Three thick Volumes Octavo—but thro' shameful neglect of the Composition & the Correction of the Press without the intended Motto—viz."

Edmund Malone's edition in 10 octavo volumes was published in 1790 (by Baldwin) and again in 21 volumes in 1821 (by Rivington); Isaac Reed's in 21 octavo volumes in 1803 (by J. Johnson) and 1813 (by J. Nichols), and in twelve volumes in 1820 and 1823 (by J. Walker and G. Offer). Malone's particular interest was in the chronological order of Shakespeare's plays and their dating, Reed's in a variorum text. At no time was Reed's edition issued in 23 volumes. C referred to an annotated reprint (1809) of Reed's edition in a notebook entry

1. the Seals] Rev 5–8.
2. Book of Life] e.g. Phil 4.3; Rev 3.5.
3. Book of LIVINGS] The editor of *The Literary Gazette*, William Jer-
dan, tried unsuccessfully to obtain a suitable benefice for Croly, who had to wait until 1835 before becoming rector of St Stephen's, Walbrook.

connected with his 1819 lectures (*CN* III 4486; also *Lects 1808–1819—CC*—II 373 and n 3), although it has not been traced (*CM—CC*—IV 869).

> Grist & Chaff, which you will!
> More Sacks on the Mill!
> Plenty! Plenty! Plenty!
> Laugh, jolly Millers, laugh!
> And reckon Wheat to Chaff,   5
> One Sack in twenty.

705. TO MISS FANNY BOYCE

[1834]

The lines were contributed to *The Athenaeum* (28 Jan 1888) by Francis G. Waugh, who introduced them as follows: "In case such a trifle should be thought worth preservation, I have Lady Wilmot Horton's permission to send you seven lines which were made on her as a small child by S. T. Coleridge. The 'cubic' is somewhat characteristic." The same letter ends: "Lady Wilmot Horton when very young was a great pet of the poet, and was staying with the Gillmans at Highgate just before his death."

SC mentions the Boyce children in a letter to HNC of 15–20 Sept 1832, now at HRC (Grantz No 560). Amelia Boyce made the drawing of the Gillmans' back garden in 1835 which is reproduced by A. W. Gillman *Searches into the History of the Gillman or Gilman Family* (2 vols 1895) II facing 168 (cf II 166).

> Little Miss Fanny,
> So cubic and canny,
> With blue eyes and blue shoes—
> The Queen of the Blues!
> As darling a girl as there is in the world—   5
> If she'll laugh, skip, and jump,
> *And not be Miss Glump!*

4². Humorous allusion to the blue-stockings, who were also known as the Blues. See **696** *Lines on Lady Mary Shepherd* 14EC.

706. DOGGEREL LETTER FOR
AN AUTOGRAPH

[Jul 1834]

The untitled lines comprise the whole of a letter addressed to William C. Saunders, c/o Harrison Latham at Liverpool (*CL* VI 988–9). Saunders does not appear in Liverpool street directories or other records. However, the *1835 Gore's Street Directory* lists a firm of general merchants by the name of Harrisons and Latham, 3 George's Dock Gates. Perhaps Saunders was connected with the firm, and he may have been an American: SC was negotiating with the American firm of Saunders and Otley for the publication of her *Phantasmion* in 1836 (Grantz No 919).

The lines are dated 10 Jul 1834 from Highgate. C died on 25 Jul.

"Rich Men, who keep accounts at various Banks,
Should not give Autographs: to *Strangers*, ne'er!"
So said a shrewd Attorney, one who ranks
High 'mongst the Jews, and in th' Old Bailey Sphere.
But I keep none: and therefore have no fear   5
In letting loose my hand-writing and name,
To gain such fair Extension to my FAME!

ANNEXES

ANNEX A

MANUSCRIPT COLLECTIONS

The manuscript collections listed below were compiled for a variety of reasons, by different copyists, at different times. They have different kinds of authority and relevance, and the list is selective. Of those collections in C's hand, some are deliberate reappraisals, interpretative selections copied carefully in the poet's best hand, with title-pages (Nos 3 and 6), and they have the status of printed collections. Others are connected with publications in various ways (Nos 7, 8, and 10), and mingle drafts and fair copies. Others are in part extempore and slight (No 12). Other collections in which C's hand appears are determined overall by their owners (No 1 and, to an extent, No 9); while others again, wholly by other copyists, preserve some versions not recorded elsewhere (Nos 2, 4, 5, 11, and 13).

The list aims to provide convenient information, not to be complete, and its focus is on "collections" in a somewhat restricted sense. It does not include the collections of epigrams in Notebooks $3\frac{1}{2}$ and 22, for example, since they are available in KC's edition (*CN* I 625, II 2224). Again, a case could be made on grounds of usefulness for a list of poems appearing in notebooks, in their numerical and alphabetical order (Notebook 1/Gutch, Notebooks Q and F, and so on), providing a system of cross-reference between the numeration of the present edition and *CN* (from whose text the readings given here sometimes differ). But such a list would describe a quite different—basically haphazard—kind of manuscript collection from the others in this annex. The list also excludes several early and late manuscripts containing groups of three and four poems, sent by C to his brothers and to editors of albums.

The annex does not include collections which have no textual significance, such as the family albums and transcripts at the BM (Add MS 47554) and HRC (MS Coleridge, S T Letters I), the poems by C included in the manuscript volume transcribed by SH in 1826–7 at Bloomington, Indiana (Lilly Library), or the transcripts by SC, EHC, and others at VCL (various classifications). The list is arranged in order of the versions each collection represents. Thus, No 2 is placed early because it was copied from early manuscripts, even though the copying was not done until 1823?; No 4 is placed between collections dating from 1791 and 1793 because its greatest value is to represent versions dating from that time; and so on. In the descriptions emphasis is given to the different features of each collection, as they bear on the establishment of C's text.

The titles are given as they appear in the manuscripts, and it should be noted that they sometimes differ from those adopted in the present edition.

1. JAMES BOYER'S *LIBER AUREUS*

BM MS Ashley 3506. Three quarto volumes. Fair copies in C's schoolboy hand of five of his poems and seven prose essays in vols I and III, the poems all in vol I.

Boyer encouraged his scholars by asking them to transcribe exercises of more than ordinary merit in a book kept for the purpose. The three volumes cover the years from 1783, when Boyer had already been headmaster for seven years, to 1799, when he retired. C's verse contributions are signed and dated, and cover the years 1787–90. They are, of course, only a selection of the best of the school exercises he wrote. CL was one of the few non-Grecians who also contributed (in 1789).

(1) ff 29^v–30^r "Nil pejus est cælibe vitâ." (=poem **6**).
(2) ff 40^r–41^r "De medio fonte leporum surgit aliquid amari." (=poem **7**).
(3) ff 41^r–41^v "Oh! mihi præteritos referat si Jupiter annos!" (=poem **8**).
(4) ff 44^r–46^v "Monody on the Death of Chatterton." (=poem **82**). Folio 46^v is reproduced in *C Bibl* (Wise *TLP*) facing p 52.
(5) f 47^r *"Nemo repente turpissimus"* (=poem **18**). Folio 47^r is reproduced in *C Bibl* (Wise *TLP*) facing p 53.

2. GREEN OTTERY COPY BOOK

VCL S LT Fl.3. Green-covered exercise book, comprising 23 leaves, 16.7× 20.0 cm; wm crown on top of a semicircle (shield?) above GR; chain-lines 2.5 cm. Transcripts by John May Jr (?), entitled on f 1^r "A Collection of Poems and Prose/~~Writings~~ by Mr Samuel Coleridge."

The transcripts are dated c 1823 in *PW* (EHC) I xxv, presumably because the back cover has the wm "M | 1822", or else on the evidence of family correspondence or tradition which has not survived. EHC's abbreviation—"MS. O.(c)"—is misleading, however, since the Green Ottery Copy Book has nothing to do with the other Ottery Copy Book. Half of the twelve poems present here are absent from the other book, and the poems common to both have been copied from different originals.

The elder John May (1775–1856) was a London wine merchant who had been a pupil of GC's. RS's friendship with him had begun in Portugal in 1795–6, and he was a particular friend also of GC's brother James ("the Colonel") and of JTC.[1] At about the time the transcript is supposed to have been made, John May Jr was paying court to SC (who in early summer 1823 was in Devonshire), but his father and the Southeys, with JTC's help, discouraged an engagement.[2] Just before C visited John May Sr at Richmond, where in Apr 1811 JTC made a record of his conversation, he became aware of not possessing one of the poems in the group that John May Jr subsequently copied (*CN* III 4055 and n). These coincidences—involving GC, SC, and JTC at Richmond and Ottery—might somehow be connected with the transcript.

John May Jr copied the poems in random, not chronological, order, though he began and ended with the earliest and latest written. He was a fairly accurate transcriber, but not good at spelling. In the Variorum apparatus transcripts are recorded only for poems of which original texts have not survived (Nos 1, 4, 6, and 12). The case for John May as copyist rests partly on an endorsement on the manuscript at VCL, partly on the circumstantial evidence cited above. Authenticated samples of his hand—e.g. Bodleian MS Eng lett c 290 ff 100^r, 104^r, 106^r—appear to be slightly different from that of the VCL copybook.

The poems by C contained in the copybook are as follows. All but four (Nos 1, 4, 6, and 12) are transcripts from original letters and manuscripts sent to GC when he was at Newcome's Academy in Hackney and C was at Christ's Hospital and Cambridge. References to the originals, where they are known, are included.

(1) f 1^r "A Sonnet." (=poem **17**). A copy from a lost original, which appears to predate the Ottery Copy Book version.

(2) ff 1^v–3^v "A Greek Poem, by which the Author gained a prize at the University of Cambridge." (=poem **48**). Copied from the version sent to GC on 16 Jun 1792, in the possession of Sir Charles Cave (1989).

  f 3^v complimentary poem on the above, by GC; ff 4^r–9^r sermon by C, written when he was 17 (*SW&F—CC—*12–17; f 9^{r-v} a definition of good writing, by GC.

(3) f 9^v "An Epitaph for Howard's Tomb on the banks of the Dnieper." (=poem **47**). Copied from the version sent to GC on 2 Apr 1792 (Eton College, School Library).

  ff 9^v–10^r translation of the above by Mr Sparrow.

(4) ff 10^r–11^v "A Monody on Chatterton, . . . written by the Author at the age of sixteen." (=poem **82**). From a lost original which postdates the version in the *Liber Aureus* and predates the version in the Ottery Copy Book.

  f 11^v comment on the above by John May.

(5) f 12^r "Nemo repente turpissimus I S. C. ætatis 16." (=poem **18**). Copied

---

[1] See *S Letters* (Curry) II 495–6 for a biographical note; also Bernard Lord Coleridge *The Story of a Devonshire House* (1905) 195, 210, 214, 216, 218, etc, and *The Letters of Robert Southey to John May, 1797 to 1838* ed Charles Ramos (Austin, Tex 1976).

[2] Griggs *Coleridge Fille* 48n.

from a manuscript perhaps sent to GC, which also includes Nos 7 and 8 (VCL S MS Fl.1).

(6) ff 12ᵛ–13ᵛ "The Nose. An Odaic Rhapsody." (=poem **11**). Differs from other known versions; original not traced. The original would appear to predate the summer of 1791, and was perhaps sent to GC in 1789.

(7) f 13ʳ "A few lines selected from some pieces written by Lee when mad." (=poem **16**). Copied from a manuscript perhaps sent to GC, which also includes Nos 5 and 8 (VCL S MS Fl.1).

(8) f 13ᵛ "Pain. A Sonnet." (=poem **15**). Copied from a manuscript perhaps sent to GC, which also includes Nos 5 and 7 (VCL S MS Fl.1).

(9) ff 13ᵛ–16ʳ "Upon the Author's leaving school and entering into Life" (=poem **30**). Copied from a letter to GC of 22 Jun 1792, which also includes No 10, in the possession of Erwin Schwarz (1989).

(10) f 16ʳ⁻ᵛ "Sonnet. | Written just after ~~he left th~~ the Author left the country in Sept: 1789 ætat: 15." (=poem **10**). Copied from a letter to GC of 22 Jun 1792, which also includes No 9, in the possession of Erwin Schwarz (1989).

2 Odes of Horace from the *Annual Register* of 1777.

(11) ff 17ᵛ–20ʳ "Prospectus and Specimen of a Translation of Euclid in a series of Pindaric Odes, communicated in a Letter by the ⱥAuthor to his Brother ~~Mr:~~ Revd: G. Coleridge" (=poem **24**). Copied from a letter to GC of 31 Mar 1791 (NYPL, Berg Collection).

ff 20ʳ–21ʳ school exercise by C, in prose (see *SW&F—CC*—5–6).

(12) f 21ʳ "On a Lady Weeping | Imitation from the Latin of Nicolaus Archius" (=poem **46**). Differs from other known versions; original untraced—apparently sent to GC some time before Jun 1792.

f 21ᵛ prose (heavily deleted).

3. OTTERY COPY BOOK

BM Add MS 47551. Exercise book with mottle-green covers, comprising 31 leaves (but foliated by the BM to include the front and back cover), 16.0× 19.5 cm; wm Britannia surmounted by crown; chain-lines 2.5 cm. Autograph selection by C from among his Christ's Hospital and early poems, entitled on f 3ʳ "Poetical Attempts | by | S T Coleridge". Folio 2ʳ has the signature of John [Taylor] Coleridge, Eton College, Bucks; also the name of Charlotte Baker. There are various notes by JTC's elder brother, James Duke Coleridge, and Latin verses and pictorial sketches are scattered throughout. Several leaves are missing: one between ff 4 and 5, another (conjugate) between ff 6 and 7, another between ff 27 and 28, another between ff 28 and 29, and three others (two of them conjugate with the last two cited) at the end. When the pages were first numbered (by JTC?) ff 4 and 5 were missing, but the leaves between ff 27 and 28 and between ff 28 and 29 (pages 47–8, 51–2) were present. Folio 30 is torn vertically in half, leaving only the inner side; f 32 is torn horizontally in half, leaving only the bottom portion.

C presumably copied the poems during the vacation he spent in Devon before he went up to Cambridge—i.e. Aug–Sept 1791, when he was staying with his brother James at Tiverton and at Ottery. The selection includes school exercises of the sort copied earlier in Boyer's *Liber Aureus*, improved versions of poems sent to GC, and poems written in the summer of 1791 (No 11 below is dated 17 Aug 1791). Some improvements appear to have been made on the spur of the moment: for example, replacing lines 90.1.1–5 of **30** *Happiness* by lines 91–2 attains dignity at the cost of rhyme and sense. Other changes—such as the fourth stanza added to **11** *The Nose: An Odaic Rhapsody*—are more properly modifications (in this case, a recension of the poem's previous political meaning). Several of the poems were first published in the enlarged category of Juvenile Poems in *PW* (1834); but the texts differ in more respects than can be accounted for by errors of transcription, and might derive from an interim transcription by JTC described below.

There is evidence that the leaves between ff 4 and 5 and between ff 6 and 7 had been removed before 1807, and that ff 30 and 32 were at that time still intact. There is also evidence which points to the identity of the missing sonnets, Nos 4 and 6; this derives from a list of C's poems made by JTC and now at DCL (MS A Coleridge J T 11). JTC sent the list to C from Oxford on 20 Jun 1809, wondering if any of the poems could be published in *The Friend*. These coincide exactly with those in the Ottery Copy Book in the form of their titles if not in their sequence, except that JTC omits Sonnet 3 (=**17** *Genevieve*) and adds at the end "Specimen of Euclid Pindaricised" (=poem **24**), which he could also have seen at Ottery. JTC notes that stanzas 2 and 3 of the "Ode on the destruction of the Bastile" (=poem **13**), which would have been contained on the missing leaf between ff 6 and 7, are not present, and he includes the sonnets "On seeing a youth affectionately welcomed by his sister" (=poem **26**) and "Anna & Harland" (=poem **19**), which one must therefore presume were the sonnets contained on the leaves between ff 27 and 28 and ff 28 and 29.

The following couplet appears at the head of f 5ʳ:

> Honor for him shall blow the Trump of Praise,
> Vigour shall brace his limbs, and Peace shall crown his days.

The missing leaf between ff 4 and 5 contained the beginning of the poem which the couplet concludes. One would guess that it was a school exercise on a moral theme, and it must have been some thirty lines long. The leaf is conjoint with the one missing between ff 6 and 7, and was therefore removed at an early date: 1807 is more likely than 1809 as a *terminus ante quem* for the mutilation of the volume because, when JTC sent C his list, he was undoubtedly copying from the notebook he prepared at Eton in 1807. This is known from the supplement to *P&DW* (RHS) II 355–60, where RHS quoted from it texts of **82** *Monody on the Death of Chatterton*, **14** *To the Evening Star*, and **19** *Anna and Harland*.

The first two of these three texts coincide with the Ottery Copy Book versions (allowing for differences caused by errors in transcription), strengthening the likelihood that the *Anna and Harland* sonnet derived from the same source— i.e. that it was originally contained in the Ottery Copy Book.

Sonnets 9 and 10 on ff 31 and 32, at the end of the sequence—Nos 20 and 21 below—are written in a less careful hand. Another fair copy of the second of these exists in C's early hand on identical paper at DCL (Letters Coleridge p 32), headed "Sonnet 9". One might reckon that C wrote the sonnet into the Ottery Copy Book, and then removed the page so as to amend the sequence. But it is difficult to see how, physically, the DCL manuscript can have been removed from the Ottery Copy Book; also, the large, rounded hand appears even earlier (1789–90?). Differently, the three leaves removed from the end of the Ottery Copy Book might have contained further sonnets.

The book contains the following poems:

(1) f 4^{r-v} "The progress of Vice—an Ode." (=poem **18**).
(2) f 5^r concluding couplet to a poem which occupied the lost leaf preceding (=poem **12**).
(3) f 5^r "*On Imitation*" (=poem **38**).
(4) ff 5^v–6^r "An Anthem" (=poem **31**).
(5) ff 6^v–8^r "An Ode on the destruction of the Bastile." (=poem **13**).
(6) ff 8^v–11^v "Monody on the death of Chatterton" (=poem **82**).
(7) ff 12^r–13^r "Monody on a Tea kettle" (=poem **21**).
(8) ff 13^v–15^r "The Nose a Rhapsody—" (=poem **11**).
(9) ff 15^v–17^v "O Curas hominum—o quantum est in rebus inane—" (=poem **29**).
(10) ff 18^r–21^r "Happiness a Poem" (=poem **30**).
(11) ff 21^v–22^r "Ode to Sleep— I Travelling in the Exeter Coach with three other Passengers over Bagshot heath after some vain endeavors to compose myself I compos'd this ode—August 17th, 1791" (=poem **34**).
(12) ff 22^v–23^r "Th' indignant bard compos'd this furious ode, I As tir'd he dragg'd his Way thro' Plymtree road. I August 18th 1799." (=poem **35,** continuing previous lines).
(13) ff 23^v–24^r "Ode on the Ottery and Tiverton Church Music." (=poem **36**).
    f 24^v "Sonnets by S. T. Coleridge" (subtitle; subsequent poems are on rectos only).
(14) f 25^r "Sonnet 1. To my Muse." (=poem **9**).
(15) f 26^r "Sonnet 2. Written Septemb^r 1789." (=poem **10**).
(16) f 27^r "Sonnet 3" (=poem **17**).
    [The folio containing Sonnet 4 is missing]
(17) f 28^r "Sonnet 5 On receiving an account that my Sister's Death was inevitable." (=poem **25**).
    [The folio containing Sonnet 6 is missing]
(18) f 29^r "Sonnet 7 Sent to M^{rs} —— with an Amelia." (=poem **32**).
(19) f 30^r "Sonnet 8 To ˻the Evening Star.˼" (=poem **14**).

(20) f 31ʳ "Sonnet 9 On quitting Christ's Hospital" (=poem **33**).
(21) f 32ʳ Bottom half of leaf only, containing the second half of **15** *Composed in Sickness*.

4. JOHN TAYLOR COLERIDGE'S COMMONPLACE BOOK

University of Pennsylvania Library (Special Collections) MS Eng 13. A folio commonplace book bound in old half calf containing 215 pages, the first 201 in the hand of JTC, the remainder in another hand; wms 1808 and 1810.

Among the authors transcribed, besides C, are Byron, P. B. Shelley, Moore, and RS, and there are poems by JTC himself dating from his years at Eton and later. The selection of material by C is different from that contained in JTC's 1807 notebook and described in his letter of 20 Jun 1809 (see No 3 above), and its sources are also heterogeneous. The transcripts were probably made between 1813 and 1817.

Nos 1–12 and 20 are copied from C's 1803 *Poems* (in random order) and have no textual significance. Of the other poems, No 18 appears to to be copied from the Ottery Copy Book and No 22 from the original letter sent to GC, but Nos 13, 16, 17, 19, and 21 are of independent interest: No 13 appears to derive from the same manuscript source from which the text of *PW* (1834) also derived, yet it omits two groups of lines; No 16 may have been copied from a newspaper, but its source has not been located; No 17 represents a version midway between the Ottery Copy Book and *PW* (1834); No 19 supplies the only complete manuscript text, the page containing the same poem in the Ottery Copy Book having been mutilated; and No 21 appears to be from a very early version indeed (perhaps from the original manuscript cited in *PW*—JDC— 563ʙ and *PW*—EHC—ɪ 17, and since lost). The fact that the "Sonnet on seeing a Youth affectionately welcom'd by his Sister" (=poem **26**) is followed by the same extract from "To a Friend, together with an Unfinished Poem" (=poem **100**) in both JTC's Commonplace Book (Nos 19 and 20 below) and *PW* (1834) ɪ 34–5 might strengthen the likelihood that one was dependent on the other, though perhaps through an intermediate version. The three remaining poems— Nos 12, 14, and 15—have been ascribed to C;[3] *PW* (EHC) ɪɪ 970 No 63 accepts only No 14, and some doubts attach even to this.

The following pieces are by or connected with C:

(1) p 3 "Epitaph on an Infant" (=poem **77**).
(2) pp 29–30 "Dedication ǀ to the Revᵈ Geo: Coleridge of Ottery ǀ Devon" (=poem **150**).
(3) p 31 "Genevieve." (=poem **17**).
(4) p 31 "Sonnet" (=poem **88**).

---

[3] Bertram Dobell "Coleridgeana" *Athenaeum* 9 Jan 1904 p 53; and in notes enclosed with JTC's Commonplace Book.

(5) p 31 "Sonnet" (=poem **103**).
(6) p 32 "To a Young Ass I Its mother being tethered near it." (=poem **84**).
(7) p 33 "To an Infant" (=poem **105**).
(8) p 33 "Lines written at the King's Arms, Ross, formerly the House of the I 'Man of Ross'." (=poem **70**).
(9) p 34 "Extracts. I from Religious musings a Desultory Poem I Written on Christmas Eve. 1794" (=poem **101**).
(10) pp 50–1 "Reflections, on having left a place of Retirement" (=poem **129**).
(11) pp 51–2 "To a Friend I Who asked me how I felt when the Nurse first presented my infant I to me" (=poem **136**).
(12) p 54 "Epitaph on an amiable Girl" (=poem **26.X1**).
(13) p 57 "Elegy on Sir J. M———sh" (=poem **267**).
     p 76 "Curious instance of Roman Catholic blindness" (prose); see *TT* 21 Apr 1811 (*CC*) I 14–15; also *TT* (*CC*) II 137fn.
(14) p 77 "On Pitt & Fox" (=poem **389**).
(15) p 95 "Est quædam flere voluptas" (=poem **61.X1**).
     No 13 of *The Friend* (prose); see *Friend* 16 Nov 1809 (*CC*) II 172–82.
     p 135 Extract from an anonymous review of *Remorse* by JTC in *The Quarterly Review* XI (1814) 177–90.
     pp 140–2 [Walter Scott] "Of Mr. Coleridge as a Poet and an Author the following correct account is given in Ed: Anniv: Reg:ʳ Vol: 1. On the living Poets". Cf *Edinburgh Annual Register, for 1808* I (1810) 427–8.
(16) p 149 "The taste of the times." (=poem **384**).
(17) p 163 "Sonnet" (=poem **10**).
(18) p 163 "Sonnet on hearing that his only Sister's death I was inevitable" (=poem **25**).
(19) p 164 "On seeing a Youth affectionately welcom'd by his I Sister" (=poem **26**).
(20) p 164 "Of his Sister he thus speaks in another Poem.—" (=poem **100**).
(21) p 165 "Sonnet composed in Sickness" (=poem **15**).
(22) pp 178–80 "Specimen of a translation of Euclid in I a series of Pindaric Odes" (=poem **24**).

5. ANN FRANCES BACON'S COMMONPLACE BOOK

VCL (uncatalogued in 1978). A commonplace book bound in quarter sheep, comprising 58 quarto leaves. Transcripts of eleven early poems by C, among much other material, in the hand of Ann Frances Bacon.

The Bacon family were not native to Ottery, but parish records name Dashwood Bacon as witness at a wedding on 24 Feb 1789; Mary Ann Elizabeth Bacon witnessed another wedding on 8 May 1797, and her own wedding to Edmund Bacon of Raveningham, Norfolk, took place at Ottery on 27 Aug 1801.

Dates at the beginning and end of her book show that it was made up between 24 Sept 1799 and 15 Jan 1801: that is, it was finished shortly before she left Ottery.

C's brother Edward was a witness at Ann Bacon's wedding, and there is other evidence of friendship between the two families. C referred to one of the Miss Bacons in jocular terms in letters to his brother GC during Aug 1792 and 1793 (*CL* I 39, 41, 61). Edward Coleridge also appears as the author of two *jeux d'esprit* in the commonplace book: "On Miss Bools and Miss Bacon having their hair I cut off" and "A Dialogue between Thomas and Anna I on les deux Amans I . . . T.N.G./l'amant.   A.F.B./l'amante" (ff 28ᵛ, 29ʳ).

The collection is made up of more than ninety pieces. They comprise verses transcribed from albums or other original sources, often with a personal connection, mixed with verses from printed sources. Most of them date from the 1780s and 1790s, but they go back in time to include pieces by John Gilbert Cooper, Mason, and Young, and come up as close to the date of transcription as Aug 1798 (the verses for the orphaned children of John Palmer). A considerable number concern holiday acquaintances made at Yarmouth, and are ascribed to army and navy officers; there are others by Robert Merry, Charlotte Smith, Mrs Robinson, and RS. They represent altogether a mixture of social, sentimental, and conventional literary interests usual for the time.

Ann Bacon's collection of poems by C centres on the months between Jul and Sept 1793, when C spent the long vacation in Devonshire, distracting himself with versified gallantries and flirtations. C wrote to GC on 5 Aug: "I stayed at Tiverton about 10 days, and got no small κῦδος among the young Belles by complimentary effusions in the poetic Way—" (*CL* I 60). Several of C's poems were adaptations of pieces written earlier, but Ann Bacon's transcripts represent versions of independent interest. At the same time, she appears to have had access to poems written and sent home earlier (to Edward Coleridge?). Her version of **51** *The Complaint of Ninathoma* almost certainly predates Jul 1793, when a different text was published in *M Chron*, and might even predate the version that C sent Mary Evans in Feb. Her version of **17** *Genevieve* likewise represents a text which is earlier than the summer of 1793. Differently, her version of **76** *The Kiss* appears to be a much later one, and was perhaps copied from *Poems* (1797). Her versions of **62** *To a Painter* and **63** *To Miss Dashwood Bacon* are the only ones known. Comparisons with other texts suggest that she was a generally accurate transcriber, but not in details.

The book contains the following pieces by C:

(1) f 7ᵛ "To Miss Dashwood Bacon of Devonshire— I Sepʳ 1793—" (=poem **63**).

(2) ff 23ᵛ–24ʳ "The Kiss." (=poem **76**).

(3) f 37ʳ "To the Moon." (=poem **61**).

(4) ff 37ᵛ–38ʳ "For an Inscription" (=poem **59**).

(5) f 38ᵛ "A Sonnet—" (=poem **17**).

(6) f 39ʳ "On Laura's weeping at taking leave of a female Friend—" (=poem **46**).

(7) ff 39ᵛ–40ʳ "Ninathóma was the daughter of the king of Cathlóma, a district in the highlands of Scotland: her father having been killed in an engagement with a neighbouring Chief, the young Princess according to the customs of the Age and Country was confined in a Cave, on the shore of a desert Island—The following is her supposed Complaint.—" (=poem **51**).

(8) ff 40ᵛ–41ʳ "To a Painter—" (=poem **62**).

(9) f 41ʳ⁻ᵛ "On presenting a moss rose to Miss Nesbitt" (=poem **56**).

(10) f 42ʳ "Cupid turn'd Chymist I A Poem" (=poem **57**).

(11) ff 42ᵛ–45ʳ "Songs of the Pyxies I On the occasion of Miss Beautfleur's &c Visit to the Pyxies Parlour near Ottery Sᵗ Mary Devon— I Sepᵇʳ 1793—" (=poem **64**).

6. ESTLIN COPY BOOK

BPL B 22189. A copybook bound in green leather, comprising 28 quarto leaves, 18.8×23.4 cm; wm crown surmounting shield device I 1794; chain-lines 2.7 cm; entitled (f 2ʳ) "Odes I with other Poems I by S. T. Coleridge I of Jesus College I Cambridge". Autograph selection by C from the poems he wrote after leaving school and after leaving Cambridge.

Folio 1ᵛ has the inscription "S: Estlin—given to her by the Author—April 1795." Mrs Estlin (fl 1785–1815) was the second wife of John Prior Estlin (1747–1817), Unitarian minister at Lewin's Mead, Bristol, and headmaster of a school at St Michael's Hill. C expressed particular affection for her and her young children in later letters (e.g. *CL* I 233: to J. P. Estlin [22 Aug 1796]; 302: to TP 6 Feb 1797; 327: to J. P. Estlin [10 Jun 1797]), and she appears to have been a woman who shared her husband's literary and liberal activities. BPL also possesses a transcript of the lines "Mrs: Barbauld to Mr: Coleridge", dated "Septr. 1797", in her hand (B 21076; see **107** *Allegoric Vision* headnote).

The arrangement of poems follows a thematic, not chronological, order. The titles, together with many of the specific personal occasions of the love poems, are generalised, and the texts represent improved versions midway between earlier manuscripts and *Poems* (1796). The selection includes a poem by CL, another by Samuel Favell, and another not certainly by C (perhaps by his Cambridge contemporary John Gaunt). The poem by CL was sent to C before 11 Dec 1794 (*CL* I 136: to RS [11 Dec 1794]), and was later published in the 1796 *Sonnets*. Samuel Favell (1775–1812) had been converted to pantisocracy while still at Christ's Hospital. C quotes another of his pantisocratic sonnets in *CL* I 100 (to RS [1 Sept 1794]), and he collaborated with C on a third (*CL* I 104: to RS 18 Sept [1794]; 134: to RS [11 Dec 1794]). S *Letters* (Curry) I 91 proves that he was with C and CL during the Dec 1794–Jan 1795 sojourn at the Salutation and Cat. (He matriculated at Pembroke College, Cambridge, in Michaelmas 1795, left without a degree—it was said because he was ashamed of his father being a house-painter in Cambridge—and later accepted a commission in the army with Samuel Le Grice, to die at Salamanca in 1812.) The poem possibly by John Gaunt of Clare Hall was published in the fourth number of *The Watchman* (25 Mar 1796) (*CC*) 141–2. It will be noticed that these three poems all have to do with the political-moral interests which distinguish the selection from its comparable predecessor, the Ottery Copy Book (No 3 above), as the Estlins differed from the Ottery Coleridges.

(1) ff 4^r–8^v "The Songs of the Pixies, an irregular Ode." (=poem **64**).

(2) f 9^{r-v} "Ode." (=poem **56**).

(3) f 10^{r-v} "Ode" (=poem **76**).

(4) f 11^{r-v} "Absence, an Ode." (=poem **39**).

(5) f 11^v "Song." (=poem **73**).
   f 12^{r-v} "Ode" (=poem **105.X1**), perhaps by John Gaunt.

(6) ff 13^r–14^v "An Effusion at Evening— | Written in August. 1792" (=poem **60**).

(7) f 15^r "Epitaph on an Infant." (=poem **40**).

(8) f 15^r "Epitaph on an Infant | (First published in the Morning Chronicle)" (=poem **77**).

(9) f 15^v "Verses to an Infant." (=poem **105**).

(10) f 16^r "Fragment | found in a Mathematical Lecture Room." (=poem **45**).
   f 16^v "On leaving a Place of Residence." Signed "F." (=Samuel Favell).

(11) f 17^{r-v} "Song." (=poem **67**). C notes at the end "Imitated from Casimir."

(12) f 18^r "Ode" (=poem **17**).

(13) f 18^v "The Compound" (=poem **57**).

(14) f 19^{r-v} "Ode" (=poem **55**).

(15) f 20 "Ode | written in snowy Weather." (=poem **88**).
   f 20^v "Written by the Sea side". Signed "Lamb" (sonnet xxv in *Sonnets from Various Authors*=poem **104**).

(16) f 21^{r-v} "Lines addressed to a ~~Forest~~ Spring in the Village of Kirkhampton near Bath." (=poem **74**).

(17) f 22^{r-v} "Lines written at the King's Arms, Ross—formerly the House of Mr Kyle, the 'Man of Ross." (=poem **70**).

(18) ff 22^v–23^v "Verses addressed to a Lady with a poem relative to a recent Event in the French Revolution." (=poem **81**).

(19) f 24^r "Sonnet" (=poem **78**).

(20) ff 24^v–25^r "Ode." (=poem **75**).

(21) f 25^v "Irregular Sonnet." (=poem **87**).

(22) ff 26^r–27^r "On the Death of Friend, who died of a Frenzy fever brought on by Anxiety." (=poem **85**).

(23) f 27^v "To Sheridan" (=poem **99**).

7. QUARTO COPY BOOK

PML MA 1916. Remains of a quarto copybook with marbled covers and leather binding, comprising 14 leaves, 20.0×24.5 cm; wm lily within a shield (?) surmounted by a shield, with GR beneath and an indecipherable printer's name | 1794; chain-lines 2.7 cm. The ms contains versions of seven poems and material for *The Watchman*, in C's hand. The first 7 leaves are filled with poems, then 39 leaves have been cut out (f 8, a fragment containing verse, has been tipped in on the first stub; another piece containing prose, to do with the aims of *The Watchman* and names, is tipped in on the last stub); then the book is filled from the back with materials for *The Watchman*.

The materials for *The Watchman* are summarised in *Watchman* (*CC*) lx; they were transcribed from the *Anthologia Hibernica*, which C borrowed from the Bristol Library between 28 Mar and 25 Apr 1796 (*Bristol LB* No 76). The main period of use of the copybook appears to be approximately nine to twelve months earlier, during the preparation of the 1796 *Poems* (pub 15 Apr). The latter had begun to go to press as early as Jul 1795, and it will be noted that the first seven leaves of the copybook contain, in order, the poems that fill the earlier pages of the printed volume (pp 14–35). Individual readings are improvements on the Estlin Copy Book (No 6 above), yet they are also provisional. That is, C appears to have used the book to experiment with revisions, not all of which he adopted, at the same time that he took care with such matters as spacing and capitals, as if preparing copy-ready versions. The same sequence of poems is missing from the Rugby Manuscript, however, and it is possible that the Quarto Copy Book served as copy, or began to serve as copy, before another version intervened. The Quarto Copy Book might indeed be "the copy book" that C requested from Joseph Cottle on 31 Jul 1795 (*CL* I 157). The tipped-in f 8 suggests the same conclusion: again it contains poems missing from the Rugby Manuscript sequence, and again C experiments with readings which were not all finally adopted. One title on the tipped-in f 8 contains a reference to a numbered note—something added at a relatively late stage in the evolution of *Poems* (1796).

Several earlier stubs of the 39 leaves which have been cut out contain traces of verse. The tipped-in f 8 is undoubtedly from one of these leaves, and other evidence confirms that the missing portion contained further poems. I purchased a holograph fragment at Christie's on 22 Oct 1980 (lot 132) which contains, on the recto, the concluding lines of **55** *Imitated from Ossian* and, on the verso, the first two stanzas of **51** *The Complaint of Ninathoma*, headed "Effusion 3̶1̶ 30". That is, it follows on directly from the tipped-in f 8 and appears to be from the same copybook. It measures 17.6×10.7 cm, the inner margin and the bottom of the leaf being irregularly trimmed away. The chain-line separation is the same (2.7 cm), and the very small portion of a watermark is compatible.

My fragmentary manuscript is accompanied by an als from SC to Mrs Auriol of 25 Nov 1845, in which she says: "I wish I could send a specimen with his signature—but my stock is now reduced very low and soon will be quite exhausted. I sent a scrap away to Lady Geo Thynne a few days ago. I am glad you applied, before it is all gone." Mrs Auriol was the youngest of three sisters, née Morris, nieces to Judge Thomas Erskine. SC met them at Tunbridge Wells in 1843. Mrs Auriol's husband, Edward, was then the new minister of St Dunstan's. SC's reference to Lady George Thynne, who died in 1836, must be a mistake: she must mean Lady John (=Mary Anne) Thynne, d 1863.

What this proves is that SC cut up the Quarto Copy Book in the 1840s, in response to requests for samples of C's handwriting. It also suggests that the copybook was never cut up by C himself, and indeed none of the leaves bound up with the Rugby Manuscript was taken from it. Perhaps the best description of it is as a book in which C began to copy out his poems for publication by Cottle, but which was or became a workbook when he began to submit copy in another form. It complements the material in the Rugby Manuscript, though the first seven leaves at least might date from a few months earlier.

(1) ff 1ʳ–3ᵛ "Songs of the Pɪxɪᴇs." (=poem **64**).
(2) f 4ʳ "Lines written at the King's ᴁArms, Ross—th formerly the House of the 'Man of Ross.'" (=poem **70**).
(3) ff 4ᵛ–5ʳ "Lines | To a beautiful Spring in a Village." (=poem **74**).
(4) f 5ʳ "On a Epitaph on an Infant." (=poem **77**).
(5) ff 5ᵛ–6ᵛ "Lines on the Dead a Friend, who died of a frenzy fever induced by Anxiety. calumnious Reports." (=poem **85**).
(6) ff 6ᵛ–7ᵛ "Lines addressed tTo a young Lady together with a Poem on the French Revolution." (=poem **81**). Folio 7ᵛ is reproduced in *Watchman (CC)* facing p 28.
(7) f 8ʳ Half-page tipped in containing untitled lines (=poem **76**.9–19).
(8) f 8ᵛ "Effusion no 30 29 | Imitated from Ossian" (half-page tipped in =poem **55**.1–8).

8. RUGBY MANUSCRIPT

HRC MS (Coleridge, S T) Works B. A volume bound in brown-olive morocco gilt, the upper hinge broken, comprising leaves mostly of folio and quarto sizes, the smaller leaves inlaid and the larger mounted along the inner edge to prepared stubs. The bookplates of S[hadworth] H[ollway] H[odgson], the metaphysician (1832–1912), and of Rugby School Library are on the front pastedown; and there are library stamps on the preliminary leaves. The volume was made up by Joseph Cottle, mainly from material submitted by C as copy for *Poems* (1796) but including other material. The manuscripts are in C's hand, with the exception of one poem in the hand of his wife, a few notes in the hand of Joseph Cottle, some lines in the hand of RS, and some annotations by EHC.

Arthur Coleridge *Reminiscences* (1921) 45 reports that Hodgson bought his copy of an annotated *Wallenstein* (annex C 11.5) from the library of his relative

DeQ, before presenting it to his old school in 1901–2. It is not known whether the present manuscript also belonged to DeQ, or, if it did, how and when he might have acquired it. If it passed through DeQ's hands, he might have acquired it in recognition of the gift of £300 he made to C through Cottle in 1807; or it could have been lent to him and he failed to return it (this is easier to believe than that Cottle lent it to him). Neither supposition is necessary, and Hodgson quite probably acquired it independently of his acquisition of *Wallenstein*. The manuscript was put together after 1837, since the engraved portraits are from Cottle's *Early Recollections*. A fairly late date for its assembly is also suggested by Cottle's shaky, spiky numbering of the separate leaves; it is quite different from his earlier writing (see on ff 1 + 1 and 40).

The suggestion that the materials were classified and brought together by Cottle at a late stage is confirmed by other evidence, and it accounts for other characteristics of the compilation. It explains the mistaken classification of lines from **110** *Contributions to "Joan of Arc"* as part of **101** *Religious Musings* (f 41), because they are largely in C's hand (a mistake Cottle made on other occasions: cf poem **110** II 442–52 VAR MS 5). It led him to include C's drafts of the lines to Thelwall (f 15), even though they were never intended to be part of the 1796 volume; to include different, overlapping drafts of **115** *The Eolian Harp* (ff 26–8) and of the conclusion to **101** *Religious Musings* (ff 52–5); he even mingles the manuscript preliminaries for the 1797 volume with the 1796 materials. It is difficult to believe that Cottle did not know what he was doing in this last instance, yet the error is surely too blatant to be intended as forgery. The volume is less sophisticated and less potentially deceiving than Cottle's combination of proof versions in BM Ashley 408.

It is important to stress that the compilation is a selection from the material that had passed through Cottle's hands, or that he still owned when he made up this volume. Thus, the conclusions to Epistles 4 and 5 (ff 37–8, 39–40), which are missing here, were both received by him in letters now at HUL. The leaf containing Effusions 15 and 16 (collaborations with RS and Favell, respectively), not present in the sequence after f 18, is divided between the Alexander Turnbull Library in Wellington, New Zealand (MS Papers 1646) and HEHL (HM 260). Two points should be mentioned in this connection. First, the Quarto Copy Book at PML contains or contained material which is not represented in the Rugby Manuscript, as indicated above. The Quarto Copy Book material dates from the first stage of preparation of the 1796 volume, and another version might or might not have intervened. Secondly, most leaves of the Rugby Manuscript carry small numbers inscribed by Cottle in a sequence extending from 80 to 133. There are gaps in the sequence, and the leaves are not always bound in their numerical order: other leaves do not have the numbers. The same numbers appear on other manuscripts endorsed by Cottle. The uncollected letter printed in *Two Letters* 313–14 (compare the facsimile in Christie's Catalogue 2 Apr 1975 facing p 13) is numbered "~~15~~ 16"; the manuscript of **145** *The Raven* at NYPL (Berg Collection) is numbered "3~~8~~7";

the manuscript of C's 1795 *Lecture on the Two Bills* now at HUL (MS Eng 947.7, reproduced in *Lects 1795—CC*—facing p 260) is numbered 145; the manuscript of the 1798 specimens of hexameters and other metres now at HEHL (HM 12123; cf poems **185–8**) is numbered 194; and so on. The few manuscripts which passed through Cottle's hands and which do not bear a number tend to be fragmentary, and the number might have been trimmed off or now be contained on a separated part.[4]

Sometimes the manuscripts numbered by Cottle fall into place in the sequence here. No 104, now at Haverford (Charles Roberts Collection No 115), is another draft of Effusion 35; the leaf containing Effusions 15 and 16, divided between New Zealand and California, is, as one would expect, No 96. In other instances, however, Cottle's numbering is wildly astray. The page of text from **101** *Religious Musings* at the Rosenbach Foundation (class No 386/21) is numbered 53 (one would expect it to be one of the missing 120s); Nos 85 and 86 (now both at HUL: fMS Eng 947.2) contain drafts of the 1797 Prefaces instead of poems from the early pages of the 1796 volume. When Cottle numbered the manuscripts, he was demonstrably uncertain and frequently changed his mind. He numbered the errata for the 1797 *Poems* (now at HUL: fMS Eng 947) first 31 and then 136, as if he came to think that they immediately followed on the materials in the Rugby Manuscript; he numbered **152** *The Foster-mother's Tale*, now at HUL (fMS Eng 870.80B) 29 and 39, and later 133, again as if uncertain as to whether it should come before or after the material assembled here.

The conclusion must be that Cottle organised his manuscripts at a late stage, when he could no longer recall the order in which he had received them or that they should fall into (note that the preliminaries are numbered at the beginning of the sequence, though they were received at the end). After he had numbered them, he made up a volume from the most connected and certain part of the sequence, leaving gaps either where he realised he had made mistakes or where he had meanwhile given away or sold the individual leaves. At the same time, he revised the sequence of some leaves and inserted others which were unnumbered. When the leaves were bound, a few further errors were made: f 21 was bound back to front, and **101** *Religious Musings* was set out in another sequence.

Because the combined manuscript is so various, each page is separately described below. There are so many complexities that in this case no attempt has been made to reproduce C's titles literatim. One last complication is the foliation. The 62 leaves are foliated 1–58 because the numeration omits three leaves at different places and numbers another leaf twice over. Page-numbers are therefore included here, beginning with the first page of the manuscript. Page measurements are given with individual poems in vol II.

---

[4] Compare the octave of Effusion 20 at Yale (In C 678 796 P); the later version of the same sonnet (poem **86**) at the Pforzheimer (Misc 74); or the various fragments of Effusion 35 since inserted into the Cottle Album at Cornell (WORDSWORTH Bd Cottle).

Not foliated (and therefore unpaged) frontispiece: engraved portrait of C by Vandyke.

f 1 (p 1) Title-page for 1797 *Poems*.
    Verso (p 2) Motto for 1797 *Poems*.
    No wm. Cottle No 80. Also numbered (recto) 1 and (verso) 2 (by C?).

f 1+1 (p 3) Motto and errata for 1796 *Poems*, with notes for the title in Cottle's early hand.
    Verso (p 4) blank.
    No wm. Cottle No 87. Also numbered (recto) $\frac{1}{2}$ (by C?).

f 2 (p 5) Divisional title-page, motto for 1797 *Poems*.
    Verso (p 6) One line of 1797 half-title motto, deleted.
    Bluish paper; no wm. No Cottle No. Also numbered (recto) 5 and (verso) 6 (by C?).

f 3 (p 7) Advertisement for 1797 *Poems*.
    Verso (p 8) Advertisement concluded.
    No wm. Cottle No 81.
                p 9 Engraved portrait of C by Hancock.
                p 10 blank.

f 4 (p 11) Table of contents for 1797 *Poems*.
    Verso (p 12) Instruction concerning Dedication to 1797 *Poems*.
    No wm. No Cottle No. Also numbered (recto) 7 and (verso) 8 (by C?).

f 5 (p 13) Preface for 1st edn, as printed in 1797 *Poems*.
    Verso (p 14) Preface continued.
    No wm. Cottle No 82.

f 6 (p 15) Preface for 1st edn, as printed in 1797 *Poems*, concluded.
    Verso (p 16) blank.
    No wm. No Cottle No.

f 7 (p 17) Preface for 1796 *Poems*, draft of first paragraph only.
    Verso (p 18) blank.
    wm Britannia in large oval. Cottle No 83.

f 8 (p 19) Preface for 1796 *Poems*.
    Verso (p 20) Preface continued.
    wm Britannia in large oval. Cottle No 84.

f 9 (p 21) Preface for 1796 *Poems* continued.
    Verso (p 22) Preface concluded by thanks to Cottle and dedication to Stanhope—both deleted.
    wm COLES | 1793. The bottom portion of the folio has been torn away. No Cottle No.
                p 23 Engraved portrait of Amos Cottle by Palmer.
                p 24 blank.

f 10 (p 25) Note added to **142** *Ode on the Departing Year* in 1797 *Poems*.
    Verso (p 26) Note concluded.
    Smaller scrap of paper; no wm. Cottle No 129.

f 11 (p 27) Draft of closing stanzas of **82** *Monody on the Death of Chatterton* for 1796 *Poems*.
  Verso (p 28) Same concluded.
  No wm. Cottle No 90.
f 12 (p 29) Another version of the same ending for 1796 *Poems*.
  Verso (p 30) Same continued.
  Faintly bluish paper; no wm. No Cottle No.
f 12+1 (p 31) Same continued.
  Verso (p 32) blank.
  No wm. No Cottle No.
f 13 (p 33) Notes for 1796 *Poems*.
  Verso (p 34) Notes continued.
  wm Britannia in large oval. Cottle No 130.
f 14 (p 35) Text of **39** *Absence: An Ode* for 1796 *Poems*.
  Verso (p 36) blank.
  Bluish paper, corner torn; wm COLES. No Cottle No.
f 15 (p 37) Draft of **130** *To John Thelwall*.
  Verso (p 38) Another draft of the same.
  No wm. Cottle No 92.
f 16 (p 39) Effusion 5 (=**89** *To the Hon Mr Erskine*); Effusion 6 (=**99** *To R. B. Sheridan*) for 1796 *Poems*.
  Verso (p 40) Effusion 7 (=**96** *To Mrs Siddons*); Effusion 8 (=**93** *To Kosciusko*) for the same.
  Faintly bluish paper; wm COLES. Cottle No 93.
f 17 (p 41) Effusion 9 (=**92** *To Fayette*); Effusion 10 (=**102** *To Lord Stanhope*) for 1796 *Poems*.
  Verso (p 42) blank.
  Faintly bluish paper; wm Britannia in small rounded oval. Cottle No 94.
f 18 (p 43) Effusion 11 (=**113** *Adaptation of "Was it some sweet device of faery land . . .?"*); Effusion 12 (=**114** *Adaptation of "Methinks, how dainty sweet it were"*) for 1796 *Poems*.
  Verso (p 44) Effusion 13 (=**104** *Adaptation of "Written at Midnight, by the Sea-side"*); Effusion 14 (=**87** *On Hope*) for the same.
  wm Britannia in large oval. Cottle No 95.
f 19 (p 45) Effusion 22 (=**100** *Together with an Unfinished Poem*) for 1796 *Poems*.
  Verso (p 46) The same concluded.
  wm Britannia in large oval. Cottle No 98.
f 20 (p 47) Effusion 25 =Effusion 24 (=**111** *In the Manner of Spenser*) for 1796 *Poems*.
  Verso (p 48) The same concluded.
  wm G P & J. Cottle No 99.
f 21 (p 49) Effusion 28 =Effusion 27 (=**56** *On Presenting a Moss Rose*) for 1796 *Poems*.

Verso (p 50) Effusion 27 = Effusion 26 (=**57** *Cupid Turn'd Chymist*) for the same.
wm Britannia in small rounded oval. Cottle No 100.

f 22 (p 51) Notes for 1796 *Poems* (continued from f 13).
Verso (p 52) Notes continued.
wm GR. The top portion of the page (and notes) has been trimmed away. Cottle No (on verso) 135.

f 23 (p 53) Note 7 for 1796 *Poems*.
Verso (p 54) Random words only.
Smaller scrap of paper, no wm. Cottle No 89.

f 24 (p 55) Effusion 32 (=**32** *With Fielding's "Amelia"*) for 1796 *Poems*.
Verso (p 56) Effusion 33 (=**84** *To a Young Ass*) for the same.
wm G P & J. Cottle No 101.

f 25 (p 57) Effusion 33 for 1796 *Poems* concluded.
Verso (p 58) blank.
wm Britannia in small rounded oval. No Cottle No.

f 25+1 (p 59) Poem **105** *To an Infant* for 1796 *Poems*.
Verso (p 60) blank.
Slightly bluish paper; wm Britannia in small rounded oval. Cottle No 102.

f 26 (p 61) Effusion 35 (=**115** *The Eolian Harp*) for 1796 *Poems*.
Verso (p 62) blank.
No wm. Cottle No 103.

f 27 (p 33) Another draft of the same for 1796 *Poems*; facsimile in *Autograph Poetry in the English Language* ed P. J. Croft (2 vols 1973) II 97.
Verso (p 64) Other draft continued.
wm G P & J. Cottle No 105.

f 28 (p 65) Other draft of the same concluded; facsimile in *Autograph Poetry in the English Language* II 98.
Verso (p 66) blank.
wm Britannia in small rounded oval. Cottle No 106.

f 29 (p 67) First draft of "Effusion" (i.e. Effusion 36) (=**60** *Absence: A Poem*) for 1796 *Poems*.
Verso (p 68) blank.
wm Britannia in small rounded oval. Cottle No 107.

f 30 (p 69) Final version of Effusion 35 (=**115** *The Eolian Harp*) for 1796 *Poems*.
Verso (p 70) Conclusion of the same.
wm crown I GR. Cottle No 109.

f 31 (p 71) Effusion 36 (=**60** *Absence: A Poem*) for 1796 *Poems*.
Verso (p 72). The same continued.
wm crown I GR. Cottle No 110.

f 31+1 (p 73) Effusion 36 continued.
Verso (p 74) The same concluded.

wm Britannia in small rounded oval. Cottle No 111.

f 32 (p 75) Poem **125** *Verse Motto to Poetical Epistles*; Epistle 1 (=**116** *Written at Shurton Bars*) for 1796 *Poems*.
Verso (p 76) Epistle 1 continued.
wm crown I GR. Cottle No 112.

f 33 (p 77) Epistle 1 continued.
Verso (p 78) The same continued.
wm Britannia in small rounded oval. No Cottle No.

f 34 (p 79) Epistle 1 continued.
Verso (p 80) The same concluded.
wm crown I GR. No Cottle No.

f 35 (p 81) Epistle 2 (=**68** *To a Friend in Answer to a Melancholy Letter*) for 1796 *Poems*.
Verso (p 82) Epistle 3 (=**49** *A Simile*) for the same.
wm Britannia in small rounded oval. Cottle No 113.

f 36 (p 83) Epistle 3 concluded.
Verso (p 84) blank.
wm Britannia in small rounded oval. No Cottle No.

f 37 (p 85) Epistle 4 (=**117** *Lines to Joseph Cottle*) for 1796 *Poems*.
Verso (p 86) The same continued.
wm Britannia in small rounded oval. Cottle No 114.

f 38 (p 87) Epistle 4 concluded; als.
Verso (p 88) Address.
wm crown I GR. Cottle No 115.

f 39 (p 89) Epistle 5 (=**119** *The Silver Thimble*) for 1796 *Poems* (in the hand of Sara Fricker Coleridge).
Verso (p 90) The same continued.
wm Britannia in small rounded oval. Cottle No 116.

f 40 (p 91) Epistle 5 concluded.
Verso (p 92) Address.
wm G P & J. No Cottle No.

f 41 (p 93) Lines for **110** *Contributions to "Joan of Arc"* II (initially in RS's hand, then C's).
Verso (p 94) The same continued.
wm COLES I 1794. Cottle No 117.

f 42 (p 95) Poem **101** *Religious Musings* for 1796 *Poems*.
Verso (p 96) The same continued.
No wm. Cottle No 118.

f 43 (p 97) *Religious Musings* continued.
Verso (p 98) The same continued.
No wm. No Cottle No.

f 44 (p 99) *Religious Musings* continued.
Verso (p 100) The same continued.
No wm. No Cottle No.

f 45 (p 101) *Religious Musings* continued.
Verso (p 102) The same continued.
No wm. No Cottle No.

f 46 (p 103) *Religious Musings* continued (after a gap of some 30 lines).
Verso (p 104) blank.
wm top of large crown (?) and Britannia (?). No Cottle No.

f 47 (p 105) *Religious Musings* continued. Verso (p 106) blank.
wm top of large crown (?) and Britannia (?). No Cottle No.

f 48 (p 107) *Religious Musings* continued.
Verso (p 108) blank.
wm bottom of rounded Britannia. No Cottle No.

f 49 (p 109) *Religious Musings* continued (after a gap of some 40 lines).
Verso (p 110) The same continued.
Bluish paper; no wm. Cottle No 119.

f 50 (p 111) *Religious Musings* continued.
Verso (p 112) The same continued.
wm Britannia in small rounded oval. Cottle No 120.

f 51 (p 113) *Religious Musings* continued.
Verso (p 114) The same continued.
Bluish paper; no wm. Cottle No 121.

f 52 (p 115) *Religious Musings* continued (after a gap of some 30 lines).
Verso (p 116) blank.
wm Britannia in small rounded oval. Cottle No 123.

f 53 (p 117) Another draft of the material for *Religious Musings* on f 52 (deleted).
Verso (p 118) The same concluded; facsimile in Sotheby Catalogue 15 May 1967 lot 261 facing p 73.
No wm. Cottle No 127.

f 54 (p 119) Another draft of the material for *Religious Musings* on f 52.
Verso (p 120) The same concluded.
No wm. Cottle No 126.

f 55 (p 121) Another draft of the material for *Religious Musings* on f 54.
Verso (p 122) The same concluded.
wm Britannia in small rounded oval. Cottle No 122.

f 56 (p 123) Notes for 1796 *Poems* (continued from f 23).
Verso (p 124) Notes continued.
wm GR. Cottle No 131.

f 57 (p 125) Notes on *Religious Musings* for 1796 *Poems*.
Verso (p 126) Notes continued.
wm GR. Cottle No 132.

f 58 (p 127) Notes on *Religious Musings* concluded.
Verso (p 128) blank.
wm Britannia in large oval. Cottle No 133.

9. SARA HUTCHINSON'S POETS

DCL MS 41. A notebook covered in red leather, comprising 83 leaves, 11.7×
18.0 cm; wm J WHATMAN I 1794. Entitled on f 1ʳ "Sarah Hutchinson's
Poets—". An anthology of poems by WW and C compiled by SH, consisting
of 25 poems by WW at the begining and 11 by C at the end, with blank pages
between these groups and between individual poems.

The WW material was probably copied between Mar and Jun 1802, soon after
the poems were composed, except for one which was composed and copied
after 1811. The C poems appear to have been copied between Apr 1802—
perhaps later (after Aug 1802, or even in 1806–7)—and the time *The Friend*
was composed (1809–10). The first ten of the eleven poems are in SH's hand,
of which three (Nos 3–5) have corrections and additions by C; the eleventh
is in C's hand entirely. Several of the poems had been published before they
were transcribed here, although the versions in this manuscript differ. It is worth
noting that SH's transcriptions are generally less careful here than elsewhere.
The selection is of considerable significance, as George Whalley described in
C&SH, which also provides a transcript (var) and selected facsimiles.

The poems by C are as follows:

(1) ff 2ʳ–3ʳ "A Soliloquy of the full Moon, She being in *A Mad Passion*—"
(=poem **290**).
(2) f 3ʳ Untitled (=**291** *Answer to a Child's Question*).
(3) ff 3ᵛ–4ʳ "Tranquillity—An Ode" (=poem **283**). Folio 4ʳ is reproduced in
C&SH facing p 16.
(4) f 5ʳ⁻ᵛ Untitled (=**275** *After Bathing in the Sea at Scarborough*).
(5) f 6ʳ "Inscription on a jutting Stone, over a Spring." (=poem **277**).
(6) ff 7ʳ–9ᵛ "The Picture, or Lovers Resolution" (=poem **300**). Folio 8ʳ is
reproduced in *C&SH* facing p 17.
(7) f 10ʳ " Song from Leesing—" (=poem **236**).
(8) f 10ʳ Untitled (=**402** *Psyche*).
(9) f 10ᵛ Untitled (=**388** *Time, Real and Imaginary*).
(10) f 11ʳ⁻ᵛ The Keep-sake—Sepʳ 17ᵗʰ 1802" (=pocm **299**). Folio 11ᵛ is repro-
duced in *C&SH* facing p 32.
(11) ff 11ᵛ–13ʳ "The Devil's Thoughts— I A Fragment from the Wreck I of
Memory.—originally revealed I to ΑΡΣΟΥΘΕΙ and ΕΣΤΗΣΕ . . ."
(=poem **214**). Folios 11ᵛ–12ʳ are reproduced in *C&SH* facing pp 32 and
33.

10. EPIGRAMS FOR *THE MORNING POST*, 1802

DCL Letters Coleridge p 27 (ff 1ʳ–2ʳ). Large folio folded to make two con-
joint leaves, each 20.9×33.4 cm; wm Britannia in oval, surmounted by crown+

countermark C (?) HALE; f 2ᵛ blank. Revised fair copies in C's hand of 12 epigrams published in *M Post*.

Nos 5, 6, 7, and 11 were published in *M Post* (23 Sept 1802), making up four of ten epigrams ("Lot I") signed "ΕΣΤΗΣΕ". The remaining 8 comprise the total ("Lot II") published in *M Post* (11 Oct 1802). Every epigram appears to adapt an original by Wernicke, with the exception of Nos 5 and 7, for which other German sources can be found, and No 12, for which no source has been traced.

(1) Poem **309** *Epigram on the Sun and Moon* pub *M Post* (11 Oct 1802).
(2) Poem **310** *Epigram on Spots in the Sun* pub *M Post* (11 Oct 1802).
(3) Poem **311** *Epigram on Surface* pub *M Post* (11 Oct 1802).
(4) Poem **312** *A Dialogue between an Author and his Friend* pub *M Post* (11 Oct 1802).
(5) Poem **313** *Epigram on Possession* pub *M Post* (23 Sept 1802).
(6) Poem **314** *Epigram on Castles in the Air* pub *M Post* (23 Sept 1802).
(7) Poem **315** *To a Vain Lady* pub *M Post* (23 Sept 1802).
(8) Poem **316** *Epigram to my Candle* pub *M Post* (11 Oct 1802).
(9) Poem **317** *From an Old German Poet* pub *M Post* (11 Oct 1802).
(10) Poem **318** *Epigram on Bond Street Bucks* pub *M Post* (11 Oct 1802).
(11) Poem **319** *Epigram on Virgil's "Obscuri sub luce maligna"* pub *M Post* (23 Sept 1802).
(12) Poem **320** *Epigram on Wisdom in Folly* pub *M Post* (11 Oct 1802).

11. REYNOLDS–HOOD COMMONPLACE BOOK

BPL B 27744. A manuscript volume in several hands, some not identified. Inscribed "J. H. Reynolds Augt. 1816" on the title-page, and by his neice "Frances Freeling Hood January 1847" on the front flyleaf. The volume contains, besides material by C, transcriptions from manuscript by Charlotte Reynolds of 17 Keats poems; autograph poems, some unpublished, by J. H. Reynolds, and cuttings of poems by J. H. Reynolds and T. Hood; copies of poems by Landor, Browning, Victor Hugo, and others.[5]

The first four pieces by C listed below are in the hand of Jane Reynolds Hood (?); the last was copied by John Hamilton Reynolds. The place of the five pieces in the sequence of other entries dates them between 1816 and 1818, and this appears to be confirmed by the fact that **178** *Kubla Khan* was copied from the 1816 text (with minor variations of spelling and punctuation). If the first three shorter poems were also copied at the same time, they would represent versions earlier than any others which are known. It is none the less difficult

---

[5] See Paul Kaufman "The Reynolds–Hood Commonplace Book: A Fresh Appraisal" *Keats–Shelley Journal* x (1961) 43–52; also Stillinger *The Texts of Keats's Poems* 46–50.

to see how **647** *Water Ballad* can be earlier than 1827, given the date of its probable original, and the reading at *Kubla Khan* 11 ("Enfolding") is a late one. The first three pieces could easily have been inserted into the book after the main part of the sequence—perhaps c 1828–32—but the available evidence leaves the question unsettled, and No 3 appears to be from a manuscript version. The fifth piece, copied by John Hamilton Reynolds, was transcribed from the 1800 printed text of *Wallenstein*, as his page reference makes clear. The same lines had been quoted in Leigh Hunt's *Literary Examiner* (22 Nov 1823) 335–6, although Reynolds here transcribed them afresh.

The pieces by C are as follows:

(1) f 4^r "Sonnet." (=poem **592:** see VAR TEXT PR 5).
(2) f 8a^r Untitled (=**647** *Water Ballad*).
(3) f 8a^r "Timepiece" (=poem **673**).
(4) ff 9^r–10^r "Kubla Khan I by I Samual Taylor Coleridge." (=poem **178**).
(5) f 12^r "Love" (=*CPic* II iv 119–38, 114–16).

12. SHORT PIECES COPIED IN 1832

Boston University Library (Special Collections). Single folio, 37.0×22.6 cm, folded to make two conjoint leaves; wm J WHATMAN I 1832; no chain-lines. Drafts and fair copies of 5 poems in C's hand, with second versions of two of them.

It is not obvious why C copied out the poems: they are not all appropriate for albums or autographs. No 1 had been published in *M Post* (22 Sept 1801); No 3 had been written two years earlier and copied several times for autographs; Nos 2, 6, and 7 are confessedly extempore. There are further folds across the paper, and there is evidence that it was once glued to something along the outer folded edge. It was bought by Boston University after the sale of the late Miss Eleanor Pocock (Sotheby's 16 Mar 1971 lot 640): an album made up of manuscripts was the first item in the same property (lot 639), and the manuscript by C might have been detached from the album to be sold separately.

(1) f 1^r "Epitaph" (=poem **221**). Followed by C's transcript of another version pub *Saturday Magazine* (10 Nov 1832).
(2) f 1^v "A guilty Skceptic's Death bed: ⟨⟨⟩or the Echo, Conscience⟨⟩⟩" (=poem **683**).
(3) f 1^v "Inscription I on a I Time-piece" (=poem **673**).
(4) f 1^v "Advice and Invitation" (=poem **684**).
(5) f 2^r "Kind Advice & Invitation" (second version of No 4).
(6) f 2^v "Specimen of pure Latinity, ex tempore" (=poem **685**(*a*)).
(7) f 2^v "Or the same more *logically*." (=poem **685**(*b*)).

13. J.M.?B.'S NOTEBOOK ALBUM

In the possession of J.C.C. Mays (1999). A paper-covered notebook comprising 132 unnumbered leaves (including one stub and both free endpapers; several other leaves are entirely missing), 10.0×17.8 cm. Wove paper, with Super Fine Bath impress; wms G CRAFTS I 1825 and HEAL MILL I 1823. The front cover has the pencilled initials "J.M.?B." and two faint pencil sketches of heads; the rear cover has an erased inscription above the date "August 19 1827".

The album contains miscellaneous material, among which is a section of transcripts of mostly late poems by C. The entries are generally in ink (a few are in pencil), and they form two sequences, written from the front and then from the back of the notebook. The earlier compilation is the more extensive, and it includes poems by Mrs Robinson, Byron, Campbell, Rogers, RS, and Robert Montgomery, as well as Milton, Pope, and others. The verse extracts are intermingled with prose extracts relating to theology (Leighton, Henry More) and classical and Anglo-Saxon history, as well as some drawings and personal memoranda. Some extracts can be dated to 1827 and 1828, and those from Montgomery's *Satan* must date from 1830. The earlier, main compilation is rounded off with two pages in a second hand—a poem by C on f 96^r and six lines transcribed from Defoe's elegy on Dr Samuel Annesley on f 96^v. The latter are quoted in Walter Wilson *Memoir of the Life and Times of Daniel Defoe* (3 vols 1830) I 9, a book which was annotated by C. This material on f 96 appears to have been added later, in a different hand from the preceding compilation.

Twenty-three blank pages follow; thereafter the volume was turned over and entries begun from the other end. Following a sketch and a note on theological and other matters in the hand of the earlier main compilation (ff 132^r, 131^v), there is a sequence of transcriptions of poems by C in the hand that appears on f 96^{r-v}, extending backwards from f 129^v to f 123^r. In addition, two lines of doggerel by C are transcribed in pencil on f 1^r; and apparently impromptu lines, perhaps by C, are transcribed in pencil on f 4^v. (There is also a transcript of "The Devils Walk by Porson. I A wrong edition" (=poem **214**) in the main sequence of entries, on ff 69^v–70^r.)

The two series of entries appear either to have been made in at least two hands, or else by someone whose handwriting underwent considerable change. Clues to the identity of the earlier transcriber (ff 1^r–95^v, 130^r) might be provided by verses from Miss Jane Hopkins to Miss Catherine Hopkins on f 36^v, by a memo on f 46^r stating that a Mr Waring's birthday fell on 28 Nov, by two sets of verses assigned to "J. P. K." on ff 73^r and 77^r (was this John Peirse Kinnaird?). The later hand (on ff 96^{r-v}, 129^v–123^r) is identical with that which made another transcript of **675** *Sonnet to my Tin Shaving-pot*, now at Cornell. George Healey *The Cornell Wordsworth Collection* (Ithaca 1957) item 2637 identified the handwriting of the transcript as SC's, but he was mistaken. The same hand appears in BM Add MS 36532 ff 6^v and 7^r, where it can be identified as that of JG's assistant, John Hartwell Bonnell Williams. It is not clear whether the pencil transcripts on ff 1^r and 4^v of the notebook are also by Williams, but it would be reasonable to assume that they are.

The earlier compilation suggests a rather conventional taste in verse. The prose extracts alternate between the educated and the childish. Some entries suggest that the compiler was involved in amusing or teaching a growing child; other more serious extracts display an interest in theology, an acquaintance with Greek and Latin, and an interest in seventeenth-century prose writers which might have a Coleridgean flavour. As for the main body of verses by C in Williams's hand, on ff 96^r and 129^v–123^r, the earliest (No 5 below) dates from Jan 1832 and the latest (No 23) from Aug 1833. Whereas the earlier, miscellaneous compilation was patently compiled at different times and in varying circumstances, the poems by C in Williams's hand look as if they might have been transcribed at a single sitting.

Williams was careless with punctuation and spelling, and his errors and omissions suggest that the poems might have been taken down from dictation. The duplication of Nos 18 and 24 might suggest likewise. The separation of the last two lines of **682** *My Baptismal Birth-day* from the body of the poem (Nos 16 and 4) occurs in no other version, and suggests either that the transcript was made from scraps or that the last two lines were taken down after the incomplete version was read back. None of the poems by C is present in the 1828 or 1829 collections, so they appear to be a conscious effort to make up a supplement some time during the months after Aug–Oct 1833, i.e. between No 23 and the publication of *PW* (1834). The singular approximation of details in Nos 4 and 21 to versions of the same poems contained in Mrs Ellis's Album (see **673** *Inscription on a Time-piece* and **682** VAR) suggests a date close to Sept 1833. Only one poem by C (No 17) directly reproduces an earlier, printed text. The others combine other recorded readings in a way which might again suggest that they were dictated by C. It is unclear why particular poems were included in the compilation and other similar poems by C omitted, unless C dictated what was at hand on a single occasion or only what Williams prompted him to remember. C was more or less room-bound in the later months of 1833, and several of the poems were not for publication.

A good deal about the purpose of the selection remains obscure. Williams was JG's medical assistant at Highgate in 1816–18, when C joined the household, and the two men enjoyed an easy relationship from the beginning (see e.g. *CL* IV 682–4: to J.H.B. Williams [24 Sept 1816]). Williams was awarded his diploma as Member of the Royal College of Surgeons in Sept 1819, and C took an interest when, in the following month, he risked offending JG for some action felt to display ingratitude (*CN* IV 4606). Williams appears in the published list of members of the Royal College from 1820 to 1833, and had set up independently as a surgeon some time before Feb 1827, when C wrote to propose that he and JG might visit him at Aldersgate Street (*CL* VI 669). Williams took down memoranda from C of philosophical and scientific subjects at Highgate (BM Add MS 3652 ff 5–20) and was the recipient of signed copies of *SL* (annex c 17.22), the Schiller translations (annex c 11.11), and *The Statesman's Manual* (*LS—CC*—237). The inscriptions in the last two are dated 12 Oct 1832, but C makes it clear that the books had been in Williams's possession for many years, so that Williams must have sent or brought them back to be signed. Might the poems in the notebook album also be an attempt on Williams's part to preserve memories of an old friend he could see was dying?

Some faint light can be thrown on the matter by comparing Williams's versions with those used in other collections. His Nos 4, 7, 11, 16, 18, 20, 21, 23, 25, and 3 were included in *PW* (1834) and *TT* (1835), but from other versions. When SC published Nos 8, 11, 12, 13, 18/24 in *EOT* (1850) and *Poems* (1852), she drew on a transcript by Henry Langley Porter, Gillman's other assistant, who also had literary interests. (The only other reported version of No 10 here was derived from Porter when George Grove met him in Jamaica in 1841: references in **653** *To Baby Bates* VAR TEXT MS 1. However, though there are connections between Porter's versions and the J.M.?B. notebook—see No 18/24 especially—and the pages of Porter's manuscript are similar to the notebook pages used by Williams—see e.g. vol II **221, 241, 242** headnotes for Porter—the versions Porter supplied are different and his hand does not appear in the notebook.) Other poems (Nos 9, 14, and 15) were not collected or published until RHS and JDC took them in, and then in different versions. Others again (Nos 5, 6, 19, and 22; also 1–2) are here published or collected for the first time (Nos 2, 19, and 22 are conjectural attributions). In short, since Williams did not pass on the transcripts, one might suppose that the supplement to *PW* (1828–9) was made for his own pleasure. It also appears that he was not in touch with the Coleridge family efforts to collect verse material; nor were he or his descendants thereafter aware of the significance of what he had transcribed. The one other collection of materials by C with which he is associated (see **625.X2** *Album Verses and Charades*) is somewhat random, in both composition and descent.

It has not proved possible to identify the presumed first owner of the album from whom Williams took over. There was no one in the Coleridge–Gillman circle with the initials "J.M.?B.", and these could be the initials of a later Victorian owner who added them to the cover. J.M.B. of Tunbridge Wells contributed short pieces on C and on antiquarian subjects to *N&Q* in the 1840s and 1850s, but the coincidence might be fortuitous. The evidence of the handwriting of the main compilation suggests also that the initials do not signify Joshua Bates or his wife, with whom C was friendly at Highgate and who both had literary interests. Nor is there anyone in the Coleridge–Gillman circle who fits the bill. JG Jr, Mrs Harding and Miss Harding (AG's sisters), and H. L. Porter are all ruled out for various reasons, as are J. H. Green, his wife, and amanuenses.

The notebook shares a few features in common with one made up by Frances Sarah Bunyan (1816–93), wife from 1846 of John William Colenso (1814–83), later bishop of Natal. This contains extracts from C's marginalia and other unpublished sources in the possession of AG, transcribed in 1842. It is described by Hilton Kelliher "A Stray Notebook of Miscellaneous Writings by Coleridge"

The British Library Journal XIV (Autumn 1988) 136–53. The background of the "J.M.?B." notebook is evidently more complicated, however, even while its versions of poems by C are of more value.

The notebook remained unnoticed until it was rescued from a London junkshop, bookshop, or roadside barrow some time in the 1930s or 1940s by a Mrs Middleton. The pencilled price of 3*s* appears on f 1ᵛ. On Mrs Middleton's death in 1977 it passed to her grandson, J. A. Hendrick of Taunton, who came to realise its significance a few years later. It was appraised by W. H. Kelliher of the BM and John Beer of Peterhouse, Cambridge, and later by Sotheby's, and Mr Hendrick sold it to me in 1988.

(1) f 1ʳ (front free endpaper, in pencil) Untitled (=**630** *Epigram on a Bitch and a Mare*).

(2) f 4ᵛ (in pencil) Untitled (=**664** *"King Solomon knew all things"*).

(3) ff 69ᵛ–70ʳ "The Devils Walk by Porson. I A wrong edition" (=poem **214**).

(4) f 96ʳ Untitled (=**682** *My Baptismal Birth-day*), with prefatory note in prose subscribed "S. T. C.". The last two lines of the same poem appear on f 126ᵛ (see No 16 below).

(5) f 129ᵛ Untitled (=**675** *Sonnet to my Tin Shaving-pot*).

(6) ff 129ʳ–128ᵛ Untitled (=**659** *Doggerel on Sir Charles Scudamore*), subscribed "S. T. C."

(7) f 128ᵛ "Jobs Luck" (=poem **239**), subscribed "S. T. C."

(8) f 128ʳ "To. Miss —— in an Album" (=poem **600**), subscribed "S. T. C."

(9) ff 128ʳ–127ᵛ "To the Daughter of an American Minister on her return home" (=poem **658**).

(10) f 127ᵛ *"To an acquaintance of the Above Lady . . ."* (=poem **653**).

(11) f 127ʳ Untitled (=**241** *Epigram on a Bad Singer*).

(12) f 127ʳ Untitled (=**242** *Epigram on a Joke without a Sting*).

(13) f 127ʳ "A Blank stone—on an atheist I An Epigram" (=poem **221**).

(14) f 127ʳ Untitled (=**227** *Epigram on an Insignificant*).

(15) f 126ᵛ Untitled (=**203** *Epigram on Kepler*).

(16) f 126ᵛ Untitled (=**682** *My Baptismal Birth-day* 13–14); cf No 4 above.

(17) f 126ᵛ Untitled (=**402** *Psyche*).

(18) f 126ᵛ "L'Envoy—" (=poem **597**); cf No 24 below.

(19) ff 126ʳ–125ᵛ Untitled (=**689** *"Oh! might I but my Patrick love"*); dated "Augᵗ 23/33."

(20) f 125ʳ "To a handsome young German who drew the authors portrait." (=poem **691**); subscribed "S. T. C. I Augᵗ 24. 1833—"

(21) f 124ᵛ "Time fleets but conscience gives immortality to the acts of fleeting time—" (=poem **673**); subscribed "S. T. C."

(22) f 124ᵛ Untitled (=**399** *"Those eyes of deep & most expressive blue"*).

(23) ff 124ʳ–123ᵛ "Loves Ghost & the evanition." (=poem **688**).

(24) f 123ᵛ "L'Envoy—" (=poem **597**); subscribed "S. T. C." Cf No 18 above.

(25) f 123ʳ "Sonnet. I An old Man's sigh." (=poem **592**); subscribed "S. T. Coleridge".

ANNEX B

PRINTED COLLECTIONS

The printed collections listed below are as various as the manuscript collections, and for similar reasons. They range from the early group of volumes published in 1796, 1797, and 1803, to *SL* in 1817, and finally to the late group of volumes published in 1828, 1829, and 1834. Individual volumes evolve from one another within the early, middle, and late groups, and there is an evolving relation between the groups. These interconnections are marked by inconsistencies and contradictions—poems are dropped and mistakes creep in, even as other poems are added and corrections are made—as has been described in the Introduction.

The annex omits pamphlets, such as *Fears in Solitude* (1798) (poem **175**), and single titles, such as the plays *Remorse* and *Zapolya*, because the aim is to show the evolution of C's *œuvre*, as far as it deserves the name, and such items are not part of that story. The preparation and development of the *LB* volumes are more properly part of Wordsworth bibliography, and are reasonably familiar. There is an argument for including the *Christabel* volume, on the grounds that it complements *SL* by including poems which might have been included in that collection, but it has not been listed here because its story is better told in annex C, describing annotated volumes, and in the Variorum headnotes to the separate poems. At the same time, C's collection of *Sonnets by Various Authors* (1796) is included. It differs from the other groups of volumes described in this annex, quite obviously, but the earlier group of poems took over its prefatory matter in 1797 and 1803; and, as long as the difference is not lost sight of, it is most conveniently described here.

There is a degree of chronological overlap with the manuscript collections. The Ottery Copy Book and the Estlin Copy Book make almost the same claims as printed collections, and there are close relations between the Quarto Copy Book and the Rugby Manuscript and *Poems* (1796) and (1797). There is also an overlap with annex C, since C's annotations continue processes initiated by the printing or, in the case of the proof copies of *Poems* (1796) and *SL*, actually precede it. The material included here under *Sonnets from Various Authors* (No 2 below) is of the same kind as that included in annex C.

Besides throwing further light on the relations between C's collections, the present annex also provides collated editions of the preliminary and prefatory materials. In the case of *Sonnets from Various Authors* notes are supplied on C's adaptations when they are not extensive enough to merit separate inclusion in vol II.

Ornaments, rules, and dotted leaders in the printed texts of introductory matter are usually not recorded, and other features of display typography, such as initial full and small capitals, or the various sizes of type in title-pages, have likewise been eliminated in accordance with the policy of the edition. Titles are otherwise given as they appear, including their sometimes irregular use of italic.

1. *POEMS* (1796)

The beginnings of C's 1796 *Poems* appear to lie in an undated entry in the Gutch Notebook: "Mem—to speak to Cottle concerning Selections &c—and setting up in printing—" (*CN* I 297). An agreement with Cottle was arrived at before the end of Jul 1795: C was to provide copy at the rate of a sheet and a half a day, written into a "copy book" supplied to him by Cottle (*CL* I 157: to J. Cottle 31 Jul 1795), and Cottle was to pay C a guinea and a half for every hundred lines of poetry (*CL* I 161: to TP [7 Oct 1795]). Later references (e.g. *CL* I 186: to J. Cottle 22 Feb 1796) show that C was paid in advance; indeed, Cottle claimed that the contract enabled C to get married (*E Rec* I 57).

C was not slow in getting down to work. A pencilled list on the cover of the Gutch Notebook (*CN* I 305)[1] is a partial review of the material to hand. The copybook supplied by Cottle, which is in fact the Quarto Copy Book described in annex A 7, is evidence that C began to copy out the poems with considerable care. On 22 Aug 1795 RS wrote with enthusiasm of the poems that he and C had been preparing together (Bodleian MS Eng letters c 22 f 158ᵛ). The work did not go according to the agreement with Cottle, however. The copybook shows that C was led into making too many changes to be able to supply the printer at the rate of a sheet and a half of material a day. The poems he was working on alongside RS are as likely to have been completely new compositions—like Effusion 35 (=**115** *The Eolian Harp*), begun on 20 Aug—as poems he had to hand and was revising. Epistles 1 and 4 (=**116** *Written at Shurton Bars* and **117** *Lines to Joseph Cottle*) were written in Sept, Epistle 5 (=**119** *The Silver Thimble*) in Oct. Meantime, C had married (4 Oct), moved back from Clevedon to Bristol, written and published political lectures (Nov), and laid plans for *The Watchman* (Dec). From 9 Jan to 13 Feb 1796 he was on tour to raise subscriptions for *The Watchman* and, given the accompanying personal difficulties (his quarrel with RS, his wife's pregnancy, various illnesses, "bread and cheese"), it is not surprising that the poems for which he had already received part payment took second place.

When the poems were set and printed is not clear. Sigs A and N were printed last, as one would expect, and they are on different paper. In an undated letter (*CL* I 162–3: to J. Cottle) C refers to six signatures as being already set—i.e. sigs B–G (up to the first page of Effusion 35 = **115** *The Eolian Harp*)—which

---

[1] Woodring 226–7 gives a more accurate transcription.

leaves four signatures to be filled (H, I, K, and M), plus sigs A and N, the prefatory material and notes. ELG dates the letter to Oct 1795 for several good reasons, and, if he is correct, half the type remained standing for about six months. It seems likely that the letter was in fact written later, following C's return from the *Watchman* tour, and that it should be moved in ELG's sequence to before letter 106, on p 186. Despite the gaps in the Rugby Manuscript, there is no evidence of an interval in the supply of printer's copy between Effusion 35, on the one hand, and its revisions and the remainder of the volume, on the other. There was more likely to have been a break in C's preparation of manuscript copy—between his return from Clevedon in Nov 1795 and his return from the *Watchman* tour in Feb 1796—than an even longer break in the processes of printing (which Cottle would surely have recorded and complained of, if it had happened, just as he recorded that the press had to be kept waiting at the end while C finished **101** *Religious Musings*: *E Rec* II 52).

The Rugby Manuscript provides detailed evidence of the difficulty C had in finishing *Religious Musings*. The poem appears at one stage to have been intended for another volume, following a first volume comprising only short poems (*CL* I 162: to J. Cottle [Oct 1795? Feb 1796?]). The first page of the Preface was drafted on 22 Feb 1796 (*CL* I 186: to J. Cottle 22 Feb 1796); and, after a delay (see C's apology in *CL* I 193: to J. Cottle [late Mar 1796]), a full version was written, which was further revised before or during the printing. The notes were added some time after 1 Mar (the note in Rugby Manuscript f 13^v refers to the first number of *The Watchman*), and the proof versions show further changes. Cottle's receipt is dated 28 Mar, and copies lacking sigs A and N were available on 1 Apr (*CL* I 196–7: to B. Flower 1 Apr 1796). The volume was finally published on 16 Apr or thereabouts. The extended, interrupted period of preparation, and its hurried conclusion, make the volume an incomplete statement on C's behalf.

Earlier manuscript collections like the Ottery Copy Book and the Estlin Copy Book are more unified because they admit fewer distractions. They are more exactly what the 1796 volume began as—"Selections" from C's previous writing—and C did not feel impelled to compose anew for them or to revise extensively. The evidence of annotated copies of the 1796 collections suggests that even as it appeared C was not satisfied with it, and preparations for a second edition continued without a very long interval.

PRELIMINARIES

Half-title. The half-title precedes the title-page, which Woodring 110 describes as unusual if not unique among volumes published by Cottle. The page perhaps held, or was meant to hold, the cancelled dedication to Lord Stanhope, which appears on f 9^v/p 22 of the Rugby Manuscript:

To Earl Stanhope
A Man beloved of Science and of Freedom
these Poems are
respectfully inscribed
by the
Author.

Charles, 3rd Earl Stanhope (1753–1816), was known as Citizen Stanhope be-
cause of his ardent advocacy of the French Revolution, even though he was
Pitt's brother in-law. He was a scientist and inventor as well as a politician. C
praised him in *The Watchman* I (1 Mar 1796) (*CC*) 46, making use of a report
published on 26 Feb, so the dedication is likely to have been cancelled some
time between then and mid-Apr, when the volume appeared. Woodring 110
suggests that the dedication might have gone as far as page proof, but the two
extant proof versions do not bear this out. C afterwards claimed that the sonnet
to Stanhope in this same 1796 volume had been included only because of a
blunder of Cottle's (*CL* III 27: to M. Cruikshank [Sept 1807]; *The Friend* II—8
Jun 1809—*CC*—II 25fn), which may or may not be true.

Title-page. C wrote out the motto, along with a list of errata (which Cottle in-
corporated), in Rugby Manuscript f 1 + 1/p 3. Cottle then added a memorandum
for the title in his own (early) hand. The motto was printed as follows:

> Felix curarum, cui non Helconia cordi
> Serta, nec imbelles Parnassi e vertice laurus!
> Sed viget ingenium, et magnos accinctus in usus
> Fert animus quascunque vices.—Nos tristia vitæ
> Solamur cantu.
> STAT. SILV. Lib. iv. 4.

The source of the Latin lines is Statius *Silvae* 4.4.46–50 (var)[2] tr Mozley (LCL)
I 233 (adapted) "Happy thou in thy labours, who carest not for the chaplets
of Helicon nor for unwarlike bays from Parnassus' summit, but thy intellect is
lean, and thy mind girt up for mighty deeds endures whatever may befall: we
beguile a sorrowful life with song." C quoted the beginning of the same lines
again in *The Watchman* IX (5 May 1796) (*CC*) 313.

Preface. The Preface appears on pp v–xi:

---

[2] C has "tristia" for Statius' "otia".

PREFACE.

Poems on various subjects written at different times and prompted by very
different feelings; but which will be read at one time and under the influ-
ence of one set of feelings—this is an heavy disadvantage: for we love
or admire a poet in proportion as he developes our own sentiments and
emotions, or reminds us of our own knowledge.   5

Compositions resembling those of the present volume are not unfre-
quently condemned for their querulous egotism. But egotism is to be con-
demned then only when it offends against time and place, as in an History
or an Epic Poem. To censure it in a Monody or Sonnet is almost as absurd
as to dislike a circle for being round. Why then write Sonnets or Monodies?   10
Because they give me pleasure when perhaps nothing else could. After the
more violent emotions of Sorrow, the mind demands solace and can find
in it employment alone; but full of its late sufferings it can endure no em-
ployment not connected with those sufferings. Forcibly to turn away our
attention to other subjects is a painful and in general an unavailing effort.   15

> "But O how grateful to a wounded heart
> The tale of misery to impart;

1 et seq. C's first attempt to begin his Preface is preserved in Rugby Manuscript f
7/p 17:

Preface

Poems on various subjects, *written* at different times, and prompted by very different
feelings; but which will be *read* at one time, and ~~under the influence of ~~*the*~~ the same
temper~~ under the influence of ~~one~~ set ~~feel~~ of feelings—~~in one state of mind /~~ a
~~unfavorable circumstance!~~ heavy disadvantage. It ~~is not uncommon~~ frequently happens
that we ⟨had⟩ thrown by slightingly a work which ⟨afterwards⟩ in more congenial mood
we ~~have~~ read with enthusiasm. Self is the basis of our censures and applauses; we love
a poet ~~in proportion~~ accordingly as he developes our own sentiments or feelings. I speak
of Poetry properly so called; not of science versified. But the remark applies equally
to poems of the latter class; we admire them in proportion to our familiarity with their
subjects. They remind us of our knowlege and we are flattered by being able to unriddle
them.

The fair copy for the Preface submitted to Cottle continues in the Rugby
Manuscript ff 8–9/pp 19–21, here designated MS 1   **2.** 1 &   **3.** 1 feelings.
This   **4–5.** 1 sentiments ~~or~~ & ~~feelings~~ emotions,   **5.** 1 Knowledge.
6. Compositions] 1 Poems   **7.** 1 ~~censured~~ condemned   1 Egotism.—But
Egotism   **7–8.** 1 condemned   **8.** 1 &   **9.** 1 Poem.—To ~~blame~~ censure
1 sonnet   **10.** 1 round.—   1 sonnets or monodies?   **11.** 1 ~~have given~~   1 could.—
12. more violent] 1 violent   1 ~~Love or~~ Sorrow   **14.** 1 connected ~~with the cause of
them.~~ with them.   **15.** 1 effort—   **16.** 1 But   **17.** 1 Tale of Misery

16–19. From Cuthbert Shaw *An   Poets* XI 564).
Evening Address to a Nightingale (*B*

From others eyes bid artless sorrows flow
And raise esteem upon the base of woe!"

The communicativeness of our nature leads us to describe our own sor- 20
rows; in the endeavor to describe them intellectual activity is exerted; and
by a benevolent law of our nature from intellectual activity a pleasure re-
sults which is gradually associated and mingles as a corrective with the
painful subject of the description. True! it may be answered, but how
are the PUBLIC interested in your sorrows or your description? We are 25
for ever attributing a personal unity to imaginary aggregates. What is the
PUBLIC but a term for a number of scattered individuals of whom as many
will be interested in these sorrows as have experienced the same or similar?

"Holy be the Lay,
Which mourning soothes the mourner on his way!" 30

There is one species of egotism which is truly disgusting; not that which
leads us to communicate our feelings to others, but that which would
reduce the feelings of others to an identity with our own. The Atheist,
who exclaims "pshaw!" when he glances his eye on the praise of Deity,
is an Egotist; an old man, when he speaks contemptuously of love-verses, 35
is an Egotist; and your sleek favorites of Fortune are Egotists, when they
condemn all "melancholy discontented" verses.

Surely it would be candid not merely to ask whether the Poem pleases
ourselves, but to consider whether or no there may not be others to whom
it is well-calculated to give an innocent pleasure. With what anxiety every 40
fashionable author avoids the word *I!*—now he transforms himself into
a third person,—"the present writer"—now multiplies himself and swells
into "*we*"—and all this is the watchfulness of guilt. Conscious that this said

19. 1 Woe! 20. 1 leads ⟨us⟩ 21. 1 describe ⟨them⟩ 22. 1 from all
them 22–3. 1 ae results 23. 1 & mingles, 24. 1 True, 1 answered—
25. 1 Public 1 in the your description? We] 1 descriptions? The PUBLIC.
We 26. 1 to some 1 Aggregates. 27. 1 Public 28. 1 similar?—
29. 1 Holy 30. 1 Mourner 1 way. 31. 1 Egotism 33. 1 [?] identity
1 Atheist 34. 1 "psha!" 35. 1 Man, 1 Love-verses, 36. 1 your well sleek
Favorites 1 Fortunes 1 egotists, 37. 1 condenmmn 39. 1 your self ourselves,
40. 1 ⟨well-⟩calculated 1 pleasure.— 1 [. . .] every 41. 1 *I*—! 42. 1 writer;
1 & swells

20–1. Cf *CN* I 62 "Poetry with-
out egotism comparatively uninterest-
ing—".
29–30. Source not located. C added

Shaw's name to the preceding quota-
tion only in 1797: perhaps he forgot
where this one came from, if indeed
he did not make it up.

I is perpetually intruding on his mind and that it monopolizes his heart, he
is prudishly solicitous that it may not escape from his lips.   45

This disinterestedness of phrase is in general commensurate with self-
ishness of feeling: men old and hackneyed in the ways of the world are
scrupulous avoiders of Egotism.

Of the following Poems a considerable number are styled "Effusions,"
in defiance of Churchill's line   50

> "Effusion on Effusion *pour* away."

I could recollect no title more descriptive of the manner and matter of
the Poems—I might indeed have called the majority of them Sonnets—but
they do not posses that *oneness* of thought which I deem indispensible in a
Sonnet—and (not a very honorable motive perhaps) I was fearful that the   55
title "Sonnet" might have reminded my reader of the Poems of the Rev.
W. L. Bowles—a comparison with whom would have sunk me below that
mediocrity, on the surface of which I am at present enabled to float.

Some of the verses allude to an intended emigration to America on the
scheme of an abandonment of individual property.   60

The Effusions signed C. L. were written by Mr. CHARLES LAMB, of
the India House—independently of the signature their superior merit would
have sufficiently distinguished them. For the rough sketch of Effusion XVI.
I am indebted to Mr. FAVELL. And the first half of Effusion XV. was
written by the Author of "Joan of Arc," an Epic Poem.   65

44. 1 &   **45.** 1 lips. ~~This modesty of phrase proceeds from selfishness: & hence~~
~~it happens that men hackneyed in the ways of the~~ *w̶i̶l̶d̶* ~~world are never Egotists.~~
46. 1 Disinterestedness of Phrase   **46–7.** 1 selfishness: ~~you~~ Men   **47.** 1 World
48. 1 Egotism.—   **49.** 1 —Of   1 ~~poems tha~~ following   1 "Effusions"—
50. 1 Line   **51.** 1 away."—   **52.** 1 I ~~have can~~ could   1 Manner and Matter
53. 1 Sonnets—;   **54.** 1 indispensable   **55.** 1 honorable Motive   **56.** 1 Title
1 Reader   **56–7.** 1 of 〈the Revd W. L.〉 Bowles—   **57.** 1 comparison ~~would~~ with
~~whose most exquisite compositions~~ whom   **57–8.** me below . . . to float.] 1 my
verses into contempt.   **58–9.** 1 has no new paragraph   **59.** 1 of ~~my~~ the Verses
60. property.] 1796 property • 1 Property.   **61.** 1 Mͬ Charles Lamb   **62.** 1 ~~their~~
signature   **63.** 1 XVI   **64.** 1 Mͬ Favell—   1 XV   **65.** 1 Arc,   1 Poem.—
65⁺. 7.5 cm trimmed away here in MS 1, at foot of f 9ʳ/p 21. The next page (f 9ᵛ/p 22)
continues with the following passage, which is entirely cancelled:

47–8. Cf *Friend* (*CC*) I 26 "O! for
one piece of egotism that presents it-
self under its own honest bare face of
'I myself I,' there are fifty that steal
out in the mask of *tuisms* and *ille-
isms!*"

51. From Charles Churchill *The
Candidate* (1764) 42, where the line
is applied to Langhorne. KC suggests
that C might also have been influ-
enced to fix on the word "Effusion"
by a review in *British Critic* v (May
1795) 554, which he read at about the
time he put together the 1796 volume
(*CN* I 48n).

61. Viz Effusions 7, 11, 12, and 13.

Contents. The table of Contents appears on pp xiii–xvi, following the Preface:

CONTENTS.

I cannot conclude this Preface without expressing my grateful acknowledgements to Mr Cottle*, Bristol—for the liberality with which (~~and~~ with little probability, I fear, of remuneration, [. . . .] from the sale) he purchased these poems, and in the ~~elegance~~ typographical elegance by which he has endeavoured to recommend them. ⟨liberal⟩ assistance, which he afforded me, by the purchase of the copy-right, ~~and the elegance~~ with little probability, ⟨I fear,⟩ of remuneration from the Sale of the Poems.

* Author of Poems published anonymously at Bristol, September, 1795.

C's cancelled dedication to Lord Stanhope, which follows at the foot of f 9^v/p 22, is given in the section "Preliminaries" above

16, 20, 21, 22. Signed "C.L."

Effusion 18, to the Autumnal Moon,	63	**61**	
Effusion 19, to my own heart,	64	**83**	
Effusion 20, to Schiller,	65	**86**	
Effusion 21, on Brockley Coomb,	66	**108**	30
To a Friend with an unfinished Poem,	68	**100**	
Effusion 23, to the Nightingale,	71	**112**	
Effusion 24, in the manner of Spencer,	73	**111**	
Effusion 25, to Domestic Peace,	77	**66**	
Effusion 26, on a Kiss,	78	**57**	35
Effusion 27,	80	**56**	
Effusion 28,	82	**76**	
Effusion 29, Imitated from Ossian,	84	**55**	
Effusion 30, Complaint of Ninathoma,	86	**51**	
Effusion 31, from the Welsh,	88	**73**	40
Effusion 32, The Sigh,	89	**75**	
Effusion 33, to a Young Ass,	91	**84**	
Effusion 34, to an Infant,	94	**105**	
Effusion 35, written at Cleveden,	96	**115**	
Effusion 36, written in Early Youth,	101	**60**	45
Epistle 1, written at Shurton Bars,	111	**116**	
Epistle 2, to a Friend in answer to a melancholy Letter,	119	**68**	
Epistle 3, written after a Walk,	122	**49**	
Epistle 4, to the Author of Poems published in Bristol,	125	**117**	
Epistle 5, from a Young Lady,	129	**119**	50
Religious Musings.	139	**101**	

Mottoes. Poems (1796) prints the following motto, from Bowles's *Monody Written at Matlock* 137–40 (*Sonnets, with Other Poems*—3rd ed Bath 1794—106 var), on p [44], the verso of the half-title "Effusions", facing Effusion 1. The motto was not reprinted in 1797 or 1803, but was included in *PW* (1828, 1829, 1834) between the title and the text of the poem:

> Content, as random Fancies might inspire,
> If his weak harp at times or lonely lyre
> He struck with desultory hand, and drew
> Some soften'd tones to Nature not untrue.
> BOWLES.

Poems (1796) prints a four-line verse motto on p [110], the verso of the half-title "Poetical Epistles", facing Epistle 1, signed "ANON.". C appears to be the author, and the poem is included in the main sequence as **125** *Verse Motto to Poetical Epistles.*

motto 1. *PW* (1834) "Content,   **motto 4.** *PW* (1828, 1829, 1834) softened *PW* (1834) untrue."   **motto 4⁺.** *PW* (1834) BOWLES.

2. *SONNETS FROM VARIOUS AUTHORS* (1796)

C describes the occasion of the printing of his pamphlet in two letters. He wrote to TP on 7 Nov 1796:

> I amused myself the other day (having some *paper* at the Printer's which I could employ no other way) in selecting 28 Sonnets, to bind up with Bowles's—I charge sixpence for them, and have sent you five to dispose of.—I have only printed two hundred, as my paper held out to no more; and dispose of them privately, just enough to pay thc printing.—The Essay, which I have written at the beginning, I like. (*CL* I 252)

When C sent a copy to Thelwall the following month, along with other material and accompanying a fourth edition of Bowles's *Sonnets* (1796), his description was more succinct: "Item—a sheet of Sonnets collected by me for the use of a few friends, who payed the printing—There you will see my opinion of Sonnets" (*CL* I 285: 17 Dec [1796]). This letter also raises the question as to whether the pamphlet contains material intended for a joint volume with Charles Lloyd or in some way resulted from cancelled plans. Some such project appears to have prompted it, as indicated in the Note on the Text below and further discussed with reference to *Poems* (1797), No 3 in this annex.

C drew both TP's and Thelwall's attention to the Preface, which explains the choice of poems with reference to the debate which had gone on during the 1780s and 1790s among writers of the sonnet, as to whether or not the Petrarchan rhyme-scheme was appropriate in English. Some argued the need to conform to the rules and practice of Boileau and Petrarch; others argued on behalf of freedom from such a complicated prescription, and for greater liberty and ease. C takes the argument for freedom to extremes, and at the same time gives it a peculiar twist. His opposition to the Petrarchan measure specifically was not unusual. Charlotte Smith was only one among several who complained that "the legitimate Sonnet is illy calculated for our language".[3]

Not unusual, either, was C's conflation of a variety of attitudes for the purposes of polemic. William Preston was a thoroughgoing, informed champion of Petrarch. Anna Seward paid no heed to the order of rhymes, only to their number: see the Preface to her *Original Sonnets* (1799). C merely exaggerates the position of one side in the contemporary debate with his claim that the sole formal requirement for a sonnet is that it should have fourteen lines. Metre and rhymes—many, few, or none—are at the author's convenience, as long as the fourteen lines make "a *Totality*". The idea of wholeness was shared with Miss Seward, for one, who wrote in 1795: "The legitimate sonnet generally consists of one thought, regularly pursued to the close."[4] "Legitimate" here means

---

[3] Preface to *Elegiac Sonnets* (1784), a collection which included a series of poems translated from Petrarch's *Can-zoniere*. Cf e.g. *Monthly Review* LXXI (1784) 368; LXXIII (1785) 306; LXXXI (1789) 366; *Universal Magazine* XCI (1792) 409, 413.

[4] Anna Seward, *Letters* (6 vols Edinburgh 1811) IV 144–5.

"sonnet proper"; in the quotation at the end of the preceding paragraph it is synonymous with "Petrarchan".

Though at least one contemporary, Capel Lofft, took C's argument about form seriously enough to answer it,[5] C's further argument in the Preface, that sonnets are distinguished by some lonely feeling, follows from his argument about their wholeness, and is idiosyncratic and important:

> In a Sonnet then we require a developement of some lonely feeling, by whatever cause it may have been excited; but those Sonnets appear to me the most exquisite, in which moral Sentiments, Affections, or Feelings, are deduced from, and associated with, the scenery of Nature. Such compositions generate a habit of thought highly favourable to delicacy of character.

This is important because, one realises, the larger part of the Preface is concerned with the argument over form and has little bearing on the choice of poems. The Preface does not anticipate contradictions among the writers included—Charles Lloyd afterwards held that Shakespearean quatrains like Charlotte Smith's had no place in sonnets.[6] It does not prepare for C's choice of two sonnets (Nos 8 and 9) with a regular Petrarchan rhyme-scheme (though each has other, metrical irregularities). It is contradicted by another (No 7) which has only thirteen lines. All of the writers included—C not least among them— demonstrably consulted a standard other than "their own convenience" when they put together their rhymes.

C's Preface in fact argues against technical distinctions in favour of other criteria. The majority of the sonnets included may be careless or peculiar in their rhyming, but qualities of feeling such as sentiment and melancholy are more important than technical conventions. In the first place, all the writers were to some extent influenced by Collins: Warton, Bowles, Brydges, and Charlotte Smith all wrote in his praise. Then again, it was not just C, Lamb, RS, and Charles Lloyd who were known to each other: Bowles had praised Thomas Russell, who had been his contemporary at Winchester and Oxford (in his *Monody on Matlock*), as he did their former tutor Thomas Warton; Egerton Brydges was affected by and continued to be interested in Bampfylde,[7] and was influenced by Charlotte Smith to write novels; H. F. Cary answered Anna Seward's sonnet with one to her which was prefixed to her *Llangollen Vale with Other Poems* (1796) v. The authors and their poems appear disparate now because they are little known; in their time, and in particular circles, they were better appreciated. RS and WW praised the Brydges sonnet (No 9) highly;[8] the second Charlotte Smith sonnet (No 23) and Thomas Russell's (No 18) were

---

[5] See *Monthly Mirror* xvii (1804) 192; *Laura; or, An Anthology of Sonnets (on the Petrarchan Model) and Elegiac Quaterzains, English, Italian, Spanish, Portuguese, French, and German* . . . (5 vols 1814) ii No 151.

[6] *Nugae Canorae* (1819) 168.

[7] *Autobiography* (2 vols 1834) i 35–6, ii 257–61.

[8] RS q Brydges *Autobiography* ii 262–3; *WL* (*L* rev) ii 604 and n.

both known and quoted by WW;[9] RS was sufficiently impressed by Bampfylde to collect his poems in manuscript.[10]

Wider issues and connections of this kind bear closely on the scope of the selection and on why C was moved to make it when he did. It should be noted that this is the only selection of other writers' verse that he put together and published. The sonnets as a group celebrate nature, withdrawal, pathos. Unlike C's earlier *M Chron* "Sonnets on Eminent Characters", these forsake public persons and events and celebrate places and scenery. Their way of dealing with politics is oblique, transforming policy into an object of contemplation. They are engaged at a distance, in a humanitarian and philanthropic spirit. "Hence, the Sonnets of B OWL E S derive their marked superiority over all other Sonnets; hence they domesticate with the heart, and become, as it were, a part of our identity" (Preface).

The make-up of the selection is thereby connected with C's decision, after the birth of his son, to leave Bristol and to move to the country near TP. The sonnets were brought together at a time when he was reckoning to leave cities and politicians behind, and "accordingly snapped my squeaking baby-trumpet of sedition" (*CL* I 240: to C. Lloyd Sr 15 Oct 1796). He invited Thelwall to condemn his *M Chron* sonnet to Pitt (*CL* I 254: 13 Nov 1796), called *To Mercy* in *The Watchman* in Apr that year (*CC* 166–7), even as he was reprinting his collaboration with Favell, celebrating an old man, "*Sweet Mercy*" (sonnet No 17=**88** *To an Old Man in the Snow*). The exaggerated, unwarranted attack on Petrarch in the Preface makes more sense with reference to the Petrarchan form of Milton's sonnets and their commitment to public, prophetic politics. At the time C sent Thelwall a copy of *Sonnets from Various Authors*, he also told TP: "My poetic Vanity & my political Furore have been exhaled; and I would rather be an expert, self-maintaining Gardener than a Milton" (*CL* I 275: 13 Dec 1796).

The binding up of the *Sonnets* with those of Bowles's fourth edition was integral to the statement that C hoped to make. *BL* describes how Bowles had, some years before, helped to rekindle "the feelings of the heart", and how C had made forty handwritten copies of Bowles's second edition for distribution among his friends (*BL* ch 1—*CC*—I 13–17). The printing of 200 copies of a selection inspired by the same author and celebrating the same values recalls the earlier occasion, and was surely intended to will the same result.

The evidence suggests that the pamphlet was put together on the spur of the moment, whatever its further background. It constitutes a gesture at a time when C's plans were more accurately hopes, not certain commitments. It takes in four poems apiece by himself, RS, CL, and Charles Lloyd, three by Bowles, two by Charlotte Smith, and one apiece by the seven other authors (plus another by Anna Seward in the Preface). Some poems—such as those by Bowles and Bampfylde, his own Nos 14=**83** *To my Own Heart* and 17=**88** *To an Old*

---

[9] *WL* (*L* rev) II 260; *WPW* IV 42–3, 407–8; *W Prose* I 163n   [10] *S Life* (CS) II 26–7.

Man in the Snow, and CL's No 25—had been to hand for a considerable time. Others—by RS, Lloyd, and Anna Seward—had only recently become available, and must have been opportunistically grasped. Some are revised very little (the Lloyd *Priscilla Farmer* poems, the Warton–Anna Seward–Russell poems, CL's No 10). Others again appear to have been revised earlier—the CL poems previously included in *Poems* (1796), the Dermody and Bampfylde poems. There is no significant pattern, though a few details add to the impression of improvisation: the incomplete, wrong, or misspelled names of Cary, Bampfylde, Brydges, and Russell; the changes to C's own sonnet on Schiller, No 28=**86** *To the Author of "The Robbers"*, which he afterwards rescinded; some variations from the originals which might not be deliberate.

To sum up, *Sonnets from Various Authors* arises from circumstances which the Preface characteristically obscures. The pamphlet commemorates a set of hopes entertained about a way of life more than an achieved position concerning the technicalities of a specific verse-form. C's attachment to those hopes was inconstant. Within a month or two he was writing the declamatory political ode which led him afterwards to explain his attitude towards pity and suffering to Bowles as more *"stormy"* than his (*CL* I 318: [16 Mar 1797]). By May 1797 he was dedicating his new volume of poems (containing the Preface, as well as several of the same sonnets) to his brother GC instead of to Bowles, in terms similar to those he had used in Oct 1796. In Mar 1798 he was repeating the same argument, including the phrase about having "snapped my squeaking baby-trumpet of Sedition" (*CL* I 397: to GC), as he had used to Charles Lloyd Sr. Given this uncertainty and inconstancy, it is not surprising that C was led himself to parody the form and qualities of the *Sonnets* pamphlet in the three Nehemiah Higginbottom sonnets of Nov 1797 (see **158** *Sonnets Attempted in the Manner of "Contemporary Writers"*). Thereafter he wrote very few sonnets indeed, and the reprinting of the Preface in 1803 was entirely due to CL.

NOTE ON THE TEXT

When C told TP that the pamphlet was printed to use up his stock of paper with the printer, it was surely understood that the printer was Nathaniel Biggs. When Biggs had printed *The Watchman*, the arrangements concerning paper were complicated and had led to argument (see *CC* lvi–lvii). But, though the pages are roughly similar in size, the papers are different: *The Watchman* is entirely on laid paper, the *Sonnets* entirely on wove paper. When C wrote of having a stock of paper with Biggs, he might therefore have had in mind the arrangement, following *The Watchman*, to publish a joint volume with Charles Lloyd.

This arrangement appears to have rested on a loose understanding, which was modified when Lloyd published *Poems on the Death of Priscilla Farmer* in the months immediately preceding C's pamphlet. It was printed by Biggs on wove paper, and indeed carried an epigraph from Bowles. A comparison of the printed versions of Lloyd's poems with those which C copied out in *CL* I 237–8, 243–4 (to TP 24 Sept, 1 Nov 1796) strengthens the probability that C helped to revise them. And this could be another background to his proprietary assumptions about the paper. There is a complication, however: the pages of Lloyd's volume, measuring 19.5×26.1 cm, are very evidently larger than C's (untrimmed) pamphlet, and it is difficult to see how the same paper could have been used.

Why no printer's name appears on the pamphlet, and why C is not identified as the compiler (the Preface is signed "EDITOR"), are moot questions. Were the names omitted to avoid the charge of piracy? Or to avoid complicating C's understanding with Cottle as the publisher of his poetry? Was C's name omitted inadvertently, Biggs being in the habit of setting C's *Watchman* pieces without identifying himself as the printer? Or was it because C was using a stock of paper which Lloyd had paid for? It may be significant that two of the five copies which have been traced originate from Lloyd, and also that Lloyd was the only author to carry forward readings which appear in this collection to later collections of his own: compare his reaction to Nos 3 and 4 below with the reactions of RS and CL to Nos 2, 12, etc. One plausible answer to the question is that Biggs received his instructions from C, used the stock of paper Lloyd had recently paid for, and divided the result.

There is another explanation altogether, which involves an almost equal number of suppositions. Bowles himself recalled much later:

> soon after this third edition came out, my friend, Mr Cruttwell, the printer, wrote a letter saying that two young gentlemen, strangers, one a particularly handsome and pleasing youth, lately from Westminster School, and both literary and intelligent, spoke in high commendation of my volume, and if I recollect right, expressed a desire to have some poems printed in the same type and form. (Introduction to the edition of 1837, in *Poetical Works* ed G. Gilfillan—2 vols Edinburgh 1855—I 3)

Bowles is writing about 1794 ("soon after this third edition came out"), C having become acquainted with the volume before Jul (cf **70.X1** *Adaptation of "I shall behold far off thy barren crest"* sec C), and C was indeed in Bath with RS during Aug. The possibility therefore arises that the beginnings of the project go back to this earlier time, owing something to RS, who was always pleased by bibliographical curiosities. Did C reserve a stock of paper then which he drew on two years later when the idea revived? Is the lack of a printer's and editor's name part of the more widespread obfuscation arising from C's involvement in the interim with a rival printer and publisher in Bristol?

Not enough is known to answer these questions with certainty, and the details that can be added do not harmonise. Thus, the notion that C's pamphlet makes use of the paper Cruttwell used in Bowles's third edition of 1794 receives slight support from the fact that the pages in both are closer to one another in size than either is to the fourth edition (1796), whose pages are both wider and taller. Against this must be set the fact that the Cornell copy of C's pamphlet (Wordsworth PR 4161 B4 1796) has the wm "1794" on sig *A* and the wm "P | 1794" on sig B, while the Cambridge University Library copy of Bowles's fourth edition (Nn 7 104) has the wm "1794" (simply). Does this suggest that both utilised stocks of the same, old paper? Bowles's recollections forty years after the event might easily have confused two editions two summers apart.

Six of the 200 copies C said were printed are known still to exist: Mrs Thelwall's, now at the V&A (Dyce Collection 4to 1298); SH's, at DCL (MS 14/2); Charles Lloyd's, at HEHL (No 123965); Rachel Lloyd's, at Oberlin (Special Collections 821.7C67 So); Sophia Pemberton's, at Cornell (WORDSWORTH PR 4161 B4 1796); Mrs Calvert's, at Princeton (Robert H. Taylor Collection). A seventh copy is known to have belonged to CL (*LL*—M—I 73–5), and a fragment of an eighth (half of p 16) is preserved at the Pforzheimer (Misc 74). It may seem curious that so few have survived. Three are bound with Bowles's *Sonnets* (1796), and other copies might be catalogued elsewhere under Bowles's name. Others again might have been catalogued under Anna Seward's name: a nineteenth-century cataloguer indexed Sophia Pemberton's copy as "Seward—Anne—Sonnets selected by her of Poets, her Cotemporaries to be added to Bowles Sonnets"; and up to 1956 the DCL catalogue described SH's copy as "proof-sheets of Anna Seward's *Original Sonnets* (1799)". The copies at the V&A and DCL contain inscriptions and annotations by C, and those at HEHL and Cornell by Charles Lloyd. The inscriptions are given, along with additional details and comments, in annex C.

The text which follows reproduces the 1796 pamphlet literatim.[11] Not only does the selection of poems itself make a statement of intent, as described above, but so likewise do C's changes to the text of individual poems. C's alterations are described in the EC, but no attempt has been made to list all of his changes to punctuation and capitals. The changes to his own poems (V = **140** *To the River Otter*; XIV =**83** *To my Own Heart*; XVII =**88** *To an Old Man in the Snow*; XXVIII =**86** *To the Author of "The Robbers"*), along with those for which versions in his hand exist (VII =**58.X1** *Adaptation of Bampfylde's "To Evening"*; XII =**113** *Adaptation of "Was it some sweet device of faery land . . .?"*; XXV =**104** *Adaptation of "Written at Midnight, by the Sea-side"*) and the adaptation of Dermody (XXIV =poem **141**), are described in detail in vol II.

I have selected the following SONNETS from various Authors for the purpose of binding them up with the Sonnets of the Rev. W. L. BOWLES.

The composition of the Sonnet has been regulated by Boileau in his Art

---

[11] Except that it corrects sonnet III.6 XXVII.5 "Patienee,". "Iv'e"; sonnet VI.11 "supended"; sonnet

of Poetry, and since Boileau, by William Preston, in the elegant preface
to his Amatory Poems: the rules, which they would establish, are founded   5
on the practice of Petrarch. I have never yet been able to discover either
sense, nature, or poetic fancy in Petrarch's poems; they appear to me all
one cold glitter of heavy conceits and metaphysical abstractions. However,
Petrarch, although not the inventor of the Sonnet, was the first who made it
popular; and *his* countrymen have taken his poems as the model. Charlotte   10
Smith and Bowles are they who first made the Sonnet popular among the
present English: I am justified therefore by analogy in deducing its laws
from *their* compositions.

The Sonnet then is a small poem, in which some lonely feeling is de-
veloped. It is limited to a *particular* number of lines, in order that the   15
reader's mind having expected the close at the place in which he finds it,
may rest satisfied; and that so the poem may acquire, as it were, a *Total-
ity*,—in plainer phrase, may become a *Whole*. It is confined to fourteen
lines, because as some particular number is necessary, and that particular
number must be a small one, it may as well be fourteen as any other num-   20
ber. When no reason can be adduced against a thing, Custom is a sufficient
reason for it. Perhaps, if the Sonnet were comprized in less than fourteen
lines, it would become a serious Epigram; if it extended to more, it would
encroach on the province of the Elegy. On this however we lay no stress.
Poems, in which no lonely feeling is developed, are not Sonnets because   25
the Author has chosen to write them in fourteen lines: they should rather
be entitled Odes, or Songs, or Inscriptions. The greater part of Warton's

4. *The Poetical Works of William
Preston* (2 vols Dublin 1793) I 257–
67. C copied some lines by Preston
into the Gutch Notebook, from a no-
tice in *Critical Review* XIII (Feb 1795)
178, which for a long while were
thought to be his own (cf **174.X1** *To
—— ——* ("l mix in life, and labour
to seem free").

6–8. In a letter to H. F. Cary dated
4 Mar 1798 (*Letters*—6 vols Edin-
burgh 1811—v 58) Anna Seward sin-
gled out this comment for approval.
C himself remarked later, in the mar-
gins of RS's copy of *Poems* (1797)
now at Yale (annex c 6.10), p 71:
"A piece of petulant presumption, of
which I should be more ashamed, if
I did not flatter myself that it stands
alone in my writings. The best of the
Joke is that at the time, I wrote it, I

did not understand a word of Italian,
& could therefore judge of this di-
vine Poet only by bald Translations of
some half dozen of his Sonnets." C's
knowledge of Italian is reviewed in
CN II appendix A; also Edoardo Zuc-
cato *Coleridge in Italy* (Cork 1996)
226–33.

17–21. C never ceased to empha-
sise the idea of wholeness as the dis-
tinguishing mark of sonnet form. Cf
CM (*CC*) I 57; *SW&F* (*CC*) 283;
"What is an English Sonnet?" q **592**
Youth and Age VAR TEXT PR *5*.

27–9. See on sonnet VIII below for
Warton; the "Greek επιγραμμα", bet-
ter known as the Greek Anthology,
contains poems of much wider scope
than the modern sense of pointedly
humorous epigrams.

Sonnets are severe and masterly likenesses of the style of the Greek επι-γραμματα.

In a Sonnet then we require a developement of some lonely feeling,   30
by whatever cause it may have been excited; but those Sonnets appear to
me the most exquisite, in which moral Sentiments, Affections, or Feel-
ings, are deduced from, and associated with, the scenery of Nature. Such
compositions generate a habit of thought highly favourable to delicacy of
character. They create a sweet and indissoluble union between the intellec-   35
tual and the material world. Easily remembered from their briefness, and
interesting alike to the eye and the affections, these are the poems which
we can "lay up in our heart, and our soul," and repeat them "when we walk
by the way, and when we lie down and when we rise up." Hence, the Son-
nets of BOWLES derive their marked superiority over all other Sonnets;   40
hence they domesticate with the heart, and become, as it were, a part of
our identity.

Respecting the metre of a Sonnet, the Writer should consult his own
convenience.—Rhymes, many or few, or no rhymes at all—whatever the
chastity of his ear may prefer, whatever the rapid expression of his feelings   45
will permit;—all these things are left at his own disposal. A sameness
in the final sound of its words is the great and grievous defect of the
Italian language. That rule therefore, which the Italians have established,
of exactly *four* different sounds in the Sonnet, seems to have arisen from
their wish to have *as many*, not from any dread of finding *more*. But   50
surely it is ridiculous to make the *defect* of a foreign language a reason for
our not availing ourselves of one of the marked excellencies of our own.
"The Sonnet (says Preston) will ever be cultivated by those who write
on tender pathetic subjects. It is peculiarly adapted to the state of a man
violently agitated by a real passion, and wanting composure and vigor of   55
mind to methodize his thought. It is fitted to express a momentary burst of
Passion," &c. Now, if there be one species of composition more difficult
and artificial than another, it is an English Sonnet on the Italian model.
Adapted to the agitations of a real passion! Express momentary bursts of
feeling in it! I should sooner expect to write pathetic *Axes*, or *pour forth*   60
extempore Eggs and *Altars!* But the best confutation of such idle rules is to
be found in the Sonnets of those who have observed them, in their inverted
sentences, their quaint phrases, and incongruous mixture of obsolete and
spenserian words: and when, at last, the thing is toiled, and hammered into

38–9. Deut 11.18–19 (var).

53–7. Preston *Poetical Works* I 268 (var).

60–1. The italicised phrases de-
rive from Preston's essay on the ir-
regular ode (*Poetical Works* II 7). C
added at the foot of the page in the

copy he sent to the Thelwalls, now
at the V&A: "The ancients little Wits
wrote many poems in the shape of
Eggs, Altars & Axes." Among Eng-
lish poets, such "little Wits" include
George Herbert and Mildmay Fane.

64. spenserian] C's coinage? Cf *BL*

fit shape, it is in general racked and tortured Prose rather than any thing   65
resembling Poetry. Miss Seward, who has perhaps succeeded the best in
these laborious trifles, and who most dogmatically insists on what she
calls the sonnet-claim, has written a very ingenious although unintentional
burlesque on her own system, in the following lines, prefixed to the Poems
of a Mr. Carey.   70

> Prais'd be the Poet, who the sonnet-claim,
> Severest of the orders that belong
> Distinct and separate to the Delphic song
> Shall reverence, nor its appropriate name
> Lawless assume: peculiar is its frame—   75
> From him derived, who spurn'd the city throng,
> And warbled sweet thy rocks and wood among,
> Lonely Valclusa! and that heir of Fame,
> Our greater Milton, hath in many a lay
> Woven on this arduous model, clearly shewn   80
> That English verse may happily display
> Those strict energic measures which alone
> Deserve the name of Sonnet, and convey
> A spirit, force, and grandeur, all their own.
>   ANNE SEWARD.   85

> *A spirit, force, and grandeur, all their own!!*
>   EDITOR.

---

ch 4 (*CC*) I 80.

71 et seq. Anna Seward's sonnet was prefixed to Henry Francis Cary's *Sonnets and Odes* (1788) 5. C has revised her text in lines 75 ("spurn'd" for "shunn'd"), 76 ("wood" for "Streams"), 78 ("in" for "by"), 81 ("which" for "that"), and 83 (originally "A grandeur, grace, and spirit, all their own."), as well as such matters as punctuation, capitals, and italic.

Anna Seward revised the poem in her volume of *Original Sonnets* (1799), but did not adopt any of C's readings. The sonnet is the first of two poems by her at the beginning of Cary's volume; and in the volume

itself (pp 8, 9) Cary addresses two poems to her. Cary was also to prefix a poem to her 1796 collection *Llangollen Vale, with Other Poems*. For a possible unacknowledged borrowing by C from Seward, see **82** *Monody on the Death of Chatterton* 104EC; for Seward on C's theorising about sonnets see on lines 6–8, 17–20 above. C met Cary on the beach at Littlehampton in 1817 (*Memoir of H. F. Cary* ed Henry Cary—2 vols 1847—II 18), and very quickly became a champion of his translation of Dante (e.g. *CL* IV 804: to F. Wrangham 10 Jan 1818; 860: to H. J. Rose [12 May 1818]; 879: to C. Brent [4 Nov 1818]).

SONNET I.

TO A FRIEND

Bereave me not of these delightful Dreams
   That charm'd my Youth, or mid the gay career
   Of Hope, or when the faintly-paining tear
Sate sad on Memory's cheek: tho' loftier themes
Await th' awaken'd mind, to the high prize   5
   Of Wisdom hardly earn'd with toil and pain
   Aspiring patient: yet on Life's wide plain
Cast friendless, where unheard some sufferer cries
Hourly, and oft our Road is lone and long.
   'Twere not a crime, should we awhile delay   10
   Amid the sunny field, and happier they
Who, as they wander, woo the charm of song
To soothe their cares, till they forget to weep,
And the tir'd sense is hush'd, and sinks to sleep.
                     W. L. BOWLES.

SONNET II.

With many a weary step at length I gain
   Thy summit Lansdown: and the cool breeze plays
   Gratefully round my brow, as hence the gaze
Returns to dwell upon the journied plain.
   'Twas a long way and tedious! to the eye   5

I. The sonnet opened Bowles's *Sonnets* (2nd ed Bath 1789) 9–10. C added capitals to several nouns and lightened Bowles's punctuation. He also amended two lines, given thus in the original:

   2 Which charm'd my youth; or
      mid her gay career
  13 To cheer their path—till they
      forget to weep,

C complained to Bowles when the sonnet was among those dropped from subsequent editions (*CL* I 318: [16 Mar 1797]). Bowles reintroduced it in the seventh edition (1800), although he did not adopt C's revisions.

C added at the head of the page above the sonnet in the copy he sent to the Thelwalls, now at the V&A: "The three Sonnets of Bowles are not in any Edition, since the first quarto pamphlet of his Sonnets."

II. Sonnet VIII in RS's *Poems* (Bristol 1797) 114, which began printing in Dec 1796 (*CL* I 275: to TP 13 Dec 1796). C must have been shown the poem either by RS or by Cottle. He changed RS's "faded" to "fading" in line 7, together with some details of punctuation. RS did not adopt the emendation when Cottle published a second edition of his 1797 *Poems* (here at p 126).

Tho' fair the extended vale, and fair to view
The falling leaves of many a fading hue,
  That eddy in the wild gust moaning by.
Even so it fared with life! in discontent
Restless thro' Fortune's mingled scenes I went,   10
  Yet wept to think they would return no more!
But cease fond heart in such sad thoughts to roam!
For surely thou ere long shalt reach thine home,
  And pleasant is the way that lies before.
                    R. SOUTHEY.

SONNET III.

TO SCOTLAND

Scotland! when thinking on each heathy hill
  O'er whose bleak breast the billowy vapours sweep,
  While sullen winds imprison'd murmur deep
'Mid their dim caves, such thoughts my bosom fill,
I cannot chuse but sigh! Oft wandering wild   5
I've trac'd thy torrents to their haunted source,
  Whence down some huge rock with fantastic course,
Their sheeted whiteness pouring, they beguil'd
  The meek dishearten'd one, in solitude
Who sought relief. Beneath some aged tree,   10
Thy white cots dimly seen yielding to me
  Solace most sweet: nor seldom have I view'd
Their low thatch wishfully, and paus'd to bless
The uncultur'd Children of lone Quietness!
                    C. LLOYD.

III. Lloyd was staying with C at the time the *Sonnets* were put together, in the process of making final arrangements to become C's pupil. In the copies now at HEHL and Cornell (annex c 4A, B) he corrected "yielding" to "yielded" in line 11, and the correction was taken forward to the STC–Lloyd *Poems* (1797) (here at p 170). C made the same correction in SH's copy of the *Sonnets* now at DCL (annex c 4.2), and he also amended "one" to "man" in line 9 (the 1797 *Poems* reads "One").

SONNET IV.

To CRAIG-MILTON CASTLE, in which MARY
QUEEN of SCOTS was confined.

This hoary labyrinth, the wreck of Time
  Solicitous with timid step I tread,
Scale the stern battlement, or vent'rous climb
  Where the rent watch-tower bows its grassy head:
These dark damp caverns breathe mysterious dread,   5
  Haply still foul with tinct of ancient crime;
Methinks some spirit of th' ennobled dead
  High-bosom'd maid, or warrior form sublime
Haunts them: the flappings of the heavy bird
  Imagin'd warnings fearfully impart,   10
And that dull breeze below that feebly stirr'd,
  Seem'd the deep breathing of an o'ercharg'd heart!
Proud Tower, thy halls now stable the lean herd,
  And Musing Mercy smiles that such thou art!

C. LLOYD.

SONNET V.

To the RIVER OTTER.

Dear native Brook! wild Streamlet of the West!
  How many various-fated Years have past,
  What blissful and what anguish'd hours, since last

IV. Lloyd made identical corrections in the copies of the *Sonnets* now at HEHL and Cornell: he abbreviated the title to "*To CRAIG-MILLAR CASTLE*" and in line 11 altered "that dull" to "the dull". The changes were carried forward to the 1797 *Poems* reprinting (p 169), which in line 8 also changed "warrior form" to "warrior-chief".

v = 140 *To the River Otter.* Lines 2–11 had previously been used (var) in **128** *Recollection*, pub *Watchman* v (2 Apr 1796) (*CC*) 167–8. The sonnet might have been composed any time between then and late Oct–early Nov 1796, when the *Sonnets* were put together; or some version of it might date from as early as 1793 (so also sonnet VII below).

C made numerous corrections in SH's copy at DCL (annex C 4.2): line 3 "blissful" to "happy" and "anguish'd" to "mournful"; line 7 "blaze" to "ray"; line 9 "margin's willowy maze" to "marge with willows grey"; line 11 "transparence to the gaze" to "transparence! on my way,"; line 13 "Lone Manhood's cares, yet" to "The cares of Manhood". These corrections date from after the time he introduced changes into the poem in Jul 1797: see poem **140** VAR.

I skimm'd the smooth thin stone along thy breast,
  Numbering its light leaps! Yet so deep imprest   5
  Sink the sweet scenes of Childhood, that mine eyes
I never shut amid the sunny blaze,
  But strait with all their tints thy waters rise,
Thy crossing plank, thy margin's willowy maze,
  And bedded sand that vein'd with various dies   10
Gleam'd thro' thy bright transparence to the gaze!
  Visions of Childhood! oft have ye beguil'd
Lone Manhood's cares, yet waking fondest sighs,
  Ah! that once more I were a careless Child!
                               S. T. COLERIDGE.

SONNET VI.

O HARMONY! thou tenderest Nurse of Pain!
  If that thy Note's soft magic e'er could heal
  Griefs which the patient spirit oft must feel,
O let me listen to thy songs again!
  Till MEMORY her fairest tints shall bring,   5
HOPE wake with brighter eye and list'ning seem
With smiles to think of some delightful dream,
  That o'er the charm'd sense wav'd its gladsome wing!
But when thou leadest all thy soothing strains
  More smooth along, the silent Passions meet   10
  In one suspended transport, sad and sweet;
And nought but Sorrow's softest touch remains
  That, when the transitory charm is o'er,
  Just wakes a tear, and then is felt no more!
                               W. L. BOWLES.

VI. C's text derives from Bowles's *Sonnets* (2nd ed Bath 1789) 30, where it is sonnet XX. C made the following changes: line 2 "If that thy note's sweet magic e'er can heal"; line 3 "may" to "must"; line 7 "on" to "of"; line 8 "That wav'd o'er the charm'd sense its gladsome wing:"; line 9 "For" to "But". He also changed punctuation and capitals.

The poem was omitted from subsequent editions of Bowles's *Sonnets*—as C complained (*CL* I 318–19: to W. L. Bowles [16 Mar 1797])—and was reintroduced only in the sixth edition (1798).

SONNET VII.

To EVENING

What numerous tribes beneath thy shadowy wing,
  O meek and modest EVENING, find delight:
First to the Grove his ling'ring fair to bring
  The warm and youthful Lover hating Light
Sighs oft for thee; and next the boisterous string   5
  Of School-Imps freed from Dame's all dreaded sight,
Round village cross in many a wanton ring
  Wishes thy stay; and last with active might,
The lusty Hinds urge the rebounding Ball;
  I, general Friend! by turns am mix'd with all,   10
Lover, and Elfin gay, and harmless Hind,
Nor heed the proud, to real wisdom blind,
So as my Heart be pure, and free my Mind!

                     BAMFIELD.

SONNET VIII.

On BATHING.

When late the trees were stript by winter pale,
  Young HEALTH, a dryad maid in vesture green,
  Or like the forest's silver-quiver'd queen,
  On airy uplands met the piercing gale;

VII. The Bampfylde lines depart considerably from the original, and because C's version here appears to date from another, earlier occasion, separate from the material he gathered in Nov 1796 (but see on sonnet v above), the versions (a holograph in C's hand, the printed text here, and the Bampfylde original) are collated separately in vol II as **58.X1** *Adaptation of Bampfylde's "To Evening"*.

It will be noted that the poem is the only one in the collection lacking the author's first name or initials and with the surname misspelled. The reason may be, again, that it is based on material from some years previously, and that C had meanwhile forgotten these details. It is also the only sonnet in the collection not to have the fourteen lines that C argued were necessary (see the Preface). The holograph manuscript is also in thirteen lines (C's line 9 merges lines 9 and 10 of the original), but the printed version here does restore part of Bampfylde's original line 1.

VIII. C's text might derive either from Thomas Warton's *Poems* (new ed 1777) 76 or from the unchanged reprinting in his *Poems on Various Subjects* (1791) 106. The one change of wording ("Iris" for "Isis" in line 10) might be a misprint, and there are fewer changes of punctuation than elsewhere in the collection.

And, ere its earliest echo shook the vale,   5
    Watching the hunter's joyous horn was seen.
But since, gay thron'd in fiery chariot sheen,
Summer has smote each daisy-dappled dale,
She to the cave retires, high-arch'd beneath
    The fount that laves proud Iris' tower'd brim;   10
And now all glad the temperate air to breathe,
    While cooling drops distil from arches dim,
Binding her dewy locks with sedgey wreath,
    She sits amid the quire of Naiads trim.

T. WARTON.

SONNET IX.

When eddying Leaves begun in whirls to fly,
    And autumn in her lap the treasures strew,
    As mid wild scenes I chanc'd the Muse to woo,
Mid glens untrod, and woods that frown'd on high,
Two sleeping Nymphs, with wonder mute I spy: 5
    And lo—she's gone! the Maid in dark-green hue!
'Twas ECHO from her Sister SILENCE flew:
For loud the Horn resounded to the Sky.
    In shades affrighted SILENCE melts away:
Not so her Sister—Hark! for onward still   10
    With far-heard step she takes her hasty way
Bounding from Rock to Rock, and Hill to Hill!
    Oh may the merry Maid in mockful play
With thousand mimic tones the laughing Forest fill.

HENRY BROOKS,
(the Author of the Fool of Quality.)

IX. The sonnet is not by Henry Brooks (i.e. Brooke), but by Egerton Brydges. It was published anonymously in his *Sonnets and Other Poems* (1785) 5, then under his name in *Sonnets and Other Poems* (1789) 5 and ibid (1795) 7, in each instance with the title *On Echo and Silence*. Brydges later reprinted it with a Latin translation by Francis Wrangham, along with a letter which praises it by RS, in his *Autobiography* (2 vols 1834) II 262–3. C might have got the name wrong either because he came across the poem in the anonymous volume or because it had been supplied to him some time before, e.g. by Wrangham or RS.

C's text draws on the 1785 or 1789 printing (both are identical: later the text was slightly revised). Brydges' original reads differently: line 1 "In eddying course when leaves began to fly,"; line 2 "treasure"; line 4 "Thro glens"; line 6 "In robe of dark-green hue"; line 8 "For quick the hunter's horn resounded to the sky."; line 9 "shade"; line 13 "Ah! mark the merry". C also changed Brydges' punctuation and capitals.

SONNET X.

We were two pretty Babes, the youngest she,
   The youngest and the loveliest far, I ween,
   And INNOCENCE her name: the time has been,
We two did love each other's company—
   Time was, we two had wept t' have been apart!   5
But when with shew of seeming good beguil'd
I left the garb and manners of a child,
   And my first Love for Man's society,
Defiling with the World my Virgin Heart,
   My lov'd Companion dropt a tear and fled,   10
And hid in deepest shades her * AWFUL head!
   Beloved! who can tell me where thou art,
In what delicious Eden to be found,
That I may seek thee the wide world around!
                CHARLES LAMB.

SONNET XI.

I knew a gentle maid: I ne'er shall view
   Her like again: and yet the vulgar eye
   Might pass the charms I trac'd, regardless by;
For pale her cheek, unmark'd with roseate hue,

---

   * Innocence, which while we possess it, is playful, as a babe, becomes AWFUL when it has departed from us.—This is the sentiment of the line, a fine sentiment and nobly expressed.   EDITOR.

   x. CL copied out the poem in a letter to C of 30–1 May 1796 now at HEHL (*LL*—M—I 8); it had been published over his name in *Monthly Magazine* II (Jul 1796) 491. The two versions differ in lines 11 and 12 ("Hiding" for "And hid"; "shall" for "can"), and the version C printed here derives from the letter, with some differences of punctuation only.

   The poem was reprinted with a further change in line 6 ("by" for "with") in the STC–CL *Poems* (1797) 223, and then in CL's *Works* (1818) I 68.

   xi. C's source is William Sotheby *A Tour through Parts of Wales, Son-*nets, Odes, and Other Poems (1794) 53, where, as sonnet VIII (in sixteen lines), the poem is entitled *A Fancy Sketch*. C's line 13 compresses lines 13–15 of Sotheby's original, which read thus:

> The lightest touch of woe her soul
>   would melt:
> And on her lips, when gleamed a
>   lingering smile,
> Pity's warm tear gushed down her
>   cheek the while:

Otherwise, besides the italicisation of "*flashed*" (line 6), C changed only a few details of punctuation.

Nor beam'd from her mild eye a dazzling glance,   5
  Nor *flashed* her nameless graces on the sight;
  Yet Beauty never woke such pure delight.
Fine was her Form, as Dian's in the dance;
Her voice was music, in her silence dwelt
  Expression, every look instinct with thought: 10
  Though oft her mind by youth to rapture wrought
Struck forth wild wit and fancies ever new,
  Yet Sorrow's lightest touch her soul would melt:
Thy like, thou gentle maid! I ne'er shall view!
                W. SOTHEBY.

SONNET XII.

Was it some sweet device of faery land
  That mock'd my steps with many a lonely glade,
  And fancied wand'rings with a fair-hair'd maid?
Have these things been? Or did the wizard wand
Of Merlin wave, impregning vacant air,   5
  And kindle up the *vision* of a smile
  In those blue eyes, that seem'd to speak the while
Such tender things, as might enforce Despair
To drop the murth'ring knife, and let go by
  His fell resolve? Ah me! the lonely glade   10
  Still courts the footsteps of the fair-hair'd maid,
Among whose locks the west-winds love to sigh:
  But I forlorn do wander, reckless where,
  And mid my wand'rings find no ANNA there!
                CHARLES LAMB.

SONNET XIII.

When last I rov'd these winding wood-walks green,
  Green winding walks and shady pathways sweet

XII. C reprinted the version of CL's poem he had included over CL's initials in *Poems* (1796) 55, with only one minor (typographical) correction. After CL protested again at C's considerable rewriting (*LL*—M—I 20, 86), the original text was restored in the STC–CL *Poems* (1797) 217 (and reprinted in CL's *Works*— 1818—I 60). C's versions are collated against CL's in **113** *Adaptation of "Was it some sweet device of faery land . . . ?"* VAR.

XIII. C undoubtedly printed the poem from the version CL sent him on 30–1 May 1796 (*LL*—M—I 7), in which he altered the punctuation and made the following changes:

Oft-times would ANNA seek the silent scene
  Shrouding her beauties in this lone retreat:
No more I hear her footsteps in the shade;   5
  Her *Image* only in these pleasant ways
  Meets me, self-wand'ring where in happier days
I held free converse with the fair-hair'd Maid!
I pass'd the little Cottage which she lov'd,—
  The cottage which did once my All contain: 10
  It spake of days that ne'er must come again,
Spake to my Heart, and much my Heart was mov'd:
  "Now fair befall thee, gentle Maid!"—said I,
  And from the Cottage turn'd me with a sigh!
                    CHARLES LAMB.

SONNET XIV.

On a Discovery made too late.

Thou bleedest, my poor HEART! and thy distress
  Reas'ning I ponder with a scornful smile
  And probe thy sore wound sternly, tho' the while
Swoln be mine eye and dim with heaviness.
Why didst thou listen to Hope's whisper bland?   5
  Or, list'ning, why forget the healing tale,
  When Jealousy with fev'rish fancies pale
Jarr'd thy fine fibres with a maniac's hand?
Faint was that HOPE, and rayless!—Yet 'twas fair
  And sooth'd with many a dream the hour of rest: 10
  Thou should'st have lov'd it most, when most opprest,
And nurs'd it with an agony of Care,
  Ev'n as a Mother her sweet infant heir,
  That wan and sickly droops upon her breast!
                 S. T. COLERIDGE.

---

line 2 "pathways shady-sweet," to "shady pathways sweet"; line 4 "the" to "this"; line 7 "better" to "happier"; line 8 "my" to "the".

  CL allowed all the changes to stand when the poem was reprinted in the STC–CL *Poems* (1797) 219, except that he restored "the" in line 4 and changed "that" to "which" in line 11. Thus improved, the 1797 version was included in CL *Works* (1818) I 62.

XIV=**83** *To my Own Heart.* C's poem had been written in Oct 1794 in response to a letter from Mary Evans, and had already been published in *Poems* (1796) under the title (in the list of contents) "*to my own heart*" (p 64). The *Sonnets* text introduces only one change of punctuation ("heir," for "heir" in line 13).

SONNET XV.

Hard by the road, where on that little mound
  The high grass rustles to the passing breeze,
  The child of Misery rests her head in peace.
Pause there in sadness: that unhallowed ground
Inshrines what once was ISABEL. Sleep on—   5
  Sleep on, poor Outcast! Lovely was thy cheek,
  And thy mild eye was eloquent to speak
The soul of Pity. Pale and woe-begone
Soon did thy fair cheek fade, and thine eye weep
  The tear of anguish for thy babe unborn,   10
  The wretched heir of Poverty and Scorn.
She drank the draught that chill'd her soul to sleep!
I pause, and wipe the big drop from mine eye—
Whilst the proud Levite scowls and passes by.
                ROBERT SOUTHEY.

SONNET XVI.

The NEGRO SLAVE.

Oh he is worn with toil! The big drops run
  Down his dark cheek! Hold—hold thy merciless hand
  Pale tyrant; for beneath thy hard command
O'erwearied Nature sinks. The scorching Sun,
As pityless as proud Prosperity,   5
  Darts on him his full beams: gasping he lies,
  Arraigning with his looks the patient skies,
While that inhuman Trader lifts on high
  The mangling scourge. Oh ye who at your ease
  Sip the blood-sweeten'd beverage! thoughts like these   10
Haply ye scorn: I thank thee, Gracious God!
  That I do feel upon my cheek the glow
Of indignation, when beneath the rod
  A sable brother writhes in silent woe.
                ROBERT SOUTHEY.

xv. C adapted the version printed in RS's *Poems* (Bristol 1797) 111, substituting "thy" for "the" in line 10 and "wretched" for "helpless" in line 11. He also made RS's punctuation somewhat more emphatic. RS ignored the changes when he reprinted the poem in *Poems* (2nd ed Bristol 1797) 123.

xvi. C's text was taken from that submitted for RS's *Poems* (Bristol 1797) 35—to which he added the title and made a few small changes of punctuation.

SONNET XVII.

Sweet Mercy! how my very heart has bled
   To see thee, poor OLD MAN! and thy grey hairs
   Hoar with the snowy blast; while no one cares
To cloathe thy shrivell'd limbs and palsied head.
My Father! throw away this tatter'd vest   5
   That mocks thy shiv'ring! take my garment—use
   A young man's arm! I'll melt these frozen dews
That hang from thy white beard and numb thy breast.
My SARA too shall tend thee, like a Child:
   And thou shalt talk, in our fire side's recess,   10
   Of purple Pride, that scowls on Wretchedness.—
He did not scowl, the GALILÆAN mild,
   Who met the Lazar turn'd from rich man's doors,
   And call'd him Friend, and wept upon his sores!
                    S. T. COLERIDGE.

SONNET XVIII.

Could then the babes from yon unshelter'd cot
   Implore thy passing charity in vain?
Too thoughtless Youth! what tho' thy happier lot
   Insult their life of poverty and pain!
What tho' their Maker doom'd them thus forlorn   5
   To brook the mockery of the taunting throng,
Beneath th' Oppressor's iron scourge to mourn,
   To mourn, but not to murmur at the wrong.
Yet when their last late evening shall decline,
   Their evening chearful, tho' their day distrest,   10
A Hope perhaps more heavenly-bright than thine,

XVII=88 *To an Old Man in the Snow.* The poem had already been published in *Poems* (1796), with the following differences of wording: line 7 "arms!"; line 12 "He did not so,"; line 13 "Lazars"; line 14 "And call'd them Friends, and heal'd their noisome Sores!". C referred to the poem in a letter to RS postmarked 11 Dec 1794 (*CL* I 134); here and in the Preface to the 1796 *Poems* (p xi) he acknowledged the help of Samuel Favell for a rough sketch and part of the first four lines (see vol II).

XVIII. C's source is Thomas Russell *Sonnets and Miscellaneous Poems* (Oxford 1789) 10. The original differs at two points: line 1 "Babes"; line 8 "his wrong!"

Russell's 1789 *Sonnets* were part of the collection of *Poetical Tracts* which C borrowed from the Bristol Library 2–10 Mar 1795 and 30 Dec 1795–28 Jan 1796 (*Bristol LB* Nos 38, 72).

A Grace by thee unsought, and unpossest,
A Faith more fix'd, a Rapture more divine
Shall gild their passage to eternal Rest.

                    THOMAS RUSSEL.

SONNET XIX.

Mild arch of promise! on the evening sky
    Thou shinest fair with many a lovely ray,
Each in the other melting. Much mine eye
    Delights to linger on thee, for the day,
Changeful and many-weather'd, seem'd to smile,   5
Flashing brief splendor thro' its clouds awhile
    That deepen'd dark anon and fell in rain.
But pleasant is it now to pause, and view
Thy various tints of frail and watry hue,
    And think the storm shall not return again.   10
Such is the smile that Piety bestows
    On the good man's pale cheek, when he in peace
Departing gently from a world of woes,
    Looks onward to the realm where sorrows cease.

                    ROBERT SOUTHEY.

SONNET XX.

Oh, She was almost speechless! nor could hold
    Awakening converse with me! (I shall bless
    No more the modulated tenderness
Of that dear voice!) Alas! 'twas shrunk and cold,
Her honour'd face! yet when I sought to speak,   5
    Thro' her half-open'd eye-lids she did send
    Faint looks, that said, "I would be yet thy friend!"

xix. The text derives from the copy submitted for RS *Poems* (Bristol 1797), where the poem appears on p 113. C amended the punctuation slightly, and substituted "Looks onward to" for "Anticipates" in the last line. He also dropped RS's title, *To the Evening Rainbow.*

RS did not adopt any of the emendations when the poem was reprinted in *Poems* (2nd ed Bristol 1797) 125.

xx. The poem is reprinted from Lloyd's *Poems on the Death of Priscilla Farmer* (1796) 16, which appeared at about the same time or very soon after C's pamphlet. C changed only some capitals and punctuation, and the poem was reprinted as in the original volume in the STC–Lloyd *Poems* (1797) 205.

And (O my choak'd breast!) e'en on that shrunk cheek
I saw one slow tear roll! My hand she took,
    Placing it on her heart: I heard her sigh,   10
    "Tis too, too much!" 'twas Love's last agony!
I tore me from her! 'twas her latest look,
    Her latest accents! O, my heart! retain
    That look, those accents, 'till we meet again!
                    CHARLES LLOYD.

SONNET XXI.

When from my dreary Home I first mov'd on
    After my Friend was in her grave-clothes drest,
    A dim despondence on my spirit press'd!
A low knell struck!—'twas friendship's latest tone!
Strange whispers parted from the entombing clay,   5
    The thin air murmur'd, each dumb object spake,
    Bidding my overwhelmed bosom ache!
Oft did I *look* to Heav'n, but could not pray!
"How shall I leave thee, quiet Scene?" said I,
    "How leave the passing breeze that loves to sweep   10
    "The holy sod where my due footsteps creep;—
"The passing breeze!—'Twas She!—The friend pass'd by!"
But the time came; the passing breeze I left!
"Farewell," I sigh'd—and seem'd of all bereft!
                    CHARLES LLOYD.

SONNET XXII.

In this tumultuous sphere, for thee unfit,
    How seldom art thou found, TRANQUILLITY!

XXI. The poem is taken from *Poems on the Death of Priscilla Farmer* (1796) 15. C rewrote line 4, where Lloyd had written "As all my pleasant days were come and gone!" The italic in line 8 is C's, and there are differences of punctuation and capitalisation.

Lloyd ignored these alterations when the poem was reprinted in the STC–Lloyd *Poems* (1797) 204; and Sophia Lloyd substituted the original reading of line 4 in her copy of *Sonnets* (1796), now at Cornell.

XXII. The poem was first printed as sonnet XLI *To Tranquillity* in Charlotte Smith's *Elegiac Sonnets* (5th enlarged ed 1789) 41; and thereafter without change in the sixth (1792) and seventh (1795) editions. C omitted the title, transposed lines 11 and 12, and made alterations to the punctuation and capitalisation.

Unless 'tis when with mild and downcast eye
By the low cradles thou delight'st to sit
Of sleeping infants—watching the soft breath   5
    And bidding the sweet slumberers easy lie;
Or sometimes hanging o'er the bed of death
    Where the poor languid sufferer—hopes to die!
Oh! beauteous Sister of the Halcyon Peace!
    I sure shall find thee in that heavenly scene   10
Where Hope alike and vain Regret shall cease,
Where Care and Anguish shall their power resign,
    And Memory lost in happiness serene,
Repeat no more, that Misery has been mine!
                CHARLOTTE SMITH.

SONNET XXIII.

I love thee, mournful sober-suited NIGHT!
    When the faint moon, yet lingering in her wane
And veil'd in clouds, with pale uncertain light
    Hangs o'er the waters of the restless main.
In deep depression sunk, the enfeebled mind   5
    Will to the deaf cold Elements complain,
    And tell the embosom'd grief however vain,
To sullen surges and the viewless wind.
Tho' no repose on thy dark breast I find,
    I still enjoy thee, cheerless as thou art;   10
    For in thy quiet gloom the exhausted heart
Is calm, tho' wretched; hopeless yet resign'd:
    While to the winds and waves its sorrows given
    May reach, tho' lost on earth, the ear of Heaven.
                CHARLOTTE SMITH.

XXIII. The poem is sonnet xxxix *To Night* in *Elegiac Sonnets* (5th enlarged ed 1789) 39 (identical in the sixth and seventh editions, 1792 and 1795). It had previously appeared (with some differences of punctuation) in Mrs Smith's novel *Emmeline: The Orphan of the Castle* (4 vols 1788) iv 147.

Apart from the omission of the title, C's text differs only in punctuation and capitals.

SONNET XXIV.

Lonely I sit upon the silent shore,
    Silent, save when against the rocky Bay
Breaks the dead Swell: the Moon soft-trembles o'er
    Ocean's broad, frownless front, with streamy ray,
    Borne in full many a dimpling wave away,   5
    Or strew'd in glittering points, and seen no more.
TRANQUILLITY has spread her raven plume
    Streak'd with faint grey, and shadowy blue, around;
    While SILENCE (catching the dull, frequent sound
Of yon dim sail whitening the distant gloom)   10
Lies in her cell abrupt, where howling SPRITE
    Starting terrific from his floating bier
Ne'er enters, nor the swart hags of the night
Who drink the sob of death with ruthless ear.
                                THOMAS DERMODY.

SONNET XXV.

Oh! I could laugh to hear the midnight wind
    That rushing on its way with careless sweep
    Scatters the Ocean waves—and I could weep,
Ev'n as a child! For now to my rapt mind
On wings of winds comes wild-ey'd Phantasy,   5
    And her dread visions give a rude delight!

XXIV. C's original was the second of four "*ORIGINAL SONNETS*". | By THOMAS DERMODY. | *Written in the 15th Year of his Age.*" pub *Anthologia Hibernica* (Dublin) I (Mar 1793) 225, which he borrowed from the Bristol Library 28 Mar–25 Apr 1796 (*Bristol LB* No 76). The original was twenty-four lines long, and the last eight lines were dropped (perhaps by accident) when the poem was reprinted in *The Watchman* IX (5 May 1796) (*CC*) 328. C rewrote and compressed lines 2–6 of Dermody's remaining sixteen lines to make the fourteen-line version here. Dermody's original is given in poem **141** headnote.

XXV. As CL protested (*LL*—M—20, 86), C considerably modified the original, which he had earlier acquired from CL, probably shortly before 11 Dec 1794 (*CL* I 136: to RS [11 Dec 1794]). C had begun to adapt it when he copied it into the Estlin Copy Book, probably in Apr 1795. The version here is the same as the one which appeared in *Poems* (1796) 57–8 over CL's initials, with one small typographical correction ("its" for "it's" in line 2). These earlier versions are collated, alongside CL's own text, in **104** *Adaptation of "Written at Midnight, by the Sea-side"* VAR.

O winged Bark! how swift along the night
Pass'd thy proud keel! Nor shall I let go by
Lightly of that drear hour the memory,
    When wet and chilly on thy deck I stood   10
    Unbonnetted, and gaz'd upon the flood,
And almost wish'd it were no crime to die!
    How Reason reel'd! What gloomy transports rose!
    Till the rude dashings rock'd them to repose.
CHARLES LAMB.

SONNET XXVI.

Thou whose stern spirit loves the awful storm
    That borne on Terror's desolating wings
    Shakes the deep forest, or remorseless flings
The shiver'd surge, if bitter griefs deform
Thy patient soul, O hie thee to the steep   5
    That beetles o'er the rude and raving tide,
    And when thou hear'st distress careering wide,
Think in a world of woe what thousands weep.
But if the kindred prospect fail to arm
    Thy peaceless breast, if Hope long since forgot   10
    Be fled like the wild blast that hears thee not,
Seek not in Nature's fairer scenes a charm;
    But shroud thee in the mantle of distress
    And tell thy poor heart—this is happiness!
W. L. BOWLES.

SONNET XXVII.

Ingratitude, how deadly is thy smart
    Proceeding from the form we fondly love!
    How light compar'd all other sorrows prove!

XXVI. C's source is sonnet XVII *In a Storm* in Bowles's *Sonnets* (2nd ed Bath 1789) 27. C expressed regret that Bowles subsequently omitted it (*CL* I 318: to W. L. Bowles [16 Mar 1797]). Besides altering punctuation and capitals, C made the following changes: line 1 "awful" (inserted); line 4 "when" to "if"; line 5 "peaceful breast" to "patient soul"; line 10 "patient" to "peaceless"; line 11 "which" to "that".

XXVII. C's text is taken from Anna Seward's *Llangollen Vale and Other Poems* (1796) 43. He lightened the original punctuation and changed some of the capitals.

Thou shed'st a night of woe, from whence depart
The gentle beams of Patience, that the Heart   5
   'Mid lesser ills illume—thy victims rove
   Unquiet as the ghost which haunts the grove
Where Murder spilt the life blood—Oh, thy dart
Kills more than life, e'en all that makes it dear!
   Till we "the sensible of pain" would change   10
For Frenzy that defies the bitter tear;
   Or wish in kindred callousness to range
Where moon-ey'd Idiocy with fallen lip
Drags the loose knee, and intermitting step!

ANNA SEWARD.

SONNET XXVIII.

To the Author of the "Robbers."

That fearful voice, a famish'd Father's cry,
   From the dark dungeon of the tower time-rent,
   If thro' the shudd'ring midnight I had sent
SCHILLER! that hour I would have wish'd to die—
That in no after moment aught less vast   5
   Might stamp me human! A triumphant shout
   Black HORROR scream'd and all her * *goblin* rout
From the more with'ring scene diminish'd past.
Ah! Bard tremendous in sublimity!
   Could I behold thee in thy loftier mood,   10
Wand'ring at eve with finely frenzied eye
   Beneath some vast old tempest-swinging wood!
   Awhile with mute awe gazing I would brood,
Then weep aloud in a wild extacy!

S. T. COLERIDGE.

* SCHILLER introduces no supernatural Beings.

XXVIII=**86** *To the Author of "The Robbers"*. The poem was probably written in Nov 1794 or soon afterwards, when C first read Schiller; and it had been printed in *Poems* (1796) 65. The *Sonnets* text rewrites the first four lines and contains other improvements, only a few of which were retained in subsequent printings: see poem **86** VAR.

In the copy C sent to the Thelwalls, now at the V&A (annex C 4.1), he deleted the comma after "time-rent" in line 2 and inserted a comma after "sent" in line 3. He also wrote at the foot of the page, following the sonnet: "I affirm, John Thelwall! that the six last lines of this Sonnet to Schiller are strong & fiery; and you are the only one who thinks otherwise.—There's a *spirit* of Author-like Vanity for you!—".

3. *POEMS* (1797)

There are several reasons for thinking that a second edition of C's poems was agreed upon even as the first was published. A letter written in early Apr 1796 contains the phrase "Two Editions would but barely repay you—" (*CL* I 201: to J. Cottle), and the way in which Cottle hurried C through the printing of *Religious Musings* in Feb–Mar might well have involved a promise of another edition. CL's letters from the end of May onwards include material of his own and revisions of C's which make sense only if another edition had been promised (*LL*—M—I 6–9, 45, 59–60, 62–3, etc), and in a letter of 9 Jun CL is explicit about the "*Editione secund:*" (*LL*—M—I 21). The fact that Cottle was able and willing to make up interleaved copies from unbound sheets (such copies make up BM Ashley 408 ff 5–35 and DCL MSS 28 and 30) again suggests that the plan for a new edition was an early one. However, such an agreement might be better termed an understanding, and it was not recalled until late Oct, when the first edition had sold out (*CL* VI 1005–7: to J. Cottle [18 Oct 1796?]; I 242–3: to TP 1 Nov 1796; 247: to B. Flower 2 Nov 1796; *LL*—M—I 62).

Another reason for believing that a second edition had been anticipated long before Oct is that C was at once ready with his plans. His aim was to be more selective and to put his juvenilia in a separate category at the end of the volume; he also intended to take in an expanded version of his contribution to *Joan of Arc* (poem **110**) at the beginning (*CL* I 275: to TP 13 Dec 1796). His instructions to Cottle on 6 Jan 1797 (*CL* I 297–300) are more elaborate, but essentially the same: the poems were to be numbered, not paginated; the offshoot from *Joan of Arc* (here called *The Progress of Liberty; or, The Visions of the Maid of Orleans*) was to begin the sequence, which was slightly expanded in its sonnets section and at the end; and CL's poems were to be explicitly included. C lists a number of emendations for the poems carried over from the first edition, and promises more copy to follow.

This promise included **101** *Religious Musings*, which C had elaborately revised on an interleaved copy, and which he eventually sent with the new sonnets (BM Ashley 408 ff 5–35; *CL* I 309: to J. Cottle [early Feb 1797]); **142** *Ode on the Departing Year*, which was set from the quarto pamphlet, revised according to his instructions (*CL* I 309 in part; *Two Letters* 313–14 in full), and which was brought forward to open the new volume when he found he could not finish *The Progress of Liberty*, the forerunner of **139** *The Destiny of Nations* (*Two Letters* 313); and drafts for the Prefaces, which are dated 27 Feb and 6 Mar (HUL fMS Eng 947.2). On 10 Mar C also instructed Cottle to include a selection of Charles Lloyd's poems (*CL* I 313), and he included a list with the *Ode* he returned on 15 Mar (*CL* I 315). The printing was not without its problems: the letter of 15 Mar asks for the *Ode* to be reset; C returned more proofs and enclosed further errata in early Apr (*CL* VI 1007–9); he was still promising further material from himself, CL, and Lloyd on 10 May (*CL* I 324); the dedicatory lines to GC were not written until 26 May (in place of the planned dedication to Bowles: *LL*—M—I 62); further errata followed on 8 Jun (*CL* I 325). The printing was completed during Jul—errata sent in late Jun and early Jul (*CL* I 329, 330–2) were not included (though Cottle was able to include an errata slip for Lloyd's poems: *C Bibl*—Wise—39)—although the exact date of publication remains elusive.

C's literary aims in the 1797 *Poems* are more ambitious and exact than in the volume it succeeds, despite accidents and distractions like the addition of Lloyd's poems and CL's. The principle of selection is more rigorously applied, and though printer's copy came from several manuscript and printed sources, it was carefully prepared and thoroughly revised in proof. The trouble which Cottle was prepared to take, in his turn, is reflected in the physical make-up of the completed volume, which incorporates several kinds of paper (see *C Bibl*—Wise—38–9; also Stephens 399–401). The same involvement is apparent in the number of copies C annotated, and in the the the extent and nature of his annotations. This is again very different from his annotation of copies of the first edition.

There is evidence in letters written by C and CL that plans for a joint volume with Charles Lloyd were afoot in Nov 1796 or thereabouts (cf *CL* I 285–6: to J. Thelwall 17 Dec [1796]; *LL*—M—I 73–5). Preparations appear to have reached the stage of collecting and cutting up already published poems (C's contribution to *Joan of Arc*=poem **110,** his newspaper poem on Burns=**133** *To a Friend Who had Declared his Intention of Writing No More Poetry*), and printing others in versions which have not survived (of **129** *Reflections on Having Left a Place of Retirement*, for one). Lloyd's *Sonnets on the Death of Priscilla Farmer* might have been intended for the collection, before or after they were published separately in 1796, and C's pamphlet anthology of *Sonnets from Various Authors* (No 2 above) also has something to do with the plan. Perhaps the pamphlet was published on the same wave of expectation which had to do with C's decision to leave Bristol for the Quantocks and another kind of life. The plans for a joint volume, apparently separate from his negotiations with Cottle and which were quickly and quietly overtaken, were probably dependent on Lloyd's promises and funds.

The relation of the 1797 *Poems* to the previous collection that never materialised is obscure and tangential. One would guess that Lloyd's poems were reintroduced in Mar 1797 because C knew from their earlier plan that they were available. The pamphlet was printed to be the same size as Bowles's 1796 *Sonnets* so that it could be bound with them, and it will be recalled that C at first intended to dedicate his new collection to Bowles (*LL*—M—I 62). The Preface to the *Sonnets* is taken forward to the 1797 collection, where the divisional title describes them as "attempted in the manner of" Bowles. It is not known whether Biggs and Cottle printed the 1796 pamphlet—no printer's name appears—so it is ironic that the paper on which the 200 copies were printed (wms "IP" and "1794") again became available in mid-Mar to print sigs D–Q of the *Poems*. For further consideration of these matters see the introduction to No 2 above.

PRELIMINARIES

Title-page: "POEMS, | BY | *S. T. COLERIDGE*, | SECOND EDITION. |
TO WHICH ARE NOW ADDED | POEMS | *By CHARLES LAMB,* | AND |
CHARLES LLOYD. | . . . | PRINTED BY N. BIGGS, | FOR J. COTTLE,
BRISTOL, AND MESSRS. | ROBINSONS, LONDON. | 1797."

The printer's copy that C sent to Cottle for the title-page is bound into Rugby
Manuscript f 1/pp 1–2. C wrote out the motto separately on the verso (p 2), and
it appears that he wanted it to be printed in the middle of the title-page verso.
As it turned out, it was printed on the title-page as follows:

> Duplex nobis vinculum, et amicitiæ et similium
> junctarumque Camœnarum; quod utinam neque mors
> solvat, neque temporis longinquitas!
> *Groscoll. Epist. ad Car. Utenhov. et Ptol. Lux. Tast.*

Tr "Double is the bond which binds us—friendship, and a kindred taste in
poetry. May neither death nor lapse of time dissolve it!" For C's comment on
how he invented the motto, "with references purposely obscure", see Cottle *Rem*
163–4. *PW* (EHC) II 1142 glosses the fictitious attribution as follows (which
in his ms directions to Cottle C emphasises should be printed on an unbroken
line):

> Carolus Utenhovius (Utenhove, or Uyttenhove) and Ptolomœus Luxius
> Tasteus were scholar friends of the Scottish poet and historian George
> Buchanan (1506–1582), who prefixes some Iambics "Carolo Utenhovio
> F.S." to his Hexameters "Franciscanus et Fratres". In some Elegiacs ad-
> dressed to Tasteus and Tevius, in which he complains of his sufferings
> from gout and kindred maladies, he tells them that Groscollius (Professor
> of Medicine at the University of Paris) was doctoring him with herbs and
> by suggestion:—"Et spe languentem consilioque juvat". Hence the three
> names. In another set of Iambics entitled "Mutuus Amor" in which he
> celebrates the alliance between Scotland and England he writes:—

> > Non mortis hoc propinquitas
> > Non temporis longinquitas
> > Solvet, fides quod nexuit
> > Intaminata vinculum.[12]

Hence the wording of the motto. Groscollius is, of course, a *mot à
double entente*. It is a name and a nickname.

It may be noted that C had borrowed Buchanan's poems during his last summer
at Cambridge (*Jesus LB* No 31).

---

[12] Tr "Neither the approach of death   bond which was tied by unsullied trust."
nor the lapse of time will loosen this

Divisional title: "𝕻𝖔𝖊𝖒𝖘, | *by* | 𝖘. 𝕿. 𝕮𝖔𝖑𝖊𝖗𝖎𝖉𝖌𝖊." followed by the Statius motto from the 1796 title-page (given in the introduction to No 1 above). However, from the printer's copy C sent to Cottle bound into Rugby Manuscript f 2/pp 5–6 it appears that C wanted the divisional title to follow the pattern of the title-page (as he originally conceived it), with the motto separately on the verso.

TABLE OF CONTENTS, PREFACES, ETC

The Contents appear on pp v–vi, the Preface to the First Edition on pp xiii–xvi (following the Dedication to GC = poem **150**), the Preface to the Second Edition on pp xvii–xx, the Introduction to the Sonnets on pp 71–4, and the Advertisement to the Supplement on pp 243–5.

CONTENTS.

4. The correct title, "Ode on the Departing Year", is given on pp 1, 5 ⁻**18.** PR pp 71–4 "Introduction to the Sonnets" is omitted from the contents

30. *Residence*] PR p 100 *Retirement*   **34.** 110] An error for 111   **42.** 364] An error for 264

35⁺. Lloyd's poems occupy pp 151–213. The contents describe **137** *Introducing Charles Lloyd's Poems on the Death of Priscilla Farmer* printed on p 193 simply as "Introductory Sonnet," (viz not as by C nor as newly collected).

CL's poems occupy pp 215–40.

42. The page-number is corrected to 264 in the copy given to William Roskilly (annex C 6.4). C's poem is missing from the list appended to the ms Advertisement (BM Ashley 408 f 4ʳ) and must have been added after 10 Mar 1797, when the list was sent (*CL* I 313: to J. Cottle).

42⁺. The Supplement continues with two poems by Lloyd and one by CL.

PREFACE

To the FIRST EDITION.

Compositions resembling those of the present volume are not unfrequently
condemned for their querulous Egotism. But Egotism is to be condemned
then only when it offends against Time and Place, as in an History or an
Epic Poem. To censure it in a Monody or Sonnet is almost as absurd as
to dislike a circle for being round. Why then write Sonnets or Monodies?   5
Because they give me pleasure when perhaps nothing else could. After the
more violent emotions of Sorrow, the mind demands amusement, and can
find it in employment alone; but full of its late sufferings, it can endure
no employment not in some measure connected with them. Forcibly to
turn away our attention to general subjects is a painful and most often an   10
unavailing effort:

> But O! how grateful to a wounded heart
> The tale of Misery to impart—
> From others' eyes bid artless sorrows flow,
> And raise esteem upon the base of Woe!   15
>   SHAW.

The communicativeness of our Nature leads us to describe our own sor-
rows; in the endeavour to describe them, intellectual activity is exerted;
and from intellectual activity there results a pleasure, which is gradually
associated, and mingles as a corrective, with the painful subject of the   20
description. "True!" (it may be answered) "but how are the PUBLIC in-

preface. The Preface is collated with the first (1796) edition = PR *1*; the holograph
version bound with the Rugby Manuscript (see EC) = MS 1   **title.** 1 Preface to the first
Edition. • *1* PREFACE.   ⁻**1.** *1* has an extra opening paragraph   **2.** *1* egotism.
But egotism   1 condenmmned   **3.** *1* time and place,   **7.** 1 Emotions
1 Sorrow   1 Mind   amusement,] *1* solace   **8.** *1* sufferings • 1 Sufferings   **9.** in
some . . . them.] *1* connected with those sufferings.   **10.** 1 Attention   general]
1 other general   1 &   most often] *1* 1 in general   **11.** 1 Effort;   **12.** *1* "But
O   1 Heart   **13.** *1* misery to impart;   **14.** *1* others   1 sorrow sorrows   *1* flow
15. *1* woe!"   **16.** SHAW.] Not in PR *1* • 1 Shaw.   **17.** The] PR *1* indents
1 nature   **17–18.** 1 Sorrows;   **18.** *1* endeavor   *1* 1 them   **19.** and from . . .
pleasure,] *1* and by a benevolent law of our nature from intellectual activity a pleasure
results • 1 & by a the benevolent law of our and from intellectual activity there results
a pleasure,   **20.** *1* associated   *1* corrective   **21.** *1* True! it • 1 True! (it
1 answered, but • 1 answered) but   how are] 1 are are

preface. See No 1 above for EC to
the version printed in 1796. Because
C redrafted much of the second half
of the Preface in 1797, he copied the
whole of it out again for Cottle on
leaves which are now bound with the
Rugby Manuscript (HRC MS (Cole-
ridge, S T) Works B) ff 5–6/pp 13–
15.

terested in your Sorrows or your Description?" We are for ever attributing personal Unities to imaginary Aggregates.—What is the PUBLIC, but a term for a number of scattered Individuals? Of whom as many will be interested in these sorrows, as have experienced the same or similar.   25

> "Holy be the lay
> Which mourning soothes the mourner on his way."

If I could judge of others by myself, I should not hesitate to affirm, that the most interesting passages in our most interesting Poems are those, in which the Author developes his own feelings. The sweet voice of *Cona   30 never sounds so sweetly, as when it speaks of itself; and I should almost suspect that man of an unkindly heart, who could read the opening of the third book of the Paradise Lost without peculiar emotion. By a law of our Nature, he, who labours under a strong feeling, is impelled to seek for sympathy; but a Poet's feelings are all strong.—Quicquid amet valde   35 amat.—Akenside therefore speaks with philosophical accuracy, when he classes Love and Poetry, as producing the same effects:

> "Love and the wish of Poets when their tongue
> Would teach to others' bosoms, what so charms
> Their own."   40
> PLEASURES OF IMAGINATION.

There is one species of Egotism which is truly disgusting; not that which leads us to communicate our feelings to others, but that which would reduce the feelings of others to an identity with our own. The Atheist, who exclaims, "pshaw!" when he glances his eye on the praises of Deity,   45 is an Egotist: an old man, when he speaks contemptuously of Love-verses, is an Egotist: and the sleek Favorites of Fortune are Egotists, when they condemn all "melancholy, discontented" verses. Surely, it would be candid

* Ossian.

---

22. *1* sorrows or your description?   **23.** *1* a personal unity *1* aggregates. •
1 Aggregates. *1* 1 PUBLIC   **24.** *1* individuals of • 1 Individuals, of? Of
25. *1* sorrows *1* similar? • 1 similar?.   **26.** *1* Lay, • 1 Lay   **27.** *1* way!"
28–41. If I . . . IMAGINATION.] not in *1*   **28.** 1 ~~may~~ could   **31.** 1 ⟨almost⟩
34. 1 Nature 1 strong.   **36.** 1 amat. 1 therefore ~~well & philosophically speaks of speaks well~~ with   **37.** 1 & 1 effects——:   **38.** 1 —Love 1 Tongue
40. 1 own.   **41.** 1 (Pleasures of Imag)   **42.** *1* egotism   **43.** 1 Feelings
45. *1* 1 exclaims 1 "pshaw"!   **46.** *1* 1 Egotist; 1 Man, *1* love-verses,
47. *1* 1 Egotist; the] *1* your *1* favorites   **48.** 1 con~~denm~~mn *1* 1 "melancholy
1 Surely [new paragraph]

36. Quicquid . . . amat] Tr "Whatever he loves, he loves passionately." C adapts what Caesar is reported to have said of Brutus, a saying that be- came proverbial: see e.g. Cicero *Ad Atticum* 14.1.2; Plutarch *Brutus* 6.
   38–40. *The Pleasures of the Imagination* (second version) 1.285–7.

not merely to ask whether the poem pleases ourselves, but to consider
whether or no there may not be others, to whom it is well-calculated to   50
give an innocent pleasure.

   I shall only add, that each of my readers will, I hope, remember, that
these Poems on various subjects, which he reads at one time and under
the influence of one set of feelings, were written at different times and
prompted by very different feelings; and therefore that the supposed infe-   55
riority of one Poem to another may sometimes be owing to the temper of
mind, in which he happens to peruse it.

S. T. C.

PREFACE

To the SECOND EDITION.

I return my acknowledgments to the different Reviewers for the assistance,
which they have afforded me, in detecting my poetic deficiencies. I have
endeavoured to avail myself of their remarks: one third of the former
Volume I have omitted, and the imperfections of the republished part must
be considered as errors of taste, not faults of carelessness. My poems have   5
been rightly charged with a profusion of double-epithets, and a general
turgidness. I have pruned the double-epithets with no sparing hand; and

49. *l* Poem   **50.** *l* others   **51⁺.** PR *l* concludes the Preface differently
52. 1 ⟨each of⟩ my readers̷   **54–5.** 1 & prompted   **57.** 1 he ⟨happens to⟩ peruseṣ̷
preface. For the text of the first draft see the appendix below. The ms for the first
two paragraphs as printed here (=MS 1), headed "Preface to the second Edition." and
signed "S. T. Coleridge | Stowey, Somersetshire.", is in a letter to Cottle which Cottle
endorsed 6 Mar 1797 (HUL fMS Eng 947.2; cf *CL* I 312–14: to J. Cottle [10 Mar
1797]). The letter includes a cancelled beginning to the Preface, not collated here. The
ms for the last paragraph as printed here (=MS 2), headed "Advertisement." and signed
"S. T. Coleridge | Stowey, | May, 1797.", is bound into the Rugby Manuscript (HRC
MS (Coleridge, S T) Works B) f 3/pp 7–8   **3–4.** 1 ⟨Volume⟩   **4.** 1 the ~~reprinting;~~
republished part   **5.** 1 considered ~~in general~~ as

6. double-epithets] C alludes to the
anonymous reviews in *English Re-
view* XXVIII (Aug 1796) 172–5; *Crit-
ical Review* XVII (Jun 1796) 209–12;
Analytical Review XXIII (Jun 1796)
610–12. He appears to have been
sensitive to the criticism before they
were published (*CL* I 207: to TP 5
May 1796), and he remained particu-
larly aware of the same feature of
style for a long time thereafter. See
Lects 1808–1819 (*CC*) I 304; *CM*
(*CC*) II 865, 1119; *BL* ch 1 (*CC*) I
6–7. The reviews of the 1796 volume
had in general been more encouraging
than this reference suggests, and the
second preface in fact addresses is-
sues raised in letters by CL, his most
attentive and intelligent critic: "Culti-
vate simplicity, Coleridge, or rather,
I should say, banish elaborateness"
(*LL*—M—I 60).

used my best efforts to tame the swell and glitter both of thought and diction. This latter fault however had insinuated itself into my Religious Musings with such intricacy of union, that sometimes I have omitted to   10 disentangle the weed from the fear of snapping the flower. A third and heavier accusation has been brought against me, that of obscurity; but not, I think, with equal justice. An Author is obscure, when his conceptions are dim and imperfect, and his language incorrect, or unappropriate, or involved. A poem that abounds in allusions, like the Bard of Gray, or   15 one that impersonates high and abstract truths, like Collins's Ode on the poetical character; claims not to be popular—but should be acquitted of obscurity. The deficiency is in the Reader. But this is a charge which every poet, whose imagination is warm and rapid, must expect from his *contemporaries*. Milton did not escape it; and it was adduced with virulence   20 against Gray and Collins. We now hear no more of it; not that their poems are better understood at present, than they were at their first publication; but their fame is established; and a critic would accuse himself of frigidity or inattention, who should profess not to understand them. But a living writer is yet sub judice; and if we cannot follow his conceptions or enter   25 into his feelings, it is more consoling to our pride to consider him as lost beneath, than as soaring above, us. If any man expect from my poems the same easiness of style which he admires in a drinking-song, for him I have not written. Intelligibilia, non intellectum adfero.

    I expect neither profit or general fame by my writings; and I consider   30 myself as having been amply repaid without either. Poetry has been to me its own "exceeding great reward:" it has soothed my afflictions, it has multiplied and refined my enjoyments; it has endeared solitude; and it has given me the habit of wishing to discover the Good and the Beautiful in all that meets and surrounds me.   35

8. 1 swell & glitter ~~of that~~ both of thought & ~~language.~~ diction.   **9.** 1 [?]into
10. 1 have ~~found it impossible~~ omitted   **11.** 1 weed ~~for~~ from   1 third &
13. 1 Justice.   **15.** 1 Poem,   **15–16.** 1 Gray; or one, that ~~conveys~~   **16.** 1 high
&   1 Collin*l*s's   **17.** 1 popular;   **18.** 1 Obscurity.   1 is ~~not~~ in the ~~author, *W*~~ not
Reader. ~~I But however unjustly, the charge *I* I will always be advanced against every *W* poet, whose imagination is warm & rapid~~ But   1 charge,   **21.** 1 Greyay   1 ~~now~~
now   1 Poems   **22.** 1 understood ~~now~~ at present,   **25.** 1 his ~~feelings~~ conceptions
26. 1 his ~~fellow~~ feelings,   **27.** 1 from ~~my odes~~ my poems   **31–2.** 1 been its
33. 1 ~~an~~ it has endeared   1 and ~~above all~~ it   **34.** 1 Good &   **35.** 1 meets &

29. Intelligibilia . . . adfero.] Tr "I offer things that are capable of being understood, not a thing [straightforwardly] understood." Not a classical source, apparently; perhaps one of the Church Fathers, or C's own.
32. "exceeding great reward"] Gen 15.1, although, as EHC pointed out (*PW* II 1146n), C might have been prompted to make the allusion by the lines on Gray in T. J. Mathias *The Pursuits of Literature* (4 pts 1794–7) dialogue 1.50, 55–6.

There were inserted in my former Edition, a few Sonnets of my Friend and old School-fellow, CHARLES LAMB. He has now communicated to me a complete Collection of all his Poems; quæ qui non prorsus amet, illum omnes et Virtutes et Veneres odere. My friend, CHARLES LLOYD, has likewise joined me; and has contributed every poem of his, which   40
he deemed worthy of preservation. With respect to my own share of the Volume, I have omitted a third of the former Edition, and added almost an equal number. The Poems thus added are marked in the Contents by Italics.

STOWEY,   S. T. C.
May, 1797.

INTRODUCTION TO THE SONNETS.

The composition of the Sonnet has been regulated by Boileau in his Art of Poetry, and since Boileau, by William Preston, in the elegant preface to his Amatory Poems: the rules, which they would establish, are founded

36. 2 Edition   **37.** 2 Schoolfellow,   **37–8.** 2 to ⟨me⟩   **38.** 2 collection
2 poems;   **39.** PR odore   **41.** 2 preservation.—   **41–2.** 2 this Volume,
42. 2 omitted ~~nearly~~ a third   **43–4.** The Poems . . . Italics.] 2 ~~The poems which appeared first in this Edition, are printed~~ The poems thus added are marked in the Contents ~~in~~ by Italics.—~~As neither of us three were present to correct the Press, and as my hand-writing is not eminently distinguished for neatness or legibility, the Printer has made a few mistakes. The Reader will consult equally his own conscience, and our credit, if before he peruses the volume, he will scan the table of Errata, and make the desired Alterations.~~   **introduction.** The Preface to No 2 above, *Sonnets from Various Authors* (1796), is collated here as PR *1*. The Introduction is preceded by a divisional title on p 69: "$onnets, I *ATTEMPTED IN THE MANNER* I OF THE I REV. W. L. BOWLES. I *Non ita certandi cupidus, quam propter amorem* I *Quod te IMITARI aveo.* I *LUCRET*."; there is no equivalent title in PR *1*   ⁻**1.** PR *1* has an extra opening paragraph

39. odere] In RS's copy, now at Yale (annex C 6.10), among notes and corrections made between 1808 and 1810 C corrected the misprint "odore" to "odere" and added the following translation and comment: "which whoever does not entirely love, *him* all the Virtues and Graces hate. N.B. This passage was referred to by the Edinburgh Reviewer as occasioning his infamously malignant Review of C. Lamb's Tragedy—a work written several years after his Poems." C's reference is to the attack on CL's *John Woodvil* by Thomas Brown in *Ed Rev* II (1803) 90–6 (cf RS's annoyance at the same review, *SL*—Curry—I 315–16).

introduction. The motto in the divisional title (see TN) is from Lucretius *De rerum natura* 3.5–6 tr Rouse and Smith (LCL) 189 "Not so much desiring to be your rival, as for love, because I yearn to copy you."

1 et seq. See No 2 above for EC to the version printed in 1796.

on the practice of Petrarch. I have never yet been able to discover either
sense, nature, or poetic fancy in Petrarch's poems; they appear to me all   5
one cold glitter of heavy conceits and metaphysical abstractions. However,
Petrarch, although not the inventor of the Sonnet, was the first who made it
popular; and his countrymen have taken *his* poems as the model. Charlotte
Smith and Bowles are they who first made the Sonnet popular among the
present English: I am justified therefore by analogy in deducing its laws   10
from *their* compositions.

    The Sonnet then is a small poem, in which some lonely feeling is de-
veloped. It is limited to a *particular* number of lines, in order that the
reader's mind having expected the close at the place in which he finds it,
may rest satisfied; and that so the poem may acquire, as it were, a *Total-*   15
ity,—in plainer phrase, may become a *Whole.* It is confined to fourteen
lines, because as some particular number is necessary, and that particular
number must be a small one, it may as well be fourteen as any other num-
ber. When no reason can be adduced against a thing, Custom is a sufficient
reason for it. Perhaps, if the Sonnet were comprized in less than fourteen   20
lines, it would become a serious Epigram; if it extended to more, it would
encroach on the province of the Elegy. Poems, in which no lonely feel-
ing is developed, are not Sonnets because the Author has chosen to write
them in fourteen lines: they should rather be entitled Odes, or Songs, or
Inscriptions. The greater part of Warton's Sonnets are severe and masterly   25
likenesses of the style of the Greek ἐπιγράμματα.

    In a Sonnet then we require a developement of some lonely feeling,
by whatever cause it may have been excited; but those Sonnets appear to
me the most exquisite, in which moral Sentiments, Affections, or Feel-
ings, are deduced from, and associated with, the scenery of Nature. Such   30
compositions generate a habit of thought highly favourable to delicacy of
character. They create a sweet and indissoluble union between the intellec-
tual and the material world. Easily remembered from their briefness, and
interesting alike to the eye and the affections, these are the poems which
we can "lay up in our heart, and our soul," and repeat them "when we walk   35
by the way, and when we lie down, and when we rise up." Hence, the Son-
nets of BOWLES derive their marked superiority over all other Sonnets;
hence they domesticate with the heart, and become, as it were, a part of
our identity.

    Respecting the metre of a Sonnet, the Writer should consult his own   40
convenience.—Rhymes, many or few, or no rhymes at all—whatever the
chastity of his ear may prefer, whatever the rapid expression of his feelings
will permit;—all these things are left at his own disposal. A sameness
in the final sound of its words is the great and grevious defect of the
Italian language. That rule therefore, which the Italians have established,   45

8. *1 his* countrymen   *1* his poems   **22.** Elegy. Poems,] *1* Elegy. On this however we
lay no stress. Poems,   **36.** *1* down

of exactly *four* different sounds in the Sonnet, seems to have arisen from
their wish to have *as many*, not from any dread of finding *more*. But
surely it is ridiculous to make the *defect* of a foreign language a reason for
our not availing ourselves of one of the marked excellencies of our own.
"The Sonnet (says Preston) will ever be cultivated by those who write   50
on tender pathetic subjects. It is peculiarly adapted to the state of a man
violently agitated by a real passion, and wanting composure and vigor of
mind to methodize his thought. It is fitted to express a momentary burst of
passion," &c. Now, if there be one species of composition more difficult
and artificial than another, it is an English Sonnet on the Italian Model.   55
Adapted to the agitations of a real passion! Express momentary bursts of
feeling in it! I should sooner expect to write pathetic *Axes* or *pour forth
extempore Eggs and Altars*! But the best confutation of such idle rules is to
be found in the Sonnets of those who have observed them, in their inverted
sentences, their quaint phrases, and incongruous mixture of obsolete and   60
spenserian words: and when, at last, the thing is toiled and hammered into
fit shape, it is in general racked and tortured Prose rather than any thing
resembling Poetry.

    The Sonnet has been ever a favorite species of composition with me;
but I am conscious that I have not succeeded in it. From a large number I   65
have retained ten only, as not beneath mediocrity. Whatever more is said
of them, ponamus lucro.

S. T. COLERIDGE

ADVERTISEMENT.

I have excepted the following Poems from those, which I had determined
to omit. Some intelligent friends particularly requested it, observing, that
what most delighted me when I was "young in *writing* poetry, would
probably best please those, who are young in *reading* poetry: and a man
must learn to be *pleased* with a subject, before he can yield that attention   5
to it, which is requisite in order to acquire a just taste." I however was fully
convinced, that he, who gives to the press what he does not thoroughly ap-

---

54. *1* Passion,"   **55.** *1* model.   **58.** *1 Altars!*   **63⁺.** PR *1* has a different
conclusion   **67⁺.** *1* EDITOR.   **advertisement.** Printer's copy was supplied by
BM Ashley 408 ff 1–4, collated here as MS 1; the Advertisement is preceded in PR by a
divisional title "S̶u̶p̶p̶l̶e̶m̶e̶n̶t̶." (p 241)   ⁻**1.** 1 ADVERTISEMENT.   **3.** 1 what
⟨most⟩ 1 me,   **5.** 1 can g̶i̶v̶e̶ yield   **7.** 1 Press

67. ponamus lucro] Tr "Let us count as profit."

advertisement. BM Ashley 408 f 1ʳ begins with an instruction from C to Cottle: "N.B. To be placed before I the poems which I have I retained." It ends (f 4ʳ) with a list of the poems to be included in the Supplement.

prove in his own closet, commits an act of disrespect, both against himself
and his fellow-citizens. The request and the reasoning would not therefore
have influenced me, had they not been assisted by other motives. The first   10
in order of these verses, which I have thus endeavoured to *reprieve* from
immediate oblivion, was originally addressed "To the Author of Poems
published anonymously, at Bristol." A second edition of these poems has
lately appeared with the Author's name prefixed: and I could not refuse
myself the gratification of seeing the name of that man among my poems,   15
without whose kindness, they would probably have remained unpublished;
and to whom I know myself greatly and variously obliged, as a Poet, a
Man, and a Christian.

The second is entitled "an Effusion on an Autumnal Evening; written in
early youth." In a note to this poem I had asserted, that the tale of Florio   20
in Mr. Roger's "Pleasures of Memory," was to be found in the Lochleven
of Bruce. I did (and still do) perceive a certain likeness between the two
stories; but certainly not a sufficient one to justify my assertion. I feel
it my duty therefore, to apologize to the Author and the Public, for this
rashness; and my sense of honesty would not have been satisfied by the   25
bare omission of the note. No one can see more clearly the *littleness* and
futility of imagining plagiarisms in the works of men of Genius; but *nemo
omnibus horis sapit*; and my mind, at the time of writing that note, was
sick and sore with anxiety, and weakened through much suffering. I have
not the most distant knowledge of Mr. Rogers, except as a correct and   30
elegant Poet. If any of my readers should know him personally, they would
oblige me by informing him that I have expiated a sentence of unfounded
detraction, by an unsolicited and self-originating apology.

Having from these motives re-admitted two, and those the longest of the
poems I had omitted, I yielded a passport to the three others, which were   35
recommended by the greatest number of votes. There are some lines too of
Lloyd's and Lamb's in this appendix. They had been omitted in the former

---

8. 1 disrespect ~~on~~ both   **9.** 1 request &   **10.** 1 motives.—   **11.** 1 Verses,
12. 1 ⟨oblivion,⟩   **13.** 1 Edition   **15.** 1 ⟨of seeing⟩   **16.** 1 kindness
17. 1 greatly &   **17–18.** 1 poet, a man,   **18–19.** Christian. | The] 1 Christian.—
The [no new paragraph]   **19.** 1 Evening,   **20.** 1 Tale   **21.** 1 Mr Rogers's
1 Memory"   **21–2.** 1 Loch leven ⟨of Bruce.⟩   **23.** 1 ⟨one⟩   **24.** 1 Duty therefore
1 & the Public   **26.** 1 ~~clearness~~ ⟨than myself⟩ the   1 &   **27.** 1 ~~the~~ the works
27–8. 1 nemo omnibus horis sapit,   **29.** 1 sick &   1 thro'   **30.** 1 ~~knowlege~~
distant knowledge   1 Mr   1 correct &   **32.** 1 inform~~er~~ing   **33.** 1 detraction by
a⟨n⟩ ~~senten~~   1 &   **34.** 1 ~~retained~~ readmitted   1 & those   **35.** 1 poems,   1 I ~~gave~~
~~a~~ yielded   1 which ~~had~~ were   **36.** 1 votes.—   1 Lines   **37.** 1 & Lambs

---

19 et seq. C's apology to Samuel
Rogers was probably prompted by
CL: see *LL* (M) I 98. His curious
and misleading acknowledgment of

his debt to Rogers is glossed in **60**
Absence: A Poem headnote.
  27–8. *nemo omnibus horis sapit*]
Tr "no one is wise at all times".

part of the volume, partly by accident; but I have reason to believe that the Authors regard them, as of inferior merit; and they are therefore rightly placed, where they will receive some beauty from their vicinity to others 40 much worse.

Appendix: First Draft of the Preface to the Second Edition

HUL fMS Eng 947.2. 2 conjoint leaves, each 20.0×25.0 cm; wm (partially obscured) large crown (in part); chain-lines 2.6 cm. f 2ᵛ blank (both leaves pasted into album). First draft, including corrections in C's hand in ink and pencil, and endorsements and corrections by Cottle.

Preface to the second Edition

I have endeavoured to avail myself of the various censures, which have been pass'd on these poems. I have omitted nearly one third, as not worth the toil of correction; and the imperfections of ~~those that I have suffered~~ the remaining part are errors of Judgment, not faults of carelessness; except indeed where the weed had climbed and *crept* around the flower 5 with such *intricacy* of union, that I could not disentangle the one without ~~snapping the~~ or hazard of snapping the other.—The blemishes, which with more or less asperity of criticism I have been imputed to my compositions, may, I believe, be reduced under three heads: the profusion of double-epithets, the turgidity both of thought and language, and their obscurity. 10 To the two former I plead guilty: the double epithets I have pruned with no sparing hand, and have endeavoured ⟨to tame⟩ the swell and glitter of diction, as much as was ~~possible~~ in my power. The⟨y⟩se were such faults as ~~were to be~~ might be expected from a young man; especially from one who had formed his opinions of poetic excellence in other schools than those 15 of Pope and Goldsmith.—Obscurity is an heavier charge; and I am not ~~equally~~ convinced, that it has been ~~justly~~ alledged ~~against my poetry~~ with equal Justice.—Obscurity consists either in dim & imperfect conceptions, ~~in~~ or in incorrect or involved phraseology. ~~Allusions to circumstances not generally known, is not~~ But a poem is not obscure, because it abounds in 20 allusions, like the Bard of Gray; nor because it exhibits ⟨those⟩ rapid transitions, and high abstractions of Fancy, which we discover in the poetry of Collins and Milton. Such poetry will indeed often appear obscure; but the deficiency is in the reader, not in the poem. "A Reader of Milton ⟨(observes an acute Critic)⟩ must be always on his duty: he is surrounded with 25 sense; it rises in every line; every word is to the purpose. There are no lazy intervals: all has been considered & demands and merits consideration. If

38. 1 volume 1 believe, **39.** 1 merit: & 1 are ~~they~~ are therefore
41. 1 worse.—

this be called obscurity, let it be remembered, it is such an one as is com-
plaisant to the Reader."—~~The truth~~ Every writer, however, whose works
are distinguished by originality of thinking, and loftiness of imagery, must   30
expect this charge from his *contemporaries*. It was adduced with virulence
against the Odes of Gray & Collins~~; but i~~. It has died away.~~N:~~ not that they
are better understood now, than they were at their first appearance; but the
man, who does not understand them, is ashamed to confess it, because he
suspects that his own ~~competency~~ powers of comprehension will be called   35
in question. But we think & speak of living writers as our equals, and when
we do not feel or understand their compositions, it is more consoling to
our pride to consider them, as lost below than as soaring above, us. If there
be any one who expects in an Ode the same easy style which he admires in
a song or satire, for him I have not written. ~~If I wished to gained money or~~   40
~~fame by the exertion of~~ ~~my poetic talent, I am not so ignorant of~~ ~~mankind~~
~~as not to know~~
     I ~~neither~~ do not expect profit or general fame ~~by~~ from my poetry; ~~but~~
& I consider myself as ⟨having been⟩ repayed without ~~either~~ them. Poetry
~~is~~ has been it's "own exceeding great reward"; it has soothed ~~severe~~ my   45
afflictions, it has increased my pleasures, it has taught me to love soli-
tude, and above all, it has given me the habit of wishing ⟨to discover⟩ the
beautiful & the good in all that meets & surrounds me.
     Stowey, ~~near Somerset~~ near Bridgwater Somerset.
     Feb. 27th, 1797   50

4. *POEMS* (1803)

C probably had an arrangement with Cottle to publish a third edition of his
poems when the second was exhausted, similar to the arrangement which must
have existed with respect to the first; perhaps "understanding" would be a better
word. C raised the question of a third edition on 18 Feb 1798 (*CL* I 387) and
began to discuss its composition in the weeks that followed (*CL* I 390–1, 399:
[7 Mar, c 13 Mar 1798]). Lloyd's poems, at Lloyd's prompting, were to be
dropped; *The Maid of Orleans* (=poem **110**) and three poems in blank verse
were to open the collection; other poems were to be dropped; **101** *Religious
Musings* was to be revised and lengthened. Juvenile poems comprising **64** *Songs
of the Pixies*, **82** *Monody on the Death of Chatterton*, and some dozen others
were to be printed at the end in a separately entitled section, but if Cottle could
wait C's preference was to replace nearly half of the 1797 volume with new
poems—presumably those he was writing in the productive spring of 1798. In
the event, Cottle published *LB* instead, while C went to Germany and never
returned to live permanently in the vicinity of Bristol. Preparations for a third
edition were not renewed until several years later, in different circumstances,
with another publisher. They appear to have been made in the spring of 1803,

when C was in London, with Longman, who had published the Bristol issue and subsequent editions of *LB* and the translations of Schiller's plays. But C left London for the North early in Apr, after making his will and in very depressed spirits, and the work of seeing the volume through the press devolved on to CL.

CL set out his role very clearly in two letters written to C while the volume was in the press, during late May 1803 (*LL*—M—II 110–12, 113–14). He placed the Preface(s) first, instead of having them acting as a barrier between the Dedication and the first poem, and thereafter set C's poems in order of composition. His own and Charles Lloyd's poems were omitted, and he moved **142** *Ode on the Departing Year* from the beginning to the penultimate position, before **101** *Religious Musings*. Despite his awareness of C's inclination to exclude a good many early poems, he took it on himself to omit only a few: "For my part I had rather all the juvenilia were kept memoriæ causa" (*LL*—M—II 111).[13] CL altered the title of **57** *Cupid Turn'd Chymist*, but was otherwise scrupulous in preserving C's text and amending it only with authority. "I am aware of the nicety of changing even so mere a trifle as a title to so short a piece, & subverting old associations, but *Two* called '*Kisses*' would have been absolutely ludicrous, & 'effusion' is no name, & these poems come close together.—I promise you not to alter *one* word in any poem whatsoever, but to take your last text, where two are" (*LL*—M—II 111). He promised to be C's factotum, "next to a *fac* nihil; at most a fac simile" (*LL*—M—II 114).[14]

A second volume of the new poems had been projected from the beginning, in 1798 (*CL* I 387: to J. Cottle 18 Feb 1798), and was intended again in 1803 (*LL*—M—II 114). But C's spirits were so low at the later time that plans for the second volume were abandoned by early Jun (*CL* II 950: to W. Godwin 10 Jun 1803). In this respect the 1803 collection was out of date when it appeared: it takes no cognisance of what C had written in the intervening five years since 1797. But it also, for the same reason, possesses a kind of retrospective authority. CL, acting on C's behalf, was not tempted to develop existing poems in new directions or to rewrite while the volume was in the press. He had been closely involved with C in the evolution of the second edition from the first, and apparently in the evolution of the texts beyond the second edition. His readings in 1803 possess authority of a kind that C's intervention at that stage would even have undermined. The 1803 text of **101** *Religious Musings*, for instance, incorporates the errata C sent to Cottle too late to be included in 1797 and other errata copied into presentation copies; the sonnet **95** *To Bowles* follows the 1797 readings, while **70** *Lines on the "Man of Ross"* goes back to 1796;

---

[13] Four poems from the 1796 collection are excluded: *To the Rev. W. J. H.* (=poem **109**); *Effusion 8, to Kosciusco* (=poem **93**); *Epistle 3, written after a Walk* (=poem **49**); *Epistle 5, from a Young Lady* (=poem **119**). Two poems from the 1797 collection are omitted: C's introductory sonnet to Charles Lloyd's *Poems on the Death of Priscilla Farmer* (=poem **137**); *On the Christening of a Friend's Child* (=poem **147**). The first of these is not listed in the 1797 Contents, so that its omission in 1803 may be an oversight.

[14] Tr ". . . do all; *do* nothing . . . do like".

other texts—e.g. **142** *Ode on the Departing Year*, the sonnet **103** *Adaptation of "Pale Roamer thro' the Night!"*—are unique and yet supported by others in several of their particulars.

Only two copies of the 1803 collection are known to have been annotated by C, and he appears not to have preserved one for himself. When he annotated RS's copy of the 1797 volume (now at Yale: In 678 797 Copy 1), perhaps at the time when he was again working on a projected two-volume collection for Longman in Apr 1809, he remarked of *Adaptation of "Pale Roamer thro' the Night!"*: "This Sonnet is much improved in the third Edition, but I cannot re-collect the alterations" (p 82). Thus, when later collections were put together in 1828 and afterwards, the peculiar authority of the 1803 volume was overlooked. Though its scope does not represent C's ambitions or achievement at the time it was published—being both unselective and curtailed—its texts rest on an intelligent winnowing of volatile possibilities. The variations in the Prefaces and the Introduction to the Sonnets are characteristically precise improvements, even if they are minor. The volume was printed by Nathaniel Biggs, who had printed *Poems* (1796), perhaps *Sonnets from Various Authors*, certainly *The Watchman*, *Poems* (1797), and *LB* (1798), all in Bristol, and after his move to London *Wallenstein* as well as later editions of *LB*—the last two titles already for Longman. The continuity of Biggs's experience must add to the authority of the volume. There is not a change of printing styles as there is, for instance, between the 1828 and 1834 *PW* volumes.

PRELIMINARIES

Title-page. The title-page uses the same wording as the 1797 divisional title: "𝔓𝔬𝔢𝔪𝔰, | BY | S. T. COLERIDGE. | [motto from Statius between paired rules]", adding: "THIRD EDITION. | LONDON: | Printed by N. Biggs, Crane-court, Fleet-street, | FOR T. N. LONGMAN AND O. REES, PATER- | NOSTER-ROW. | [rule] | 1803." Wise *C Bibl* 64 claims that the title-page (sig A1) is a cancel-leaf pasted in on a stub, but this is not the case in all copies and no example of a cancelled title has been discovered.

Contents. The Contents list is given on pp iii–iv, before the verse Dedication to GC (=poem **150**):

CONTENTS.

	1796	1797	*CC*
Preface	v	v	v
Dedication	1	—	vii	**150**
Songs of the Pixies| 11	15	29	**64**

The Rose	19	80	41	**56**
Kisses	21	78	260	**57** 5
To Sara	23	82	43	**76**
The Sigh	25	89	49	**75**
Genevieve	27	62	—	**17**
Absence, a Farewell Ode	29	40	—	**39**
Lines to a beautiful Spring	31	28	54	**74** 10
Written in Early Youth	34	101	249	**60**
To a young Lady	42	36	61	**81**
Imitated from Ossian	46	84	—	**55**
The Complaint of Ninathoma	49	86	—	**51**
Imitated from the Welch	51	88	—	**73** 15
To a young Ass	52	91	45	**84**
To an Infant	55	94	262	**105**
Epitaph on an Infant	57	31	51	**77**(a)
Domestic Peace	58	77	48	**66**
Lines on the Man of Ross	60	26	52	**70** 20
To a Friend, with an unfinished Poem	62	68	65	**100**
Lines on a Friend who died of a frenzy fever, induced by calumnious reports	65	32	57	**85**
Monody on Chatterton	71	1	17	**82**

SONNETS

Introduction	81	—	71	25
Sonnet 1,	85	45	75	**95**
2,	86	64	76	**83**
3,	87	59	77	**87**
4,	88	—	78	**140**
5,	89	61	81	**88** 30
6,	90	60	82	**103**
7,	91	46	—	**90**
8,	92	47	—	**94**
9,	93	48	—	**91**
10,	94	49	—	**89** 35
11,	95	50	—	**99**
12,	97	51	224	**96**
13,	98	53	—	**92**
14,	99	66	79	**108**
15,	101	65	83	**86** 40
16,	103	54	—	**102**

37. CL included Sonnet 12, *"As when a child on some long winter's night"*, as if it were C's, even though it is signed "C. L." in 1796 and appears in the section of CL poems in 1797. The mixed authorship is discussed in **96** *To Mrs Siddons* headnote.

17,	104	—	85	**135**
18,	106	63	—	**61**
19,	107	—	87	**136**
To the Nightingale	109	71	—	**112**	45
In the Manner of Spencer	111	73	256	**111**
To the Author of Poems, &c.	115	125	246	**117**
Ode to Sara	119	111	88	**116**
To a Friend	126	119	—	**68**
Composed at Clevedon	129	96	96	**115**	50
Reflections, &c.	133	—	100	**129**
To an unfortunate Woman	138	—	105	**149**
Lines on a Blossom	140	—	107	**124**
The Hour when we shall meet again	143	—	109	**123**
To a Friend, on his proposing to domesti-					55
cate with the Author	145	—	111	**138**
Ode on the Departing Year	153	—	1	**142**
Religious Musings	171	135	117	**101**

Prefaces. The 1803 volume pp v–xi reprints the 1796–7 Prefaces (given in Nos 1 and 3 above) as they appeared in 1797. Only the first is headed *"PREFACE."* in 1803, and only the first is signed ("S. T. C."); they are separated simply by rules. There are some variations from the 1797 texts:

preface to the first edition. 1797 **11** (also 1796). effort:] 1803 effort.   1797 **24** (also 1796). scattered Individuals?] 1803 scatter'd individuals?   1797 **29.** those,] 1803 those   1797 **37.** accuracy,] 1803 accuracy

preface to the second edition. 1797 **1–5.** I return . . . carelessness.] Not in 1803 1797 **17.** character;] 1803 character,   1797 **36–44.** Not in 1803

Introduction to the Sonnets. The sonnets have a separate divisional title, simply "Sonnets." There is no reference to Bowles and the motto from Lucretius is omitted (see No 3 above). The Introduction follows on pp 81–4, headed *"INTRODUCTION TO THE SONNETS."*, and is not signed. The text follows that of 1797, with the following variations:

1797 **4–5.** to discover either sense,] 1803 to discover sense,   1797 **30.** the scenery of Nature.] 1803 the Scenery of Nature.   1797 **31.** a habit of thought] 1803 a kind of thought   1797 **36.** when we rise up."] 1803 when we rise up".   1797 **58.** *Eggs and Altars!*] 1803 *Eggs and Altars!*   1797 **61.** spenserian] 1803 Spenserian   1797 **66.** retained . . . not] 1803 retained such only as seemed not 1797 **67.** ponamus lucro.] 1803 *ponamus lucro.*

5. *SIBYLLINE LEAVES* (1817)

SL descends directly from C's earlier collections, despite the long interval and changed and changing circumstances, and its material beginnings may be traced to events which happened at least ten years before it appeared. On 1 May 1807 Longman's house journal, *The Athenaeum: A Magazine of Literary and Miscellaneous Information*, announced that "Mr Coleridge has sent two volumes of Poems to the press, which will shortly make their appearance"; and there is evidence that C began to entertain hopes for a collection resembling WW's at this time (*CL* III 15–16: to W. Sotheby [5 May 1807]; see also Preface 10EC). However, although the *Literary Panorama* II (Jun 1807) para 653 repeated the *Athenaeum* announcement, C's interest appears not to have lasted beyond the excitement of watching WW's volumes appear and was soon overtaken by other, moneymaking commitments.

In Apr 1809, at a time when C's spirits had revived somewhat, he returned to Longman to propose again that the volume published in 1803—in effect, "Poems written chiefly from the age of 17 to 25"—should be followed by two further volumes of the same size, comprising (vol II) "Poems from 25 to 33" and (vol III) separately entitled longer poems like **155 Continuation of *"The Three Graves"*** and presumably **176 Christabel**. The volume covering the years 1797–1805 would collect poems already written or in print, from *M Post*, *LB*, and other newspapers and collections, anything in length from 10 to 1,000 lines, all "completed, & corrected for the Press" (*CL* III 203–4: to T. N. Longman [27 Apr 1809]; see also 191: to J. Brown [c 9 Apr 1809]). When Longman offered only £100 for the copyright (*CL* IV 561: to Lord Byron Easter week 1815; cf *WL—M* rev—I 359), C declined, but in May 1811, under conditions of severe financial distress, C renewed the offer on Longman's terms. It was again for two volumes to collect the poems he had written since 1797. One would include material from *LB* and scattered elsewhere, and the other would be made up of original poems, only 200 lines of which had previously been published as a fragment (*CL* III 324–5: to T. N. Longman [2 May 1811]; perhaps this was **110 Contributions to *"Joan of Arc"***). C felt able to promise the first of these volumes "to be delivered within a fortnight", and received £20 or £22 on account (cf *CL* IV 562: to Lord Byron Easter week 1815; 797: to J. J. Morgan [7 Jan 1818], from which it appears that the money was owing on the *Friend* account anyway). Mrs C sent the manuscript down from Keswick in 1811 (*WL—M* rev—I 489, 495), but no more was done, and on 7 Mar 1815 C renewed the offer, this time to Cottle (*CL* IV 546) and soon afterwards to William Hood (see *CL* IV 551: to J. Cottle 10 [=11] Mar 1815). Though his offers in 1815 were less specific—"I have collected my scattered & my Manuscript Poems sufficient to make one volume—Enough I have to make another" (*CL* IV 546), "Mss Poems equal to one volume of 250 to 300 pages" (*CL* IV 551)—a letter soon afterwards to Lord Byron makes it clear that C has in mind the same project he had mooted earlier. That is, he proposed two volumes to collect what he had written since 1796, one for poems already published (besides those added in 1797) and the other for longer poems still in manuscript and unfinished (*CL* IV 560–1).

Cottle declined the offer with a £5 note (*Rem* 388) and the project was taken up by William Hood, Morgan, Gutch, and other Bristol supporters. At this point C's plans began to be modified. Since Longman was somehow understood to hold the copyright on the 1796 volume but not on the poems added in 1797 (even though the latter were included in the Longman volume of 1803), the 1797 additions were included in the group of previously published poems. In addition, the planned two volumes shrank to one, comprising those which were to hand or immediately available (*CL* IV 565: to Lady Beaumont 3 Apr 1815): that is, the volume of longer unpublished poems was postponed. Then, in a way which had not been foreseen, the critical preface which C had always had in mind but as something which would fill only thirty pages (*CL* III 204: to T. N. Longman [27 Apr 1809]; 324: to T. N. Longman [2 May 1811]; IV 561: to Lord Byron Easter week 1815) developed rapidly in length and importance to become *BL*. This came consciously to be regarded as "the *main* work" (*CL* IV 585: to J. M. Gutch [17 Sept 1815]), and meanwhile the hope of adding to the single volume of poems was displaced. The original purpose was obscured as other unpublished titles were added, and the single volume acquired the character of an omnium gatherum.

The decision to exclude **176** *Christabel* was taken early (*LL*—M—III 188; *CL* IV 585: to J. M. Gutch [17 Sept 1815]), but **155** *Continuation of "The Three Graves"* was included. Although C told John May Sr (*CL* IV 588–9: 27 Sept 1815) and Daniel Stuart (*CL* IV 591: 7 Oct 1815) that all the poems he thought worthy of publication since his first collection would be brought in, and that manuscript poems would make up a third of the whole, this is not what actually happened. Besides including nine of the eleven poems added in 1797, it takes in **115** *The Eolian Harp* from 1796; and besides thirty-eight poems from previously published sources, it takes in only ten hitherto unpublished ones. Care is taken to provide a strong opening and ending (as in previous collections), with **161** *The Rime of the Ancient Mariner* and **139** *The Destiny of Nations*, and to organise the other poems into groups of political, love and meditative poems, and odes.

None the less, despite C's evident intentions, the groupings are not everywhere clear, and are further obscured by separate divisional titles for **167** *Fire, Famine, and Slaughter* and **155** *Continuation of "The Three Graves"*. It is difficult to see why some poems are grouped with the love poems and others with the poems in blank verse, in particular, and why there is not a separate divisional title for *The Destiny of Nations* as for *The Rime of the Ancient Mariner*. In addition, the volume is less rigorously selective and carefully organised than one might have been led to expect. C told Gutch that he approved of only two of the ten poems appearing between pp 145 and 160 (sig L), "the others being either sickly or silly or both" (*CL* IV 619: [c 25 Jan 1816]). The *SL* Preface describes the contents in terms and phrases that C had used to Longman in 1809 and 1811, and the contents follow on the 1796 collection as vol II to vol I. At the same time, the character of *SL* is, as CL said, that of a volume of fugitive poems (*LL*—M—III 211), and the continuity of purpose is obscure.

SL developed its character as a volume not just as the printer's copy was being assembled, in the months following Mar 1815, but also later as it was being printed. Sigs B–U were printed between Oct–Nov 1815 and Jun 1816, and ELG (*CL* IV 618n) provides a summary analysis of when each surviving proof was dispatched. The bound collection of returned proofs is now at Yale (In C678 817 sa), and they suggest that C revised the texts as extensively when they were in type as he did before he submitted them. Take *The Rime of the Ancient Mariner*, in sigs B–D. Sig B is so lightly revised that it might be a second proof; the date on it in Gutch's hand, Sunday 26 Nov, does not help. Sig D is the only missing signature from among those printed in Bristol. The puzzles here are sufficient to lend weight to C's repeated claim, in the Wrangham/ "Peter Morris" and JG copies, that disagreements over printing arose very early in the volume, starting with the printing of the very first poem (see **161** *The Rime of the Ancient Mariner* VAR 198.1.1–4, 199–202 commentary). It was a time (Nov and early Dec 1815) when C was seriously ill, suffering partly from exhaustion, partly from the growing congestive heart disease that was to trouble him increasingly henceforth, partly from laudanum. Thereafter, during the printing, he was distracted by the composition of *Zapolya* and hopes for its acceptance by a London theatre.

At the other end of the stage of Bristol printing, it would appear from a letter of Morgan to Gutch postmark 6 May 1816 (q *BL*—*CC*—II 286–7) that some time after 1815 *Christabel* had been reintroduced, to close the volume. The fact that it was removed again at a later stage bears on the randomness of poems in sigs T and U (e.g. the inclusion of a poem by Washington Allston) at the end of the Odes section, the need for two proofs of sig U, and the continuing heavy revisions of *The Destiny of Nations*. C complained to Gutch that the printer had introduced changes on his own authority, when it is demonstrable that the change he specifically complained of had been initiated by him, the author (*CL* IV 645–6: [6 Jun 1816]; cf **180** *The Nightingale* 61 VAR commentary).

Gutch's bills (*BL*—*CC*—II 289–90) prove that even more changes were made during the printing of *SL* than of *BL*. Gutch understated the extent of the cancellations when he listed only four pages: he meant to set down four cancelled signatures, 32 pages.[15] Indeed, the preservation not just of the original proofs to support the printer's side of the argument but of a second "waste-office copy" shows how tangled and acrimonious the situation became. Sig A was not added

---

[15] Gutch wrote the bill properly when he copied it out again for his friend J. B. Nicolls in Feb 1817 (he had turned to Nicolls for advice as to how to cope with Gale and Fenner). The correspon-dence, which recapitulates Gutch's deal-ings with C and clarifies and augments the account given in *BL* (*CC*), is in the Bodleian (MS Eng lett b 11 ff 134–40).

until the printing transferred from Bristol to London, between May and Jul 1817, and was *ad hoc* and inadequate. It should have been filled with the special preface C promised for *The Rime of the Ancient Mariner*, comprising an essay on the supernatural in poetry and of which indeed he wrote at least the opening.[16] It turned out to contain three miscellaneous poems, one an adaptation of Ben Jonson (**486** *Adaptation of "A Nymph's Passion"*), arbitrarily yoked together by an unconvincing explanation, and a list of emendations and errata. It even fails to provide a list of contents.

By the time *SL* was published, eight years after the idea was conceived and two years after it had begun to go to press, the collection was curiously unrepresentative. Owing to what proved to be a misunderstanding about Longman's claims, it included some poems but excluded others from previous volumes. As a result of Byron's encouragement and Murray's readiness with cash, it excluded *Christabel*, as well as **178** *Kubla Khan* and **335** *The Pains of Sleep*, which were published separately while it was in press. It eventually appeared at a time when C's writings were attracting a good deal of notice, even notoriety, and was very much more widely reviewed than any earlier collection. C was willy-nilly more aware of the poems as a statement of his achievement than he was in 1809, 1811, or originally in 1815, and he became more deeply involved in the book's fortunes after publication than with any of his earlier collections. He annotated copies over a number of years to an extent without precedent or parallel.

SL is by its nature, and admittedly, more various than other volumes. It is also clear that individual texts were in a less ready state than C pretended when he offered the volume for publication. He perhaps knew what sources he wanted to draw on, but he left his friends to locate many of them (as Morgan's letter to Gutch makes clear: q *BL—CC*—II 286–7). The sources of different texts can be determined through a comparison of variants, and they are not always what one would expect. The *SL* version of **148** *To an Unfortunate Woman at the Theatre*, for instance, goes back to the version in *M Chron*, not to the manuscript or to the *Annual Anthology*. Poem **174** *France: An Ode* goes back to a text C had himself criticised for its misprints, not to the later version which incorporates his revisions, and the earlier text is only partly emended to bring it into line with his improvements. Other versions which appear to be faulty because of badly chosen or ill-prepared copytext include **482** *Human Life* and **467** *The Visionary Hope*, for both of which no earlier versions are known; and there are others again which suffer from Evans's impatience at C's changes (e.g. **172** *Lewti*, which has patent misprints in lines 9 and 53 and which, according to C, Evans promised to reset: see **172**.53 VAR commentary). With these and a few other exceptions, individual texts are none the less considerably improved. The proofs show that C exercised control over details of spacing and typography, as well as spelling and punctuation, in a way he was not to do again. With a

---

[16] *SW&F* (*CC*) 401–2; cf *CL* IV 561:   13 (*CC*) I 306; annex C 17.6 below.
to Lord Byron Easter week 1815; *BL* ch

few obvious exceptions like those described, and apart from a few other poems
C continued to work on (e.g. *The Rime of the Ancient Mariner*), *SL* provides
authoritative versions of texts which the late collections only contaminate.

TITLE

C intended a two-volume collection, preface plus poems, from the beginning
(*CL* IV 560–1: to Byron Easter week 1815). He received WW's *Poems* in two
volumes in Apr–May 1815, and this also influenced his plans. The story of how
it influenced the preface, which developed into *BL*, has been told by D. M.
Fogel "A Compositional History of the *Biographia Literaria*" *SB* XXX (1977)
219–34. By early Aug both John and Mary Morgan were insisting, on C's be-
half, that both of his volumes should mimic "Wordsworth's last edition" in
their typography and format (John Morgan q *BL*—*CC*—I 1–li; Mary Morgan
q *LL*—M—III 192. The *SL* title describes the scattered poems which C, unlike
Virgil's Sybil in *Aeneid* 3.441–52, is himself here collecting, and it therefore
supplies an equivalent for his earliest conception: "my scattered & my Manu-
script Poems" (*CL* IV 546: to J. Cottle 7 Mar 1815). At the same time, it would
not be inappropriate for it to allude to WW's subtitle ("Miscellaneous Pieces"),
raising to prominence what WW relegated.

The title possesses other meanings which C may have intended. It could ack-
nowledge a degree of obscurity and need for interpretation (cf *Aeneid* 6.100),
as, for instance, in **176** *Christabel*, which was originally part of the collection.
It could claim a measure of prophetic insight, as suggested by the damsel with
a dulcimer of **178** *Kubla Khan*, which was also part of the original collection;
or, differently, in political poems like **174** *France: An Ode*. For C on Sibylline
prophecy cf *SM* (*CC*) 26–7; **596** *Heraclitus on the Sibyl's Utterance*.

PRELIMINARIES

Sig A was printed a year after the rest of the volume and by another printer,
as described above. And whereas C intended that the signature should include
a critical preface to *The Rime of the Ancient Mariner* on the supernatural in
poetry, it turned out to have an *ad hoc* and random character. Besides a title and
a half-title, and a list of errata which are as much second thoughts and revisions,
it comprises three poems and a Preface. The poems are miscellaneous, and part
of the Preface offers an unconvincing explanation of how two of them might be
construed as schoolboy poems. The earlier part of the Preface repeats phrases
from descriptions of the collection in letters from 1809 onwards. The list of
contents appears to have been omitted by oversight.

Preface. The Preface appears on pp i–iii:

PREFACE.

The following collection has been entitled SIBYLLINE LEAVES; in allusion to the fragmentary and widely scattered state in which they have been long suffered to remain. It contains the whole of the author's poetical compositions, from 1793 to the present date, with the exception of a few works not yet finished, and those published in the first edition of his   5
juvenile poems, over which he has no controul. They may be divided into three classes: First, A selection from the Poems added to the second and third editions, together with those originally published in the LYRICAL BALLADS, which after having remained many years out of print, have been omitted by Mr. Wordsworth in the recent collection of all his minor   10
poems, and of course revert to the author. Second, Poems published at very different periods, in various obscure or perishable journals, &c. some with, some without the writer's consent; many imperfect, all incorrect. The third and last class is formed of Poems which have hitherto remained in manuscript. The whole is now presented to the reader collectively, with   15
considerable additions and alterations, and as perfect as the author's judgment and powers could render them.

In my Literary Life, it has been mentioned that, with the exception of this preface, the SIBYLLINE LEAVES have been printed almost two years; and the necessity of troubling the reader with the list of errata, which follows this preface, alone induces me to refer again to the circumstance, at   20
the risk of ungenial feelings, from the recollection of its worthless causes.

4. from 1793] C means 1796. At other times he wrote 1795 (*CL* IV 560: to Lord Byron Easter week 1815; 589: to J. May 27 Sept 1815) and 1794 (*CL* IV 591: to D. Stuart 7 Oct 1815).

10. recent collection] WW's *Poems* were published in two volumes by Longman in Apr 1815. C was almost certainly encouraged to propose his two-volume collection to Longman in 1809 by WW's two-volume collection of 1807 (also published by Longman), and there is evidence that he indeed began to gather and revise materials at the earlier date, prompted also by an offer from Longman (e.g. *CN* II 2780, 2880, 2882, 2900, 3157; cf *CL* III 15–16: to W. Sotheby [5 May 1807]; 21: to J. Wedgwood [25 Jun 1807]; 25: to J. Wade [Aug 1807]; 31: to H. Davy [9 Sept 1807]; 57: to RS 10 [=9] Feb 1808; 203: to T. N. Longman [27 Apr 1809]; and the first paragraph of the present entry).

WW's 1815 collection was also pretty much much what C had in mind for himself: revised reprints of poems which had appeared in *LB* and elsewhere, supplemented by manuscript poems written since the previous collection. C wanted *BL* physically to resemble the WW volumes (*CL* IV 585: to J. M. Gutch [17 Sept 1815]; *BL—CC—*II 283, 284), and the question arises whether he was at all influenced in his grouping of poems in *SL* by WW's far more elaborate classifications, even negatively.

A few corrections of later date have been added.—Henceforward the author must be occupied by studies of a very different kind.

> Ite hinc, CAMŒNÆ! Vos quoque ite, suaves,   25
> Dulces CAMŒNÆ! Nam (fatebimur verum)
> Dulces fuistis!—Et tamen meas chartas
> Revisitote: sed pudenter et raro!
> VIRGIL. Catalect. vii.

At the request of the friends of my youth, who still remain my friends,   30
and who were pleased with the wildness of the compositions, I have added
two school-boy poems—with a song modernized with some additions from
one of our elder poets. Surely, malice itself will scarcely attribute their
insertion to any other motive, than the wish to keep alive the recollections
from early life.—I scarcely knew what title I should prefix to the first. By   35
imaginary Time, I meant the state of a school boy's mind when on his
return to school he projects his being in his day dreams, and lives in his
next holidays, six months hence: and this I contrasted with real Time.

Contents. The following list gives the titles as they appear in the body of *SL*
itself, there being no contents list in the volume. Poems previously published in
newspapers, pamphlets, and joint collections but first collected by C in 1817 are
marked with an asterisk. Poems published for the first time in 1817 are marked
with a dagger. The remainder are taken from C's collections of 1796 and 1797.

37. and lives] *SL* [AG (annex C 17.17), C's hand] and ⟨by anticipation⟩ lives
8–9. p 2 contains a motto from Burnet; p 3 repeats the title, the first six words in
gothic script

25–8. pseudo-Virgil *Catalepton*
5.11–14 (var: "suaves" for "iam
sane") tr (var) Fairclough (LCL) II
491 "Get ye hence, ye Muses! away
even with you, ye gentle, sweet
Muses! For the truth we must avow—
ye have been sweet. And yet, come ye
back to my pages, though with mod-
esty and but seldom!"

⁻12. p 47 contains divisional title "POEMS \| OCCASIONED BY POLITICAL EVENTS \| OR \| FEELINGS CONNECTED WITH THEM."; p 48 contains a motto from WW 12⁺. p 49 repeats the poem-title and gives a motto from Aeschylus; p 50 contains an argument to the poem 19⁺. p 88 contains mottoes from Claudian and Ecclesiasticus; p 111 repeats the poem-title ⁻20. p 117 contains a divisional title "LOVE-POEMS."; p 118 has a motto from Petrarch ⁻41. p 163 contains a divisional title "MEDITATIVE POEMS" \| IN \| BLANK VERSE; p 164 contains a motto from *CWal* I viii 42–9

⁻20. The motto from Petrarch on p 118 had previously been transcribed into a notebook (*CN* III 4178), and was also quoted (var) in a personal context in *BL* ch 10 (*CC*) I 222.

62⁺. p 216 is blank; p 217 repeats the poem-title and subtitle   ⁻63. p 235 contains
a divisional title "ODES | AND | MISCELLANEOUS POEMS."; p 236 is blank

6. *POETICAL WORKS* (1828, 1829, 1834)

Thomas J. Wise (*C Bibl*—Wise—148) refers to the 1834 collection as the seventh edition of C's *Poetical Works*. In effect, it is: the seven collections beginning with 1796 make up a developing series. Other publications such as *Fears in Solitude* (1798) and *Poems* (1812) are separate in their scope and purpose, and the volumes of *Wallenstein* (1800), *Christabel* (1816), *Remorse* (1813), and *Zapolya* (1817) are best seen as adjuncts to the main sequence of collections (though all are included in the list of annotated copies in annex C).

The title-pages of the 1796, 1797, and 1803 volumes state C's working premiss, that they hang together as a group, being the first, second, and third editions of the same collection. The first was somewhat hurried into print, after characteristic delays. The second was more carefully prepared as a revision of the first, and what was excluded constitutes as ambitious a gesture as what was added. The third embraces most of the material from the two earlier collections, and was put together in the cause of friendship by CL. Though its inclusiveness contradicts C's inclination to be selective and shaping in the make-up of his volumes, it incorporates a number of authoritative revisions in the text of individual poems. *SL* complements the earlier group in that it attempts to collect the material written and published in the interval following *Poems* (1796–7)—not *Poems* (1803), since that volume was out of date as a collection even as it appeared. *SL* excludes **176** *Christabel* and **178** *Kubla Khan*, which were published separately as a result of a spur-of-the-moment arrangement while *SL* was in press. Despite the variety of sources it drew upon, C was able to make considerable improvements and impose a unity of style.

The three later collections evolve from the earlier ones, but differently, and

94–5. This is by Washington Allston.

they make up a different grouping of their own. They are not described on their title-pages as the fifth, sixth, and seventh editions of *PW*, but they are together from the same publisher, all in three volumes in a similar format. The contents are grouped around *SL*, and add the two published plays and the translations of Schiller. All three volumes add the same sections of early (Juvenile) poems and recently written (Miscellaneous) poems, as well as incorporating *Kubla Khan* into *SL*, and including *Christabel*.

C's control over the content and preparation of the late collections was less than it had been on earlier occasions; indeed, his intervention was demonstrably sporadic. The difficulties caused by his deteriorating health from 1818 onwards, together with the distraction of many non-literary interests, are constant determining factors, and none of the late collections—not even, or especially, the final one—possesses authority that should not be questioned, either as a whole collection or as an assembly of individual texts. The enlargement of the final collection, as well as much of its character, owes much to HNC. If *PW* (1834) and the idiosyncrasies of HNC's controlling hand are most fully discussed here, it is because the collection has provided the basis of the standard scholarly edition (EHC's) for the best part of a century.

C considered a new collection of his poems in the early 1820s, but the plans came to nothing. In May 1820 he wrote to RS to say that since *SL* was sold out, "& neither the Zapolya nor the Christabel are on sale", he was thinking of an edition of all his poetic works (*CL* v 51). The only outcome at this time was that RS obtained Longman's permission for C to make whatever use he wanted of the *Wallenstein* volume (*CL* v 269: to W. Godwin [28 Feb 1823]. In Jun 1823 C made a more considered attempt to get a new edition published, when he asked JTC to speak to Murray on his behalf (*CL* v 276: to JTC [5 Jun 1823]); cf *S Life*—CS—v 142). The collection was to include *Remorse* but not, apparently, *Wallenstein*, which C wished to adapt for the stage. C hoped for two independent volumes, one containing a selection of his poems and the other containing *Remorse*, an altered *Zapolya*, and "a free Imitation of a Tragedy of Calderon's" (*CL* v 283, 291–3: to C. A. Tulk [Jul, 14 Aug 1823]). Murray was welcoming, but the terms he proposed were not acceptable: he insisted that H. H. Milman should have control over the editing—"to select, and make such omissions and corrections as should be thought advisable" (*CL* v 279: to T. Allsop [c 12 Jun 1823]; 423: to JTC [8 Apr 1825]; vi 902–3: to HNC [7 May 1832]).

C's resentment at what he called Murray's "smooth *courtierly* insolence" must have combined with other commitments, so that hopes for a new collection were set aside. They revived in Feb 1827 (or earlier), when JG and an Ambleside friend of HC, Robert Jameson, now a London barrister, took it upon themselves to supervise a new edition for William Pickering. Jameson had been a visitor to Highgate from the early 1820s, and was probably the link with Pickering, from whom the initiative might have come. Jameson and Pickering were protégés of Basil Montagu, who also appears to have acted as intermediary between C and Pickering (e.g. *CL* VI 760: to A. A. Watts 14 Sept 1828; 914: to HNC [endorsed 10 Jun 1832]). Pickering's concern to insert some of C's recent album verses, the format of the volumes, and their small print-run suggest that he saw a way to exploit the new literary fashions of the later 1820s.[17]

It was a time when C's interest in verse was reviving, but the evidence suggests that the burden of editorial work fell to JG (and perhaps AG). Several annotated copies of *SL* contain revised readings in JG's hand (annex C 17.14, 15; see also 17.11–13). While they are not as closely connected with the new edition as they might at first appear to be, they are certainly part of the background preparation. C himself became involved in editorial preparations to the extent of writing to Stuart for a copy of the *M Post* containing **214** *The Devil's Thoughts* (*CL* VI 672–3: [25 Feb 1827]), and in other ways which will be described below. But he had no control over printing and business matters, and his attitude towards the edition which appeared in Jun–Jul 1828 was detached and critical.

C's original hope had been for a collection containing only previously published poems, "written in youth & earliest Manhood", but this had been eroded by Pickering's obtaining other poems by false pretences. For example, **592** *Youth and Age*, which C had sold to Alaric Watts for inclusion in *The Literary Souvenir*, was previously published in Pickering's annual *The Bijou*, and then inserted in the collection along with other manuscript poems obtained from JG on the pretext of a mistake in casting off (*CL* VI 699–700, 710–11, 758–60: to A. A. Watts [Aug 1827], 24 Nov 1827, 14 Sept 1828). Though there is evidence that C excised **623** *The Improvisatore* in proof (*CL* VI 760; to A. A. Watts 14 Sept 1828), too many new poems remained. The fact that C at one time envisaged a collection in two volumes (*CL* VI 760) might even suggest that he planned, as in 1823, to exclude *Wallenstein*. Only 300 copies were printed; they were reviewed in the *Literary Gazette* (23 Aug 1828) 535–6; all were sold by Oct (*CL* VI 760; 766: to D. Stuart 14 Oct 1828).

The extent to which the 1828 collection blurs C's inclination to be selective, to produce a retrospective rather than a current collection, is something more easily appreciated than the modification of individual texts. C writes of being given a list of his printed poems and "marking those which, I thought, ought to be omitted"; he also writes of making corrections in proof (*CL* VI 759–60: to A. A. Watts 14 Sept 1828). The initial choice of texts none the less determined features which were to persist through and despite later revisions. The section of Juvenile Poems at the beginning of vol I draws mainly on *Poems* (1796). The texts were revised, but even those which were based on 1797 versions ignored improvements, like those taken forward to the 1803 text of **101** *Religious Musings*. The *SL* section of vol I is of course based on the 1817 volume, but it takes in only a few of the many revisions C made at the time of publication—even from among the several copies he and JG had to hand.

---

[17] Bernard Warrington "William Pickering: His Authors and Interests" *Bulletin of the John Rylands Univer-sity Library of Manchester* LXIX (Spring 1987) 572–628 at 593–6, 628 sets Pickering's dealings with C in context.

Thus, from among those poems JG emended in the part copy at HUL (*EC8 C6795 817s (D)), covering sigs G4–O3, the emended version of **156** *This Lime-tree Bower my Prison* provides the basis of the 1828 text, but only one of the emendations to **129** *Reflections on Having Left a Place of Retirement* was carried forward, and all the emendations to **300** *The Picture* were ignored. Similarly with the copies of **176** *Christabel* and *Zapolya* that passed through the two editors' hands: only a selection of the revisions that C made were adopted, and not in a consistent manner. It is not known whether either editor possessed copies of *Remorse* or *Wallenstein*. AG had given away her lightly corrected copy of *Remorse* in 1826, and perhaps the Gillmans were not interested in the theatre. At all events, the result is the same. The 1828 *Remorse* was based on the second edition of 1813, and no attempt was made to remove errors and incorporate improvements, as in the several annotated copies.

The section of Juvenile Poems in the 1828 collection takes in two poems from sig A of the original *SL* (**145** *The Raven* and **388** *Time, Real and Imaginary*), and otherwise represents a selection from C's early volumes. The *SL* section omits only poems **177** *The Story of the Mad Ox* and **162** *Parliamentary Oscillators* from Political Poems, and *Ode to the Rain* (=**280** *Lines Written in Bed at Grasmere*) from Odes, and it ends with **178** *Kubla Khan*, **335** *The Pains of Sleep*, and the transferred Apologetic Preface to **167** *Fire, Famine, and Slaughter*. Vol II opens with the transferred **161** *The Rime of the Ancient Mariner*, followed by **172** *Christabel*, and then miscellaneous pieces written, with one exception (**160** *The Wanderings of Cain*), in the 1820s; it continues and ends with *Remorse* and *Zapolya*. Vol III contains the *Wallenstein* translations. The Preface is the version of 1797 as modified in 1803. This was repeated with only slight modification for the next edition, preparations for which followed almost without a break after the 1828 edition had sold out. C corrected the 1828 volumes and began to return them to Pickering in Jan 1829 (*CL* VI 782–3). He instructed him to make a correction in an added poem—**652** *The Garden of Boccaccio*—early in Mar (see VAR TEXT PR 2). The volumes were reset for the most part line for line and page for page, by the same printer (Thomas White), and they were advertised in the *Literary Gazette* (23 May 1829) 351 at the unusually high price of £1 16s for the three-volume set.

C was not moved by motives of financial gain, and in fact earned little or nothing from either edition (*CL* VI 760: to A. A. Watts 14 Sept 1828; 913–14: to HNC [endorsed 10 Jun 1832]). Instead he hoped to make his poems more widely and cheaply available, and at the same time took the opportunity to make some minor changes. Poems **82** *Monody on the Death of Chatterton*, **171** *Frost at Midnight*, and **517** *Glycine's Song* were revised, in particular, in 1829; two small poems were dropped from the section of miscellaneous poems in vol II (**633** *"Tho' hid in spiral myrtle Wreath"* and **624** *The Alienated Mistress*); and three pieces were added (**107** *Allegoric Vision*, **623** *The Improvisatore*, and **652** *The Garden of Boccaccio*). None the less, the peculiarities that had already entered the collection willy-nilly were preserved and added to, and this subtle kind of modification of C's meaning is the more important because it is pervasive.

These features are separate from actual errors: though a good number crept into the 1829 collection, most were corrected in 1834. Thus, of the errors in **139** *The Destiny of Nations* 15, 90, 115, 195, 323, 399, 462, or in the Apologetic Preface to **167** *Fire, Famine, and Slaughter* ¯1.201 et seq (*PW*—1829—ɪ 345), only the mistake at line 399 was later repeated. Take instead *Zapolya*. Three changes of wording were introduced in 1829 (Prelude i 20; ɪɪ i 75⁺; ɪv i 44–7). The last two can be proved to have authorial backing, and so presumably has the first. But besides carrying forward the process of regularisation begun in 1828 (expanding contractions, not capitalising certain nouns, introducing *-ou*-spellings, putting apostrophes in the correct place, regularising punctuation, normalising stage directions), *PW* (1829) introduces further changes of style as well as errors. The alterations can be proved to be contrary to C's intentions as certainly as the errors, even though he did not intervene to prevent them.

At the beginning of *Zapolya* ɪ i phrases like "What tired Glycine?" (line 2), "The good strength, nature gave me" (4), "Compared with those, the royal court affords" (31) are heard differently according to whether commas are supplied or removed. A semicolon at the end of a line (37) enables a transition to the next different from that suggested by a colon. Changing an exclamation to a question and vice versa (182, 246) gives whatever one speaks or hears before the punctuation a different tone and note, either less certain or more peremptory, either tender or abrupt. The importance of these matters and others related to them is dealt with in part ɪɪ of the Introduction. The modifications which began in the 1828 versions, and are confirmed in 1829 and extended in 1834, are one of the most important features of this group of collections. They subtly change the texture of the verse, and with it the movement of mind and the values therein embodied.

It is significant that no copies have been traced of the 1828 or 1829 collections which were annotated by C as they were published. Those that are known—two large-paper copies of *PW* (1828)—contain extensive corrections, but these were not made till Apr? 1832. That is, while they contain changes introduced into *PW* (1829), these were inserted afterwards. C's retrospective interest in the 1828–9 collection in the spring of 1832 might none the less have prompted or reflected thoughts of its republication yet once more, this time with the help of HNC. It is not known whether the initiative came from C or his nephew, but by Jul–Aug a new, cheaper, and enlarged edition was under way (*CL* vɪ 923 and n: to HNC [28 Aug 1832]; *Minnow* 168). C and indeed his family and friends appear to have been more directly and amicably involved than before, as a series of letters attests (*CL* vɪ 923; 974–5: to HNC [early Dec 1833]; 980: to HNC [Mar 1834]; *Minnow* 174); and HNC's role as editor was certainly greater than Jameson's or JG's had been, as will become apparent. The collecting and preparing of the materials proceeded slowly enough, and the three volumes were set and printed afresh by another printer (Charles Whittingham the younger). The initial print-run was again not large—a reprint was called for in 1835—but this did not matter since it was set in stereotype and the price was low (5*s* per volume, like the scarce 1828 edition). The first volume was available in late Mar–early Apr; vol II followed two or three weeks afterwards; and vol III was delayed until mid-Jul, a week or so before C died.[18]

Whether or not the idea of the collection was HNC's, he without doubt determined its scope. His aim was to be as comprehensive as possible, and he enlarged the 1829 collection wherever he could find new material. A large number of early poems, from manuscript sources such as the Ottery Copy Book and from JTC, were inserted into the sequence of Juvenile Poems; and a few poems were added to the Sibylline Leaves section. The largest number of additions, from C's own manuscripts and fugitive printed sources, from all periods, were inserted in the Miscellaneous Poems section of vol II. It will be recalled that C had opposed Pickering's enlarging of this same section with new poems in 1828. What HNC discovered too late to insert in its proper place, he added to the tail of vol III (*Love, Hope, and Patience in Education* = poem **656**); thereafter in an appendix of seven poems added to vol II of *TT* (1835); then further in vol I of *LR* (1836).

There are two things to say about HNC's effort to be comprehensive. First, it takes further a tendency of the two other late collections, initiated by JG and Pickering, to be less selective than C himself was inclined to be. Of course, HNC acted with C's consent, but it was benevolent tolerance on C's part rather than active encouragement. In 1832 C privately appended exculpatory dates to the Juvenile Poems already printed, along with comments like "Very like one of Horace's Odes, *starched*" (on **68** *To a Friend in Answer to a Melancholy Letter*). In 1834 he wrote in the margins of the later collection: "Genuine Della Cruscan!" and "Little Potatoes in the *Manner* of Pine Apple" (on **64** *Songs of the Pixies* and **111** *In the Manner of Spenser*). Afterwards SC was quite clear why a much more rigorously selective collection would have better represented her father:

> My dear Henry found these poems in old MS. books & in all the ardour of first love, would insert them in the new edition. He had in him the strangest mixture of high taste and low taste, passion & unselectness, delicacy (or *particularity*) and exceeding freeness—dignity and familiarity. I think by this time he would have been ready to discard these *puerilia*. . . . The fact must have been that my Father never troubled his head about the edition of 1834—left it entirely to Henry—Had he given the matter a thought, he never COULD have sanctioned the publication of poems he scorned in 1796.[19]

---

[18] Vol i was advertised in the *Literary Gazette* (29 Mar 1834) 231, and vols I and II were reviewed ibid (17 May 1834) 339. Vol III was reviewed posthumously ibid (9 Aug 1834) 537–8. C's annotations in the copy now at HEHL are confined to vol I: they do not prove that he saw all three volumes before he died.

[19] SC to DC (als of 23 Jan 1852) (HRC); given in part by Grantz No 96. Cf SC Preface to *Poems* (1852) xi–xii.

This sense, that it was their judgment against HNC's, not their judgment against C's, led SC and DC in their 1852 edition to deny that the collections of 1828, 1829, and 1834 had canonical status, and to omit almost twice as many poems as they included afresh.

The other thing to be remarked about HNC's attempt to be comprehensive is the way he set about it. HNC later realised—as the poems added in *TT* and *LR* show—that *SL* omits poems from the 1796 and 1797 collections, even as he came across and added poems from *M Post* and *Watchman*, and manuscript and other sources. And he appears to have realised also at the later time, but incompletely, that *PW* (1828) and (1829) were similarly selective—that they omitted **162** *Parliamentary Oscillators*, **177** *The Story of the Mad Ox*, **280** *Lines Written in Bed at Grasmere*, **633** *"Tho' hid in spiral myrtle Wreath"*, and **624** *The Alienated Mistress*. Several of these poems were not collected until *EOT*, in 1850. The point is that HNC's attempt to enlarge the canon started from the later group of collections, and their peculiarities dawned on him only much later.

The decision to base the 1834 collection on *PW* (1829), which is in turn based on *PW* (1828), is of particular importance not just because of the omissions, which HNC more than counterbalanced by the poems he added, but because of the implications for the individual texts included. The three collections do not stand alone: a mistake in one tends to be repeated either exactly or in modified form in the next, so that there is a knock-on effect. For instance, the epigraph to the Epistles section of the 1796 *Poems* was misconstrued as an epigraph to **116** *Written at Shurton Bars* first in *PW* (1828), and consequently in 1829 and 1834. *PW* (1834) usually rectifies such obvious mistakes, though not always, but, for example, it is not so good at restoring paragraph-divisions and stanza-breaks which have been lost. The division between lines 58 and 59 of **102** *Religious Musings* occurs between two pages in *PW* (1828) and (1829) (I 86–7): *PW* (1834) I 84 misunderstands and prints the lines without division. The same happens with **145** *The Raven* 38–9, at *PW* (1828) I 26–7, (1829) I 28–9, and (1834) I 19. For further examples see **172** *Lewti* 14–15; **85** *Lines on a Friend Who Died of a Frenzy Fever* 18–19; **111** *In the Manner of Spenser* 37–8; **39** *Absence: An Ode* 16–17; **190** *The Visit of the Gods* 18–19.

Poem **176** *Christabel* is a particularly striking example of this kind of misunderstanding, compounded by the dependence of one edition on another without reference to the original or prior versions—in this case the misconstruing of the 1816 text by the compositor of *PW* (1828), of *PW* (1828) by *PW* (1829), and of *PW* (1829) by *PW* (1834): see lines 54–5, 128–9, 183–4, etc. Such mistakes accumulate because they are not obvious, and they are pervasive.

Further instances and variations of the same knock-on effect are supplied by *Remorse*, in which *PW* (1828) follows the second edition of 1813 with only a handful of modifications. At I ii 355 *PW* (1828) drops the exclamation-mark at the end of the line, and has no punctuation; *PW* (1829), obviously without reference to the original, supplies a comma; which *PW* (1834) then carries forward. The accompanying table lists a selection of similar phenomena. Sometimes *PW* (1834) strikes lucky and emends *PW* (1829) in a way which restores the 1813 reading (e.g. at II i 102 and IV i 19), but the principle (or lack thereof) remains unaltered.

	1813	1828	1829	1834
II i 7	suicide,	suicide	suicide	suicide:
II i 98	parley—	parley	parley.	parley.
II i 106	yours—	yours	yours;	yours;
II i 118	life—	life	life,	life,
II i 125	now—	now	now	now.
II ii 90	friend—	friend	friend,	friend,
II ii 91	again"—	again,"	again,"	again;"
IV ii 47	fear,	fear,	fear.	fear
IV ii 66	him	him	him,	him,
V i 11	mountebanks;	mountebanks;	mountebanks:	mountebanks;—
V i 192	off—	off—	off	off,
V i 193	am;	am?	am?	am,
V i 255	Heaven!	Heaven	Heaven	Heaven,
Appendix				
II ii 42fn	his	this	this	an

Although C had more control over the putting together of the final collection, the evidence suggests that he more gratefully abrogated responsibility to his literary nephew. HNC wrote to JTC on 20 Mar 1834, as the first volume appeared: "I have endeavored to collect every thing, & the arrangement & corrections give me much trouble" (BM Add MS 47557 ff 103^r–104^r). The 1828 and 1829 editions progressively regularised many features of C's texts which had remained closer to his intentions, as expressed in manuscript, in early collections. HNC took the process further, and put his own stamp on the Whittingham–Pickering house style. A certain literal-mindedness might be thought to be the accompaniment to the assiduous collecting and inclusion of C's juvenilia and miscellanea—at least, when applied to a living poet and in the nineteenth century.

This attitude affects other poems in such instances as the 1834 version of **82** *Monody on the Death of Chatterton*: the addition of the original ending, which HNC retrieved from the Ottery Copy Book, to the version that C had brought to completion in 1829 is inappropriate. It juxtaposes styles which are at variance with each other, supposing falsely that more lines mean that C is better served. The substance of the eleven lines had been assimilated into the revised second stanza, so that they are now redundant; their jerky schoolboy rhythms are at odds with the developed elegiac strain of the 1829 version. Or, differently, one might point to the correction of factual errors in poems like **11** *The Nose: An Odaic Rhapsody* (VAR 30.1.9), **395** *A Lesson on Metrical Feet* (7), *A Mathematical Problem*=**24** *Translation of Euclid* (38, 57). Or, differently again, a corresponding moral and political attitude which is made evident by the inclusion of such poems as **678** *Cholera Cured Beforehand* at the expense of others like **589** *The Bridge Street Committee* (which Allsop characteristically did include); or by omitting the names from **620** *Sancti Dominici Pallium*—which makes it softer and blander, but actually pointless.

HNC's selection, full though it is to the point of striking some reviewers as indiscriminate, omits what is funny and subversive; and its soberness has further implications for the texture of style. As SC remarked later, HNC was careful always to write "-ed", and to put an accent where the "-ed" was to form a separate syllable (als to DC 9 Feb [1852?]—HRC; Grantz No 106). The expansions in *PW* (1834) are consistent enough to make the exceptions noticeable: e.g. **623** *The Improvisatore*; **11** *The Nose: An Odaic Rhapsody*; **182** *The Ballad of the Dark Ladiè*; **9** *To My Muse*; **656** *The Accomplishments Most Desirable in an Instructress*; **665** *Love and Friendship Opposite*. One wonders if these poems came in late, or what other reason there might be for their not being revised.

HNC is likewise careful about grammar—changing "will" to "shall" (**625** *Last Words of Berengarius* III 28)—and smoothes out incongruities (**623** *The Improvisatore* 32). He continued the processes of normalisation (spelling, cap-italisation, punctuation) begun in 1828–9, but took them further. The few cap-itals that remain within verse lines conform to later usage, not to C's own; the punctuation is characteristically heavier and more logical, emphasising the separateness of rhyming and rhythmical units (see e.g. **688** *Love's Appari-tion and Evanishment*). An exception—*Introduction to the Tale of the Dark Ladiè* (=**253** *Love*)—where the 1828–9 punctuation has been restored to earlier, lighter modes (see lines 48, 56, 60, 64)—is one that heightens one's awareness of the 1834 rule. HNC regularised the Greek, especially by the correction of breathings, accents, and subscript iotas, in ways which were not always entirely correct even by the conventions of the time (see **48** *Sors Misera Servorum* VAR 1–16).

Of course, C intervened in the process described above. A marked-up page of the 1829 text of **139** *The Destiny of Nations* at VCL (S MS Fl.13) proves that he did prepare at least part of the 1834 collection in detail. There is a copy of *PW* (1829) at NYPL (Berg Collection) containing corrections which possess authority, but these are not in C's hand. Other revisions, such as the correction of "yellow" to "quiet" in *Remorse* III i 79, made after "yellow" had survived uncorrected in so many copies of the 1813 *Remorse* and in *PW* (1828, 1829), can be proved to be authoritative by comparison with manuscript sources and with the copies of *PW* (1828) which C corrected in 1832. Many other changes and improvements—in **161** *The Rime of the Ancient Mariner*, to take one further example—are undoubtedly his; but his intervention appears to have been sporadic, and he seems to have made little attempt to reverse the process of change affecting punctuation, capitalisation, and the like.

The fact that C annotated detached pages containing the poems he contributed to *Friendship's Offering* some time after they appeared in Oct 1833 is unconnected with the preparation of *PW* (1834). Only a selection of *Friendship's Offering* poems were taken forward, and those same poems incorporated C's corrections only in part. The fact that he corrected a copy of vol I of the 1834 *PW*, taking care to amend instances of HNC's capitals and paragraph-divisions (in **39** *Absence: An Ode* 16–17; **101** *Religious Musings* 321; **190** *The Visit of the Gods* 18–19), proves only that he noticed that the tendency of HNC's editing diverged from his own practice. In the same annotated copy C passed over patent errors: e.g. **214** *The Devil's Thoughts* 39; **293** *Dejection: An Ode* 39; the mistaken renaming of **186** *English Duodecasyllables* as *English Hendecasyllables*; **174** *France: An Ode* 66; **678** *Cholera Cured Beforehand* 41; and so on. The errors are no less obvious for being in most cases minor.

Some texts—like **652** *The Garden of Boccaccio*—carry over mistakes from previous printings and introduce others. Others—like **688** *Love's Apparition and Evanishment*—are revised and improved. It is sometimes difficult to distinguish between new legitimate readings and new errors (e.g. in the Apologetic Preface to **167** *Fire, Famine, and Slaughter* or in **81** *With a Poem on the French Revolution* 24); or between C's intervention and HNC's (e.g. in poems introduced into the Juvenile Poems section, such as **31** *Anthem for the Children of Christ's Hospital*, **9** *To My Muse*, **31** *Ode on the Destruction of the Bastile*, **18** *Nemo Repente Turpissimus*). Each poem has to be taken separately, and considered in relation to other versions of it. Enough has meanwhile been said to make it clear why *PW* (1834) does not enjoy special status, any more than the two previous late collections. The versions of poems in all three are frequently less authoritative than in earlier collections, manuscripts, and separate publications.

The impression to be gained from *C Bibl* (Wise) and other sources is that later impressions of *PW* (1834) are uncorrected reprints. They are not. Though a casual comparison might suggest that they are page for page the same, typographical errors are silently corrected in the later impressions, and small corrections made; while at the same time a few small errors creep in. Punctuation is dropped from the Schiller translations in vol III, in particular.

PRELIMINARIES AND FORMAT

No manuscript or proof material connected with the three late collections as a whole has survived. The preliminaries are very similar. In 1828 and 1829 the table of contents to all three volumes follows the title-page, and the Prefaces come next. In *PW* (1834), by a different printer, the Prefaces follow the title-page and then we have the table of contents for vol ɪ (only). The table of contents for vol ɪɪ is given separately in that volume, and there is no table of contents in vol ɪɪɪ.

Prefaces. The 1828 Prefaces derive from either the 1803 or the 1797 volume (curtailing the 1797 text in exactly the same way as in 1803), with a few small variations in punctuation. *PW* (1829) and (1834) add a footnote (var) from *BL* (1817) and introduce further minor variations. The text given here is that of *PW* (1829) = PR *2*, collated with *PW* (1828) = PR *1* and *PW* (1834) = PR *3*. The extra footnote in PR *2 3* is annotated in *BL* ch 3 (*CC*) ɪ 50–1n. For EC on the remaining quotations etc see No 3 above.

PREFACE*

Compositions resembling those of the present volume are not unfrequently condemned for their querulous Egotism. But Egotism is to be condemned then only when it offends against time and place, as in a History or an Epic Poem. To censure it in a Monody or Sonnet is almost as absurd as to dislike a circle for being round. Why then write Sonnets or Monodies?   5
Because they give me pleasure when perhaps nothing else could. After the more violent emotions of Sorrow, the mind demands amusement, and can find it in employment alone: but full of its late sufferings, it can endure no employment not in some measure connected with them. Forcibly to turn away our attention to general subjects is a painful and most often an   10
unavailing effort:

> "But O! how grateful to a wounded heart
> The tale of Misery to impart—
> From others' eyes bid artless sorrows flow,
> And raise esteem upon the base of Woe!"   15
>   Sʜᴀᴡ.

The communicativeness of our Nature leads us to describe our own sorrows; in the endeavour to describe them, intellectual activity is exerted; and from intellectual activity there results a pleasure, which is gradually associated, and mingles as a corrective, with the painful subject of the   20

* To the First and Second Editions.

title fn. *3* first and second editions.   **2.** *3* egotism. But egotism   **3.** *1* Time and Place,   *1* as in an   **3–4.** *3* history or an epic poem.   **4.** *3* monody or sonnet.
7. *3* sorrow,   **8.** *1* alone;   **13.** *3* misery   **15.** *3* woe!"   **16.** *3* Sʜᴀᴡ.
17. *3* nature

description. "True!" (it may be answered) "but how are the PUBLIC in-
terested in your Sorrows or your Description?" We are for ever attributing
personal Unities to imaginary Aggregates. What is the PUBLIC, but a term
for a number of scattered individuals? Of whom as many will be interested
in these sorrows, as have experienced the same or similar.   25

> "Holy be the lay
> Which mourning soothes the mourners on his way."

If I could judge of others by myself, I should not hesitate to affirm, that
the most interesting passages are those in which the Author developes his
own feelings? The sweet voice of Cona* never sounds so sweetly, as when   30
it speaks of itself; and I should almost suspect that man of an unkindly
heart, who could read the opening of the third book of the Paradise Lost
without peculiar emotion. By a Law of our Nature, he, who labours under
a strong feeling, is impelled to seek for sympathy; but a Poet's feelings
are all strong. Quicquid amet valde amat. Akenside therefore speaks with   35
philosophical accuracy when he classes Love and Poetry, as producing the
same effects:

> "Love and the wish of Poets when their tongue
> Would teach to others' bosoms, what so charms
> Their own."   40
>   PLEASURES OF IMAGINATION.

There is one species of Egotism which is truly disgusting; not that which
leads us to communicate our feelings to others, but that which would
reduce the feelings of others to an identity with our own. The Atheist,
who exclaims, "pshaw!" when he glances his eye on the praises of Deity,   45
is an Egotist: an old man, when he speaks contemptuously of Love-verses,
is an Egotist: and the sleek Favorites of Fortune are Egotists, when they
condemn all "melancholy, discontented" verses. Surely, it would be candid
not merely to ask whether the poem pleases ourselves, but to consider
whether or no there may not be others, to whom it is well calculated to   50
give an innocent pleasure.

I shall only add, that each of my readers will, I hope, remember, that
these Poems on various subjects, which he reads at one time and under
the influence of one set of feelings, were written at different times and
prompted by very different feelings; and therefore that the supposed infe- 55

---

* Ossian.

21. *1 2* are • *3* is   *3* Public   **22.** *3* sorrows or your description?"   **23.** *3* unities
3 aggregates.   *3* Public,   **29.** *1 2* passages are • *3* passages in all writings
are   *3* author   **33.** *3* law   *3* nature,   **34.** *3* poet's   **41.** *3* PLEASURES
OF IMAGINATION.   **42.** *3* egotism   **44.** *1* Atheist, • *3* atheist,] *2* Athiest,
46. *3* egotist: **47.** *3* egotist: *3* favorites   *3* fortune are egotists,   **53.** *3* poems

riority of one Poem to another may sometimes be owing to the temper of
mind, in which he happens to peruse it.

My poems have been rightly charged with a profusion of double-
epithets, and a general turgidness. I have pruned the double-epithets with
no sparing hand; and used my best efforts to tame the swell and glitter both   60
of thought and diction.* This latter fault however had insinuated itself into
my Religious Musings with such intricacy of union, that sometimes I have
omitted to disentangle the weed from the fear of snapping the flower. A
third and heavier accusation has been brought against me, that of obscu-
rity; but not, I think, with equal justice. An Author is obscure, when his   65
conceptions are dim and imperfect, and his language incorrect, or unap-
propriate, or involved. A poem that abounds in allusions, like the Bard
of Gray, or one that impersonates high and abstract truths, like Collins's
Ode on the poetical character, claims not to be popular—but should be
acquitted of obscurity. The deficiency is in the Reader. But this is a charge   70
which every poet, whose imagination is warm and rapid, must expect from
his *contemporaries*. Milton did not escape it; and it was adduced with vir-
ulence against Gray and Collins. We now hear no more of it: not that their
poems are better understood at present, than they were at their first publi-
cation; but their fame is established; and a critic would accuse himself of   75
frigidity or inattention, who should profess not to understand them. But a
living writer is yet sub judice; and if we cannot follow his conceptions or
enter into his feelings, it is more consoling to our pride to consider him as
lost beneath, than as soaring above us. If any man expect from my poems
the same easiness of style which he admires in a drinking-song, for him I   80
have not written. Intelligibilia, non intellectum adfero.
    I expect neither profit or general fame by my writings; and I consider
myself as having been amply repaid without either. Poetry has been to

---

* Without any feeling of anger, I may yet be allowed to express some
degree of surprize, that after having run the critical gauntlet for a certain class
of faults, which I had, viz. a too ornate, and elaborately poetic diction, and
nothing having come before the judgement-seat of the Reviewers during the
long interval, I should for at least seventeen years, quarter after quarter, have   5
been placed by them in the foremost rank of the *proscribed*, and made to abide
the brunt of abuse and ridicule for faults directly opposite, viz. bald and prosaic
language, and an affected simplicity both of matter and manner—faults which
assuredly did not enter into the character of my compositions.
Literary Life, i. 51. Published 1817.   10

56. *3* poem   **61fn.** Not in PR *1*   **fn2.** *3* surprise,   **fn4.** *3* judgment-seat
fn6. *3* proscribed,   **fn10.** *3 Literary Life*,   **65.** *3* author   **66–7.** *3* inappropriate,
70. *3* reader.   **72.** *3* contemporaries.

me its own "exceeding great reward:" it has soothed my afflictions; it has multiplied and refined my enjoyments; it has endeared solitude; and it has   85 given me the habit of wishing to discover the Good and the Beautiful in all that meets and surrounds me.

S. T. C.

Contents. The following list reproduces the contents pages of *PW* (1834). In the apparatus the collections of 1828, 1829, and 1834 are designated PR *1–3*.

PW (1828) has a good many mistakes in the table of contents, many but not all of which were corrected in 1829. It fails to list **61** *To the Autumnal Moon* on p 10; it gives **388** *Time, Real and Imaginary* out of sequence; it gives altogether wrong page-numbers for **540** *Fancy in Nubibus*, the Appendix to *Remorse*, and *The Death of Wallenstein*. These mistakes were corrected in 1829, except that the altered page-number of the Appendix to *Remorse* was still wrong; **175** *Fears in Solitude* was again given as "Tears . . ."; more seriously, **180** *The Nightingale* and **335** *The Pains of Sleep* were again omitted from the contents list. *PW* (1834) corrects all of these errors, and its pagination is correct; but it repeats one small error present in the two previous collections, and exacerbates another in a characteristic way. Like *PW* (1828, 1829), it lists the first line of Sonnet IV (=poem **89**) as "When British Freedom from a happier land" (instead of "for"), and in vol II it drops the title *Reason for Love's Blindness* (=poem **359**), presumably because the lines are untitled in the text (the title had been included in the two previous collections). *PW* (1834) also removes the rule dividing the lines from those that precede them at vol II p 78 (=**492** *To a Lady, Offended by a Sportive Observation that Women Have No Souls*), thereby making one rather odd poem out of two.

Divisional titles are not given in any table of contents. *PW* (1828) and (1829) retain them for the various sections and some of the poems of *SL*.[20] and supply them for *Kubla Khan* and *Christabel*. *PW* (1834) does not give these divisional or poem-titles separate pages in the body of the text.

CONTENTS.

VOLUME I.

	1828	1829	1834	*CC*
JUVENILE POEMS.			Page	
Genevieve	9	11	3	**17**

⁻**1.** PR *1–3* do not record the Preface (PR *1 2* pp 1 et seq, PR *3* pp v et seq)

[20] Political Poems; Love Poems, etc; *on the Departing Year*; *The Three* *The Rime of the Ancient Mariner*; *Ode* Graves.

Sonnet. To the Autumnal Moon	10	12	3	**61**	
Anthem for the Children of Christ's Hospital	—	—	4	**31**	5
Time, real and imaginary	11	13	5	**388**	
Monody on the Death of Chatterton	12	14	6	**82**	
Songs of the Pixies	19	21	13	**64**	
The Raven	25	27	18	**145**	
Music	—	—	20	**36**	10
Devonshire Roads			21	**35**	
Inside the Coach	—	—	22	**34**	
Mathematical Problem	—	—	23	**24**	
The Nose	—	—	27	**11**	
Monody on a Tea-kettle	—	—	29	**21**	15
Absence, a Farewell Ode	28	30	30	**39**	
Sonnet. On Leaving School	—	—	31	**33**	
To the Muse	—	—	32	**9**	
With Fielding's Amelia	—	—	33	**32**	
Sonnet. On hearing that his Sister's Death was inevitable	—	—	33	**25**	20
On Seeing a Youth affectionately welcomed by a Sister	—	—	34	**26**	
The same	—	—	35	**100**	
Pain	—	—	35	**15**	25
Life	—	—	36	**10**	
Lines on an Autumnal Evening	30	32	36	**60**	
The Rose	35	37	40	**56**	
The Kiss	37	39	41	**76**	
To a Young Ass	39	41	43	**84**	30
Happiness	—	—	44	**30**	
Domestic Peace	41	43	48	**66**	
The Sigh	42	44	48	**75**	
Epitaph on an Infant	43	45	49	**77**(*a*)	
On Imitation	—	—	50	**38**	35
Honor	—	—	50	**29**	
Progress of Vice	—	—	53	**18**	
Lines written at the King's Arms, Ross	44	46	54	**70**	
Destruction of the Bastile	—	—	55	**13**	40
Lines to a beautiful Spring in a Village	46	47	57	**74**	

3. Sonnet. To the Autumnal Moon] Not listed in PR *1* contents the title wrongly following *Monody on the Death of Chatterton* only lines 12–19 of this poem **6.** PR *1* positions **24.** PR *3* prints

53. PR *3* omits final quotation-marks   **55.** for] *1–3* from

85. Fears] *1 2* Tears   86. PR *1 2* wrongly give the page-number as 155
117. Reflections] *1 2* Recollections

129. PR *1 2* omit this title from the contents   **159.** PR *1 2* omit this title from the contents

VOLUME II.

164 et seq. PR *1 2* give vol II table of contents in vol I; PR *3* gives in vol II   **176⁺.** PR *1 2* have section-heading "PROSE IN RHYME; OR EPIGRAMS, MORALITIES, &C."; PR *3* repeats the section-heading "MISCELLANEOUS POEMS." (at the top of p vi, headings being routinely repeated on new pages); the motto to this section (PR *1 2* p 75, PR *3* p 55=poem **631**) is not recorded in the contents **185⁺.** PR *1* Song   78 • PR *2 3* omit [=poem **633**]

⁻**199.** *1 2* Reason for Love's Blindness   86 [*2* 85] • *3* omits from contents but includes in text (p 78) [=poem **359**]   **199.** *2 3* Words] *1* Word's   **202⁺.** *1* The Alienated Mistress   93 • *2 3* omit [=poem **624**]   **211.** 102] *1* 120 [an error] **215.** PR *2 3* also use this title in the running headlines of the text, but head the text "THE IMPROVISATORE; | OR 'JOHN ANDERSON, MY JO, JOHN.'"

219–20. By J. H. Green. The authorship these two poems is given in a headnote on p 133, but not in the contents.

250. PR *1 2* wrongly give the Appendix page-number as 132 and 156 respectively **256 et seq.** PR *1 2* give vol III table of contents in vol I; PR *3* does not provide a table of contents in any volume, and titles are given here as they appear on the half-title pp of the text   **256.** PR *1 2* THE PICCOLOMINI, OR THE FIRST PART OF WALLENSTEIN.   **261.** THE DEATH OF WALLENSTEIN. PR *1* wrongly gives the page-number as 429   **263⁺.** PR *3* contents fails to list "Love, Hope, and Patience in Education" [=poem **656**], printed on p 331

244. By HNC. The poem is signed "By a friend." SC identifies the author in her annotated copy of PR *3* (annex C 24A).

263⁺. Poem **656** (see TN) is printed facing the last page of *The Death of Wallenstein*; p 332 contains a single erratum, to **682** *My Baptismal Birthday* 7 (*PW*—1834—II 152), followed by the colophon.

ANNEX C

ANNOTATED COPIES

This annex has obvious connections with those describing manuscript and printed collections. It lists annotated, inscribed, and corrected copies of titles in order of publication. The titles embrace all those on which the texts of this edition rest—pamphlets and plays as well as larger printed collections. It also includes titles to which C only contributed, when the corrected texts have some status in the collation of variants: *The Fall of Robespierre*, *Joan of Arc*, *Sonnets from Various Authors*, *LB*, *Annual Anthology*, *Israel's Lament*, *The Tears of a Grateful People*, *Friendship's Offering for 1834*. Some of these titles appear in *CM* (*CC*), and the descriptions given here are curtailed accordingly. Poems by C appear in the "margins" of other titles, and one corrected copy of *The Friend* (1812) contains corrections to verses, but these instances do not warrant separate description.

The general background to C's annotations is described below in order to suggest why they took the course they did. In kind they range from being largely corrections (e.g. the 1797 *Poems*), to possessing a retrospective and detached character (the translations of Schiller), to indicating a self-protective and defensive mood (*Christabel*), to forming the preparation for another edition (e.g. *PW* (1828)). The changes in the text of individual poems differ from copy to copy of the same title, and need to be weighed against circumstances (when they were made, who they were made for). The volumes annotated after C moved to Highgate in 1816 form into groups on several occasions, when JG and AG transferred corrections and comments from copy to copy.

Each known annotated copy is arranged in the order in which it was annotated. Sometimes this has to be deduced from internal relations or otherwise guessed at, sometimes it can be exactly determined. Known copies are listed whether or not they have been located, and all the available information is provided, including details of sale prices and binding. The reason is that several such copies have been confused with each other in the past, and this confusion might persist or multiply if the details are not borne in mind. They were often necessary in identifying the copies listed here, and will continue to be necessary in discriminating and placing further copies as these come to light. It can indeed be expected that more will be added to this list, since volumes are particularly prized by private collectors, are likely to have been preserved, and regularly appear (and disappear) at book auctions.

There is sometimes a section of copies identified by letter preceding the main

1274

numbered list (see e.g. No 3 below). These comprise copies which are not truly described as "inscribed" or "annotated", and/or copies of related interest.

1. *THE FALL OF ROBESPIERRE* (1794),
WITH ROBERT SOUTHEY

C said that he made presents of six copies (*CL* I 117: to RS 21 Oct [1794]), some or all of which may have been inscribed and none of which has been located. One of the six was presented to Ann Brunton, with a poem (*CL* I 117–18: to RS 21 Oct [1794]; see **81** *With a Poem on the French Revolution*), another to Francis Wrangham (*CL* I 121: to F. Wrangham 24 Oct 1794), and another to GC (see *CL* I 125–6: to GC 6 Nov 1794).

RS's copy, with his signature, was sold with his books at Sotheby's 10 May 1844 (lot 628 to Kerslake).

2. CONTRIBUTIONS TO ROBERT SOUTHEY'S
JOAN OF ARC (1796)

The copy which C marked up for William Hood in Jun 1814 to indicate his own contributions is at NYPL (Berg Collection Copy 2). Poem **110** *Contributions to "Joan of Arc"* records only those annotations which bear directly on C's contribution, the full set being given in *CM* (*CC*) v. Most annotations are in red pencil; others are in ordinary pencil and others (not cited in poem **110**) are in ink.

Some notes by JDC are loosely inserted into the NYPL copy. Another copy, at DCL (SOU (a) 1796), contains JDC's transcriptions from the Hood copy. JDC's notes and his copy are of no independent textual interest, though the first help with the identification of C's contributions and the second with readings in the Hood copy which have become faint or rubbed.

Hood's copy carries the bookplates of William Hood and Jerome Kern. From William Hood it passed to Herbert Coleridge (1831–61), from whom it passed to John Taylor Brown (before 1864). It was sold with Brown's library at Sotheby's 20 Apr 1903 (lot 361 to Hopkins for £19); then again at Sotheby's 2 Jul 1924 (lot 345 to Sawyer for £37); then in the Kern Sale, Anderson Galleries 7–10 Jan 1929 (lot 282 for $1150). It was acquired by NYPL with the collection of Owen D. Young in 1941. JDC's copy, meanwhile, was purchased by Gordon Wordsworth at the JDC Sale, Sotheby's 13 Jun 1904 (lot 427 for 4*s*). In 1961 it was in the possession of Mrs Dorothy Wordsworth Dickson of Rydal; it was acquired by DCL before 1973.

WW's library contained two copies of the 1796 edition which are marked as belonging to C, though there is no indication that either was annotated or inscribed.[1] A copy which belonged to RS was sold in a lot with a presentation copy of *Madoc* from J. H. Green's library, Sotheby's 27–9 Jul 1880 (lot 869 to Edward William Stibbs for 6*s*). A copy listed in the Scribner and Welford *Catalog of Scarce and Valuable Books, Including a Remarkable and Unique Collection of Coleridgeana* (New York 1884) item 37 is referred to by *C Bibl* (Haney) 129, in a chapter headed "Marginalia", as if the copy was annotated by C. These references are conflated by Ralph J. Coffman *Coleridge's Library* (Boston, Mass 1987) 197 to describe a "presentation [copy] from Southey to S.T.C." The grounds of the conflation and Coffman's inference are unclear.

3. *POEMS* (1796)

The printing history of C's first collection is complicated and protracted, as described in the two previous annexes. This history bears on the several annotated copies in a number of ways.

In the two known (incomplete) proof copies the annotations are more in the nature of corrected drafts: see copies 3.1 and 3.2 below. It may be assumed that further proofs were printed whose text differed from the published version, but none has come to light.

C either inscribed very few copies of this, his first collection, or at least very few inscribed copies have been preserved: see copies 3.3, 3.4, and 3.6 below. Nor did he amend or annotate these same copies. Instead, beyond inscriptions, he intended to write sonnets on the blank leaves of presentation copies. It cannot be proved that he did this, although there is evidence that he wrote verses in the copy he sent to John Thelwall (3.5). The only other copy containing autograph verses which is known to exist, or to have existed, contains these verses on a loosely inserted leaf, and was made up by Joseph Cottle from superseded manuscript copy (see 3.8 below).

Perhaps C failed to send copies to all his friends because he wanted to save Cottle undue expense (see *CL* I 201: to J. Cottle [early Apr 1796]); he did not even send a copy at once to CL (*LL*—M—I 3; cf copy 3H below). And perhaps he did not correct the copies he gave away because, even on the eve of publication, he and Cottle had agreed on a second edition. The fact that Cottle was willing and able to make up interleaved copies from unbound signatures might again confirm that plans for a new edition were agreed on early (cf also *CL* I 201).

A single extant copy (3.7) contains corrections in C's hand, but these are not extensive and C began again on a different scale when he reworked the materials for *Poems* (1797). The corrections and reworkings in the interleaved copy of the 1796 *Poems*, part of which is included in BM Ashley 408, are more properly described as part of the printer's copy for *Poems* (1797) than as an annotated copy of *Poems* (1796).

---

[1] Shaver 354.

3A. Copy containing C's inserted receipt for 30 guineas for the copyright of his poems, dated 28 Mar 1796
Not located.

The copy was sold at Sotheby's 3 Jun 1896 (lot 126 to Pearson for £20); at Sotheby's 4 Oct 1971 (lot 116 to Seven Gables Bookshop for £500); and at Parke–Bernet 19 Nov 1974 (lot 99 "The Stockhausen Copy" for $1300). The full text of the receipt is quoted in *CL* I 195n.

3B. Copy containing a misfolded sig C, and into which a ms fair copy of Effusion XV (=poem **103**), beginning "Poor Wanderer of the Night!", is loosely inserted
Alexander Turnbull Library, Wellington, New Zealand MS Papers 1646.

The endpapers of the copy bear traces of erasures, but these cannot now be deciphered. The inserted leaf is of the same paper as that submitted as printer's copy for the volume, and it is endorsed by Cottle with the number 96, which places it where one would expect in relation to the Rugby Manuscript sequence. Traces of glue and/or fragments of paper around the edge, and the renumbering of some adjacent Rugby Manuscript leaves, suggest that Cottle inserted it in the album sequence and then removed it. See **103** *Adaptation of "Pale Roamer thro' the Night"* VAR TEXT MS 2.

It has been supposed that Cottle himself preserved the manuscript in the defective copy, or perhaps made a gift of them together, since Effusion XV has a particular interest as a joint composition by RS and C. The volume was sold with the manuscript at Sotheby's 9 Dec 1902 (lot 1034 to Pickering for £13 15*s*). Pickering and Chatto sold them together to Alexander Turnbull on 8 May 1907. See June Starke "Effusion XV: A Memory of Pantisocracy" *The Turnbull Library Record* XI (May 1978) 18–25. However, the manuscript previously appeared in Henry Southeran's Catalogue 12 (1899) item 36 (at £5 5*s*), by itself alone. In other words, it was not Cottle who inserted it into the defective copy of *Poems* (1796), but the vendor at the Sotheby sale.

Copy 3.8 below contains a similar manuscript insertion, which may genuinely originate from Cottle.

3C. Copy presented by C to the Bristol Library Society on 17 May 1796
BPL Accession No 7676.

The copy is not inscribed or marked in any way; it is bound up with *Conciones ad Populum* and *On the Present War*, and *The Plot Discovered* (=*Lects 1795—CC*—25–74, 283–318). Was it presented in lieu of the recently terminated *Watchman*? A number of copies were distributed soon afterwards, at a guinea each, to compensate C "for his disappointment in The Watchman" (*CL* I 219 and n: to John Fellows 31 May 1796). The persons to whom they were distributed—predominantly of a liberal/radical persuasion—are glossed by Paul Magnuson "Subscribers to Coleridge's *Poems* (1796), or

Duckings and Drubbings in Nottingham" *The Coleridge Bulletin* NS XII (Winter 1998) 57–78.

3D. Presentation copy to Dora Wordsworth
Not located.
The copy was sold by Puttick and Simpson 30 Jan–3 Feb 1902 (lot 659 to Bumpus for £2 11*s*). The catalogue does not say whether the inscription was by C. One presumes not, since Dora W—WW's and MW's second child and first daughter—was not born until 16 Aug 1804. (She died 9 Jul 1847.)

3E. James Dykes Campbell's (first) copy
Not located.
The catalogue of the John A. Spoor Sale, Parke–Bernet 27 Apr 1939 (lot 173 for $30), describes it as "apparently a copy used by the poet while preparing a second edition. With autograph notes and corrections by him on a number of the pages. On page (138) is a manuscript poem of 26 lines in the poet's hand, at the foot of which he has written: '*This faces p.* 141.' In all about 1,250 words." Also, as "J. Dykes Campbell's copy, with a number of autograph notes by him, and his signature and date '1859'."
It seems likely that the autograph notes and corrections are all by JDC, and that the twenty-six lines copied on to the blank verso of the Argument to **101** *Religious Musings* are JDC's transcript of C's development of the text—either from the 1797 *Poems* or from the proof version then in the possession of R. A. Potts. There is no mention of such an extensively corrected copy either in JDC's correspondence at the HRC or in his type facsimile of the proof version, or in his 1893 *PW*, or by EHC, with whom JDC shared his discoveries. JDC possessed no other richly annotated volume, but he was in the habit of transcribing variants and annotations into his own copies. The low price fetched by the copy—the next item in the sale, a clean copy of *Poems* 1797, fetched $105—strongly suggests that the cataloguer's attribution was questioned. Indeed, the copy is likely to be the same copy, uncut in original boards—"*with numerous interesting* MS. memoranda, corrections, and alterations"—sold at the JDC Sale, Sotheby's 13 Jun 1904 (lot 81 to B. J. Stevens for £2 18*s*).
This copy is not to be confused with the one that JDC acquired later than 1859 at Sotheby's (10 Aug 1883 lot 72 for £1 10*s*), which he marked up solely with reference to R. A. Potts's interleaved version used for *Poems* (1797). The later copy is bound in marbled boards, with leather corners and spine, and is not uncut. It was acquired by the BM on 15 Jul 1968 (C 132 c 16): see copy 3.1 below.

3F. Green paper copy
Not located; perhaps non-existent.
In a letter to T. J. Wise of 30 Jan 1913 (BM Ashley B 2879 f 96ᵛ) EHC

says, apropos of offering to help Wise with his bibliography of C: "I have an edition of 1796–*Poems* on *green paper*—the proper paper having run short—& a few other rarities & oddities." The volume has not survived, either in Wise's or in EHC's or in any other known collection. Although some of Cottle's papers had a bluish tinge, it seems probable that EHC was teasing.

3G. Interleaved copies

At least two interleaved copies have survived in part. They may be presumed to have been prepared by Joseph Cottle with a second edition in mind, though perhaps before this was finally settled on. One such copy containing pp 141–75 (=sigs K7–M8) constitutes ff 6–35 of BM Ashley 408. It contains the revised text of **101** *Religious Musings* with its notes. The *JDC facsimile* does not record the blank interleaves (which have not been foliated by the BM) or the signatures; Stephens 395–7 gives further details of the manner of interleaving. One interleaf, between pp 156 and 157 of the printed text, contained corrections or redrafting in C's hand and appears to have been removed by Cottle; see **101** *Religious Musings* VAR TEXT MS 13.

Another copy is divided between two manuscripts at DCL: MS 28 and MS 30. The first of these consists of *Poems* (1796) pp 131–75 (=sigs K2–M8) interleaved, and the second of pp 33–64 (=sigs D1–E8) interleaved. The interleavings in both cases were used by WW for his own writing, in Oct–Dec 1800 and perhaps in 1806, and contain nothing in C's hand. Reed II 90–1n and 627 comments on the dating of WW's usage; cf "*Lyrical Ballads", and Other Poems, 1797–1800* ed James Butler and Karen Green (Ithaca 1992) xxiv–xxvi, 604–93.

Whether such interleaved copies are amended by C or not, they are part of the background to the preparation of *Poems* (1797) and are not annotated copies in the sense in which the term is used here.

3H. Charles Lamb's copy

CL's copy and his copy of *Poems* (1797) were sold together as part of the Frederic Dannay collection, Christie's (New York) 16 Dec 1983 (lot 77 for $1300). CL's ownership is attested in neat inscriptions by George Daniel (1789–1864) of Canonbury Square, book collector and poet, on the half-title of *Poems* (1796) and the blank flyleaf of *Poems* (1797). The Christie sale catalogue does not suggest that either copy contains C's inscriptions or corrections.

If CL received his copy from C, it arrived late. Cf *LL* (M) I 3 and the discussion in the headnote above. See also No 6E below for another copy or copies of the later volume belonging to CL.

3.1. Joseph Cottle's proofs of sig N (only)
BM Ashley 408 ff 36ʳ–57ᵛ.

The sophistication of Joseph Cottle's compilation—in which he mixed corrected and uncorrected proofs for *Poems* (1796) with copy submitted for *Poems* (1797) with proofs for **142** *Ode on the Departing Year*—is described by Stephens. The material concerning *Poems* (1796) is confined to three pulls of sig N: an extensively revised pull of the first seven pages of the signature (N1–N7); another pull, missing the first page (comprising N2–N8), much less heavily revised; and a third pull, this time of the complete signature (N1–N8), on a different kind of paper and not revised at all.

It should be noted that the *JDC facsimile* contains several errors in its transcription of the first pull, and omits to mention the presence of the second and third. JDC's marked-up copy of the 1796 *Poems* now in the BM (C 132 c 16) contains his transcription for this part of the type facsimile. He acquired the copy he used for marking up at Sotheby's on 10 Aug 1883 (lot 72 for £1 10*s*), and there is evidence that the type facsimile was ready as early as 1885 (see the letter by Simon Nowell-Smith to T. J. Wise of 23 May 1935, in BM Ashley B 2893 f 92^{r-v}).

Sig N is the last in the volume. Rugby Manuscript f 58/p 127 instructs Cottle to take the note for the sonnet to Burke (=poem **90**) from the first copy of *The Watchman*, which Cottle did and which C then in part cancelled. The proofs and the cancellation probably date, therefore, from early Mar 1796. The two corrected proofs are on paper watermarked Britannia, with a countermark comprising a circle containing three (?) plumes, which appears nowhere else in the compilation of *Poems* (1796). The paper on which the third pull of uncorrected proofs is printed—wm "WHATMAN I 1794"—was used for sigs N and A (and, in some copies, sig M) in the published volume.

Joseph Cottle died in 1853, and the compilation which includes these proofs was sold with many other of his books and manuscripts at Sotheby's 13 Mar 1865 (lot 121 to Willis for 15*s*). It soon afterwards passed into the hands of W. G. Cottersell, and then to R. A. Potts (by 1885). It was acquired by T. J. Wise from Potts, probably between 1905 and 1908; and it came into the possession of the BM in 1938.

3.2. Mary Hutchinson's copy of the proof version, missing sig A

Alexander Turnbull Library, Wellington, New Zealand R Eng COLE Poems (1796).

MH's name is written on the front free endpaper. There are annotations and deletions in C's hand on p 124 (sig I) and throughout the Notes (sig N). The revisions in sig N are less extensive than the first pull of sig N included in Joseph Cottle's incomplete copy (3.1 above), and they have been heavily cropped in rebinding. A transcript of **129** *Reflections on Having Left a Place of Retirement*, in MH's hand, is inserted between sigs M and N.

C did not, of course, know MH at the time the volume was published (she and WW were married on 4 Oct 1802). Is this the copy he might have sent WW, either just before or just after publication? See *CL* I 215–16: to J.

Thelwall 13 May 1796; also Reed I 179, 181. *Reflections on Having Left a Place of Retirement* had been written during the time the 1796 volume was being put together, and the original of the transcript might have been sent with the copy sent to WW (as C included verses in the copy sent to Thelwall and perhaps to others: see 3.5 below, and cf *CL* I 201: to J. Cottle [early Apr 1796]).

The evidence of the text of the MH transcript, however, suggests that it represents a version later than that first published in the *Monthly Magazine* in Oct 1796, and earlier than *Poems* (1797). MH might have transcribed the poem while she was at Racedown (between c 28 Nov 1796 and 4 Jun 1797), since, during the time C visited Racedown later in Jun, the poem had an important influence on WW's own *Lines Left upon a Seat in a Yew-tree.* Further details are given with poem **129** VAR.

Whoever first owned the copy, J. F. Tattersall describes in an inserted note how he discovered the volume in a Tunbridge Wells bookshop in 1899, and it bears his bookplate. Tattersall described it as still in his possession in a letter to the *TLS* (13 Jan 1916 p 21), which makes more puzzling the sale of what is apparently the same copy at Sotheby's on 17 Jun 1910 (lot 252 to Black for £1 10s). Tattersall presumably bought it back through a dealer. The Tattersall copy came to the Turnbull Library in the period 1950–5.

3.3. Thomas Poole's copy

NYPL Berg Collection Copy 6.

The copy is not strictly an inscribed/annotated one, since C's inscription is tipped in (before the half-title) on a piece of paper 1 cm taller than the page-size. Thus:

To T. Poole

My very dear Friend! I send these poems to you with better heart than I should to most others, because I know that you will read them with affection however little you mightay admire them. I love to shut my eyes, and bring up before my imagination that arbour, in which I have repeated so many of these compositions to you—. Dear Arbour! an Elysium to which I have so often passed by your Cerberus, & Tartarean tan-pits!

God bless ⟨you,⟩ my dear Poole!
& your grateful &
affectionate Friend
S. T. Coleridge

Thursday
April 11th 1796

Did C write the letter for Cottle to include and send with the poems as they became available? It is otherwise difficult to see why he did not write on the front flyleaf, where the same inscription would easily fit (cf copy 3.4).

CL I 204 prints from a transcript in the BM, which misleadingly describes the original as being written on "the first Page" of the volume; see also *Poole* I 202. The half-title carries TP's signature only. There are no annotations or insertions into the text.

The copy was sold at Sotheby's on 18 Apr 1921 (lot 570 to Maggs for £9); and again at the Jerome Kern Sale at Anderson Galleries 7–10 Jan 1929 (lot 269 for $700). It was acquired by NYPL with the collection of Owen D. Young in 1941.

3.4. Joseph Cottle's copy
   NYPL Berg Collection Copy 2.
   Inscribed by C on the front flyleaf (*CL* I 204 var):

> Dear Cottle! on the blank Leaf of my Poems I can most appropriately write my acknowledgements to you for your *too disinterested* conduct in the purchase of them, & the elegance with which you have given them to the Public. Indeed if ever they should acquire a name & character, it might be truly said, that the World owed them to you— Had it not been for you, none perhaps of them would have been published & many not written—
>
> God bless you & your affectionate Friend
>
> April 15th 1796   S. T. Coleridge

The copy was subsequently inscribed by Joseph Cottle for his great nephew, Joseph Cottle Green. It was acquired by NYPL with the collection of Owen D. Young in 1941.

3.5. John Thelwall's copy
   Not located.
   C sent a copy of the 1796 *Poems* to accompany the first letter he ever wrote to Thelwall (*CL* I 204–5). ELG dates the letter late Apr 1796, and Thelwall's reply is dated 10 May (BM Add MS 35444 ff 184–5). The presentation copy appears to have been of the kind C described to Cottle, with a sonnet on one of its blank leaves (see *CL* I 201: [early Apr 1796]). In this instance the copy appropriately contained a transcript of C's irregular sonnet to Thelwall. Two drafts of the poem are preserved among Cottle's papers associated with the 1796 volume, and Thelwall quoted from a more finished version in his reply of 10 May and again on a later occasion. Thelwall must have received the poem at the time of C's first letter and the presentation copy, since it was never published. Texts and further details are given with **130** *To John Thelwall*.

3.6. Mrs Elizabeth Evans's copy
   Cornell WORDSWORTH PR 4478 A1 1796.

Inscribed on the front flyleaf in C's hand: "Mrs Evans from the Author."

C had received an invitation to tutor the children of Mrs Elizabeth Evans of Darley Abbey, Derbyshire, in May 1796. She, the daughter of the inventor Jedediah Strutt (1726–97) and the widow of William Evans (d 1795), had proposed £150 annually and wished C to live in her residence. He was interested, but her (unidentified) father-in-law and brothers were opposed to the idea, and by Aug she had deferred to them. She gave C £95 and gave Mrs C her children's baby clothes, for their trouble. See *LL* (M) I 27–8n; *CL* I 227–35. The book might have been presented to Mrs Evans when C and Mrs C travelled to Darley to be interviewed, during Jul. There are no further annotations.

Mrs Evans of Darley Abbey appears to have no connection with the Evans families C knew in London during his schooldays and later in Bristol. The volume contains the bookplate of E. and F. Evans, and was presented to Cornell on 18 Mar 1914 by Prof James Morgan Hart.

3.7. C's own copy

NYPL Berg Collection Copy 7.

There is no inscription, but there are corrections and a brief instruction in C's hand, all in pencil, on pp 22, 24, 74, 126, 127, 128, and 168. The corrections simply take in the list of errata printed on the last page of the volume. The additional instruction on p 168—"No Notes to this to be printed"— applies to **101** *Religious Musings*, and is more likely to be a memorandum than a direction to Cottle. The 1796 notes were curtailed in 1797, but not omitted.

The copy has EHC's bookplate, and was acquired by NYPL with the collection of Owen D. Young in 1941.

3.8. Another copy, with corrections not certainly by C

Not located.

A copy which is apparently not inscribed, but which contains "several corrections in text, apparently in the author's autograph . . . Inserted is a sonnet in Coleridge's autograph, marked 'First Version.' It appears in this volume in somewhat different form as 'Effusion I.'"—i.e. **95** *To Bowles*. The copy has the half-title and page of advertisements, and is bound in "full crushed levant morocco, gilt top, uncut, by C. Cross." The quotations and details are from the catalogue of the Winston H. Hagen Sale, Anderson Galleries 13–16 May 1918 (lot 253 to Drake for $95).

The corrections in the text are not certainly in C's autograph presumably because they are minor; they could merely take in the errata. On the other hand, the presence of an early version of the sonnet to Bowles argues some connection either with C or with Joseph Cottle. Considered alongside the other copies, and taking into account the mysterious provenance (it was probably not "discovered", in England, until the late decades of the 19th century, when C.—for George?—Cross, binder to Queen Victoria, was active), the circulation of the volume probably originates with Cottle. Cottle is also more likely than C to have given away a copy with an early draft tucked inside. The corrections might even be markings by someone other than C, making this a spoiled copy like the one containing a draft of Effusion xv= **103** *Adaptation of "Pale Roamer thro' the Night!"* (see 3B above).

The book does not appear in any of the catalogues of James F. Drake, the American bookseller, in the years 1918–19—if it was he who bought it at the Hagen Sale in 1918.

4. *SONNETS FROM VARIOUS AUTHORS* (1796)

The circumstances of the printing of C's pamphlet *Sonnets from Various Authors* are described in annex B. Of the five copies known still to exist, four contain annotations, two by C and two (4A–B below) by Charles Lloyd.

4A. Charles Lloyd's copy
HEHL No 123965.

C's pamphlet is bound up with W. L. Bowles's *Sonnets, with Other Poems* (3rd ed Bath 1794) = HEHL No 123964. Lloyd signed his name on the front free endpaper of the Bowles volume, and there are pencil markings on pp 60–1 and 86–7. Lloyd also signed his name on the first page of C's pamphlet—"Charles Lloyd Jr"—and made corrections to his Sonnets III and IV, both on p 4. There is a facsimile of p 4 in *Coleridge's "Sonnets from Various Authors"* ed P. M. Zall (Glendale, Calif 1968) 32. Henry E. Huntington purchased the copy with the Church Collection in Apr 1911.

4B. Sophia Pemberton's copy
Cornell WORDSWORTH PR 4161 B4 1796.

C's pamphlet is bound up between W. L. Bowles *Sonnets, and Other Poems* (4th ed 1796) and Charles Lloyd *Poems on Various Subjects* (Carlisle 1795). The front free endpaper of the combined volume is signed "Sophia Pemberton | 1796". In the pamphlet Lloyd has corrected his Sonnets III and IV, both on p 4, and his Sonnet XXI on p 13. There are numerous notes and corrections in Lloyd's hand, in ink and pencil, throughout *Poems*.

The possibility that other copies exist—perhaps corrected—bound up with copies of Bowles's *Sonnets* or catalogued under Anna Seward is discussed in annex B. The fifth known copy, without annotations, is bound up with Mrs Calvert's copy of *Poems* (1812) (see 14.2 in the present annex). CL records receiving a copy (*LL*—M—I 73–5), which has not survived; nor have the five copies that C sent to TP (*CL* I 252: to TP 7 Nov [1796]).

A portion of p 16, corrected in C's hand, the lower half containing Sonnet XXVIII = **86** *To the Author of "The Robbers"* (with Sonnet XXVI, by Bowles, on the verso), is in the Pforzheimer (Misc 74). The 1796 *Sonnets* text has been corrected in a way which suggests that it was used as copy for *Poems* (1797) (it is also endorsed by Joseph Cottle), and the corrected version is better treated as part of the history of the particular poem than as part of an annotated copy. See poem **86** VAR.

4.1. Mrs Thelwall's copy
   V&A Dyce Collection 4to 1298.
   C's pamphlet is bound up with W. L. Bowles's *Sonnets, and Other Poems* (4th ed 1796). C has inscribed the flyleaf of the Bowles volume as follows (*CL* I 287 var; *CM—CC—*I 717):

> Dear Mrs Thelwall
>   I entreat your acceptance of this Volume, which has given me more pleasure, and done my heart more good, than all the other books, I ever read, excepting my Bible. Whether you approve or condemmmn my poetical taste, this Book will at least serve to remind you of your unseen, yet not the less sincere,
>
> Friend
Samuel Taylor Coleridge
>
> Sunday Morning   December the eighteenth
>   1796

There are comments in C's hand on *Sonnets* pp 2, 13, and 16.

4.2. Sara Hutchinson's copy
   DCL MS 14/2.
   Inscribed by C at the head of p 1: "The Editor to Asahara, the Moorish Maid I Dec. 1800 I Greta Hall, I Keswick." There are corrections in C's hand on pp 4 (Charles Lloyd's sonnet *To Scotland*) and 5.

5. *ODE ON THE DEPARTING YEAR* (1796)=poem **142**

There are at least three states of the printed version. The differences are in sig D and affect the last two pages of text (pp 15, 16). An early, uncorrected state is represented by V&A Dyce L° 2293, where a variant on p 16 affects **143** *Lines to a Young Man of Fortune* 9. A later, trial state is represented by BM Ashley 4766, where a variant p 15 constitutes a rearrangement of **142.**158–70. The second state, which combines the Dyce L° 2293 text of poem **142** with the Ashley 4766 text of poem **143**—viz the combination of readings found in BM C 59 e 14(1) and C 126 k 6—would seem to be the most common.
   Besides the two known inscribed copies, two others are worthy of note. First, lot 121 in the Joseph Cottle Sale, Sotheby's 13 Mar 1865, was *Ode on the Departing Year* ("*two copies, with Corrections and Additions by the author*").

This was sold to Willis for 15s, bound in one volume with a corrected part of *Poems* (1796); from which it is clear that it is in fact what now makes up BM Ashley 408. In other words, this item constitutes two sets of proofs of sig A of *Poems* (1797) rather than a pair of annotated copies of *Ode on the Departing Year*: see No 6.1 in the present annex.

The second is James Losh's copy, marked up in ink and pencil, at DCL (COL (a) 1796). Losh's diary, now at Tullie House Library, Carlisle (front pastedown), reveals that Losh sent WW this copy of C's pamphlet on 20 Mar 1797, along with other books and magazines. From previous references in the diary it appears that he had read some of what he sent WW—indeed, that some of the books and pamphlets were his own and that he had finished with them. Losh sent the book from Bristol, where C arrived between 16 and 23 Mar to meet Cottle, with whom he was arranging to include a revised version of the ode in the new edition of his poems. C and Losh had of course met previously—in Bath and in Bristol—and had corresponded, but there is no evidence that they met during Mar.

C had been revising the ode in the months since its publication in Dec 1796. But the underlinings and markings appear to have nothing to do with the revisions he was making at the time, or with any he made afterwards, and they seem to be in Losh's or someone else's hand. It seems probable that Losh sent his own copy of the poem to WW on 20 Mar because he had no further use for it, and that the markings have nothing to do with C.

5.1. Unascribed copy
Not located.
A copy bearing an inscription in C's hand on the title-page—"From the author December 30, 1796"—was sold at the John Pearson Sale, Sotheby's 7 Nov 1916 (lot 95). There are no annotations. The blank portion of the title has a small defect, which has been repaired; and the volume is bound in green morocco extra, with gilt edges. Pearson was a knowledgeable collector of C's manuscripts and printed books, as well as being the publisher of Richard Herne Shepherd's 1873 edition of *Osorio . . . As Originally Written in 1797*; the inscription is almost certainly genuine.

5.2. Samuel Reid's copy
Not located.
A copy bearing an inscription in C's hand on the title-page—"To Mr. S. Reid from the Author"—was listed in Blackwell's Rare Books Catalogue No A-77 (Feb 1985) item 40 (for £900). The copy, in frayed blue wrappers, had a consistent tear laterally through the centre of each leaf, and the catchword on p 15 together with C's printed signature following the text on p 16 had been torn away. It was repaired and rebound before being offered for sale by Blackwell's.

Samuel Reid appears to have been a contemporary of George Burnett

(1776–1811), and likewise a common Dissenting friend of C and John Prior Estlin (see *CL* I 578: to J. P. Estlin 1 Mar [1800]). He might also have been the Mr Reed whom RS described as "an intimate friend" of Charles Lloyd, or his brother (see *S Letters*—Curry—I 132). Inscribed copies of *Conciones ad Populum* (1795) and *The Plot Discovered* (1795) (=*Lects 1795*—*CC*— 25–74, 283–318), the first with a correction on p 51, were sold at Christie's (London) 19 Sept 1984 lots 102 and 104 (both to Taylor, for £2200 and £2400 respectively).

6. *POEMS* (1797)

The printing history of what C thought of as the second edition of his *Poems* is as complicated as that of the first collection (1796). It is described in annex B above, and bears on his annotations in several ways.

Copy submitted by C to the printer might be confused with proofs furnished by the printer to C, since C in some instances submitted marked-up or interleaved pages from the 1796 collection. The confusion is encouraged by Joseph Cottle's muddled combination of material connected with the two separate collections—into the Rugby Manuscript (see annex A 8) and in copy 6.1 below. Cottle was able to incorporate changes sent to him as late as 8 Jun 1797 (*CL* I 325).

Publication of the 1797 collection was curiously delayed even after it was printed, and there are conflicting accounts of its availability. It was available for Charles Lloyd to inscribe a copy on 4 Jul (see copy 6D), and for RS to tell correspondents on 11 Jul that it was "published now". RS discussed its contents with C at about the same time, in terms that suggest both of them possessed or had seen copies (see copy 6.10). It was reviewed with lengthy quotations in the *Monthly Visitor* II (Aug 1797) 169–80. On the other hand, Lloyd waited until the end of Sept before telling his brother Robert that it was available at Robinson's, the London booksellers,[2] and it was not advertised as published until 28 Oct (in *M Post*).

The explanation of these apparent contradictions bears on the corrections in the bulk of annotated copies (6.2–7 below). C at first hoped that Joseph Cottle would pay a boy to make by hand the corrections he had sent during early Jul instead of inserting a loose errata slip (*CL* I 330–2: to J. Cottle [c 3 Jul 1797]). When Cottle did not, one must suppose that the unresolved issue delayed distribution and sales outside Bristol through Jul–Sept, while C was busy with visits from the Wordsworths, the Lambs, and John Thelwall, with the completion of *Osorio* and the writing of other poems, and with absences and illnesses, while Cottle was occupied with the second edition of RS's *Poems*. It may be significant that C visited Bristol on 25 Oct (*Bristol LB* No 97), a

[2] E. V. Lucas *Charles Lamb and the Lloyds* (1898) 43.

few days before the *M Post* announcement. It may also be significant that in correspondence with Cottle during Feb–Mar 1798 C was referring to a third edition as a matter previously agreed upon (*CL* I 387, 391, 399): the agreement may well have been reached at the earlier time, in the same spirit and for the same reasons which had prompted Cottle's agreement to publish a second edition when he was bringing out the first, as a way of resolving the dilemma arising from C's instinct for revision. As indicated above, Cottle did not employ anyone to insert the errata by hand, and the only errata slips which are known to have been inserted concern Lloyd's poems and no others (*C Bibl*—Wise—39).

The main body of annotated copies appears to date from Aug–Oct 1797. The corrections are almost entirely a selection of the errata that C had sent Cottle, and must have been written in as it became clear that Cottle was not going to do so himself. The corrections in four of the copies concentrate on **101** *Religious Musings* (copies 6.2–4, 6.7), and it may be no accident that three of the four are known to have been given to clergymen, who might have heightened C's awareness of the poem's theological implications. The internal sequence of this main body of annotated copies is uncertain, since only one of them (6.3) is dated. It will be noted that this date—17 Oct—precedes that of the London announcement in *M Post*.

The 1797 collection was superseded almost at once in C's mind by other interests—*Osorio*, his collaborations with WW and *LB*, Germany, indeed by a "third edition". It is therefore not surprising that only a few annotated copies demonstrably date from after Oct 1797. One of them is of doubtful authenticity (6.8), and another was given to Thomas Hutchinson in 1800 (6.9). The copy with the most extensive corrections and comments of all (6.10) dates from several years later still, and its relation to the others is oblique. This is the copy that RS apparently acquired as soon as copies became available in Jul 1797, probably directly from Cottle, and which C must have rediscovered at Greta Hall—probably around Apr 1809.

6A. Presentation copy to R. B. Sheridan

    Not located.

    C apparently sent a copy to Sheridan through Bowles, along with the manuscript of *Osorio*, on 16 Oct 1797 (*CL* I 356). It is not known whether it was inscribed or corrected, though it would be remarkable if it had not been.

    This entry can meanwhile stand for the copies almost certainly given to TP, WW, and perhaps Bristol friends and others, which are likely to have been inscribed and/or corrected but which have not been recorded. They may be any one of the unseen, unlocated copies described below (6.6–8).

6B. Presentation copy to Dr Parr

    Not located.

    C told Cottle that he intended to send a copy to Parr "with a sonnet" (*CL* I 331: [c 3 Jul 1797]). Samuel Parr (1747–1825), "the Whig Johnson", had subscribed to C's projected "Imitations of the Modern Latin Poets" (*CL* I 101: to RS [11 Sept 1794]; see poem **50.X1**). He was also, at the time, sympathetic to radical causes like the one concerning Joseph Gerrald, which also involved C (see *Lects 1795—CC—*14n). Even so, C's consciousness of the differences dividing them[3] might have overtaken a passing resolve, and the copy might never have been prepared.

6C. Sara Coleridge's copy
HRC (uncatalogued in 1978).
This copy is annotated by SC with variant readings, and interleaved with transcriptions by her in ink and pencil from the 1796 *Poems*. It is inscribed "Sara Coleridge January 1852" on the second title-page, and "Edith Coleridge" on the front flyleaf.

6D. Charles Lloyd's copy
HEHL has the part of the 1797 volume (pp 151–214) that belonged to Lloyd, but it contains no annotations. A copy said to be Lloyd's, with his signature on the title-page, was sold at Hodgson's 20 Feb 1930 (lot 539 to Stonehill for £42). A copy inscribed by Lloyd to Mary Lloyd, dated 4 Jul 1797, was sold by Parke–Bernet 15 May 1941 (lot 599). A copy with an inscription by Lloyd to Susan Hawker, dated 1812, was sold by Puttick 12 Jan 1921 (lot 169 to Lawson for £3 10*s*).

6E. Charles Lamb's copy.
Boston Public Library.
The Boston copy contains no annotations. See also copy 3H above for another said to have belonged to CL. CL's presentation copy to Marmaduke Thompson, dated 3 May 1798 and annotated, was sold by Puttick 30 Jul–1 Aug 1913 (lot 105 to Dobell for £26); by Henkels of Philadelphia 18 Apr 1922 (lot 1 for $200); by Parke–Bernet 23 Jan 1941 (lot 399). Another (?) presentation copy by CL, with many corrections in his hand, was sold by Parke–Bernet 17 Apr 1945 (lot 208).

6F. James Losh's copy
Not located.
This copy, with Losh's pictorial bookplate and a long pencil note asserting that it came from the library at Rydal Mount, was offered for sale by Wm Reese Co, New Haven, Conn, Catalogue 134 (Jun 1994) item 260 for $600. It contains no annotations.

6.1. Joseph Cottle's proofs of sig A (only)
BM Ashley 408 ff 58^r–72^v.
The sophistication of Cottle's compilation has already been described with

---

[3] See *CN* I 101, 112; also **2** *Fragments of an Ode on Punning.*

reference to *Poems* (1796): copies 3G and 3.1 above. The material concerning *Poems* (1797) comprises the manuscript Advertisement and an interleaved version of **101** *Religious Musings*, consisting of the 1796 printed text with revisions, both submitted as printer's copy. These are properly part of the pre-publication history of the volume (see annex B 3, and copy 3G in the present annex). In addition, there are two sets of annotated proofs of sig A, which are included here.

Sig A embraces pp 1–16 of the printed text, i.e. **142** *Ode on the Departing Year* in its entirety. Both sets of proofs are identical, though the Argument is missing from the second, and both contain corrections and comments by C, many of which coincide. The second set also contains Cottle's responses to C's instructions, which prove that while the printed texts are identical they were annotated on separate occasions. *Ode on the Departing Year* had been published as a separate quarto pamphlet in Dec 1796. It replaced **139** *The Destiny of Nations*, which C originally planned as the first poem in the new collection, some time in Jan–Feb 1797. References in C's letters make it clear that the proofs were printed and corrected in early Mar 1797 (*CL* I 313, 315: to J. Cottle [10, 15 Mar 1797]). C introduced further changes into the ode in a letter to Cottle which ELG dates 8 Jun (*CL* I 325). The watermark of the proof signatures is "DURHAM AND SON", the same as in sigs B and C of the printed volume; the revised sig A, printed after 8 Jun, is watermarked "IP | 1794", the paper on which Cottle had printed sigs D–Q.

JDC facsimile, the type facsimile of BM Ashley 408, contains several minor errors in its transcription of the two proofs. Four pages are reproduced photographically in *C Bibl* (Wise *TLP*) 63, facing p 63, and facing p 64. Details of the provenance of the original are given with copy 3.1 in the present annex.

6.2. Rev William Lisle Bowles's copy

In the possession of Erwin Schwarz (1983).

The copy is not inscribed, but on the verso of the first flyleaf is written "Lucy Benett | given her by the Rev^nd W. L. Bowles", and there is the library stamp of Pyt House Library, Tisbury, Wiltshire. The copy is corrected and revised in C's hand on pp 16, 22, 33, 78, 97, 105, 109, 114, between 122 and 123 (a single leaf tipped in to p 123, containing a rewritten version of **101** *Religious Musings* 64–77 on the recto, verso blank), 123–4, and 145. The corrections and revisions are close to the list of errata C sent Cottle in early Jul 1797 (*CL* I 331–2), and also to the Barbey and Roskilly copies (6.3–4 below). They were made hurriedly, since there is blotting on some facing pages. There is slight evidence that the copy might be an early state of the edition: see **149** *Allegorical Lines on the Same Subject* 5–7 VAR commentary.

Crease-lines impressed on the pages before and after show that the leaf tipped in to p 123 was originally 10.5 cm in overall width. The position of C's (cropped) description—"Page 123."—at the head suggests that he folded and so described the leaf immediately after he had copied the rewritten passage of *Religious Musings*, so that it would fit inside the pages of the book. The paper broke at the fold (the pressure on the book in the rebinding process appears, from the crease-lines, to have been excessive), the detached RH side was lost, and with it the end of the verse-lines. The leaf does not have any watermark or chain-lines, and appears to be made up of slightly lighter stock than the pages of the book. The instruction at the foot of p 123 is at first puzzling: "See the blank page of this volume: at the end." It has blotted on to p 122 (i.e. was written before the extra leaf was inserted). The blank page at the end (S4) has been roughly torn out, and there are again traces of ink-blotting at the top of the facing page (278). At the same time the extra, inserted leaf was on wider paper, different from the missing S4. One explanation is that C first drafted his revision on the blank S4, headed it when he finished (say) "Insert on p 123" (the vestiges of this being left as the blotting on p 278), then drafted another revision, or a fair copy of the first, on a separate leaf, which he folded and inserted at p 123, tearing out the superseded draft. The book was rebound at an early stage, before (or perhaps when) Bowles inscribed it to Lucy Benett, at which point the extra leaf was tipped in to p 123. The new first flyleaf of the rebinding has the wm "180" (in the gutter). There are stubs in the front and rear flyleaves of the rebinding: they probably have nothing to do with the tipped-in leaf or the removed S4, but are instead relics of the incompetent country binder whose pressure on the book seems to have been responsible for the loss of part of the inserted leaf and the very shaky condition of the binding today.

The copy was presumably given to Bowles when C visited him at Donhead some time between 6 and 14 Sept 1797 (*WL*—E rev—192; **157** *Sonnet: To William Linley*). Lucy Benett was either the Lucy Lambert of Boyton, near Warminster, who married John Benett of Norton Bavant and Pythouse (the adversary of Henry "Orator" Hunt and William Cobbett) in 1801 and who died on 7 Feb 1827; or her daughter, Lucy Harriet Benett, who was born in 1802 and married on 27 Aug 1827 the Rev Arthur Fane. It seems most likely that the book was given to the elder of the two: if given to the younger, it would not have remained at Pythouse (she died at Torquay on 5 or 6 Apr 1845); and if it was given away by Bowles at the time it was rebound, this is likely to have been during or soon after the first decade of the century (see the watermark on the rebound first flyleaf). The book might have left the Pythouse library any time during the late 19th or early 20th century. It was in the possession of the Sherman Haight family of New York from the early 1930s to the later 1960s, at least, and contains the Haight bookplate on the front pastedown. Mr Schwarz acquired it from the New York dealer John Fleming during the 1970s.

6.3. The Abbé Barbey's copy
BM C 126 b 1.

Inscribed by C on the front free flyleaf: "Mr Barbey from S. T. Coleridge, in token of his unmingled esteem.—Oct. 17th, 1797". The copy has corrections in C's hand to pp 105, 127, 135, 145, and 147—in all but one instance to the text of **101** *Religious Musings*.

Mrs Sandford records that the Abbé Barbey escaped the September Massacres and took up residence in Stowey in Aug 1795. He made a living by teaching French and became a particular friend of the Poole family; "a good old man in appearance, and speaking but little English" (*Poole* I 116–17, 164–6; II 35). There are also comments on him in the early pages of the diary of the Rev William Holland, Vicar of Over Stowey, covering the period 1799–1819 (photocopy of a typescript at Somerset Record Office, Taunton: T PM ay 1), from which it appears that Barbey taught Holland's children French, usually in return for vegetables and a meal, that he was a canon of Lisieux, and that Holland thought him a good Latin scholar and well-read in divinity and history: "the best of all Emigrants I ever met with".[4] Barbey was quite independent of and separate from the small, short-lived, and problematic community of French Carthusian monks at Lord Arundell's house of Coombe Priory, at Donhead St Mary nearby.[5] Bellenger 145 indicates that Barbey's full correct name was Guillaume Le Barbey, a detail supplied from the Winchester collection of passports issued to French priests.

The volume was given by Barbey to a Mr T. Gill "as a mark of Kinship" in 1802, as a pencil note in Gill's hand records, and Gill in turn presented it to Mr Justice Coleridge (=JTC) in 1839. Another flyleaf bears the name and date of the first Lord Coleridge, Apr 1875, to whom the book had been given by his father. It was acquired from the third Lord Coleridge by the BM in 1951.

6.4. Rev William Roskilly's copy
     In the possession of J.C.C. Mays (1999).

The copy has "Wm Roskilly" written on the title-page, and corrections by C on pp vi, 22, 78, 87, 97, 105, 107, 109, 113, 124, 145, 146, and 147. The Roskilly copy is—along with the Bowles copy (6.2 above)—closest to the errata list C sent Cottle in early Jul 1797 (*CL* I 331–2). The corrections were made either in late summer/early autumn 1797, when the volume was published, or in early Jun 1800, when C presented Roskilly with a copy of *Wallenstein*. Comparison with other known corrected copies makes it clear that the corrections were made not later than 1800, and supports the likelihood that they were made soon after publication.

William Roskilly was curate in charge of Stowey in 1797, and was pro-

---

[4] Holland's remarks on the Coleridges are at the same time scathing. The version published as *Paupers and Pig Killers* ed Jack Eyres (Gloucester 1984) is selective and includes only one reference to Barbey.

[5] See Dominic Aidan Bellenger *The French Exiled Clergy in the British Isles after 1789* (Downside Abbey 1986) 94–5.

moted to be rector of Kempsford in Gloucestershire very soon after C left for Germany in 1798. Berta Lawrence supplies brief notes on his life in "The Cornish Curate" *Coleridge Bulletin* NS II (Autumn 1993) 2–4.

I purchased the copy from the Ravenstree Company of Wellton, Arizona, in Jan 1980, who in turn had it from Deighton Bell of Cambridge. These and previous dealers had not recognised the corrections as being in C's hand.

6.5. Rev George Coleridge's copy
Princeton Robert H. Taylor Collection.
Inscribed by C on the title-page: "The Author's Present to his Brother. George Coleridge—". C corrected the text on pp 22, 78, and 105. It had previously been sold by Parke–Bernet 20 Feb 1950 (lot 118).

6.6. Unascribed copy
Not located.
A copy containing pencil corrections in C's hand on pp 78, 82, and 97— i.e. to Sonnet IV *To the River Otter* (=poem **140**), Sonnet VII *Pale Roamer thro' the Night!* (=poem **103**), and *Composed at Clevedon* (=**115** *The Eolian Harp*). Four lines are altered in the first poem, two in the second; in the third four lines are crossed through and four others substituted. It is bound in contemporary calf, slightly worn and mottled, rebacked, with a new leather label, in a cloth case. It is described in Sotheby's catalogue 1 May 1946 (lot 935 to King for £5); Sotheby's catalogue (Arthur Randle Sale) 11 Oct 1948 (lot 43 to Schwartz for £9); Parke–Bernet catalogue 20 Feb 1950 (lot 120 for $22); and Hodgson's catalogue 4 Aug 1950 (lot 847 to Schwartz for £8). The low prices at each sale are not evidence that the corrections were discovered to be inauthentic: other prices were comparably low. Arthur Randle's ownership might be thought to weigh slightly in favour of their authenticity, since he was a knowledgeable Coleridge collector. If the corrections are by C, the fact that they are in pencil suggests that the copy was C's own, or was intended to be when the corrections were made. It might indeed be among the first of the copies he corrected.

6.7. Unascribed copy
Not located.
A copy owned and described by J. Rogers Rees as C's own: "Coleridge Items" *N&Q* ser 10 IX (25 Jan 1908) 63–4 at 63. The only annotation which Rees gives details of is on p 145. It affects **101** *Religious Musings* 370–3, which are emended (though a little differently) in other copies. Rees was a knowledgeable collector—for example, he owned West's marked-up stage version of *Remorse* (copy 15.5 below) and the copy of *SL* that C gave to J.H.B. Williams (copy 17.22 below)—but some doubt remains over C's authorship of the annotation.

6.8. Unascribed copy
Not located.

"With a two-line note in Coleridge's hand on the verso of the fly-title: *'Fears in Solitude/Frost at Midnight'*." The copy is so described in Blackwell's Centenary Antiquarian Catalogue A-1 (1979) item 75. It is bound in brick-red morocco, with gilt lettering and ornaments, signed by T. J. Cobden-Sanderson at the Doves Bindery in 1907. It was from the library of Charles Walker Andrews, with his bookplate on the front pastedown, and listed at £1200. *American Book Prices Current, 1977–1978* LXXXIV (New York 1979) 249 lists this same copy as sold at Christie's (New York) 7 Apr 1978 (lot 303 for $1300), but it has not been possible to confirm the transaction.

The note is of a kind without parallel in other known annotated copies—of *Poems* (1797) or indeed of any C title—and for this reason doubts might be entertained concerning its authenticity. Poem **171** *Frost at Midnight* was not written until Feb 1798, and **175** *Fears in Solitude* before Apr 1798; both were first published, in a pamphlet together with **174** *France: An Ode* (also written in Feb 1798), following C's departure for Germany in September of the same year.

6.9. Thomas Hutchinson's copy
In the possession of Jonathan Wordsworth (1979).

Inscribed by C on the title-page: "T. Hutchinson from S. T. Coleridge". C corrected and annotated the text on pp 14, 15, 78, 80, 82, 85, 96, and 181. The corrections were probably made in Dec 1801, when C also presented a corrected copy of *Wallenstein* to Hutchinson; the ink and the handwriting, indeed the whole manner of correction, are very similar. The annotation on p 181—to Charles Lloyd's *Lines Addressed to S. T. Coleridge*—is quoted in **138** *To Charles Lloyd, on his Proposing to Domesticate with the Author* headnote.

6.10. Robert Southey's copy
Yale In 678 797 Copy 1.

The copy contains no inscription, but there are corrections and comments by C on pp viii, ix, x, xii, xix, 5, 11, 13, 14, 15, 22, 49, 50, 51, 53, 55, 57, 66, 71, 78, 82, 87, 88, 96, 97, 98, 99, 103, 105, 113, 114, 115, 128, 135, 137, and 139. The corrections on pp 113, 114, 115 (in **138** *To Charles Lloyd, on his Proposing to Domesticate with the Author*), and 135 are not certainly in C's hand—it could be RS's or Charles Lloyd's. Lloyd added notes and dates to his own poems (pp 168, 169, 170, 171, 172, 174, 175, 176, 177, 178, and 186; the corrections on pp 200 and 201 might be by RS). A note on p 261 is signed "C. B." (=Caroline Bowles), who might indeed have made the corrections here tentatively ascribed to RS.

It is likely that the annotations by Lloyd were made first, and those in what appears to be RS's hand at about the same time or soon afterwards. RS had asked Cottle about the volume as early as 2 May 1797 (*S Letters*—Curry—I 127), and received an advance copy from him before 11 Jul (see *S Life*—CS—I 319; *S Letters*—Curry—I 134), so that by c 17 Jul C was responding to his congratulations (*CL* I 333, 334). Lloyd meanwhile spent the summer and early autumn with RS, first at Burton and then at Bath. C's comments and corrections date from much later. Those on pp 82 and 87 refer to a "third edition" of C's poems, i.e. to the edition of 1803; they appear to have been made after C's return from Italy in 1806 (cf p 71); indeed, they refer to the estrangement from WW, which took place between 1807 and Oct 1810 (cf p 88).

The corrections differ from those in copies corrected earlier in that some repeat changes made in *Poems* (1803) and thus anticipate changes made in *SL*, while others have no parallel. They are most likely to have been made between Dec 1808 and Oct 1810, when C was staying at Allan Bank—perhaps about Apr 1809, when he negotiated yet again with Longman for a new edition of his poems (*CL* III 191; VI 1022–5; III 238; cf III 324–5). Caroline Bowles's comment might have been inserted any time after 1823, when she first visited RS at Keswick, and before she married him in 1839 (she died in 1854). A copy of C's 1797 *Poems* was sold with RS's books at Sotheby's 10 May 1844 (lot 628 to Kerslake): it was apparently not inscribed, but the catalogue does not separately notice annotated copies.

The volume bears the bookplates of Frederick Locker(-Lampson) and C. B. Tinker. While it was in the possession of Locker-Lampson it was described and quoted several times: see Frederick Locker-Lampson *The Rowfant Library* (1886) 148; *P&DW* (RHS) I 82, 129, 160, 163, 164, II 379; *PW* (JDC) 542B, 577B, 588B; *PW* (EHC) I 173, II 1147, etc. C. B. Tinker acquired it at the James B. Clemens Sale, Parke–Bernet 8 Jan 1945 (lot 179 for $160). RHS transcribed the annotations—including those by Charles Lloyd, RS, and Caroline Bowles—into a copy of the 1797 *Poems* now at HUL (*EC8 C6795 796 pb (C)). This volume was acquired by HUL in Jul 1943, and has no textual significance.

7. *LYRICAL BALLADS* (1798)

There are two issues of the first edition, the Bristol and the London printings. There is also a cancelled state of the first issue containing **172** *Lewti* (replaced in the later state by **112** *To the Nightingale*). The copy of the later state in the Ashley Library, containing (besides *To the Nightingale*) a poem by Thomas Beddoes called *Domiciliary Verses*, printed on a separate leaf and paginated 62* and 63*, has been proven to be one of Wise's forgeries.

Loose type in the imposition of the Bristol issue affects the poor positioning of one word (in WW's *Tintern Abbey*) in some copies; and many copies of the London issue have the misprint "Oft" in **161** *The Rime of the Ancient Mariner* on p 19 (see VAR **161**.202.1) neatly corrected to "Off", evidently by the printer or publisher. The second issue differs from the later state of the first only in its title-page. Convenient summaries of the bibliographical details are provided by *The Cornell Wordsworth Collection* ed George Harris Healey (Ithaca 1957) 3–5 and *The Rothschild Library* (2 vols Cambridge 1954) II 703–4. See also R. A. Potts "*Lyrical Ballads*, First Edition" *The Academy* LXX (6 Jan 1906) 20–1; John Edwin Wells "*Lyrical Ballads*: A Variant?" *RES* IX (1933) 199–201 on the effects of loose type.

Further details of the evolution of the volume and its subsequent enlargement are provided, along with a wealth of illustrative matter, in *"Lyrical Ballads", and Other Poems, 1797–1800* ed Butler and Green. This also gives details of copies of *LB* (1800, 1802, 1805) which contain corrections of WW's contributions in the hands of DW, WW, MW, and RS (see e.g. pp xxxiv–xxxvi, xxxix).

The errata listed on p [211] bear on several of C's corrections.

7.1. Martha Fricker's copy

Not located.

PW (EHC) II 1030, 1032, 1039 nn describes a copy of the cancelled state of the first issue (containing **172** *Lewti*) which C presented to his sister-in-law Martha Fricker. It contains corrections on pp 9, 11, and 29—i.e. to the text of **161** *The Rime of the Ancient Mariner*—and could be the same copy as 7.4 below.

7.2. C's own copy?

Trinity College Cambridge TCL RW 38 28–29.

The volume, which is a first issue containing **112** *To the Nightingale*, is bound up in mid-19th-century calf, with a first issue of *Lyrical Ballads* (1800) vol II. Only the 1798 volume is annotated by C, in ink on pp 18 and 19, in pencil on p 43. The ink annotations are illustrated in *The Rothschild Library* II facing p 704. The pencil annotation (which is passed over in the *Rothschild Library* description) is now faint. The partially obliterated readings are supplied in *P&DW* II 54 by RHS, to whose publisher, Basil Montagu Pickering, the volumes once belonged.

The annotations are all to **161** *The Rime of the Ancient Mariner*, whose textual history suggests that they were made soon after the book was printed. C's emendation of "those" to "these" twice on p 18, as noted in the Errata (see lines 185, 187), was forgotten very soon after. The manuscript stanza inserted after line 189 was afterwards forgotten, and instead lines 189.1.1–5 were dropped. C's emendations must have been made before WW began to articulate his dissatisfaction with "the old words and the strangeness of it" (*WL*—E rev—264). The revised text of 1800 amends the poem at the same points, but as if approaching them anew, and was arrived at by Jul 1800 (*CL* I 598–602: to Biggs and Cottle [mid-Jul 1800]).

This copy was in the possession of B. M. Pickering when it was cited by

RHS. It was sold by Sotheby's 28 Jun 1912 (lot 417); it was in the possession of H. T. Butler in 1927–30 (when it was cited by J. L. Lowes in *RX*), in whose sale it was sold at Hodgson's 14 Jun 1934 (lot 447 to Quaritch for £460); and it was sold in the Harmsworth Sale, Sotheby's 24 Oct 1944 (lot 1759).

7.3. Another such copy?
Not located.
The copy is described thus in *C Bibl* (Haney) 107: "A copy of the first edition bound up with the second volume of the second edition, with an inserted A.L.S. of Wordsworth and many additions and alterations to *The Ancient Mariner* in Coleridge's autograph. Sold at Bangs' for $200.00 on January 31, 1895 (Foote Sale), to W. A. White, Esq., of New York City." A similar description of the unlocated copy is given in *American Book-prices Current* I (1895) item 2048.
It is just possible that the copy is the same as 7.2 above, having travelled in America for some twenty or thirty years.

7.4. Another such copy?
Not located.
The copy is described thus in Hodgson's sale catalogue 23 Oct 1924 (lot 599): "(Wordsworth—W.—and Coleridge—S.T.—) Lyrical Ballads, *First Edition, with a few corrections in MS., apparently in Coleridge's hand (bdg. bkn.)*". *Book-auction Records for 1924–5* XXII (1926) 175 gives the purchaser as Sanger, for £9 10s. This could be the same copy as 7.1 above.

8. *LYRICAL BALLADS* (1800)

The bibliographical complexities of this edition, which are even more extensive than in the case of the 1798 edition, do not affect C's contributions or annotations.

8.1. C's copy? later Edward Irving's?
Victoria State Library, Melbourne * 821.71 L.
The copy, of vol I only, contains C's signature on the front flyleaf and at the end of **152** *The Foster-mother's Tale* (p 28), **153** *The Dungeon* (p 84), **112** *To the Nightingale* (p 100), and **253** *Love* (p 144), as well as on the half-title of **161** *The Rime of the Ancient Mariner*. It also contains corrections and additions in C's hand on pp xi (Preface), 5 (WW's *The Tables Turned*), 26, 27 (*The Foster-mother's Tale*), 141 (*Love*), 153, 179, 196 (*The Rime of the Ancient Mariner*). The title-page, the half-title of *The Rime of the Ancient Mariner*, and pp 153 and 179 are reproduced by Geoffrey Little "Coleridge's Copy of *Lyrical Ballads*, 1800 and his Connection with the Irving Family" *The Book Collector* XXXIII (Winter 1984) 457–69.

The additions to *The Rime of the Ancient Mariner* might be in response to WW's criticism in his note on the poem in the same edition; or they might accompany C's tinkering with the poem in 1806–7, as he projected a new collection with Longman. The annotation to the other poems is similarly inconclusive: three of the four corrections to C's own poems are adopted in the 1802 and 1805 editions of *LB* (though they were ignored in *SL*); the fourth correction is adopted in the 1813 text of *Remorse* and afterwards, though it was ignored in the 1802 and 1805 *LB*. The corrections and additions might have been made before 1802, or they might have been written after 1805.

The copy was given to Victoria State Library in 1900 by Professor M. H. Irving, who had emigrated to Melbourne in 1856. He was the son of C's friend Edward Irving, for whom see **602** *Lines on Edward Irving* headnote; also *CN* IV 4963n. A copy of *LB* vol II only—"S. T.COLERIDGE'S COPY, SIGNED BY HIM ON FLY-LEAF AND WITH ALTERATIONS TO THE TEXT IN HIS HAND *on about* 20 *pages, contemporary calf, spine and lower cover missing, upper cover detached.*"—was sold at Sotheby's 14 Apr 1959 (lot 331 for £380). The cataloguer notes that "Coleridge has corrected with his own hand most of the errata listed on the last page, and has made a few other changes in the text besides deleting several passages." This second volume has not been located: if it is the partner of the Irving copy, it might help determine more exactly when the annotations were made.

8.2. Another, related copy?
Not located.

The Doris L. Bentz sale at Christie's (New York) 16 Nov 1984 (lot 403 for $1300) comprised the following: a copy of the second edition, revised, of vol I, with the usual cancels, and of the first edition, second issue, of vol II; "original blue boards, uncut, spines repaired and worn with handwritten labels added, rear free endpaper in vol. 2 removed, maroon quarter-morocco gilt box-case." Tipped in at the front endpaper of vol I is a slip with the following inscription in C's hand: "Magna dabit qui magna potest: Mihi parva potenti, Parvaque poscenti, parva dedisse sat est. S. T. C." tr "He will give much who can give much; for me, who can give little and ask little, it is enough to have given little" =**493** *Latin Distich on Giving and Receiving.*

The volumes bear the signature of "Lillies Campbell | July 2, 1805" on each title-page. C was in Malta at that time, but is not known to have been acquainted with such a person. The tipped-in inscription would seem to have been composed—if it was indeed composed by C—in 1811–12 (*CN* III 4122). C used it again when he made a gift of his "literary labours" to the Lord Chief Justice, Charles Abbott, in Nov 1819 (*CL* IV 964).

9. *LYRICAL BALLADS* (1805)

A copy in the BM, C 58 bb 23, is inscribed on the title-page of vols I and II: "W. Wordsworth I and I S. T. Coleridge I to R. Southey". Reed II 300n suggests that the inscriptions are in C's hand, but it is in fact DW's. The ink revisions to the text of a number of poems are in RS's hand (cf *"Lyrical Ballads", and Other Poems, 1798–1800* ed Butler and Green xxxv–xxxvi etc).

**10. *FEARS IN SOLITUDE . . . FRANCE, AN ODE . . .
FROST AT MIDNIGHT* (1798)=poems 175, 174, 171**

Jonathan Wordsworth has suggested that the quarto pamphlet should be taken alongside *LB* (1798), which was published very shortly before. Whereas *LB* was intended to reach a wide audience and was issued anonymously, the pamphlet was issued by the radical publisher Joseph Johnson over C's own name; the names of the publisher and author claimed an interest in advance of what the pamphlet contained. Indeed, whatever the revolutionary implications of the earlier volume, the pamphlet is arranged explicitly to describe how personal faith can emerge from conditions of political despair. See Jonathan Wordsworth Introduction to *Fears in Solitude 1798* (Oxford 1989) v–vi; cf **171** *Frost at Midnight* 15EC for the significance of Cowper in the concluding poem and the advertisement which follows. Gerald P. Tyson *Joseph Johnson: A Liberal Publisher* (Iowa City 1979) 171–4 describes C's dealings with Johnson and some further connections with *LB* (1798).

Another argument connects *Fears in Solitude* with *LB* in a different but related way. It can be argued that WW's last-minute insertion of *Tintern Abbey* into a volume which began as a joint experiment was a partial appropriation which was extended and confirmed by his subsequent actions. If C felt this at the time they left England, the separate publication of three poems written while the *LB* experiment got under way amounts to a mild riposte. C's compositions represent different kinds of poetry from the one WW settled towards as he began work on *The Recluse*. It will be noted that C returned to annotate *Fears in Solitude* when a new collection of his poems was under consideration, in 1807, at a time when WW was engaged in publishing his own new collection (see on *SL*, No 16 below); also, that *Fears in Solitude* was reprinted in 1808 and in 1812 while C continued negotiating for a new collection.

C complained about the printing of the pamphlet, which took place while he was in Germany (*CL* I 417–18: to Mrs C 18 Sept 1798; manuscript note on **174** *France: An Ode* 46). The fact that it appeared in his absence undoubtedly explains why there are not more corrected copies; but the bid to make an explicit political statement, even of such a quietist kind, might also have a bearing. He told RS, "There were not above two hundred sold" (*CL* I 550: [19 Dec 1799]). Only one corrected copy is known, and that dates from almost ten years after publication; C probably came across it at Coleorton by chance. A copy bound up with other poetical tracts by Charles Lloyd, WW, and others—the whole described as "Full of corrections and variations of the text, MS. Contents, &c., by C. L."—was sold at the sale of CL's books by Bartlett and Welford (New York) Feb 1848 (lot 37).

10.1. Sir George Beaumont's copy
PML No 47225.

Annotated by C on pp 8, 8–9, 10, 11, 15, 16, 17, 18, and 23. There is also some pencil scansion of the opening of *Fears in Solitude* on pp 1 and 2, apparently not in C's hand. The Beaumonts were absent from Coleorton between 3 Nov 1806 and 3 Jun 1807, and C stayed there with WW between 21 Dec and about 17 Apr (Reed II 343, 351). The book is likely to have been annotated at that time, and it remained at Coleorton until it was noticed by B. Ifor Evans in *TLS* (18 Apr 1935) 255. It was acquired by PML in 1954.

11. *THE PICCOLOMINI* AND *THE DEATH OF WALLENSTEIN* (1800)

The publication history of the two titles and the background to C's annotation are described in the introduction to the texts in vol III, which provides references for the following summary and explains why the two titles are taken together. All of the following annotated copies combine *CPic* and *CWal*, separately paginated within a single volume. Whereas C's general comments on collections as a whole are usually quoted in this annex, in the case of the two Schiller plays they are given at the beginning of the text (introduction c2).

C began translating Schiller's plays for Longman c mid-Feb 1800. He completed *CPic* in the earlier part of Mar, and it was published separately during Apr or May. He then continued with *CWal*, which he completed in May and which was published in Jun bound up with *CPic*. The translation was done under pressure, so as to be published ahead of rival versions, and it so exhausted C that he did not attempt to translate *Wallensteins Lager*, the prelude to the two plays he had completed.

C said that he received six copies from Longman upon publication, but in the exhausted and depressed state of his mind at the time he seems not to have stirred himself to circulate them beyond the immediate group of friends where he was at the time, around Bristol. He told William Godwin that he had not thought it worthwhile to send copies back to London, and instead gave them to West country friends like William Roskilly and John Chubb (11.1 and 11.2 below). It is likely that other copies from the half-dozen were given to TP and Humphry Davy, though they have not been traced. It is not known whether RS's copy and the copy C later gave to Thomas Hutchinson (11.3 and 11.4 below) are from this same number, or indeed the copy that WW sent to DC in 1817–18 (copy 11B below).

The annotations in copies 11.1–4 reflect C's dim view of his achievement as he finished it. They are not extensive. The copies given to Roskilly and RS are inscribed only; the copy given to Chubb contains minor corrections; the copy given to Hutchinson contains, besides minor corrections, a comment which answers the criticisms made in a review.

C appears to have received further copies from Longman when he returned from Malta in 1806, at a time when Longman was disposing of unsold stock and C was engaged on a new collection of verse for Longman to publish. He annotated a group of three of these copies (11.5–7 below) in an interconnected way and quite differently from his annotation of 11.1–4. The copies contain corrections as before, but, more interestingly, the comments manifest a new, independent interest in Schiller's dramatic technique and values, aroused by C's preparation for his Shakepeare lectures. Indeed, they appear to confirm the suggestion made in sec v of the Introduction above, that Schiller was instrumental in drawing C to Shakespeare in the first place. It was inevitable that C should go back to Schiller to articulate his impression that Shakespeare's dramaturgy is different and superior. One of the three copies is inscribed to WW; the two uninscribed copies were given to or found their way into the possession of DeQ and Sir George Beaumont. Three other copies (11.8–10) appear to have been inscribed about a year later (c Apr 1808). Copy 11.8 contains minor corrections on two pages, copy 11.9 might contain similar corrections, while copy 11.10 contains no corrections or annotations at all.

Though C's confidence in the worth of his translations increased thereafter, and though he drew on them in writings published during the next decade, copies of the publication became increasingly hard to come by. He mentions not having a copy to hand on at least three occasions between 1819 and 1834. Copy 11.11 below appears to have been presented to be inscribed by the recipient, and, as it is, the inscription exists separately from the book. It is evident that C himself took little interest in the translations after 1823.

11A. Charles Lamb's copy
    Not located.

W. Carew Hazlitt *Mary and Charles Lamb: Poems, Letters, and Remains* (1874) contains an appendix, "Catalogue of CL's Library, for Sale by Bartlett and Welford, New York, Feb 1848". Hazlitt 304/catalogue item 39 lists the two parts of C's *Wallenstein* bound up with plays by Joanna Baillie in one volume, with "*MS. notes*" by CL.

C stayed with CL while he worked on the translation, and CL afterwards recalled the visit vividly. "I am living in a continuous feast," he wrote (*LL—* M—ɪ 189). He also appears to have corrected the proofs of *CPic* after C left London for Grasmere (*LL—*M—ɪ 192). Though C told Godwin that he did not return any of the complimentary copies he received from Longman to

London friends, it seems inconceivable that he would not have arranged for one to go to CL. If the present copy did reach CL via C, it is possible that it contains corrections in C's hand.

11B. Derwent Coleridge's copy
Not located.

Shaver 351 lists two copies of *The Piccolomini and The Death of Wallenstein* in WW's library. One is marked in WW's hand as belonging to DC: "1 Copy sent to Derwent at Mr Hopwoods . . . his Fathers desire".

DC became tutor to two sons of a Mr Hopwood of Lancashire, to prepare them to go to Eton, when he was only just turned 17, at a salary of 50 guineas a year (see *Minnow* 51–2). It is not known whether the copy was corrected, or how long it had been in WW's care—i.e. whether it is one of the copies C might have carried with him when he migrated northwards in Jun 1800.

DC's edition of *The Dramatic Works of Samuel Taylor Coleridge* (1852) 426–7 records a number of mistranslations which were first pointed out by G.H.E. "Schiller's Wallenstein. Translated by S. T. Coleridge. Bohn's Standard Library" *Westminster Review* LIII (Jul 1850) 349–65. The publisher of the 1852 *Dramatic Works*, Edward Moxon, had sent a copy of the article to SC in Nov 1851 (?), and SC had discussed it in a letter to DC of 4 Jan [1852?], questioning the propriety of "giving the scribbler importance by referring to him" (Grantz Nos 427 and 83). A manuscript page at HRC is described in the catalogue as "Notes on *The Death of Wallenstein* in STC's hand" (MS Coleridge, S T Works). In fact the notes are in SC's hand, concern mistranslations in both plays, and derive directly from the later part of the *Westminster* article (pp 358–65).

11C. William Charles Macready's copy of *The Piccolomini* and *The Death of Wallenstein*
V&A Forster Collection 48.F.55.

18 folio pages, pasted up on single sides, each with three columns of printed material cut and rearranged from the Smith's Standard Library edition of 1844, with manuscript deletions and minor inserts. Half-bound in green leather, with tooled spine: "*Wallenstein* as marked for acting by W. C. Macready"; with the bookplate of John Foster, Inner Temple.

Macready had been an attentive auditor at C's lectures in Jan–Mar 1818.[6] He read two acts of *Wallenstein* in Aug 1834, and had been "much struck with many of the thoughts, the language, and dramatic situation".[7] He returned to the plays two years later, and recorded in his diary for 15 Aug 1836:

---

[6] Note *hors du texte* in the manuscript of his reminiscences at Princeton, cited by Alan S. Downer *The Eminent Tragedian: William Charles Macready* (Cambridge, Mass 1966) 353, 379 n 42.
[7] *Reminiscences and Selections* ed Sir Frederick Pollock (2 vols 1875) I 429–30.

Looked through Coleridge's translation of "Wallenstein" to see if it were possible to turn it to account in representation, but, though abounding with noble passages and beautiful scenes, it is spread over too much space to be contracted within reasonable dimensions. (*Reminiscences and Selections* ed Pollock II 45)

The V&A volume is evidence that Macready took his 1836 speculations at least as far as working out a radical five-act abridgement of the two plays for theatrical use and at a fairly late stage. His version might be compared with the abridgements by William Poel, published as *War*, using C's translations (1934), and the Royal Shakespeare Company, entitled *Wallenstein*, trans Francis Lamport, adapted by Tim Albery (1993).[8]

11.1. Rev William Roskilly's copy
NYPL Berg Collection Copy 3.
Inscribed by C on the joint title-page: "S. T. Coleridge to the Revd Mr Roskilly." There are no notes or corrections by C. The copy also bears the name M. E. Roskilly, and the bookplate of Alfred Trapnell, who appears to have acquired it from George's Bookshop in Bristol in 1904. It was acquired by NYPL with the collection of Owen D. Young in 1941.
   On Roskilly see No 6.4 above. Mrs C and HC stayed with the Roskillys at Kempsford in Gloucestershire during Mar 1800, while C stayed in London translating Schiller; C was to have joined them there. It is reasonable to assume that the present copy was given to Roskilly at the time of publication, before the Coleridges left the West country.

11.2. John Chubb's copy
Princeton Robert H. Taylor Collection.
Inscribed by C on the joint title-page: "S. T. Coleridge to Mr Chubb. | June 2, 1800". C corrected the text on pp 43, 48, 177, 186, and 189 of *CPic* (only). The corrections are minor and were for the most part adopted in *PW* (1828). The copy was once owned by Harry Bache Smith.[9]
   John Chubb lived at Bridgewater, and C stayed with him several times. He was a well-to-do merchant, a former mayor, a close friend of C. J. Fox, and well known for liberal opinions. His son Morley attended Roskilly's boarding-school at Stowey (Lawrence 93–4).

11.3. Robert Southey's copy
NYPL Berg Collection Copy 2.
Inscribed by C on the joint title-page: "S. T. Coleridge to Robert Southey". There are no notes or corrections by C. The copy is also inscribed "A. H.

---

[8] Prompt-copies of Poel's productions in London and Oxford during Jun 1900 and Aug 1911 respectively are now at the Theatre Museum, Covent Garden, S 1181h–1983.
   [9] *A Sentimental Library* (New York 1914) 55.

Hallam to Robert J. Tennant", and carries the bookplates of Maurice Baring and W. Van R. Whitall. It was acquired by NYPL with the collection of Owen D. Young in 1941.

11.4. Thomas Hutchinson's copy
In private hands (Dec 1998).
Inscribed by C on the joint title-page: "T. Hutchinson from his friend, S. T. Coleri₍dge₎ I Dec. 1801." C corrected the text of *CPic* at pp 22, 29, and 186, and of *CWal* at pp 132 and 156, as well as adding a long note to *CWal* on p 128. The book is bound in calf with marbled endpapers, and has been rebound and rebacked. It is marked with the price "12/6", which appears to refer to the rebinding, since there is no reason to think it left the possession of the Hutchinson–Wordsworth families until its recent sale.

11.5. Thomas De Quincey's copy
Birmingham University Library, Rugby School Collection (on deposit).
There is no inscription on the title-page, but the copy is heavily corrected and annotated. There is a note on the front flyleaf, which is completed on a leaf set into the front pastedown. The note originally comprised a paragraph only, and was subsequently expanded. *CPic* contains further notes and corrections on pp 26–7, 38–9, 45, 48, 50, 70, 72, 76, 80, 83, 86, 92, 96, 186, and 204. *CWal* has corrections on pp 136 and 156, and two portions of verse on the rear flyleaf (see **402** *Psyche* VAR TEXT MS 2; **427** *"Or like the Swallow"* VAR). The copy carries the Rugby School Library bookplate, with a ticket recording it as the gift of Shadworth H. Hodgson, an Old Rugeian and a metaphysician. Arthur Coleridge *Reminiscences* (1921) 45 says that Hodgson bought it from the library of his relative DeQ before presenting it to his old school in 1901–2.

The reasons for dating the annotations to the period 1807–8 are as follows. (1) The text of *Psyche* which C copied on to the rear flyleaf of *CWal* is the same as the version in *SH's Poets*, which was most probably inscribed at Coleorton in the winter of 1806–7. (2) The annotations in part overlap with C's first set of Shakespeare lectures, as if he was annotating as he prepared the lectures. (3) The volume belonged at some stage to DeQ, who did not meet C until Aug 1807 and who followed him to London to hear the Shakespeare lectures. This set of considerations would, with modifications, also support the date 1811–12, but, taking into account the relation between this copy and 11.6–7 below, the earlier date is more likely.

The nature of C's annotation suggests that the copy might be regarded as one of several which came into his possession in 1807, which he used to work out ideas which were pressing on him at the time, in a rather random way, and which he afterwards passed on to friends. The sequence in which he used and annotated these copies is not the same as the sequence in which he gave them away. Thus, while it is likely that he annotated copies 11.5–7 in the order in which they are listed here, he appears to have given them away in the reverse order, over a period of two months or longer. Perhaps he held on longest to the copy in which he first began to work out his ideas.

11.6. William Wordsworth's copy

DCL COL (a) 1800.

Inscribed by C on the title-page of *CPic*: "For W Wordsworth I from I S. T. Coleridge— I Vale!" C also wrote previously, on the verso of the *CPic* half-title: "How much might be well and usefully written on this Play by a truly philosophic Scholiast." He corrected and annotated *CPic* at pp 88, 116, 152–3, 157, 186, 189, and 195; and *CWal* at pp 84, 91, 92, 94, 95, 96, 98, 103–4, 106, 107, 109 (he also deleted the whole of iv ii, covering pp 98–109), 128, 129, and 157.

The corrections and annotations in this copy are closely related to those in 11.5 above. Each contains commentary rather than corrections. Only one correction overlaps (*CPic* p 186), and no commentary. It is as if C began with the DeQ copy, used it up to approximately p 96 of *CPic*, and made only a few corrections to the volume thereafter. It would appear that he resumed reading in the present copy, picking up at about *CPic* p 88 and continuing through to the end of *CWal*. In other words, the commentary in the two copies is continuous, the WW copy completing what the DeQ copy had begun.

The note on p 157 of *CWal* after v x 54 suggests that the annotations were made in 1807. Taken with C's inscription, one might reckon that the book was presented to WW as a going-away present when WW left London in May of that year (Reed ii 354). It is important to bear in mind that this copy, like 11.5, was annotated by C for his own use before he thought of giving it away.

11.7. Sir George Beaumont's copy

Cornell Wordsworth PT 2473 W3 C69 1800.

The volume is not inscribed and carries no bookplates, but the Cornell catalogue records that it came from Sir George Beaumont's library. It was given to Cornell by Victor Emmanuel between 1931 and 1957. A one-page manuscript commentary on the two plays in C's hand was folded in, and is now catalogued separately under the shelfmark "WORDSWORTH". The annotations, which are all minor emendations, occur in the *CPic* Dramatis Personae and on pp 22, 83, and 186, and in *CWal* pp 54, 55, 60, 128, and 156.

There are also pencil lines on the inner and outer margins of a good many pages, which are heavier on those pages which C recommends in his manuscript commentary and for this reason might have been made by him. They occur at *CPic* pp 16–17, 18, 21, 22–6, 37–40, 49–51, 56, 74–86, 93, 127–36, 139, 152, 154, 156–8, 160, 170–80, 184–94, and 211–14, and *CWal* pp 13,

17, 24–5, 28, 34, 36, 42, 43, 47, 50, 54, 63, 64, 73, 74, 76, 93, 95, 111, 112, 113, 114, 118, 120–5, 130, 136–8, 146, and 156.[10]

The one-page commentary derives from that on the flyleaf and pastedown of copy 11.5 above: it is an abbreviated version, cast in positive terms. The corrections in the text of the plays, on the other hand, display a different kind of interest from copies 11.5–6, and might date from an earlier time (cf 11.2, 11.4 above). The copy may have come into Sir George Beaumont's possession as or soon after C left Coleorton, in the spring or summer of 1807.

11.8. Mary Evans Todd's copy
University of Kansas, Lawrence Special Collections C2407.

Inscribed by C on the title-page of *CPic*: "To Mrs Todd | from the Trans,lator,". There are minor corrections at *CPic* p 186 and *CWal* p 128, which remained unnoticed by cataloguers until Jun 1988. Mary Evans, with whom C had been in love in his last year at Christ's Hospital and early years at Cambridge, had married Fryer Todd in 1795. She wrote to C on 6 Apr 1808 after seeing him lecture at the Royal Institution, and they met soon after. C was shocked at her circumstances (see *CL* III 85–6: to Mary Evans Todd [7 Apr 1808]; 91: to D. Stuart [c 18 Apr 1808]). He probably took the book with him, or sent it round afterwards.

11.9. Dr William Babington's copy
Not located.

Inscribed on the joint title-page: "Dr. Babbington from his obliged and grateful S. T. Coleridge." It is described ("uncut, polished calf, gilt top") in the catalogue of the library of William F. Johnson of Boston, Mass, sold by Bangs & Co., New York, 27 Jan 1890 (item 298). It is possible that the copy contains minor corrections, like 11.8 above, which have not been noticed by cataloguers. William Babington (1756–1833) was an eminent physician attached to Guy's Hospital. He was also an eminent mineralogist, and thereby associated with G. B. Greenough, whom C had known in Germany. C refers to him in a letter to RS postmarked 14 Dec 1807 as one of Humphry Davy's doctors (*CL* III 41), was in correspondence with him during Mar–Apr 1808 concerning SH's illness (*CL* III 81, 91; cf *WL*—M rev—I 216), and on 21 May 1808 cited him in a letter to WW with regard to an assurance policy (*CL* III 109).

11.10. John Anastasius Russell's copy
Yale In C678 800S.

Inscribed by C on the joint title-page: "To Mr John Anastasius Russell from the Translator, S. T. Coleridge 1808.—" The copy contains a single note at the head of the Preface.

---

[10] Because the pencil lines have transferred themselves on to facing pages, some of these may be spurious.

John Anastasius Russell is not identified, unless he is related to Thomas Russell, whom C met in Rome in 1806. Thomas Russell's father was a banker in Exeter, who also ran a freight service between Exeter and London, and his acquaintance with C continued at least until 1809, when he subscribed to *The Friend* (*CC* II 455–6); cf also **176** *Christabel* VAR TEXT MS 5.

The collector Richard Heber acquired the volume for 4*s*, and it was sold after his death for £1 2*s* to a Mr Molteno; see **619** *Virgil Applied to the Hon Mr B and Richard Heber*. The manuscript note is quoted in the Sotheby sale catalogue *Bibliotheca Heberiana* pt IV, 20 Dec 1834 (lot 2307).[11] It was quoted in *P&DW* (RHS) III 45n; the citation in *PW* (JDC) 647B makes it obvious that JDC had not seen the copy; W. Hale White relied on a letter from R. A. Potts for a transcription in May 1909.[12] It was sold at Sotheby's 6 Jun 1929 lot 634 (to Last for £4 5*s*), and now bears the bookplate of C. B. Tinker.

11.11. J.H.B. Williams's copy
Not located.
A dedicatory letter to Williams is extant on a flyleaf which has been separately preserved at Cornell (shelfmark "WORDSWORTH"; *CL* VI 926: to J.H.B. Williams 12 Oct 1832):

Grove, Highgate.
Octr. 12, 1832

My dear Williams,
This Work has risen in public estimation, since the time that it fell apparently dead-born from the Press, and for a series of years continued in a state of suspended Animation—the greater part of this Edition having been sold off by the Desponding Publishers for *waste paper*. Such has not been the case, my dear Friend! with *your* character in *my* respect and regard. The best compliment, I can pay you—and it is a high compliment—is, that what you *were* when you first received these Tragedies, you *continue* to be. And so likewise do the Regard and Respect of your old Friend

S. T. Coleridge.

Williams was JG's assistant at Highgate, and C had been on friendly terms with him since 1816 (see e.g. *CL* IV 682–4: to J.H.B. Williams [24 Sept 1816]). The letter suggests that Williams had been in possession of the copy since the early days of their friendship; indeed, by Nov 1819 C had no more spare copies to hand (*CL* IV 970: to the Author of "Peter's Letters to his Kinsfolk"; cf V 287: to EC 23 Jul 1823; VI 980: to H. N. Coleridge [Mar 1834]). The copy of *SM* that C inscribed for Williams on the same day (*LS*—

---

[11] Prices are given from the Bodleian copy, Mus Bibl III 8° 722–5, 728–31*, the buyer from BM 11904 g 25.

[12] See White's annotated copy of *PW* (JDC) 226A, in BM C 60 g 7.

CC—237) also appears to have been in Williams's possession previously. It is not known whether the copy from which the letter has been removed contained corrections or further comments.

C also inscribed copies of *SL* and *SM* to Williams: see copy 17.22 below; and *LS* (*CC*) 237.

12. *ANNUAL ANTHOLOGY* (1800)

Two volumes of the *Annual Anthology*, edited by RS, were published—the first in Bristol in 1799 and the second in London in 1800. Vol I does not contain any contributions by C, and its bibliographical peculiarities (a missing leaf, sig B8 = pp 31–2, in every copy but those at the V&A and the Berg Collection, NYPL) are not relevant. C contributed the following poems to vol II, although only the *Recantation* (p 59) bears his name, the remainder having a single initial, a pseudonym, or no indication of authorship at all. (An asterisk indicates the existence of annotations in C's hand in copy 12.1 below; the titles are given as they appear in the body of the text, not the contents list.)

		CC	
LEWTI,	*Or the CIRCASSIAN LOVE-CHANT*	23	**172**	
To a *YOUNG LADY*,	*On her first Appearance*	*AFTER A*			
DANGEROUS ILLNESS.	*Written in the Spring*, 1799.	32	**173**	
RECANTATION,	*Illustrated in the STORY of the MAD*			
OX.	*By S. T. COLERIDGE.*	59	**177**	5
LINES	*Written in the Album at Elbingerode, in the*	*Hartz*			
Forest.		74	**200**	
A CHRISTMAS CAROL.		79	**260**	
To a *FRIEND*	*Who had declared his intention of writing*			
no more Poetry.		103	**133**	10
THIS LIME-TREE BOWER MY PRISON.	*A POEM*,	*Ad-*			
dresed to CHARLES LAMB, of the India-House,	*London.*	140	**156**	
SONNET XII.	*To W. L. Esq. while he sung a Song to*			
Purcell's Music.		156	**157**	
The BRITISH STRIPLING's WAR-SONG.		173	**212**	15
Something childish, but very natural.	*Written in GER-*			
MANY		192	**189**	
HOME-SICK.	*Written in GERMANY.*	193	**196**	
ODE	*To GEORGIANA, DUTCHESS of DEVONSHIRE,*			
On the 24th Stanza in her "Passage over Mount				20
Gothard."		212	**254**	
FIRE, FAMINE, & SLAUGHTER.	*A WAR*			
ECLOGUE.	*The SCENE, a desolated Tract in La Ven-*			
dee.—*FAMINE is*	*discovered lying on the ground: to*			
her enter FIRE	*and SLAUGHTER.*	231	**167**	25

A copy of related interest is RS's, now at HUL (10493 27 25*), where in vol II RS indicated the authorship of several poems. His comments on the authorship of *Lewti* are given at **172** VAR TEXT PR *3*.

12.1. C's copy

Yale Tinker 1953 2.

Inscribed on the title-page of vol II in RS's hand: "S. T. Coleridge from Robert Southey." Vol II contains annotations in several hands, but mainly C's, in ink. A large number of his annotations are attributions, and there are also comments on poems by others. There are emendations of his own poems on pp 23, 26, 59, 74, 75, 82, 140, 141, 142, 143, 156, 174, 213, 214, 215, 267, 268, and 292. The full set of C's annotations—including a note on the annotations in vol I (not by C)—is given in *CM* (*CC*) I 88–99.

The fact that vol I is not inscribed, and not annotated by C, suggests that the two volumes might not always have made up this particular set. In a letter to GC of 29 Sept 1799 C refers to a copy of vol I left behind with GC in Devon (*CL* I 532), which it is not known if he recovered. He might have annotated vol II at any time between its publication and when he left Greta Hall (Oct 1810). The corrections to the poems would appear to have been made in the earlier part of that period, though some of the other annotations (identifications) were probably made later. A letter from JDC to EHC of 11 Jul 1888 (HRC: uncatalogued in 1978) reveals that vol II was in EHC's possession at that time. EHC quoted from the annotations in his edition of 1912 (*PW*—EHC—I 299, 337 nn), but in the meantime it had passed into the hands of Stuart M. Samuel (*C Bibl*—Haney—128), with whose library, along with the copy of vol I which makes up the present set, it was sold at Sotheby's 1 Jul 1907 (lot 34 to Shepherd for £10 10*s*). The two volumes were sold again at Sotheby's 2 Jun 1908 (lot 184 to Maggs for £15), and were described by Harry Bache Smith in *A Sentimental Library* 54 as belonging to him. They were in Professor Tinker's possession by 1948.

12.2. Thomas Poole's copy
Not located.
Signed by TP on the endpaper of vol I; with corrections in C's hand at II 23–5, 74–5. The corrections must have been made after 15 Feb 1803, when C wrote to RS to say that TP had not received the second volume (*CL* II 924). Sold in the James B. Clemens Sale, Parke–Bernet 8 Jan 1945 (lot 180). The volumes were bound in "full contemporary tree calf, leather labels, marbled edges; worn, hinges cracked. In a full morocco double solander case by SANGORSKI & SUTCLIFFE . . . A former owner has written pencilled identifications of the authors and subjects of many of the poems. On the front end-paper of each volume is a library shelf number, and the bookplate of William Summers." Sangorski & Sutcliffe are a London firm founded in 1901, and still in business; William Summers has not been traced.

13. *POEMS* (1803)

The peculiar status of what C described as the third edition of his *Poems* has been described at annex B 4 above. His lack of direct involvement in its preparation bears on the paucity of annotated copies, though it is in any case a less common collection than either of its predecessors.

13A. John Taylor Coleridge's copy
BM C 126 b 3.
This copy contains annotations in pencil and pen on pp 38, 92, 104, 106, 159, and 161. These are all by JTC, made by him when he was still a schoolboy, between 1804 and 1809. The copy is signed on the title-page: "J. T. Coleridge I Eton Coll. I Bucks." and also carries the bookplate of Bernard, Lord Coleridge.
A couple of the annotations are of interest because they suggest parallels and sources. In themselves they also attest to the rediscovery of C by the younger generation of the Coleridge family.

13B. Inscribed by Charles Lamb
Sold at Parke–Bernet 28 Feb 1974 (lot 631 for $350).

13C. A copy of C's *Poems* "(1802)"[13] in boards, uncut—"Inserted is a Poem in Coleridge's autograph, 'KNOW THYSELF,' *signed and dated*"—was sold at Sotheby's 5 Mar 1891 (lot 1223). The catalogue is thus explicit—inserted,

[13] A mistake for 1803? It is much less likely to be a mistake for 1812.

not inscribed—and it seems probable that the autograph manuscript is the same as the one collected into an album by W. K. Bixby at about this time (see **700** *"E Cœlo Descendit"* VAR TEXT MS 1).

13D. Sara Coleridge's copy

This was discovered in a Manchester bookshop and described by Bernard G. Hall "Sara Coleridge's Notes" *TLS* (29 Jan 1925) 71. It contained "one or two notes" in SC's hand. In the note on **82** *Monody on the Death of Chatterton* the earlier version is compared favourably with the later, revised one—an opinion contrary to the one expressed in DC's and SC's edition of C's *Poems* in 1852.

13E. A copy inscribed on the front free endpaper for Rev James Duke Coleridge (1788–1857), eldest son of James Coleridge ("the Colonel") and elder brother of HNC, from Rev Charles Yonge, Lower Master of Eton, on 28 Apr 1819 is described by Ewen Kerr Books (Kendal) Catalogue 47 (Sept 1994) item 396 (for £1500). The same page contains a further inscription for Deborah Owen from Fanny Patteson, niece of the original recipient, dated 20 Mar 1889.

The five rear endpapers contain a transcript of the *SL* text of **253** *Love* in the same hand which made the first inscription (James Duke Coleridge rather than Charles Yonge?). Two pages are reproduced in the Ewen Kerr catalogue, where it is wrongly suggested that there are similarities with C's own hand. The transcript has no textual significance.

13.1. Sara Hutchinson's copy

Cornell WORDSWORTH PR 4252 B91R9 1813 Copy 2.

The copy is inscribed on the title-page, in SH's hand: "S. Hutchinson". There are corrections and comments on pp 99, 103, 104, and 117. The comment on p 103 is in C's hand, and signed; the other corrections are small, and might or might not be in C's hand.

The copy also carries the signature of Thomas Carr of Hill Top, Ambleside, dated 1835, who was given it by Mary Wordsworth (MH) in memory of his attendance on the dying SH. It was sold at Sotheby's 18 Apr 1932 (lot 45 to Dobell for £12), and again at Parke–Bernet 29 Jan 1951 (lot 121, the property of a New York collector).

14. *POEMS* (1812)

This pamphlet, entitled *Poems by S. T. Coleridge, Esq.*, bears a relationship— not always understood—to C's earlier publications *Fears in Solitude . . . France, an Ode . . . Frost at Midnight* (the 1798 quarto) and the same group of three poems included in *The Poetical Register and Repository of Fugitive Poetry for 1808–09* (vol VII in the series, published in 1812). The relationship can be explained as follows. C almost certainly submitted his three poems to the *Poetical Register* at the time he annotated Sir George Beaumont's copy of the 1798 quarto, i.e. in 1807 or soon thereafter. The *Poetical Register* text is clearly based on the 1798 version; it takes in some revisions first evident in the 1798 publication, introduces more, and otherwise follows the details of the earlier text. What arrangement existed between C and the editor and publishers of the *Poetical Register* (R. A. Davenport, and Henry Law and Robert Gilbert, respectively) is not known; nor is it known whether the pamphlet preceded, accompanied, or followed the *Poetical Register* publication. Vol vii of the *Register* covers the years 1808–9, and the separate pamphlet might have been prompted by the unusual delay before publication, or it might have been made up as a keepsake for an eminent and previous contributor. The pamphlet uses the same type and paper (wm 1810), but differences of punctuation and spacing in each of the three poems, and the fact that the pages in the pamphlet hold more lines of type, prove that it was not merely an offprint.

The 1812 pamphlet is described in *C Bibl* (Wise) 56 as "of very considerable rarity". Wise doubted whether more than half a dozen copies exist, but he was too cautious. Besides the located copies listed below (at V&A, Princeton, and Indiana), there are further copies at HEHL, HUL, Cambridge University Library, and BM (under the heading "*Fears in Solitude* 1812 ed": C 131 d 23). This last mistake—in which the 1812 pamphlet is titled and catalogued incorrectly as if it were the 1798 publication—is not uncommon: see e.g. *National Union Catalogue: Pre-1956 Imprints; with Supplement* (754 vols 1968–81) cxv 861; Scribner catalogue *Superb Collected Sets of the First Editions of Milton, Coleridge, Swinburne, Wordsworth* (New York 1914) 9; the Mark P. Robinson Sale, Anderson Galleries 26 Feb 1918 (lot 135). The 1798 and 1812 pamphlets are most obviously distinguished by their different size and bibliographical collation and their different printers (quarto printed for J. Johnson, and octavo printed by Law and Gilbert, respectively).

14A. Robert Southey's copy
V&A Forster Collection P 97.

The copy is bound up with other pamphlets owned by RS, and contains corrections in his hand on pp 11, 12, 13, 15, and 16. The emendations to **174** *France: An Ode* bring the text closer to C's revised text for *M Post* (1802), though not systematically. The coincidences might suggest that the emendations have C's authority, though it is not clear in what way. The three small emendations to **171** *Frost at Midnight* are without parallel in other texts.

14B. Fanny Godwin's copy
Not located.
Signed on the first page of text (p 3) "Fanny Godwin | April 14th | 1814".

There are no further annotations. Described in *C Bibl* (Wise *TLP*) 66, with facing illustration.

14.1. William Hood's copy
Indiana University, Bloomington Lilly Library, Special Collections.
Inscribed on the title-page: "W. Hood, Esqre | from his obliged Friend. | S. T. Coleridge". There are no other annotations.
William Hood was one of C's good Bristol friends, like Morgan but more affluent and less intimate. He assisted with the promotion of *The Friend* and with the financial backing of *SL* and *BL*. C annotated a copy of RS's *Joan of Arc* for him (see **110** VAR TEXT PR *1*); cf **509** *To a Lady, with Falconer's "Shipwreck"*. The copy came into the possession of Frederick Locker-Lampson.[14] It was sold at the James B. Clemens Sale, Parke–Bernet 8 Jan 1945 (lot 186); and again at Parke–Bernet 26 Feb 1952 (lot 83 for $180).

14.2. Mrs Calvert's copy
Princeton Robert H. Taylor Collection.
Inscribed on the title-page: "Mrs Calvert | from her obliged Friend | S. T. Coleridge". There are no other annotations. The copy is bound with a copy of C's *Sonnets from Various Authors* (1796). They are inscribed on the combined flyleaf: "Joshua Stanger from his attached Brother Raisley Calvert. St. Ann's Hill, 23 Oct. 1837", and carry the bookplate of Stephen Coleridge. The volume was sold at Sotheby's 9 Apr 1957 (lot 339 to Quaritch for £220).

14.3. Miss Hillier's copy
Not located; perhaps no longer extant.
C says in a letter to R. H. Brabant of 13 Mar 1815 from Calne: "I have inclosed my fears in solitude, with two other poems, written in 1798—which as I hope soon to present Mrs Brabant with my poems collectively, I could wish you to present in my name to Miss Hillier, as a mark of my respect" (*CL* IV 553). C almost certainly enclosed a copy of the pamphlet published in 1812 (rather than that published in 1798); it is also likely that he inscribed it on the title-page. It appears from other letters of Mar 1815 to Brabant (e.g. *CL* IV 550, 555, 556) that Miss Hillier lived with the Brabants at Devizes; possibly she was Mrs Brabant's sister.

15. REMORSE (1813)

The first edition of *Remorse* was issued in early Feb 1813, following the success of the play at Drury Lane on 23 Jan and afterwards. Five of the six known

---

[14] Frederick Locker-Lampson *The Rowfant Library* (1886) 149.

annotated copies of the first edition are inscribed to or belonged to persons attached to the theatre, who, it may be assumed, had been especially helpful or friendly in the evolution of the Stage version. Indeed, four of the copies are addressed to persons connected with the management, and only one to an actor. The annotations are almost wholly made up of corrections and emendations of the text, though there are some comments on the Introduction. The annotations overlap, and together look towards the second edition.

The second and third editions are properly different impressions of the second edition, differing only in their title-page. The fact that C waited to give the second edition to his friends suggests that it had been planned even as the first edition became available. C promised to send copies to RS, TP, John Rickman, and WW (*CL* III 432: to RS 8 [=9] Feb 1813; 438: to TP [13 Feb 1813], to John Rickman [16 Feb 1813]; *CRC* I 71, 73), but only two inscribed copies of the second edition have survived—to SH (part at HUL, part at Brandeis—a copy cannibalised by Stuart M. Samuel) and to Sir George Beaumont. The copy given to Robert Owen is listed as a second edition, but this is not certain. Although the third edition was contemporaneous with the second, all three extant annotated copies were given and inscribed later (1816–19). Each contains only a few comments and no annotation.

As indicated above, the annotations and corrections in these copies are distributed between different sections of the present edition: that is, the Raymond and Dibdin copies of the first edition, the SH copy (Brandeis part) of the second, and the Tieck copy of the third all contain notes given with the Prologue in the Stage version in vol III; the note on the Prologue in SH's copy (HUL part) is also given there. Some notes in Raymond's and RS's copies of the first edition and in SH's copy (HUL part) of the second are given at *Remorse* (Stage) III iii 89–95EC; IV i 24–5EC. The notes on *The Foster-mother's Tale* in SH's copy (HUL part) and in the Beaumont copy of the second edition are cited at **152** VAR commentary. Otherwise—with the exception of a note in West's prompt-copy and a note in AG's/EC's copy—the remaining notes and corrections are given in the EC to the Printed version.

15A. C. A.'s copy of the first edition
  University of Chicago PR 4480.08 Rare Book Room.
  This copy has the following note on the title-page: "Was at the first representation of this play. Went with Benjn Thomson and Mr. Hook. Complimented Mr. Coleridge who was at the theatre on its success—who was flooded with tears at its success. C. A."
  C. A. could have been Charles Aders or, indeed more likely, HCR's friend Charles Aikin.

15B. Charles Lloyd's copy of the second edition
  Jackson Library, Tullie House, Carlisle M 107.

The copy is signed by Lloyd on the title-page, with the date 14 Mar 1813. There are no annotations.

15C. Miss John's copy of the first edition
NYPL Berg Collection Copy 3.
The copy is inscribed by CL on the title-page: "Miss John. With Compts of a Friend of the Author." There are no annotations.

The book carries the bookplates of Winston Hagen and Jerome Kern. It was sold at the Jerome Kern Sale, Anderson Galleries 7–10 Jan 1929 (lot 272 for $1850) and presented to NYPL in 1941 by Owen D. Young.

15D. Barron Field's copy of the third edition
Not located.
The copy, inscribed by CL to Barron Field, was sold by Henkels' of Philadelphia 22 Nov 1921 (lot 5 for $80). In 1961 it was in the possession of Walter S. Taintor of Oak Park, Illinois, and it was sold again at Parke–Bernet 28 Feb 1974 (lot 631 for $350).

15E. Charles Lamb's copy (edition unknown)
Not located.
The copy was sold bound up with four other pieces (including Godwin's *Antonio* and Barron Field's farce *Antiquity*) at the sale of CL's library by Bartlett and Welford (New York) Feb 1848 (lot 26), and was later in the possession of Harry Bache Smith (*A Sentimental Library* 147–8). It appears not to have contained any kind of annotation. *Lamb and Hazlitt: Further Letters and Records Hitherto Unpublished* ed W. C. Hazlitt (1900) xxii lists a copy of the third edition among additional works thought to have been in CL's library during his lifetime.

15F. Basil Montagu's copy of the first edition
Bodleian Arch AA e 20.
The copy is signed by Montagu on the title-page. It is not inscribed or annotated.

15G. Copy of the first edition
University of Melbourne Baillieu Library Bald 821 72R.p Copy 1.
The copy is marked up for the Theatre Royal at York and at Hull. The play was performed at Hull on 2 Mar 1813 (also 12 Nov) and at York on 29 Apr 1813. The relation between the marking up and W. West's prompt-copy (15.5) makes it clear that this copy is based directly on West's. Further details are given in the introduction to *Remorse* (Stage). However, the copy does not contain any annotations by C.

15H. Two copies of the 1813 New York edition (based on the second London edition) owned by William B. Wood

NYPL Lincoln Center. NCOF; HUL Theatre Collection * 71T-29.

Both copies were marked up by Wood for the stage. The first was used in the Philadelphia and Baltimore productions, the second was used in the New York production. Neither contains annotation by C, and neither has any connection with the DL production. For further details see the introduction to *Remorse* (Stage) sec H.

15.1. Samuel James Arnold's copy of the first edition

Not located.

The copy was inscribed by C on the title-page: "A Corrected Copy. I Mr Arnold from his greatly obliged Friend, S. T. Coleridge. 'Più vorrëi: più non posso.'" tr "I would like to do more, but more I cannot do". C copied down the Italian phrase while he was in Malta or Italy (*CM—CC*—III 978). Samuel James Arnold (1774–1852) had written comedies and tragedies, and had been involved with opera and musical plays, before he joined DL as director when it reopened in 1812. He had been instrumental in confirming the acceptance of C's play and in reshaping it for the stage.

The copy is interleaved throughout, like W. West's prompt-copy (15.5). It contains numerous corrections and notes in C's autograph. On the front flyleaf there is a long inscription concerning the play in another hand, and the volume bears Robert Hoe's and an identified bookplate. The binding is old half-calf, uncut.

The copy is known only from four sales catalogues. It was sold in the Lonsdale Sale, Sotheby's 6 Nov 1897 (lot 380 to Maggs for £15); in the Robert Hoe Sale, Anderson Auction Company 24 Apr 1911 (lot 777 for $310); in the John A. Spoor Sale, Parke–Bernet 27 Apr 1939 (lot 183 for $140); in the Chrysler Sale, Parke–Bernet 26 Feb 1952 (lot 85 for $180). The last of these has a facsimile of the inscribed title-page, facing p 19.

15.2. James Grant Raymond's copy of the first edition

HRC Wn C678 813r Cop 1.

The copy was inscribed by C on the title-page (cropped): "A Copy corrected by the Author: 5 Feb^{ry}1813. I Mr Raymond I in record of zealous I kindness shewn to I the Author I and of Gratitude I due to him I from S. T. Coleridge". Raymond (b 1768) was stage manager at DL when *Remorse* was produced there, and had, according to Leigh Hunt, something of a literary air.[15] He died suddenly in Oct 1817.

The copy has corrections and annotations in C's hand, of a kind similar to but not identical with those in Dibdin's and Pope's copies (15.3–4), on every page of the Preface and on every page of the text *except* pp 1, 11, 14–16,

---

[15] Leigh Hunt *Critical Essays on the Performers of the London Theatre* (1807) 31–2.

22, 25, 27, 33–4, 36, 42–7, 50, 52, 55, 58–61, 64, 68, 70, and 72. It would appear to be the earliest, as it is the richest of the annotated copies of the first edition (though it has not been possible to compare it with the Arnold copy, 15.1). Some lines written on p 49 are in another hand—apparently J. J. Morgan's—and seventeen brief appreciative comments have been written in pencil mostly in the earlier half of the text, the first of them (p 2) signed "R R". Some of the annotations—like the inscription on the title-page—have been cropped in binding, and in vol III of the present edition these are supplemented from the transcript made by JDC into his own copy in 1892 (VCL S MS 37).[16]

J. G. Raymond's books were sold, along with other of his theatrical property, in 1818,[17] after which the copy passed to the publisher William Pickering (note by SC in HRC). A letter from JDC to EHC of 5 Jul 1892, also at HRC (uncatalogued in 1978), describes it as in the possession of Stuart M. Samuel; JDC must have copied the annotations into the copy now at VCL at this time. It continued in Samuel's possession when Haney made his bibliography (*C Bibl*—Haney 1903—108), and was sold with other of Samuel's books at Sotheby's 1 Jul 1907 (lot 36 to Wise for £15 10s). Wise acquired it as agent for John Henry Wrenn of Chicago, whose collection became part of the HRC.

15.3. Thomas John Dibdin's copy of the first edition
Wellesley College Special Collections.

The copy is inscribed in C's hand on the title-page (cropped): "*Corrected Copy* | Mr Dibden with respectful ackno.wledgment, from his obliged Fr.iend, S. T. C,oleridge,". T. J. Dibdin (1771–1841), actor and dramatist, had worked for Elliston at the Surrey (Royal Circus) Theatre in 1809–11, and had been engaged by S. J. Arnold when DL reopened in 1812, as prompter and writer of pantomimes. He was involved with C in various projects for pantomimes (*CL* IV 605: to Lord Byron 22 Oct 1815; cf e.g. 644: to J. Murray [endorsed 6 Jun 1816]); and later, as manager of the Surrey, he was to stage his own melodrama version of *Zapolya*.

The copy has corrections and annotations in C's hand, of a kind similar to but not identical to those in Raymond's and Pope's copies (15.2, 15.4), on pp iv, v, 2, "6" (for 3), 4, 5, 7, 8, 9, 10, 12, 13, 17, 19, 22, 23, 28, 31, 32, 35, 37, 39, 40, 41, 49, 53, 54, 56, 57, 58, 60, 62, 63, 65, and 71. The relationship of the corrections and annotations to those in the other copies suggests that this was annotated after Raymond's copy, at about the same time as the copy given to Pope. Some time after C emended the text someone else—perhaps Dibdin, more probably W. West—marked it up with reference

---

[16] Some words had already been lost by cropping before JDC made his transcript, as he notes on pp. v, vi, and vii.

[17] See Robert W. Lowe, James Fullarton Arnott, and John William Robinson *English Theatrical Literature 1559–1900: A Bibliography* (1970) item 123.

to the prompt-copy "Mark'd and Altered from the Manuscript" (15.5 below), showing entrances and exits and deletions, but not writing in the new scenes. These deletions on several occasions (pp 4, 7, 13, 17, 37, 39, and 62) override C's own changes. Several of C's annotations and some of West's (?) have been cropped in binding. C's annotations to the text are given with *Remorse* (Printed); the annotations to the Preface and West's (?) annotations to the text are given with *Remorse* (Stage).

The copy is contained in the first of seven volumes which belonged to Dibdin and carry a binder's title "PRESENTS FROM AUTHORS". *Remorse* is the second of the six plays in the volume. The seven volumes contain 47 plays in all, 23 of which (including *Remorse*) have been inscribed to Dibdin by the author or publisher, and several of which are annotated in different hands. They carry the bookplate of Mr and Mrs Henry Fowle Durant, founders of Wellesley College in 1875. They might have been bequeathed to Durant by his maternal aunt, Mrs Charlotte Fowle Wiggin, or purchased by him, perhaps from Willis and Southeran. They have been in the Wellesley College collections since 1875.

15.4. Alexander Pope's copy of the first edition
BM Ashley 2847.

The copy is inscribed by C on the title-page: "*Corrected* Copy | ——— Pope, Esqre with the Author's sincere Thanks." Alexander Pope (1763–1835) played Valdez in the DL production. He had been the principal tragic actor at CG for many years before he joined DL, and he played at other theatres besides. As an actor, he was known for his mellifluous voice; as a man, for his gluttony.

The copy is less fully annotated than the one C gave to Raymond (15.2), and does not contain any such personal statements as are found in that copy. In this respect it is closer to the Dibdin copy (15.3), and comparison of the three suggests that the Pope and Dibdin copies were annotated a little later (after 5 Feb 1813). There are corrections and emendations on pp iii, iv, v, "6" (for 3), 4, 5, 6, 7, 8, 9, 10, 12, 13, 15, 16, 17, 18, 19, 20, 21, 22, 23, 24, 25, 26, 27, 28, 29, 30, 31, 32, 35, 36, 37, 38, 39, 40, 41, 49, 53, 54, 55, 56, 62, 65, and 71. Most of the corrections are in C's hand; others appear to have been made by the same hand that appears in the Dibdin copy, and their coincidence with corrections in other copies confirms their authority. Frequently (pp 65 and 71 provide clear examples) the corrections are partly in C's hand, partly in the other. Some minor corrections cannot be attributed with certainty, but in citing the annotations a distinction is made between "C has emended" and "The word has been emended".

The title-page and p 54 (wholly in C's hand) are reproduced in *C Bibl* (Wise *TLP*) between pp 72 and 73. Page 54 (only) is reproduced in *C Bibl* (Wise) 85. Nothing is known of the provenance of this copy before it was acquired by T. J. Wise.

15.5. W. West's prompt-copy of the first edition
    HUL HCL 19475.65 *.

The copy is interleaved and marked up with reference to the DL production. An inserted manuscript title-page reads: "The. | REMORSE | Mark'd and Altered | from | the | Manuscript at by | W. West | A. Domini 1813. | S. T. Coleridge. author". As even this version betrays, West was not the regular copyist at DL (who was a Mr Stokes): he held a fairly low position as a messenger. There is no record in the DL accounts books, at the BM or the Folger, of West being paid for making the copy. It appears to have been made unofficially, perhaps on behalf of the prompter Thomas Dibdin and with C's knowledge, for theatres like Hull which wanted to stage the play while it was enjoying its London success.

The altered text is the basis for the Stage version in the present edition, where further details of the connections with Dibdin's copy and the Hull prompt-copy (15.3 and 15G above) are given. There are indications that West made his revisions on at least two separate occasions. On some pages (6, 26, 28, 42, etc) there are different styles of deletion, and on p 48 an added SD describing Ordonio's movements is superseded by the cancellation of the whole passage. The altered version is not the one played on the first night, since it gives a later form of the ending, and there are reasons for thinking that it represents a version arrived at by the end of the second week of February.

Corrections on a number of pages (9, 30, 58, 60, and 63) look as if they might be in C's hand, but the balance of probability is that they are not. However, the rear pastedown is filled with a note by C, in ink. The writing has been almost completely erased, and only individual words and phrases can be deciphered (in several cases only conjecturally) with the aid of ultraviolet light. Thus:

> Mr Editor,
> Wh . . . . to inform you
> of . . p . . . es? . . . .
> . . . .
> you will . . . . ly account
> it pas . . . the . . . . .
> in . . . .
> . . . . . he . . . . suited
> . . . age . . . . I at last
> . . . . he
> . . . . to Imitate the Management
> by . . . . Men in . . . . so . . .
> him . . . again. E . . . h Well
> by him . . . .
> the . rish feast . . . . !!!
> I leave . . . to . . . t
> is . . . . lth—

Was the note a comment on the alterations by C, addressed to West, whom C did not know personally ("Mr Editor")? Was the reference to "the ₁Irish feast" a repetition of C's complaint against Sheridan, maintaining that he had always been ready to accept such changes? Or was it a complaint against the copyist for making such a copy without permission, for repeating Sheridan's shoddy business practices? Whatever the case, the note must have been obliterated because of its inappropriateness in a copy prepared for the use of provincial theatre managers, such as John Wilkinson of Hull.

The title-page carries the signature of W. West. The front endpapers carry the signatures of W. H. West and J. Rogers Rees (with notes by Rees, who wrongly assumes, perhaps, that it was the DL prompt-copy). The volume was given to Harvard College Library by Norton Perkins on 4 Sept 1924.

15.6. Robert Southey's copy of the first edition
DCL (uncatalogued Nov 1993).
The copy is inscribed by C on the title-page: [top LH] "*Corrected Copy.*" and [top RH] "Robert Southey, Esqre I from the I Author I 4 Feb.^ry, 18^r. .^?". There are corrections in C's hand on the following pages (a number are cropped): [iii], iv, v, 4, 5, 6, 8, 9, 10, 13, 17, 22, 23, 25, 28, 31, 32, 39, 40, 48, 49, 53, 56, 62, 65, 69, and 71. They closely resemble the corrections in the copies C gave to Raymond, Dibdin, and Pope (15.2–4), and might predate them. On the other hand, a note which C added to p 5 concerning *Remorse* (Printed) I i 115–16 (q EC) is matched only in SH's copy of the second edition.

The volume is bound up in 19th-century buckram with six other plays, the earliest being George Colman the younger's *Feudal Times* (1808) and the latest James Sheridan Knowles's *The Rose of Arragon* (1842). One play— George Stephens's *Gertrude and Beatrice* (1839)—is inscribed by its author on the title-page to RS; another—Jacob Jones's *Longinus* (2nd ed 1827)—is inscribed by its author to "——. Barrow Esqr". The volume was discovered at a country sale in the south of England by the York bookseller Richard Axe early in 1992, and sold to another bookseller soon afterwards, who in turn sold it on to a waiting collector, from whom it was acquired by DCL in 1993.

C also promised RS the first copy of the second edition he could procure (*CL* III 432: 8 [=9] Feb 1813); it seems that he hoped RS might review the play for the *Quarterly Review*, and was anxious that RS should use the "corrected & augmented" edition (*CL* III 438: to J. Rickman [16 Feb 1813]). While there is no record that such a second corrected copy was prepared for RS, it might indeed exist.

15.7. Sara Hutchinson's copy of the second edition
Part at HUL HEW 2.1.18, part at Brandeis University Library Henry Hofheimer Collection.
The HUL copy is inscribed on the title-page: "Miss Sara Hutchinson I

from I S. T. Coleridge". At the foot of the title-page C wrote and then deleted: "20 Feb^{ry} 1813. I 71, Berners' S^t I Oxford S^t I London". It contains plentiful annotation and correction, from CL's Prologue onward, throughout the text and Appendix, but it has no annotation to the Preface. The Brandeis copy is not inscribed and has no annotations or corrections whatsoever to the text or Appendix. The Preface, however, is annotated with detailed personal comments addressed to someone whose sympathy C could count on. The HUL copy is odd in that it does not contain any annotation to the Preface, given the extent of the subsequent annotations, and the Brandeis copy is unique in containing no annotations beyond the Preface. These peculiarities are of a complementary kind.

The suspicion that the HUL and Brandeis copies were manufactured from a single annotated copy combined with another clean copy is confirmed by other evidence. The JDC–EHC correspondence at HRC proves that they examined the SH copy in Dec 1888, when it belonged to Stuart M. Samuel. JDC made a transcript which is now at VCL (LT 67), and this contains the HUL and Brandeis annotations as if they belonged to one copy. *PW* (EHC) II 814–15nn quoted two of the three annotations in the Brandeis Preface, reporting that they were to be found in SH's copy. (In *PW*—EHC—II 819 EHC reports that he had seen only two annotated copies of *Remorse*, the SH and Raymond copies of the first edition: both were owned by Stuart M. Samuel.) Although the copy at Brandeis shows no evidence of sophistication, the copy at Harvard does. The stabbings that are clearly visible in the title-page and throughout the rest of the book do not appear at all on the two Preface pages (one can only suppose that the binder of the Brandeis copy took care to stitch through the stab-holes). Also, in all other copies of *Remorse* that I have seen CL's Prologue precedes the Dramatis Personae: in the HUL copy these are mistakenly transposed. (The small pencil marks in the inner margins of the unsigned preliminary leaves of the HUL copy are not significant: they appear also in the Raymond copy at HRC, also bound for Samuel by Rivière.)

The fabrication must have taken place between Dec 1888, when Samuel showed the SH copy intact to JDC and EHC, and 1892, when the HUL copy was bound by Samuel's usual binder, Rivière. It is not known whether the Brandeis copy was made up at this time or a little later, but it was bound in London (by Zaehnsdorf) some time before 1903, when it was in the possession of Harry Bache Smith of New York (*C Bibl*—Haney—108; cf Smith *A Sentimental Library* 57). Samuel's way with books was not always straightforward, and neither JDC nor EHC would have been surprised if he had separated the SH copy specially to make a private sale to an American eager to collect materials associated with the play (as Harry Smith was in the early 1890s). One might note again that the copy Samuel parted with shows no trace of recombination; the copy he kept for himself does, when one knows what to look for. Cf copy 17.7 below.

The HUL copy was sold at the Samuel Sale, Sotheby's 1 Jul 1907 (lot 37 to Quaritch for £16 10*s*); Quaritch sold it to Harry Elkins Widener in 1909, from whom it passed to Harvard in 1915. The Brandeis copy was sold at Parke–Bernet 4 Dec 1962 (lot 49 for $375). The catalogue describes it as having been the property of an "English Gentleman", and reproduces p v in facsimile. It was given to Brandeis by Henry Hofheimer in 1975.

15.8. Sir George Beaumont's copy of the second edition
    Yale In C678 813B.

The copy is inscribed by C on the front free endpaper: "Sir G. Beaumont I from I the Author." C made minor corrections and emendations on pp 12, 14, 15, 16, 17, 54, 58, 70, and 77. Their relation to other such emendations suggests that they were made soon after publication, perhaps at about the time C sent copies to RS, TP, John Rickman, etc.

Beaumont had read *Osorio* in the summer of 1803, on his and C's first meeting at Greta Hall, and commented on the play from a practical point of view (see *CL* III 14: to D. Stuart [c 5 May 1807]; cf *CL* II 958: to WW [23 Jul 1803] q *Osorio* II i 32–6EC). He and Lady Beaumont had previously appeared on many occasions in the private theatre of their friend Sir Oldfield Bowles at North Aston, as *Jackson's Oxford Journal* duly reported (see the typescript index by E. C. Davies in the Local History Section, Oxford County Library, Oxford). C's annotations to the printed text do not in fact advert to the earlier history of the play, or any aspects of its production.

The copy bears the bookplate of Hannah D. Rabinowitz.

15.9. Robert Owen's copy (edition unknown)
    Not located.

The copy is described by ELG in a footnote to *CL* III 426 as being in "private possession". It is inscribed by C: "R. Owen, Esq., from his sincere admirer, S. T. Coleridge." ELG does not say whether it contains any corrections, nor what edition it is.

C appears to have received an advance copy of Owen's *A New View of Society* (1813) during Dec 1812, while *Remorse* was in rehearsal (*CL* III 426: to D. Stuart [22 Dec 1812]). C's acquaintance with Owen, the social reformer (1771–1858), had begun when he visited the Manchester Academy in Nov 1793. See *The Life of Robert Owen by Himself* (1920) 49–50; John Unsworth "Coleridge and the Manchester Academy" *The Charles Lamb Bulletin* NS XXXII (Oct 1980) 149–58.

15.10. Mrs Morgan's copy of the third edition
    VCL Book No 37a.

The copy is inscribed on the title-page: "⟨To⟩ M‧ʳˢ Morgan with the Author's kindest respects". The hand that wrote the bulk of the inscription seems more like JG's than C's; the hand that added "To" looks like AG's. If this is correct, the book was given to Mrs Morgan after Apr 1816, perhaps as a replacement. It might also explain why there are no other annotations, indeed why it is a copy of the third edition.

The book first appears at Sotheby's 14 Jul 1914 (lot 264 to Dobell for £1 10*s*). It was acquired by VCL, together with other material from EHC's grandson, in 1954.

15.11. Anne Gillman's/Edward Coleridge's copy of the third edition
Brandeis University Library Henry Hofheimer Collection.

The copy is inscribed by C on the title-page: "Mrs Gillman | from the Author." C subsequently deleted this, and wrote: "⟨To⟩ The Revd Edward Coleridge | this Duplicate of the Remorse with Mrs Gillman's best respects | 8 Feby 1826." EC attempted to obtain a copy of the play in 1823, but evidently failed to do so (see *CL* v 287: to EC 23 Jul 1823; cf vi 566: to EC [8 Feb 1826], which evidently accompanied the present copy). EC inscribed it to Frederic W. Farrar of Eton, later Dean Farrar, on 11 Oct 1874. The volume contains ink annotations by C on pp ii and 78 and pencil annotations on pp 3 and 4.

The brevity of the inscription to AG might suggest that it was written not long after C arrived at Highgate, in Apr 1816. The annotations are likely to have been made at this time or later. The pencil annotations cite *SL* (in type since 1815, pub 1817), and the annotation on p 78 must have been made after the death of Sir George Beaumont in 1814. The annotation on p ii (title-page verso) is associated with feelings strongest during 1818 and 1819, and since it is of general import and bears especially on the dating is given here complete:

> It is scarcely worth noticing; but as an instance of damning with faint praise, one might refer to the criticism on this play in the Quarterly Review—the only work ~~which~~ of mine which the Quarterly ever condescended to notice.—As a notable *improbability* gross even to absurdity the Reviewer gives the surprize of Valdez's Castle by a party of Morescoes!—Within the space of ⟨the⟩ 18 months preceding the publication of this criticism no less than five perfectly parallel incidents had taken place in Ireland.—But what should render it improbable, or why the Reviewer conceived it to be such, I cannot even conjecture—.
>
> The concluding Paragraph of this Review, far more injurious to me than all the Malignities of the Edingburgh, affords an instance of insolent intrusion into the sacredness of private Life, surpassed only by the detestible attack on my dear friend, Charles Lamb, perpetrated ~~on~~ by the same Aristarchus, Mr J. Gifford.
>
> S. T. Coleridge.
>
> N.B. The great and serious defect in this Play is the representation of a solemn Shew of Magic with not a single Believer in it's reality among

the supposed Spectators. Each in a different way indeed but yet all alike know or presume it to be a Trick, Alvar, Valdez, Ordonio and Teresa./

C's sense of injury over the *Quarterly*'s delayed and unfair review of *Remorse* was compounded as it became evident that the journal was not even going to notice *Christabel, SL, BL,* and *Zapolya* (*CL* IV 701, 716–17, 813, 889, 949; cf C's annotation of SH's copy of *Remorse* q *Remorse* (Printed) I ii 329EC). The postscript here makes a criticism of the play not found elsewhere, which might even suggest that it was added as late as 1826, when C dedicated the volume to his clerical nephew.

The review of *Remorse* appeared anonymously in *Quarterly Review* XI (Apr 1814) 177–90. C originally hoped that RS might write such a review— see on 15.6 above—but in the end it was written by his nephew, JTC.[18] Whether or not C knew this, he blames the editor William Gifford, and the allusion to Aristarchus of Samothrace—notable for his critical rescension of Greek texts—implies that Gifford mutilated whatever passed through his hands. Gifford mutilated CL's review of WW's *Excursion* in *Quarterly Review* XII (Oct 1814) 100–11 (for Lamb's outraged protest see *LL*—M—III 128–30), though C refers here to Gifford's cruel treatment of CL in an earlier review: see *Remorse* (Printed) I ii 329EC. The last paragraph of the Apr 1814 review, which so offended C, referred to his supposed private habits and reproved him for not publishing. See *CL* III 532: to D. Stuart 12 Sept 1814; IV 604: to Lord Byron 22 Oct 1815; *BL* chs. 1, 3, etc for C's further protests.

The volume was sold—along with the EC/Dean Farrar copy of *Zapolya* (18.9 below)—at Sotheby's 12 Dec 1903 (lot 724 to Kenneth for £5). It was listed in the John Pearson *Catalogue of a Unique Coleridge Collection* 38–9, and again in the Scribner catalogue *Superb Collected Sets of the First Editions of Milton, Coleridge, Swinburne, Wordsworth* 13–14. It was sold in the Mark P. Robinson Sale, Anderson Galleries 26 Feb 1918 (lot 152); in the Jerome Kern Sale, Anderson Galleries 7–10 Jan 1929 (lot 273 for $900); in the James B. Clemens Sale, Parke–Bernet 8 Jan 1945 (lot 187 for $400); at Parke–Bernet 26 Feb 1952 (lot 86 for $220). It came into the possession of Henry Hofheimer of New York, who bequeathed it to Brandeis University on his death in 1975.

15.12. Ludwig Tieck's copy of the third edition
Princeton Robert H. Taylor Collection.
    The copy is inscribed by C on the title-page: "To L. Tieck, Esqre from S. T. Coleridge, 'parvum μνημοσυνον hic sodalis.'" tr "This is a little memento of your friend." C annotated pp iii–iv and 45–6. The second is dated Jul 1817. Tieck left England on 21 Jul and the book, bound with a copy of the second

---

[18] Hill Shine and Helen Chadwick Shine *The "Quarterly Review" under*   *Gifford: Identification of Contributors 1809–1824* (Chapel Hill 1949) 42.

edition of *Christabel* (also presented to Tieck), was probably in the nature of a going-away present, as suggested by the sentence in Latin and Greek. The provenance of the book is described at 16.7 below.

16. *CHRISTABEL . . . KUBLA KHAN . . . THE PAINS OF SLEEP* (1816)

The first edition of *Christabel* was issued on 25 May 1816, but copies were available before that. Besides copies 16.1–2 below, one might note that the copy belonging to Mrs Calvert of Greta Bank is inscribed (in her hand) "May 10th 1816" (HRC: uncatalogued in 1978). The copies inscribed or corrected by C are distinctive in several respects. There is no record of copies being presented to close personal or literary acquaintances, as there is in the case of *SL*. The copies C is known to have presented on publication were all given to what can be described as accidental acquaintances, and carry no markings other than C's inscriptions. The extant corrected (as distinct from inscribed) copies, which bring the text of *Christabel* closer to the version reported by J. D. Collier and introduce further revisions which became the basis of *PW* (1828) (see **176** *Christabel* VAR TEXTS MS 6, PR 2), all appear to date from several months after publication, and were given away almost at random. The first of these corrected copies was presented, indeed, to a person with a contemporary reputation for resembling one of Shakespeare's fools.

The corrections in the eleven corrected copies are concerned almost exclusively with *Christabel*, and three of those among the earlier to be corrected contain corrections transcribed by JG and AG. One must suppose that C did not begin to amend copies until he went to Mudeford (19 Sept 1816), where he hoped to pick up work again on the poem (cf *CL* IV 663: to Thomas Boosey 31 Aug 1816) and where he was materially aided by the Gillmans. Vol II figs 5–6 reproduce AG's, JG's, and C's emendations of two pages (7 and 10). The copying out of corrections might have proceeded in any order: the Hinves copy (16.5) might have been done first among those extant, other copies taking over and developing a selection of its emendations; or it might have been done after the Green copy and the first version of C's (?) own (16.6, 16.9), C (and JG) expatiating for Hinves's benefit. The pencil corrections in Tieck's copy (16.7) might represent the earliest stage; or possibly C's (?) own (16.9) (or some lost master copy) is the earliest, from which all the others derive.

It must be borne in mind that the correction of *Christabel* took place against the background of the hostile reception described in *BL* ch 24. The review in *Ed Rev*, which C believed was by Hazlitt, appeared in Sept, the month in which C began to make changes to the text after his (for him) curiously long spell of inactivity. The larger number of C's changes were made in direct response to the misrepresentation of his critics. The same impulse is demonstrably still at work in copies he corrected in 1818–19 and afterwards gave to his school and university friend Bishop Middleton, and to his son DC (16.8 and 16.10).

The latest corrected copy, dating from Ramsgate 25 Nov 1824 (16.11), is another matter again. While it appears to have been corrected for no specially intimate acquaintance, and while the changes conform to the pattern established by the other corrected copies, the marginal glosses add a new perspective altogether. The Middleton copy (16.8) contains the seeds of these glosses, in three brief (unfortunately cropped) notes, but, taken with other corrections and against the background of the corrected copies as a whole, the glosses appear more like a reappraisal than a revision of the fuller version. The several changes made to the text of this copy are significantly close to, or directly connected with, parts of the gloss material.

16A. J. P. Collier claimed that C gave him "a printed copy when Christabel first came out, I think in 1816: it had his autograph and a few words on the title-page, but I have in some unaccountable way lost it": *Seven Lectures on Shakespeare and Milton by the Late S. T. Coleridge* (1856) xl n.

The BM copy of the third edition, bound up with a copy of *Zapolya* (C 61 c 10–3), into which a letter from C to J. P. Collier is inserted (see *CL* IV 825–6: [2 Feb 1818]), is not inscribed. On the other hand, this BM volume may never have been Collier's, so the possibility remains of an unlocated or lost inscribed copy.

The BM copy of the first edition (11642. d. 60), which the catalogue describes as containing "minor corrections in C's hand", contains some annotation related to the metre, but none of it is in C's hand.

Because there is no difference, beyond the title-page, between the three editions, and because the sequence of editions bears such slight relation to the sequence of annotation beyond the first four copies, the sequence of editions is ignored in the list that follows.

16.1. Miss Wayte's copy of the first edition

Not located.

The copy is inscribed by C on the half-title: "Miss Wayte | with the Author's | kindest respects. | 7 May, 1816". It was sold at Hodgson's 20 Jun 1929 (lot 160 for £190); again in the Robert J. Hamershlag Sale, American Art Association–Anderson Galleries 18 Jan 1935 (lot 23 for $500); and again in the Doris L. Benz Sale, Christie's (New York) 16 Nov 1984 (lot 64 for $3700). It was offered for sale in the Beeleigh Abbey Books Catalogue No BA/39 (Spring 1985) (lot 67 at £5250). The catalogues describe it as disbound, in a full red levant morocco case, and carrying the bookplates of Robert J. Hamershlag and of Doris Louise Benz. The Christie's catalogue (p 31) incorporates a photograph of the inscription.

Miss Wayte is unknown. Perhaps she was the sister of "young Wayte", one of C's and Morgan's neighbours, perhaps a doctor, at Calne in 1815 (see *CL* IV 568: to R. H. Brabant [17] May 1815). Alternatively, since the volume first came on the market at Hodgson's with the property of Lucy E. Watson (née Gillman), Miss Wayte might have been a Highgate neighbour.

16.2. James Harding's copy of the first edition
HUL * EC8 C 6795 816 c.
The copy is inscribed by C on the front flyleaf: "Mr Harding with the Author's respectful Wishes.—Highgate, 20 May, 1816.—" James Harding, AG's brother, was a public notary in the City, and frequently gave C the benefit of legal advice; cf copy 16.4 below. The front wrapper carries the signature of M. A. Knight; the copy subsequently belonged to Amy Lowell, who bequeathed it to Harvard in 1925.

16.3. Neville White's copy of the first edition
Not located.
A copy of the first edition, inscribed by C "on fly-leaf": "Mr. Neville White, from the obliged Author, S. T. Coleridge, Highgate, May, 1816." Sold, bound with an uninscribed copy of *SL*, the property of J. E. Maitland, Esq., Sotheby's 20 Jun 1903 (lot 854 to Dobell for £6 6*s*). Neville White is unknown.

16.4. Miss Lucy Harding's copy of the first edition
Yale In C678 816 Copy 2.
A copy of the first edition, inscribed by C on the half-title: "Miss Lucy Harding with the high Respect of the grateful Author, S. T. Coleridge High-gate, 4 June 1816." Lucy Harding was one of AG's two sisters, and a frequent visitor to the Gillman household; cf copy 16.2 above. Nothing is known of this copy before it was acquired by Chauncey B. Tinker, who bequeathed it to Yale.

16.5. David Hinves's copy of the second edition
In the possession of John Murray (1979).
The half-title contains the following letter-inscription in C's hand (*CL* IV 691 var):

Dear Hinves
    Till this Work is concluded, and with it "Gundimoor, a Poem? by the same Author", accept of this *corrected* Copy of Christabel as a *small* testimonial of Regard, yet such a testimonial as I would not pay to one, I did not esteem, tho' he were an Emperor. Be assured, I will send for your private Library every work, I have published (~~of which~~ if there ⟨be⟩ any to be had) and whatever I shall publish—. Keep steady to the

FAITH: if the Fountain-head be always full, the stream cannot be long empty.—Your's sincerely,

S. T. Coleridge

11 Nov.ᵗ 1816
Mudiford.

It is difficult to know how seriously to take C's words. David Hinves was the eccentric literary valet of William Stewart Rose, a sometime Methodist preacher with the reputation of a natural fool. For example, one knowledge-able reader of Scott's *Waverley* in 1814 took him to be the model for Davie Gellatly, the "motley follower' of Baron Bradwardine of Tully-Veolan.[19] Gundimore was a half-acre on the seashore at Mudeford which gave its name to the weird house Rose had built there; in a note to his *Rhymes* (Brighton 1837) 92 Rose explained that it was also the title of a poem C pretended to be working on. For a description of Rose and Hinves at Gundimore at about this time see E. R. Vincent *Ugo Foscolo: An Italian in Regency England* (Cambridge 1953) 38–41; also *CL* IV 683–4: to J.H.B. Williams [24 Sept 1816].

There are ink corrections and additions in C's hand on pp [3], 4, 5, 6, 7, 8, 10, and 18; in JG's hand on pp 5, 9, 12, 13, 17, 18, 19, 21, 47, and 54; and pencil corrections on pp 5 and 56, apparently by C. JG had returned to Highgate before 10 Nov (see C's letter to him of that date, *CL* IV 688–90), so the volume must have been annotated some days at least before C gave it to Hinves. The annotations are roughly and untidily made, though they are fuller than in all other copies except the Ramsgate one (16.11), with its glosses. There are signs that it is among the earliest of such copies. C appears to be feeling his way towards readings which the other copies simply record, e.g. on pp [3]–4 (lines 1–13). The reading "bed" inserted on p 10 (line 122) is shared only with J. H. Green's copy (where the emended reading was copied out by JG) and DC's; "couch"—as in Tieck's copy, the copy sent to Middleton and AG's transcript, and the Ramsgate copy—was the reading adopted in *PW* (1828). Later copies selected from the alterations worked out in this copy, and added to them (for instance, the Hinves copy does not include the emendation on p 13 = **176** *Christabel* 166, which is found in Middleton's, C's, and J. H. Green's copies). Did C give the working copy, in which he and JG had worked out revised readings, to Rose's valet after they had transcribed the readings into other copies?

C told Murray on 26 Mar 1817: "The corrections and additions to the two first Books of the Christabel may become of more value to you when the work is finished" (*CL* IV 716). There is no need to suppose that C was referring to this copy at this date. William Rose Stewart was able to quote the

---

[19] J.B.S. Morritt, cited by J. G. Lock-hart *Memoirs of the Life of Sir Walter Scott, Bart* (7 vols Edinburgh 1837–8) III 298.

inscription in 1837, and it must have come into the possession of the Murray family after this date. Pages 7 and 10 are reproduced in vol II figs 5–6.

16.6. Joseph Henry Green's copy of the first edition
NYPL Berg Collection.

An uninscribed copy which belonged to J. H. Green. There are corrections and additions in the hand of JG on pp [3], 4, 5, 7, 8, 9, 10, 12, 13, 18, and 19. The annotations are closely related to those in the copies given to Bishop Middleton (16.8) and DC (16.10), though they are not a transcript of either, and perhaps this copy derives from a lost original close to the Hinves copy. Thus, the substitution on p 10 has Middleton's "strove" and "and", but DC's "bed". The same combination of readings is found only in Hinves; but Hinves does not include the same emendation on p 13 (=**176** *Christabel* 166) (it appears elsewhere in Middleton's copy and in AG's transcript of the same). The emendation of *Christabel* 166.1.1 appears to be unique. Was this a spare master copy which C gave to Green, or which Green inherited?

The copy was given to the Berg Collection in 1941 by Owen D. Young. Pages 7 and 10 are reproduced in vol II figs 5–6.

16.7. Ludwig Tieck's copy of the second edition
Princeton Robert H. Taylor Collection.
The copy is inscribed by C on the half-title:

To Ludwig Tieck, Esqre

Dear Sir
    If I ever finish this Poem, I shall be very ungrateful if I omit to mention your honored name in the conclusion as the unexpected Breeze of Hope. when I had altogether desponded—

S. T. Coleridge
July 16, 1817.—

It is inscribed on the title-page: "S. T. Coleridge to Ludwig Tieck."

C had met Tieck, the German poet and critic, in Rome in 1806, and the acquaintance was renewed in Jun 1817, when Tieck visited England. The present copy is bound up with a copy of *Remorse*, inscribed to Tieck at the same time, and the volumes were probably in the nature of a going-away present (Tieck left England on 21 Jul). It was a time when copies of *BL* and *SL* were becoming available, and it is possible that C gave or sent Tieck copies of these two volumes as well, although they have not been traced. The evidence is a letter to C from Tieck, postmarked 20 Feb 1818, in which he discusses all four volumes.[20]

The present copy of *Christabel* appears to have been one that just came to

---

[20] E. L. Griggs "Ludwig Tieck and Samuel Taylor Coleridge" *Journal of* *English and Germanic Philology* LIV (Apr 1955) 262–8 at 267.

hand. The annotations are of two kinds and were undoubtedly made at two different stages. There is a series of pencilled directions and comments in C's hand, apparently addressed to a printer or perhaps to Murray for the further edition that was never published. These appear on pp 4, 8, 9, 10, 18, and 48. They are sketchy, indicating where the text would be altered or expanded, and by how much, but making no attempt to provide the substance of the changes. Then there is a further selection of emendations by C in ink, on pp [3], 4, 5, 9, 10, 18, and 19. They follow the emendations to be found in other known copies, adding nothing new, and the handwriting, as well as some of the punctuation, suggests haste. The explanation of "Assay" on pp 18–19 (=**176** *Christabel* 258) might suggest that the second set of emendations were made specifically, and hurriedly, for Tieck at the time the book was given to him.

Library stamps on the title-page reveal that the copy was owned in turn by the Graf von York at Kloels, and then by the library of the English Seminar at the University of Kraków. In the period 1958–60 it was sold on behalf of the Jagellonian University by Frank Tuohy to Maggs Bros of London (?for £400).

16.8. Thomas F. Middleton's copy of the first edition

Not located; photocopy in BM (RP 2438 ii).

A copy inscribed on the front free flyleaf: "From the Author | to Bishop Middleton | velut prati | Ultimi Flos, praetereunte postqua͵m͵ | Tactus Aratro es͵t͵".[21] Beneath the inscription is the following note, which continues on to the verso (several letters have been cropped from the outer margin and one or two lines from the bottom of the recto):

> Sir Walter Scott, after repeating with grea͵t͵ animation a portion of the Christabel, in the pre͵sence͵ of Sir George and Lady Beaumont, Mr Rogers and others, desired it *expressedly* to be understoo͵d͵ that it was his perusal of Christabel tha͵t͵ had suggested and the enthusiasm, it had excit͵ed͵ in his mind, that had sustained him in the composition, manner, &c of the Lay of the last Minstrel. Never, perhaps, was a Poem so enthusiastically praised by the *Laudatissimi* of ͵the͵ Age, as Scott, Southey, Lord Byron, M͵ʳ Rogers, Sir H. D.͵, the H͵ᵒⁿ J. D. Frere, M͵ʳ Canning, Sir J. Malcolm &c &c, so us͵ed͵ ͵ʳ....ꞌ Ingratitude, W. Hazlitt) to review it as likewise the ͵L͵ay-sermon which was reviewed in an Article written ͵for the͵ greater part before it's appearance, and on the ͵s͵upposition of it's being on the subject afterwards ͵rel͵ated of in the second Lay-Sermon. It was this ͵w͵retch whom the Author had for 3 years ⟨housed, maintained,⟩ treated ͵as͵ a Brother, & afterwards with M͵ʳ Southey & M͵ʳ ͵Wo͵rdsworth saved him from injury if not from the

---

[21] Catullus 11.22–4 tr F. W. Cornish (LCL rev 1962) 17 "like a flower on the meadow's edge, when it has been touched by the plough passing by".

ˌgˌallows, & had never injured by word or deed except to keeping at a distance from him when his own ⌈. . .⌉ ?aniposter Vices had made it a necessary duty—it was he who gave out that to his knowledge Geraldine ˌwˌas meant to be a man in disguise & the whole Poem was disguised Obscenity—Speaking of this ˌaˌnd of me, he observed—How it will make C ˌsˌtare! It is the only Lie that could sting him.—And why? said one of the persons present, who ⟨afterwards⟩ openly ˌinˌformed him that he should communicate the accusation ˌtoˌ some of my friends—Why would you sting him?—Because ˌIˌ hate him. And why do you hate him?—Because *I am obliged to him!*

S. T. C.

C refers to the unsigned review of *Christabel* in *Ed Rev* xxvII (Sept 1816) 58–67 and to the unsigned review of the first *Lay Sermon* in *Examiner* (8 Sept 1816) 571–3, only the second of which is now thought to be by Hazlitt. He wrote in similar terms against Hazlitt to various correspondents between Sept 1816 and Feb 1818 (*CL* IV 669–70, 692–3, 699–700, 735–6, 813, 831), and complained to RS in late Jan 1819 about Hazlitt spreading the rumour that Geraldine was a man in disguise (*CL* IV 918); on 19 Sept 1830 he described to HNC how Hazlitt had to flee from Keswick (*TT—CC*—I 198).

There are emendations and comments by C on pp [3], 4, 5, 7, 9, 10, 11, 13, 15, and 18. There is extensive overlapping between this copy (the comment quoted above and the emendations) and copy 16.10, which C appears to have sent to DC on 3 Feb 1819 (the comment on the front flyleaves and the subsequent emendations), suggesting that they were annotated at about the same time. C inscribed two other titles to Thomas Middleton—*SL* (pub Sept 1817) and *The Friend* (pub Nov 1818). It appears that C sent the volumes to Middleton early in 1821, along with a letter introducing the son of his friend H. F. Cary, who was going out to India in the army (*CL* V 131: to H. F. Cary 31 Dec 1820). The inscriptions to Middleton may have been made at this time, i.e. later than the corrections and annotations. The parcel of books was evidently made up in haste.

The Middleton copy is also related to C's (?) own (16.9), into which AG copied C's emendations (though not his preliminary comments on Hazlitt, nor his explanatory notes on Geraldine). This other copy supplies several lines which have been cropped from the foot of several pages. The Middleton copy also anticipates several emendations to be found only in the 1824 Ramsgate copy (16.11), as well as aspects of the marginal glosses which that copy contains.

The copy contains a pencil note by W. Carr of Ditchingham Hall, Norfolk, who says it was given to him by his cousin, Lady Hobart. She received it from her father, Bishop Carr of Bombay, to whom it had been given by Bishop Middleton. It was rebound by Ramage, apparently after the severe cropping which affects parts of words at the outer margins and two lines of C's annotations at the bottom edge. It was sold at Sotheby's 15 Dec 1982 (lot

122 to Quaritch for £6820); p 50 of the catalogue contains a facsimile of p 10 of the copy, which is said now to be in the possession of a private collector in Chicago.

16.9. C's copy (?) of the first edition
HUL *EC 8 C 6795 817s (c).

The copy is described in pencil on the title-page as "Coleridge's own-proofsheets-corrections-handwriting page 18", which is slightly misleading. There are corrections and markings on pp [3], 4, 5, 7, 8, 9, 10, 11, 12, 13, 18, and 56. The markings and a single word on pp 11 and 12—all in pencil—may be C's; an insertion on p 18 and perhaps an emendation on p 56 are in his hand; all the remaining emendations are in the hand of AG. Pages 7 and 10 are reproduced in vol II figs 5–6.

AG's emendations appear to be careful transcriptions of the larger part of those found in other copies. The relation to the copy sent to Middleton is particularly close, though there are minor differences. C himself inserted **176** *Christabel* 255–6 in the revised version of the passage on p 18, thereby proving that this copy passed through his hands at a time when the transcription was being made. This insertion is paralleled only in the Middleton copy, 16.8 (annotated in 1819?), and (var) in the Ramsgate copy, 16.11 (annotated in 1824). The correction to *Christabel* 174 on p 13 is paralleled only in the same pair of copies. Taken together, the manuscript additions constitute the difference between the 1816 and 1828 texts of the poem, and this emended copy is likely to have served as the basis for what was printed.

There is a line copied on to p 18 in a third hand, which is not distinctive and may belong to RHS, JDC, or some other person. The same line is also to be found in the Fitzwilliam Museum copy of *PW* (1828) only (21.1 below; see **176** *Christabel* 252 VAR commentary). The correction on p 56, to the text of **178** *Kubla Khan* 11 ("Enfolding" for "And folding"), may or may not be in C's hand or the same hand as on p 18; the correction is matched only in the Hinves copy (16.5), and it brings the 1816 text into line with that published in 1828.

This copy is bound up with an annotated copy of *SL* (JG's copy), the provenance of which appears to be separate (see 17.3 below). The combined volume was presented to Harvard by Norton Perkins in Sept 1924.

16.10. Derwent Coleridge's copy of the first edition
St John's College, Cambridge, Class 15 Shelf 53.

The copy is inscribed by C on the front free flyleaf (preceding the half-title) as follows:

> I still cherish the hope of finishing this poem. and if by any means I can command two months' actual leisure at the sea side, I hope to finish it in the course of the present year. Enough at present to assure you, that Geraldine is *not* a Witch, in any proper sense of that word—That

she is a man in disguise, is a wicked rumour sent abroad with malice prepense, and against his own belief and knowlege, by poor Hazlitt. Unhappy man! I understand that when one of his Faction had declared in a pamphlet ("Hypocrÿisy unveiled") the Christabel "*the most obscene poem in the English Language*" he shrugged himself up with a sort of sensual orgasm of enjoyment, and exclaimed—How he'll stare! (i.e. meaning *me*) Curse him! I *hate* him.—When I reflect on such things, and know that to be *real* which otherwise I could not have believed possible, it is an unspeakable Comfort to me that I can with my *whole* heart obey the divine precept, Matth: V. 43, 44, 45, 46.—

S. T. Coleridge.

Feb.ʸ 3. 1819

Highgate.

There are corrections and annotations in C's hand on pp. [3], 4, 5, 7, 8–9, 10, 13, 16–17, and 18.

There are corrections and parallels between C's note quoted above together with the subsequent corrections, and the note and corrections inscribed in copy 16.8, which he sent to Thomas Middleton at about the same time. See 16.8 on C's remarks concerning Hazlitt. The pamphlet *Hypocrisy Unveiled, and Calumny Detected: A Review of Blackwood's Magazine* (Edinburgh 1818) was written anonymously by Macvey Napier, who condemned *Christabel* on p 24 on moral grounds. C's corrections to the text are also close to the corrections in J. H. Green's copy (16.6 above), which are copied out in JG's hand, but which do not include the note he added on pp 8 and 16 (see **176** *Christabel* 81–98, 231–6 VAR commentary). The corrections in this copy might indeed have been made before C wrote the note on the flyleaf, perhaps in 1817–18. A few emendations to *Christabel* (lines 11, 254, 254.1.1) are unique

C repeated several phrases from the note quoted above in a letter to RS of 31 Jan 1819 (*CL* IV 916–18). In the same letter he says that he would be sending some books for DC: this copy of *Christabel* was presumably among them. The front pastedown carries the inscription, in DC's hand: "The Gift of Derwent Coleridge | To Thomas Fisher." Fisher was a neighbour of DC's in Cornwall. From him it passed into the hands of the Acland family, who sold it to St John's in 1982.

16.11. Ramsgate Circulating Library copy of the second edition
Princeton Robert H. Taylor Collection.

In this copy C added a dash following the words "SECOND EDITION" on the title-page, and inserted underneath: "with MSS. corrections and additions by the Author. | 25 Nov.ʳ 1824 | Ramsgate.—" C also made alterations and additions in ink, in a neat and careful hand, on pp [3], 4, 5, 7, 8, 9, 10, 11, 13, 15, 18, 30, 34, 35, and 37. The changes in the text of the poem are similar to those found in other copies, but they appear to be from memory:

the variant of *Christabel* 167.1, inserted on p 13, is unique to this copy, and there are a few other, minor variants that are peculiar to it; yet the blotting of facing pages (evident on pp 4, 8, and 14) suggests that the emendations were made without pause. What makes the copy especially interesting is the developed form of the marginal glosses, on pp 10, 11, 15, 18, 30, 34, 35, and 37, annotating *Christabel* 112–22, 129–32, 141–2, 204–9, 262–8, 383–6, 451–6, 463–6, and 493–7.

The copy contains the bookplate, deliberately defaced, of a Ramsgate circulating library, which must have been its first or second owner. It is reasonable to suppose either that C found the book in such a library during his holiday, at a time when he was confined indoors by unusually perverse weather, or that he presented it to such a library shortly before his departure later in Nov (see *CL* v 396: to JG 23 Nov 1824; 399, 402: to JG [26 Nov 1824]). The inscription on the title-page is in a form without parallel in the other copies, which were inscribed to individuals. The developed glosses suggest a unique, even odd, occasion, perhaps one in which C was able to assume a certain detachment from his poem. Could he have been moved by memories of his Ramsgate holiday the year before, when he met SH there and perhaps completed **412** *The Pang More Sharp than All*?[22] Whether this was the case or not, annual seaside holidays with the Gillmans, first at Muddiford and then at Ramsgate, had become deeply associated with his hopes of completing it. It is possible that *Christabel* was the "Ballad" he told JG that he hoped to complete at Ramsgate during Oct 1824, and that the present annotated copy is somehow connected with this (*CL* v 375; cf **598.X1** *Ballad*).

The copy also contains the name-plate of E. F. Stratton Reader of Sandwich, identifying the "alterations, emendations, & notes" as by C. Stratton Reader (c 1786–1872), a banker who lived at Sandwich, Kent, throughout his life, had no known connection with C or C's family, and is not known as a book collector. He is likely to have obtained the copy locally rather than from a dealer. It was in the library of H. L. Bradfer-Lawrence of York during the 1960s and 1970s, until it was sold by Quaritch in 1981.

17. *SIBYLLINE LEAVES* (1817)

The evolution of *SL* from C's earlier plans to follow on and complement his earlier collections has been described in annex B, as have the material difficulties with printers and publishers between submission of the copy in late 1815 and publication in Jul 1817. C's anxieties and hopes for the collection were intensified by the difficulties and the long delay, during which time he also became increasingly aware of reviewers and of the way the volume might be

---

[22] *The Letters of Sara Hutchinson from 1800 to 1835* ed Kathleen Coburn (1954) 262, 263, 264, 266–7; cf p xxxi n.

received. This background bears in an obvious way on the large number of annotated copies: they were annotated for various purposes, at different times, and sometimes with the help of AG and JG. They are arranged below in approximate chronological sequence, with comment on differences and groupings. Two pages of the edition are particularly significant in establishing this sequence: p 133 (=**300** *The Picture* 113–40), on which C in most cases deleted a series of lines and in many cases experimented with draft substitutions; and p 176 (=**115** *The Eolian Harp* 17–43), which in many cases C emended in accordance with the errata or versions of it. The difference between C's hand and that of his two helpers, AG and JG, is also most obvious on these two pages (cf vol II figs 1, 10).

Few copies are inscribed with dates, but evidence can be assembled to suggest that annotations were made in two separate phases. The first embraces the months immediately before and after publication, from about May 1817 to Jan 1818. C appears first to have added comments and elucidatory remarks, in pencil and ink, in several copies as they came to hand—copies which he afterwards passed on to friends, without inscribing them. Then, on publication in Jul, he appears to have given away copies to a few friends, with corrections, and at the same time to have arranged for AG and JG each to prepare more systematically corrected copies. Though each copy differs slightly from all the others, they derive from a common original, and they were sent to friends and acquaintances. After 18 Aug 1817, when C's contract with Gale and Fenner superseded his agreement with Gutch, copies became less freely available (though not so severely as C pretended to Wrangham on 10 Jan 1818: *CL* IV 800–1).

The second phase of inscription and annotation dates from after Fenner's bankruptcy in Sept 1819, when copies again became more easily available to C (*CL* IV 948–9: to F. Wrangham 28 Sept 1819). The pattern of annotation differs from that adopted in the first phase: C did not seek help from the Gillmans, and the annotations differ more widely from copy to copy. He told RS in May 1820 (*CL* V 51) that all copies of *SL* had been sold, and there is no evidence of his distributing the book after that date.

17A. *Rosenbach Catalogue* XXIV (1916) lists "Coleridge's own copy . . . with corrections in the author's own handwriting", in half-morocco, uncut, at $75. The catalogue contains books which "formed part of the collection of Mr. Harry B. Smith", a collector of other annotated copies (see *C Bibl*—Haney— 105, 106, 109, etc). The same copy is listed at the same price in *Rosenbach Catalogue* XXV (1920).

Rosenbach Catalogue XXXIII (1942) "Selections from our Shelves" lists a copy which might be the same. It is offered at exactly half the price ($37.50), and the description is fuller: "some MS. corrections by the author. Most corrections of typographical errors in Coleridge's hand are found on pp 78, 80, 81, and 83." With half-title and errata; half blue morocco, top edges gilt, other edges uncut. The concentration of corrections on **177** *The Story of the Mad Ox* (pp 75–82) is odd.

17B. "With an autograph note in pencil signed by the author, inserted." Sotheby's 8–12 Apr 1918 (lot 1369 to Dobell for £1 15*s*).

17C. Writing from Calne to Dr Brabant at Devizes on 13 Mar 1815, C promised to send a copy of the *SL* collection when it was published (*CL* IV 553). C continued to correspond with Brabant at least until the year in which *SL* eventually appeared; but whether he remembered his earlier promise remains doubtful. Even if he did, it is not known if the volume was inscribed or corrected.

17D. Alaric A. Watts's copy
VCL Book No 138.
H. O. Dendurent "The Coleridge Collection in Victoria University Library, Toronto" *TWC* v (1974) 229 describes this as an "author's presentation copy". It does not bear any inscription, though it does carry Watts's name and extended annotations in Watts's hand.

17E. Copies containing manuscript transcripts of **540** *Fancy in Nubibus*
A copy containing the poem transcribed "in Coleridge's hand", as well as other annotations, was sold by Anderson Galleries 14 Dec 1909 (lot 387). The hand was subsequently identified as CL's, and the same copy was sold thus (at substantially higher prices) by Henkels' of Philadelphia 26 Jan 1921 (lot 295), and in the Gribbel Sale, Freeman's of Philadelphia 16–17 Apr 1945 (lot 208).
Another copy of *SL*, presented by CL to an acquaintance in 1828, contains his transcription of the same poem (with a different title). It was described by Major S. Butterworth "Coleridge's Marine Sonnet" *The Bookman* LVIII (Jul 1920) 134–6 at 135. Carl Woodring sent me an undated clipping (from the London *Times*?) in which the same copy is described as for sale from Bertram Dobell.
It seems that CL liked to transcribe ms poems by C into copies of books of C's works—both his own copies and those he presented to others. A copy of *BL* is also extant in which CL transcribed **592** *Youth and Age* (see VAR TEXT PR 1).

17F. A copy in levant morocco, gilt edges and in a cloth case, with an autograph manuscript fragment of "an intended third stanza to the Poem 'Youth and Age'" inserted, was sold in the C. B. Darrow Sale, National Art Galleries (New York) 12–13 Jan 1933 lot 133 (for $52.50). The catalogue description states unambiguously that the poem is inserted, not inscribed, and the manuscript might be one of several reported in **592** *Youth and Age* VAR.

17G. Unascribed copy
   Biltmore House Library, Asheville, NC 4.18 R13/S1/9.
   The copy bears no inscription or name, but there are annotations on pp 15, 35, and 195 and at least one marking elsewhere (p 133). It was reported by Peter Applebome in an article on the little-known collection of 23,000 volumes made by George Washington Vanderbilt (d Mar 1914) at Biltmore ("Dusting off the Pages of a Bookish Vanderbilt's Passion" *The New York Times* 11 Mar 1999 Arts Section p 2). An earlier bookplate of John Walker is present (beside the Vanderbilt plate), and a bookseller's note reads "1st ed. of Ancient Mariner etc. with notes and corrections in the hand writing of Coleridge, one of them signed with his initials."
   Page 15 contains the instructions "erase this S. T. C." written against **161** *The Rime of the Ancient Mariner* 198.1.1–4; and pp 35 and 195 take in errata (to **161**.533 and **133** *To a Friend Who Had Declared his Intention of Writing No More Poetry* 25a). Page 133 contains a small pencil mark "x" in the margin of **300** *The Picture* 126 = the beginning of the erratum which extends to line 135. The copy resembles those inscribed to Frere, Middleton, and Miss Ford (Nos 17.8, 17.9, and 17.21) in its sparse annotation, as well as the deletion (only) of the "gust of wind" stanza on p 15 and the lack of annotation on p 133. Other known unascribed copies (17.5, 17.13) contain completely different patterns of annotation.
   The sample of handwriting on p 15—the only one I have seen, in an indistinct photocopy—might be in JG's hand: it is certainly not C's. The phrasing "erase this" also seems uncharacteristic of C (cf "To be struck out" and "Omitted" in other copies). Taking this into account, alongside the unusual pattern of annotation, despite the *New York Times* assertion that this is "perhaps the most important book in the [Biltmore] collection", it could at best be a copy containing memoranda inserted by JG, at worst a copy annotated by a reader who marked a few words and passages revised in subsequent editions (*PW* 1828, 1829, 1834). The annotations and markings have not been recorded in the vol II apparatus.

17.1. John Evans's proof copy
   Yale In C678 817sa.
   A bound copy of proofs and revises printed at Bristol, heavily corrected by C and bearing letters to J. M. Gutch, together with complaints, directions, and comments from C to the printer, John Evans, with Evans's reactions. The proofs embrace sigs B–U. Sig A is of course not present, because it was not added until after the printing passed out of Evans's hands in May 1817; sig D is missing; and there are two stages of sig K. Postmarks and other endorsements on each signature date the sequence of printing and correction between Nov 1815 and Jul 1816 (ELG gives a summary in *CL* IV 618n). The amount of correction varies from signature to signature and from poem to poem. Only significant corrections or additions are recorded in the VAR texts.

It is important that the proofs came to be preserved by the printer, from motives of self-justification in the dispute that developed between himself and C. C complained to Gutch of Evans's failure to follow instructions several times in the margins of later signatures (e.g. *CL* IV 618–19: [c 25 Jan 1816]; 645–6: [6 Jun 1816]), and claimed afterwards that the trouble had begun in sig B, the first to be printed (see **161** *The Rime of the Ancient Mariner* 198.1.1–4 VAR commentary and VAR TEXT PR 5). An earlier stage of sigs B and C (covering *The Rime of the Ancient Mariner*), as well as all stages of sig D (covering the completion of the poem), may not have been preserved for the same reason. Evans's transcription of the first printed version of a stanza from **155** *Continuation of "The Three Graves"* in his "waste office copy" (17.2 below: see VAR TEXT PR 2) makes it clear that an early stage of sig Q has not been preserved; and so on. It should be noted that Gutch's bill specifically mentions "4 pages cancelled in proof" (see ELG's headnote in *CL* IV 658)—cancelled pages which are not included in the proof copy.

The proofs must have been bound by John Evans, their first owner, whose notes defending himself against C's complaints fill the endpapers, where they are dated Oct 1817; his signature is on the front pastedown. The volume remained in the Evans family until 1879, when Lord Coleridge, according to the memorandum on the front free endpaper, received it as a gift from a Miss Evans. It was acquired by Yale as part of the Albert H. Childs Memorial Collection in 1961.

17.2. John Evans's "waste office copy"

Not located.

This copy is quite separate from the bound proofs now at Yale (17.1), although John Evans was involved in both and this copy is based largely (not entirely) on the other.

It was in the possession of James Taylor Brown in 1864, and was sold with his library in 1903: "Bibliomania" *North British Review* XL (Feb 1864) 70–92 at 72n; Sotheby's 20 Apr 1903 (lot 355 to Riley for £2 8*s*). It is listed in the John Pearson *Catalogue of a Unique Coleridge Collection* 48 and again in the Scribner catalogue *Superb Collected Sets of the First Editions of Milton, Coleridge, Swinburne, Wordsworth* 17. It was sold as part of the library of Mark P. Robinson of Honolulu, Anderson Galleries 26 Feb 1918 (lot 164 for $15).

The details overlap to provide the following description. When the copy was sold by Sotheby's it was "half bound", but by the time it was sold by the Anderson Galleries, it was bound in "full red straight-grain morocco, gilt top". It is somewhere entitled "Waste Office Copy", and is signed "J. Evans" on the "first leaf". Page 207 has Evans's note "See the proof returned to Mr. Coleridge for the justice of 'Gratuitous Emendation' on my part." Page 225 contains Evans's transcript of a different stanza—evidently the original one— from **155** *Continuation of "The Three Graves"*. And Evans has also written here and there the original lines as they appeared in the material C submitted. All of what Evans printed appears to be present—i.e. all signatures except the first (sig A).

No sales catalogue or other source suggests that the copy contains any annotation in C's hand. None the less, in at least one instance (p 225) it contains material not elsewhere recorded.

17.3. C's/James Gillman's copy
HUL *EC8 C6795 817s.

The copy is bound up with what appears to be C's own copy of *Christabel* (16.9 above). The title-page carries the signature "James Gillman. | 1817", together with a pencil note: "S. T. C.'s own copy, before publication given to his friend James Gillman." There are numerous annotations in C's hand, in pencil and ink. Those in pencil have been gone over again in another hand, and one (on p viii, at the end of **145** *The Raven*) has been erased. Others are in the hand of JG. There are also markings and comments in the hands of members of the Gillman family in pencil, and on the flyleaves in ink.

Annotations by C appear on pp v, vi, vii, viii, x, 14, 15, 18, 44, [88], 94, 95, 98, 118, 119, 126, 157, 168, 185, 191, 192, 195, 211, 212, 213, 219, 238, 240, 283, 290, 291, 293, 298, and 300. They mingle correction and comment, and not all of the corrections are carried over to later copies. The deletion of the "gust of wind" stanza on p 15 (**161** *The Rime of the Ancient Mariner* 198.1.1–4) is accompanied by a complaint about the printer (only); no corrections appear on p 133 (**300** *The Picture* 113–40), which C also revised in most other copies. The copy might be compared to the Hinves copy of *Christabel* (16.5), along with copies 17.4–5 below, in its relation to subsequent annotated copies.

The front pastedown is inscribed by Lucy Elinor Watson to her uncle, S. B. Watson. The copy was apparently in the possession of Stuart M. Samuel during the 1890s;[23] but it is not the Samuel copy seen and cited by JDC, nor the copy of which Samuel passed on a selective transcript to Thomas Hutchinson and Richard Garnett (see 17.5 below). Nor does it bear Samuel's bookplate, and it was not included in the Samuel Sale, Sotheby's 1 Jul 1907. It is bound up with a copy of *Christabel*, corrected so as to serve as copy for *PW* (1828), and the double volume was presented to Harvard by Norton Perkins in 1924.

SC's copy of *SL* at NYPL (Berg Collection Copy 5) contains a selection of annotations from the JG copy, as well as a number of notes in ink and pencil by SC. The annotations have mistakenly been taken to be in C's own hand (American Art Association Sale 14 Feb 1927 lot 261 for $400), but they have no independent significance. SC's copy belonged to Maurice Baring and to

---

[23] He quoted from it in "The Source of the Ancient Mariner" *The Athenaeum* 19 Mar 1890 p 40; see also *C Bibl* (Haney) 108.

W. Van B. Whitall before it was bought in 1927 by Owen D. Young, who donated it to the Berg Collection in 1941.

17.4. C's/Henry Nelson Coleridge's copy
     HUL *AC85 L 8605 Zy 817c.

A note on the verso of the front free endpaper says: "Coleridge's own copy with his corrections & some notes by H N C". There is no inscription by C, but there are numerous annotations and corrections by him throughout. Four annotations are in pencil, and have been gone over again (also by C) in ink, which suggests at least two stages of emendation. There are also a few emendations and comments in other hands (HNC's on p 260; DC's (?) on p 159). Some comments have been cropped.

Annotations by C appear on pp 8, 10, 15, 18, 88, 89, 90, 118, 119, 126, 133, 145, 157, 158, 168, 176, 185, 191, 197, 207, 211, 212, 213, 234, 240, 255, 257, 261, 266, 268, 269, 276, 301, and 302. There are connections in format (pencil and ink) with JG's corrected copy (17.3 above), suggesting that this might also be an early annotated copy. Not all the errata are written out, but references are given to the list of errata in a way that suggests it had recently become available (pp 133, 176); no gloss has been added on p 15. A proportion of C's comments identify persons referred to in the poems— perhaps at a later stage of annotation, for HNC's benefit. C wrote a footnote to the title of *America to Great Britain* on p 276: "by Washington Allston, a Painter born to renew the 15th Century."

The copy bears the bookplate of Henry Wadsworth Longfellow; as an inserted list makes clear, it was one of several books given to him in 1869 by Robert Ferguson of Carlisle.[24] In 1954 it was placed on deposit at HUL from the Longfellow Collection at Craigie House.

17.5. Copy belonging to C (?), Francis Wrangham (?), "Peter Morris" (?)
     Not located.

The richest of the three early copies annotated by C (17.3–5), apparently for his own purposes, and afterwards given to friends. Several annotations appear to predate those in the other two copies, although others were made several years afterwards. It lacks sig A and carries no inscription or sign of early ownership. For this reason it might be presumed to be a proof copy; or possibly it is the copy shown to J. H. Frere in loose sheets (a note in Frere's hand appears on p 268); or it may be the copy promised to Francis Wrangham on 5 Jun 1817 (*CL* IV 737), promised again as "my own copy" on 10 Jan 1818 (*CL* IV 802), and perhaps the copy containing "numerous M.S.S. corrections . . . peculiar to that set" sent finally on 28 Sept 1819 (*CL* IV 949). It was not, however, listed among the copies of C's works

---

[24] See also Samuel Longfellow *The Life of Henry Wadsworth Longfellow* (3 vols Boston 1891) III 139–40.

owned by Wrangham in 1826.[25] Quite differently, the tenor of at least one of C's remarks—concerning **115** *The Eolian Harp* on p 175—suggests that the copy was in part annotated with Wilson, Lockhart, or some other person connected with *Bl Mag* particularly in mind. For this reason it might be the copy C sent to "Peter Morris" (=John Gibson Lockhart, though C did not know this, and might even have thought that Peter Morris was J. H. Frere: see 17.19 below).

Annotations by C appear on pp 15, 18, 35, 44, 51, 98, 126–7, 128, 133, 134, 157, 168, 175–7, 207, 211, 217–18, 257, 262, 268, 269–70, and 282–3. Less of the annotation comprises correction than in JG's and HNC's copies, obvious errors are left unamended, and there is more plentiful extended comment. All of it is in ink, though not all in the same sort of ink, and some has been lost by trimming. Pages 176 and 269 are reproduced by Mary Lynn Johnson "How Rare is a 'Unique Annotated Copy' of Coleridge's *Sibylline Leaves*?" *BNYPL* LXXVIII (1974–5) 451–81 at 457, 459. Page 15 contains a complaint against the printer, like JG's copy, but also a marginal gloss in an apparently early form; the emendations on p 133 appear to precede the errata as they were eventually published in sig A, and might therefore date from any time after mid-Jun 1816, when C came to think that an errata sheet would be necessary (*CL* IV 645fn: to J. M. Gutch [6 Jun 1816]); p 269 contains lines on Donne, as does HNC's copy less fully; the emendations to the text of **139** *The Destiny of Nations* (pp 281–303) seem also to have been made before the errata were drafted.

On the other hand, C's reference to Henry Francis Cary on p 51 must postdate autumn 1817, when C made Cary's acquaintance; the reference to the *M Rev* critique on p 127 is proof that at least this note was written after Jan 1819; and DC transcribed the notes on pp 98 and 269 into his own copy some time after late Nov 1819 (?). The fact that the volume was annotated over several years, up to early 1819 at least, increases the likelihood that it was the one C promised Wrangham. C had known Wrangham at Cambridge (see **79** *To Ann Brunton* headnote; also the headnotes to poems **80–1**). Their friendship continued while Wrangham developed into a bibliophile who, at the time of his death in 1842, owned over 15,000 volumes. One might be tempted to think that C wrote several comments with Wrangham's interests in mind, in order to increase the value of the promised gift. Alternatively, the late date of some of the annotations as well as their tenor might suggest that C had "Peter Morris" in mind. Because the copy does not contain a letter to "Peter Morris", of which a draft survives, and because one wonders whether C would have sent an incomplete copy to him, the "Peter Morris" copy has been given a separate entry as an unlocated item at 17.19 below.

If the copy was Wrangham's, it might have been among the "upwards of 70" poetical and miscellaneous tracts in the 1843 Hunmanby Sale (see

[25] *The English Portion of the Library* 1826) 190.
of the Ven. Francis Wrangham (Malton

BM Sale Catalogue 248 (5) lot 2410). It was in the possession of Stuart M. Samuel when it was cited by Garnett in 1898 (*PW*—RG—286, 293, 295, etc), until it was sold by Sotheby's 1 Jul 1907 (lot 41 to Quaritch for £45). It was in the possession of H. T. Butler when Lowes cited it in 1927–30 (*RX* 471, 483, 504, 505, 580), until it was sold by Hodgson's 13 Jun 1934 (lot 470 to Pickering for £68). It was in the possession of Arthur A. Houghton Jr in the 1970s, until it was sold at Christie's 13 Jun 1979 (lot 126 to Fleming for $6500). The Christie's catalogue reproduces p 269 as pl 18.

17.6. Incomplete copy
   Not located.
   A copy of *SL* pp 3–74, "Inscribed by the author on the first page: 'An Essay on the use and abuse of the Supernatural in Poetry precedes the volume, and about 4 sheets of the Poetry are missing at the end.' With four marginal notes in an unknown hand, and a stanza on p. 15 has been inked over": John Gribbell Sale, Parke–Bernet 16 Apr 1945 (lot 101). This copy may have been a sort of mock-up for the essay on the supernatural in poetry to be prefixed to *The Rime of the Ancient Mariner*, which C mooted before and during the writing of *BL* (*CL* IV 561: to Lord Byron Easter week 1815; *BL* ch 13—*CC*—I 306), a fragment of which is preserved at VCL (LT 13) in J. J. Morgan's hand (*SW&F*—*CC*—401–2; cf *C Life*—G—279–80). The original plan grew out of C's intention to review Scott's *Lady of the Lake* (1810)—*CN* III 3952 f 72ᵛ, 3970—and was of course overtaken by *BL* itself. The present copy must represent an effort to retrieve the planned essay, before or after the delayed publication of *SL* in Jul 1817.
   This copy was sold in the Stuart M. Samuel Sale, Sotheby's 1 Jul 1907 (lot 42); and again, as the property of John Cresswell, by Sotheby's 12 Dec 1907 (lot 531), where, though the first page is described as having a note in C's hand, the other "numerous notes" are described as being "in another hand". Dobell was the buyer on each occasion, and the quick resale at a much lower price (£3 7*s* 6*d* instead of £10 10*s*) was undoubtedly caused by the reattribution of the handwriting. However, if the notes are in the hand of JG or AG or some other amanuensis (even J. J. Morgan?), their interest is hardly less.

17.7. Another copy owned by C?
   Not located.
   A copy with annotations by C is quoted in *PW* (JDC) 564–5, 588, 608, 610, 619, 628. The annotations are to the following poems, in the sequence in which they appear in *SL*: **145** *The Raven* on p viii; *Mutual Passion* (=**486** *Adaptation of "A Nymph's Passion"*) on p ix; **142** *Ode on the Departing Year* on p 58; **174** *France: An Ode* on p 61; **175** *Fears in Solitude* on p 65; **300** *The Picture* on p 131. The annotations are of particular interest: two of them are textual emendations, the remaining four comment on the text, and

all six are unique to this copy. One would guess, from their content and their relation to annotations in other copies, that the present copy is early.

JDC repeatedly identifies Stuart M. Samuel as the owner of the copy (*PW* 564B, 619B, 628B), and other references (e.g. *PW* 610B) imply that this was the only copy belonging to Samuel he had seen or knew of. This raises interesting questions. JDC's correspondence with EHC at HRC reveals that JDC became aware that Samuel owned an annotated copy of *SL* following Samuel's letter in *The Athenaeum* 19 Mar 1890 p 40. However, as JDC told EHC (10 Apr 1890), Samuel ("the Jew") refused to lend it to him. In a later letter (5 Jul 1892) JDC reported that Samuel had so far relented as to lend him the annotated *SL*, and an annotated copy of *Remorse* as well. What is odd is that Samuel did not lend JDC the copy he had quoted in his *Athenaeum* article, which prompted JDC's original request—i.e. JG's copy (17.3 above). The notes in *PW* (JDC) show that he never saw it.

Samuel afterwards lent the Wrangham copy to Garnett, who cited it (only) in *PW* (RG), and to Thomas Hutchinson, who cited C's comment on *The Three Graves* in his 1898 edition of WW's poems; or, more probably, he gave them a transcript, which they shared. One might have wondered, given Samuel's duplicity at this time over SH's copy of *Remorse*, whether he also lent JDC a transcript of the *SL* marginalia which was a forgery or fabrication. But the annotations quoted by JDC strike an authentic note, and his transcript proves that he did see the complete, undivided copy of SH's *Remorse*. Although JDC's letters to EHC show that he did not strike up any rapport with Samuel, Samuel appears not to have tried to cheat him.

Thus, the copies of *SL* belonging to Samuel, described in *C Bibl* (Haney) and in the Sotheby sale catalogue of 1 Jul 1907, appear not to include the present copy. Nor does it appear to have been seen by EHC, who cites only two notes from it, each accompanied by the rubric "*MS. Note by S. T. C.*" (*PW*—EHC—I 168, 171), and who was undoubtedly dependent on JDC for them. EHC does cite marginalia from the Wrangham/"Peter Morris" copy not included by Garnett (*PW*—EHC—I 425), but since he fails to cite marginalia of considerable pertinence from the same copy, he must have depended on the selective transcript made for or used by Garnett and Hutchinson. Cf also *Remorse* copy 15.7 above.

A copy of *SL*, said to contain JDC's transcript of the annotations in Samuel's copy as well as JDC's own notes, was sold at Sotheby's 13 Jun 1904 (lot 97 to B. S. Stevens for 18*s*).

17.8. John Hookham Frere's copy
    Princeton Robert H. Taylor Collection.
    Inscribed on the half-title, in C's hand: "With the Author's | grateful Respects". There are corrections in C's hand on pp 15, 126, 207, and 240.
    The copy was sold with the library of John Tudor Frere at Sotheby's 14 Feb 1896 (lot 103 to Robson for £3 7*s* 6*d*). Lot 104 was another of J. H.

Frere's copies, presumably uncorrected. It was perhaps in the possession of John A. Spoor in 1927–30 (see *RX* xiii—though Lowes had no need to cite it), and sold with his library at Parke–Bernet 27 Apr 1939 (lot 188 for $205). It was sold again at Parke–Bernet, as the property of a New York private collector, 29 Jan 1951 (lot 123 for $110).

17.9. Thomas F. Middleton's copy
Not located.

A copy inscribed by C on the title-page: "To the Right Reverend | the Bishop of | Calcutta from the | Author.—" Described in Sotheby's catalogue 4 Aug 1939 (lot 325 to Stonehill for £48), with a facsimile reproduction of the inscription. Also corrected by C on p 15.

The Sotheby cataloguer assumed that C inscribed the copy for Reginald Heber, the hymnologist and bishop of Calcutta. It is almost certain that C inscribed it for his friend from Christ's Hospital and Cambridge days, Thomas F. Middleton, bishop of Calcutta from 1814 until his death in 1822. C presented Middleton with an extensively corrected copy of *Christabel* and a copy of the 1818 *Friend*; the present volume was probably included with them in a hastily assembled package which C put together at the end of 1820 (*CL* v 131: to H. F. Cary 31 Dec 1820). The annotations in the *Christabel* volume appear to date from a year or so before the inscription (see *Christabel* copy 16.8), and possibly the annotations in the present volume likewise.

The Frere and Middleton copies resemble one another in their inscriptions and their very sparse annotation, as well as in their deletion (only) of the "gust of wind" stanza on p 15 (**161** *The Rime of the Ancient Mariner* 198.1.1–4) and their lack of any emendation on p 133. In respect of pp 15 and 133 they resemble the early JG and HNC copies (17.3–4).

17.10. Another copy owned by C?
Not located.

The only records of this copy are photocopies of pp 133 and 176, each corrected in C's hand, given to me by George Whalley in 1977. Whalley could not recall how the photocopies came into his possession, but each carries a comment on C's hand by KC, who also could not recall where they came from. They have a peculiar interest because, on the basis of C's emendation of **300** *The Picture* on p 133 (see 126–35 VAR commentary), this copy appears to be the original or at least the counterpart of the copies given to WW (17.11), TP (17.12), Martha Fricker (17.15), William Hood (17.14), and an unknown person (17.13). In none of the five copies is the hand C's: it is either AG's or JG's. Only these have the same variant substitution (and they are closely related, though not identical, in other ways too). The two pages of C's original, together with AG's and JG's transcripts (in copies 17.12 and 17.15), are reproduced in vol II figs 1 and 10. (KC's notes on the photocopies have been erased.)

C's substitution for **115** *The Eolian Harp* on p 176 (see 26–33 VAR commentary) does not have variant words which differentiate it from the errata, as *The Picture* has. In fact, it is verbally the same. But details of punctuation and capitalisation suggest again that this copy—rather than the printed errata sheet—may be the original of the emendations of the five copies named above.

It is possible that the photocopies are from the copy sold with a "Booklover's Fine Library", City Book Auction (New York) 20 Oct 1954 (lot 67 for $150). The copy is described as "Unique . . . with many corrections in the author's hand throughout the text. Deleting and adding words as he read his own work probably in preparation for another edition. On p. 133, he adds six lines to the bottom of the text. Not only single words, but in many cases whole sentences are crossed out." The copy is (or was) bound in old, worn calf. It has proved impossible to trace.

17.11. William Wordsworth's copy
Cornell WORDSWORTH PR 4480 S5 1817 Copy 1.
Large-paper copy bearing the name on the half-title in AG's (?) hand: "Wm Wordsworth." The flyleaf is inscribed in WW's hand: "John Wordsworth from his affectionate Uncle Wm Wordsworth". There are annotations and corrections in AG's hand on pp 15, 18, 35, 44, 57, [88], 93, 98, 119, 126, 130, 133, 134, 138, 168, 176, 191, 192, 195, 207, 211, 212, 213, 240, 242, 257, and 287. There are also some pencil underlinings and markings, probably by one of the Wordsworths.

AG's annotations and corrections largely amount to an incorporation of the errata, though not all are taken in, especially towards the end of the volume. In addition, some emendations are not derived from the errata: the addition of a gloss on pp 15, 44, and 133 (where the emendation coincides with the untraced copy 17.10). This copy, among the group of five closely related copies emended in the hand of AG and JG, contains the largest number of emendations.

Listed in Southeran & Co's catalogue Nov–Dec 1902 (item 172), from which it was acquired by Mrs Henry St John (see *C Bibl*—Haney—108). Following her death in 1919 it was purchased by Victor Emanuel, who presented it to Cornell in 1925.

17.12. Thomas Poole's copy
Brown University PR 4478 A1 1817 Koopman Collection.
Inscribed on the half-title, in JG's hand: "Thomas Poole from his friend | S. T. Coleridge." There are annotations and corrections in the hand of AG on pp 15, 18, 44, 57, [88], 96, 119, 126, 130, 133, 134, 138, 157, 176, and 207. There is also a comment in TP's hand on p 73, and some markings in pencil—probably made later—on pp 192, 195, 198, 199, 206, and 212. Pages 133 and 176 are reproduced in vol II figs 10 and 1 respectively.

AG's annotations and corrections overlap those she made in the copy sent to WW (17.11): they constitute an even more selective incorporation of errata and add to the errata the emendations on pp 15, 44, and 133. Furthermore, the present copy takes in an erratum on p 96, which the WW copy does not, and it makes corrections on pp 130 and 157.

The copy is undoubtedly the one C sent to TP on 22 Jul 1817 (*CL* IV 754). The front pastedown carries, besides TP's own signature, that of J. C. Collins and the bookplate of Philip D. Sherman, from whose library it passed into Brown's possession in 1958.

17.13. Unascribed copy
Yale In C 678 817S Copy 2.

The copy bears no inscription or name, and is largely uncut, but there are annotations and corrections in the hand of AG on pp 15, 18, 44, 57, [88], 119, 126, 130, 133, 138, 176, 207, and 240. The annotations in this copy might seem to be copied selectively from TP's (17.12), except that the latter has a mistake on p 15 which this copy does not take over, and the correction on p 240 does not appear in TP's copy. Nor is it derived from WW's copy (17.11), because it follows TP's (not WW's) on p 130, and it shares a slight mistake with TP's (and no other copy) on p 207—if indeed this last is evidence. The shared readings on pp 15, 44, and 133, taken along with such other evidence, reinforce the impression that AG copied her annotations from a single original, such as the unlocated copy 17.10.

The copy bears Chauncey B. Tinker's bookplate. Correspondence with J. L. Lowes inserted into the copy proves that it was in his possession in Jun 1926 (cf *RX* xiii, 505 n 61).

17.14. William Hood's copy
Columbia X 825C67 W3 1817.

Inscribed on the title-page: "W. Hood, Esqre | from the obliged Author." There are annotations and corrections in the hand of JG on pp 15, 18, 44, 57, [88], 96, 119, 126, 130, 133, 134, 138, 176, 207, 240, and 302. The annotation on p 15 is reproduced in Parke–Bernet catalogue 29 Jan 1952 (lot 110), and in Carl Woodring "A Coleridge Miscellany" *Columbia Library Columns* XXIV (May 1975) 26–32 at 27.

The peculiar emendations on pp 15, 44, and 133 establish connections between this and the four preceding copies. This copy takes in many of the same errata also, but the emendation on p 302 (see **139** *the Destiny of Nations* 438fn25 VAR commentary) is paralleled only by HNC's copy (17.4) and is proof of an independent transcription. *RX* 166 reports that the inscription is accompanied by the date "Sept^r, 1817," which it is not—though it is likely to have been inscribed at that time or a little before. Hood, along with Gutch and other Bristol friends, had of course sponsored the publication of *SL* and *BL* in the first instance.

The copy was in the possession of James B. Clemens in the earlier part of this century, when it was described in *C Bibl* (Haney) 109 and *RX* 166. It was sold at the Clemens Sale, Parke–Bernet 8 Jan 1945 (lot 194 for $380); and again, as the property of Jacob J. Podell, Parke–Bernet 29 Jan 1952 (lot 110). It was acquired by Columbia in 1965.

17.15. Martha Fricker's copy
HUL Lowell *EC8 C6795 817s.

Inscribed in C's hand on the half-title: "Miss Fricker I in mark of high regard I from her affectionate I Brother, I S. T. Coleridge I Aug. 1817". There are annotations and corrections in the hand of JG on pp 15, 18, 44, 57, [88], 96, 119, 126, 130, 133, 134, 138, 157, 176, 207, and 240. The emendations on pp 15, 44, and 133 establish connections with the preceding five copies; but they are not identical, and the form of the marginal gloss on p 15 is unique. The ink-blots on facing pages suggest that the corrections were made quickly. Martha Fricker was C's favourite among his wife's sisters—"the Angel of the Race, self-nibbling Martha" (*CL* III 518: to J. J. Morgan 7 Jul 1814), "the only one of the Brood that I had any regard for, & who deserved it" (*CL* IV 673: to R. H. Brabant 21 Sept 1816; cf *CL* III 431: to Mrs C [27 Jan 1813]; 435: to RS 8 [=9] Feb 1813). She had settled in London in the autumn of 1812 or early in the winter of 1812–13, as a mantua-maker.[26]

Curiously, the copies C claimed to have sent to the Greta Hall household, "The Aunt-Hill"—i.e. to RS and to his own family (*CL* IV 800–1: to F. Wrangham 10 Jan 1818; cf *Minnow* 105)—have not survived. It is also strange that this apppears to be the only book C inscribed to Martha Fricker. The added gloss on p 15 differs from others in the set copied by the Gillmans, perhaps being (as Lowes argued: *RX* 165–6) in an earlier form. C possibly gave her a copy containing an earlier, unrevised form of the gloss because he assumed that she would be less likely than the other recipients to notice or care.

Nothing is known of the provenance of this copy until its sale at Sotheby's 31 May 1907 (lot 31). It was subsequently owned by Harry Bache Smith (*A Sentimental Library* 58) and by Amy Lowell, who bequeathed it to Harvard in 1925. Pages 133 and 176 are reproduced in vol II figs 10 and 1 respectively.

17.16. Unascribed copy, reported by John Livingston Lowes; possibly John Matthew Gutch's copy
Not located. Possibly a phantom copy, or perhaps Duke University R. B. R. A-29 C693 SM.

Lowes cites a copy "in the collection of the late Miss Frances Bennett", whose collection passed to Professor Phillip Ogden (*RX* xiii), containing on p 15 a unique form of the marginal gloss: "Within the Tropics there is no Twilight" (*RX* 167, 505 n 62; see **161** *The Rime of the Ancient Mariner*

---

[26] See *LL* (M) III 86–7 and n; Collier *An Old Man's Diary* II (3) 80.

198.1.1–4 VAR commentary). The gloss thus cited forms the first sentence of the different, longer glosses in AG's and Miss Ford's copies (17.17, 17.21). No further annotations from the Frances Bennett copy are recorded in *RX* or elsewhere.

It is possible that Lowes's notes became confused, and that the copy does not exist as he describes it. Duke University has a copy which carries the bookplate of Frances E. Bennett and contains contemporary pencil annotations. Duke acquired the copy in 1935. The front pastedown carries the following two notes (in a 19-century hand): "Sold by Sotheby Mar 17. 1859" and "Coleridge's Copy with his corrections for a new Edition/ compare later editions." This is odd because the sale at Sotheby's on 17 Mar 1859 was the first of a three-day sale of drawings, engravings, and plates, in which no books were included. The pencil annotations follow the errata only, and no gloss has been added on p 15. The only addition to the incorporated errata appears on p 304, where the annotator has added beneath the imprint (again in pencil): "for I John Matt. Gutch I who paid him for the printing I & J. M. G. found the paper." The hand might be that of Gutch, or it might be that of JG: both varied considerably, depending on how hard they tried to be clear.

17.17. Anne Gillman's copy
Stanford V 821.6 C69s.

Inscribed on the title-page: "⌜. . .⌝ with equal Respect and Regard I from his obliged and gratefully I affectionate I Friend, I The Author." Approximately 6 cm have been trimmed away at the head of the page, above the inscription, so that only a couple of downstrokes remain of the recipient's name. The same title-page carries two further inscriptions. The first is in AG's hand: "H A Gillman I The Gift of his Mother." The second reads: "The Notes and Alterations in manuscript are in S. T. Coleridge's own hand-writing—H A Gillman."

An unidentified hand, on a sheet of writing-paper tipped in to face the first preliminary leaf, claims that C presented the copy to AG. AG copied on to pp [305–6] a note by C relating to her and to the poem on p 186 (**277** *Inscription for a Fountain on a Heath*), dating from a manuscript of 1832—perhaps at the time she passed on the copy to her younger son. The copy was not the one from which AG copied errata into copies 17.11–13 above, and it was annotated by C relatively late in the sequence.

There are corrections and annotations by C on pp iii, 15, 16, 44, 51, [88], 119, 126, and 187. The marginal gloss on p 15 has something in common with the glosses to be found in the Wrangham/"Peter Morris" copy (17.5) or Miss Ford's copy (17.21); the note on p 51 (**142** *Ode on the Departing Year*) is matched only in the Wrangham/"Peter Morris" copy, and proves, in its reference to H. F. Cary, that the copy was not annotated until after autumn 1817, when C and Cary met at Littlehampton. The relation of the other annotations to those in other copies suggests any date between late 1817 and 1820.

The tipped-in note states that the copy was purchased from H. A. Gillman by Basil Montagu Pickering. The staff at Stanford conjecture that they acquired the volume in about 1936–8. It had previously been in the possession of Mrs Timothy Hopkins, and she may have acquired it from Molly Latham, whose library the Hopkinses took over when they bought the Latham estate.

17.18. Derwent Coleridge's copy
HRC (uncatalogued in 1978).

The copy is not inscribed, but it carries the bookplate of DC and notes on the front endpapers by EHC (dated 1908) and Anthony D. Coleridge (dated 1945). There are corrections and comments in C's hand on pp [88], 93, 94, 95, 97, 98, 100, 105, 106, 109, 168, 240, and 269. There are also annotations in DC's hand on pp 98, 186, and 269, the first and last taken from the Wrangham/"Peter Morris" copy (17.5); there are many more, in pencil and ink, by EHC.

C's annotation in this copy concentrates almost exclusively on perfecting the text of **167** *Fire, Famine, and Slaughter* (pp 88–109), which is unusual. This may be linked to the claim he made to DC in late Nov 1818 (?), that the Preface "is my happiest performance in respect of *Style*" (*CL* IV 885). The annotations might have been written at about the same time.

The copy was acquired by HRC from Anthony Coleridge in 1964.

17.19. Copy belonging to "Peter Morris" (=John Gibson Lockhart)
Not located.

In his letter to "Peter Morris" in Nov 1819 C wrote: "I intreat your acceptance of all my works, of which I possess a copy. I flatter myself their value will not be diminished by their having been corrected, and, I hope, sometimes amended, by myself, or by the number of of MSS. comments." (*CL* IV 970).[27] "Peter Morris" had come to C's defence and singled out C's verse for praise, in particular, in *Bl Mag*. C appears to have been uncertain as to his identity at the time, and here calls him "Brother Bard" (as in **560** *To a Comic Author*). For the annotated copies of *Zapolya* and *LS* presented to "Peter Morris" see 18.8 below and *LS* (*CC*) 236, 238.

Copy 17.5 above contains remarks on **115** *The Eolian Harp* (p 175) which might have been inscribed with someone connected with *Bl Mag* particularly in mind, and can be proved not to have left C's possession until after Jan 1819 at the earliest. However, there are good reasons for thinking that copy 17.5 might be the one sent to Francis Wrangham.

---

[27] Cf Eric W. Nye "Coleridge and the Publishers: Twenty New Manuscripts"   *MP* LXXXVII (1989) 51–73 at 61–4 for an improved text of the letter.

17.20. Thomas Allsop's copy
Not located.

C appears to have sent Allsop a mutilated copy c 18 Jan 1820: "I should have sent a corrected Copy of the Sibylline Leaves; but for a two-legged little *Accident's* having torn out two leaves at the Beginning, & I will no longer delay this parcel, but will transcribe at another time what I had written in them—" (*CL* v 16; the "little *Accident*" was probably Henry, the Gillmans' younger son). Allsop owned a heavily annotated copy of *The Friend* (*CC* II 389). It is possible that the copy described here is the one described by Haney as being in Stuart M. Samuel's possession, which also lacked a title-page (*C Bibl*—Haney—109); but Haney was not always accurate, and his descriptions do not enable precise identification. Besides, the Allsop copy as C describes it did not appear in the Samuel Sale, Sotheby's 1 Jul 1907.

17.21. Miss Ford's copy
HUL *EC8 C 6795 817s (A).

Inscribed by C on the half-title: "Miss Ford | in testimony of respect | and regard from | S. T. Coleridge | Highgate, | 29 July 1820." Miss Ford is unknown; she can be presumed to be a visitor to Highgate, or a neighbour. There are annotations by C on pp 15 (the longest form of the added marginal gloss), 168, and 207. The pencil annotations on pp 180–1 are not in C's hand.

There are no indications as to who owned the copy after Miss Ford and before Sept 1924, when Norton Perkins bought it in a bookshop (*RX* 505 n 60) and gave it to Harvard.

17.22. J.H.B. Williams's copy
Not located.

J. Rogers Rees possessed a copy "which C gave to his friend J.H.B. Williams": "Coleridge Items" *N&Q* 10th ser IX (25 Jan 1908) 63–4 at 64. Williams was JG's young assistant, and C inscribed copies of *Wallenstein* and *SM* to him in 1832 (see *LS—CC*—237; 11.11 above). He also made a manuscript collection of C's late poems in J.M.?B.'s Notebook Album (annex A 13). KC records in *CN* IV 4606n that a gift copy of *SL* inscribed to J.H.B. Williams was on sale in Valparaiso, Indiana, in 1978. She does not say whether the volume is annotated.

17.23. Emended part copy, pp [87]–196
HUL *EC8 C 6795 817s (D).

The part copy contains numerous annotations and corrections, all of them in JG's hand, on pp [88], 93, 94, 95, 96, 98, 105, 108, 119, 126, 130, 131, 133, 134, 138, 139, 155, 157, 158, 160, 168, 171, 176, 177, 179, 180, 187, 189, 191, 192, and 195. The pencil note on p [87] is in EHC's hand.

It is difficult to know how to explain these emended pages. They are not proofs; nor were they used as printer's copy for *PW* (1828), since the emendations of only one poem (**156** *This Lime-tree Bower my Prison* on pp 189–93) were consistently carried forward. The full annotation of **167** *Fire, Famine, and Slaughter* is approached only in DC's copy (17.18), and the comment on Joanna Baillie's borrowing from **172** *Lewti* on p 126 is similar only to the comment in the Wrangham/"Peter Morris" copy (17.5). At the same time, the pages contain a number of emendations which have no parallel. The redrafting of p 133 (**300** *The Picture*) is particularly odd, since, after an alternative was worked out in the copy C gave to Wrangham/"Peter Morris", the emendation remained more or less stable in corrected and later versions. On the evidence available, there is no way of deciding whether the emended pages date from 1817, when the final copy of *SL* became available, or from the time when JG began preparations for *PW* (1828). The later possibility seems more likely, and some of the emendations might in fact be JG's rather than C's.

The emended pages were sold by Anderson Auction Co 31 Mar 1904 (lot 160 for $4.25), and again in the Arnold Sale, American Art Association (New York) 30 Mar–1 Apr 1925 (lot 253 for $90). They were given to Harvard by Norton Perkins in Jun 1925.

18. *ZAPOLYA* (1817)

The annotated copies of *Zapolya* form a distinctive group in several ways. The emendations and corrections are in most cases very small, and there are very few comments of a reflective or explanatory nature. They also overlap very little, and only a small number are carried forward to the collected editions of 1828, 1829, and 1834. These peculiarities are perhaps a result of the text appearing some two years after it had been written; indeed, it stood in type for some six months before it was printed. The few coincidences and relations there are between individual annotations shed light on the question of their authenticity and date. The corrections and emendations are noticeably concentrated in the earlier part of the play.

18.1. Sara Hutchinson's copy
DCL COL (a) 1817.
Inscribed by C on the title-page: "ΕΣΤΗΣΕ | Miss Hutchinson | from | S. T. Coleridge". C also added, following his name and above "*LONDON:*" "Egenus feci, Musis et Apolline nullo." After the first two words, "I have written this in want" (*egenus* being applicable to poverty of mind as well as goods), C quotes Martial 2.89.3 tr Ker (LCL) I 159 "aided by no Muse and no Apollo". C also used the Martial quotation in the copies given to J. G. Lockhart and EC (18.8–9); *CL* v 436 (to JTC [8 May 1825]). There are annotations on pp 21, 22, 35, 37, 45, 57, 59, 67, 68, 73, 75, 76, and 77. The corrections on pp 35 and 73 are paralleled in SC's copy (18.2), and the

correction on p 57 is paralleled in Henry Erskine Johnston's copy (18.3). Only two (obvious) corrections—on pp 21 and 35—were carried forward to *PW* (1828).

18.2. Sara Coleridge's copy
VCL Book No 31.
Inscribed apparently by SC on the title-page: "Sara Coleridge August 18—1825". There are eight annotations or corrections to the text: in the Advertisement and on pp 7, 21, 35, 39, 43, 53, and 73. Only one of these—a note on metrics on p 53—is certainly in C's hand, and the others are too minor to be attributed to him with certainty. Two corrections—on pp 35 and 73—are paralleled in the copy given to SH (18.1); two—on pp 21 and 35—are paralleled in the copy given to Robert Jameson (18.10); but only the correction on p 35 was taken forward to the later, collected versions of the play.

18.3. Henry Erskine Johnston's copy
HUL * 19475.50 A.
Inscribed by C on the title-page: "to H. Johnstone, Esqre I from S. T. Coleridge I respectfully." There are corrections on pp 31, 35, and 57. The emendation on p 31 (=Prelude ii 91) does not appear to be in C's hand; and, though it was carried forward to *PW* (1828, 1829, 1834), it is without parallel in the annotated copies. The corrections on p 35 are not certainly in C's hand, but they are—together with the emendation on p 57—paralleled in other annotated copies.

H. E. Johnston (1777–?1830), actor, had been stage manager at DL for some time after 1817. An uncollected letter by C to the actor George Bartley, dated 16 Feb 1818, reveals that C had sent the present copy with a letter to Johnston before this date, and that Johnston had acknowledged neither (*Two Letters* 315).

This copy was acquired by Harvard under the Charles Minot Fund, on 8 Mar 1884.

18.4. J. H. Green's copy
BM Ashley 2859.
Inscribed by C on the title-page: "J. H. Green, Esqre I in testimony of sincere respect I from S. T. COLERIDGE". There are no annotations or corrections. The inscription is reproduced in *C Bibl* (Wise *TLP*) 80 and facing.

The copy had been sold, bound with a copy of *Remorse*, at the Green Sale, Sotheby's 27 Jul 1880 (lot 107 to Riggall for 13*s*).

18.5. Washington Allston's copy
Indiana University, Bloomington Lilly Library, Special Collections.
Inscribed by C on the half-title: "W. Allston, Esqre I as a feeble expression I of the I high respect, esteem, and most I affectionate regard of the Author, I

S. T. Coleridge I Highgate, Jan.ᵧ 1818". There are no annotations or correc-
tions. C had met Allston (1779–1843), the American artist, at Rome in 1805.
The acquaintance was renewed in the years Allston spent in England between
1812 and 1818, when he returned to America. It was particularly close in the
year before *Zapolya* was written, when C nursed Allston through a serious
illness and wrote his essays in *Felix Farley's Bristol Journal* prompted by
Allston's exhibition at Bristol. Allston, meanwhile, painted the portrait of C
which now hangs in the National Portrait Gallery, and contributed a poem
(*America to Great Britain*) to *SL*.

18.6. Uninscribed (?) copy
Not located.
The copy has an alteration to the text and several lines added on p 107
(*Zapolya* IV ii 4⁺), all in C's hand, in ink. The emendation was described and
quoted in *P&DW* (RHS) IV 270n; the page is reproduced in the catalogue of
the John F. Fleming Sale, Christie's (New York) 18 Nov 1988 p 51, though
not very clearly. The emendation has no parallels in other known annotated
copies, nor was the passage revised in the later, collected versions. It appears
to have been drafted on the spot and forgotten.
When RHS quoted the emendation in 1877, the copy was in the posses-
sion of his earlier publishers, John Pearson & Co. It was sold at Sotheby's 6
Jun 1929 (lot 636 to Thorp for £3); and again at the John F. Fleming Sale,
Christie's (New York) 18 Nov 1988 (lot 81 for $5000). The Sotheby's cata-
logue describes the copy as lacking the four leaves of advertisements at the
end of the text and as being in polished calf, gilt, with gilt edges; the Christie
catalogue adds that the calf binding is late 19th century, that the front hinge
has been repaired, and that the copy is enclosed in a quarter-blue morocco
folding case.

18.7. Robert Southey's (?) copy
NYPL Berg Collection.
There are corrections and notes in C's hand on pp 54 and 55 (both in ink)
and on p 57 (in ink and in pencil); they constitute extensive redraftings of part
of act I sc i. Only the revisions on p 57 have any parallels in other annotated
copies, and none was carried forward to the later, collected editions. The
relation between p 57 in this copy and the copy C gave to J. G. Lockhart
(18.8) suggests that this copy was annotated earlier, before Nov 1819. There
is no inscription, but the other books by C acquired by Sir George Grove all
previously belonged to RS (see Christie's 15 Mar 1901 lots 397, 401, 402).
It was not, however, part of the sixteen-day sale of RS's books by Sotheby's
8–26 May 1844.
A letter by SC to DC of 9 Feb [1852?] (HRC; see Grantz No 106) proves
that the copy was in the hands of Sir George Grove at this time. Grove
made the corrections available to SC, and later loaned the copy to EHC,

who transcribed the annotations afresh.[28] Although SC, DC, JDC, and EHC all knew of the corrections, they did not make them public. Perhaps Grove asked them not to.

The volume was sold with Grove's other books by C at Christie's 15 Mar 1901 (lot 398 to Sabin for £11 10s). It was sold again at Hodgson's 26 Mar 1903 (lot 428 to Ellis for £11 15s), and in the Stuart M. Samuel Sale, Sotheby's 1 Jul 1907 (lot 40 to Dawes for £14). It was included in the John Pearson *Catalogue of a Unique Coleridge Collection* 46 and in the Scribner catalogue *Superb Collected Sets of the First Editions of Milton, Coleridge, Swinburne, Wordsworth* 16; and sold in the Mark P. Robinson Sale, Anderson Galleries 26 Feb 1918 (lot 162). It came into the possession of John Drinkwater in 1921, who published the corrections in his *Books for Bookmen* (1926) 95–9. It was acquired by the Berg Collection in 1941, as part of the collection of Owen D. Young.

18.8. Copy belonging to "Peter Morris" (=J. G. Lockhart)
Not located.
The copy is inscribed in the form of a letter written on the front flyleaves in Nov 1819: "To the Author of Peter's Letters to his Kinsfolk from his obliged S. T. C." The letter was printed in *PW* (RG) 315–18, and, from a transcript by EHC, in *CL* IV 971–2. In it C recommends the following passages to "Peter Morris's" attention: pp 21, 22, the last five lines of p 25, pp 26–31, 38, 39–44, and 106. Garnett also cites four minor alterations to the text, at pp 7, 7–8, 57, and 126. Only the third of these is paralleled in the other extant annotated copies (18.7 above).

PW (RG) 315 says that the copy was sold at Sotheby's in 1895, to Pearson & Co. Both Garnett and EHC made their transcripts at the time of the sale, but it has not been possible to trace the copy in the Sotheby's sales catalogues or any later references to it.

See 17.19 (also 17.5) for another title presented to "Peter Morris".

18.9. Edward Coleridge's copy
PML No 17971.
Inscribed by C on the half-title: "Edward Coleridge from his Uncle | S. T. Coleridge"; and thereafter, below the half-title (trimmed), "Ehu! Musis et Apolline null₍ₒ₎,". *Eh(e)u* means "alas"; for the rest, from Martial 2.89.3, see 18.1 above. There are no annotations or corrections.

The copy was given by EC to Dean Farrar, and sold at Sotheby's 12 Dec 1903 (lot 726 to Kenneth for £4). It was acquired by PML from J. Pearson & Co in Aug 1911.

---

[28] Grove to EHC, 22 Jun, 30 Jun, 31 Jul 1889 (HRC). EHC's copy of *Dramatic Works* ed DC (1868), with his transcription on to half a sheet of notepaper, was listed in Blackwell's Catalogue No 531 (Spring 1948) item 58 at 15s.

18.10. Robert Jameson's copy
> HUL * 19475. 80 B.
> Inscribed by C on the title-page: "To Robert Jameson I from S. T. Co-
> leridge". There are only two emendations by C, both on p 21. The first is
> unique, and the second is paralleled only by SC's copy (18.2)—though it is
> not certain that the emendation in SC's copy is in C's hand.
> Robert Jameson (d 1854) was a native of Ambleside and a schoolboy friend
> of HC. He was patronised by Basil Montagu, became a successful barrister
> with literary leanings, and eventually (after 1829) a judge in the Colonies.
> He visited Highgate frequently during the 1820s, and with JG supervised the
> publication of *PW* (1828).
> This copy was given to Harvard by Norton Perkins on 4 Sept 1924.

19. *A HEBREW DIRGE* (1817)

Princess Charlotte's funeral was on 19 Nov 1817. C promised Hyman Hurwitz
that he would begin and perhaps finish work on the translation on Monday
24 Nov (see *CL* IV 784). It must have been printed and published during the
following two weeks.

19.1. Mrs Green's copy
> HEHL No 114453.
> Inscribed on the title-page by C: "Mrs Green I with S. T. Coleridge's I
> respectful Complements I 12 December, 1817." There are corrections in C's
> hand on pp [5] and 9. C refers to having sent the copy to Mrs Green in a letter
> to J. H. Green of 23 Dec 1817 (*CL* IV 793). Henry E. Huntington acquired it
> at the Mark P. Robinson Sale, Anderson Galleries 26 Feb 1918 (lot 159).

19.2. Unascribed copy
> HRC An C678 817h.
> Inscribed on the outside of the original brown-paper wrapper, in C's hand:
> "With the Authors respectful Comp^s". There are no further annotations.

20. *THE TEARS OF A GRATEFUL PEOPLE* (1820)

George III died on 29 Jan 1820 and was buried on 16 Feb. The pamphlet was
written and published in the following months. It is not known how many of the
white-satin, interleaved, and specially bound copies were made up, nor whether
it is an accident that the only four copies to survive should be of this kind—two
of them being inscribed, separately, by each author.

20A. The special copy inscribed by Hyman Hurwitz has an ornamental manuscript dedication to King George IV. Once in the possession of R. A. Potts, and described in *C Bibl* (Wise) 128, it was listed in the John Pearson *Catalogue of a Unique Coleridge Collection* 52–3, and the Scribner *Superb Collected Sets of the First Editions of Milton, Coleridge, Swinburne, Wordsworth* 18–19. It was sold again in the Mark P. Robinson Sale, Anderson Galleries 26 Feb 1918 (lot 169). Its present location is unknown. HEHL has another copy printed on white satin (No X80668), but it is not inscribed.

20.1. J. H. Green's or Mrs Green's copy
   BM Ashley 2867.
   Inscribed on the rear free endpaper by C: "S. T. Coleridge | e dono Auctoris | 15 March, 1820" (tr "the gift of the author"); and, on the title-page beneath the description "Translated into English Verse, by a friend", C has written "S. T. C." The page containing C's initials is reproduced in *C Bibl* (Wise *TLP*) facing p 85. The copy was sold with Green's library at Sotheby's 28 Jul 1880 (lot 379 to Pickering for 18*s*), from whence it passed into the possession successively of William Bell Scott, H. Buxton Forman, and T. J. Wise.

21. *POETICAL WORKS* (1828)

21A. *PW* (EHC) I iii–iv, 131n cites "a proof-sheet of the edition of 1828" containing an emended version of the first paragraph of **139** *The Destiny of Nations*. This is now at VCL (S MS Fl.13) and in fact is a single leaf from *PW* (1829) (I 104–5 = **139** VAR TEXT PR 5), emended to read as the lines were printed in *PW* (1834). The leaf can be proved to be from *PW* (1829)—not (1828)—by small peculiarities of the typeface. Taken along with other peculiarities of the 1834 text of *The Destiny of Nations*, it suggests that copy was provided by a marked-up copy of 1829; but the VCL leaf is not a proof-sheet.
   The two known annotated copies of *PW* (1828) are related, but a good deal about them remains unclear.

21B. *PW* (EHC) I 198n, 206n cites a copy of *PW* (1828) containing minor pencil corrections to **161** *The Rime of the Ancient Mariner* 300, 511 (at II 21, 32), possibly in C's hand. This copy is untraced. It has not been possible to examine AG's copy in person (21.2), and it is conceivable that it contains the two corrections.

21.1. C's copy?
   Fitzwilliam Museum, Cambridge, Marlay Bequest 1912.
   The copy is No 9 of the twelve large-paper copies. Annotations by C appear at I 9, 10, 11, 12, 13, 14, 15, 16, 17, 24, 82, 83, 87, 92, 96, 97,

100, 101, 102, 121, 122, 123, 124, 125, 224, 352; II 83, 97, 100, 101, 257, 260, 262; there are no annotations in vol III. In addition, two annotations in vol I (pp 143 and 236) are in the hand that copied the larger part of C's annotations into the other annotated copy, which belonged to AG; and three pencil annotations in vol II—on pp 48, 54, and 73—are in a second unknown hand. Like some further pencil markings in vol II—pp 276, 277, 299, 301, and 349—they may have no particular authority.

C's annotation is mainly reflective: that is, it was not undertaken in preparation for another edition. It appears to have been made after *PW* (1829), since a note at I 12 refers to "the 2nd Edition". The stanza added to **592** *Youth and Age* (II 83 = VAR 38.1.1–4; cf **593** *"Dewdrops are the Gems of Morning"*) is very close to a version of the lines current between late Jan and late Apr 1832 (see poem **592** VAR TEXTS MSS 11, 12), and perhaps the majority of C's notes were written then. One of the two notes C made in the other annotated copy is also dated, significantly, 1832. The revisions and emendations were not used in the preparation of *PW* (1834).

The volumes bear no trace of ownership or provenance. At the same time, their relation to the other annotated copy suggests that they passed through the hands of the Gillman family at an early stage. They were not known to JDC or EHC, and were donated to the Fitzwilliam in 1912.

21.2. Anne Gillman's copy
In the possession of Erwin Schwarz (1983).

The copy is No 4 of the twelve large-paper copies. The front free endpaper of vol II is signed (in pencil): "To my beloved Godchild I My dear Lucy I A. G." The title-pages of all three volumes are signed "Lucy Eleanor Gillman." There is a correction in C's hand at I 143; another note in his hand, concerning AG and dated 1832, at I 236–7; and a third note in his hand, in pencil, at II 175.

The hand that transcribed C's correction and his note concerning AG from this copy to the Fitzwilliam copy (21.1) also transcribed from the Fitzwilliam copy into the present one the bulk of C's comments and emendations in vol I (in fact, all but two very small emendations on pp 24 and 82). The transcription is made with great care; the hand bears a family resemblance to AG's. (This set of transcriptions is not recorded in the commentary.)

Vol II contains, besides C's pencil note on p 175, a few pencil markings (pp 77, 81), which have also been omitted from the commentary. On p 104 some lines are added to **618** *The Two Founts* in AG's (?) hand. They were perhaps taken in from N 26 f 157ʳ (= *CN* IV 5368), possibly after C's death. *PW* (JDC) 642A quotes the addition, adding that it dates from 1826. Since it is not dated here in AG's copy, JDC must have added the date from the notebook, or perhaps it was supplied by EHC. There are no annotations, apart from Lucy Gillman's signature, in vol III.

The copy was known to JDC and EHC as the Gillman copy. JDC wrote to

EHC about it on 3 Nov 1888, citing its comments on three early poems (als at HRC, uncatalogued in 1976); and JDC appears to have copied the annotation into a set of his own (see Sotheby's, 13 Jun 1904, lot 115 to Stevens for 8*s*). JDC quoted from this copy in his own edition (*PW*—JDC—642A and 650B: the annotations are not contained in the Fitzwilliam copy). Though JDC was dependent on EHC for his use of this copy in 1888, EHC appears to have depended on JDC later, when he prepared his own edition. AG's copy was sold at Hodgson's 13 Dec 1928 (lot 185 to Elkin Matthews for £68); and later at the Prescott Sale, Christie's (New York) 6 Feb 1981 (lot 61 for $2800). Mr Schwarz acquired it soon afterwards from the New York dealer John Fleming.

22. *POETICAL WORKS* (1829)

22.1. James Gillman's copy?
NYPL Berg Collection.
This copy contains corrections at I 35, 56, 58, 60, 92, 133, 141, 148, 149, 163, 306, 344, 345, 349, and 352. The corrections are not in C's hand and are minor, but they appear to be contemporary and to possess some measure of authority. In themselves, they manifest an attention to the vagaries of the text, which strongly suggests authorial or editorial interest. In addition, while a large number might be reckoned to have a logical basis (those on pp 56, 58, 92, 133, 149, 306, 344, 345, and 349), others (on pp 35, 60, 141, 148, and 163) restore earlier readings and seem to have been prompted either by recollection or to be the result of collation. The emendation to the Apologetic Preface to **167** *Fire, Famine, and Slaughter* on p 352 is particularly significant. It is matched in only two other instances—in DC's copy of *SL* (17.18 above) and C's (?) own copy of *PW* (1828) (21.1 above)—both of which were annotated by C himself. Cf **167** *Fire, Famine, and Slaughter* VAR ⁻1.383.

The tentative ascription of this copy to JG rests in part on the fact that the hand which wrote the emendations on pp 56, 141, and 352 resembles his: compare *Christabel* copy 16.5 and *SL* copy 17.23. In addition, *PW* (1828) copy 21.1, which contains the overlapping emendation to p 352, is associated with the Gillman family. The connection with JG thus rests on very slight evidence, which could be interpreted differently, and it is suggested here with diffidence.

The emendation on p 352 and the corrections on pp 35, 148, and 349 were incorporated in *PW* (1834). The second correction on p.163 was made in a different way in *PW* (1834). It would therefore seem that the corrections in the present copy were made with a future edition in mind, perhaps with JG's aid, but that they were forgotten or overlooked by HNC. At 21A above a copy of *PW* (1829) is described which is corrected in C's hand and indubitably served as copy for *PW* (1834).

22.2. John Pridham's copy
   Not located.
   John Pridham was the father of Mary Pridham, whom DC married on 6 Dec 1827. The volumes evidently contain a note to the Apologetic Preface of **167** *Fire, Famine, and Slaughter*, at I 353 (see *PW*—JDC—600A; *PW*— EHC—II 1108). EHC lent the volumes to JDC in 1888, and refers to them again in a letter of 26 Jul 1891 (HRC, uncatalogued in 1976). EHC mentions only that they contain "a note" which is "not very important". It is likely that JDC's working copy of *PW* (1829) "with numerous pencil corrections in the margins"—which was sold at Sotheby's 13 Jun 1904 (lot 117 to Hopkins for 9s)—contained a transcript from John Pridham's copy.
   ELG (*CL* VI 782n) cites a copy inscribed by C, dated May 1829, which is perhaps this one.

22.3. Emma Duke Coleridge's copy
   BM C 126 c 3.
   All three volumes are inscribed, on the front free endpaper or half-title: "S. T. Coleridge to his unseen but not unloved Grand-neice, Emma Duke. May 13, 1833. Grove, Highgate" (in the third volume the date and place are omitted). The half-title of vol I carries the additional inscription: "Aunt & Godmamma Henry, & Uncle Henry present these volumes to dear little Emma Duke Coleridge, hoping & trusting, with their tenderest love, that she may live to read them with pleasure & profit, when the author & the givers are all gone. 15 May 1833."
   There are no annotations. Each volume bears the bookplate of Bernard, Lord Coleridge. The BM acquired them from Lord Coleridge in 1951.

23. GALIGNANI EDITION (1829, 1831)

The 1829 Paris edition was reprinted in Philadelphia in 1831, and C was acquainted with the text of both (*CL* VI 903–4: to HNC [7 May 1832]).

23A. The single copy of the Paris edition said to have been annotated by C is of doubtful authenticity. It was sold at Sotheby's 14–16 Jun 1937 (lot 438), the property of R. M. Nealon. It contains on the front endpaper C's epitaph on himself (poem **693**) and his epigram on Cologne (poem **648**). The poems are written in pencil "in the handwriting of Coleridge, each being signed 'S. T. C.'."
   The texts are discussed in the General Notes at poems **648, 693** VAR. They

might have been copied carelessly from *PW* (1834) by someone other than C. The copy is in "stained, original boards, uncut, badly worn".

23B. Another copy of the Coleridge pages (only) of the Paris edition containing an als to Basil Montagu, dated 3 Jan 1827 (=*CL* VI 661) and pasted in to the front free endpaper, is now at Jesus College Cambridge (JES COL 11). It was previously offered for sale in Blackwell's Catalogue No 531 (Spring 1948) item 22. The letter must have been pasted in after publication of the volume, which might or might not have belonged to Montagu and is in no way inscribed or annotated.

24. *POETICAL WORKS* (1834)

24A. The copy at Coleridge's Cottage, Nether Stowey, now in the care of the National Trust, contains notes and comments in all three volumes by SC. Her annotations are in pencil and ink, and mainly in her late hand. The rear flyleaves of vols I and II also contain her transcript of several epigrams and other verses, which are cited in the Variorum sequence. The volumes carry the ownership signatures of Ellen Coleridge (1861) and Edith Coleridge (1909). They were given to the National Trust by the Rev Nicholas Coleridge.

24B. The copy "with numerous MS. notes, emendations, corrections and interpolations, printed slips, etc. 'PRINTER'S PROOFS,' prepared for a new edition, half calf, uncut" which was sold with JDC's books at Sotheby's 13 Jun 1904 (lot 119 to Lyle for £2 4*s*) was almost certainly one emended by JDC himself. Such was his practice, and if the annotations had been by C both JDC and EHC would have made use of them in their editions. The price fetched in the sale would also have been higher. However, the Sotheby cataloguer did not describe the annotations as JDC's, as he did elsewhere, and the copy remains untraced.

24.1. C's copy?
HEHL No 109531.
There are manuscript notes and corrections in C's hand throughout vol I (only), on pp 14, 15, 31, 71, 87, 92, 94, 152, 201, 205, 206, 259, and 260. The note on p 71 is dated Apr 1834, a date which is in part confirmed by the note on p 201. The volume is not a proof copy, but it might have been annotated in an unbound state. None of the three volumes (the last of which appeared after C's death) is inscribed, and there are no bookplates.
C Bibl (Haney) 108 describes these volumes as being in the possession of Stuart M. Samuel. Samuel must have allowed EHC only a cursory inspection of them, since EHC quotes only one annotation (*PW*—EHC—I 178, citing p 201) and does not refer to the corrected copy as a whole, as one would

expect, in his preface. The volumes were sold in the Samuel Sale, Sotheby's 1 Jul 1907 (lot 44 to Dawes for £10), and were listed in the John Pearson *Catalogue of a Unique Coleridge Collection* 74—which reproduces the annotation on p 201 in type facsimile—and in the Scribner *Superb Collected Sets of the First Editions of Milton, Coleridge, Swinburne, Wordsworth* 23. They were sold at the Mark P. Robinson Sale, Anderson Galleries 26 Feb 1918 (lot 184 to Henry E. Huntington for $85).

25. *FRIENDSHIP'S OFFERING FOR 1834*

PML possesses two sets of detached pages containing C's contribution to *Friendship's Offering for 1834*—i.e. pp 163–8 (once) and 355–60 (repeated)—corrected in C's hand (PML No 49359). C contributed the following poems (the titles are given as they appear in the body of the text, not the contents list):

7⁺. The title is followed by a prose note subscribed "S.T.C."

17–18. Subscribed on p 356 "S. T. COLERIDGE, I *August*, 1833."

The editor of *Friendship's Offering* was Thomas Pringle, who had spent the years 1820–6 in South Africa, was appointed Secretary of the Anti-slavery Society in 1827, and became editor of *Friendship's Offering* in 1829. C sent his contribution to him on 6 Aug 1833 (*CL* VI 950–1), and subsequent letters reveal that proofs were ready later in the month. The album was reviewed in *Athenaeum* for 19 Oct, and C had been paid by 24 Oct (*CL* VI 962: to T. Pringle). It would seem that the corrections were made at about this time, the pages being perhaps a contributor's offprint. Thus, the revisions to **688** *Love's Apparition and Evanishment* are closer to MS 5 (sent to Charles Aders on 18 Aug 1833) than to MS 6 (sent to Lockhart on 5 Nov).

Not all the poems C corrected here were included in *PW* (1834), nor were all the corrections he made incorporated. It is therefore incorrect to suggest that these corrected pages are evidence that C "was at work on his poems in 1834, and more than helped to prepare that edition for the press", as EHC does in a note dated Mar 1908 bound up with the *Friendship's Offering* pages. Some notes by JDC accompany the notes by EHC.

ADDENDUM

433A. LINES TO CHARLOTTE BRENT

[Late 1807–early 1808; or any time thereafter up to 1816]

The unpublished manuscript was in the possession of Clifton College, Bristol, for some years but became available only when it was put up for auction in Nov 1999. It is here presented in an incomplete state—with four lines represented by asterisks—because the purchaser also declined to make the text available. C wrote similar doggerel verses to the Morgan sisters in late 1807–early 1808, when he was ill, which Mary Morgan endorsed with the same numbering system (see poems **431–3**; also *CL* III 46–8: to Mary Morgan [22] Jan 1808; 49–50: to J. J. Morgan [1 Feb 1808]). Alternatively, the present verses may be those C described to Mary Morgan on 5 Nov 1813 as "the inclosed piece of Nonsense, the only Object of which was to make you laugh" (*CL* III 450). Or they might have been handed to Charlotte Brent at any of the times C was domiciled with the Morgan household. In a letter of 7 Jul 1814 (CL III 518fn) he appealed to the whole family on behalf of a trisyllabic pronunciation of his name as if it were a familiar shared joke.

The first line might hint at C's dependence on laudanum, about which the Morgans were both sympathetic and concerned. The lines altogether prefigure what became almost a genre of patient–doctor doggerel in C's later Highgate years (cf e.g. poems **679–81**).

> Double Dose of the Med'cine—Quere?
> *   *   *   *   *   *
> *   *   *   *   *   *
> Lest Tyrant Pain should grow surlier
> *   *   *   *   *   *   5
> *   *   *   *   *   *
> None so weak and uneasy
> When in pain, as S. T. C.

4. The line positioned here could turn out to be line 3, 5, or 6.

8. C wrote "*Esteesi*" in the RH mar-gin, which is a transliteration of his name into "Punic Greek" (see **561** *A Character* 71–3EC).

1363

But below & above
Pain & Sorrow lives Love,   10
Till Life reach it's goal or Ridge,
I' th' Heart of S. T. Coleridge.

11–12. C used a variant of the same   *cott's Album* 1–2.
rhyme in **637** *Written in William Up-*

INDEX OF TITLES AND FIRST LINES

Greek entries are given at the end. For variant forms of titles and first lines see the index to volume II.